Emerging Trends in ICT Security

Emerging Trends in ICT Security

Edited by

Babak Akhgar

Hamid R. Arabnia

AMSTERDAM • BOSTON • HEIDELBERG • LONDON
NEW YORK • OXFORD • PARIS • SAN DIEGO
SAN FRANCISCO • SINGAPORE • SYDNEY • TOKYO

Morgan Kaufmann is an imprint of Elsevier

Acquiring Editor: *Steve Elliot*
Editorial Project Manager: *Kaitlin Herbert*
Project Manager: *Punithavathy Govindaradjane*
Designer: *Maria Inês Cruz*

Morgan Kaufmann is an imprint of Elsevier
225 Wyman Street, Waltham, MA 02451, USA

Library of Congress Cataloging-in-Publication Data
Emerging trends in ICT security / edited by Babak Akhgar, Hamid R. Arabnia.
    pages cm
  Includes bibliographical references and index.
  ISBN 978-0-12-411474-6 (alk. paper)
1. Information technology—Security measures. 2. Computer crimes—Prevention.
3. Cyberterrorism—Prevention. 4. Electronic surveillance. I. Akhgar, Babak, editor. II. Arabnia, Hamid, editor.
  QA76.9.A25E467 2013
  005.8—dc23
                2013034381

British Library Cataloguing-in-Publication Data
A catalogue record for this book is available from the British Library

ISBN: 978-0-12-411474-6

Printed and bound by CPI Group (UK) Ltd, Croydon, CR0 4YY
Transferred to digital print 2013

Working together
to grow libraries in
developing countries

www.elsevier.com • www.bookaid.org

For information on all MK publications visit our website at *www.mkp.com*

Contents

PART 1 INFORMATION AND SYSTEMS SECURITY

SECTION 1 Theory/Reviews of the field

CHAPTER 1 System Security Engineering for Information Systems 5

CHAPTER 2 Metrics and Indicators as Key Organizational Assets for ICT Security Assessment.. 25

SECTION 9 Methods

SECTION 12 Methods

Acknowledgments

We wish to thank everyone who has contributed to this book. In particular, we would like to acknowledge the contribution of CENTRIC (Centre of excellence in terrorism, resilience, intelligence & organised crime research, at Sheffield Hallam University, UK). We would also like to take this opportunity to express our gratitude to the following as members of the book review board for their contributions to the final publication.

Review Board

Babak Akhgar
Hamid R. Arabnia
Ben Brewster
Richard Hill
Hamid Jahankhani
Kayleigh Johnson
Eleanor Lockley
Reza Nasserzadeh
Simon Polovina
Jawed Siddiqi
Andrew Staniforth

About the Editors

Babak Akhgar

Babak Akhgar is Professor of Informatics and Director of the Centre of excellence in terrorism, resilience, intelligence & organised crime research (CENTRIC) at Sheffield Hallam University, and a Fellow of the British Computer Society. Professor Akhgar graduated from Sheffield Hallam University in Software Engineering. After gaining considerable commercial experience as a Strategy Analyst and Methodology Director for several companies, he consolidated this experience by obtaining a masters degree (with distinction) in Information Systems in Management and a PhD in Information Systems. He has more than 100 referred publications in international journals and conference proceedings. He is on the editorial boards of three international journals, and is chair and programme committee member of several international conferences. He has extensive hands-on experience in development, management, and execution of large international KM and security initiatives (e.g., combating terrorism and organized crime, cybersecurity, public order, and cross-cultural ideology polarization). He also has an established network of collaborators in various academic and law enforcement agencies locally, nationally, and internationally. The impact of his research on e-security, manifested in a multi-lingual portal for business crime reduction, and his research on combating organized crime and terrorism led to an international research project with partners such as Europol and a number of LEAs (with a project value of 3.2 M Euro). He has recently written and edited a number of books on intelligence management and national security.

Hamid R. Arabnia

Hamid R. Arabnia received his Ph.D. degree in Computer Science from the University of Kent (Canterbury, England) in 1987 and since October of that year has been a Full Professor of Computer Science at the University of Georgia (Georgia, USA). Professor Arabnia's research interests include parallel and distributed processing techniques and algorithms, supercomputing, interconnection networks, and applications. He is is Editor-in-Chief of the *Journal of Supercomputing* (one of the oldest journals in computer science), published by Springer, and has been Associate Editor of *IEEE Transactions on Information Technology in Biomedicine* (2008–2011). He is also on the editorial and advisory boards of over 35 other journals. Professor Arabnia is the founding chair of the annual World Congress in Computer Science, Computer Engineering, and Applied Computing (WORLDCOMP), and editor of *Transactions on Computational Science and Computational Intelligence* (Springer), and *Transactions on Computer Science and Applied Computing* (Elsevier). Prof. Arabnia has edited/co-edited over 100 books; his most recent co-edited book (*Software Tools and Algorithms for Biological Systems*) is among the top 25 percent most downloaded Springer e-books. Prof. Arabnia has published extensively in journals and refereed conference proceedings. He has over 350 publications (journals, proceedings, editorships) in his area of research. He has been a PI/Co-PI on approximately $7.5 M worth of externally funded projects/initiatives. During his tenure as Graduate Coordinator/Director of Computer Science (2002–2009), Dr. Arabnia secured the largest level of funding in the history of the department for supporting graduate students (PhD, MS).

List of Contributors

Zair Abdelouahab
Federal University of Maranhão, São Luís, MA, Brazil

Maher Aburrous
Al Hoson University, Abu Dhabi, UAE

Eyidayo Adebola
Prairie View A&M University, Prairie View, TX, USA

Babak Akhgar
Sheffield Hallam University, Sheffield, UK

Sayed Alireza Hashemi Golpayegani
Amirkabir University of Technology (Tehran Polytechnic), Tehran, Iran

Ja'far Alqatawna
The University of Jordan, Amman, Jordan

Omar Al-Kadi
The University of Jordan, Amman, Jordan

Rizik Al-Sayyed
The University of Jordan, Amman, Jordan

Faisal T. Ammari
University of Huddersfield, Huddersfield, UK

Annamalai Annamalai
Prairie View A&M University, Prairie View, TX, USA

Manoj Apte
Tata Consultancy Services Limited, Pune, MH, India

Hamid R. Arabnia
University of Georgia, Athens, GA, USA

Vladimir B. Balakirsky[†]
State University of Aerospace Instrumentation, St-Petersburg, Russia

Maros Barabas
Brno University of Technology, Brno, Czech Republic

Gerald Baumgartner
Laboratory for Telecommunications Science, College Park, MD, USA

[†]Deceased

Petra Saskia Bayerl
Erasmus University, Rotterdam, The Netherlands

Timothy Bowden
Jacksonville State University, Jacksonville, AL, USA

Ben Brewster
Sheffield Hallam University, Sheffield, UK

Roman Busse
Fraunhofer Institute for Open Communication Systems (FOKUS), Berlin, Germany

Petr Chmelar
Brno University of Technology, Brno, Czech Republic

Seonho Choi
Bowie State University, Bowie, MD, USA

John M. Colombi
United States Air Force Institute of Technology, Wright-Patterson AFB, OH, USA

Guillermo Covella
National University of La Pampa Engineering School, Santa Rosa, LP, Argentina

Miles Crabill
Lewis & Clark College, Portland, OR, USA

Evan Damon
Lewis & Clark College, Portland, OR, USA

David de Andrés
Universitat Politècnica de València, Valencia, Spain

Alberto De la Rosa Algarín
University of Connecticut, Storrs, CT, USA

Leonidas Deligiannidis
Wentworth Institute of Technology, Boston, MA, USA

Nikolaos L. Dellas
SingularLogic Software and Integrated IT Solutions, Nea Ionia, Greece

Steven A. Demurjian
University of Connecticut, Storrs, CT, USA

Alexander Dieser
National University of La Pampa Engineering School, Santa Rosa, LP, Argentina

Steven Drager
US Air Force Research Lab, Rome, NY, USA

Michal Drozd
Brno University of Technology, Brno, Czech Republic

Hyeonsang Eom
Seoul National University, Seoul, Korea

Diogo A.B. Fernandes
University of Beira Interior, Covilhã, Portugal

Guillermo Francia, III
Jacksonville State University, Jacksonville, AL, USA

Mário M. Freire
University of Beira Interior, Covilhã, Portugal

Kaleb Ganz
Lewis & Clark College, Portland, OR, USA

Qigang Gao
Dalhousie University, Halifax, NS, Canada

Anahit R. Ghazaryan
State University of Aerospace Instrumentation, St-Petersburg, Russia

João V. Gomes
University of Beira Interior, Covilhã, Portugal

Geff Green
Sheffield Hallam University, Sheffield, UK

Michael R. Grimaila
United States Air Force Institute of Technology, Wright-Patterson AFB, OH, USA

Petr Hanacek
Brno University of Technology, Brno, Czech Republic

Mohammad Hassanzadeh
Tarbiat Modares University, Tehran, Iran

Peng He
University of Maryland, Baltimore, MD, USA

Douglas D. Hodson
United States Air Force Institute of Technology, Wright-Patterson AFB, OH, USA

Ivan Homoliak
Brno University of Technology, Brno, Czech Republic

Mihai Horia Zaharia
"Gheorghe Asachi" Technical University, Iaşi, Românᵃia

Claire Humbeutel
Lewis & Clark College, Portland, OR, USA

Pedro R.M. Inácio
University of Beira Interior, Covilhã, Portugal

David Jacques
United States Air Force Institute of Technology, Wright-Patterson AFB, OH, USA

Narges Jahangiri
Ministry of Education, Tehran, Iran

Kayleigh Johnson
Sheffield Hallam University, Sheffield, UK

Dimitra I. Kaklamani
National Technical University of Athens, Athens, Greece

Maria N. Koukovini
National Technical University of Athens, Athens, Greece

Sofiane Labidi
Federal University of Maranhão, São Luís, MA, Brazil

Ville Leppänen
University of Turku, Turku, Finland

Georgios V. Lioudakis
National Technical University of Athens, Athens, Greece

Eleanor Lockley
Sheffield Hallam University, Sheffield, UK

Denivaldo Lopes
Federal University of Maranhão, São Luís, MA, Brazil

Pascal Lorenz
University of Haute Alsace, Colmar, France

J. Lu
University of Huddersfield, Huddersfield, UK

Jianbing Ma
Bournemouth University, Bournemouth, UK

Jens Mache
Lewis & Clark College, Portland, OR, USA

Nicolás Macia
The National University of La Plata, La Plata, BA, Argentina

Logan O. Mailloux
United States Air Force Institute of Technology, Wright-Patterson AFB, OH, USA

Héctor Marco
Universitat Politècnica de València, Valencia, Spain

Maria Angel Marquez-Andrade
York University, Toronto, ON, Canada

William McKeever
US Air Force Research Lab, Rome, NY, USA

Davud Mohammadpur
University of Zanjan, Zanjan, Iran

Seyyed Mohammad Reza Farshchi
Ferdowsi University of Mashhad, Mashhad, Iran

Falkner Moraes
Federal University of Maranhão, São Luís, MA, Brazil

Jeffrey D. Morris
United States Air Force Institute of Technology, Wright-Patterson AFB, OH, USA

Anas Najdawi
Princess Sumaya University for Information Technology, Amman, Jordan

Samir M.R. Nasserzadeh
University of Tehran, Tehran, Iran

Holger Nitsch
Fachhochschule fur Offenttliche Verwaltung und Rechtspflege in Bayern, Bavaria, Germany

Abiodun Olaluwe
Prairie View A&M University, Prairie View, TX, USA

Emerson Oliveira
Federal University of Maranhão, São Luís, MA, Brazil

Luis Olsina
National University of La Pampa Engineering School, Santa Rosa, LP, Argentina

Girish Keshav Palshikar
Tata Consultancy Services Limited, Pune, MH, India

Eugenia I. Papagiannakopoulou
National Technical University of Athens, Athens, Greece

Paul R. Prucnal
Princeton University, Princeton, NJ, USA

Tran Quang Thanh
Fraunhofer Institute for Open Communication Systems (FOKUS), Berlin, Germany

Victor Raskin
Purdue University, West Lafayette, IN, USA

Sampsa Rauti
University of Turku, Turku, Finland

Yacine Rebahi
Fraunhofer Institute for Open Communication Systems (FOKUS), Berlin, Germany

Mohammad Reza Movahedisefat
Amirkabir University of Technology (Tehran Polytechinc), Tehran, Iran

Ismael Ripoll
Universitat Politècnica de València, Valencia, Spain

Hamzeh Roumani
York University, Toronto, ON, Canada

Juan Carlos Ruiz
Universitat Politècnica de València, Valencia, Spain

Sébastien Salva
University of Auvergne, Clermont-Ferrand, France

Maryam Shahpasand
Amirkabir University of Technology (Tehran Polytechnic), Tehran, Iran

Bhavin J. Shastri
Princeton University, Princeton, NJ, USA

Jawed Siddiqi
Sheffield Hallam University, Sheffield, UK

Liliana F.B. Soares
University of Beira Interior, Covilhã, Portugal

Andrew Staniforth
North East Counter Terrorism Unit, West Yorkshire Police, West Yorkshire, UK

Nary Subramanian
University of Texas at Tyler, Tyler, TX, USA

Kun Sun
George Mason University, Fairfax, VA, USA

Fahimeh Tabatabayi
MehrAlborz University, Tehran, Iran

Julia M. Taylor
Purdue University, West Lafayette, IN, USA

Cenidalva Teixeira
Federal University of Maranhão, São Luís, MA, Brazil

Ariel Teles
Federal University of Maranhão, São Luís, MA, Brazil

David Thornton
Jacksonville State University, Jacksonville, AL, USA

Fernando G. Tinetti
The National University of La Plata, La Plata, BA, Argentina

Monica Trifas
Jacksonville State University, Jacksonville, AL, USA

Sanjai Veetil
Dalhousie University, Halifax, NS, Canada

Lakovos S. Venieris
National Technical University of Athens, Athens, Greece

Natalija Vlajic
York University, Toronto, ON, Canada

Richard Weiss
Evergreen State College, Olympia, WA, USA

Charlie Wiseman
Wentworth Institute of Technology, Boston, MA, USA

Ben Wu
Princeton University, Princeton, NJ, USA

Mira Yun
Wentworth Institute of Technology, Boston, MA, USA

Stassia R. Zafimiharisoa
Blaise Pascal University, Clermont-Ferrand, France

Preface

The multi-billion-dollar information and communication technologies (ICT) security market is one of the fastest growing in the world. The ICT security field is a highly complex cross-disciplinary domain that includes computer science, management science, software engineering, information systems, network management, policy making, and management of infrastructures.

ICT security is becoming increasingly important for global business and for society in general. ICT is having an ever-increasing impact upon many aspects of our lives, bringing with it a growing reliance upon ICT networks, data, and services. This reliance makes the protection and security of ICT assets critical. However, as the rapid evolution of technical innovation brings increased complexity of systems and networks, effectively securing ICT assets is becoming ever more challenging. Society's dependence on ICT infrastructure has made it vulnerable to individuals, organizations, and others who may seek to exploit this dependency to further their own interests, be that for financial or political gain.

These ICT vulnerabilities can be considered threats to national security and can have a profound impact upon individuals, communities, businesses, and societies. The task of preventing, mitigating, and supporting resilience in the face of such threats remains a major role for nation-states.

To effectively protect society and reduce these vulnerabilities, ICT security is required to be innovative and dynamic in its approach. It needs to anticipate, detect, deter, and respond to all levels of threats while simultaneously operating in line with current legal, governance, regulatory, and ethical frameworks.

This book is a compilation of chapters that address emergent topics related to ICT and security from both theoretical and applied perspectives. It is arranged into five parts. Part 1 addresses a range of current topics around information and systems security, Part 2 focuses on network and infrastructure security, Part 3 takes a look at mobile and cloud computing security, Part 4 discusses cyber-crime and cyber-terrorism, and Part 5 addresses online radicalization and online financial crime.

Information and Systems Security

Theory/Reviews
of the Field

System Security Engineering for Information Systems

Logan O. Mailloux[1], Michael R. Grimaila[1], John M. Colombi[1], Douglas D. Hodson[1], and Gerald Baumgartner[2]

[1]*United States Air Force Institute of Technology, Wright-Patterson AFB, OH, USA*
[2]*Laboratory for Telecommunications Science, College Park, MD, USA*

INFORMATION IN THIS CHAPTER

- A concise history of system security engineering is provided;
- Established system security engineering methods, processes, and tools are described with emphasis on United States Department of Defense program protection planning; and
- Modern and emerging system security engineering methods, processes, and tools for complex information-centric systems are described.

INTRODUCTION

The benefits of embedding information and communications technologies (ICT), also known as "cyber systems," into core business processes are well understood as a means to increase operational efficiency, improve decision quality, and reduce costs. Information systems and technologies permeate almost every aspect of life, from hand-held smart phones to massive smart grids; they enable modern 21st-century lifestyles. However, security and assurance of these systems proves elusive. Understanding and controlling risks in an ICT System-of-Systems (SoS) environment is difficult due to the complex nature of modern information-centric systems and a dynamic, often hostile operational environment. This problem is further exacerbated by the nature of cyber system operations, which involve numerous interactions between people, processes, and technologies that is difficult to account for in present security efforts.

Large, widely distributed organizations especially struggle with this ICT security problem. The United Stated (US) Department of Defense (DoD) is an excellent example of a large organization with multi-level security requirements that continues to struggle with risk management, assurance, and security despite massive outlays of financial and personnel resources. Conservative estimates place federal cyber security spending at roughly $10 billion for 2012, with projections up to $14 billion in 2017.

Like many large organizations, parts of the US DoD are primarily focused on providing mission-essential services in any operating environment or condition. Whether relying on a commercial financial service or a tactical intelligence system, users cannot tolerate security compromises or extended outages. Furthermore, military missions often involve dynamically changing, time-sensitive, complex, cooperative, and coordinated ventures among multiple organizations (e.g., units, services, agencies, coalition partners) who may not share in a complete view of their roles within the overall mission, which creates the need for a structured means to collect and evaluate security requirements from a diverse set of stakeholders, each with different goals and objectives. These non-trivial complex security issues would ideally be addressed through a holistic systems engineering (SE)—based approach, known as system security engineering (SSE), to manage or reduce system complexity while providing continuous improvement and cost-effective security solutions.

In this chapter, we provide a concise history of SSE followed by a detailed description of long-standing US DoD SSE methods, processes, and tools (MPT) used to limit vulnerabilities in operational environments. Next, SSE modern and emerging MPTs to manage critical shortfalls in the development and fielding of complex information-centric systems are described. Finally, conclusions and recommendations are provided to promote the discovery and shared understanding of complex system security problems and solutions through multidisciplinary efforts by those trained in the art and science of systems engineering, security engineering, and risk management to assure critical missions and secure modern ICT implementations.

System security engineering history

The field of systems security engineering is extremely young when compared to traditional engineering disciplines. System security engineering was first defined in 1989 by US DoD Military Standard 1785 and superseded in the otherwise unchanged 1995 edition of the Military Handbook 1785 [1]:

> *Systems Security Engineering. An element of system engineering that applies scientific and engineering principles to identify security vulnerabilities and minimize or contain risks associated with these vulnerabilities. It uses mathematical, physical, and related scientific disciplines, and the principles and methods of engineering design and analysis to specify, predict, and evaluate the vulnerability of the system to security threats.*

A number of observations can be made from the historic definition. First, SSE is an element or specialty of systems engineering. Second, the primary purpose of this engineering specialty is to identify, minimize, and contain vulnerabilities and their associated risks. Third, SSE is a multidisciplinary effort that uses scientific disciplines, principles, and methods to identify and assess vulnerabilities. Lastly, the SSE handbook's stated objective is to reduce system vulnerabilities prior to system fielding which lends itself to early design and development initiatives.

The system security engineering process

The foundation of SSE rests on cost-benefit decision tradeoffs focused on engineering out vulnerabilities and designing in security countermeasures as long-term cost saving measures [1]. The SSE process was originally considered for the design and development of systems with respect to the

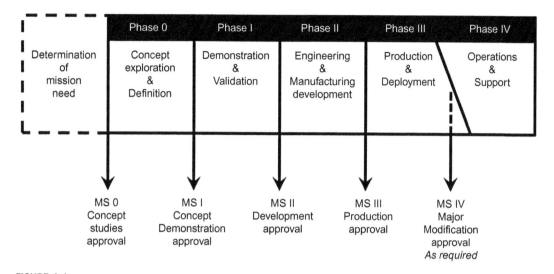

FIGURE 1.1

DoD Acquisition management phases [2].

acquisition life cycle phases shown in Figure 1.1, while program protection addresses operations and support in phase IV:

- Phase 0. Develop system security criteria, describe the baseline security system design, and conduct security threat and vulnerability studies.
- Phase I. Analyze and validate the system security baseline, prepare preliminary performance specifications for security hardware and software, and process identified threats and vulnerabilities through system design modifications and risk management techniques.
- Phase II. Design and integrate the security system, acquire or develop security system hardware and software against the specifications.
- Phase III. Implement the security system design via production and conduct deployment planning.
- Phase IV. Address operational and support security concerns through continual risk management via the program protection process.

From this description we note fundamental items of interest that constitute core SSE MPTs. Risk management forms the crux of US DoD system security and protection efforts through threat identification and vulnerability analysis serving as the basis for all SSE decisions. Of great importance, system security requirements are also emphasized from initial concept exploration to implementation and production. Lastly, integrated throughout the acquisition process is the system security baseline, which serves as the foundation for security tradeoffs.

In the 1990s, industry and government supported the development of a System Security Engineering—Capability Maturity Model (SSE-CMM) to help standardize and assess SSE practices. The SSE-CMM was accepted by the International Organization for Standardization/Intentional Electrotechnical Commission in 2002 and revised again in 2008 [3]. The SSE-CMM formalizes

SSE into three separate process areas: risk, engineering, and assurance. The SSE-CMM provides SSE goals consistent with MIL-HDBK-1785 [1], while further attempting to address and clarify difficult security concepts such as assurance and trust:

- Gain understanding of the security risks associated with an enterprise;
- Establish a balanced set of security needs in accordance with identified risks;
- Determine that operational impacts due to residual security vulnerabilities in a system or its operation are tolerable (i.e., determine acceptable risks);
- Transform security needs into security guidance to be integrated into the activities of other disciplines employed on a project and into descriptions of a system configuration or operation;
- Establish confidence or assurance in the correctness and effectiveness of security mechanisms; and
- Integrate the efforts of all engineering disciplines and specialties into a combined understanding of the trustworthiness of a system.

Over the next decade, information system functionality was chiefly emphasized over security, leading to a general neglect of the art and science of SSE [4]. However, during this period some works on security engineering were published, including Bruce Schneier's *Secrets & Lies* in 2000 [5], and Ross Anderson's *Security Engineering* in 2001 [6]. Additionally, during this timeframe the International Information Systems Security Certification Consortium $(ISC)^2$ created the Certified Information Systems Security Professional (CISSP) and later, in conjunction with the National Security Agency, added the Information System Security Engineering Professional (ISSEP) credential to focus specifically on engineering processes.

The revitalization of system security engineering

A number of recent high-profile commercial and DoD-related security compromises have caused a renewal of interest and widespread acceptance of SSE as a specialized domain of expertise in both the US government and industry [7,8]. The International Council On Systems Engineering (INCOSE) officially recognized SSE as a specialty domain in August 2011 and committed to writing a dedicated SSE section in the 2013 INCOSE Handbook rewrite [9]. The Stevens Institute is responsible for hosting the online Systems Engineering Book of Knowledge (SEBoK) [10] and recently produced a US DoD sponsored System Security Engineering Technical Report [11]. These international and academic organizations are helping to reinstitute and advance SSE as a multidisciplinary specialty domain combining systems engineering (SE), information assurance (IA), and critical knowledge of established security domains (i.e., the CISSP common body of knowledge) to overcome the elusive ICT security problem [12,13].

Established system security engineering methods, processes, and tools

In this section, we detail existing SSE MPTs, with particular focus on the US DoD program protection planning process. The established SSE MPTs will be further considered, in view of a holistic SSE approach selectively applied throughout the system life cycle, in order to manage system complexity and provide cost-effective security solutions for ICT systems.

Acquisition program protection planning

Under Secretary of Defense for Acquisition, Technology, and Logistics Frank Kendall recently released a directive that "reflects the integration of the Acquisition Information Assurance (IA) Strategy and recognizes Program Protection as the Department's holistic approach for delivering trusted systems" [14]. To a great extent, SSE has been conducted in the US DoD through a multifaceted program protection planning framework, as shown in Figure 1.2. The framework depends upon the risk-based identification and mitigation of potential vulnerabilities, which continue to be refined as understanding and expertise grow. For example, detailed accompanying program protection guidance was recently added to the Defense Acquisition Guide (DAG), via a new chapter, in November 2012 [16].

At the highest level, program protection for large acquisition programs is driven by laws and regulations within the defense acquisition management system [17], which drives a cost-based life cycle decision approach. Depending on the purpose, expense, and sensitivity of a given acquisition system, a scalable level of protection should be conducted to meet sponsor needs and government requirements.

Identification and protection of critical program information and technology (CPI/T) is defined in DoD Instruction 5200.39 [18]. Program protection for hardware and software

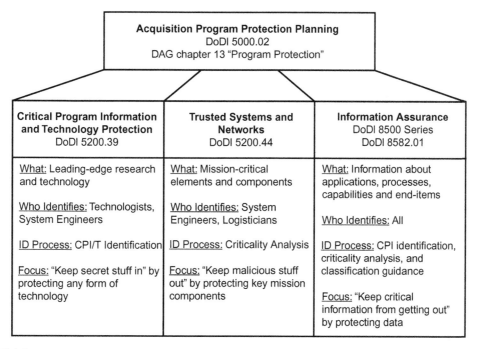

FIGURE 1.2

Acquisition program protection planning [15].

components is defined in the Trusted Systems and Networks DoD Instruction 5200.44 [19], which dates back to the celebrated "Orange Book" of 1985 [20]. More recently, the role of Information Assurance (IA) has been formalized through the risk-based DoD Information Technology Security Certification and Accreditation Process (DITSCAP), and later updated to the DoD Information Assurance Certification and Accreditation Process (DIACAP) [21].

The protection process begins with identifying leading-edge research and technologies that support US DoD mission areas, as shown in Table 1.1 [16]. Examples of CPI/T may be as specific as engine designs for supersonic flight, software assurance techniques for information systems, or unique manufacturing processes for low observable composite wings.

Criticality analysis is used to provide a mission-oriented analysis of system functions and components, which are prioritized into four criticality levels, listed in Table 1.2 [16]. The defined criticality capture the consequence or potential loss of critical system components. Defined levels also allow for consistent system risk and mission assurance analysis across competing systems and missions.

Figure 1.3 demonstrates the program protection process and is described with respect to Table 1.1. The results of CPI/T identification and component-level critical analysis (step 1) are combined, forming consequence ratings for individual mission capabilities, while threat analysis (step 2) and vulnerability assessment (step 3) define the likelihood of losing a particular mission capability for the initial risk assessment. Threat and vulnerability identification, analysis, and assessment must be conducted for all potential actors or activities, hostile and non-hostile. Most

---

Table 1.1 The Program Protection Planning Process [16]

Step 1: Identify CPI/T and Component-Level Criticality Analysis
Step 2: Threat Analysis
Step 3: Vulnerability Assessment
Step 4: Risk Assessment
Step 5: Countermeasure(s) Implementation
Step 6: Horizontal Protection (i.e., internal protections to the DoD)
Step 7: Foreign Involvement (i.e., external protections to the DoD)

Table 1.2 Criticality Levels [16]

Level I: Total Mission Failure	Program protection failure that results in total compromise of mission capability.
Level II: Significant/ Unacceptable Degradation	Program protection failure that results in unacceptable compromise of mission capability or significant mission degradation.
Level III: Partial/ Acceptable Degradation	Program protection failure that results in partial compromise of mission capability or partial mission degradation.
Level IV: Negligible Degradation	Program protection failure that results in little or no compromise of mission capability.

often DoD risk assessments (step 4) result in an initial risk posture composed of a 5×5 categorization of high, medium, and low risks. Example program risks are shown as R1 and R2. The program protection risk assessment needs to be a detailed holistic mission-oriented capability analysis against all known and postulated threats, vulnerabilities, and weaknesses. Consideration for risk mitigation strategies (risk reduction, avoidance, transfer, or acceptance) and additional countermeasures is made until agreeable levels of risk are achieved within programmatic cost-benefit limitations (step 5). The results of risk mitigation decisions are shown as lower risks R1′ and R2′, with reduced consequence and likelihood postures.

Although it is still developing, the program protection process seems to have a physical component orientation, while perhaps neglecting the holistic nature of modern missions and systems; that is, the interactions of people, processes, and technology produce the desired capability. Ideally, system security engineers can leverage this existing process to select and implement multidisciplinary cost-effective security solutions.

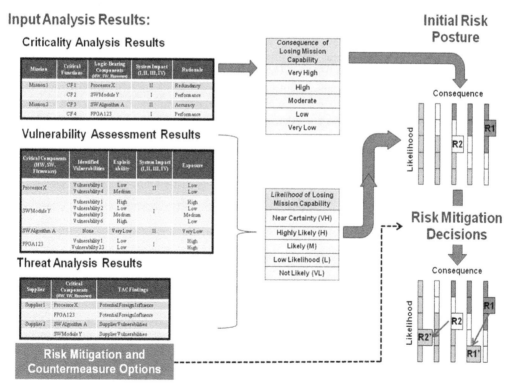

FIGURE 1.3

Risk assessment methodology [16].

Information assurance

Returning to Figure 1.2, we see that the US DoD utilizes a complete system life cycle risk-based methodology for information assurance, certification, and accreditation through the DIACAP approach, which is largely based on information classification levels. DIACAP describes a step-by-step approach to assure that DoD systems are protected by addressing confidentiality, integrity, availability, authentication, and non-repudiation. The US DoD's approach to information assurance continues to improve through collaborative initiatives with other federal organizations, such as the ongoing transformation initiative between the US DoD and the National Institute of Standards and Technology (NIST). This effort seeks to provide common terminology, processes, acceptance, and architectures using NIST Special Publication 800-53 as a baseline framework for standardizing risk management approaches [22].

For ICT implementations, DIACAP serves primarily as a formal way to identify and document risk before authorizing connectivity to the broader DoD network. For large information-centric acquisition programs, multiple critical design and development activities should occur throughout the system life cycle. Design and development activities are typically run as specialized teams with multiple representatives from the sponsor, responsible program office, testing organizations, user communities, and various other subject matter experts. Information assurance testing events are most often realized through system security assessments and penetration testing events conducted by highly training cyber security and software professionals.

For conventional weapon systems, the difficulty of information assurance and software testing has come to a head with one of the most complex systems ever developed—the Joint Strike Fighter. The newly appointed program executive officer, Air Force Major General Bogdan, recently stated, "The 'gorilla in the room' is testing and securing the 24 million lines of software code for the plane and its support systems, a mountain of instructions that goes far beyond what has been tried in any plane" [23]. Early program testing efforts for the Joint Strike Fighter reflect a significant shift in capability delivery from hardware-based systems to software-oriented functionality.

Information assurance and, more fully, system assurance efforts, such as component verification and system validation provide SSE requirements traceability. This helps the DoD achieve its goal of assured systems through program protection [24].

Systems engineering critical reviews

The DoDI 5000.02 defense acquisition management system describes a formal process for developing and fielding desired capabilities for sponsors and users [17]. A critical aspect of its success is the integration of system engineering efforts in key technical reviews and decision points, as shown in Figure 1.4. These key points represent ideal opportunities for system security engineers to address security, risk, and program protection issues in a formalized and iterative fashion and to work in a multidisciplinary, collaborative environment to simultaneously address multiple interest groups [16].

A successful risk-based SSE approach lies in the identification and correct assessment of risks across all involved people, processes, and technologies that contribute to the desired capability(ies) while selecting and implementing appropriate safeguards. Experienced program managers, system engineers, and especially system security engineers need to thoroughly understand the desired capability(ies), requirements, and operational environment in order to make correct decisions and properly informed recommendations [3].

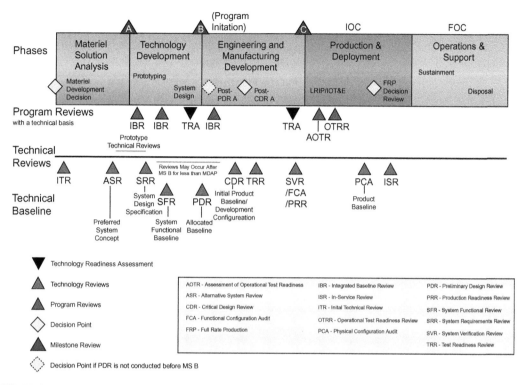

FIGURE 1.4

Systems engineering critical reviews [16].

Modern and emerging system security engineering methods, processes, and tools

Many modern and emerging SSE MPTs exist to assess and manage critical shortfalls in the development and fielding of complex information systems. This section describes SSE MPTs, which aid in understanding and controlling system complexity for secure ICT implementations.

Discovery and understanding of complex systems for security

While advanced hardware and software implementations along with extensive interoperability are often the very enablers of desired critical mission functionality, their intrinsic complexity is diametrically opposed to the required security of those missions and systems. However, this is precisely where security engineers can leverage SE MPTs to perform complex system analysis, functional decomposition, and system integration activities to dissect complex systems into manageable parts [25].

Consider, for example, the interoperability requirements and resulting dependencies for a vast classified Command and Control (C2) system as the Combined Air Operations Center (CAOC), which can employ hundreds of personnel across elaborate suites of over 50 software applications and sensors responsible for controlling thousands of aircraft for a large geographical area. More complex still are Command, Control, Communications, Computers, Intelligence, Surveillance and Reconnaissance (C4ISR) systems such as the Distributed Common Ground Station (DCGS), configured to store, analyze, and pass real-time classified intelligence information across globally distributed operational nodes while directly interfacing with live intelligence gathering assets. Lastly, Figure 1.5 demonstrates the collaborative interoperability provided by the Global Information Grid (GIG) for which the National Security Agency provides a robust information assurance program [26].

Modern weapon systems are an amazing collaboration of people, processes, hardware, software, and firmware that must function correctly to enable mission-essential capabilities; they are large, complex SoS implementations. To address these SoS problems, the DoD published the SE guide for SoS in 2008 [27]. However, even though SE and SoS SE practices have been established for a number of years, they have not been widely accepted or applied to the security domain. Some SE best practices for consideration are:

• Following a formalized system development process, such as Agile software development, Spiral development (Boehm), Rational Unified Process (RUP), Test-driven development (TDD), or evolutional acquisition process (DoD);

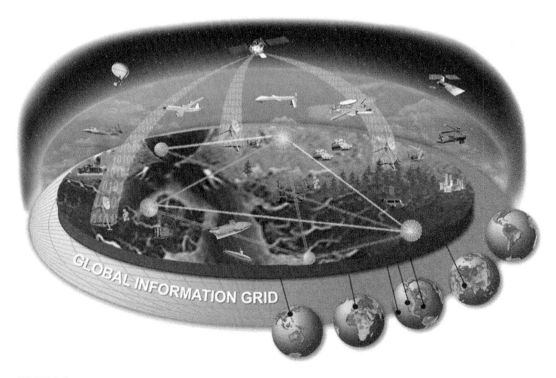

FIGURE 1.5

Global information grid architecture [26].

- Following a logical series of developmental activities such as the V-Model;
- Using model-based systems engineering (MBSE) tools and best practices;
- Utilizing concept of operations visualization;
- Early prototyping and testing;
- Systems-thinking practices;
- Addressing human-system integration (HIS) issues; or
- Implementing tailored and lean processes.

Novel complex system analysis approaches include: game theory, agent-based models, and nonlinear dynamics [28]. SSE must leverage these MPTs to first understand and then implement cost-effective security solutions.

Mission assurance

The US DoD faces the daunting challenge of executing military operations against an array of adversaries and environments across the globe—from isolated nationalistic countries to dispersed networks of terrorist cells. This uniquely difficult and dynamic task has spawned an operationally focused, mission-oriented view to address poorly understood risks and interactions, formally defined in [29]:

> *Mission Assurance. A process to protect or ensure the continued function and resilience of capabilities and assets—including personnel, equipment, facilities, networks, information and information systems, infrastructure, and supply chains—critical to the execution of DoD mission-essential functions in any operating environment or condition.*

Inherent in mission assurance is the holistic ability to perform risk management through the identification, assessment, and protection of critical people, processes, and technologies responsible for ensuring mission-essential functions. An excellent example of the linkage between mission assurance and information system risk management is demonstrated by the Mission Assurance Categories (MAC) (Table 1.3) [30].

The information assurance MACs are broken down by identification, analysis, and mitigation technique, consistent with risk management strategies. The MACs clearly define identification and analysis criteria, as well as what risk mitigation steps are necessary. Although the MAC levels are defined with respect to information systems, other mission types can be similarly identified, analyzed, and mitigated to include people and processes.

The US DoD's movement toward mission assurance demonstrates a greater understanding of the risk modern warfighters face. Although still maturing, mission assurance holds potential as an effective tool for addressing mission risk and overcoming operational complexity through a holistic (people, processes, technologies) risk management approach. Additionally, mission assurance identification and analysis provides an effective way to quickly prioritize operational-based risk and security concerns. Lastly, as an identified best practice, system security engineers should address changing operational environments and attempt to consider unexpected system modifications that may occur during fielding to support evolving mission needs [31].

Table 1.3 Mission Assurance Categories [30]

Category	Identification	Mission Assurance Analysis	Mitigation
Mission Assurance Category I (MAC I)	Systems handling information that is determined to be vital to the operational readiness or mission effectiveness of deployed and contingency forces in terms of both content and timeliness.	The consequences of loss of integrity or availability of a MAC I system are unacceptable and could include the immediate and sustained loss of mission effectiveness.	Requires the most stringent protection measures.
Mission Assurance Category II (MAC II)	Systems handling information that is important to the support of deployed and contingency forces.	The consequences of loss of integrity are unacceptable. Loss of availability is difficult to deal with and can only be tolerated for a short time. The consequences could include delay or degradation in providing important support services or commodities that may seriously impact mission effectiveness or operational readiness.	Requires additional safeguards beyond best practices to ensure assurance.
Mission Assurance Category III (MAC III)	Systems handling information that is necessary for the conduct of day-to-day business, but does not materially affect support to deployed or contingency forces in the short-term.	The consequences of loss of integrity or availability can be tolerated or overcome without significant impacts on mission effectiveness or operational readiness. The consequences could include the delay or degradation of services or commodities enabling routine activities.	Requires protective measures, techniques, or procedures generally commensurate with commercial best practices.

Formalized security requirements

Initial concept definition and requirements analysis efforts allow system security engineers the opportunity to develop formal security requirements, which can then be effectively incorporated into system design efforts. Formalized security requirements should address conventional security attributes such as confidentiality, integrity, availability, authorization, and non-repudiation. Further, defined security requirements should contain desired levels of security or assurance [24]. The SEBoK offers nine requirement areas for consideration (Table 1.4) [10].

These security requirement areas set the stage for well-understood and formalized system-level requirements that can be easily understood, accepted, and correctly implemented. Furthermore, defining the requirements upfront allows for clear system-level requirements that lend themselves to easier requirements traceability throughout system development and also provides an effective means to embrace the "build-in not bolt-on" security best practice.

Table 1.4 SSE Requirement Areas [10]

• Physical	• Transmission
• Personnel	• Cryptographic
• Procedural	• Communications
• Emission	• Operations
• Computer Security	

Early design considerations

Early involvement by system security engineers examines the widest solution space possible, and therefore, the best opportunity to positively affect the system development for successful fielding. This is especially true for complex ICT SoS implementations, which have many technical issues to manage. Further, system security engineers should take a top-down design strategy when approaching new system development, traditionally considered a strength of the SE discipline [32]. Expert guidelines, lessons learned, and best practices should be taken into consideration early in system design, when they have the best opportunity to be accepted and implemented. Some overarching security engineering-oriented guidelines for system design are offered [33]:

1. Simple is better, but no simpler than necessary is prudent (unwarranted complexity, over-coupling, and unnecessary dependencies);
2. Having contingencies is a good idea (defining failure and response);
3. Using "watchdogs" distributed throughout the system to monitor and report;
4. Configuring for reduced functionality or graceful shutdown;
5. Modularity of functions to enable isolation of offending operations;
6. Shifting functions based on threats; and
7. Configuring the system for failure (whether accidental or malicious).

Traditional fields of security engineering include security protocols, trust relationships, access controls, and cryptology, with each supplying a vast set of best practices and helpful resources, which should be explored for applicability early in the design phase. For example, defense-in-depth has long been considered a key principle of security engineering and should be applied whenever possible. While this principle remains true, system security engineers must design in detection capabilities and not just prevention tools. There is a subtle difference between detection and prevention requirements; however, the cost and difficulty to implement them can be substantial. System thinking approaches can also aid the development of protection schemes when identifying, defining, and addressing mission-essential tasks, operational environment(s), and system boundaries within the system solution trade-space.

Plan for failure

Given the complexity of modern ICT systems and the rapidly changing threat environment, the system security engineer must plan for system failure. Well-known security engineer Ross Anderson states, "Failure recovery is often the most important aspect of security engineering, yet it is one of the most neglected" [6]. But first, organizations must learn to accept system failure. In order to facilitate organizational change, system security engineers should promote shared understanding through educating decision makers on successful fail-safe strategies and mitigating MPTs. Such strategies generally include a number of technical and non-technical design considerations for fault avoidance, fault tolerance, error recovery, failure recovery, and system resiliency. Fail-safe strategies should then be fully integrated as part of the complete design solution trade-space.

Designing fail-safe, resilient ICT systems is a difficult multidisciplinary endeavor, which system security engineers must become increasingly aware of in high-threat environments [34]. Further, fail-safe engineering requires a detailed understanding of the subject system such that extensive domain expertise may be required.

Security and system patterns

Since 1995, object-oriented software design patterns have proven to be a valuable resource for the software engineering community [35]. The information system community has attempted to develop their own security patterns, defined as "a particular reoccurring security problem that arises in specific contexts, and presents a well-proven generic solution" [36]. These security patterns range from conceptual topics such as risk management to detailed implementation issues like programming language-specific Web-based application security. Formalized patterns have also been extended to system design [37]. While security and system pattern research is still in early development, there could be great benefits in a formalized approach that provides a reusable library of solutions to specific ICT security problems.

Leveraging system architectures for security

System security engineers can evaluate preliminary or proposed system or enterprise architectures to identify and assess security considerations between systems, operators, and networks [38]. System architectures identify and define the system's interactions between people, processes, and various ICT systems including key interfaces and dependencies. DoD Architecture Framework (DoDAF) viewpoints may also help understand and analyze the security trade-space [39].

Specifically, operational views are helpful to identify and understand critical nodes, organizations, and information exchanges while illustrating critical functions along with their dependencies. System and service views help to understand and define system boundaries, inputs, outputs, controls, and supporting mechanisms. The combination of viewpoints supports the identification, understanding, and definition of critical interfaces throughout the system design and development phases. Lastly, the DoDAF offers the possibility of both security views, which facilitate identification and understanding of security points of interest, and verification views, which support system assurance efforts.

Agile and self-organizing system security

An up-and-coming field for SSE is agile system security, which considers designing systems that can detect and proactively respond during unexpected conditions such as cyber attacks. The concept goes well beyond intrusion prevention system responses and enables systems to dynamically respond to uncertain incidents, ensuring continuing operation [40]. Self-organizing systems imply an extremely agile and readily adaptable system configuration capable of reorganizing in response to unexpected system or environmental changes [41,42]. These advanced system designs hold promise for system security engineers.

Security metrics and evaluation

The ability to accurately determine the effectiveness of security solutions is a non-trivial problem that is receiving increased attention as security experts continually attempt to understand the ICT security problem [43]. Security metrics to assess the effectiveness of security solutions is a prevalent area of research both formally and informally [44]. Academic experts and security practitioners have the difficult task of recommending and justifying security expenditures in a cost-constrained, resource-limited environment.

System security engineers need to thoroughly understand the complete risk environment to ensure that recommended and selected security solutions will provide the desired capability. Furthermore, a significant research area exists in measuring and assessing information-centric SoS performance and security metrics [45].

Identified SSE research areas

Ongoing basic research efforts by the INCOSE SSE Working Group are attempting to identify, define, share, and advance modern systems security solutions where no agreed-upon solutions exist. Furthermore, the SSE Working Group is using a commonly understood life cycle approach to promote awareness and adaptability to existing system development efforts [46].

- Conceptual: Explore and advance technology trends and strategies that identify potentially beneficial technologies, advance promising security strategies, or protect desired system capabilities.
- Development: Ensure that security concepts are translated into verifiable requirements with defined levels of effectiveness. Provide functional designs with integrated system solutions facilitating necessary security characteristics.
- Production: Provide insight into security considerations during fabrication, implementation, and integration to ensure security settings and configurations are properly initialized and delivered.
- Operations and Support: Monitor and maintain security effectiveness during the entire system lifetime, including considerations for changes in the operational, user, and threat environments. Ensure security features are updated and effective such that system capabilities are supported or enhanced. Continually assess security features for effectiveness.

Beyond community wide standardization, Steven's Institute has identified a list of potential SSE research areas for further exploration: scalable trustworthy systems; enterprise-level metrics; system evaluation life cycle; combating insider threats; combating malware and botnets; global-scale identity management; survivability of time-critical systems; situational understanding and attack attribution; provenance of information, systems, and hardware; privacy-aware security; and usable security [11].

CONCLUSION

The US DoD continues to have significant challenges and successes in terms of addressing risk, system security, and mission assurance. Modern information-centric systems contain millions of lines of source code controlling critical mission functions through a vast suite of interconnected and distributed systems, sensors, and operators. These complex systems present the difficult challenge of understanding a dynamic integrated suite of people, processes, and technologies in a resource-constrained environment. The US DoD has invested billions of dollars in government, industry, and academic organizations to study, address, and refine this difficult task, with many insights and lessons to be gleamed.

- Performing risk analysis for missions and systems leads to a more complete understanding of the subject system and its associated risks while also identifying potential areas for further mitigation;
- The dynamic nature of modern systems and mission demand continuous monitoring;
- Resource limitations necessitate the utilization of proven best practices for risk analysis techniques and mitigation strategies;
- Continuous process improvement lends itself to the rapidly evolving nature of holistic systems; that is, constantly changing people, processes, and technologies; and
- Determining the effectiveness of risk management, and specifically security solutions, is both an art (i.e., qualitative) and a science (i.e., quantitative).

Recommendations

From this review of established, modern, and emerging SSE MPTs, a number of recommendations can be made for the broader community struggling with ICT system security.

- Foster the development of multidisciplinary professionals trained in the art and science of systems engineering, security engineering, and risk management; these professionals are best situated to understand today's complex systems to holistically manage the dynamic risk environment and provide cost-effective security solutions.
- Promote the discovery and shared understanding of complex systems through awareness, education, training, shared lessons learned, and documented best practices to enable improved security postures of complex ICT systems.
- Further explore identified SSE research areas. In the authors' opinion, the research and application of security-oriented metrics, interoperability performance, and system architectures for security show promise.

Disclaimer

The views expressed in this paper are those of the authors and do not reflect the official policy or position of the United States Air Force, the Department of Defense, or the US Government.

Acknowledgments

This work was supported by the Laboratory for Telecommunications Sciences (grant number 5713400-301-6448).

References

[1] DoD. Military Handbook 1785. System security engineering program management requirements. Washington, DC: Department of Defense; 1995.

[2] Schmoll JH. Introduction to defense acquisition management. 2nd ed. Fort Belvoir: Department of Defense Systems Management College; 1993.

[3] ISO/IEC 21827 ISO/IEC 21827:2008(E) Systems security engineering: Capability maturity model (SSE-CMM), security techniques, information technology. 2nd ed. Geneva, Switzerland: ISO/IEC; 2008.

[4] Irvine C, Nguyen TD. Educating the systems security engineer's apprentice. IEEE Security & Privacy 2010;8(4):58−61.

[5] Schneier B. Secrets and lies: Digital security in a networked world. New York: John Wiley & Sons; 2000.

[6] Anderson R. Security engineering. Indiana: Wiley Publishing; 2008.

[7] Baldwin K, Miller J, Popick P, Goodnight J. The United States Department of Defense revitalization of system security engineering through program protection. Pap presented at the Systems Conference (SysCon), 2012 IEEE International, 2012;1−7.

[8] Lewis JA. Raising the bar for cybersecurity. Center for Strategic and International Studies: Technology & public policy; 2013.

[9] Dove R. Something wicked this way comes … SE responsibility for system security. Unpublished PowerPoint presentation. INCOSE Enchantment Chapter Meeting; 2012 Sep 12.

[10] Pyster A, Olwell D, Hutchison N, Enck S, Anthony J, Henry D, et al. Guide to the systems engineering body of knowledge (SEBoK) Version 1.0. Hoboken, NJ: The Trustees of the Stevens Institute of Technology©; 2012.

[11] Hamilton D, Horowitz B, Neuman C. Systems security engineering final technical report SERC-2010-TR-005. Hudson, NJ: Stephens Institute; 2010.

[12] Baldwin K. Systems security engineering: A critical discipline of systems engineering. Insight 2009;12 (2):113.

[13] Baldwin K, Dahmann J, Goodnight J. System of systems security: A defense perspective. Insight 2012;14(2):113.

[14] Kendall F. Document streamlining—program protection plan (PPP). Washington, DC: Principal Deputy Under Secretary of Defense for Acquisition, Technology, and Logistics; 2011.

[15] Baldwin K. DoD trusted systems and networks (TSN) update. [PowerPoint presentation]. NDIA Cyber Division Breakfast Meeting, Office of the Deputy Assistant Secretary of Defense for Systems Engineering, OUSD(AT&L); 2013.

[16] Defense Acquisition Guide Defense acquisition guidebook [Internet]. Version 16. Oct 2012 [cited 2012]. Retrieved from https://dag.dau.mil.

[17] DoD. DoD Instruction 5000.02. Operation of the Defense Acquisition System. Washington, DC; 2008.

[18] DoD. DoD Instruction 5200.39. Critical Program Information (CPI) Protection Within the DoD. Washington, DC; 2010.

[19] DoD Instruction 5200.44. Protection of mission critical functions to achieve trusted systems and networks (TSN). Washington, DC: DoD Chief Information Officer/Under Secretary of Defense, Acquisition, Technology, and Logistics; 2012 Jul 16.

[20] DoD. DoD 5200.28-STD. Trusted Computer System Evaluation Criteria. 1985 Dec.

[21] DoD Instruction 8510.01. DoD information assurance certification and accreditation process (DIACAP). Washington, DC: Assistant Secretary of Defense for Networks and Information Integration/DoD Chief Information Officer; 2007.

[22] Cussatt, D. DoD IA policy portfolio update. [PowerPoint presentation]. Information Assurance Symposium; 2011.

[23] Drew, C. The next war, costliest jet, years in making, sees the enemy: Budget cuts. [Internet]. New York Times [cited 2012 Nov 29]. Retrieved from: http://www.nytimes.com.

[24] National Defense Industrial Association. Engineering for systems assurance. Assurance Committee. Arlington, VA: National Defense Industrial Association (NDIA); 2008.

[25] Bayuk JL. Systems security engineering. Security & Privacy, IEEE 2011;9(2):72−4.

[26] Global Information Grid [Internet] 2008 Nov 14 [updated 2012 Apr 23; cited 2013 July 9]. Available from: http://www.nsa.gov/ia/programs/global_information_grid/index.shtml.

[27] Systems engineering guide for systems of systems. Version 1.0. Washington, DC: Office of the Deputy Under Secretary of Defense for Acquisition and Technology, Systems and Software Engineering; 2008.

[28] Calvano CN, John P. Systems engineering in an age of complexity. Sys Eng 2004;7(1):25−34.

[29] DoD. DoD Directive 3020.40. DoD Policy and Responsibilities for Critical Infrastructure. Washington, DC; 2012.

[30] DoD Instruction 8500.2. Information assurance (IA) implementation. Washington, DC: Assistance Secretary of Defense for Command, Control, Communications and Intelligence; 2003.

[31] Dove R. Systems of systems and self-organizing security. Insight 2011;14(2):7−10.

[32] Sutton SJ. Securing a system of system: Start with the threats that put the mission at risk. Insight 2011;14(2):15−8.

[33] DeSpain MJ. Toward a dynamic system architecture for enhanced security. Insight 2009;12(2):18−9.

[34] Rieger C. Resilient control systems: A basis for next-generation secure architectures. Insight 2009;12(2):20−1.

[35] Gamma E, Helm R, Johnson R, Vlissides J. Design patterns: Elements of reusable object-oriented software. Boston: Addison-Wesley; 1994.

[36] Schumacher M, Fernandez-Buglioni E, Hybertson D, Buschmann F, Sommerlad P. Security patterns: Integrating security and systems engineering. West Sussex, England: John Wiley & Sons; 2006.

[37] Cloutier RJ, Verma D. Applying the concept of patterns to systems architecture. Sys Eng 2007;10(2):138−54.

[38] Wirsbinski J, Boardman J. Establishing security strategy using systems thinking. Insight 2009;12(2):41−3.

[39] DoD Architectures Framework DoDAF architecture framework. Version 2.0. Washington, DC: DoDAF Working Group; 2009.

[40] Bayuk JL. Systems-of-systems issues in security engineering. Insight 2011;14(2):22−4.

[41] Dove R. Embedding agile security in system architecture. Insight 2009;12(2):14−7.

[42] Nichols C, Dove R. Architectural patterns for self-organizing systems-of-systems. Insight 2011;14(2):42−4.

[43] Chew E, Swanson M, Stine K, Bartol N, Brown A, Robinson W. NIST Special Publication. Performance measurement guide for information security. Gaithersburg, MD: National Institute of Standards and Technology; 2008; sp800-55:Rev1.

[44] Metricon. Seven metrics challenges. [Internet]. In: Proceedings of The Eighth Annual Meeting of Metricon 2013 Mar 1 [cited 2013 Jun 26]. Retrieved from: http://www.securitymetrics.org

[45] Ford TC, Colombi JM, Jacques DR, Graham SR. A general method of measuring interoperability and describing its impact on operational effectiveness. The Journal of Defense Modeling and Simulation: Applications, Methodology, Technology 2009;6(1):17−32.

[46] Dove R. DRAFT System security engineering handbook section. Paper presented at the 2013 INCOSE International Workshop, System Security Engineering Working Group; 2013 Jan 26−29; Jacksonville, FL.

Further reading

INCOSE. INCOSE system engineering handbook. Version 3.2.2. INCOSE-TP-2003-002-03.2.2. San Diego, CA: International Council on Systems Engineering (INCOSE); 2011.

Meier JD, Mackman A, Wastell B, Bansdone P, Taylor J, & Araujo R. Microsoft's Security Engineering Explained. [Internet] 2005. [cited 2013 Aug 23]; Available from: https://www.securityinnovation.com/uploads/SecurityEngineeringExplained.pdf.

Stuart J. Engineering Information Security: The Application of Systems Engineering Concepts to Achieve Information Assurance. Vol 14. Wiley.com; 2011.

Metrics and Indicators as Key Organizational Assets for ICT Security Assessment

Luis Olsina, Alexander Dieser, and Guillermo Covella

National University of La Pampa Engineering School, Santa Rosa, LP, Argentina

INFORMATION IN THIS CHAPTER

- Added value of supporting the ICT Security/Risk assessment area with a well-established measurement and evaluation strategy
- Foundations for a consistent specification of metrics and indicators for Security characteristics and attributes
- Illustration of metrics and indicators from an actual ICT Security and Risk evaluation study

INTRODUCTION

Data and information are basic inputs for many processes. While data usually comes from facts, measures, formula calculations, and so on, information is the meaningful interpretation of data for a given purpose, user viewpoint, and context. Recall the saying, "If you do not know where you are, a map will not help you reach your destination." In the same way, lack of data and information to understand a given situation prevents any effort—even with enough resources—from helping you reach your ultimate goal, such as improvement. We cannot improve what we cannot understand, and we cannot appropriately understand without analyzing consistent data and information. In this chapter, we state that metrics and indicators are basic, yet key, organizational assets to provide suitable data and information for analyzing, recommending, controlling, and monitoring.

With the aim of performing measurement and evaluation (M&E) projects and programs in a systematic way, software organizations should clearly establish an M&E strategy that includes a set of principles, activities, methods, and tools to specify, collect, store, and use trustworthy metrics and indicators and their values [1]. Moreover, in order to make the analysis and decision-making processes more robust, it is necessary to ensure that measures and indicators values are repeatable and comparable among the organization's projects. Therefore, it should be mandatory to store not only M&E data but also metrics and indicators metadata such as, for example, measurement procedure, scale, scale type, unit, elementary indicator model, and acceptability levels.

As a matter of fact, metrics and indicators should be seen as designed and versioned by-products or resources stored in an organizational repository [2]. A metric is the specification of a measurement process description that transforms an entity attribute (i.e., a single quality) into a measure (i.e., data). An elementary indicator is the specification of an evaluation process description, which has as input a metric's measure and produces an indicator value (i.e., contextual information). However, when we look at recognized literature [3−6,1,7], we see that what a metric and an indicator mean and how they fit in for a given M&E project, as well as issues such as why, what, who, when, where, and how (W5H) to measure and evaluate, are very often poorly linked and specified. To make things a bit more complicated, we have often observed a lack of consistent consensus among M&E terminological bases in different recognized standards and manuscripts, or sometimes terms are absent altogether [8]. This is also true for other areas, such as security.

The particular contributions of this paper are: (i) a thorough discussion of the specification of metrics and indicators as versioned by-products for M&E process descriptions; (ii) the illustration of metrics and indicators from an actual ICT security and risk evaluation study, highlighting the importance of recording not only data but also the associated metadata of information needs, context, attributes, metrics, and indicators to ensure repeatability and consistency among an organization's projects; and (iii) the added value of supporting the ICT security/risk assessment area with an M&E strategy, which is based on metrics and indicators. This integrated strategy, named GOCAME (Goal-Oriented Context-Aware Measurement and Evaluation) [2,9], can be used to understand and improve the quality or capability quality of any organizational entity or asset. Specifically, we discuss metric and indicator specifications for vulnerability attributes regarding the "security" characteristic [10] for an information system as the target entity.

It is worth mentioning that vulnerabilities can be seen as inherent weaknesses in a target entity that could be exploited by a threat source. Most of the vulnerable capabilities/attributes of a target system can be identified, for instance, with security controls either that have not been applied or that, while applied, retain some weakness [11]. Hence, understanding the current quality acceptability level met for each vulnerability attribute can help to assess the risk and planning actions for improvement—that is, risk reduction—by implementing the risk treatment from the impact viewpoint. The underlying hypothesis is that each meaningful attribute associated with the target entity to be controlled should show the highest quality satisfaction level as an elementary non-functional requirement. The higher the security quality indicator value achieved for each attribute, the lower the vulnerability indicator value and so also the potential impact.

Following this introduction, we provide an overview of the GOCAME strategy, focusing on its M&E conceptual framework and process (including the W5H issue) to better understand the designing of metrics and indicators. We then analyze concrete metrics and indicators for security, fleshing out their specification templates. Data and metadata stemming from a practical case are analyzed following an abridged presentation of how to link vulnerability attribute values with risk assessment. We review related work and then draw the main conclusions and outline future work.

GOCAME strategy overview

Measurement and analysis is an example of a basic CMMI process area at level 2 of the staged representation [3] intended to support other process areas by means of measures. Therefore, in CMMI measures and their interpretation for a given information need are considered key inputs to assist and analyze all other process areas. Moreover, in order to support consistency in different M&E projects, well-established M&E strategies are also needed. For instance, GOCAME is based on three main principles or capabilities: (i) a conceptual framework utilizing a robust terminological base, (ii) a well-defined M&E process, and (iii) evaluation methods and tools.

GOCAME's first principle is that designing and implementing an M&E program requires a sound M&E conceptual framework. Often, organizations conduct measurement programs that start and stop because the organization doesn't pay enough attention to the way non-functional requirements, contextual properties, metrics, and indicators should be designed, implemented, and analyzed. This endeavor requires an M&E framework built on a rich conceptual base, that is, on an ontological base, which explicitly and formally specifies the main agreed concepts, properties, relationships, and constraints. To accomplish this, we developed the C-INCAMI (Contextual-Information Need, Concept model, Attribute, Metric, and Indicator) framework and its components [2] based on our metrics and indicators ontology [8].

GOCAME's second principle requires a well-established M&E process in order to guarantee repeatability in performance of activities and consistency of results. A process prescribes a set of phases, activities, inputs and outputs, sequences and parallelisms, roles, check points, and so forth. In [12], a process model for GOCAME was proposed that is compliant with both the C-INCAMI conceptual base and its components.

GOCAME's third principle is methods and tools, which can be instantiated from both the conceptual framework and the process. While activities state "what" to do, methods describe "how" to perform these activities, which in turn can be automated by tools.

Next, we outline GOCAME's conceptual framework and general process (and the W5H mnemonic rule) for better understanding the metric and indicator modeling described later in the chapter.

GOCAME conceptual framework

GOCAME is a multi-purpose strategy that follows a goal-oriented and context-sensitive approach in defining and performing M&E projects. GOCAME is a multi-purpose strategy because it can be used to evaluate (i.e., understand, improve, etc.) the quality of entity categories, such as product, system, or resource, by using their instantiated quality models. Moreover, the evaluation focus can vary, ranging, for example, from external quality and non-vulnerability to cost.

GOCAME's first principle is its conceptual framework, which has six components, namely: (i) M&E project, (ii) non-functional requirements, (iii) context, (iv) measurement, (v) evaluation, and (vi) analysis and recommendation. The components shown in Figure 2.1 are described below. For more details, see [2].

The *non-functional requirements* component (the requirements package in Figure 2.1) allows for specifying the information need of any M&E project. It identifies the purpose (e.g., understand, improve, control, etc.) and the user viewpoint (e.g., developer, security administrator, etc). In turn, the component focuses on a calculable concept, such as quality, security, or reliability, and specifies the entity category to evaluate, for example, a resource, a system, and so on. The leaves of an instantiated model (a requirements tree) are attributes associated with an entity category. Thus, information need is defined as "insight necessary to manage objectives, goals, risks, and problems," entity as "a concrete object that belongs to an entity category," and attribute as "a measurable physical or abstract property of an entity category."

The *context* component (the context package) uses a key term, "context," which is defined as "a special kind of entity representing the state of the situation of an entity, which is relevant for a particular information need." Context is a special kind of entity in which related relevant entities are

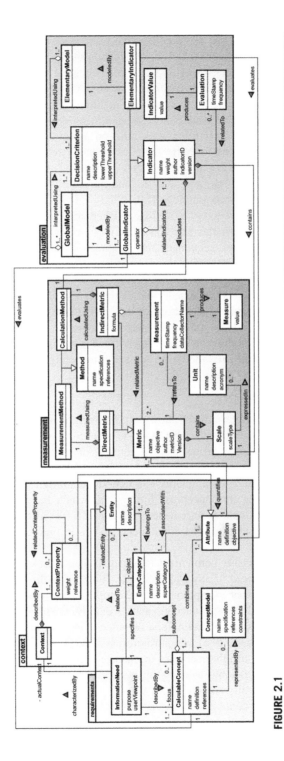

FIGURE 2.1

Main concepts and relationships for the C-INCAMI requirements, context, measurement, and evaluation components.

involved. Related entities can be resources such as a network or security infrastructure, the project itself, and so on. To describe the context, attributes of the relevant entities are used, which are called "context properties" (see details in [13]).

The *measurement* component (the measurement package) allows for specifying the metrics that quantify attributes. To design a metric, the measurement and calculation method (or procedure) and the scale should be defined. Whereas a measurement procedure is applied to a direct metric, a calculation procedure is applied to the formula of an indirect metric. A measurement produces a measure. Measurement is defined as "an activity that uses a metric definition in order to produce a measure's value," while a measure is "the number or category assigned to an attribute of an entity by making a measurement." Hence, for designing a direct metric, two aspects should be clearly specified as metadata, namely, its measurement procedure and its scale. Note that the scale type depends on the nature of the relationship between values of the scale, such as keeping the order and/or distances among categories, in addition to the existence of the zero category (or class), which means absence of the measured attribute. The scale types mostly used in software engineering are classified into nominal, ordinal, interval, ratio, and absolute. Ultimately, each scale type determines the choice of suitable mathematical operations and statistics techniques that can be used to analyze the data.

The *evaluation* component (the evaluation package) includes the concepts and relationships intended to specify the design and implementation of elementary and global evaluations. It is worth mentioning that the selected metrics are useful for a measurement activity as long as the selected indicators are useful for an evaluation activity.

"Indicator" is the main term that allows for specifying how to calculate and interpret the attributes and calculable concepts of a non-functional requirements tree. There are two types of indicators: elementary indicators and partial/global indicators. Elementary indicators evaluate lower-level requirements, namely, attributes. Each elementary indicator has an elementary model that provides a mapping function from the metric's measures (the domain) to the indicator's scale (the range). The new scale is interpreted using agreed-upon decision criteria (also called "acceptability levels"), which help to analyze the level of satisfaction reached by each elementary non-functional requirement; that is, by each attribute. Partial/global indicators evaluate mid-level and higher-level requirements, that is, sub-characteristics and characteristics in a quality model (see, e.g., the instantiated "Security" model in Table 2.1). Different aggregation models (global models) can be used to perform evaluations. The global indicator's value ultimately represents the global degree of satisfaction in meeting the stated information need for a given purpose and user viewpoint. Lastly, an evaluation represents the activity involving a single calculation, following a particular indicator specification—either elementary or global—to produce an indicator value.

GOCAME process and the W5H rule

GOCAME's second principle is its general process, which embraces the following core activities: (i) define non-functional requirements, (ii) design the measurement, (iii) design the evaluation, (iv) implement the measurement, (v) implement the evaluation, and (vi) analyze and recommend. These high-level activities, as well as sequences, parallelisms, inputs, and outputs, are shown in Figure 2.2. Note that a repository is represented by the << datastore >> stereotype. The proposed M&E process follows a goal-oriented approach (see [12] for process details).

Table 2.1 Requirements Tree Specification for "Security"

1. **Security** (see definition in [10])
    1.1. **Confidentiality** [10]
        1.1.1. **Authentication Schema Protectability**
            1.1.1.1. *Authentication Schema Bypass*
        1.1.2. **Session Data Protectability**
            1.1.2.1. *Session Data Theft Protectability*
    1.2. **Integrity** [10]
        1.2.1. **Cross-Site Scripting Immunity**
            1.2.1.1. *Reflected Cross-Site Scripting Immunity*
            1.2.1.2. *Stored Cross-Site Scripting Immunity*
            1.2.1.3. *DOM-based Cross-Site Script. Immunity*
            1.2.1.4. *Cross-site Request Forgery Immunity*
        1.2.2. *Session Data Tampering Protectability*
    1.3. **Authenticity** [10]
        1.3.1. **Session ID Protectability**
            1.3.1.1. *Session ID Theft Protectability*
            1.3.1.2. *Session ID Tampering Protectability*
        1.3.2. **Session Impersonation Protectability**
            1.3.2.1. **Session Management Protectability**
                1.3.2.1.1. *Session ID Expiration*
                1.3.2.1.2. *Session Expiration Due to Idle Timeout*
                1.3.2.1.3. *Re-authentication Mechanism Availability*
                1.3.2.1.4. *Session ID Regeneration Availability*
                1.3.2.1.5. *Keep-me-logged-in Mechanism Availability*
            1.3.2.2. *Session Non-Replay Protectability*
            1.3.2.3. *Session Fixation Protectability*
        1.3.3. **Password Protectability**
            1.3.3.1. *Password Aging Policy*
            1.3.3.2. *String Password Strength*

Once the requirements project has been created, the Define Non-functional Requirements (A1) activity has a specific goal, problem, or risk as input and a nonfunctional specification document as output (which contains the M&E purpose, user viewpoint, focus, entity, instantiated (sub-)characteristics and attributes, and context information). Next, the Design the Measurement (A2) activity allows for selecting the metrics from the Metrics repository to quantify attributes; the output is a metrics specification document. (Each metric specification describes the measurement procedure, scale, and other metadata, as depicted in Table 2.2.)

Once this task is done, the evaluation design and the measurement implementation activities can be performed, in any order or in parallel. The Implement the Measurement (A3) activity uses the specified metrics to obtain the measures, which are stored in the Measures repository. The Design the Evaluation (A4) activity allows for selecting indicators from the Indicators repository. The Implement the Evaluation (A5) activity can now be carried out. Finally, the Analyze and Recommend (A6) activity has as inputs the values (i.e., data) of measures and indicators, the requirements specification document, and the associated metrics and indicators specifications (i.e., metadata) in order to produce a Conclusion/Recommendation report.

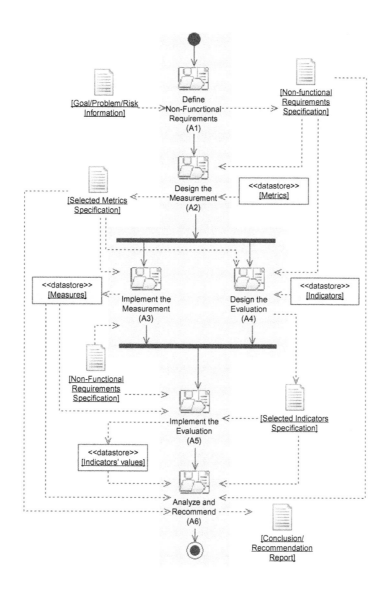

FIGURE 2.2

High-level activities for the GOCAME M&E process (Note that legend "A" means "activity").

Nelson [14] asserts that a "discussion of the why, who, what, where, and when of security metrics brings clarity and further understanding because it establishes a framework for implementing a framework to implement security metrics in your organization" ([14] p.14). We want to reinforce this idea and make it more definitive. GOCAME's three principles mentioned previously—the M&E conceptual framework, process, and methods—help to illustrate the rationale for the W5H mnemonic rule. In the following summary we rely on the general process depicted in Figure 2.2, which in turn is compliant with the terminological framework shown in Figure 2.1.

Table 2.2 Specification of All Metrics Involved in Quantifying the "1.2.1.2. Stored Cross-Site Scripting Immunity" Attribute

Attribute:
    Name: *Stored Cross-Site Scripting Immunity;* **Coded:** 1.2.1.2
    Definition: Stored XSS occurs when a Web application gathers potentially malicious input from a user, then stores that input in a data store for later use (persistent data), so the input that is stored is not correctly filtered. As a consequence, the malicious data will appear to be part of the Web application and run within the user's browser under the privileges of the application.
    Objective: Determine the degree of protection to prevent the execution of offending code through stored data on Web browsers.
Indirect Metric:
    Name: *Ratio of Stored Cross Site Scripting (%SXSS)*
    Objective: Determine the ratio between the number of SXSS vulnerable persistent-data variables and the total number of persistent-data variables taken from the *set of pages* sub-entity.
    Author: Dieser A.; **Version:** 1.0; **Reference:** [15]
Calculation Procedure:

$$\%SXSS = \left(\frac{\#VPDv}{\#PDv} \right) * 100 \;\; if \;\; \#PDv \neq 0$$

Formula:

$$\%SXSS = 0 \;\; if \;\; \#PDv = 0$$

Numerical Scale:
    Representation: Continuous; **Value Type:** Real
    Scale Type: Ratio
    Unit/Name: Percentage; **Acronym:** %
Related Metrics:
    1) *Number of vulnerable persistent-data variables (#VPDv);* and 2) *Total number of persistent-data variables (#PDv)*
Attribute: Amount of vulnerable persistent-data variables
Direct Metric: Name: *Number of vulnerable persistent-data variables (#VPDv)*
    Objective: Count the total number of SXSS vulnerable persistent-data variables within the *set of pages* sub-entity.
    Author: Dieser A.; Version: 1.0; Reference: [16]
Measurement Procedure/Type: Objective
Specification:
#VPDv = 0
For each persistent-data variable within the *set of pages*:
Set or replace the persistent-data variable value with any javascript code that triggers a response from the Web browser (as per [16] <script > alert(document.cookie) </script>); perform the corresponding action to store the value into the back end.
If the browser executes the injected javascript code instead of displaying the value of the persistent-data variable
then #VPDv = #VPDv + 1
Numerical Scale:
    Representation: Discrete; **Value Type:** Integer
    Scale Type: Absolute
    Unit/Name: vulnerable persistent-data var.; **Acronym:** PDv
Attribute: *Amount of persistent-data variables*
Direct Metric: Name: *Total number of persistent-data variables (#PDv)*

(Continued)

Table 2.2 (Continued)

Objective: Count the total number of persistent-data variables in the *set of pages* sub-entity;
Author: Dieser A.; Version: 1.0; Reference: [16]
Measurement Procedure/Type: Objective
Specification:
Note: A persistent-data variable is a user input that is stored into the back end (e.g., a database) and displayed by the application.
$\#PDv = 0$
For each page within the *set of pages* sub-entity:
Identify all text fields or text areas longer than X_{min} characters (e.g., 40 characters as per [16]) where the user input is stored into the back end; fill them with test data (i.e., any javascript code that triggers a response from the Web browser; see [16]), and store them into the back end.
For each test data already stored: *If* is displayed in at least one page from the *set of pages*, *then*
$\#PDv = \#PDv + 1$;
Numerical Scale:
Representation: Discrete; **Value Type:** Integer;
Scale Type: Absolute;
Unit/Name: Persistent-data variable; **Acronym:** PDv

Why should an organization tackle the M&E endeavor? The answer might be depicted in the M&E project definition and instantiation and supported by a broader quality assurance policy. Basically, there is a problem or an issue (see the goal/problem/risk input to A1, in Figure 2.2) that requires a solution driven by analysis and decision-making. For instance, the organization needs to reduce some particular entity vulnerabilities; however, as stated earlier, it cannot improve what it cannot understand, and it cannot appropriately understand without consistently analyzing data and information. The *why* aspect therefore embraces the concrete information need and purpose for M&E such as understand, improve, and control some relevant objective, regarding a specific user viewpoint.

What is to be measured and evaluated? This embraces the concrete target entity—and related entities including context—that belongs to an entity category. In addition, a given information need is described by a focus (e.g., the security calculable concept) to which attributes are combined. Moreover, entities cannot be measured and evaluated directly but only by means of their associated attributes and context properties. Ultimately, the non-functional requirements specification artifact (see Figure 2.2) documents to a great extent the why and the what.

How are the metric and indicator specifications developed? Metrics and indicators are reusable, versioned assets stored in organizational repositories and are selected by the A2 and A4 activities, respectively, at design time, then implemented by the A3 and A5 activities accordingly. As we analyze later in the chapter, metric and indicator specifications should be considered metadata that must be kept linked through metricID and indicatorID (for consistency reasons) to measure and indicator values produced for the A3 and A5 activities. Metadata and data sets are consumed by the A6 activity, as well.

Who is responsible for the different stages of an M&E project? Certainly, there are different levels of responsibilities and roles. In the C-INCAMI M&E project definition component (not shown in Figure 2.1), related project concepts allow for recording the responsible information. In addition, "author name" is a common field for both metric and indicator specifications and represents their creator as a piece of design. The "data collector name" (see the "measurement" term in Figure 2.1) allows for recording the name of the person responsible for data gathering for the A3 activity.

When do components of the M&E project occur? *When* is also recorded for each enacted measurement and evaluation. Basic questions to ask include (among others): When are metrics collected? How often are they collected? When are evaluations and analysis performed? For example, the time stamp and frequency fields under the measurement and evaluation terms allow for recording measurements and evaluations when A3 and A5 are executed.

Where is the M&E project running? Where is the entity under evaluation placed? In which context is the target entity measured and evaluated? Where is data collection for metrics performed? Some of these questions can be taken into account by the C-INCAMI M&E project definition component, including the recorded context and its associated context properties and values.

Next, we use the W5H rule to illustrate some security attributes, metrics, indicators and their outcomes for a Web application. We also discuss how to link security with risk.

Security evaluation for a web system: A proof of concept

One of the stated contributions of this chapter, as discussed in the introduction, is that metrics and indicators are key organizational assets for providing relevant data and information for analyzing, recommending, controlling, and ultimately making decisions. From the specification standpoint, metrics and indicators are designed by-products stored in an organizational repository and can be reused. For this aim, in this Section we illustrate some metrics and indicators from a practical ICT security and risk evaluation case, highlighting the importance of recording not only values but also the associated metadata, among other aspects.

Target entity and information need

One item of the above-mentioned W5H mnemonic rule considers *what* is to be measured and evaluated. In this study, we use a fictitious name for an actual concrete target entity, the "XYZ register system," a student management Web system used widely in Argentinean universities. It is a Web application or system (from the entity category standpoint) commonly used by students, professors, and faculty members.

So, *why* should it be evaluated? Because a concrete information need was raised in early 2012 by the responsible ICT department in the ABC organization—again, a fictitious name for a real-world organization. This information need arose because of security risks from various potential threats such as students using system vulnerabilities to change their poor grades. Note that if this threat materialized, the impact on the institution's credibility could be high.

Thus, the purpose of this information need is first to understand the current satisfaction level achieved for the external quality of the XYZ Web application, particularly for non-vulnerabilities regarding the security quality focus, from the security administrator user viewpoint. Once the indicators are analyzed and the values are measured, the current security quality satisfaction level can be determined. The purpose is then to improve the system in the areas with weakly performing indicators. The ultimate purpose is to reduce security risks by improving vulnerable attributes in the Web system by risk treatment. (Note that this paper deals primarily with the documentation of the first purpose. However, change actions were taken after yielded outcomes.)

Security characteristic specification

There is abundant literature in the ICT security area ([5,14,7,15], to mention a few), and often "security" refers to the CIA (confidentiality, integrity and availability) triad (from the non-functional viewpoint). In the ISO 25010 external (system) quality model [10], security is one of eight characteristics, which in turn is split into five sub-characteristics, namely: confidentiality, integrity, non-repudiation, accountability, and authenticity. Availability is a sub-characteristic of the reliability characteristic. Security is defined as the "degree to which a product or system protects information and data so that persons or other products or systems have the degree of data access appropriate to their types and levels of authorization" [10]. We use this ISO characteristic and three sub-characteristics for the XYZ case study. (Note that in [9] we have extended/updated some ISO 25010 (sub-)characteristics.)

Recall Figure 2.2, which shows that the output of the A1 activity is the non-functional requirements specification artifact, which mainly documents the *why* and *what* aspects. Table 2.1 represents the requirements tree instantiated for the security characteristic and its sub-characteristics such as confidentiality (coded 1.1), integrity (1.2) and authenticity (1.3). For example, integrity is defined in [10] as the "degree to which a system, product or component prevents unauthorized access to, or modification of, computer programs or data." Moreover, we have identified all sub-sub-characteristics such as cross-site scripting immunity (1.2.1), which we define as the "degree to which the system ensures the integrity of data by providing cross-site scripting immunity capabilities" [10]. Also, we have specified 18 measurable attributes, which are italicized in Table 2.1.

As proof of concept, we illustrate the 1.2.1.2 attribute named "Stored Cross-Site Scripting Immunity" (XSS), which is described in Table 2.2. The objective for evaluating it is to determine the degree to prevent the execution of offending code trough stored data on Web browsers. Stored XSS is particularly dangerous in application areas where a user with high privileges has access. Thus, when the administrator visits the vulnerable page, its browser automatically executes an attack. This might expose sensitive information such as session authorization tokens [16]. Below, the attribute's metrics and elementary indicator are thoroughly specified.

Metric and indicator specifications

As discussed in the section titled "GOCAME Process and the W5H Rule," the W5H rule's *how* aspect deals with the metric and indicator specifications. Once the non-functional requirements are specified, the A2 activity is performed. This consists of selecting the meaningful metrics from the Metrics repository (Figure 2.2) that quantify attributes. One metric should be assigned per each attribute of the requirements tree respectively; for example, the indirect metric named "Ratio of Stored Cross-Site Scripting" was selected for quantifying the 1.2.1.2 attribute. Table 2.2 shows that this indirect metric is composed of two related direct metrics, which are also fully specified in the template. Note that an indirect metric usually has attributes of related metrics that may not be part of regular attributes shown in the requirements tree; they are necessary to quantify indirect metrics, so this information should also be linked.

While an indirect metric has a calculation method for its formula specification, a direct metric has a measurement method or procedure. For instance, the measurement procedure for the #VPDv direct metric is objective; that is, it does not depend on human judgment when the measurement is performed. The measurement method represents the counting rule, as shown in the template's specification tag. Here, the "set of pages" sub-entity is a collection of pages chosen by evaluators from the XYZ entity according to its relevance regarding potential security impact; that is, each page is chosen given that potential vulnerabilities on it could compromise the application security.

Lastly, in many cases, a software tool can automate the measurement procedure, so this field can be added to the metric template, as well.

The metric template (see Table 2.2), as a designed and stored by-product/resource used by the A2 and A3 activities, includes metadata such as scale, scale type, unit, measurement/calculation procedure specification, tool, version, author, etc. These metric metadata allow for repeatability among M&E projects and consistency in the further analysis of data sets.

Once all metrics are selected for quantifying the 18 attributes in Table 2.1, then the A4 activity should be performed, which deals with designing the evaluation. As discussed in the section titled "GOCAME Conceptual Framework," an elementary indicator evaluates the satisfaction level reached for an elementary requirement, that is, an attribute of the requirements tree. At the same time, a partial/global indicator evaluates the satisfaction level achieved for partial (sub-characteristic) and global (characteristic) requirements.

Table 2.3 specifies the "Performance Level of the Stored Cross-Site Scripting Immunity" (P_SXSS) elementary indicator. This indicator will help to determine the quality satisfaction level reached by the 1.2.1.2 attribute, considering the measured value of its indirect metric (as we analyze in the section titled "Implementing the M&E"). Conversely to metrics, indicators have decision criteria for data interpretation, which ultimately means information in context. As shown in Table 2.3, three acceptability levels useful for the interpretation of indicator values in percentage are employed after an agreement with evaluation stakeholders. A value between 0 and eighty represents an "Unsatisfactory" level and means that change actions must be taken with high priority; a

---

Table 2.3 Elementary Indicator Template Used for Interpreting the "Stored Cross-Site Scripting Immunity" Attribute

Attribute: *Stored Cross-Site Scripting Immunity* **Coded:** 1.2.1.2 **Elementary Indicator:**
    Name: *Performance Level of the Stored Cross-Site Scripting Immunity (P_SXSS)*
    Author: Dieser A. **Version:** 1.0
Elementary Model:
    Specification: the mapping is: P_ SXSS = 100 iff %SXSS = 0; P_ SXSS = 90 iff %SXSS < %SXSS$_{MAX}$;
    P_ SXSS = 0 iff %SXSS >= %SXSS$_{MAX}$ where %SXSS is the indirect metric in Table 2.2. Note that the
    %SXSS$_{MAX}$ is an agreed parameter (threshold) of 2% for the XYZ case study.
Decision Criterion: [Three Acceptability Levels]
    Name 1: Unsatisfactory; **Range:** if 0 ≤ P_SXSS ≤ 80
      Description: Indicates change actions must be taken with high priority
    Name 2: Marginal; **Range:** if 80 < P_SXSS ≤ 98
      Description: Indicates a need for improvement actions
    Name 3: Satisfactory;Satisfactory **Range**: if 98 < P_SXSS ≤ 100
      Description: Indicates no need for current actions
Numerical Scale:
    Value Type: Real; **Scale Type:** Ratio
    Unit/Name: Percentage; **Acronym:** %

value between 80 and 98 represents a "Marginal" level and means improvement actions should be taken; a value between 98 and 100 corresponds to the "Satisfactory" acceptability level.

Each elementary indicator has an elementary model specification (see Table 2.3) that provides a mapping function from the metric's measures (the domain) to the indicator's scale (the range). In this evaluation all indicator scales are normalized to the percentage unit.

Consider the *how* for a global indicator, which evaluates characteristics and sub-characteristics in a requirements tree: it has similar metadata, as shown for the elementary indicator template. But instead of an elementary model it has a global (aggregation) model. An example of a global model is LSP (Logic Scoring of Preference) [17], which was used in many studies [9,18]. LSP is a weighted multi-criteria aggregation model, which has operators for modeling three kinds of relationships among inputs (that can be attributes, sub-characteristics, and characteristics of a requirements tree), namely: simultaneity (i.e., a set of C [conjunctive] operators), replaceability (i.e., a set of D [disjunctive] operators), and neutrality (i.e., the A operator). For instance, the CA moderate conjunction operator is used (as can be observed in the third column of Table 2.4) for modeling the simultaneity criterion among the 1.1, 1.2, and 1.3 security sub-characteristics. At evaluation time, if one input were zero, the output will yield zero, given the mandatory nature of the CA operator. Ultimately, an aggregation model may impose weight and operator constraints over quality model elements. The equation below follows the specification of the LSP aggregation model:

$$P/GI(r) = (W_1 * I_1^r + W_2 * I_2^r + ... + W_m * I_m^r)^{1/r} \tag{1}$$

where P/GI represents the partial/global indicator to be calculated; I_i stands for the (elementary) indicator value and the following holds $0 <= I_i <= 100$ in a percentage unit; W_i represents weights, where the sum of weights for an aggregation block must fulfill: $W_1 + W_2 + \cdots + W_m = 1$, and $W_i > 0$, for $i = 1$ to m, where m is the number of elements (sub-concepts) at the same level in the tree's aggregation block (note that "weights" represents relative importance of elements in a given aggregation block); and r is a parameter selected to achieve the desired logical simultaneity, neutrality, or replaceability relationship.

As result of carrying out the whole M&E design and selection process—activities A1, A2, and A4 in Figure 2.2—the following artifacts are yielded: the nonfunctional requirements specification, the metrics specification, and the indicators specification documents.

Implementing the M&E

Aspects of the W5H rule's *when* and *where* are strongly related to the Implement the Measurement and Implement the Evaluation activities. Particularly, for each executed M&E project, the A3 and A5 activities produce measure and indicator values, respectively, at given moments in time and at specific frequencies.

Considering the W5H rule, we can indicate that data collection for direct metrics was performed by September, 2012, over the XYZ's "set of pages" sub-entity (which were 20 relevant pages), in the context of the ABC institution.

In our example case, the calculated %SXXS indirect metric value yields 25%. This value comes from gathering the data of both direct metrics—resulting in #VPDv = 3 and #PDv = 12 respectively, following their specified measurement procedures—and using its (Table 2.2) formula. In a preliminary analysis, we observe that three well-identified persistent-data variables on "XYZ" are

Table 2.4 Indicator Values in [%] for Security.

Characteristic and Attribute	W	Op.	EI	PI	GI
1. Security		CA			17.67
1.1. Confidentiality	0.33	C--		100	
1.1.1.	0.6				
1.1.1.1.	1		100		
1.1.2.	0.4				
1.1.2.1.	1		100		
1.2. Integrity	0.33	C--		10.54	
1.2.1.	0.8	C-		1.08	
1.2.1.1.	0.25		100		
1.2.1.2.	0.25		0		
1.2.1.3.	0.25		100		
1.2.1.4.	0.25		0		
1.2.2.	0.2		100		
1.3. Authenticity	0.33	C--		12.47	
1.3.1.	0.45	C-		3.51	
1.3.1.1.	0.5		50		
1.3.1.2.	0.5		0		
1.3.2.	0.45	C--		32.75	
1.3.2.1.	0.3	A		40	
1.3.2.1.1.	0.3		100		
1.3.2.1.2.	0.2		0		
1.3.2.1.3.	0.2		0		
1.3.2.1.4.	0.2		0		
1.3.2.1.5.	0.1		100		
1.3.2.2.	0.35		0		
1.3.2.3.	0.35		100		
1.3.3.	0.1	A		0	
1.3.3.1.	0.4		0		
1.3.3.2.	0.6		0		

W Stands for Weight; Op. Stands for LSP Operator; EI Stands for Elementary Indicator; P/GI Stands for Partial/Global Indicator
Light gray represents a value that falls between 98–100; black represents a value that falls between 80–98 (as none of the values fall between this range it is not shown in this table); and dark gray means a value that falls between 0–80.

vulnerable for this kind of attack (see 1.2.1.2 attribute definition in Table 2.2). (Note that we could use the #VPDv direct metric alone instead of the %SXXS indirect metric for quantifying 1.2.1.2, but an indirect metric, as proportion, conveys a bit of information).

While measurement produces data, evaluation produces contextual information. Hence, the level of quality (non-vulnerability) achieved by the 1.2.1.2 attribute should be appropriately interpreted by applying the elementary indicator specified in Table 2.3. Enacting the P_SXSS elementary model, the 25% metric value maps to the 0% indicator value, as shown in the fourth column of Table 2.4. This outcome falls at the bottom of the "Unsatisfactory" acceptability level, meaning that a change action with high priority must be taken for this attribute, because it represents an actual security vulnerability.

Once all measurements and elementary evaluations for interpreting the 18 attributes are performed, the aggregation model (see Equation 1) using the agreed-upon weights and LSP operators should be executed. This model yields partial and global indicators values, as shown in the last two columns of Table 2.4.

The A6 activity (analyze and recommend) has inputs of: the values of measures and indicators (e.g., information shown in Table 2.4), the non-functional requirements specification document, and the associated metrics and indicators specifications (i.e., metadata as shown in Tables 2.1, 2.2, and 2.3) in order to produce the conclusion/recommendation report.

In the next section we give some clues on how to link the security quality M&E approach with the risk assessment and treatment issues. We also introduce some basic concepts for the ICT risk area.

Risk and security vulnerability issues

There are abundant standards and much research in software risk management (SRM), risk assessment processes, and techniques, as well as in risk vocabularies, including [19,3,20,21,11], among others. However, an ontology for the risk domain as we have specified for metrics (measurement) and indicators (evaluation) is, to the best of our knowledge, still missing. Here, without entering in specific discussions of the risk terminological base, some terms defined in the section titled "GOCAME Conceptual Framework," such as as "entity" and "attribute," are used.

Entity categories such as software development/service project, product, and system and its components involve risks at different developmental or operative stages that can be identified, assessed, controlled, treated, and monitored using a systematic SRM approach. A risk can be defined as an undesirable consequence of an event on a target entity. This target object represents an organizational asset, where an asset is an entity with added value for an organization. Potential losses affecting the asset are also called the "impact" of the risk. Also, the term "vulnerability" is commonly used in the security area, which refers to a weakness of an entity that can be exploited by a threat source (entity).

SRM suggests actions to, for example, prevent risk or reduce its impact on a target entity instead of dealing with its further consequences. Thus, we can identify the most relevant attributes associated with an entity that can be more vulnerable (weak) from triggered external/internal events. Then, by understanding the relevant attributes' strengths and weaknesses,—by using an evaluation-driven approach such as GOCAME, for example—actions for change can be recommended and planned for further treatment implementation.

Usually, SRM includes a set of policies, processes, methods, techniques, and tools to identify and analyze risks, understand weaknesses, prepare preventive/perfective actions, and control risks on the target entity. Particularly, for risk assessment three general activities are proposed in [21], namely: (i) Risk Identification, (ii) Risk Analysis, and (iii) Risk Evaluation. Additionally, Establishing the Context, Risk Treatment, Risk Monitoring and Review, and Communication are common processes for a well-established SRM strategy.

For example, the Risk Evaluation activity is defined as "the process of comparing the results of risk analysis with risk criteria to determine whether the risk and/or its magnitude is acceptable or tolerable," and it assists in the decision about risk treatment, which is defined as "the process to modify risk" [20]. In fact, risk treatment can involve: (i) avoiding the risk by deciding not to start or continue with the activity that gives rise to the risk, (ii) taking or increasing risk in order to pursue an opportunity, (iii) removing the risk source, (iv) changing the likelihood (probability), (v) changing the consequences, (vi) sharing the risk with another party or parties, and (vii) retaining the risk by informed decision.

Returning to our example case, if we apply item (v) to designing the measurement, evaluation, and improvement plan, then the plan should describe actions to understand the current situation on the target entity vulnerabilities, then try to reduce the risk consequences of it. Following the GOCAME strategy, the system (target entity) vulnerability attributes, metrics, and indicators should be identified and selected in order to manage the risk status and determine whether the risk is reduced after treatment. The underlying hypothesis is that each meaningful attribute to be controlled should meet the highest quality satisfaction level as an elementary non-functional requirement. Therefore, the higher the security quality indicator value achieved for each attribute, the lower the vulnerability indicator value and, consequently, the potential impact. In percentage terms, we can easily transform the quality elementary indicator value to the vulnerability elementary indicator value as follows:

Vulnerability Indicator value for Attribute $A_i (VI\_A_i) = 100 -$ Quality Indicator value A_i;   (2)

Note that the elementary model and acceptability levels shown in Table 2.3 can be also transformed accordingly for the new vulnerability indicator, if needed. So for each relevant attribute A_i of the requirements tree (as in Table 2.1), we can calculate the risk elementary indicator value (magnitude) by slightly adapting the well-known formula:

Risk Indicator value for Attribute A_i (RI_A_i) = Probability of Event occurrence for $A_i * VI\_A_i$;

(3)

Let us suppose that for the 1.2.1.2 attribute, the probability of an attack occurrence is determined to be 0.7; then the risk magnitude is calculated as $RI\_A_{1.2.1.2} = 0.7 * 100 = 70\%$, where 100 stems from $VI\_A_{1.2.1.2}$ (see Equation 2 and the $A_{1.2.1.2}$ value in Table 2.4). Moreover, the aggregation model specified in Equation 1 can be used for calculating the current state of partial and global risk indicators based on risk elementary indicator magnitudes. It is worth mentioning that GOCAME methods for evaluation are based on multi-criteria (attribute) decision analysis, which can also be used for risk assessment, as indicated in [21].

In short, our approach allows accomplishing the above plan with specified actions to first understand the current situation on the target entity vulnerabilities, and then to try to reduce the impact on it by performing improvement change actions on weakly benchmarked attributes/capabilities. So as the reader may surmise, the risk reduction—per each vulnerability attribute or per aggregated characteristic—can be calculated after improvement actions (risk treatment) and re-evaluation are performed.

The purpose of this discussion is to provide a starting point for how to intertwine our quality M&E approach with security and risk assessment and treatment issues. The topic will be thoroughly analyzed in future writings.

Metrics and indicators for repeatable and consistent analysis: a discussion

We have shown in Tables 2.2 and 2.3 the specification of security metrics and a quality elementary indicator, which are seen as reusable resources and versioned by-products for M&E process descriptions. It is worth restating that metric and indicator specifications should be considered metadata that must be kept linked, for the sake of analysis comparability and consistency, to measures (i.e., data) and indicator values (i.e., information shown in Table 2.4).

Let's suppose, as proof of the concept, that the same "Stored Cross-Site Scripting Immunity" (1.2.1.2) attribute can be quantified by two metrics. (Note that, in Figure 2.1, an attribute can be quantified for many metrics, but just one must be selected for each concrete M&E project.) One direct metric (DM_1) in the Metrics repository is the "Number of Vulnerable Persistent-Data Variables" (#VPDv), as specified in Table 2.2. The other metric (DM_2) has a different measurement method and scale type; that is, DM_2 considers the criticality of existing vulnerable persistent-data variables as a measurement procedure and a categorical scale, specifically, an ordinal scale type with values ranging from 0 to 3, where 3 represents the higher criticality (catastrophic category), and 0 the lower. After many M&E projects using the same security (sub-)characteristics and attributes are executed, all collected data are recorded in the Measure repository. In some projects, DM_1 was used, and in others, DM_2 was used for quantifying the same 1.2.1.2 attribute. Then, if metric metadata of recorded data were not linked appropriately—say, to the measured value of 3, which can stem from both metrics in different projects—the A6 activity will produce inconsistent analysis if it takes all these related projects as inputs. The inconsistency is due to the 3 value, which, depending on the metric used, has different scale properties. (Recall that each scale type determines the choice of suitable mathematical operations and statistics techniques that can be used to analyze data and datasets.) In summary, even if the attribute is the same, the two metric measures are not comparable.

We have discussed the fact that metric and indicator (metadata) specifications can both be regarded as versioned by-products. That is, each metric specification must have unique metricID fields and versions in order to keep traceability, repeatability, and comparable accuracy in different analyses. Let's suppose two metrics have the same ID, since both share most of the same metadata specification—for example, the same measurement procedure, scale, scale type, unit, etc.—but differ from each other only in the tool that automates the same measurement procedure specification. We suggest that, to ensure comparable accuracy, both metrics should share the same ID but differ in the metric version (e.g. v1.0 and v1.1). However, in other cases with more meaningful metadata variations, in order to guarantee repeatability and accuracy, the version field should be a must. Furthermore, metrics in many cases are different; that is, they must not share the same ID, although they are intended to quantify the same attribute. This is so for the abovementioned DM_1 and DM_2, which are different metrics.

Here we analyze some of the values of the indicators shown in Table 2.4 with respect to the usefulness of data and information for the A6 activity. Security as a global quality indicator value (17.67) falls in the lower threshold of the "Unsatisfactory" acceptability level, so an urgent action of change is recommended. We see that, at the sub-characteristic level, 1.1 (confidentiality) is satisfactory (100%), but both 1.2 (integrity) and 1.3 (authenticity) partial indicator values are at the bottom of the "Unsatisfactory" range. As a general conclusion, it emerges that XYZ should strengthen these two sub-characteristics. To improve them, we have to analyze and plan which change actions should be prioritized, considering, for instance, the poorly benchmarked elementary quality indicators and their potential risk consequences.

For instance, for Integrity, and particularly for the 1.2.1 sub-characteristic, the 1.2.1.2 ("Performance Level of the Stored Cross-Site Scripting Immunity"), and the 1.2.1.4 elementary indicator values are 0%, whereas all attributes in the group must satisfy 1.2.1 simultaneously due to the C- operator. In order to analyze the cause of the 1.2.1.2 bad indicator performance, we have to look at data coming from its indirect metric value. The %SXXS value is 25%, which was calculated using the formula in Table 2.2 from #VPDv = 3 and #PDv = 12, respectively. So there are three identified vulnerable persistent-data variables to be improved within the concrete set of pages for XYZ.

Ultimately, by using our strategy based on metrics and indicators, it was possible, first, to understand at that moment (by September, 2012) the situation on the XYZ vulnerabilities, and then, by the end of 2012, to reduce their impact by performing improvement actions on weakly benchmarked attributes/capabilities. As the reader can surmise, in order to increase the 1.2.1.2 indicator value to 100%, the three vulnerable persistent-data variables identified must be fixed. So metric specifications also help to design and implement the change actions for the improvement plan.

Related work

Considering the research literature, what metrics and indicators mean and where they properly fit in with regard to specific M&E processes and strategy have often been understated or neglected. Furthermore, there are abundant standards and much research in areas such as measurement and analysis [22,3,4,6,1], and ICT security and risk assessment [19,5,21,11,7], but issues such as why, what, who, when, where, and how to measure and evaluate have often been poorly intertwined and specified.

For instance, as quoted in the section titled "GOCAME Process and the W5H Rule," Nelson states that a "discussion of the why, who, what, where, and when of security metrics brings clarity and further understanding because it establishes a framework for implementing a framework to implement security metrics in your organization." Nevertheless, in our opinion, Nelson fails to discuss the W5H mnemonic rule with more robust conceptual grounds, as we did based on GOCAME first and second principles introduced in the section titled, "GOCAME Strategy Overview." Moreover, the *how* issue, which precisely deals with metric and indicator specifications, is also left aside when the author remarks "How is left as an exercise for the reader" ([14], p.14).

We have developed an integrated M&E strategy that we call "GOCAME," which is made up of three capabilities: the conceptual framework, the process, and the methodology. The metric and indicator ontology used by the C-INCAMI conceptual framework has similarities to the one presented in [23] and then slightly refined in [24]. However, in [8], we have modeled some terms (e.g., elementary indicator, global indicator, etc.) and some relationships (e.g., measurement and measure, metric and indicator, among others) that differ semantically with those proposed in [24]. In addition, we have enlarged the metric and indicator ontology with context terms and relationships [13], while in [24] these are missing. Moreover, GOCAME exhibits a terminological correspondence between the C-INCAMI conceptual framework and process specifications.

Lastly, in order to support repeatability and consistency of results among different evaluation and analysis projects, well-established M&E strategies are needed. In [18], two integrated strategies,

GQM$^+$Strategies [22] and GOCAME, were thoroughly assessed and analyzed. The study drew GQM$^+$Strategies' performance lower than GOCAME regarding the suitability of the conceptual base and framework. Note that GQM$^+$Strategies enhances the GQM (Goal-Question-Metric) approach [25], though GQM$^+$Strategies completely reuses the GQM. Authors in [1] pointed out that GQM is not intended to define metrics at a level of detail suitable to ensure that they are trustworthy; in particular, whether or not they are repeatable. In addition, contrary to the GOCAME strategy, GQM lacks a sound conceptual base; therefore, it cannot assure that M&E values (and their associated metadata) are consistent and trustworthy for further analysis among projects.

Ultimately, the sound and complete specification of metrics and indicators, as shown in Tables 2.2 and 2.3, outperforms the examined ones in related research works.

CONCLUSION AND FUTURE WORK

To conclude this chapter, we would like to highlight the main contributions listed in the introduction. To provide a thorough discussion about the specification of metrics and indicators as versioned by-products or resources for M&E process descriptions is one of the main drivers of the chapter. We argue that metrics and indicators are reusable organizational assets for providing suitable and consistent data and information for analyzing, recommending, improving, monitoring, and, ultimately, decision-making processes. Toward this end, we discuss why metric and indicator specifications should be considered valuable metadata that have to be linked by means of their IDs (and versions) to measure values (i.e., data and datasets) and indicator values (i.e., information). Additionally, we illustrate specific metrics and elementary/global indicators for a real security/risk M&E case, highlighting the importance of recording not only data but also the associated metadata of information needs, context (not exemplified here for space reasons), attributes, metrics, and indicators to ensure repeatability and comparability of analysis among an organization's projects. This illustration is made considering the six key items raised by using the W5H rule.

Lastly, metrics and indicators are designed assets useful for supporting M&E for any entity category and domain. They are not isolated by-products or resources, but rather the building blocks used, for example, by the integrated GOCAME strategy, which is based on three main pillars, namely: (i) a conceptual framework utilizing a robust terminological base, (ii) a well-defined M&E process, and (iii) evaluation methods and tools. The added value of specifically supporting the ICT security/risk area with a quality M&E strategy is highlighted, as well.

Regarding future work, an ontology for the security/risk assessment area is, to the best of our knowledge, missing yet, so we are considering its further development. This can benefit the instantiation of more robust strategies, processes, and methods.

References

[1] Kitchenham B, Hughes R, Linkman S. Modeling software measurement data. IEEE Transactions on Software Engineering 2001;27(9):788−804.
[2] Olsina L, Papa F, Molina H. How to measure and evaluate web applications in a consistent way. In: Springer, HCIS Series; Web engineering: Modeling and implementing web applications. Rossi G, Pastor O, Schwabe D, Olsina L, editors. 2008;385−420.

[3] CMMI Product Team. CMMI for development. Version 1.3. CMU/SEI-2010-TR-033, USA; 2010.

[4] Goethert W, Fisher M. Deriving enterprise-based measures using the balanced scorecard and goal-driven measurement techniques. Software engineering measurement and analysis initiative, CMU/SEI-2003-TN-024. [Internet]. 2003. http://repository.cmu.edu/cgi/viewcontent.cgi?article=1541&context=sei.

[5] ISO/IEC 27004. Information technology − security techniques − information security management − measurement; 2009.

[6] ISO/IEC 15939. International standard, information technology − software engineering: Software measurement process. Geneva, Switzerland; 2002.

[7] NIST SP 800-55. Performance measurement guide for information security. [Internet]. July 2008 [cited Jan 2013]. Available from: <http://csrc.nist.gov/publications/PubsSPs.html>.

[8] Olsina L, Martín M. Ontology for software metrics and indicators. In: Journal of Web Engineering. Rinton Press: New Jersey. 2004;2(4)262−81.

[9] Olsina L, Lew P, Dieser A, Rivera B. Updating quality models for evaluating new generation web applications. In: Journal of Web Engineering, Special issue: Quality in new generation web applications. Rinton Press: New Jersey. 2012;11(3):209−246.

[10] ISO/IEC 25010. Systems and software engineering − systems and software product quality requirements and evaluation (SQuaRE). System and software quality models; 2011.

[11] NIST SP 800-30. Guide for conducting risk assessments. [Internet]. 2011 Sep [accessed Jan 2013]. Available at http://csrc.nist.gov/publications/PubsSPs.html.

[12] Becker P, Molina H, Olsina L. Measurement and evaluation as quality driver.In: ISI Journal (Ingénierie des Systèmes d'Information), Special Issue: Quality of Information Systems. Lavoisier: Paris. 2010; 15(6):33−62.

[13] Molina H, Rossi G, Olsina L. Context-based recommendation approach for measurement and evaluation projects. In: Journal of Software Engineering and Applications (JSEA). Irvine: CA. 2010;3(12):1089−1106.

[14] Nelson C. Security metrics: an overview. In: ISSA Journal. 2010;12−18.

[15] OWASP testing guide. Version 3.0. [Internet]. 2008 [cited 2013 Jan]. Available from: <https://www.owasp.org/index.php/OWASP_Testing_Project>

[16] OWASP testing guide. Version 3.0 [Internet]. Stored XXS. 2008 [cited 2013 Feb]. Available from: <https://www.owasp.org/index.php/Testing_for_Stored_Cross_site_scripting_(OWASP-DV-002)>.

[17] Dujmovic JJ. A method for evaluation and selection of complex hardware and software systems. 22nd Int'l Conf for the Resource Management and Performance Evaluation of Enterprise CS. CMG 96 Proceedings. 1996;368−378.

[18] Papa F. Toward the improvement of an M&E strategy from a comparative study. In: Current Trends in Web Engineering, ICWE Workshops. Grossniklauss M, Wimmer M, editors. LNCS 7703, Springer. 2012;189−203.

[19] Alberts C, Dorofe A. OCTAVE: method implementation guide. Version 2.0. Carnegie Mellon SEI: Pittsburgh; 2001.

[20] ISO/IEC Guide 73. Risk management − Vocabulary − Guidelines for use in standards; 2009.

[21] ISO/IEC 31010. Risk management: risk assessment techniques; 2009.

[22] Basili V, Lindvall M, Regardie M, Seaman C, Heidrich J, Jurgen M, et al. Linking software development and business strategy through measurement. IEEE Comput 2010;43(4):57−65.

[23] García F, Ruiz F, Bertoa M, Calero C, Genero M, Olsina L, et al. An ontology for software measurement. Technical Report UCLM DIAB-04-02-2. Computer Science Department, University of Castilla-La Mancha, Spain; 2004 [In Spanish].

[24] Garcia F, Bertoa M, Calero C, Vallecillo A, Ruiz F, Piattini M, et al. Towards a consistent terminology for software measurement. Inf Softw Technol 2005;48(4):631−44.

[25] Basili R, Caldiera G, Rombach HD. The goal question metric approach. In: Encyclopedia of Software Engineering. 1994;1:528−532.

A Fresh Look at Semantic Natural Language Information Assurance and Security: NL IAS from Watermarking and Downgrading to Discovering Unintended Inferences and Situational Conceptual Defaults

Victor Raskin and Julia M. Taylor

Purdue University, West Lafayette, IN, USA

INFORMATION IN THIS CHAPTER

- Early breakthroughs in NL IAS
- A sketch of ontological semantic technology
- Mature semantic NL IAS

INTRODUCTION

The goal of this chapter is to revisit, update, and advance significantly the issue of a possible and necessary contribution from natural language processing to information assurance and security. First, it will review the early motivation for natural language information assurance and security (NL IAS), its program, and its implementations. For some reason, until now this has never been published in a dedicated and concentrated publication. The closest we have ever come to that was a COLING 2004 tutorial [1], never presented as a cohesive text but rather only as a huge collection of PowerPoint slides, even though it was distributed widely throughout the security community. This paper will selectively borrow some pertinent factual material from that tutorial, mostly the descriptions of the implemented software because, of course, those facts—the reality on the ground, as it were—have remained the same, although their interpretation and theoretical basis have been rethought significantly since, often as clarifications rather than rebuttals to subsequent citations.

Different from the still-dominant statistical machine learning strand in Natural Language Processing (NLP) since the early 1990s, the NLP approach we have applied to IAS has been rule- and meaning-based. Its theoretical basis remains the Ontological Semantics theory developed in the 1990 s and applied to the level of academic proof-of-concept implementations. Since roughly 2005, it has been significantly revised on a continuous basis, gaining considerable momentum in the 2004–2011 proprietary implementations of product-level systems. Leaving that IP behind and persistently expanding the coverage domain as well as improving the quality of the methodology, since 2011 OST has made qualitative jumps, mostly within academia again, toward developing a new set of resources, potentially for open source use as an alternative to the currently common opportunistic resources such as WordNet [2].

Early work in NL IAS took advantage of the access to meaning of NL texts. Its fullest semantic application was semantic forensics, where the system could automatically flag contradictions as potential deception [3], but it was not until 2010 that even more sophisticated semantic techniques led to a qualitatively higher level of penetration into semantic clues revealing what is not being said. While still short of full-fledged NL inferencing and deliberately staying away from reasoning proper, this initiative has a far-reaching potential, in particular in security work.

Accordingly, the rest of the chapter consists of three major sections corresponding to early NL IAS ("Early Breakthrough in NL IAS"), the semantic foundation of this work ("A Sketch of Ontological Semantic Technology"), and new advances in NL IAS ("Mature Semantic NL IAS"). The conclusion and future work are briefly outlined in the last section.

Early breakthrough in NL IAS
The conceptual foundation of NL IAS

Information Assurance and Security is the CERIAS designation, shared by many in the 2000 s, of the general enterprise to protect computer systems and information in them from attacks. Within IAS, Information Security (IS) was often understood as protection from intrusion and unauthorized use, the area that has been recently referred to as Cyber Security, folding neatly into the domains of computer science, computer engineering, and computer technology. Information assurance (IA) has focused on ensuring the authenticity of stored and transmitted information, and it is inherently multidisciplinary: the Purdue Center for Education and Research in Information Assurance and Security (CERIAS), a leading IAS organization in the world and the first ever multidisciplinary center, includes some 80 faculty from at least 12 different departments in six colleges. Now much of the information in IA is in the form of NL texts, and that brings the necessity to handle this enormous massive of text computationally. So, as early as 1999, CERIAS started funding and encouraging a joint effort by an NLP expert (Raskin) and a computer scientist (Atallah) on what has become a new front in the IAS effort, namely, NL IAS.

By that time, NLP had progressed since the early 1950 s from machine translation (MT) to information retrieval (IR) in its various forms, such as information extraction (IE), data and text mining, question answering (QA), Internet searching, and abstracting and summarization. The rationale for NLP to move into IAS was based on the following arguments [4]:

- Information assurance and security needs make it an important and growing area of application for NLP.
- The new area of application is a healthy mix of recycling the existing modules and systems and of new adjustments and adaptations.
- One exciting innovation is the clearly identified need of "lite" versions of tools and resources, which are incremental but non-adhoc meaning-based enhancements for bag-of-words applications.

The symmetrical rationale for IAS to be receptive to NLP listed these arguments:

- Inclusion of natural NL data sources as an integral part of the overall data sources in InfoSec applications.
- Analysis of NL at the level of meaning, that is, with the knowledge-based methods, such as Ontological Semantics.
- Re-use of already implemented and tested systems of MT, IR, IE, QA, planning and summarization, data mining, information security, intelligence analysis, etc.

Within NL IAS, NL IA has been understood as the global task of protecting NL information on computer systems by guaranteeing its authenticity and preventing its misuse and abuse; as such, it has largely been a part of the digital rights protection effort. NL IA applications centrally include:

- NL watermarking
- NL tamper-proofing
- NL sanitizing/downgrading/desensitizing
- NL steganography and steganalysis

Somewhat symmetrically again, NL IS has been seen as using NL and/or ontological clues for the traditional tasks of information security, such as network protection, intrusion detection, trusted computing, etc. Its applications largely include:

- NL intrusion detection
- NL ontological support for rapid response to new attacks
- NL Web crawler support for attack planning and prevention

NL IA applications

In this subsection, we briefly describe a selection of central NL IA applications.

NL watermarking

This is the most cited, emulated, criticized, and attempted-to-improve-on application, most probably because it spent a year on a provisional patent and was then abandoned, both actions initiated by the authors' institution. We discuss here the more advanced and hard-to-emulate semantic version of it rather than the simpler syntactic version [6]. The main principle was that we created a 128-bit hash of the entire document, selected at random 64 sentences in the text to carry two bits each, and applied a published traversal procedure [7] to a semantic representation of the meaning of the carrying sentence produced by Ontological Semantics as its text-meaning representation (TMR).

At the time, there had been a few attempts to watermark an NL text. The approach that had gained the most currency was based on watermarking text on the same principle as an image. It was obviously harder to do with the letters, so they tweaked the proportional spacing. A smart idea it was; however, it was easily defeated by OCR software. Embedding the watermark in an automatically generated text that followed the rules of the English sentence, another smart low-hanging fruit of an idea, made it impossible to detect by computers equipped only with syntactic rules, but it also made these texts stand out for any smarter computer as well as for any human speaker or reader of English. Such attempts violated at least some of the principles of efficient watermarking that had been developed in a highly successful enterprise of watermarking images: those provided a lot of pixels to play with in the margins of an image without the human eye noticing any difference when a lot of them from, say, the human face on a portrait, were deliberately switched from blue, for example, to red.

The watermark technology we developed lived up to the standard requirements of image watermarking, which include:

- undetectability
- verifiability
- robustness
- resilience
- authenticity/quality
- holding up in court

We watermarked the digital NL text itself—in fact, its meaning, not the form—and most certainly not its printed, video, audio, or any other image, nor any particular format, such as MS Word, Adobe PDF, XML, etc. It survived anything but the most radical meaning changes, namely:

- translation into any NL
- reorganization
- paragraph reshuffling
- limited addition
- limited omission
- any sentence paraphrase
- any syntactic changes

Very simplistically, the overview of the watermarking algorithm can be represented as follows:

- Choose subset $t_1, \ldots, t_m$ of sentences from the text being watermarked to carry a watermark in a k-based procedure.
- Represent text as a sequence of TMR (semantic) tree representations $T_1, \ldots, T_n$ for each of its sentences $s_1, \ldots, s_n$.
- "Arborize" each TMR; that is, turn it into a tree in case it is not one already.
- Use secret key k (large prime number).
- Map each tree into a bit string $B_1, \ldots, B_n$ using keyed hash $H_k(T(s))$.

Transform the subset such that $\beta \leq 8$ bits of each $B_{t1}, \ldots, B_{t\alpha}$ correspond to the watermark W: if the transform already carries the necessary two bits (about 25 percent of all cases, on the average, obviously), leave it as is; if not, apply any one of the three prescribed techniques to transform the sentence, and hence its tree, until the targeted pair of bits is achieved.

The three prescribed procedures, grafting (adding), pruning (dropping), and substitution, each operating algorithmically with the prescribed lists and tables, create minor changes in the carrying sentences, such as adding something like "generally speaking," dropping similar expressions, or substituting, say, "Kabul" with "the capital of Afghanistan"—or vice versa. To mask the carrying sentences further, it is optionally recommended to perform similar transformations in a number of non-carrying sentences as well to fake a stylistic feature and thus further hide the watermark-carrying sentences. (Because the procedure is designed mainly for government- or corporation-generated papers, verbose and stylistically garbled on their own, our minor changes did not affect the readers' perception of the styles.)

NL tamperproofing
The NL watermarking technique can be interestingly reversed from the search for the most robust, indestructible watermark to that for the most brittle one, so that any tampering with a document, other than mere formatting, would invariably lead to the removal of the watermark. It shares the Ontological Semantics basis with NL watermarking, but it adds the chaining algorithm, so that the slightest change in the original breaks the watermark and thus signals tamper-proofing.

The chaining of sentences according to secret ordering includes:

* Semantic "mini-watermark" of b bits inserted in each sentence
* Dependence of the watermark on all predecessors of that sentence in the chain ("fragilization")

This makes the probability of a successful attack on a sentence equal $2^{-\beta}$, where β is the distance from the end of the chain. After applying this preliminary scheme, we repeat it but now chain sentences according to the reverse of secret ordering, including:

* *Syntactic* "mini-watermark" of β bits per sentence
* Dependence of the watermark on all *successors* of that sentence in the secret ordering

This makes the probability of a successful attack on a sentence $2^{-\beta}$ that is $1 +$ the total length of the chain. Then, at the first pass of a semantic marking scheme, we need to state precisely which β bits are to be the inserted as a "mini-watermark" in each sentence. Let H denote a keyed hash function. We do the following

* Compute $x_1 = H_k(1\ldots1) =$ the keyed hash of all 1's (e.g., 100 ones)
* Insert (as a watermark) in s_1 the leftmost β bits of x_1
* Then for $i = 2, \ldots, n$ we do the following:
* Compute $x_i = H_k(x_{i-1}, T_{i-1})$, where x_{i-1}, T_{i-1} denotes the concatenation of x_{i-1} and T_{i-1}, and T_{i-1} is the TMR tree obtained from the already marked version of sentence s_{i-1}
* Insert (as a watermark) in s_i the leftmost β bits of the just-computed x_i

The verification phase that corresponds to the first pass is a similar pass, except that instead of inserting β watermark bits in an s_i, we read them and compare them to the leftmost β bits of x_i. Because of the "forward chaining" from 1 to n, the probability that a modification of s_i goes undetected by this "first pass verification" is $2^{-\beta(n-i+1)}$.

The second pass is a syntactic marking scheme (so it does not change any of the TMRs resulting from the first pass). We need to state precisely which β bits are to be the inserted as a "mini-watermark" in each sentence. As before, H_k denotes a keyed hash function. We then do the following:

- Compute $x_n = H_k(1\ldots1) =$ the keyed hash of all 1's (e.g., 100 ones)
- Insert (as a watermark) in s_n the leftmost β bits of x_n
- Then for $i = n-1, \ldots, 1$ we do the following:
- Compute $x_i = H_k(x_{i+1}, T_{i+1})$, where x_{i+1}, T_{i+1} denotes the concatenation of x_{i+1} and T_{i+1}, and T_{i+1} is the syntax tree obtained from the already marked version of sentence s_{i+1}
- Insert (as a watermark) in s_i the leftmost β bits of the just-computed x_i

The verification phase that corresponds to the second pass is a similar pass, except that instead of inserting β watermark bits in an s_i, we read them and compare them to the leftmost β bits of x_i. Because of the "backward chaining" from n to 1, the probability that a modification of s_i goes undetected by this "second pass verification" is 2^{-i}.

The probability that a modification to s_i escapes detection by both the first-pass verification and the second-pass verification is, therefore, $2^{-\beta(n-i+1)}2^{-\beta i} = 2^{-\beta(n+1)}$.

NL sanitizing/downgrading

The need to suppress certain information from documents that have to be published or shared with less than fully trustworthy or authorized parties is ubiquitous. Governments have to monitor the distribution of classified information; businesses must protect their trade secrets and other proprietary forms of their intellectual property.

In the late 1990 s, the US Department of Energy, guarding primarily nuclear secrets, had over 700 rules of declassification, mostly listing words and phrases that could not be listed, and it took their human analysts a very long time to redact texts manually and then getting the authorization— up to two person-months for a 20-page document. So the idea of computing the process was natural.

Non-semantic NLP can only operate on character strings, and without understanding the meaning of a text, it is very hard to add, delete, or substitute the sensitive material. Attempts were made to create lists of synonyms for classified terms, but this rarely worked smoothly. Statistical methods, with their admitted 15−20 percent error rate, are not typically employed for this task.

To complicate matters, downgrading rules rarely ban the use of a term and stop there. In a mock-up but realistic example, a term like *nuclear submarine* will be allowed, but any information about the location of any particular vessel and its fuel capacity, which is essential for calculating the speed of its getting to the next location from the previous one, cannot be mentioned.

The OST Lexicon entry for *nuclear submarine*, in significantly simplified form, is as follows. The declassification rule will not allow the system to fill the location and speed slots.

```
nuclear submarine
(isa    warship)
(theme-of build, commission, decommission, deploy, destroy, attack)
(instrument-of attack, support, transport, threaten)
(manned-by naval crew)
```

```
(propel-mode     surface, sub-surface)
(engine-type     nuclear-engine)
(range     N < x < M)
(speed     K < y < L)
(current-location body-of-water and/or geographic point and/or coordinates and/or rela-
  tive, time-range)
(prior-location...)
(next-location ...)
(current-mission   ...)
```

An advanced OST procedure is capable of filling a location slot by running into a report that a couple of US sailors were involved in a bar brawl in Manila on a certain date, if the system's InfoStore has no other American vessel in port.

A proof-of-concept downgrading system based on Ontological Semantics was implemented at the master's thesis level [8].

NL steganography and steganalysis

Steganography is the ancient art of concealing a secret message in an innocuous text. It has been widely used in the world of intelligence and terrorism: in fact, after 9/11, it was revealed [9] that several steganographic messages in Arabic had been intercepted by US agencies (but not deciphered until after the attack). Steganalysis, discovering the hidden message, is heuristic rather than algorithmic, and we have not implemented any OST approach to it [5].

Since watermarking is essentially a specific case of steganography, the OST-based algorithms for steganography follow the OST watermarking techniques for the existing texts. We have demonstrated, however [10], that OST can significantly advance the mimicking technique, that is, generating the cover text to hide the message. The original technique was based only on syntax, and using context-free grammar, it created cover texts that looked syntactically well-formed and thus could fool the computer-based detection programs that were not meaning-based. Obviously, reversing analysis into generation, OST can mimic texts that are semantically correct and thus fool non-expert humans.

A sketch of ontological semantic technology

The architecture of the Ontological Semantic Technology (OST—see [11–16]) is shown in Figure 3.1. The engineered language-independent ontology is acquired semi-automatically, with a minimum of "human computation," to use a gimmicky new term (see [17] and references there) for a hybrid human-computer effort that we have been using for over two decades. The language-specific lexicons contain lexical entries for all senses of all words and phrasals of the language, and their meanings are anchored in the appropriate concepts of the ontology, with all of the concepts' properties assigned a concept or literal filler. The POST (Processor for/in OST) uses all of these and other resources to convert each sentence of a text into a text meaning representation (TMR).

The oval centerpiece is the language-independent property-rich ontology, whose two main branches are event and object, connected by properties. In each language-specific lexicon, such as

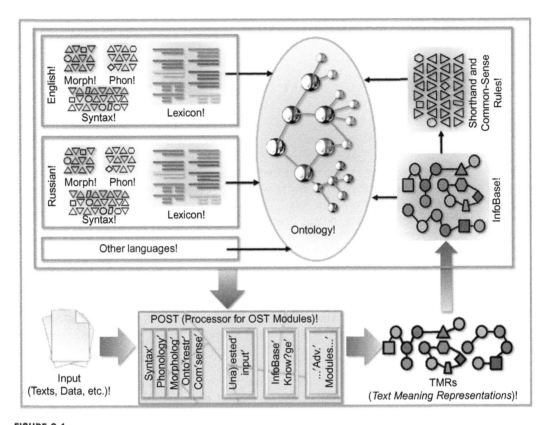

FIGURE 3.1

OST architecture.

English, Russian, Korean, etc., every sense of every word is represented in ontological terms. Besides, the lexicon contains the morphosyntactic information about every word, such as where and in what syntactic context it occurs in sentences. When a sentence in a natural language is input, the system reads every word linearly, finds in the lexicon, and generates the ontological structure of the sentence, mostly and most ubiquitously by fitting the objects in the event as agent, theme, instrument, etc. (see [18]: Chs. 6, 7.1−2, and 8.1−2 on these basics). The result is the text-meaning representation (TMR) of the disambiguated meaning of the sentence.

Each successfully processed TMR is stored, along with the exact wording information, in the InfoBase. Along with the running, the testing and evaluation procedure of "blame assignment" identifies cases when a failure to disambiguate or even to generate a TMR is due to a missing common sense information, and a procedure of identifying this information, similar to that for understanding such unattested input as words that are not in the lexicon, is then activated (see, for instance, [16]).

Below is an example of an OST concept drive in the XML format, one of the many basically isomorphic formalisms, with all of which the OST resources are fully compatible:

```
<concept-def>
    <name>drive</name>
    <date>2013-02-14T20:06:38.704-05:00</date>
    <anno><def>to operate a motor vehicle</def></anno>
    <is-a>
        <concept>
            <name>move-vehicle</name>
        </concept>
    </is-a>
    <property>
        <name>agent</name>
        <filler facet="sem">
            <concept><name>human</name></concept>
        </filler>
    </property>
    <property>
        <name>instrument</name>
        <filler facet="sem">
            <concept><name>vehicle</name></concept>
        </filler>
    </property>
</concept-def>
```

Formally, the OST ontology is a lattice of conceptual nodes. In other words, the ontology can be looked at as a graph with labeled nodes, with the labels ignored by the machine and used only for identification, and edges named with the properties, one property per edge, corresponding to the concept-property filler connection between any two nodes.

In the example above, since DRIVE is a SubClassOf MOVE-VEHICLE, along with LAND, DOCK, TO-PARK, and TAKE-OFF-PLANE, a number of properties for DRIVE, such as time and instrument, are inherited from MOVE-VEHICLE. The IS-A relationship is based on the simple subsumption: "A property p subsumes q if and only if, *for every possible state of affairs*, all instances of q are also instances of p" [19]. If not for the multiple parenthood possibility, making the ontological graph into a lattice, the inheritance would be simply monotonic; as it happens, in cases of multiple parenthood, the child inherits from all parents.

Several versions of the ontology and lexicons, significantly upgraded between versions, have been used in academic, proof-of-concept ([18]: Ch. 1), and commercial applications. The largest version used under 10,000 concepts and under 400 properties to define over 100,000 English word senses.

While statistical approaches to NLP still dominate the field, seriously constraining the achievable level of precision in application implementations well below the users' tolerance levels, some creeping semanticalization has been taking place. Lacking the credentials and resources to aim for comprehensive meaning representation, researchers try to patch up their systems with shallow ontologies—often automatically extracted and thus not very informative word lists—and, quite popularly, WordNet, a loose thesaurus that was originally created for psychological association experiments [2].

In this spirit of NLP semanticalization and, hence, better results in applications, we would like to take the semantic information used in NLP work to a finer grain size, beyond semantic types and synonymy/antonymy, to the level of explicitly represented concepts and properties that define the meaning of words in all of their senses. The existing semantic resources, such as WordNet, stop short of this level of representation. One could argue that WordNet synsets, when organized well, do—or at least should—correspond to a property that is the basis for the similarity. But, in our experience, a lexicon that uses these properties explicitly, while they come from a tight hierarchical structure of all properties and their fillers, does present a finer-grained representation of meaning. This is how the ontological semantic resources are organized.

An immediate advantage of the OST grain size of semantic representation is that it can support inferences, such as (1b), that have words not used in the premise (1a), are not synonyms or antonyms of those words, and do not even belong to the same semantic types.

(1a) Mary drove off from New York to Boston around 10 a.m. this morning.
(1b) Then it was not her Honda I saw on Broadway at noon.

The OST lexicon anchors the English verb *drive* in the concept DRIVE, from which it obtains VEHICLE as the INSTRUMENT. VEHICLE has CAR as a SUBCLASS, and CAR has a large numbers of fillers for the property BRAND-NAME, of which HONDA is one, and it will anchor the lexical entry *Honda* in the OST English lexicon. OST also has the DEFAULT facet for its properties, which turns out to be useful to mark situational defaults that are essential for understanding the unsaid.

Example (1) opens the way to a discussion of implicit meaning, unintended inferences, and conceptual defaults in the next section. But first, equipped with some basic information on OST, we briefly review the most semantic NL IAS application of the early 2000s, semantic forensics [3].

Mature semantic NL IAS

In this section, a brief review of the most semantically advanced application of the earlier period in NL IAS, semantic forensics, the algorithmic calculation and representation of unintended inferences, other implicit meanings, and finally, conceptual defaults are introduced and discussed in the aspect of their recent applications to NL IAS.

Semantic forensics

After minimal experience, people learn to produce lies, "white" and otherwise, as well as to expect and detect them. They do it by processing meaning, building expectations, and comparing the received content against those expectations. They detect contradictions (easy), omissions (harder), glossing over (harder still), and sophisticated lying (by inference, very hard). Can we emulate those abilities computationally? Semantic forensics was an early attempt to answer this question [3].

The application was triggered by a real-life event: a 10,000-word investigative profile of Howard Dean in a *Sunday Times* issue during a tumultuous Democratic primary in the US 2004 presidential election. The *New York Times* ran such a profile on each of the nine high-profile candidates on nine consecutive Sundays. Howard Dean, the former governor of Vermont, led the pack for a short while, and his family background was rather prominently Republican. The reporter did not seem to spare a single compromising detail: hereditary Republicanism, a (rich) Park Avenue childhood, the $7 million that Howard's father left him and his somewhat troubled brother. Moreover, that father and his father (Dean's grandfather) had both been presidents of a country club that, until recently, had not admitted Blacks or Jews. What I, a text-processing human, with enough motivation and alertness, could not help noticing was that the father's profession was never mentioned. What could it have been that it was unmentionable in a sympathetic report? And could that omission have been detected computationally?

Actually, yes: ontological semantics could accommodate it pretty easily (using the alternative, early, easy-to-read LISP-like format):

```
human-1
    name          Howard Dean
    age           adult
    relation      self
    occupation    physician, politician

human-2
    name          Judy Dean
    age           adult
    relation      spouse
    occupation    physician

human-3
    name          Papa Dean
    age           adult (deceased)
    relation      father
    occupation    unknown
```

This is, of course, the most elementary case of finding an omission, which is still harder than a direct contradiction, which is flagged by the system when a new TMR directly contradicts a previously processed TMR that is stored in the system's InfoBase.

Unintended inferences and the meaning of the unsaid

The first mature NL IAS contribution was unintended inference [14,20], a sketch of an algorithmic process that catches unsolicited remarks, usually in relaxed private conversations, and derives information these remarks divulge, to a high degree of confidence, that the speakers neither intend to divulge nor become normally aware that they have. This is reiterated and exemplified later in this section in a more substantive fashion, albeit briefly, in the much broader context of the meaning of the unsaid, to which that venture finally led.

Understanding and processing information contained in natural language text has been the major challenge for natural language and information processing. The extent to which a computational system can comprehend and absorb the information similarly to what humans do determines how well it can implement any number of past, current, and future applications that use natural language as input. This is a tall enough order by and of itself, but it is complicated enormously by the fact that a human does not limit his or her understanding to what the text actually says.

A considerable part of the information that a human gets out of the text is not expressed there explicitly: it is considered too obvious and too well-known to the hearer or reader to be stated; it may be inferred from the text absolutely or with high enough probability; it may be hinted or insinuated; it may be presupposed, entailed, or inferred.

Humans uses their backgrounds, general and specific knowledge of how things are, domain experience, familiarity with a situation and/or its participants, etc. to understand a text, and the better informed the hearers or readers are, the more informed they are by what is unsaid, if we assume—rather counter-factually at a finer grain size—that they all interpret what is said differently. The huge divergence between the "minimum" and "maximum" comprehender is the latter's ability to populate the unsaid with all the pertinent background information enabling its calculation.

The examples are ubiquitous, varying from such a primitive case as understanding (2) as John's having used a key, without any need to mention the instrument of his action; to assessing (3) as a complaint, based on the never-mentioned notion that the (or even, a) line does not—or should not—normally take so long; to realizing that the observed and reported deployment of an enemy army division without any visible presence of the Corps of Engineers—with their bobcats, bulldozers, and other digging and construction equipment—is very likely to indicate the offensive, not defensive, intentions of the deployment because it is engineers that build trenches, bunkers, antitank barriers, etc.; to, finally, correctly interpreting the absence of military brass in a top-level US delegation to Israel as removing the controversial issue US F35 sales to Israel from the meeting agenda.

Let us consider the following English sentences:

(2) John unlocked the door.
(3) I spent over an hour in the check-out line.
(4a) John unlocked the door with the key.
(4b) John unlocked the door with a key.
(5a) John unlocked the door by inserting the key and turning it.
(5b) John unlocked the door by entering the code.
(5c) John unlocked the door by entering his personal code.
(5d) John unlocked the door by entering the appropriate code.
(6a) John unlocked the door, and Mary invited him in.
(6b) John unlocked the door for Mary, and she invited him in.

We claim that (4a and 4b) are more appropriate and likelier to be heard or read than (2). A key is what one normally opens a locked door with, and the definite article *the* indicates that the key should be the one for that very lock. If we replace it with *a*, we will assume that John did not know which key of several corresponded to that door and tried several, or he did not have the correct key and wanted to check if some other key might fit. The sentence (5a), in the same situation, is extremely obvious, to the point of absurdity and non-acceptability, while (5b) is perfectly appropriate. In (5c), *his personal* seems redundant, as indeed is *the appropriate* in (5d).

We equally claim that (7a) raises a question, while (7b) does not. Equally—or perhaps slightly less—obviously, it is normal for the host to unlock his or her own door and to let a companion in. So the second clause of (7a) raises the question why, which *for Mary* settles, doubling up as the introduction of a companion to the scene.

We introduce the term "default" for those bits of information that the speaker and hearers both take for granted and consider unworthy to be mentioned. We are interested in the hypothesis that people communicate felicitously when they omit defaults, while considering a deviation from them to be worthy of relaying. See more on defaults below.

Situational conceptual defaults
The term, its origins, and the canonical case

Examples 2 through 6 above present perhaps one of the simplest, most canonical, and archetypal cases of defaults. To reflect this fact, the OST concepts of LOCK and UNLOCK make KEY the filler of the INSTRUMENT property on the DEFAULT facet. In researching the meaning of the unsaid, we use the term "default" to mark all kinds of information that it is unnecessary and, in many cases, inappropriate to make explicit because it is obvious and therefore both uninformative and uninteresting to the hearers. This sense of default is also compatible with the terminology of the logic of default reasoning [21], also known as default logic, which allows the use of implicit propositions—such as that birds can fly—in the calculation of logical inferences. By the same token, default logic also introduced probabilistic reasoning [22] because, while most birds do indeed fly, chickens and ostriches do not. In our usage, defaults are situational because they occur in specific semantic situations, and they are conceptual because they are contained in, or follow from, the OST ontology.

Default reversal

Not only will failing to omit *with the key* in (4a) be perceived by the hearers as redundant, tautological, and boring, but it may also offend them because of the speaker's possible implication that something that should be obvious is not part of their cognitive and/or intellectual baggage. Alternatively, guided by Grice's [23] Co-Operative principle, the hearer(s), instead of dismissing the speaker as deficient or incompetent, may consider an alternative, somewhat more sophisticated but still easily accessible interpretation: that the reason the default is verbalized when it should not be is that it is not the default. What if John is a burglar (or a locksmith) who usually unlocks doors without having access to the correct keys and uses two paper clipsor a credit card instead? This default reversal was analyzed as an invaluable clue for detecting and representing the meaning of an unintended reference [24], often the last resort in detecting and exposing an inside traitor [22].

In a real-life example in the unintended inference research, a professional woman calls her cousin and angrily relates to her cousin that her boss wants her to fly to Frankfurt, Germany, from the United States by coach. Now, flying coach is a default for all but the very few, so when someone (of the "99 percent") reports that he or she has just flown to Frankfurt, coach class is assumed unless explicitly indicated otherwise. In the cousins' conversation, the traveler explicitly verbalizes that she traveled by coach, thus changing the default to first or business class. This happened to be factually true, in her case; she is an executive in a large company, but not an inside traitor at all. She naively gave away the fact that the company was cutting down on its travel expenses in a pretty drastic way, and that could be heard and interpreted as a signal to get rid of its stock.

Are defaults really common sense knowledge?

We found ourselves in disagreement with a somewhat careless statement in passing in an abstract by Raghavan [25], which said that "[h]uman readers naturally use common sense knowledge to infer ... implicit information from the explicitly stated facts." This is true only partially; going back to the numbered (and the two unnumbered) situations above, example (2), the key example, is the only one that can be referred to as common sense knowledge (a legitimate OST component presented by us at WI-IAT 2011 [16]). The two unnumbered situations deal with specialized domain knowledge—military and political, respectively—the latter of which is, in addition, highly time-sensitive. Example (3) is an element of situational knowledge shared by all, independent of their education and/or special knowledge, who have lived in the world of check-outs. We selected the adjective "situational" to use with our term—if and when an adjective is necessary to separate the term from the non-terminological uses and specific ones in different domains.

What is fair to say is that situational defaults may be based on any shared knowledge and work when used among those who share that knowledge. The real picture is much more complicated than the concentric circle figure representing individual, private knowledge inside, the group knowledge including it, and common sense knowledge as the larger circle ([26]: Ch. 2), but every individual is indeed encircled by those layers—except that one belongs to various groups and thus is encircled by various group knowledge circles.

Underdetermination of reality by language

The ubiquitous problem of underdetermination of reality by language remains surprisingly unexplored (see, however, [27–29]) with regard to natural language, because humans use natural language usually blissfully unaware of the problem—except when reporting on a piece of news to somebody and discovering that they cannot answer many questions about the piece. Thus, the sentence *Two men walked into the room* leaves out tons of information about them. HUMAN has tons of properties in the OST ontology; some of them are physical, such as age, height, mass, eye color, and hair color; and none of them are provided in the sentence. Humans have professions, they wear clothes, and they self-propel themselves, as those two men apparently did. They had not been born yesterday, so they had done things prior to walking into the room. They may have slept the night before at their homes or hotels. They may have eaten breakfast or lunch or even dinner, depending on the time of the day—which is also, by the way, not indicated.

The coverage of all these properties depends on the grain size of the statement, and if the listener or reader wants to refine the grain size in any respect they will ask the speaker or writer additional questions. But no matter how many questions they ask, they will never cover all of the properties, and they will be satisfied with a description of the situation that is partial and selective. In the context of the unsaid, implicit information, the acceptance of such undetermining statements is possible because of the defaults—some of them absolute, such as wearing clothes in public—and most probabilistic, such as having had breakfast. For humans, the defaults bridge the gap between whatever they may potentially want to know about the situation and what is actually, stated explicitly.

It is clear, of course, that requests for more details may be completely fatuous. Thus, it would be pretty weird to want to know if the men liked Quentin Tarantino's movies unless there is some obvious connection between the director and the room (such as, for instance, the men have shot people in the room, covering the floor with pools of blood, and there is one person who inquires about the murderers' cinematic preferences), but the ability to produce pertinent questions is cognitively important for humans, and the fact that they can answer these questions themselves, without asking them of their interlocutors, is invaluable.

Humans are enabled in this respect by defaults, and this is why it is essential for any form of Web intelligence—in fact, for any computational processing of information—that default knowledge be made available to the computer. Some of it may be present in the form of stated facts, but most will result from applying rules to the explicit statement, with some of these rules being based on the available knowledge and others—lacking the requisite knowledge—on learning algorithms.

Scripts

Finally, the last issue to consider in this subsection is that most of our knowledge, and hence, default knowledge, comes in scripts. Everybody knows about the script of going to a restaurant from the early and naïve attempt to treat it computationally in Schank and Abelson [30]. A typical script is a chronological and/or causal sequence of events that constitute a standard way of doing things or of how things happen. Raskin et al. [31] present an early attempt to accommodate the script of approaching bankruptcy in Ontological Semantics (not yet OST); incidentally, the inadvertent give-away in the coach/first class statement by that executive in a large and (still) prosperous company is a possible component of the script of approaching bankruptcy.

Anonymization

Referring to essentially a form of sanitizing or downgrading a text (see the section on early NL IAS above), the term "anonymization" has been widely used to designate the US law concerning privacy, especially an individual's guaranteed protection from revealing private data to those unauthorized by law or the individual's consent to access them. In a standard computer application, anonymization is achieved by removing all human names, addresses, social security or other identifying numbers, and often geographic locations. It is harder to generalize this to all named entities, because some statistical data, pooled from many private records, may be necessary to preserve.

Much of the research and application work has been invested in protecting health records, especially in connection with centralizing them, as per new legislation. In fact, this work has replaced many other IAS concerns of the recent past as the leading area in security. The state of the art shows, again and again, that statistical and other pre- and non-semantic approaches fall short of preventing reidentification after all the obvious identifying data are removed. Thus, if it follows from the record that the patient was a female African American senior army officer who lost a leg in action, this combination of features will probably uniquely identify one individual. A typical target in anonymization, marked by the variable k, is preset at $k = 3$.

The way humans reidentify anonymized data is by using all the semantic clues left intact in the text. These clues are based on explicit text meaning, with its basis in conceptual structures and properties, as well as on implicit meaning, inadvertently divulged inferences, scripts, and everything else discussed in the previous subsection. We are now implementing a major anonymization draft, for which OST is accordingly implemented and extended (see Acknowledgments).

Summary

This chapter provides an updated view of Natural Language Information Assurance and Security, an effort in porting Ontological Semantics and, later, Ontological Semantic Technology, to previously existing assurance and security applications as well as to those that this approach has uniquely enabled. An argument is presented, in multiple facets, that computational access to meaning is necessary for any chance to implement successful IAS applications. Most of the chapter is devoted to the newest methods for enabling the computer to access natural language meaning, especially implicit meaning, using situational conceptual defaults, that is, the most obvious information that is typically omitted by speakers and writers. The significance of the approach to successful anonymization of health records is mentioned as a significant current application being implemented on its basis.

Many of the mentioned applications need to be implemented beyond the proof-of-concept level to a full-fledged off-the-shelf product level. Others have to be advanced from algorithms to fully implemented code. Even more importantly, we have to be on constant alert for new applications and new functionalities of the existing ones that the meaning-based approach uniquely enables.

Acknowledgments

This research has been partially supported by the National Science Foundation research grant "TC: Large: Collaborative Research: Anonymizing Textual Data and Its Impact on Utility." The authors also wish to express their gratitude to their co-authors in the cited works and students participating in the classroom discussions of and research projects in NL IAS, especially in Taylor's class, Spring 2013 CNIT 623: Natural Language in Information Assurance and Security.

References

[1] Raskin V. Tutorial on natural language information assurance security. COLING 2004.

[2] Fellbaum C, editor. WordNet: An electronic lexical database. Cambridge, MA: MIT Press; 1998.

[3] Raskin V, Hempelmann CF, Triezenberg KE. Semantic forensics: An application of ontological semantics to information assurance. In: Hirst G, Nirenburg S, editors. Proceedings of the Second Workshop on Text Meaning and Interpretation. Barcelona, Spain: ACL; 2004 Jul. p. 25−6.

[4] Raskin V, Nirenburg S, Atallah MJ, Hempelmann CF, Triezenberg KE. Why NLP should move into IAS. In: Krauwer S, editor. Proceedings of the Workshop on a Roadmap for Computational Linguistics. Taipei, Taiwan: Academia Sinica; 2002. p. 1−7.

[5] Atallah MJ, Raskin V, Hempelmann CF, Karahan M, Sion R, Topkara U, et al. Natural language watermarking and tamperproofing. In: Petitcolas FAP, editor. Information Hiding. Berlin-New York: Springer Verlag; 2002. p. 196−212.

[6] Atallah MJ, Raskin V, Crogan M, Hempelmann CF, Kerschbaum F, Mohamed D, et al. Natural language watermarking: Design, analysis, and a proof-of-concept implementation. In: Moskowitz IS, editor. Information Hiding. Berlin-New York: Springer Verlag; 2001. p. 193−208.

[7] Atallah MJ, Wagstaff SS. Watermarking data using quadratic residues. Working Paper, Department of Computer Science. Purdue University; 1996.

[8] Mohamed D. Ontological semantics methods for automatic downgrading [unpublished thesis]. W. Lafayette (IN): Linguistics and CERIAS, Purdue University; 2001.

[9] Hersh SM. Missed messages: Why the government didn't know what it knew. New Yorker. 2002 June 3.

[10] Bennett K. Ontological semantic generation for mimicking texts in steganography. The Purdue Ontological Semantic Project, MCLC. Bloomington: Indiana University; 2004.

[11] Raskin V, Hempelmann CF, Taylor JM. Guessing vs. knowing: The two approaches to semantics in natural language processing. Annual International Conference Dialogue; 2010a. p. 642−50.

[12] Raskin V, Taylor JM, Hempelmann CF. Meaning- and ontology-based technologies for high-precision language in information-processing computational systems. Advanced Engineering Informatics 2013.

[13] Hempelmann CF, Taylor JM, Raskin V. Application-guided ontological engineering. International Conference on Artificial Intelligence; 2010.

[14] Taylor JM, Hempelmann CF, and Raskin V. On an automatic acquisition toolbox for ontologies and lexicons in ontological semantics. International Conference on Artificial Intelligence; 2010a.

[15] Taylor JM, Hempelmann CF, Raskin V. Post-logical verification of ontology and lexicons: The ontological semantic technology approach. International Conference on Artificial Intelligence; 2011a.

[16] Taylor JM, Raskin V, Hempelmann CF. From disambiguation failures to common-sense knowledge acquisition: A day in the life of an ontological semantic system. Web Intelligence Conference; 2011.

[17] Law E, von Ahn L. Human computation. San Rafael: Morgan & Claypool; 2011.

[18] Nirenburg S, Raskin V. Ontological semantics. Cambridge: MIT Press; 2004.

[19] Guarino N, Welty CA. An overview of OntoClean. In: Staab S, Studer R, editors. Handbook on Ontologies. Berlin: Springer; 2004. p. 151−9.

[20] Raskin V, Hempelmann CF, Taylor JM. Ontological semantic technology for detecting insider threat and social engineering. Concord, MA: New Security Paradigms Workshop; 2010.

[21] Reiter. A logic for default reasoning. Artificial Intelligence 1980;13:81−132.

[22] Wheeler and Damasio. An implementation of statistical default logic. Proc. 9th European Conference on Logics in Artificial Intelligence (JELIA 2004). LNCS Series, Springer; 2004. p. 121−123.

[23] Grice HP. Logic and conversation. In: Cole P, Morgan JL, editors. Syntax and Semantics, Speech Acts. New York: Academic Press; 1975. p. 3.

[24] Taylor JM, Raskin V, Hempelmann CF, Attardo S. An unintentional inference amd ontological property defaults. IEEE SMC 2010.

[25] Raghavan S, Mooney RJ, Ku H. Learning to "read between the lines" using Bayesian logic programs. ACL 2012.

[26] Raskin V. Semantic mechanisms of humor. Dordrecht: Reidel; 1985.

[27] Taylor JM, Raskin V. Fuzzy ontology for natural language. Toronto, Ont, Canada: NAFIPS 2010; 2010.

[28] Bonk T. Underdetermination: An essay on evidence and the limits of natural knowledge. Bost Stud Phil Sc. Dordrecht: Springer; 1981. p. 261

[29] Quine WVO. Word and object. Cambridge, MA: MIT Press; 1960.

[30] Schank R, Abelson R. Scripts, plans, goals, and understanding.Hillsdale, NJ: Erlbaum.

[31] Raskin V, Nirenburg S, Hempelmann CF, Nirenburg I, Triezenberg KE. The genesis of a script for bankruptcy in ontological semantics. Hirst G, Nirenburg S, editors. Proceedings of the Workshop on Text Meaning, NAACL-HLT; 2003. p. 27−31.

Methods

An Approach to Facilitate Security Assurance for Information Sharing and Exchange in Big-Data Applications

Alberto De la Rosa Algarín and Steven A. Demurjian
University of Connecticut, Storrs, CT, USA

INFORMATION IN THIS CHAPTER

- Policy modeling
- Policy integration
- Big-Data application security
- Policy definition

INTRODUCTION

Security assurance for an application is the guarantee that a security officer seeks to provide regarding the utilized access control model, its defined security privileges, and their enforcement over time as users simultaneously interact with the system. For a big-data application constructed as a meta-system (system of systems) that shares and exchanges a wide variety and high volume of information in potentially different formats (e.g., XML - http://www.w3.org/XML/, RDF-http://www.w3.org/TR/2004/REC-rdf-concepts-20040210/, JSON-http://www.json.org/, etc.), security assurance must address the different and potentially conflicting security capabilities of constituent systems, the diverse set of stakeholders, and the overall security logic to be attained. A security approach to control the how, what, and when of stakeholders accessing a big-data application must insure that the local security policies of constituent systems are reconcilable with one another to yield a consistent and usable global security policy. From the perspective of information integration that allows the big-data application to be constructed, translations among the data formats of the constituent systems that maintain the structure and semantics of the local systems must be available. From a security perspective, these data formats must be reconciled to allow data sharing and exchange to occur in a secure fashion as users of the big-data application indirectly access local systems. The main objective of this chapter is to present and explain a role-based access control (RBAC) [1] approach to integrate and reconcile local security policies of the systems that comprise a big-data application, thereby providing a means to define a global security policy that contains the roles, privileges, and rules of the constituent systems. For security enforcement, this approach can generate a global policy for the big-data application, targeting the information shared by each constituent (local) system using rules that define security assurance on internal and shared resources.

To facilitate the discussion in this chapter, we focus on an area of law enforcement that has the potential for many different big-data applications. Law enforcement in the United States is organized in a very hierarchical fashion. For example, in the state of Connecticut, cities and larger towns have their own police forces. From a road management perspective, the local police forces concentrate on their local roads, while the state police force manages all of the state highways and interstate highways. For smaller towns that do not have their own police force, resident state troopers manage the roads. State and local police forces can also work with the Federal Bureau of Investigation at the national level when crimes cross state boundaries.

Other states have a similar hierarchical structure of law enforcement personnel. Each law enforcement official, from the lowest to the highest ranking, generates information regarding criminal activities, traffic accidents, and so on. As a result, there is a wide range of information that can potentially be linked within and across states. An example is the Integrated Automated Fingerprint Identification System (IAFIS, http://www.fbi.gov/about-us/cjis/fingerprints_biometrics/iafis/iafis), which is in a national database that already includes criminal histories, pictures, physical traits, and so on, as well as fingerprints from civilian (that is, governmental, ranging from local to state to federal) and military sources. Another example is the National Missing and Unidentified Persons System (NamUs, http://www.namus.gov/) of the US Department of Justice (DoJ).

In this chapter, we focus on the collection of data on motor vehicle crashes by law enforcement personnel that are then made available to a wide range of stakeholders. For example, faculty and graduate students in the departments of Civil Engineering and Computer Science and Engineering at the University of Connecticut have worked under the leadership of the State of Connecticut Transportation Department and the Department of Public Safety to establish a Connecticut Crash Data Repository (CTCDR, http://www.ctcrash.uconn.edu/) that contains data back to 1995 on crashes on state roads. Many other states have similar repositories: Florida (http://www.flhsmv.gov/ddl/ecrash/), Indiana (http://www.in.gov/cji/2481.htm), Wisconsin (http://transportal.cee.wisc.edu/services/crash-data/), Louisiana (http://datareports.lsu.edu/), and New Jersey (http://www.state.nj.us/transportation/refdata/accident/), to name a few.

From a security perspective, many stakeholders are interested in doing research and discovery using these large date sets (e.g., to identify road locations that have more accidents, study the impact of road work on traffic, etc.). For instance, a Department of Transportation (DoT) employee at the local, state, or federal level could read and curate (correct) the crash data; a police officer could enter new crash reports; a researcher might be interested in aggregate and other trend-oriented queries; while an attorney representing a client in an accident may want to see if prior accidents occurred at that location (akin to an FOI request). What is not supported is the ability to marshal information across all crash data for all states (local repositories) to form a crash report big-data application (global repository) that allows queries that cross state boundaries, enabling stakeholders to explore crashes and accidents across an area larger than a state. In fact, such a scenario is actually being explored. The Governors Highway Safety Association (http://www.ghsa.org/html/media/pressreleases/2012/20120702_mmucc.html) is promoting a unification of format on crash data collection (http://www.mmucc.us/). Once unified, the result will be a big-data application of crash data.

A big-data application is constructed by marshaling information from multiple sources to form an information exchange repository application that, as shown in Figure 4.1, includes data from multiple state sources that warehouse crash data (road accidents). The multiple data sources are brought together to create a big-data Crash Repository to support access across multiple sources in a secure manner for three types of users: police officers (denoted with a role of PoliceOfficer), DoT workers (DOTWorker), attorneys (Attorney), and data researchers (Researchers). This big-data Crash Repository can support the consolidation of accident data, included meta-data (driver, road, time of accident, cars involved, etc.) for research purposes (e.g., to find out which roads are more susceptible to crashes) to better allocate resources.

To illustrate, in Figure 4.1, States 1 and 3 might utilize a proprietary or state-recommended XML schema as their format for structuring information, while the States 2 and 4 might have already adopted the national MMUCC standard (http://mmucc.us/sites/default/files/MMUCC_4th_Ed.pdf). Each State/system in the figure has its own role-based access control (RBAC [1,2]) policies, in which different stakeholders have permissions defined at the local level to access the constituent systems. A new big-data Crash Repository using data from the four states in Figure 4.1 would have to consider the differences in permissions of logically equivalent roles (PoliceOfficer, DOTWorker, Attorney and Researcher), which may be different in different systems, and data provided by systems that may not match user needs. Our focus is on the security policies that dictate which resources can be accessed by whom, when, where, and how. We assume each local system has its own security policy for supporting the big-data Crash Repository with potential complementary and conflicting requirements. We also assume that each of the constituent systems provides data in either XML or a format that can be easily converted to XML so the big-data Crash Repository application has a unifying data format.

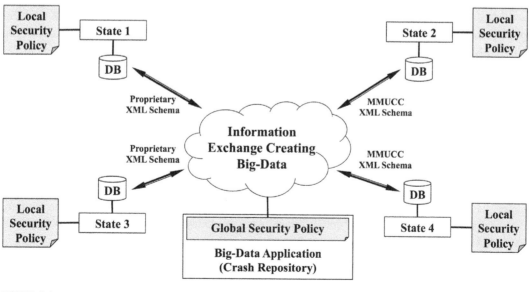

FIGURE 4.1

An information exchange scenario and intended policy integration for a big-data application.

This chapter extends our prior work on a security modeling framework for XML schemas and documents achieved via Unified Modeling Language (UML) extensions to model generic security policies and generate extensible markup access control language (XACML, https://www.oasis-open.org/committees/tc_home.php?wg_abbrev = xacml) policies [3,4] with an approach that reconciles multiple local security policies (policies for States 1 through 4 in Figure 4.1) in support of global security for a big-data application (Crash Repository in Figure 4.1). In our work, we assume that the constituent applications (e.g., States) that support a big-data application (e.g., Crash Repository) are each composed of a set of XML schemas and associated instances, such that when a user attempts access, the instance will be customized and filtered based on privileges. This chapter significantly extends [3,4] by providing the ability for more precise definitions of security policies. This allows local security policies (or portions thereof) to be enforceable for a big-data application, like Crash Repository, that is capable of obtaining, sharing, and changing information found in the constituent systems, thereby attaining a global security policy. We envision these policies to operate within a publish/subscribe model, where local systems as data owners decide which portion of their information (for their state) can be exposed (published) for use by other systems (in this case, the big-data Crash Repository application). While we use the Crash Repository for the example, this work is applicable to all big-data applications used in varied domains (science, engineering, biomedical informatics, finance, e-commerce, telecommunication, etc.) that seek to bring together and control access to data stored in multiple locations.

The main objective of this chapter is to model RBAC security of local systems regardless of their form and structure (XACML policy, database table with security definitions, etc.) while simultaneously integrating these local security policies acting on independent systems. The end result is a global security policy for a big-data application that is heavily structured around information sharing, using resources from its constituent systems, and provides a degree of security assurance. With this as its basis, this chapter focuses on both policy definition and integration processes to link the local policies (states) into a global context for the Crash Repository (country) as shown in Figure 4.1. The intent is to provide a means to reconcile the local polices of the constituent systems to allow their use for information exchange without sacrificing security assurance of those local systems. In the process, the security of a big-data application (e.g., Crash Repository) can leverage and integrate existing local security, resulting in a global policy that respects and privileges of the constituent systems.

The remainder of this chapter has five sections. The first section, "UML Extensions for XML Security," provides a brief overview of our XML framework for RBAC [3,4]. The second, "Extensions for Policy Modeling and Integration," extends this work to capture local and global security policies in support of the security for a big-data application. The third section, "Integrating Local Security Policies into a Global Security Policy," details the process of integrating multiple local security policies into a global policy for a big-data application, including reconciling conflicts across local systems, roles, and permissions in order to attain a global policy that can be assured. The next section, "Related Work," details related work on policy/security modeling and policy integration. The chapter ends with concluding remarks.

UML extensions for XML security

In this section, we provide a brief summary of our XML security framework [3,4] that utilizes schemas and instances to separate the security policy definition from the application's XML schema. It

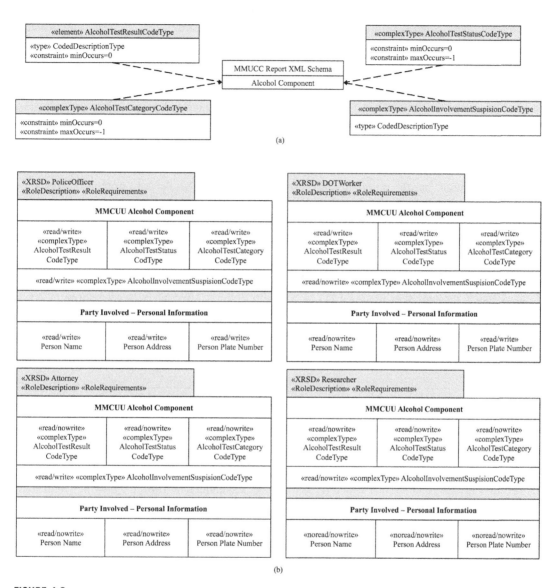

FIGURE 4.2

XML Schema Class Diagram (a) and XML Role Slice Diagram (b).

accomplishes this by using two new UML diagrams for modeling XML schemas and roles along with a mapping algorithm that places the XACML policies in the same layer of conceptual design as UML diagrams. The XML Schema Class Diagram (XSCD), in the top of Figure 4.2(a), is an artifact produced with a custom UML profile that holds all of the architecture and characteristics of the XML schema, including structure, data type constraints, and value constraints. In Figure 4.2(a), a crash report's alcohol component (following the MMUCC standard) can include the *mmucc: AlcoholInvolvementSuspisionCodeType* (whether there is a suspicion of alcohol involvement in the accident), the *mmucc:AlcoholTestCategoryCodeType* (what type of alcohol test was given e.g., blood, breath, etc.), the *mmucc:AlcoholTestResultCodeType* (whether the test results are pending), and the *mmucc:AlcoholTestStatusCodeType* (whether the person involved refused to take the test or not). The same crash report can include other information, such as the involved parties' information (name, address, license plate number, etc., not pictured in the XSCD), location (GPS or road markings).

The XML Role Slice Diagram (XRSD), shown in Figure 4.2(b), defines permissions such as read, no read, write and no write, to the attributes modeled in the XSCD. In the figure, PoliceOfficer and DOTWorker have the same read/write permissions on the alcohol and involved parties information, but the Attorney and Researcher differ on the alcohol attribute (an Attorney might be able to update this information as a result of a federal investigation, but the Researcher might not be able to write under any circumstances).

By utilizing these diagrams for security definition (the XSCD and the XRSD), a system's information security can be included as part of the overall software engineering process. Once defined, the XSCDs and XRSDs are used to generate an XACML policy that targets the initially modeled XML schema, and in turn all the respective instances, from the perspective of the local system (e.g., States 1 through 4 in Figure 4.1). As a result, policies affecting a large number of XML instances can change and be updated without incurring an overhead of updating each instances [4], unlike security methods that embed the security in the data itself.

Extensions for policy modeling and integration

This section details the three proposed extensions to the model described in the preceding section and in [3,4] to support local policy modeling and their global integration. These extensions are: the Master Role Index (MRI), which is an XML schema to track roles across systems; a new UML Policy Slice Diagram (PSD) that models a specific segment of an established security policy with respect to a role, its permission, and the entities on which the permissions act; and a new UML Security Policy Schema Set (SPSS) that represents the complete security policy as an interconnection of the PSDs.

To begin, the Master Role Index (MRI) is an XML schema that keeps track of the many different roles across all the constituent local systems that are exchanging information to provide services to the IE big-data application. The MRI schema (left side of Figure 4.3) allows each role to have a unique identifier, a name, and a role description, and to indicate the type of information that the role can read and/or write. Instances (right side of Figure 4.3) are created for each role, as shown for the PoliceOfficer role.

The second extension, the Policy Slice Diagram (PSD), shown in Figure 4.4, is a new UML diagram that models a segment of the local security policy of an application (e.g., State 1 in Figure 4.1) from the perspective of representing security rules (SR) as triples. These triples have the form: $SR = <Role\ (r),\ Permission\ (p),\ Entities\ (ents)>$, where an entity can be an object, an XML attribute, an XML complexType, an XML XQuery, an XML schema, and so on; this is left very general to allow for all of the types of access that the different systems could provide (see Figure 4.1). In Figure 4.4(b), the PoliceOfficer PSD links to the PSD for the application and

```
<?xml version="1.0" encoding="utf-8"?>
<xs:schema id="MRI" xmlns="" xmlns:xs="http://www.w3.org/2001/
XMLSchema">
<xs:element name="MRI" msdata:IsDataSet="true"
msdata:UseCurrentLocale="true">
  <xs:complexType>
   <xs:choice minOccurs="0" maxOccurs="unbounded">
    <xs:element name="Role">
     <xs:complexType>
      <xs:sequence>
       <xs:element name="RoleID" type="xs:string"
                      minOccurs="0" />
       <xs:element name="RoleName" type="xs:string"
                      minOccurs="0" />
       <xs:element name="RoleDescription" type="xs:string"
                      minOccurs="0" />
       <xs:element name="RoleRequirements" type="xs:string"
                      minOccurs="0" />
      </xs:sequence>
     </xs:complexType>
    </xs:element>
   </xs:choice>
  </xs:complexType>
</xs:element>
</xs:schema>
```

```
<?xml version='1.0' encoding='ISO-8859-1' ?>
<MRI>
<Role>
  <RoleID>1234 </ RoleID>
  <RoleName>PoliceOfficer</ RoleName>
  < RoleDescription>Direct involvement with vehicle accidents and
                      other law requirements.
  </ RoleDescription >
  <RoleRequirements>All crash information that they are first
                      responders to. Can write/modify any portion of
                      the crash report to record progress in the
                      investigation.
  </RoleRequirements >
</Role>
</MRI>
```

FIGURE 4.3

Master role index schema (*left*) and instance (*right*).

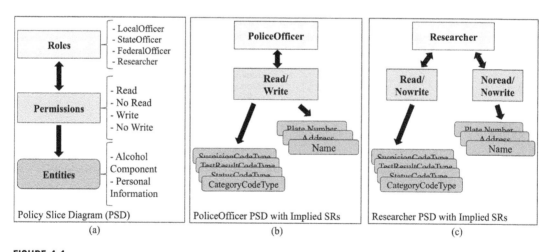

FIGURE 4.4

Policy slice diagram (a), policeofficer slice example (b), and researcher slice example (c).

indicates that PoliceOfficer can read the attribute *mmucc:AlcoholInvolvementSuspisionCodeType*. Figure 4.4(b) represents a total of 14 security rules: Read and Write in combination with *AlcoholInvolvementSuspisionCodeType*, *AlcoholTestCategoryCodeType*, *AlcoholTestResult CodeType*, *AlcoholTestStatusCodeType*, Person Name, Person Address, and Person License Plate. In comparison, the Researcher PSD in Figure 4.4(c) would have a Read and Nowrite with the

```xml
<?xml version="1.0" encoding="utf-8"?>
<xs:schema id="SRs" xmlns=""
        xmlns:xs="http://www.w3.org/2001/XMLSchema" >
<xs:element name="SRs" msdata:IsDataSet="true"
             msdata:UseCurrentLocale="true">
  <xs:complexType>
    <xs:choice minOccurs="0" maxOccurs="unbounded">
      <xs:element name="SecurityRule">
        <xs:complexType>
          <xs:sequence>
            <xs:element name="Role" type="xs:string"
                  minOccurs="0" />
            <xs:element name="Permission" type="xs:string"
                  minOccurs="0" />
            <xs:element name="Entity" type="xs:string"
                  minOccurs="0" />
          </xs:sequence>
        </xs:complexType>
      </xs:element>
    </xs:choice>
  </xs:complexType>
</xs:element>
</xs:schema>
```

```xml
<SRs>
<SecurityRule>
  <Role>PoliceOfficer</Role>
  <Permission>Read</Permission>
  <Entity>mmucc:AlcoholInvolvementSuspisionCodeType </Entity>
</SecurityRule>
<SecurityRule>
  <Role>PoliceOfficer</Role>
  <Permission>Read</Permission>
  <Entity>mmucc:AlcoholTestCategoryCodeType </Entity>
</SecurityRule>
<SecurityRule>
  <Role>PoliceOfficer</Role>
  <Permission>Read</Permission>
  <Entity>mmucc:AlcoholTestResultCodeType </Entity>
</SecurityRule>
<SecurityRule>
  <Role>PoliceOfficer</Role>
  <Permission>Read</Permission>
  <Entity>mmucc:AlcoholTestStatusCodeType </Entity>
</SecurityRule>
...
<SecurityRule>
  <Role>PoliceOfficer</Role>
  <Permission>Write</Permission>
  <Entity>mmucc:AlcoholTestStatusCodeType </Entity>
</SecurityRule>
<SecurityRule>
  <Role>PoliceOfficer</Role>
  <Permission>Write</Permission>
  <Entity>Person Name</Entity>
</SecurityRule>
<SecurityRule>
  <Role>PoliceOfficer</Role>
  <Permission>Write</Permission>
  <Entity>Person Address</Entity>
</SecurityRule>
<SecurityRule>
  <Role>PoliceOfficer</Role>
  <Permission>Write</Permission>
  <Entity>Person License Plate</Entity>
</SecurityRule>
</SRs>
```

FIGURE 4.5

Security rules schema (*left*) and instance (*right*).

alcohol components (eight security rules) and Noread/Nowrite on the personal components (six security rules). A sample security rule from Figure 4.4(b) is $< PoliceOfficer, << read >>,$ $AlcoholInvolvementSuspisionCodeType >$, which indicates that PoliceOfficer can read the attribute *AlcoholInvolvementSuspisionCodeType*.

In practice, the set of PSDs define all of the security rules for a local application (e.g., State 1 in Figure 4.1) that are published, which may be fewer than the rules available in the local system. Security rules are also defined using an XML schema (left side of Figure 4.5) and an instance for the security rules of PoliceOfficer (right side of Figure 4.5, shortened due to space limitations).

The union of all PSDs for a system (e.g., State 1 in Figure 4.1) defines a local security policy that is represented in the third extension, a new UML Security Policy Schema Set (SPSS). In the policy integration process, to be discussed in the next section, the SPSS (as shown in Figure 4.6) is

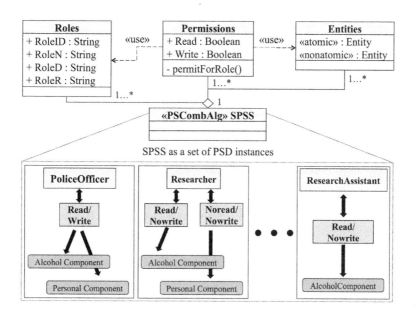

FIGURE 4.6

Example of a local security policy schema set.

published as the local security policy (e.g., State 1's local security policy). At the top of Figure 4.6, UML classes represent: Roles, with RoleID, RoleN, RoleD. and RoleR as string type members (defined in the MRI schema); Permissions, with read and write as Boolean members; and Entities with two generic object members, one extended with the «atomic» stereotype and the other with a «nonatomic» stereotype. Since entities can exhibit structural differences (e.g., an element in an XML schema can have multiple node children, or the XML element might be a leaf in the XML schema tree), we categorize utilizing two stereotypes, «atomic» and «nonatomic».

The Permissions class has a dependency relationship between the Roles and Entities classes to grant permission and verify the role and entity of the permission targets. All three classes have an instance level relationship of composition with the parent local security policy SPSS, which is shown at the bottom of Figure 4.6, where SPSS is a union of the various PSDs.

Note that the union of PSDs that yields the local security policy is not performed as a traditional mathematical set union. In order for security policies to maintain a proper degree of semantics, policy combination algorithms exist to determine the result of a policy evaluation when one or more rules (or policies in the case of policy sets in XACML) is inconsistent. For example, the XACML specification offers combination algorithms such as: *Deny-overrides*, in which a policy is denied if at least one of the rules is denied; *Permit-overrides*, in which a policy is permitted if at least one of the rules is permitted; *First-applicable*, in which the result of the first rule's evaluation is treated as the result of all evaluations; and *Only-one-applicable*, in which the combined result is the corresponding result to the acting rule. To maintain an equivalent level of knowledge in the SPSS, the union of its PSDs must be performed in a similar manner (to respect the local system's enforcement definitions). Towards this end, four corresponding policy slice combination algorithm stereotypes («deny-overrides», «permit-overrides», «first-applicable», «only-one-applicable») are assigned to the SPSS, which specifies which combination policy is enforced by local security policy (not shown due to space limits). In Figure 4.6, one of these four stereotypes would take the place of the «PSCombAlg».

Integrating local security policies into a global security policy

With the constituent security policies modeled as Local SPSS (LSPSS, with their granular segments with respect to roles represented as PSDs with the implied security rules), policy integration can be performed at the model level for a Global SPSS (GSPSS). In this section, we present a process for integrating a set of LSPSSs (for different states) into a GSPSS for the new big-data Crash Repository by using the MRI and security rules for each local SPSS. The four subsections discuss the following topics, respectively: our assumptions and various new concepts; the integration process of LSPPSs into a GSPSS; the security rule conflict resolution process; and the GSPSS that is generated for the big-data IE repository from the integration process that can be used via the big-data Crash Repository to provide access to constituent systems.

Assumptions and equivalence finding

The intent of the LSPPS is to allow each constituent local system (e.g., State 1 in Figure 4.1) to define one or multiple LSPSSs that contain different PSDs in order to tailor the information they are interested in publishing for inclusion in the GSPSS, which supports the big-data Crash Repository used by various stakeholders. In support of these ideas, there is an associated three-step development process as shown in Figure 4.7:

1. Local systems create one or more security policies (or specialized security policies) for information exchange that are publishable for public use by the big-data Crash Repository, which wants to subscribe to some or all of the information, functionality, or other entities governed by local security policies. This is shown in the leftmost box of Figure 4.7.
2. A new big-data application, like Crash Repository, is developed that will utilize resources from the local systems (specific LPSSs for states) by examining the exposed (published) instances, that is, the available LPSSs per constituent system. The new big-data application can subscribe to any policies exposed for public use that are relevant.
3. The new global security policy GSPSS for the new big-data application (Crash Repository) needs to integrate the exposed (published) local policies (LSPSSs of states) that have been subscribed to and merge them appropriately with the new security requirements of the new big-data application. This is shown in far right of the fourth box of Figure 4.7.

The publisher/subscriber paradigm (second and third boxes from left in Figure 4.7) provides an ideal way for the data source owner (local system) to decide what to present to whom, in order to reconcile the naming conventions of roles and their permissions and to clearly understand the way information can be shared and the scope of roles and their permissions against that information (entities). We assume that each LSPSS has its own set of security rules captured as XML instance triples $<role, permission, entity>$, and that the local application (e.g., State 1 in Figure 4.1) may

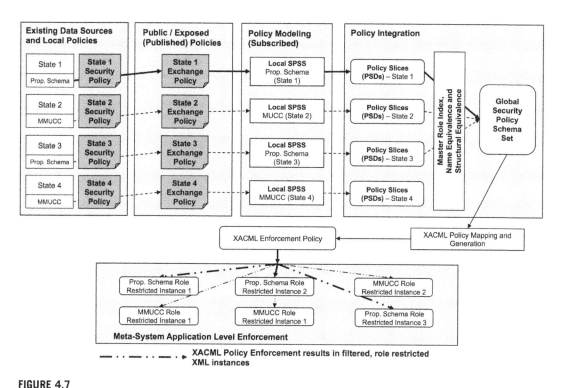

FIGURE 4.7

Processes to integrate local security into global security.

have multiple policies (see Figures 4.4, 4.5, and 4.6 again). We further assume that it possible in an automated fashion to attempt to match across a given set of LSPSSs to determine which policy slices (or portions of policy slices) have some level of equivalence. To accomplish this, we apply two types of equivalence used in programming language typing: name equivalence and structural equivalence, as shown in the Policy Integration box (upper right of Figure 4.7).

In name equivalence, recall that the MRI schema (discussed in the previous section 'Extensions for Policy Modeling and Integration) is a shared resource instantiated with an initial set of roles (in our case, for IE Repository, the roles PoliceOfficer, DOTWorker, Attorney, and Researcher). As each State/system (see Figure 4.1) establishes its own LSPSS (publishes a PSD or portion thereof), it is free to use existing instances (roles) in MRI, or to define new roles, thereby expanding this shared role repository. Notably, State 1 or State 2 may wish to expose only some of its PSDs, and, for each PSD, may want to limit the security rules even further. For name equivalence, if State 1 (from Figure 4.1) has a PSD with RoleID "1234" (PoliceOfficer) with RoleDescription and RoleRequirements (see Figure 4.2), and State 2 has a PSD with Role "1234" (PoliceOfficer) with the same RoleDescription and RoleRequirements values, these are clearly equivalent by name. This means they have the potential to also be structurally equivalent, but only to some degree. This is because the security rules are unique for each system: State 1 has its own set of security rules, and the ones for the PoliceOfficer role might be different from the security rules for the PoliceOfficer role in State 2. To see if the rules are the same, an algorithm for structural equivalence needs to be executed. We ask ourselves, does PoliceOfficer, as given in Figure 4.4(b) for State 1, have the exact same list of 14 security rules as the PoliceOfficer PSD for State 2? The hierarchies do not have to be identical, but the security rules that are constructed from each PSD must be equivalent, namely:

$$STATE_A \cdot PSD_{POLICEOFFICER} \cdot SRSet \equiv STATE_B \cdot PSD_{POLICEOFFICER} \cdot SRSet,$$

The level of structural equivalence can vary, if for instance:

$$STATE_A \cdot PSD_{POLICEOFFICER} \cdot SRSet \subset STATE_B \cdot PSD_{POLICEOFFICER} \cdot SRSet,$$

meaning that there are some rules in PoliceOfficer PSD for State 2 that are not present in State 1.

These equivalences (and containment) at the structural level are crucial to allow sharing among systems in a consistent manner. A GSPSS can be constructed for Crash Repository by its subscription to the available LSPSSs of the constituent systems (states). Unlike integrating homogeneous policies (policies utilized on the same application, with roles, permissions, rules, and so on that target a limited, unchanged set of resources), our process aims to integrate heterogeneous policies (which contain equivalent and nonequivalent roles and permissions) that act on different resources utilized and provided by different local systems. To successfully create the GSPSS for a new system like Crash Repository, the SPSSs need to be integrated via similarity finding (name equivalence and structural equivalence) and other techniques that analyze PSDs and their security rules across a set of published LSPSSs requested by the GSPSS.

Integration process for local SPSS

The integration process among multiple LSPSSs that are made available to the big-data application (Crash Repository) involves a name equivalence (among roles), utilizing the MRI, and structural equivalences (between security rules). Name equivalence verification among roles of heterogeneous local systems can be achieved by utilizing the MRI, where two roles are name equivalent if and only if their respective RoleName, Role Description, and RoleRequirements are the same (see right side of Figure 4.2 for XRSD). The formal definition is as follows:

DEFINITION 1

Local System A and Local System B with $L-SPSS_A$ and $L-SPSS_B$, $PSD_A \cdot Role$
$\subset L-SPSS_A$ *and* $PSD_B \cdot Role \subset L-SPSS_B$, *with* $PSD_A \cdot Role \cdot RoleName$
$= PSD_B \cdot Role \cdot RoleName$, *are name equivalent if f* $PSD_A \cdot Role \cdot RoleDescription$
$= PSD_B \cdot Role \cdot RoleDescription$ *and* $PSD_A \cdot Role \cdot RoleRequirements$
$= PSD_B \cdot Role \cdot RoleRequirements$

Finding name equivalences results in two sets of roles, an equivalent set (*EqualRoles*), which satisfy the above definition, and an unmatched set of roles (*DistinctRoles*), which do not match any other roles. The PSDs that correspond to the roles in the set *DistinctRoles* can automatically become part of the new GSPSS (if the LSPSS is subscribed to), as there is no risk of conflict with other roles and their respective security rules. Note that two roles that are name equivalent may still have differing sets of security rules in their respective PSDs. As a result, structural equivalence must also be quantified.

Structural equivalence is a process that assumes name equivalence is met and then proceeds to examine the actual security rules for each of the involved PSDs of LSPSSs. To verify structural equivalence, it is necessary to examine the security rules set (SRSet) of each involved PSD. Four possible combinations can result from comparing two security rule sets (SRSets):

- *Equality*, where the SRSets of two systems are contained within one another;
- *Containment*, where the SRSet of one PSD fully contains the SRSet of another PSD (proper containment, hence not equal);
- *Intersection*, where the SRSets of two PSDs have at least one SR rule in common (intersection is not empty); and
- *Disjoint*, where the SRSets of two systems with equivalent roles have no security rules in common (intersection is the empty set).

These relationships can result from either security rules overlapping with one another or different entities being available as resources on one system but not the rest (recall the security rule triple discussed in the section on extensions for policy modeling and integration).

Successfully integrating these SRSets while maintaining a proper level of security that complies with the local security requirements of constituent systems depends on the resulting relation between SRSets. Equality between SRSets is trivial; since no conflict can arise, both security rule sets can be consolidated and made part of the GSPSS. Handling SRSets that have a containment relation (proper subset) results in a subset of security rules being added to the GSPSS (all of the security rules of the contained smaller set), leaving the complement of the contained set in a state of conflict. There are two cases of intersection between two SRSets: When null, the SRSets are disjoint, both SRSets are in a state of conflict and there are two options: either include them both or omit them both from the GSPSS. When non-null, only the intersection is included, which means that security rules not in the intersection must be excluded.

Resolving conflicts of integrated security rule sets

This subsection discusses alternatives to resolve conflicts between intersected sets (security rules not in the intersection) and disjoint sets (SRSets that have no rules in common). Conflict resolution can be achieved through either a fully automated approach, which makes hard assumptions in order to provide the highest level of access control, or a human-guided approach, where human intervention is necessary to select which security rules will become part of the GSPSS, due to the intersection and disjoint cases. For an automated approach, there are different options capable of maintaining a proper sense of security:

- *Safe and lazy approach*: The GSPSS (e.g., Crash Repository) utilizes the most restrictive security rules, with respect to the entity involved, ensuring that no destructive operations (write) or breach in access (reading) can be performed; security rules are excluded if not held in common.

- *Data Owner over Requester*: The GSPSS utilizes the security rules specified by the data owner (e.g., a repository, and only if available), disregarding other, conflicting security rules.
- *Hierarchical approach*: A hierarchical order is given to the constituent local systems (and their LSPPSs of state repositories) to determine which security rules takes precedence over others. This order of priority results in security rules for a local system that can cover a wide spectrum in terms of the information to be published. That is, the granularity of data could range from a detailed patient record (lower level of a hierarchy) to an aggregation of records from a patient cohort (group that shares similar characteristics) for a population study (higher in the hierarchy).

While these automated approaches maintain a robust level of security, they also present limitations. In the case of the safe and lazy approach, there could be automatic denials of access that might have been authorized in the local system via human intervention. The data owner approach makes it possible to grant access to an otherwise secured request. In our example, State 1 can allow read permissions to Researchers in a localized manner (only when using the local system), but the big-data Crash Repository may want to limit the number of reads to a subset of the information or to the entire operation. The hierarchical approach offers the best alternative for resolving conflicts, but the implementation depends highly on the information published by LSPSSs being ranked by some process (or human). While there are natural hierarchies of information and its granularity in some domains such as health care, this is not necessarily the case in others.

Clearly, the safest approach to conflict resolution relies on human intervention in order to more create the appropriate GSPSS for a big-data application like Crash Repository. This is not an unreasonable requirement, given our modeling and engineering approach to policy integration, since the human designer of the new application is already examining the published PSDs for each LSPSS in order to decide which ones are relevant for the new information exchange/sharing application. The only additional task for the designer would be to make a final decision regarding any conflicting security rules. Potentially, if no name equivalence or structural equivalence exists between SRSets, the designer has to select each security rule that will become part of the system.

Creating the global SPSS

The software engineer who is creating the big-data Crash Repository will use the capabilities and the potential integration of LSPPs discussed in the preceding two subsections to arrive at a GSPSS that contains all of the relevant security rules for Crash Repository, with respect to the roles, packaged into respective Global Policy Slices. Using the approach discussed in this chapter, we deconstruct the local security policies by modeling them as SPSS (higher level), PSD (intermediate level), and SRSet (lower level), and we build the GSPSS following a bottom-up approach (from SRSets to Global PSDs to Global SPSS). Assuming that all of the SRSet conflicts have been resolved, whether using a human-guided or an automated approach that satisfies the new system's security requirements, the process of building the GSPSS involves three steps.

In the first step, Global Policy Slice Diagrams are built utilizing the SRSets with respect to roles. This is done with the aid of the MRI, following Definition 1 (see the subsection on integrating the local SPSS), ensuring that name equivalence is correct and that we are packaging the properly equivalent SRSets.

In the second step, a translation between the security rules represented in the PSDs (recall the triple $SR = < Role\ (r),\ Permission\ (p),\ Entities\ (ents) >$ and see Figures 4.4 and 4.6) and UML class members for the Global Policy Slice Diagrams is performed. To achieve this, we group the security rules by Role and Entities, and propose the following equivalence:

- The combination of possible permissions (read, write) and entities from the SR will result in a class method with a stereotype that determines whether execution of the method is permitted («allow») or denied («deny»).

   The third and final step is structuring the UML GSPSS artifact with respect to roles, as shown for the Crash Repository in Figure 4.8. This involves several rules and steps:

- Roles that will be part of the GSPSS (e.g., Crash Repository) are represented as UML subclasses of the GSPSS class (Figure 4.8). The role classes are named after their respective roles.
- Each role class will have descriptive string members, RoleDescription and RoleRequirements, per the MRI.
- Each role class will have methods as given in the second step of the integration. This means that two methods per targeted entity of each role will be given, as dictated by the SRs.

As an example, assume that multiple PoliceOfficer, DOTWorker, Attorney, and Researcher PSDs were integrated from State 1 and State 2 (from Figure 4.1). Roles are represented as subclasses of the parent GSPSS class of Crash Repository as shown in Figure 4.8. The subclasses named after the respective roles (PoliceOfficer, DOTWorker, Attorney, and Researcher) have two string members, which are instantiated to the MRI values of the RoleDescription and RoleRequirements. In turn, these classes have one method per each security rule, and their permissions are given as attached UML stereotypes. The DOTWorker and Attorney roles are structured similarly.

Note that the structure of the GSPSS is different from the local (L) SPSS structure (shown in Figure 4.6). The justification for this lies in the end use of each of these structures. In the case of the LSPSS (Figure 4.6), it tries to model an already existing security policy in order to obtain the policy slices (and in turn, security rules) without the loss of structure or information. The GSPSS for Crash Repository, on the other hand, is the result of integration that will be utilized as a blueprint for the generation of an actual enforcement policy. For this reason, we chose to structure the GSPSS in a role centric way, which simplifies the mapping process for the enforcement policy generation.

Finally, as shown in the bottom portion of Figure 4.7, the generation of XACML Enforcement Policy from the GSPSS follows a process similar to the one we used in our earlier research [4], where XACML policies were generated from modeled Role Slice Diagrams (see Figure 4.2 again). The benefit of utilizing the GSPSS as the blueprint for generating an XACML policy is that a similarity finding does not need to be performed (since it was done as part of the name and structural equivalence); instead, we are provided with an already organized diagram that only requires direct translation to code. As also shown in the bottom of Figure 4.7, the generated XACML policy, when applied to instances of the XML Schema (modeled as an XSCD in Figure 4.2), yields a set of role-restricted instances for the Crash Repository that interact with the LPSSs of the states. This means that the instances for each stakeholder are filtered by role prior to delivery for use via a combination of the XACML enforcement policies at both the LSPSS and GSPSS levels.

Global SPSS : Big-Data Application (Meta-System)

«GlobalPSDS» PoliceOfficer

- RoleName: String = "PoliceOfficer"
- RoleDescription : String = "Direct involvement with vehicle accidents and other law requirements."
- RoleRequirements : String = "All crash information that they are first responders to. Can write/modify any portion of the crash report to record progress in the investigation."

«allow» +readCategoryCodeType()
«allow» +readStatusCodeType()
«allow» +readTestResultCodeType()
«allow» +readSuspisionCodeType()
«allow» +readName()
«allow» +readAddress()
«allow» +readPlateNumber()
«allow» +writeCategoryCodeType()
«allow» +writeStatusCodeType()
«allow» +writeTestResultCodeType()
«allow» +writeSuspisionCodeType ()
«deny» +writeName()
«deny» +writeAddress()
«deny» +writePlateNumber()

«GlobalPSDS» DOTWorker

- RoleName: String = "DOTWorker"
- RoleDescription : String = "Local, state or federal level worker that handles crash data information."
- RoleRequirements : String = "Can read and curate data, make corrections."

«allow» +readCategoryCodeType()
«allow» +readStatusCodeType()
«allow» +readTestResultCodeType()
«allow» +readSuspisionCodeType()
«allow» +readName()
«deny» +readAddress()
«allow» +readPlateNumber()
«allow» +writeCategoryCodeType()
«allow» +writeStatusCodeType()
«allow» +writeTestResultCodeType()
«allow» +writeSuspisionCodeType ()
«deny» +writeName()
«deny» +writeAddress()
«allow» +writePlateNumber()

«GlobalPSDS» Attorney

- RoleName: String = "Attorney"
- RoleDescription : String = "Legal proxy of a party member involved in a vehicle accident."
- RoleRequirements : String = "Can read the crash data report for analysis, including (but not limited to) area statistics, alcohol report, etc."

«allow» +readCategoryCodeType()
«allow» +readStatusCodeType()
«allow» +readTestResultCodeType()
«allow» +readSuspisionCodeType()
«allow» +readName()
«allow» +readAddress()
«allow» +readPlateNumber()
«deny» +writeCategoryCodeType()
«deny» +writeStatusCodeType()
«deny» +writeTestResultCodeType()
«deny» +writeSuspisionCodeType ()
«deny» +writeName()
«deny» +writeAddress()
«deny» +writePlateNumber()

«GlobalPSDS» Researcher

- RoleName: String = "Researcher"
- RoleDescription : String = "Secondary involvement with crash data."
- RoleRequirements : String = "Can read and aggregate directly unidentifiable data for consolidation and statistic operations."

«allow» +readCategoryCodeType()
«allow» +readStatusCodeType()
«allow» +readTestResultCodeType()
«allow» +readSuspisionCodeType()
«deny» +readName()
«deny» +readAddress()
«deny» +readPlateNumber()
«deny» +writeCategoryCodeType()
«deny» +writeStatusCodeType()
«deny» +writeTestResultCodeType()
«deny» +writeSuspisionCodeType ()
«deny» +writeName()
«deny» +writeAddress()
«deny» +writePlateNumber()

FIGURE 4.8

Example of a global security policy schema set.

Related work

In this section, we describe and compare related research work done in three areas: big-data security, policy and security modeling, and policy integration methods. Big-data security is often aimed at the data storage system, the back end of the system. For example, security approaches for big-data are often aimed at the data warehouses or storage systems (https://securosis.com/assets/library/reports/SecuringBigData_FINAL.pdf). While this information is important, we have instead focused on the front end, the users of the big-data application, in this case, control access to IE Repository. Another common approach to relating big-data with security is to exploit the former to improve the latter. Big-data repositories can serve as knowledge bases to create more robust reactive and proactive security mechanisms (http://codeascraft.com/2013/06/04/leveraging-big-data-to-create-more-secure-web-applications/). As a matter of fact, the nature of the big-data security problem reduces the importance of security at the user level, and encourages problem-solving efforts to be focused instead on performance and reliability of operations (http://www.darkreading.com/applications/security-implications-of-big-data-strate/240151074), as well as the development of applications devoted to efficient data exploration and discovery (http://www.ibm.com/developerworks/library/bd-exploration/).

While the motivation for security in big-data scenarios is well defined (http://unm2020.unm.edu/knowledgebase/technology-2020/14-are-you-ready-for-the-era-of-big-data-mckinsey-quarterly-11-10.pdf; http://www.stanfordlawreview.org/online/privacy-paradox/big-data) [5,6], at the time of this writing, despite extensive literature research, we were unable to find any related work on big-data security from the meta-system perspective, for example, defining and controlling what the stakeholders of IE Repository are allowed to do at what times. We believe that the work presented in this chapter is one of the earliest attempts at interpreting big-data security from the perspective of the application (IE Repository) and its stakeholders.

For security and policy modeling, SecureUML [7], an approach based on RBAC and UML, combines a graphical notation for RBAC with constraints. It allows policies to be expressed using RBAC permissions, and complex security requirements can be done with a combination of authorization constraints. In our work, we take a similar graphical approach but concentrate on modeling and securing XML via the XSCD and XRSD diagrams (see Figure 4.2). A later effort [8] presents a model-driven security approach for designers to set security requirements along with system models to automatically generate an access control infrastructure. This approach combines UML with a security modeling language defining a set of modeling transformations; the former produces infrastructures for JavaBeans, and the latter can generate secure infrastructures for Web applications. Our work is done at a higher conceptual level. With respect to Web service security, [9] utilizes the model-driven architecture paradigm to achieve security for e-government scenarios with inter-collaboration/communication. This is achieved by describing security requirements at a high level (models), with relevant security artifacts being automatically generated for target architectures. This removes the otherwise present learning curve concerning specifying security requirements by domain experts with no technical know-how. This is dramatically different from our work, which is focused on information exchange and its security assurance. Similar to our presented work, [10] uses aspect-oriented programming and a generic security meta-model for the automatic generation of platform specific XACML. In contrast, our approach's objective is to model security policies for eventual integration for a distributed scope.

Policy integration approaches vary from similarity finding to specialized algebraic approaches. For example, [11,12] present a policy integration methodology to find similarity of policies on distinct levels (rule effects, targets, roles), and to integrate a set of defined rules with regard to policy decision conflicts. This is similar to our work, but differs in that our integration is done at the instance level (XACML) and involves homogeneous policies, while heterogeneous policies (LSPSSs) are integrated into a global one (GSPSS). Another approach [13] addresses the problem of integrating complex security policies at a detailed granular level using an algebraic solution that consists of five unary operations (three binary and two unary). This algebra is utilized as part of a framework for generating an instance policy automatically. Like [12], this approach also focuses on the instance level, creating a dependency on the OASIS XACML specification and policy structure to achieve proper results. These methods could not be used on security requirements defined in any other method (e.g., a database table with security rules, policies modeled with a different language, etc.).

CONCLUSION

In this chapter, we have presented a local policy integration process for sharing and exchanging XML that leverages UML as a policy-modeling tool, which has also been integrated into our prior work of security at a modeling level (Section 2 and [3,4]) and allows definition of a global security policy that supports a role-based access control approach for the stakeholders of a big-data application. We began by briefly reviewing our prior work [3,4] and introducing the XML schema class diagram (XSCD) and XML role slice diagram (XRSD) as given in Figure 4.2. Next, we introduced new modeling artifacts to support security policy definition in XML. These are a Master Role Index (MRI) that tracks the roles by names that can occur in multiple constituent systems that are used by a big application, and,two new UML diagrams to represent security policies for both the local and global systems: the Policy Slice Diagram (PSD) to track roles across systems, and the Security Policy Schema Set (SPSS) to represent the security policy for a set of interconnected PSDs. Using this as a basis, we are able to define local, heterogeneous SPSSs and integrate them into an all-encompassing global SPSS that contains all of the logic and semantic information of the constituent LSPSSs. In turn, this GSPSS can be utilized as a blueprint to automatically generate an enforcement XACML policy that can be readily deployed to a newly developed meta-system that uses data from across distinct repositories, such as the big-data Crash Repository example. Throughout the chapter we have employed an Crash Repository big-data application but focus the security on stakeholders and their access to the information.

The work presented in this chapter dovetails with our other three related research efforts. First, in [3] we proposed role-based access control extensions to UML that are capable of modeling XML schemas as a class level via the XSCD and capturing their role-based privileges via XRSD; as a result, security can be represented as a set of rules and permissions that a role has with respect to a specific element of an XML schema. Second, in [4], we presented the automatic generation of XACML security policies from the XML Role Slice Diagram, which can be used to model the XML security for a single local system, the predecessor of LSPSS in this chapter. Finally, in [14], we applied our work in [3,4] to a distributed, information exchange context where each local system in a group provides a set of resources that can define applications to use one or more of the local systems, with security enforced against XML using our approach in [3].

References

[1] Ferraiolo DF, Sandhu R, Gavrila S, Kuhn DR, Chandramouli R. Proposed NIST standard for role-based access control. ACM Transactions on Information and System Security (TISSEC) 2001;4:224–74.

[2] Liebrand M, Ellis H, Phillips C, Ting T. Role delegation for a distributed, unified RBAC/MAC. In: Proceedings of Sixteenth Annual IFIP WG 11.3 Working Conference on Data and Application Security King's College; 2002. p. 29–31.

[3] De la Rosa Algarín A, Demurjian SA, Berhe S, Pavlich-Mariscal J. A security framework for XML schemas and documents for healthcare. Proceedings of 2012 International Workshop on Biomedical and Health Informatics 2012. p. 782–9.

[4] De la Rosa Algarín A, Ziminski TB, Demurjian SA, Kuykendall R, Rivera Sánchez Y. Defining and enforcing XACML role-based security policies within an XML security framework. Proceedings of 9th International Conference on Web Information Systems and Technologies (WEBIST 2013) 2013. p. 16–25.

[5] Boyd D, Crawford K. Critical questions for big-data: Provocations for a cultural, technological, and scholarly phenomenon. Information, Communication & Society 2012;15:662–79.

[6] Chaudhuri S. What next?: A half-dozen data management research goals for big-data and the cloud. Proceedings of the 31st symposium on Principles of Database Systems 2012. p. 1–4.

[7] Lodderstedt T, Basin D, Doser J. SecureUML: a UML-based modeling language for model-driven security. «UML» 2002—The Unified Modeling Language; 2002. p. 426–441.

[8] Mouelhi T, Fleurey F, Baudry B, Le Traon Y. A model-based framework for security policy specification, deployment and testing. Model Driven Engineering Languages and Systems 2008. p. 537–52.

[9] Basin D, Doser J, Lodderstedt T. Model driven security: From UML models to access control infrastructures. ACM Transactions on Software Engineering and Methodology (TOSEM) 2006;15:39–91.

[10] Breu R, Hafner M, Weber B, Novak A. Model driven security for inter-organizational workflows in e-government. E-Government: Towards Electronic Democracy 2005. p. 122–33.

[11] Mazzoleni P, Bertino E, Crispo B, Sivasubramanian S. XACML policy integration algorithms: Not to be confused with XACML policy combination algorithms! Proceedings of the eleventh ACM symposium on access control models and technologies 2006. p. 219–27.

[12] Mazzoleni P, Crispo B, Sivasubramanian S, Bertino E. XACML policy integration algorithms. ACM Transactions on Information and System Security (TISSEC) 2008;11:4.

[13] Rao P, Lin D, Bertino E, Li N, Lobo J. An algebra for fine-grained integration of XACML policies. Proceedings of the 14th ACM symposium on access control models and technologies 2009. p. 63–72.

[14] De la Rosa Algarín A, Demurjian SA, Ziminski TB, Rivera Sanchez YK, Kuykendall R. Securing XML with role-based access control: Case study in health care. In: Ruiz Martínez A, Pereñíguez García F, Marín López R, editors. Architectures and Protocols for Secure Information Technology. p. 334–65. IGI Global; 2013.

Gamification of Information Security Awareness Training

## 5

Guillermo Francia, III, David Thornton, Monica Trifas, and Timothy Bowden

Jacksonville State University, Jacksonville, AL, USA

INFORMATION IN THIS CHAPTER

- Information security and awareness
- Gamification of training
- Game design and implementation
- Student learning
- Information security awareness metrics

INTRODUCTION

The need for well-trained Information Security and Assurance (ISA) professionals, as well as general information security awareness, has never been more pronounced, as shown by current news reports. To address this need, both industry and academia have been driven to innovative approaches. The use of digital games and game mechanics to further education has received growing attention and respect in the last several years. Numerous indications suggest that thoughtful employment of gaming elements can improve motivation and understanding. In this chapter, we describe our on-going project toward the gamification of information security awareness training.

Teaching concepts to children through digital games has received increased attention over the last few years. In fact, a school called Quest to Learn, which educates children in almost every subject through gameplay, opened in 2009 in New York. Even at the college level there has been an increased level of research and attention paid to learning in gaming environments such as Second Life. In the July 2007 issue of Communications of the ACM, Michael Zyda stated that youth spend a great deal of time playing video games, with some game developers claiming from 18,000 to 180,000 years of aggregate in-game play for their games [1].

One of the more vocal proponents of game-enhanced pedagogy is James Gee. He lists 13 principles employed in game design that are also good principles of teaching and learning: co-design, customization, identity, manipulation, well-ordered problems, pleasantly frustrating problems, cycles of expertise, just-in-time and on-demand information, fish tanks, sandboxes, skills as strategies, system thinking, and meaning as action image [2].

Many of Gee's principles can be mapped directly onto the educational psychology literature, which has a great deal to say about what components should be incorporated into an ideal game-enhanced pedagogy based on the findings of best practices in teaching [3,4]. First, challenging (pleasantly frustrating) goals are essential for increasing student motivation [5]. However, students must be given a great deal of scaffolding (well-ordered problems and just-in-time information) to help them reach these goals. That is, instructors must adjust the amount of guidance they give to fit the student's current performance level. When the task or concepts are new, the instructor is more likely to give directive feedback and explicit instruction, but as the student's competence increases, the scaffolds are removed and less guidance is given. Instructors also must set smaller, proximal goals, which students can more easily reach on their way to larger goals [6]. Feedback has also been found to be one of the most essential tools in increasing student persistence and understanding in courses [5].

As the video game industry grows to rival the movie industry, many wonder whether digital games can be anything more than an amusing time sink. Merrilea J. Mayo, director of the Government-University-Industry Research Roundtable at The National Academies, argues that video games could provide effective science and engineering education for the following five reasons:

- Sophisticated video games appeal to a wide audience.
- Students are not limited to the classroom setting and can play games any time.
- Video games are compelling and engaging.
- Video games stimulate chemical changes in the brain that promote learning.
- Initial studies show teaching effectiveness through games to be more effective than the classic lecture.

Several well-known gamification proponents have applied the approach at the secondary as well as post-secondary education levels. Paul Andersen, AP Biology instructor, received the 2011 Teacher of the Year award at the Montana Professional Teaching Foundation, in part for his gamified classroom. He presented a TED talk entitled *Classroom Game Design* [7], in which he describes how the use of leaderboards, points, and leveling helped to increase motivation and improve learning. Lee Sheldon, associate professor and co-director of the Games and Simulation Arts program at Rensselaer Polytechnic Institute, has employed gamification techniques in his university courses with great success. His book, *The Multiplayer Classroom* [8], outlines strategies for converting a standard course into a "gamified" course.

Jane McGonigal, author of *Reality Is Broken* [9], believes that games have the power to not only entertain but improve the world. She claims that multiplayer games teach people how to work more effectively in teams and that games allow people to sublimate stress. Further, McGonigal believes that the problem-solving components of games can be leveraged to make us innovators in truly important global issues like poverty and climate change.

Literature review
General concepts

In [10, p. 2], Quitney and Rainie define "gamification" as "interactive online design that plays on people's competitive instincts and often incorporates the use of rewards to motivate action that may include, among other things, virtual rewards such as points, payments, badges, discounts, and free gifts." Gamification—applying the mechanics of gaming to nongame activities—is a new strategy used for influencing and motivating groups of people. The business community started to realize the power it has to improve customer engagement, build loyalty, and offer incentives to employees and partners to perform at high levels. This concept has the potential to solve a variety of problems outside the business world as well, in areas such as:

- Health and wellness: health care cost containment, obesity programs, and smoking cessation
- Education and training: e-learning, corporate and vocational training, and on-line testing
- Public policy and government: education reform, climate change, and welfare reform

The technology consultancy firm Gartner projected that 50 percent of corporate innovation will be "gamified" by 2015. Another consulting firm, Deloitte, cited gamification as one of its top 10 technology trends for 2012 and predicted that serious gaming simulations and game mechanics such as leaderboards, achievements, and skill-based learning will be embedded in day-to-day business processes [11].

According to Quitney and Rainie [10], digital games generated $25 billion in sales in 2010, and their popularity is regarded as driving the Internet adoption of elements of gamification.

The rapid development of social networks, currently used by 70 percent of American Internet users, provides reward and status elements, which are embedded in implicit and explicit forms in the users' interactions with online communities.

Other applications of gamification, in addition to marketing, status and community building, and skills development, include education and problem solving. Games like Foldit, designed by a group of researchers at the University of Washington [12], have helped to produce real-world benefits. In this game, players generated a crowd-sourced discovery of a key protein component that may be helpful in HIV research.

Gamification, while a slightly ambiguous term, is probably best described as the use of design elements that are characteristic to digital games in non-gaming contexts. Common game elements include, but are not limited to, the following:

- Leaderboards
- Points (XP)
- Leveling (often with titles)
- Achievements
- Loot (or spendable resources)
- Instant feedback
- Clearly defined work/reward cycles
- Social elements
- "Boss" battles

Some popular examples of gamification include Microsoft's Ribbon Hero, which awards users with points, levels, and achievements for completing tutorial sequences. Other popular games, like Fitocracy and Chore Hero, convert activities that are often perceived as arduous into an entertaining diversion by leveraging social aspects, leveling up, and competition (via leaderboards). In pedagogy, gamification can be applied to at least three different approaches: (1) playing educational games, (2) making educational games, and (3) making the program of study itself "game-like."

Serious games

Though many games are entertaining by nature, a well-designed game has the potential to confer serious benefits. Clark Abt, a war-games and simulation-training specialist, said the following in his 1968 book *Serious Games*: "[Games] have an explicit and carefully thought-out educational purpose and are not intended to be primarily for amusement. This does not mean that serious games are not, or should not be, entertaining" [13, p. 9]. While there is no clear-cut definition of serious games, a primary component of a serious game is the delivery of learning objectives through engaging and interactive gaming components.

Games adoption in multiple domains

Military training and learning have a long history of using immersive 3D technologies and gaming methods to improve learning outcomes. For the past several years, the US military has recognized the value of using video games for training to accommodate the media preferences of the military personnel and to leverage the fidelity of the technology. Middle Eastern cultural training is a key component of this initiative. The Institute for Creative Technology (ICT) at the University of Southern California (USC) is a major developer of interactive military training modules. The Enhanced Learning Environments with Creative Technologies (Elect) suite of products utilizes the PsychSim social simulation system, which seeks to understand social simulations [13,14]. Elect employs an intelligent coach and tutor to provide the student with pedagogical feedback about social and cultural issues.

The training system Virtual BattleSpace 2 is a fully interactive, three-dimensional gaming system used by the UK army for customized training. It can be used to simulate real terrains and equipment for a multitude of training exercises. The training applications include convoy driving, unmanned vehicle flying, and soldier training and debriefing, among others [15].

The application of serious games dealing with health issues is another area of considerable growth. The Annual Conference on Games for Health is experiencing a steady increase in participation [16]. Health games for practitioners, like the Hollier Simulation Centre pilot program in the United Kingdom, allow junior doctors to experience and train for a variety of medical scenarios by employing computerized mannequins as patients [17]. The learning process occurs through hands-on experiences and session reviews of digital recordings.

According to IBM, serious games will be used by between 100 and 135 of the Global Fortune 500 by 2012. In a study of the relationship between leaders in massively multiplayer online role-playing games (MMORPGs) with real-world leadership, IBM stated the following: "The organizational and strategic challenges facing players who serve as game leaders are familiar ones: recruiting, assessing, motivating, rewarding, and retaining talented and culturally diverse team members; identifying and capitalizing on the organization's competitive advantage; analyzing multiple streams of constantly changing and often incomplete data in order to make quick decisions that have wide-ranging and sometimes long-lasting effects" [18, p. 1].

Digital games can play an important role in education or training. Some instructors have been using immersive environments and gaming technology in order to reach their students. This shift in teaching practices has been supported by advances in gaming technology and realism. Nowadays, it is less expensive to develop digital games because of availability of game engines, games middleware, and mods (modified versions of existing games); these tools make it possible for people with little or no programming experience to develop digital games. Instructors who are interested in creating educational digital games can focus on the educational features rather than the underlying technology.

Benefits of digital games

Digital games can develop cognitive, spatial, and motor skills. Teachers can use games to emphasize facts, principles, and complex problem solving. Games can also be used to increase creativity or to provide practical examples of concepts and rules that may be difficult to illustrate in the real world. Teachers can make use of games to perform experiments that could be dangerous when performed in real life, such as experiments that use hazardous materials and equipment. While games are often not explicitly educational, they possess intrinsic qualities that challenge learners' cognitive abilities. Playing well-designed games has the potential to increase the time students spend learning, increase difficulty along with their ability, and allow them to fail without fear.

Gamification system
System architecture

A basic gamification system architecture is shown in Figure 5.1. The two servers facing the Internet are publicly accessible for registered users. The Game Server is a main file transfer

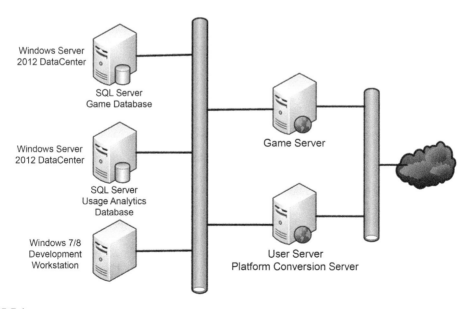

FIGURE 5.1

Information security awareness gamification system architecture.

machine where games, which are categorized by platform, can be downloaded. The Platform Conversion Server serves as a conversion system for users to convert their games to a desired operating system platform. The three servers on the backend serve three functions: (1) as a repository for all the games that were developed, (2) as a user and system data collection system, and (3) as a development and testing platform for games and other applications.

Software tools

GameMaker is an easy-to-learn, multiplatform, highly configurable game engine produced by YoYo Games. It supports fast application development through built-in libraries and functions relevant to digital gaming. It was created by Professor Mark Overmars, head of the Center for Advanced Gaming and Simulation at Utrecht University. GameMaker's features include the following: AI path-finding, advanced collision detection, animated graphics, built-in image editor, particle effects, joystick/gamepad support, multi-channel audio/video playback, and a powerful scripting language.

One of the most useful features of GameMaker is its multi-format export feature. Once a game is developed, it can be released for multiple platforms, including Apple iOS, Android, and HTML5. The engine is well documented, and the company website (www.yoyogames.com) features a vast library of tutorials and sample games, many of them user-submitted.

Best of all, GameMaker features a graceful learning curve because of its visual programming style and its scripting language, GML. Students can create a bare-bones prototype in hours and a working game in just a few weeks. One of the authors of this chapter has employed this engine since 2007 in his game design courses. Student teams have completed over 75 games under his supervision. He also teaches numerous game programming seminars each year with middle and high school students.

Game design

Our design methodology is guided by Zichermann and Cunningham's work on game design elements [19]. Each of these elements is briefly described as follows:

Point Systems are perhaps one of the important components of a gamification system. They provide measures to track the progress of the game, the skill of the player, the interaction between the player and the game, and the status of the player.
Levels provide a measure of the status of difficulty. A good gaming system must provide a seamless transition for the player to transition to each level of difficulty with a reasonable amount of challenge.
Badges provide tokens of achievement toward the goal, indicating and encouraging progress.
Leaderboards provide a ranking of players and a quick comparison. This component may also be a motivational tool for the player to keep on improving in order to attain certain a certain status.
Challenges and quests keep the player engaged by providing the player with activities and pursuits that will constantly challenge the player's skills.

Onboarding provides a way to delicately usher a novice player into the gamification system. The system must facilitate this transition because the first few minutes of the game are the most critical in determining whether the player embraces the system or not.

Engagement Loops get the player engaged into the system, determine the manner in which the player disengages from the system, and gets the player re-engaged with the system.

Storyboards

Password awareness game

Figure 5.2 depicts the main menu for Brute Force, an educational game that focuses on teaching good password habits. From this menu, the user can choose to learn the rules of the game or start playing immediately. Random passwords fly around the screen, helping to set the theme of the game and draw users in.

Figure 5.3 provides users with the basic knowledge needed to play and enjoy the game. Personal information is used as a resource that players must defend throughout the game. The constant threat of identity theft motivates players to keep playing. The game's controls are fairly simple (mouse and keyboard), so the game is accessible to all ages and skill levels.

The storyboard on Figure 5.4 represents a general gameplay scenario, demonstrating the level design and core mechanics behind the game. Ease of use is paramount here; the interface is clean and intuitive, which keeps focus on the game. The adversaries are shown walking toward the pool of personal information, passing through the password sockets along the way. The password bank is shown on the left side of the screen.

Should a user choose a weak password, or one that has already been tried, the storyboard shown in Figure 5.5 encapsulates the progress of the game. This is only a sample screen, as the in-game

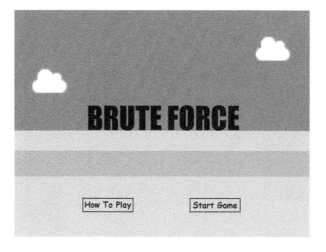

FIGURE 5.2

Main menu.

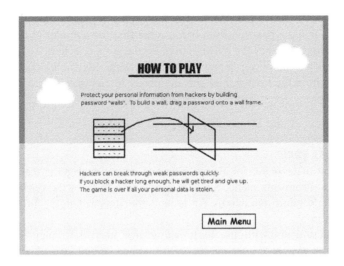

FIGURE 5.3

Rules of the game.

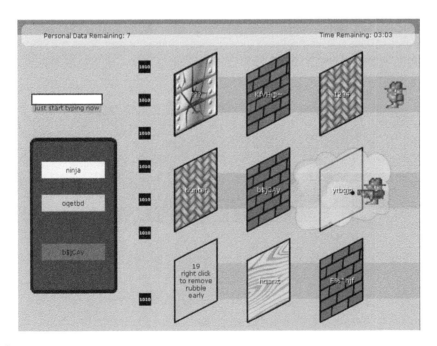

FIGURE 5.4

The gameplay scenario.

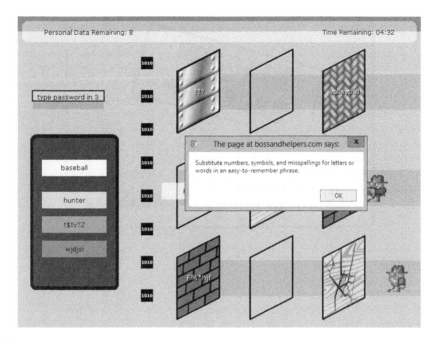

FIGURE 5.5

The informational scenario.

message will change depending on the context of the game (bad password, repeat, etc.). The purpose of in-game messages is to educate the user without the user having to read too much at once. The tutorial manager employs a geometric back-off with regard to help pop-ups. Thus, a player is notified about a misstep less and less often in order to provide gradually decreasing scaffolding. The user learns gradually, in an enjoyable manner, as the game progresses.

Phishing awareness game

This game carries the same focus on an educational and enjoyable experience that is accessible regardless of skill level. Message Received aims to inform users on what phishing is and how to avoid it. From the title screen shown in Figure 5.6, the user can learn the controls or start a game immediately.

The core concept behind the game is that the airplane base that must be defended from enemy planes. Players must inspect the messages (e-mails, websites, etc.) sent by each plane and decide whether or not to accept them. Over time, players will learn to discern legitimate e-mails and websites from phishing attempts.

The storyboard shown in Figure 5.7 shows a typical scenario in the game. Airplanes are flying overhead, each carrying either a bomb or a soldier. The user interface consists of a readout displaying the current plane's message, a base health monitor, and two buttons for deciding whether the current message is good or bad. As long as the player makes good decisions, the base will remain undamaged.

FIGURE 5.6

The *message received* main screen.

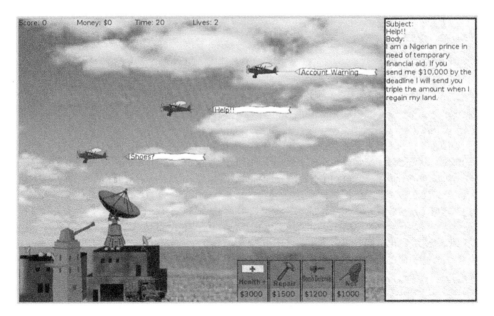

FIGURE 5.7

A typical game scenario.

Figure 5.8 depicts a sample popup that displays when a player accepts a bad message. These screens change based on the context of the game and will help explain why the message was bad. As the players progress through the game, they will become better at filtering out phishing attempts.

FIGURE 5.8

Informational screen.

Information security awareness games

The information security awareness training games are currently implemented and deployed. The testing and evaluation phase will commence during the Fall 2013 term. The planned game-based training modules include: Password Protection, Phishing Scam, Spam, Spyware, ID Theft, Wireless Vulnerabilities, Anti-Virus Protection, Digital Forensics, and Critical Infrastructure Protection.

Information security awareness metrics

Kark and Stamp published a Forester Research survey [20] documenting the struggle of organizations to provide a meaningful report for managers to make decisions on the security of their information systems. Security metrics can be effective tools for discerning the effectiveness of various components of a security program [21]. A well-known saying states, "What cannot be measured cannot be improved."

Our gamification system facilitates the monitoring of the state of information security awareness within an organization through the point system and leaderboard components. A Web-enabled database will be enabled and utilized for data collection and analytics. A Web-based reporting system will be designed and implemented to generate comprehensive reports on the state of information security awareness.

CONCLUSION AND FUTURE PLANS

The critical need for Information Security and Assurance (ISA) professionals is becoming more pronounced, as evidenced by past and current news pertaining to cyber-espionage, cyber-intrusion, cyber-warfare, and even cyber-crimes. There are numerous calls to both the industry and academia to address this need, as well as government initiatives that highlight both the national and global importance of cybersecurity. We have presented an overview of an ongoing project in gamification of information security awareness training as a modest contribution to this area of national importance. We envision this project as a catalyst for expanding the information security curriculum from the secondary to the graduate level of education. An opportunity to instill ISA concepts into the mindset of the next generation of professionals exists and we intend to take leadership in this process.

Future plans to enhance and expand the gamification project include:

- adding vulnerability and system penetration tools into the gaming scenarios;
- exporting Web-based information security games; and
- expanding the ISA training games to address the business, industrial, and government sectors' needs.

Acknowledgments

This chapter is based on a project partly supported by the Department of Defense-National Security Agency under grant number H98230-12-1-0427 and the National Science Foundation under grant award OCI-0959687. Opinions expressed are those of the authors and not necessarily of the granting agencies.

References

[1] Zyda M. Creating a science of games. Communications of the ACM; 2007 July.

[2] Gee J. Learning by design: games as learning machines. Interact Educational Multimedia 2004;8:15−23.

[3] Donovan S, Brandsford J. How students learn: History, science, and mathematics in the classroom. [Internet]. Available from: <http://www.nap.edu/catalog.php?record id=10126>; 2005 [accessed 8.02.13].

[4] Bell P, Lewenstein B, Shouse A, Feder M. Learning science in informal environments: People, places, and pursuits. [Internet]. Available from: http://www.nap.edu/catalog.php?record id=12190; 2009 [accessed 08.02.13].

[5] Hattie J. Visible learning: A synthesis of over 800 meta-analyses relating to achievement. New York, NY: Routledge; 2008.

[6] Stipek D. Motivation and instruction. Handbook of educational psychology. NY: MacMillan; 1996; p. 85−113.

[7] Anderson P. Classroom game design. [Internet]. Available from: <http://www.youtube.com/watch?v=4qlYGX0H6Ec>; [Accessed 13.06.13].

[8] Sheldon L. The multiplayer classroom: designing coursework as a game. Cengage; 2011.

[9] McGonigal J. Reality is broken: Why games make us better and how they can change the world. Penguin Books; 2013.

[10] Anderson JQ, Rainie L. Pew Research Center. [Internet]. Available from: <http://www.pewinternet.org/~/media/Files/Reports/2012/PIP_Future_of_Internet_2012_Gamification.pdf>; 2012 [accessed 30.01.13].

[11] Gartner Newsroom. [Internet]. Available from: <http://www.gartner.com/newsroom/id/1629214>; 2011 [accessed 02.02.2013].

[12] Khatib F., Cooper S., Tyka M. D., Xu K., Makedon I., Popovic Z., Baker D., FoldIt Players. Algorithm discovery by protein folding game players, Proc. Natl. Acad. Sci. USA; 108:47; 18949 −18953; 2011.

[13] Abt CC. Serious games. Viking Press; 1970.

[14] USC Institute for Creative Technologies. [Internet]. Available from: <http://ict.usc.edu/news/two-ict-projects-win-army-modeling-and-simulation-awards-for-fy08/>; 2013 [accessed 02.02.13].

[15] Ulicsak M. Games in education: Serious games. [Internet]. Available from: <https://www.evernote.com/shard/s18/res/3d58cb23-d313-4364-bff3-d5bb733e601f/Serious-Games_Review.pdf>; 2010 [accessed 30.01.13].

[16] Games for health. [Internet]. Available from: <www.gamesforhealth.org>; 2013 Feb [accessed 06.02.13].

[17] Hollier Simulation Centre. [Internet]. Available from:< www.hollier-simulation-centre.co.uk>; 2012 [accessed 30.01.13].

[18] Reeves B, Malone T, O'Driscoll T. Leadership's online labs. [Internet]. Available from: <http://hbr.org/2008/05/leaderships-online-labs/ar/1>; 2008 [accessed 30.01.13].

[19] Zichermann G, Cunningham C. Gamification by design: Implementing game mechanics in web and mobile apps. Sebastopol, CA: O'Reilly Media, Inc.; 2011.

[20] Kark K, Stamp P. Defining an effective security metrics program best practices. Forrester Research; 2007.

[21] Payne SC. A guide to security metrics. [Internet]. Available from: <http://www.sans.org/reading_room/whitepapers/auditing/guide-security-metrics_55>; 2006 [accessed 15.11.12].

A Conceptual Framework for Information Security Awareness, Assessment, and Training

6

Mohammad Hassanzadeh[1], Narges Jahangiri[2], and Ben Brewster[3]
[1]Tarbiat Modares University, Tehran, Iran
[2]Ministry of Education, Tehran, Iran
[3]Sheffield Hallam University, Sheffield, UK

INFORMATION IN THIS CHAPTER

- Dimensions of information security awareness
- The role of human factors in information security
- The Information Exchange Environment
- Information security policies

INTRODUCTION

The increased advancement and integration of information and communication technology (ICT) applications within business processes have made ICT a significant part of management, supervision, and service delivery. Consequently, a large proportion of staff members' organizational life is spent working with computerized information systems, thus shaping their information exchange environment (IEE). The IEE is constantly exposed to electronic and physical threats such as organized crime for the purpose of content defalcation, information flow monitoring, database disruption, and violation of intellectual property rights.

Despite security arrangements, the vulnerability of the IEE has increased as threats become more widespread and intricate. Because of this, information security has become a fundamental issue for businesses, organizations, and governments. Much of the increased emphasis on information security can be attributed to an increase in security breaches, many of which have resulted in significant losses for the affected enterprises. Effective countermeasures, technologies, and solutions usually exist for many of these breaches and contributing threats. However, in most cases they are not deployed correctly nor effectively [1]. This is because technological solutions cannot deal with all information security risks, and the people in the organizations are, in fact, the primary and most critical line of defense [2,3].

Traditionally, the primary focus has been on the technical aspects of information security, with less emphasis placed upon human resources and the people affected by and exposed to information security threats. However, this flawed reliance on technology seems to be changing; managers, security experts, and other decision makers are now increasingly focused on people rather than technology.

When it comes to "human factors," there are various controls available related to training and awareness. No longer is just the technical security training of IT staff considered sufficient; information security awareness training and other awareness campaigns have become mandatory requirements for everyone [1]. This is proving to be a compulsory principle in international information security management system standards and the related codes of best practices [4—6].

People are the key factor in both the success and the failure of information security management in organizations. Every security breach or security problem is, in fact, frequently associated with human input, not only with technology. Any organization thinking of mitigating information security risks through purely technological countermeasures is likely to eventually fail [7]. In any type of organization, each and every employee should be convinced of and taught to contribute to and comply with information security rules, implementations, and controls in order to achieve successful and effective information security management [8,9]. Studies have shown that for employees to contribute in this way, they must be exposed to proper awareness education and other awareness mechanisms and tools on a regular basis [10,11]. They learn what is necessary for protection of information security as related to their particular roles and responsibilities [12—15].

An awareness of information security can lead to changes in behavior and an enhancement of suitable security activities, allowing people to be responsive with regard to information security and enabling a gradual cultural change within organizations [1,14—18]. Together with technical solutions for information security, it is necessary to make revisions to regulations and policies based on the new requirements of IEE and secure deployment of IT applications. It is also critical to promote information security awareness in organizations and society through training.

Background and literature

A large amount of information is stored and retrieved digitally with speed and precision. The development of networks and the digitization of documents have exposed knowledge repositories to various kinds of threats, theft, and destruction. One of the most important problems in the information era is protecting the security of information [1]. Since the 1980s, various standards have been developed for information security, such as: BS7799, ISO/IEC TR13335, and ISO/IEC 27001. Many organizations have implemented information security management systems (ISMS) to evaluate the security of their information systems. Since the start of the third millennium, various studies have dealt with the assessment and awareness of information security management. Maconachy et al. [19] considered important aspects of information security, placing specific focus on security services (availability, integrity, authentication, confidentiality and nonrepudiation), security countermeasures (technology, policy, practice, and people), and security status (transmission, storage, and processing) to achieve information security objectives.

Kruger and Kearney [14] assessed the information security awareness of users at an international gold mine company and discovered important factors regarding the different dimensions of information security awareness of users. They investigated information security awareness in three aspects: knowledge, attitude, and behavior. They also investigated several sub-areas including: adherence to policies, password secrecy, Internet and email safety, security of mobile equipment in information transmission, reporting of security related events, and suitable actions and consequences.

Chang and Lin [20] proved that organizational culture has a direct effect on information security culture. Some organizational factors, including cooperation, innovation, consistency, and effectiveness on the principles of information security (confidentially, integrity, availability, and accountability), were investigated. The findings indicated that organizational culture factors have a positive impact on information security settings. Taheri [21] proposed a conceptual framework for the human factors in information security systems. In this framework, the impact of factors such as top manager support, self-efficacy, skill, experience, awareness, and training users on information security were examined. Namjoo et al. [22] found that managerial information security awareness (MISA) is directly and positively related to managerial actions toward information security (MATI Security). Kritzinger and Smith [23] presented a conceptual view of an Information Security Retrieval and Awareness (ISRA) model for industry to enhance information security awareness among employees. They provided a common body of knowledge for information security suited to industry that would ensure that technical information security issues did not overshadow the nontechnical, human-related information security issues. The proposed common body of knowledge also focuses on both professionals and low-level users of information.

Shaw et al. [15], in an article titled "The Impact of Information Richness on Information Security Awareness Training Effectiveness," divided information security awareness into three levels: conception, comprehension, and projection (similar to Kruger's work). They investigated the richness of the information in online training based on hypertext, multimedia, and hypermedia by studying 250 Managerial Information Security (MIS) students using electronic education and concluded that there is a positive relationship between these levels. By enhancing information richness, information security awareness increased, such that the effect of hypermedia contents would be more than that of multimedia and hypertext contents. Nikrerk and Solms [17] indicated that the lack of "people knowledge" concerning information security is the main threat. It has become widely accepted that the establishment of an organizational subculture of information security is key to managing the human factors involved in information security.

Mete et al. [1] carried out an information security awareness project by training and subsequently auditing the effectiveness and success of this training. Each employee took part in information security training. Results showed the effectiveness of the project and the impact of human awareness on the success of information security management programs in all organizations, regardless of their size, location, culture, or type of business. Veiga and Eloff [18] found that components of information security, such as leadership and governance in an organization's technology protection and operation, security policies, security program management, and user security management, influence information security behavior and develop information security culture.

Kruger et al. [16] found that the use of vocabulary tests to assess a security awareness level is beneficial. A significant relationship between knowledge of concepts (vocabulary) and behavior was observed. Regarding the background presented, the issue of information security awareness is one of nontechnical and human factors, although in organizational information security, less attention is paid to this issue than is paid to technical solutions. Within any organization, when authorities pay more attention to accurate programming, they can institutionalize good security behavior in employees and enhance the culture of information security [1]. By deploying a strategy of information security, organizations and commercial institutes can benefit from advantages such as [21]:

- Reduced possibility of inactivation of systems and programs (opportunity loss)
- Effective use of human and nonhuman resources within an organization (increased efficiency)
- Reduction of the costs of data loss and information by harmful viruses or security holes (protection of valuable data)
- Improvement of intellectual property protection

It should be noted that the cost of preventing a security problem is always much less than the cost of recouping the resulting losses.

Human factors and information security

As the literature has indicated, technology, people, and processes are three dimensions that have been identified as critical success factors for information security strategy deployment [1]. Physical access and control of IT systems are examples of the technological aspects that provide support for others. These systems usually provide services that are vital for the definition of access controls. Security processes indicate how companies conduct themselves in formal and informal manners. This is demonstrated throughout the company and includes all procedures, routine activities, trends, and instructions, as well as interactions with customers, suppliers, and commercial partners. Even the plans required for the discovery of any critical situation are included. Eventually, human factors define the development of people, in line with organizational systems and processes. Of course, human factors are usually ignored, perhaps because they are not measurable and cannot be quantified [21].

Investigations into the erroneous use of IT emphasize the role of human factors in information security deficits. In security plans for information systems, the human factor is usually considered as the core component [14]; even if all technical arrangements and security policies are developed and well established, lack of user awareness may make all technical solutions ineffective [13,15]. However, users with security awareness will significantly reduce security risks in the workplace [13–15], improve the safe information behavior of users, and provide a foundation for the enhancement of information security effectiveness throughout the organization [24,14,17,15,18].

Information security learning continuum

Rather than being viewed as a product, the components that make up information security mean that it is more suitable to instead treat it as an organizational process. Each component has its own weight and function. An element should not be considered more than what it is; nor should another parameter be neglected or underestimated just because a particular aspect of information security (e.g., hardware security) is being dealt with. However, new emergent technologies bring with them new and often unique threats. What must we do to effectively utilize technologies and prevent direct or indirect threats? Undoubtedly, direct users of these technologies have very important roles and can be considered as the front line of defense [2,3]. According to the National Institute of

Science and Technology (NIST) definition, the IT security-learning continuum of users is divided into levels of awareness, training, and education (NIST, SP 800-50).

The IT security learning continuum (NIST, SP 800-50) provides a visual representation of how education in regards to information security can disseminated to users. Learning at the first level begins with awareness and training for all employees and then builds upon this through information security literature that relates information security to user's roles and responsibilities in regards to IT systems. This then evolves through special education and experience delivered by information security specialists (NIST, SP 800-16).

Awareness

Security awareness efforts are designed to change behavior or reinforce good security practices. The purpose of awareness presentations is simply to focus attention on security. They focus on reaching a broad audience, often using attractive packaging techniques. Awareness presentations are intended to help individuals to recognize IT security concerns and respond accordingly. In an awareness presentation, the learner simply receives information; this is in contrast to a training environment, where the learner has a more active role. A few examples of IT security awareness materials and activities include:

- Promotional or specialty trinkets with motivational slogans
- A security reminder banner on computer screens, which appears when a user logs on
- Security awareness videotapes
- Posters or flyers

Training

The NIST Special Publication 800-16 (p. 16—17) states with regard to training: "The 'Training' level of the learning continuum strives to produce relevant and needed security skills and competencies by practitioners of functional specialties other than IT security (e.g., management, systems design and development, acquisition, auditing)." The most significant difference between training and awareness is that training seeks to teach knowledge and skills that allow a person to perform a specific function and enhance job performance, while awareness seeks to focus an individual's attention on an issue or set of issues. However, the skills acquired during training are built upon a foundation of awareness—in particular, upon security basics and literacy material. A training curriculum does not necessarily lead to a formal degree from an institution of higher learning; however, a training course may contain much of the same material found in a course that a college or university includes in a certificate or degree program (NIST, SP 800-16).

Education

The NIST Special Publication 800-16 (p. 17—18) says regarding education: "The 'Education' level integrates all of the security skills and competencies of the various functional specialties into a common body of knowledge, adds a multidisciplinary study of concepts, issues, and principles (technological and social), and strives to produce IT security specialists and professionals capable of vision and pro-active response."

Education is an essential aspect of the human factors that influence information security management within any organization. When human factors, such as education are not considered, technical solutions have little impact on information security management [14,23]. Education incorporates other human factors including the provision of training and the increasing of awareness in the development of effective information security management [12,13,25,14,15,1].

Generally, an effective security structure must be composed of both technical and functional elements in order to have mutual impact on the risks that are developed due to omissible information. Because of the increasing speed of technological changes, the need for flexible security measures is felt more than ever before. These rapid changes increase the requirements for accurate management of omissible information and employee awareness about that management. Remedies and methods of using it should be part of security policies along with suitable policy-making. Employees who work with vital information must know the concept of omissible information security. If we consider security education and awareness as a part of our job, we feel more responsibility regarding our role and tasks, which results in a reduction of information security risks. The overall strategy of information security awareness and training for users is presented in Figure 6.1.

Dimensions of information security awareness

The weak security behavior of users (for example, security errors, lack of accuracy, lack of attention) has played a part in many security events [13−15]. Increased security awareness on the part

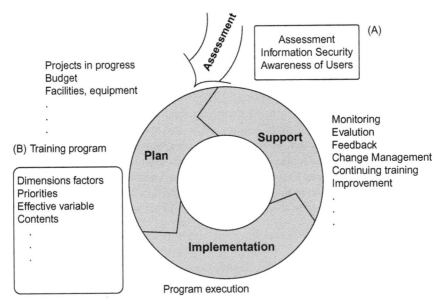

FIGURE 6.1

The overall strategy for improving information security user awareness.

of end users can lead to the emergence of a security culture and, in turn, the creation of increased security competence. Although there is no single method for programming security awareness that is compatible with all situations across all organizational and human levels, determining a specific method for implementing a security awareness program based on security awareness dimensions is necessary for every organization [15].

Many organizations are aware of the importance of implementing a program for informing employees about information security [15]. For these programs to be successful, it is important that employees reach acceptable levels in three dimensions of awareness about security risks. These three dimensions are: knowledge, attitude, and behavior [14,15].

Knowledge

The first step for securing an organization is to be able acquire knowledge of and also track the security risks of the working environment. Knowledge means identifying the presence of a threat and developing an awareness of it. The advantages of forming an accurate image of an environmental security threat can be enhanced by optimizing observation and security awareness perception [15].

Attitude

To have enough knowledge about occurring security events and their impact is not helpful in isolation. A positive attitude is needed for this knowledge to be used effectively. If users reach a sufficient level of perception regarding information security, it can prove beneficial to both them and the organization [14].

Behavior

Behavior is the third dimension of security awareness. In this dimension, when employees develop good security behaviors and habits, a strong information security culture within the organization is established. Timely decisions can be made through preparation, projection, and behavior. The ultimate objective of an effective program of security awareness is making the users prepared to react to potential security risks [15]. Prevention is better than treatment. In order to prevent security risks, end users must be able to predict and deal with future security attacks.

A field study

Here we report findings of applied research. User information security awareness was assessed in nine categories: email, spam, and attachments; backup; passwords; social engineering; mobile security; malware (e.g., viruses, worms, and Trojans); Internet, reporting security events; and adherence to organizational policies. These nine were assessed in three dimensions: knowledge, attitude, and behavior. The relationship and values of seven independent variables were investigated.

The independent variables include: gender, job experience, education, familiarity with IT, professional field, occupation, and job category. Data was collected via a questionnaire based on relevant subject literature and the ideas of experts. The questionnaire consisted of 70 questions that were grouped into nine factors of information security awareness in three dimensions of information security (knowledge, attitude, and behavior). The results were expressed in the Likert scale, where 1 represents "strongly disagree" and 5 represents "strongly agree." The questionnaires were manually distributed and collected.

The research sample was selected from employees of a financial organization estimated to consist of 1400 staff distributed across branches all over the country. We selected a sample of the population via random sampling. Five hundred employees were selected. Of the 530 questionnaires distributed, 500 questionnaires were returned and also qualified for investigation. During distribution of the questionnaires, the participants received verbal and written explanations about the subject of the questionnaire and its importance within the organization. Normality of distribution was justified using a Kolmogorov-Smirnov test. The validity of the questionnaire was confirmed by expert practitioners of information security affairs and by using Cronbach's Alpha Coefficient (0.8452). The scores and priorities of elements in each of the three components are presented in Table 6.1. (Percentage)

As Table 6.1 shows, the total information security awareness of employees, analyzed in the three dimensions (knowledge, attitude, and behavior) was average. Employees were lower in knowledge than in the other two dimensions (attitude and behavior). An employee's attitude toward information security was more positive and effective than exhibited behaviors regarding security considerations would suggest. An awareness score of less than 60 was indicated as unsatisfactory,

Table 6.1 Results of the Evaluation of Information Security User Awareness (Percentage)

IS Factors	Knowledge	Attitude	Behavior	Total Awareness of Factors	Priority Factors for Training
Email, Spam	68.250	53.00	68.00	63.132	5
Backup	79.180	68.560	69.167	72.354	9
Password	73.457	83.375	57.500	71.445	8
Social Engineering	66.375	59.000	59.875	61.750	2
Mobile Security	58.937	62.357	82.957	68.09	7
Malware	69.270	69.375	67.620	67.90	6
Internet	48.98	70.625	67.220	62.275	4
Reporting	55.832	65.000	53.083	57.972	1
Adhere to Policy	61.25	63.500	64.000	62.017	3
Total Awareness/ Dimensions	64.59	65.867	65.470	65.310	

☐ 10-59: Unsatisfying-action required ☐ 60-79: Monitor-action potentially required ☐ 80-100: Unsatisfying-no need for action.

suggesting that action was required. Cases where the score was between 60 and 80 indicated the need for more attention and monitoring. In areas where the score was higher than 80, no action was required. The average total information security awareness of employees was 65.31, indicating that the organizational managers and information security authorities should begin a comprehensive effort to create a suitable program, based on research results, to enhance employee information security awareness.

The last column identifies the priority of factors in an education program. Among these factors, the need to educate and consider reporting was ranked higher than other factors. The need to educate and consider password and backup factors was ranked lower than other factors. The priorities of factors calling for further attention and training are shown in Table 6.1. In order to test the results, Kramer and Spearman's correlation coefficient was used. The results are shown in Table 6.2.

As shown in Table 6.2, the correlation between demographic and organizational variables was not considerable. Despite this, some of the variables do show correlation with information security awareness components (in particular, IT skills and job category). Based on the detailed results of interconnectivity of variables, a conceptual framework was prepared to articulate the basic components of a training program on information security awareness in organizations.

The proposed framework is composed of two steps. The first step deals with users' information security awareness in three dimensions: knowledge, attitude, and behavior. The conclusions from the assessment phase can be used for prioritizing the factors and their dimensions in regard to demographic and organizational factors. In turn, priorities obtained in the second phase can be functionalized in the assessment phase. As shown in Figure 6.2, the priorities of dimensions in each factor are varied. Improving employee awareness can be achieved through the required dimensions and the priority of the determined factors of information security.

As depicted in the framework, the components for each individual task differ. For example, reporting needs to be trained by prioritizing behavior first, then knowledge, and then attitude, but backup needs to be enhanced by prioritizing attitude first, then behavior, and then knowledge. Making appropriate policies for information security requires considering the organization's overall

Table 6.2 Correlation Coefficient Between the Independent Variables and the Dependent Variable (Information Security Awareness)

	Independent Variable	P Value	Correlation Coefficient
1	Gender	0.699	−0.085
2	Education level	0.308	0.072
3	Familiarity with IT	0.002	0.216
4	Job experience	0.109	−0.109
5	Organizational degree	0.010	0.182
6	Field	0.002	0.324
7	Job category	0.006	0.212

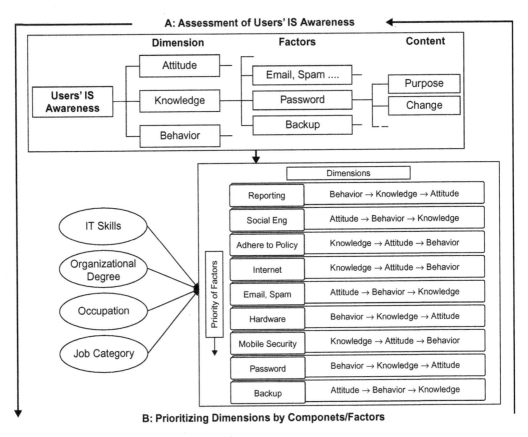

FIGURE 6.2

Conceptual framework of information security awareness, assessment, and education.

priorities and formulating the policies accordingly. By doing this, the objectives of creating a good information security policy can be reached.

CONCLUDING REMARKS

Most organizations invest in technical solutions to providing information security while investing little in the human aspects of information security. This is because there is no appropriate estimation of the information security awareness of staff members in organizations. IT managers should consider nontechnical and human factors in information security, such as enhancing employees' awareness of it. For this purpose, it is valuable to evaluate employees' awareness of and training in information security concepts and behaviors. The conceptual framework proposed in this chapter draws on the prioritization of three key dimensions (knowledge, attitude, and behavior) relevant to each factor. This framework could be a starting point for articulating and improving users' awareness of information security as well as designing an education program for use in organizations.

References

[1] Mete E, Erdem U, Saban E. The positive outcomes of information security awareness training in companies. Information Security Technical Report 2009;14:223−9.

[2] Tipton HF, Krause M. Information security management handbook. Auerbach Publications; 2007.

[3] IT Governance Institute. Information security governance: Guidance for information security managers. ITGI Publishing; 2008.

[4] Scholtz T. Structure and content of an enterprise information security architecture. Gartner Res 2006; January 23.

[5] International Organization for Standardization. ISO/IEC 27001: ISO; 2005.

[6] Wood CC. Information security policies made easy. Penta Safe Security Technologies; 2002.

[7] Mitnick KD, Simon WL. The art of deception. John Wiley & Sons, Inc; 2003.

[8] Ashenden D. Information security management: A human challenge? Elsevier Information Security Technical Report 2008;13:195−212.

[9] Williams P. In a 'trusting' environment, everyone is responsible for information security. Elsevier Information Security Technical Report 2008;13:207−215.

[10] Lacey D. Managing the human factor in information security: how to win over staff and influence business managers. Wiley.com; 2011.

[11] Gehringer EF. Choosing passwords: security and human factors. In: ISTAS'02 International Symposium on Technology and Society; 2002. p. 369−373.

[12] Thomson ME, Von Solms R. Information security awareness: Educating your users effectively. Information Management & Computer Security 1998;6(4):167−73.

[13] Wilson M, Hash J. Building an IT security awareness and training program. National Institute of Standards and Technology 2003;sp800-50:20−79.

[14] Kruger HA, Kearney WD. A prototype for assessing information security awareness. Computer & Security 2006;25:289−96.

[15] Shaw RS, Charlie C, Harris, Albert, Huang H. The impact of information richness on information security awareness training effectiveness. Computer & Education 2009;52:93−100.

[16] Kruger HA, Drevin L, Steyn T. A vocabulary test to assess information. Information Management & Computer Security Journal 2010;18(5):316−9.

[17] Nikrerk JF, Solms V. Information security culture: a management perspective. Computer & Security 2009;5:142−4.

[18] Veiga AD, Eloff JHP. A framework and assessment instrument for information security culture. Computer & Security 2010;29(2):196−200.

[19] Maconachy V, Schou CD, Ragsdale D, Welch D. A model for information assurance: An integrated approach. Workshop on Information Assurance and Security. United States Military Academy; West Point, NY; 2001 Jun 5−6.

[20] Chang E, Lin CS. Exploring organizational culture for information security management. Industrial Management & Data Systems 2007;107:1−10.

[21] Taheri M. The role of human factors in the security of information systems [thesis]. Tehran, Iran: Tarbiat Modares University, IT management, Dept; 2007.

[22] Namjoo C, Dan K, Goo J. Knowing is doing: An empirical validation of the relationship between managerial information security awareness and action. Information Management & Computer Security 2008;16:484–5.

[23] Kritzinger E, Smith E. Information security management: An information security retrieval and awareness model for industry. Computer & Security 2008;27:224–31.

[24] Stanton JM, et al. Analysis of end user security behaviors. Computers & Security 2005;24.2:124–33.

[25] Wilson M, et al. IT security training requirements: A role- and performance-based model. National Institute of Standards and Technology 2003;sp800-16:22–6.

Further Reading

Shaw SC, Charlie C, Chen RS. Mitigating information security risks by increasing user security awareness: case study of an information security awareness system. IT, Learning, and Performance Journal 2002;24:132–3.

Security Projects for Systems and Networking Professionals

7

Leonidas Deligiannidis[1], Charlie Wiseman[1], Mira Yun[1], and Hamid R. Arabnia[2]

[1]Wentworth Institute of Technology, Boston, MA, USA
[2]University of Georgia, Athens, GA, USA

INFORMATION IN THIS CHAPTER

- Overview of encryption techniques
- Example projects utilizing encryption technologies
- Overview of wireless security
- Towards the development of a Cyber Security Management framework
- Example of subverting wireless security

INTRODUCTION

Despite the growing demand for security professionals in all areas of computing and information technology, relatively few schools offer degree programs that incorporate hands-on security training. The result is that most security-oriented positions are filled either by security veterans or by fresh graduates who have little or no working security knowledge. A small number of free online resources are available (e.g., http://opensecuritytraining.info), but most security education ultimately happens on the job and only as needed.

This chapter provides an overview of introductory systems and network security by way of several projects and demonstrations. Clearly, this one chapter cannot serve as a complete picture of the vast field of security. Rather, it aims to be a starting point for newcomers to the security field who want to bridge the gap between concept and practice.

The materials presented in this work are derived from undergraduate courses taught in the Department of Computer Science and Networking at Wentworth Institute of Technology (WIT). That department offers two degree programs: one in computer science and one in computer networking. While the computer science degree program is a typical, traditional CS program, the computer networking program is more hands-on and exposes students to a broad skill-set in networking, computer science, and management.

One of the courses now offered regularly at WIT is a cryptography and network security course. The book used in the class is *Cryptography and Network Security: Principles and Practice*, by

William Stallings, Prentice Hall. This is an excellent book and is highly recommended to anyone interested in learning more about network security. There are several programming assignments that cover from the ground up symmetric encryption, digital signatures, digital certificates, and RSA public key cryptography. More recently, wireless network security has been incorporated into the curricula at WIT in several different courses, including the network security course, cryptography and network security, and wireless networking courses.

This chapter describes and discusses a selection of the projects, demonstrations, and future materials from these courses.

Background

It is suggested that hands-on, investigative teaching with associated exercises improves the learning performance of students [1]. It is also shown that engaging students in hands-on exercises promotes active learning and helps students develop critical thinking skills [2,3] better than simply covering lecture material in class and leaving students with many unanswered questions. This improves their learning performance and, as a result, increases the likelihood of programs to retain their students [2–9]. A three-year study was performed to determine why Science, Technology, Engineering, and Mathematics (STEM) majors switch to non-STEM majors [10]. They found that students switch majors because of lack of interest, teaching methodology ineffectiveness, and because they feel overwhelmed with the curriculum demands. Successful completion of the introductory courses for the first year is crucial in retaining students in a program, and most lecture courses are notoriously ineffective in engaging students [11].

DefEx is a set of hands-on cyber-defense exercises that focuses on undergraduate development through understanding and problem solving related to security [12]. These exercises include code and system level hardening, problem detection, digital forensics, wireless access point security, cross-site scripting, command and SQL injection, file uploading, and a wireless access point treasure hunt game based on wardriving that requires students to utilize all their skills from throughout the course.

Cryptography

In the cryptography course, the students are given two exams during the semester and a final at the end of the semester. The students are also required to attend every lecture and complete six assignments. Extra credit assignments are provided for students who are interested in learning more. In the next section we describe the major programming assignments and demonstrations we perform to motivate our students.

Assignment in symmetric encryption

The Data Encryption Standard (DES) algorithm used to be the most widely used symmetric cryptosystem in the world. It is a block cipher that was selected by the National Bureau of

Standards as an official Federal Information Processing Standard for the United States in 1976. DES is now considered insecure and has already been superseded by the Advanced Encryption Standard (AES) [13].

The DES algorithm takes a 64-bit plaintext block and a 64-bit-long secret key and transforms them into a 64-bit-long ciphertext block. Decryption must be performed using the same key as was used for encryption and the same algorithm in reverse to reproduce the original plaintext block.

The students learn about symmetric encryption algorithms, and they complete one assignment where they use DES to encrypt and decrypt a memory-mapped file. In another assignment, the students compare the performance of DES and AES by plotting how fast different-size files are encrypted and decrypted.

Assignment in hash functions

Cryptographic hash functions play an important role in modern communication technology. The input to a hash function is a file or stream of any size and the output is a fixed-size digital representation of the file that is normally less than 1KB and serves as the fingerprint of the original file (often called the message digest). It is impossible to reconstruct the original file with only the fingerprint. Moreover, changing a single bit of information in the input would result in a significantly different fingerprint. These algorithms are designed to avoid collision. In other words, it is very unlikely for two messages, M and M', to produce the same fingerprint using the cryptographic hash function H: $H(M) != H(M')$. Many cryptographic hash functions are based on the so-called MD4 algorithm initially proposed in [14], and they have received the greatest attention.

Students write a program to compute the message digest given different input streams. Then they modify the input in order to produce substantially different digests. The students are challenged to find two inputs that produce the same message digest. We then demonstrate how they can break MD5 using the techniques described in [15,16]. Specifically, we produce two different executable files that have significantly different purposes yet whose MD5 digests are identical. This shows that it is possible to have two different files with the same MD5 message digest and that using MD5 hashing to verify file downloads is not safe.

Extra credit assignment on steganography

Steganography is a technique used to conceal information so that only the communicating parties know about the existence of the information in any form [17]. Steganography uses a cover image, which is an image that has information embedded in it. Then there is the actual information itself, which could be anything from plain ASCII text or another image to pdf files, sound files, etc. After the information has been embedded into the cover image using any of the steganography techniques (such as Least Significant Bit Insertion), a Stego image [18] is obtained. It is also possible to encrypt the information before embedding it, thereby adding another level of security [19].

We demonstrate two applications that use steganography. Both of them are written in Java and are accessible via Web Start technology: HAE (Hide at End) [20] and Stego [21]. HAE demonstrates how one can hide any document of any size at the end of a PNG picture. The output looks exactly like the input, but the file is bigger in size. This tool relies on the fact that PNG viewers ignore everything after the end-tag of the PNG image. So, right after the end-tag, any other file or information can be appended. Students can use HAE to interactively hide pictures inside other pictures, retrieve them, and check file sizes. HAE inserts metadata (seven bytes) at the end of the first image, which describe the data that it hides after the end of this file. This way, HAE can easily retrieve the hidden information. One can experiment with hiding information after the end of an image by simply running the following command in Windows:

```
copy /B a.gif + p.pdf output.gif
```

This command copies a binary (/B flag), a.gif, appends to it the p.pdf file, and produces the output.gif file. Viewers will open the output.gif file and display the image stored in a.gif. However, we know that the hidden information in this case is after the end of the a.gif file.

Stego, shown in Figure 7.1, is an interactive graphical interface that allows one to hide text or images into other images, retrieve the secret text or image, and display it, all in the same window. Stego uses the Least Significant Bit insertion technique. This means that every bit of the secret is

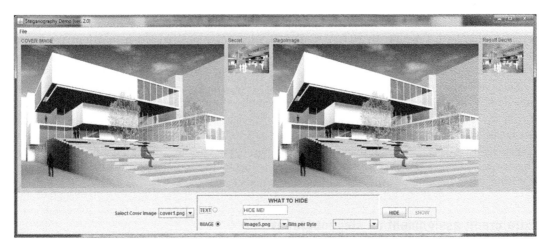

FIGURE 7.1

Graphical interface of the Stego steganography demonstration. application. Four images at the top, from left to right: the cover image, the secret image, the Stego image (output image containing the secret image), and the resulting secret image retrieved from the Stego image. At the *bottom*, the user first selects a cover image, then selects what to hide (text or image) and either types in the text or selects a secret image. The user then selects the number of least significant bits to be used to hide the secret image. Finally, the user can click on the "HIDE" button to create the Stego image and "SHOW" to retrieve the secret image hidden in the Stego image. The user can use the menu bar to save to the disk the intermediate steps (Stego, image, and result image). The user can then compare the images bit by bit with the original images.

inserted in the least significant bit of a byte that represents either the red, green, or blue color of the RGB pixel of the original image (the cover image). Stego also allows the students to hide more than one bit per byte. The effect can instantly be seen on the graphical interface. A user can also save each image on the system to inspect the file size, run a hash function on it, etc., or even load saved Stego images. This feature is provided from the pull-down menu. Figure 7.2 shows how the Stego image looks when the five least significant bits per byte are used to hide the secret image.

For an extra credit problem, we give the students the source code of Stego with one of the functions removed. The function is used to retrieve a secret image from the Stego image. This is the function that the students need to implement for extra credit.

Assignment in a key exchange algorithm

One of the questions students have with symmetric encryption algorithms concerns key distribution. One of the simplest algorithms that we illustrate and describe with real numbers is called Diffie-Helman. The students write a program to show how a "key" can be distributed to two entities without actually transmitting the key itself. The students have the option to work on an extra credit component. The extra credit problem is to use the Diffie-Helman key exchange algorithm to exchange keys in a secure client/server "chatting" application. They exchange a key, then use a symmetric algorithm to establish a secure connection and transmit text and images over the Internet. Later in the semester, after we cover asymmetric encryption and begin talking about Pretty Good Privacy (PGP), they can modify their program so that the key exchange is implemented using RSA.

FIGURE 7.2

A cover image (*left*) and a Stego image (*right*), side-by-side where the five least significant bits per byte are used to hide a secret image. Visible alterations can be observed at the top of the Stego image.

Assignment in asymmetric encryption

RSA [22] and elliptic curve [23] are two popular public key cryptosystems. Public key systems are the standard choice for sending secure information over an insecure channel or network connection. For example, a customer wants to send their credit card information to a website. There is no way for the customer and the Web vendor to share a secret key, as in symmetric encryption systems, without the risk of a third party overhearing the secret key. Instead, public key systems use two keys: a public key that is shared with everyone and a private key that is kept secret by the receiving party. The public key and the private key share a mathematical link, but it is not possible (or is at least computationally very difficult) to derive either key from the other.

RSA is one of the most commonly used public key cryptosystems on the Internet today. It is based on the premise that factoring very large numbers is difficult. "Large" numbers, in modern practice, are 1024-bit or 2048-bit numbers. That is, they are numbers on the order of 2^{1023} ($\sim 10^{307}$) or 2^{2047} ($\sim 10^{615}$). One of these large numbers is chosen to serve as the modulus for encryption and decryption and then a public key exponent and private key exponent are chosen following certain number theory principles. This is the general procedure for generating the associated public and private keys:

1. Choose two prime numbers: p and q.
2. Compute the modulus n: $n = pq$.
3. Compute Euler's totient function $\varphi(n)$: $\varphi(n) = (p-1)(q-1)$.
4. Choose the public key exponent e, such that $1 < e < \varphi(n)$ and e is co-prime with $\varphi(n)$.
5. Compute the private key exponent d, where $(de) \bmod \varphi(n) = 1$.

Step 4 is easily done by selecting a random prime number less than $\varphi(n)$ and then checking that it is not a factor of $\varphi(n)$. Step 5 is somewhat more computationally intensive, but can be computed with the Extended Euclidean algorithm. When this is completed, the public key is the pair (n, e) and the private key is the pair (n, d). Going back to the credit card example above, the Web vendor would send the customer their public key so that the customer can encrypt the credit card information. The private key is kept secret by the vendor. The customer uses standard encoding and padding schemes to produce the message, m, to be sent from the credit card information. To encrypt the message and produce the ciphertext, c, the customer uses this formula:

$$c = m^e \bmod n \tag{1}$$

The encrypted message c is then sent over the Internet and received by the Web vendor, who decrypts the message with this formula:

$$m = c^d \bmod n \tag{2}$$

There are a few different approaches to an RSA assignment. We implement three main components: generating the keys, encrypting and decrypting data, and sending information over a network. The full assignment has students completing all three phases to send a single encrypted file over the network. They first generate the public and private keys, then write a client/server application that allows a user to select a file and transmit it from the client to the server. The server stores the keys and transmits the public key to the client. The client encrypts the file, sends it, and then the server decrypts it.

The first and last steps can be omitted due to time constraints, if necessary. For example, instead of having students write code to generate the keys, they could compute one key pair by hand and use that directly. Alternatively, they could use existing tools such as OpenSSL [24] to generate the RSA keys. The file transfer could also be optional. Students could simply encrypt the file on the local system with one program and decrypt it with another. This would alleviate the need to have code that actually transmits the file, but loses the key exchange between two systems.

Demonstrations

Every student who takes this class is interested in knowing how a virus is written and how viruses work. We demonstrate to the students how four different keyloggers[1] work. We explain the code, which is written in C, and they can experiment with the programs. We also demonstrate three viruses. One of them attacks the browser, another attacks the operating system; of course, we only simulate the deletion and modification of system files. The third virus is a self-replicating virus that infects a machine when a user opens a file. We also demonstrate and explain how to copy DVDs and how they are protected. The code given is written in Java.

Another demonstration involves sending fake email messages (messages where the sender information is modified). A user can hide his or her identity to send emails to others, pretending being someone that the recipient knows. This way, a virus can be distributed. We also write code and utilize open source software to crack passwords and eventually gain system access. Throughout the course, we have the opportunity to talk about ethical issues. However, the students should learn about these techniques so that they can protect themselves in the real world.

Wireless network security

In our course on cryptography and network security, we provide students with solid security fundamentals and hands-on exercises that are focused on wired networks. As a next step, we plan to incorporate wireless security issues into our course. Since wireless networking and communication systems are already fundamental in typical day-to-day use of the Internet, teaching wireless networking and security issues is a demanding task [25,26]. A recent trend in the use of wireless technologies to improve current law enforcement networks demonstrates that wireless security is emerging as a premier research and development issue [27,28]. As the demand increases in law enforcement, hospitals, industry, and the military, so does the importance of wireless and security education for systems and networking professionals.

---

[1]Keyloggers are special purpose hidden programs that record every keystroke, and sometimes mouse movements, of a user without their knowledge. They then have the capability of sending those keystrokes to a malicious operator so that the user's passwords, credit card numbers, and other personal information can be compromised.

802.11 Wireless security

Despite the popularity of the topic, courses on wireless and security are not frequently offered at the undergraduate level; this is mainly due to the fact that the topic is relatively new and requires further research. Unlike teaching graduate students, teaching a wireless security course to undergraduate students can be a difficult task because the study requires the students to have strong knowledge in both technical implementation and theoretical concepts. Thus, continuous research has been made to develop effective teaching methods [29−33]. Following this trend, we present an overview of hands-on wireless security materials for undergraduate students, with specific examples of 802.11 wireless security experiments.

The first generation of the 802.11 standard included security protection in the form of Wired Equivalent Privacy (WEP) [34]. WEP was found to be vulnerable to various statistical weaknesses, especially in the encryption algorithm it employed to scramble data passed over the Wireless Local Area Network (WLAN) [35,36]. While attempts were made to correct the problem, it is still a relatively simple procedure to crack the protocol. Essentially, one can pull the password right out of the air. In response, the Wi-Fi Alliance stepped up to the challenge and created an interim standard called Wi-Fi Protected Access (WPA). However, WPA's pre-shared key (PSK) mode is also crackable due to a flaw that exists in the authentication procedure [37]. For the most part, a system that involves a password and a user is flawed. The fact that most users select poor passwords provides an opportunity that can be exploited.

802.11 WEP Key cracking experiment

The purpose of this experiment is for the students to learn how to exploit 802.11 wireless security properties. In this project, students use a variety of devices and tools that are widely used in the real market, including Linksys WRT54G series access points (802.11 g broadband routers), OpenWRT [38] firmware, Wireshark [39], and Aircrack-ng [40]. The overall goal is to crack the key of the WEP protocol defined in the 802.11 standard.

To begin this experiment, students have to figure out detailed information about the target wireless network, which includes the MAC address, clients associated with the target access point (AP), security features, etc.

The next step requires students to capture the data traffic on the target network. At this stage, students should have enough information (i.e., weak IVs [41]) to crack the WEP key and be able to associate and utilize the wireless network. Tools such as Airodump-ng [42] can be used. In this experiment, students need to collect enough WEP-encrypted data. For a 64-bit WEP key, between 20,000 and 50,000 packets are required [41,37]. While collecting packets, the WEP key cracking program (aircrack-ng) can be run at the same time. Figure 7.3 shows the cracking output of aircrack-ng.

However, this is a passive approach and requires large amounts of data traffic and data collection time. A more efficient technique is to inject Address Resolution Protocol (ARP) request packets through fake authentication and association [43]. The only known effective way to crack WPA-PSK is to force a re-authentication of a valid client. By forcing the connected client to disconnect, we capture the re-connect and authentication packets (i.e., the four-way handshake), as shown in Figure 7.4.

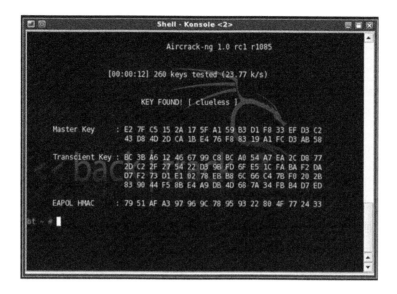

FIGURE 7.3

Cracking output of Aircrack-ng.

No..	Time	Source	Destination	Protocol	Info
5275	55.703027	Fon_a2:70:32	IntelCor_55:5c:d0	EAPOL	Key
5276	55.703040		Fon_a2:70:32 (RA)	IEEE 802	Acknowledgement
5277	55.703554	IntelCor_55:5c:d0	Fon_a2:70:32	EAPOL	Key

▶ Frame 5275 (155 bytes on wire, 155 bytes captured)
▷ IEEE 802.11 Data, Flags: ......F.
▷ Logical-Link Control
▽ 802.1X Authentication
    Version: 2
    Type: Key (3)
    Length: 119
    Descriptor Type: EAPOL WPA key (254)
  ▷ Key Information: 0x01c9
    Key Length: 32
    Replay Counter: 2
    Nonce: FDC5DE9DC8C75DF0C4E8FCF7CBC86B2E8A872CD81C80CCBE...
    Key IV: 00000000000000000000000000000000
    WPA Key RSC: 0000000000000000
    WPA Key ID: 0000000000000000
    WPA Key MIC: 7182499BCA8A2F68D7AD38ACD74B3A67
    WPA Key Length: 24
  ▷ WPA Key: DD160050F20101000050F20201000050F20201000050F202

FIGURE 7.4

Wireshark screenshot of a WPA authentication frame.

CONCLUSION

The projects and demonstrations presented in this chapter are excellent activities for students, computing professionals, and law enforcement personnel to begin building practical security experience. In particular, projects are discussed in detail from two major areas of security: cryptography and wireless security.

Cryptographic methods underlie protocols and mechanisms in order to provide secure data transmission and storage. Projects from the three major areas of encryption (hashing, symmetric key, and asymmetric key) are described, showing how they allow students to learn how they work, when it is appropriate to use them, and how they might be vulnerable.

Wireless security is addressed separately, as transmitting signals over the air opens up several different security vectors to consider. The most important one is that wireless signals are broadcast in such a way that any receiver in range can hear and interpret the signal. It is vital that such signals be encrypted and protected at all times. Older techniques such as WEP are susceptible to statistical-based exploits, as demonstrated to students in one project, whereas newer protocols like WPA are more robust.

Together, these two areas cover a broad base of security principles that any computing IT or law enforcement professional should be familiar with, regardless of particular specialization. The projects described are ways to gain that knowledge first-hand by implementing, testing, and sometimes breaking the relevant protocols and services.

References

[1] Yates JK, Voss M, Tsai K. Creating awareness about engineering careers: innovative recruitment and retention initiatives. 29th ASEE/IEEE Frontiers in Education Conference. 1999 Nov;3. San Juan Puerto Rico.

[2] Tester JT, Scott D, Hatfield J, Decker R, Swimmer F. Developing recruitment and retention strategies through "Design4Practice" curriculum enhancements. 34th ASEE/IEEE Frontiers in Education Conference; 2004 Oct; Savannah, GA, USA.

[3] Tester JT, Hatfield J. The Design4Practice sophomore design course: Adapting to a changing academic environment. ASEE Annual Conference Proceedings; 2005 June.

[4] Anderson-Rowland MR, Blaisdell S, Fletcher S, Fussel P, Jordan C, McCarthey MA, et al. Comprehensive programmatic approach to recruitment and retention in the college of engineering and applied sciences. In: Ptoc of the 29th Annual Frontiers in Education Conference. 1999;1.

[5] Courter SS, Millar SB, Syons L. From the students' point of view: experiences in a freshman engineering design course. Journal of Engineering Education 1998;87(3):283–7.

[6] Wang H. From C to Python: Impact on retention and student performance. In: Proc of The 2008 International Conference on Frontiers in Education: Computer Science and Computer Engineering (FECS'09); 2009 Jul 13-16; Las Vegas NV, USA. p.170–4.

[7] Tanaka JC, Gladney LD. Strategies for recruiting and retaining minorities in physics and biophysics. Biophys J 1993;65:552–8.

[8] Hatfield JM, Tester JT. LEGO plus. Proceedings of the 2005 American Society for Engineering Education Annual Conference & Exposition; 2005.

[9] Parcover JA, McCuen RH. Discovery approach to teaching engineering design. Journal of Professional Issues in Engineering Education and Practice 1995:236−41.

[10] Seymour E, Hewitt NM. Talking about leaving: Why undergraduates leave the sciences. Boulder, CO: Westview Press; 1997.

[11] Twigg CA. Using asynchronous learning in redesign: Reaching and retaining the at-risk student. JALN 2004;8(1):7−15.

[12] Glumich SM, Kropa BA. DefEX: Hands-on cyber defense exercises for undergraduate students. In: Proc of the 2011 Int Conf on Security and Management (SAM'11); 2011 July; USA.

[13] US Department of Commerce/National Institute of Standards and Technology, FIPS PUB 197; Advanced encryption standard (AES). Federal Information Processing Standards Publication, 2001. [Internet]. Available at: http://csrc.nist.gov/publications/fips/fips197/fips-197.pdf.

[14] Rivest RL. The MD4 message-digest algorithm. Crypto, LNCS 1991;537:303−11.

[15] http://www.codeproject.com/Articles/11643/Exploiting-MD5-collisions-in-C.

[16] MD5 Collision Demo [homepage on the Internet]. [Updated Oct. 11 2011; cited 2013 Sep. 11]. Available from: < http://www.mscs.dal.ca/selinger/md5collision/ >.

[17] Kipper G. Investigator's guide to steganography. Print ISBN: 978-0-8493-2433-8 eBook ISBN: 978-0-203-50476-5. Auerbach Publications; 2004.

[18] Ptzmann B. Information hiding terminology. First Workshop of Information Hiding Proceedings. Lecture Notes in Computer Science. 1996 May 30-Jun 1; Cambridge, UK. Springer-Verlag. 1996;1174:347−50.

[19] Choche A, Arabnia HR. A methodology to conceal QR codes for security applications. Proceedings of the International Conference on Information and Knowledge Engineering (IKE'11); 2011 Jul; USA.

[20] Hide At End Demo Software [homepage on the Internet]. [Cited 2013 Sep. 11]. Available from: < http://faculty.cs.wit.edu/Bldeligia/PROJECTS/HAE/index.html >.

[21] Stego Demo Software [homepage on the Internet]. [Cited 2013 Sep. 11]. Available from: < http://faculty.cs.wit.edu/Bldeligia/PROJECTS/Stego/index.html >.

[22] Rivest R, Shamir A, Adleman L. A method for obtaining digital signatures and public-key cryptosystems. Commun ACM 1978;21:2.

[23] Black I, Seroussi G, Smart N. Elliptic curves in cryptography. Cambridge University Press; 1999.

[24] OpenSSL Project [homepage on the Internet]. [Cited 2013 Sep. 11]. Available from: http://www.openssl.org/.

[25] Ma D, Tsudik G. Security and privacy in emerging wireless networks. [Invited Paper]. Wireless Commun IEEE 2010;17(5):12−21.

[26] Shiu YS, Chang SY, Wu HC, Huang SCH, Chen HH. Physical layer security in wireless networks: a tutorial. Wireless Commun. IEEE 2011;18(2):66−74.

[27] Thomas P, Cloherty J, Ryan J. ABC News. After $350 million, law enforcement wireless network success still doubtful. [Internet]. 2012 Jan. Available at http://abcnews.go.com/.

[28] Seth M, Kasera SK, Ricci RP. Emergency service in Wi-Fi networks without access point association. In: Proceedings of the first International Conference on Wireless Technologies for Humanitarian Relief (ACWR '11). ACM, New York, NY; 411−19.

[29] Sarkar NI, Craig TM. Teaching wireless communication and networking fundamentals using Wi-Fi projects. IEEE Transactions on Education. 2006;49(1):98−104.

[30] Güzelgöz S, Arslan H. A wireless communications systems laboratory course. IEEE Trans Educ 2010;53 (4):532−41.

[31] Lin Y. An ultra low cost wireless communications laboratory for education and research. IEEE Transactions on Education 2012;55(2):169−79.

[32] Chenard JS, Zilic Z, Prokic M. A laboratory setup and teaching methodology for wireless and mobile embedded systems. IEEE Transactions on Education 2008;51(3):378−84.

[33] Mateo Sanguino TJ, Serrano Lopez C, Marquez Hernandez FA. WiFiSiM: an educational tool for the study and design of wireless networks. IEEE Trans Educ 2013;56(2):149—55.

[34] IEEE standard for information technology - telecommunications and information exchange between systems- local and metropolitan area networks - specific requirements -Part II: Wireless LAN medium access control (MAC) and physical layer (PHY) specifications. ANSI/IEEE Std 802.11. 2003.

[35] Boland H, Mousavi H. Security issues of the IEEE 802.11b wireless LAN. Canadian conference on electrical and computer engineering; 2004. 333—36.

[36] Fluhrer SR, Mantin I, Shamir A. Weaknesses in the key scheduling algorithm of RC4. In: Vaudenay S, Youssef AM, editors. Revised Papers from the 8th Annual International Workshop on Selected Areas in Cryptography (SAC '01). London, UK: Springer-Verlag; p. 1—24.

[37] Berghel H, Uecker J. WiFi attack vectors. Commun ACM 2005;48(8):21—8.

[38] OpenWRT [homepage on the Internet]. [Cited 2013 Sep. 11]. Available from: https://openwrt.org/.

[39] Wireshark, [homepage on the Internet]. [Cited 2013 Sep. 11]. Available from: http://www.wireshark.org/.

[40] Aircrack-ng key craking program, [homepage on the Internet]. [Cited 2013 Sep. 11]. Available from: http://www.aircrack-ng.org/.

[41] Reddy SV, Sai Ramani K, Rijutha K, Ali SM, Reddy CP. Wireless hacking - a WiFi hack by cracking WEP. 2010 Second international conference on education technology and computer (ICETC); 2010. 189—93.

[42] Airodump-ng tool, [homepage on the Internet]. [Updated: 2013 Aug. 16; Cited 2013 Sep. 11]. Available from: http://www.aircrackng.org/dok u.php?id5airodump-ng.

[43] Yuan X, Wright OT, Yu H, Williams KA. Laboratory design for wireless network attacks. In: Proceedings of the fifth annual conference on information security curriculum development (InfoSecCD '08). ACM, New York, NY; 5—12.

Further Reading

Deligiannidis L. Classroom experiences: Disallowing laptops during lectures improves student learning. In Proc of The 2011 International Conference on Frontiers in Education: Computer Science and Computer Engineering (FECS'11); 2011 Jul 18—21; Las Vegas, NV. p. 217—221.

Case Study

Assessing the Role of Governments in Securing E-Business: The Case of Jordan

Ja'far Alqatawna[1], Jawed Siddiqi[2], Omar Al-Kadi[1], Rizik Al-Sayyed[1], and Anas Najdawi[3]

[1]*The University of Jordan, Amman, Jordan*
[2]*Sheffield Hallam University, Sheffield, UK*
[3]*Princess Sumaya University for Information Technology, Amman, Jordan*

INFORMATION IN THIS CHAPTER

INTRODUCTION

According to the Global Information Technology Report (GITR), e-business adoption in Jordan is still in the early stages although the country has been very successful in leveraging information and communication technology (ICT) [1]. However, the report also points out that there is rapidly increasing demand for adopting e-business and that the government lags behind when compared with businesses' and individual's readiness to participate. While GITR is one of the few public reports providing valuable data on the diffusion of ICT in many countries, including Jordan, it offers limited information on security aspects of ICT. For instance, it does not assess the government's contribution in securing a national ICT infrastructure or building a public security awareness. This gap can be filled by exploring how policymakers at the national level should tackle security during the transition into the digital environment. To this end, this study aims to determine the effectiveness of the Jordanian government as a stakeholder in providing security for e-business.

Numerous previous studies in e-business identify government as an important stakeholder [2,3]. Roberts and Toleman [4] speculate that government involvement will affect several dimensions of e-business security, particularly technical, organizational, and legal. From our empirical work involving several case studies in Jordan [5], we have identified three important themes agreed upon by both business and customer stakeholders:

- Security for e-business is overlooked; it comes as an afterthought or is perceived purely as a technical issue.
- It is essential that the government plays an effective role in security.
- Government must put out more effort to meet the expectations of business and customer stakeholders.

The rest of the chapter is organized as follows: The next section provides a review of the literature concerning the role of government in e-business security, Jordan's Electronic Transaction Law (ETL), and the National e-Commerce Strategy (NCS). The section after that presents the investigation of ETL and NCS in relation to e-business security requirements and discusses the findings. The chapter closes with a brief conclusion and recommendations.

Literature review
The role of government in E-business security

The literature on e-business adoption appears to consider a wide range of stakeholders [6–9]. However, a comprehensive review reported in [8] reveals that in practice researchers are likely to focus on just a few stakeholders, predominantly customers. Hence, they stress the importance of paying more attention to stakeholders such as regulators, suppliers, and investors.

Clearly, government is also an important stakeholder, and a number of studies have explored its role in the context of developed countries. An early paper by Julta et al. [10] investigates the effect of governmental legislation concerning electronic signatures to promote the use of electronic communications on building the public's confidence in electronic transactions. Van Baal [11] examines the government's role in devising measures for supporting small and medium-sized enterprises that could stimulate e-business in the trade sector. Roberts and Toleman [4] discuss how governments could improve regulations and compliance effectiveness in order to promote more secure services. A more recent study in the developing world by [3] investigates the effect of support provided by national government institutions and commercial infrastructure on e-business outcomes in Latin America and Sub-Saharan Africa. The findings reveal the need for ICT policies specific to the needs of e-business.

In Jordan there is a paucity of studies involving the role of government in building a secure and trustworthy e-business environment. Abu-Samaha and Abdel Samad [12] studied the reasons why most organizations and individuals in Jordan refrain from using the Internet to exchange products and services or funds online. They concluded that the primary reasons are lack of an advanced and secure technical infrastructure, low volume of Internet users, and limited use of digitized payment methods in Jordanian society (like credit cards). Obeidat and Abu-Shanab [13] identified different categories of barriers to adopting electronic government services among business organizations in Jordan; these were: strategic, technological, organizational, policy, legal, and human factors. Interestingly, the findings of these studies, particularly the latter, concur with our own finding based on empirical work [5]. Similarly Alsmadi [14] has identified many security threats in several Jordanian e-government portals that provide e-services to citizens and businesses. Clearly these weaknesses and problems hinder the expansion of e-government services in Jordan to becoming fully active in e-business in terms of G2C (Government to Consumer) and G2B (Government to Business).

Despite these limitations, through the past decade the Jordanian government has been working hard to increase the country's electronic readiness to benefit from today's information society and has recognized the potential benefits that ICT diffusion and e-business adoption can bring to the country. Indeed, Jordan was one of the first countries in the region to pass a special law for online transactions [15]. In 2007 the government policy for ICT called for more efforts to encourage local companies to offer e-services, especially e-commerce services [16]. In response to this policy, the Ministry of Information and Communications Technology (MoICT), in cooperation with other governmental bodies and stakeholders, introduced the National e-Commerce Strategy for 2008 to 2012 in order to provide the necessary framework for implementing those recommendations [17].

Since our research focuses on security relating to e-business adoption strategy, we aim to explore how and to what extent security is addressed in the Electronic Transactions Law [15] and in the government's National e-Commerce Strategy. In the following subsection, we provide a detailed overview of [15] and the National e-Commerce Strategy.

Overview of the Electronic Transaction Law (ETL): Law No. 85 of 2001

Al-Omari and Al-Omari [18] point out that Jordan was one of the first countries in the region to recognize the importance of legislation that facilitates e-business transactions and pass a special law for online transactions. This temporary law is called Electronic Transactions Law (ETL) No. 85 and represents the single legal reference that can be applied to e-business transactions [15]. Instead of amending existing legislation to recognize online transactions, this law was introduced to be applicable to any transactions that involve electronic processing, transmitting, and storing of data. The law attempts to regulate a number of aspects of e-business such as: electronic contracts, records, messages, and signatures. It also provides a set of articles related to electronic transfer of funds and authenticity of electronic documents. It therefore represents a first effort toward prevention of certain sorts of cybercrime. However, ETL does not provide comprehensive legislation that can ensure the security and trustworthiness of the online environment.

According to article (3) of the ETL, the law was introduced to enable electronic means of conducting online transactions for both governmental and commercial sectors. ETL consists of 7 chapters and 41 articles that cover four areas relevant to secure e-business: electronic documents, including records, contracts and messages; electronic transfer of funds; electronic signatures and digital certificates; and penalties for some kinds of online abuse.

First, regarding the use of electronic documents, the law acknowledges the legal power of different forms of electronic documents and considers them acceptable sources of evidence that cannot be denied just because they are conducted by electronic means. Indeed, according to article (7/a) of ETL "*the electronic records, contracts, messages, and signatures shall be considered to produce the same legal consequences resulting from the written documents and signatures in accordance with the provisions of the Laws in force in terms of being binding to the parties concerned or in terms of fitness thereof as an evidential weight.*" Similarly, article (8/a) of the law sets the conditions for considering an electronic record to have the same legal effect as its original form. These conditions mainly concern availability, accessibility, and integrity of the data contained in the digital record as well as identification of the originator.

Second, at the core of e-business is the notion of electronic transfer of funds. ETL stipulates a number of provisions for facilitating e-payment. For instance, article (25) recognizes electronic transfer of funds as an acceptable payment method. Only two general conditions are set on financial institutes providing e-payment services: they must comply with other relevant laws of banking as per the Central Bank of Jordan, as well as regulations and instructions that the Central Bank issues to regulate e-payment in the country; and they must ensure the security of the services provided to clients and maintain banking confidentiality.

Third, the law defines "electronic signature" as the only mechanism which provides security and acceptability of the "electronic record," which the ETL defines as *"a record, contract or data message generated, sent, received or stored by electronic means."* It stipulates that the electronic record is valid and deemed secure from a legal point of view only if it is signed by a secure electronic signature generated during the validity period of its digital certificate, which needs to be obtained from an accredited certificates authority. This implies the existence of a Public Key Infrastructure (PKI) for implementing this law.

Finally, in terms of secure e-business, some means is required to prevent related abuse. The ETL stipulates provisions related to some cybercrimes which mainly focus on illegal use of digital certificates. Both imprisonment and fines have been introduced as penalties for illegal online acts such as the creation of security certificates for fraudulent purposes. Penalties have also been introduced for organizations involved in the process of securing electronic records. For instance article (37) stipulates that *"any entity engaged in the practice of securing documents which submits false information in a registration application, or discloses confidential information of any of its clients, or violates the regulations and instructions issued pursuant to this Law documents shall be subject to a fine of no less than (5000) five thousand dinars."* In article (38) the law goes further, introducing punishment for any act considered a crime committed by electronic means.

Overview of the National E-commerce Strategy

The National e-Commerce Strategy represents the governmental plan for developing e-commerce in Jordan. The strategy defines e-commerce as *"transactions between consumers and businesses or between businesses associated with the development or trade of goods and services over telecommunications or broadcast network,"* which implies that this strategy is intended to cover all e-business modes, including business to customer, business to business, and internal business automation. The strategy was drawn up based on a SWOT analysis (of Strengths, Weaknesses, Opportunities, and Threats) carried out between July and October 2007 to assess the current state of e-business in the country. The strategy's vision, goals, and objectives have been set with the intention of making Jordan *"a leading e-commerce centre in the region through the exploitation of its information technology capacity and the creativity of its people"* [17]. Five major factors were identified as reasons why e-commerce had not taken off in Jordan:

- lack of e-payment systems
- lack of supportive legislation
- lack of e-commerce awarenes;

Table 8.1 Enablers of the National e-Commerce Strategy [17]

Enablers	Enabling Actions
The Law	Provide an effective legal framework for the development of e-commerce including the validity of digital signatures, consumer protection, cybercrime, and various changes to the e-transaction law.
Security	Increase general awareness of the need for information and personal security among companies that trade electronically.
Electronic payments	Develop fully operational payment gateway and associated banking services for use with internet and mobile phone payments.
Tax	Develop systems and processes for simplified tax audits.
Awareness	Encourage general awareness throughout society, and specifically among lawyers, judges, SMEs, government officials, and banking staff.
Skills	Develop commercial and technical e-commerce skills among SMEs and ICT firms; develop commercial and legal e-commerce skills among lawyers, judges and tax officials.
Customs	Introduce rapid customs clearance via associated IT systems.
Employment	Provide employment opportunities to meet youth aspirations.
The IT sector	Develop capacity in e-commerce, e-commerce software, and services for fixed and mobile sectors; promote sector skills.
Availability and use of ICT infrastructure and services	Encourage competitive supply and widespread adoption of broadband; improve affordability of ICT; introduce 3 G mobile services; support competition and diversity in international telecommunications.
Logistics and transport infrastructure	Develop warehousing and packing facilities; remove impediments to the development of air and land freight hubs.
Catalogues and content	Establish capacity in e-commerce content development.
Finance and investment	Improve links between investors and entrepreneurs.
Government	Advance the use of e-procurement in government.

- unaffordable broadband access and PCs
- arbitrary tax changes

To overcome these impediments a set of enablers and their associated actions were identified. These are shown in Table 8.1.

In the next section we assess to what extent these government initiatives, namely, the Electronic Transaction Law and the National e-Commerce Strategy, meet the requirements for e-business security. We show that they have a number of limitations that make them inadequate to provide the required legal setup.

Security in Jordan's E-business initiatives: An analysis
Analysing ETL in relation to E-business security

The Electronic Transaction Law (ETL) is clearly an important step toward increasing the adoption of e-business in the Jordan because it provides a suitable legal framework for such activities.

However, our analysis reveals that several issues related to e-business as well as security are not addressed in this law. These limitations render the current legal situation inadequate for providing a secure e-business environment.

One major drawback we identified is that the law is not mandatory; therefore, it is applicable only if participating parties agree to apply it. Indeed, article (5/a) states: *"unless a provision in this Law states otherwise, the provisions of this Law shall apply to the transactions on which the parties thereto agree to implement the transactions thereof through electronic means."* Similarly, article (5/b) requires a new agreement between the parties for every new transaction. According to Al-Ibraheem and Tahat [19], this is because ETL uses as its model the United Nations Commission on International Trade Law (UNCITRAL [20]), which requires explicit consent from the parties that are going to perform transactions by electronic means. While this provides some sort of flexibility for the parties transacting online, it also means that the law might never be implemented, hence failing to regulate e-business.

A further factor making a large part of this law ineffective is the lack of regulations and instructions on how to implement and enforce some of its provisions. For instance, the validity of an electronic signature is linked, under this law, to the validity of the digital certificate, which needs to be issued by a competent and licensed certificate authority. According to article (40/b) the Cabinet will issue the necessary regulations for implementing the provision related to *"the procedure for issuing security certificates, the authority competent to do such and the application fees."* As another example, article (29), relates to the security of electronic transfer of funds. It specifies that the Central Bank of Jordan is responsible for maintaining and ensuring the safety of the banking environment in Jordan. Unfortunately, as of this writing, regulations to support both of these articles have still not been issued [21].

This lack of supportive regulations concerning the security of online transactions hinders the establishment of a secure e-business infrastructure and increases the legal uncertainty for both businesses and citizens. Furthermore, the absence of these regulations makes it impossible to establish even a basic security infrastructure. In the contrary, many developed countries such as the UK, the United States, and most of the European Union states have established a set of directives and regulations for digital signatures and certificates authorities that support the adoption of online transactions in those parts of the world [22].

ETL is also very limited with regard to cybercrime, mainly addressing the illegal use of digital certificates. It introduces a penalty of up to one year's imprisonment for any illegal act conducted online. However, the law does not distinguish among the many forms of cybercrime, which differ in terms of type, intention, and severity. Under the current law there is no difference between a simple computer penetration targeting any machine over the Internet, which can be committed by an individual, and an organized denial of service attack targeting large e-business portals. Considering the nature and diversity of cybercrime, these provisions fail to recognize the wide range of real risks associated with e-business environments and fail to deal with each type of these crimes according to its nature and impact.

The Jordanian constitution appears to respects citizens' privacy in the physical world; however, there is no equivalent treatment for online privacy. For instance, Internet cafés, which are very popular in the country, are requested by law to collect personal data from the Internet users and must disclose this data if the government so requests: "In March 2008, Jordan began increasing restrictions on the country's Internet cafés. Under the pretext of maintaining security, Internet cafés were installed with cameras to monitor users, and Internet café owners were required to register the IP number of the café, the users' personal data, the time of use and the data of Web sites explored" (see [23] p. 3).

According to the Economic and Social Commission for Western Asia (ESCWA) [24,25], lack of data protection laws and absence of disclosure control mechanisms are the major cause of privacy problems in many countries, including Jordan: "While most advanced countries have devised laws that protect privacy and data, all ESCWA member countries still lack standards and regulations to protect personal privacy and data, with the exception of general laws that are applied in certain cases" ([24] p. 38).

Furthermore, the absence of laws and regulations to protect the rights of customers engaging in e-business transactions represents a serious obstacle to building customer trust in this form of transaction. Consumer protection includes many issues such as product liability, privacy rights, fraud and misrepresentation [24]. Unfortunately, these issues are not covered under the current legal framework, which contributes to the legal uncertainty of the e-business environment. The authors of [19] point out the obvious absence of legislation that covers standards, procedures, techniques, infrastructures, and security guidelines for e-business that the commercial sector should follow in order to ensure security.

We therefore conclude that the current legal framework is inadequate to provide a secure e-business environment. It has failed to address several fundamental issues: enforcement, supportive regulations for establishing security infrastructure, cybercrimes, privacy, and online customer protection. Moreover, from our empirical research [5] we know that these issues are of significant concern for a wide range of stakeholders. Addressing these issues is essential for providing the comprehensive legal framework required for today's complex e-business environment.

Analyzing security within the National E-commerce Strategy

The government's strategy to develop e-business covers a wide range of areas, including legislation, local ICT industry, infrastructure, and financial services, and its actions target a wide range of stakeholders, including customers and service providers as well as government departments. It appears that all of these stakeholders' requirements could be fulfilled. However, some important questions remain: How and to what extent is security addressed by the National e-Commerce Strategy? Is it comprehensive enough to fulfill the requirements? Here we explore these questions.

Clearly, there has been an attempt to address two barriers to the lack of confidence in e-business: the absence of an adequate legal framework and the absence of security awareness among potential online users. The government's National e-Commerce Strategy incorporates two action plans to address these two limitations. The inadequate legal framework especially relates to customer protection and the security of e-transactions; as we have discussed, the Electronic Transaction Law (ETL) is not able to ensure sufficient online security. One of the government's action plans was to amend the current ETL to cover issues such as confidentiality of e-transactions, spamming prevention, dispute resolution, and effective enforcement measures. Moreover, the action plan included promulgating three new laws: a cyber crime law, a consumer protection law, and a law to establish credit bureau facilities in Jordan. The second action plan, intended to leverage security for e-business, focused on increasing security awareness among potential online companies, including publishing security guidelines for online companies. The target was to have 90 percent of online merchants conforming to these guidelines two years from the issuing date. Unfortunately that date was left unspecified!

The government's National e-Commerce Strategy with its proposed action plan is clearly a significant step in assuring e-business security and eliminating the relevant stakeholders' concerns. It has addressed some important issues, especially in relation to legislation that promotes a secure online environment. However, the strategy still has a number of interrelated deficiencies, which can be observed at the strategic,governance, and action levels of the strategy. We now discuss these deficiencies and their possible implications.

Looking at the strategy's goals and objectives, it appears that securing the e-business environment was perceived not as a strategic goal but as an obstacle that could simply be removed by offering security guidelines to online companies and passing a certificate authority law and other relevant laws and regulations. This limited understanding of the role of security and its implications could be the reason that the strategy does not take a comprehensive and systematic approach to addressing wider security issues. Not having security as a strategic goal can increase the chance that it will be overlooked in many areas associated with the implementation of the strategy. We illustrate with three notable examples.

At the infrastructure level, the government seems to want to invest heavily in providing citizens with physical ICT infrastructures without paying much attention to how to secure these infrastructures, which are required by e-business adopters. For instance, the strategy emphasizes the availability and affordability of e-payment systems, broadband, and wireless services, but does not require service providers, such as ISPs and telecommunication companies, to secure these services. This means that security could be overlooked in these critical infrastructures. The ICT infrastructure section of the action plan states that MoICT, in collaboration with telecommunication operators and local ISPs, would ensure the availability of the ICT infrastructure necessary for e-business services; unfortunately, none of the actions relates to the security of ICT infrastructure.

In the second and fourth goals of the strategy, the government aims to make Jordan a regional leader for IT services and a strong competitor in the digital economy. Yet security is not integrated into the process of achieving these goals and unfortunately is not considered as a competitive advantage. Therefore, we think that these goals are unlikely to be achieved, since security of IT services is an important factor for companies who want to provide their customers with a high quality, reliable service. This lack of security could lead to Jordan being excluded from the benefits of such opportunities, thereby negatively impacting its strategic goals. Moreover, even though the government owns this strategy, the absence of a governance framework for information security shows that the government does not want to take responsibility toward ensuring security. Indeed the strategy clearly states that *"as an implementer of e-commerce strategy, however, Government's roles and responsibilities are limited. This strategy lays down objectives for Government to meet in areas such as the law associated with e-commerce, taxation and customs. Government can facilitate, promote, propose, recommend and sometimes fund, but seldom command or require action by the private sector."*

The action plan PLURAL? associated with the National e-Commerce Strategy includes many actions to raise e-business awareness in different sectors and among a wide range of stakeholders. However, in practice these actions focus only on the benefits of e-business; none of them emphasizes the need to build information security awareness especially among stakeholders such as

customers, judges, lawyers, and government officials. This limited focus on raising security awareness in the business community means that it is failing to fulfill the government own ICT policy
which states: *"Government requires that users (both residential and small business) be supported
by the provision of advice on the safe use of the Internet and the protection of children, in order to
promote consumer confidence in the use of ICT, while avoiding risks and protecting human rights.
This function should be led by the MoICT and should include participation by other relevant public
and private stakeholders"* [16]. As a consequence, it has not been possible to build citizens' security awareness, which could increase their levels of confidence and equip them with skills for protecting their online security, thereby elevating their trust in e-business. Our empirical work [5]
strongly suggests that all stakeholders need to be involved and therefore the strategy needs to recognize the importance of information security awareness at different levels of society for cultivating a security culture, which, we propose, would contribute to enhancing the security of e-business.

Discussion

The analysis of our study revealed that the Jordan government's limited view of security has
impacted its plans and initiatives to promote an attractive e-business climate. The first government
attempt to address security was through the Electronic Transaction Law (ETL). Our analysis
revealed that EFL is, however, inadequate to provide a secure e-business environment, since it fails
to address several security issues that are concerns of a wide range of stakeholders. These issues
include online privacy and data protection, online customer protection, and security of e-business
infrastructure. Besides, the lack of supportive rules and regulations to implement and enforce some
provisions in ETL, especially the ones relating to establishing certificate authorities, render a large
part of ETL inactive and therefore unable to fulfill its goal.

The National e-Commerce Strategy, introduced seven years later, represents acknowledgment by
the government that the existing legal framework was hindering the adoption of e-business in the
country and its attempt to correct this situation through actions to reform the current legal setup to
better facilitate e-business. These actions include promulgating three new laws: a cyber crime law, a
consumer protection law, and a law to establish credit bureau facilities in Jordan. Nevertheless, the
strategy fails to perceive security outside the legal dimension. While the government has acknowledged the relation between security and citizens' trust in e-business, its proposed action plan does
not go beyond providing security guidelines to online companies, and the legal role predominates.

Our analysis suggests that security was not viewed as an essential part of the strategy or as a
competitive advantage. This has had two major implications. First, security has been overlooked in
many areas at the implementation level of the strategy. This is notable in the action plan which
covered areas such as stakeholders' awareness and ICT infrastructure but lacked any plan to
address associated security aspects. Second, there is no national security governance framework to
establish a set of roles and responsibilities that the government and other relevant stakeholders
need to exercise to ensure security of the e-business environment. In such a situation, it is difficult
to know who is in charge of what, and security is left to the judgment of the individual parties
involved in e-business.

This analysis highlights the absence of an effective governmental role with respect to government's responsibility to regulate the digital environment to protect both businesses and customers.

Accordingly, we recommend that the government should contribute in building awareness of security issues at both organizational and individual levels. For instance, our study found that the lack of a government monitoring role has two implications. On the business side, nobody checks whether or not private companies are capable from a security point of view of doing business online, which can impact negatively on a business's perceived responsibility toward security. On the other hand, lack of monitoring increases customers' feelings of distrust in the electronic environment, especially in the absence of a legal setup to protect online customers [26].

CONCLUSION AND RECOMMENDATIONS

This chapter has attempted to describe and analyze the current role of the government in the security of e-business in Jordan. Based on the findings, our study suggests that the government should recognize the full range of socio-technical implications that security and the lack of security may have on the adoption of e-business. This can be achieved by understanding the real security needs and concerns of the various stakeholders at different e-business stages. The government then needs to align and integrate these requirements with its policy and plans. Our findings also suggest that in order for the government to be an effective partner in developing a secure e-business environment, it is not enough to limit its role to promulgating laws and regulations addressing security issues; rather, government should take a multifaceted role, which might include, in addition to legislation, increasing security education and awareness, monitoring, ensuring compliance with security standards and regulations, and protecting the country's critical ICT infrastructure.

There have been numerous previous studies highlighting the role of governments and policy makers in the diffusion of e-business; however this study has scrutinized the role of government in the adoption of e-business particularly with respect to security-related actions. An early paper by Molla and Licker [27] argues that government must have an important role in encouraging the private sector in the country to adopt e-business by providing supportive infrastructure, legal and regulatory frameworks, policies, and strategies. However, in practice government support varies from country to country, and it is below the threshold in many developing countries [25]. We therefore strongly argue that the government represents an important if not the primary security stakeholder in the adoption of e-business, with a number of responsibilities that need to be fulfilled to ensure security and protect online customer rights. Its responsibility starts with regulating e-business in the country and enacting the laws that protect customer privacy and security. It can force online merchants to follow best practices in security and to provide their customers with some level of security assurance. For instance, in many developed countries laws force online retailers to disclose their privacy and security practices to their customers in order to increase transparency and trust levels. Our findings also suggest that government needs have greater a stake in building public knowledge of security related matters through national awareness.

References

[1] World Economic Forum. Global information technology report 2008−2009. Mobility in a networked world; 2009.

[2]   Papazafeiropoulou A, Pouloudi A, Currie, W. Applying the stakeholder concept to electronic commerce: extending previous research to guide government policy makers. In: Proceedings of the Annual Hawaii International Conference on System Sciences; 2001. p. 122−122.

[3]   Okoli C, Mbarika V, McCoy S. The effects of infrastructure and policy on e-business in Latin America and Sub-Saharan Africa. Eur J Inf Syst 2010;19(1):5−20.

[4]   Roberts B, Toleman M. The role of government in e-business adoption. In: Al-Hakim L, editor. Global e-government: Theory, applications and benchmarking. Information Quality Management. Hershey, PA, United States: IGI Publishing (IGI Global); 2007. p. 65−84.

[5]   Alqatawna J. Multi-stakeholders inquiry for securing e-business environments: a socio-technical security framework [PhD thesis]. England: SHU; 2010.

[6]   Pouloudi A. Aspects of the stakeholder concept and their implications for information systems development. Hawaii International Conference on System Sciences. Citeseer; 1999. p. 254−254.

[7]   Shankar V, Urban GL, Sultan F. Online trust: a stakeholder perspective, concepts, implications, and future directions. J Strateg Inf Syst 2002;11(3):325−44.

[8]   Chua CEH, Straub DW, Khoo HM, Kadiyala S, Kuechler D. The evolution of e-commerce research: a stakeholder perspective. J Electron Commerce Res 2005;6(4):262−81.

[9]   Flechais I, Sasse MA. Stakeholder involvement, motivation, responsibility, communication: How to design usable security in e-science. Int J Hum-Comput Stud 2009;67(4):281−96.

[10] Jutla D, Bodorik P, Dhaliwal J. Supporting the e-business readiness of small and medium-sized enterprises: approaches and metrics. Internet Res 2002;12(2):139−64.

[11] Van Baal S. Governmental support for e-business in Germany: the trade sector's perspective. Workshop on the Role of Government in Promoting Electronic Business, hosted by the German Institute for Economic Research, Berlin; 2005.

[12] Abu-Samaha AM, Abdel Samad Y. Challenges to the Jordanian electronic government initiative. J Bus Syst, Governance Ethics 2007;2(32007):101−4.

[13] Obeidat RA, Abu-Shanab EA. Drivers of e-government and e-business in Jordan. J Emerg Technol Web Intell 2010;2(3):204−11.

[14] Alsmadi I. Security challenges for expanding e-governments. Int J Adv Sci Technol 2011;37(5):47−60.

[15] ETL. Electronic transactions law no. 80 of 2001. Jordan; 2001.

[16] ICT-policy. Statement of government policy on information and communication technology and postal sectors Jordan. [Internet] [Cited 2012 Jun 1]. Retrieved from: <http://www.moict.gov.jo/>; 2007.

[17] MoICT. Jordan national e-commerce strategy 2008−2012. Jordan, Ministry of Information and Communication Technology (MoICT). [Internet]. [Cited 2013 Apr 24]. Retrieved from: <http://www. moict.gov.jo/MoICT_National_E-Commerce_Strategy.aspx>; 2008.

[18] Al-Omari A, Al-Omari H. E-government readiness assessment model. J Comput Sci 2006;2(11):841−5.

[19] Al-Ibraheem M, Tahat H. Regulating electronic contracting in Jordan. 21st BILETA Conference: global-isation and Harmonisation in Technology Law; 2006.

[20] The United Nations Commission on international trade law (UNCITRAL). [Internet]. Retrieved from: <www.uncitral.org>.

[21] NIS. The National Information System. [Internet]. [Cited 2013 Apr 24]. Retrieved from: <http://www. lob.gov.jo/ui/main.html>; 2013.

[22] Wang M. Do the regulations on electronic signatures facilitate international electronic commerce? A critical review. Comput Law & Secur Rev 2007;23(1):32−4.

[23] OpenNet (2009). Internet filtering in Jordan. OpenNet initiative. [Internet]. [Accessed on 2012 June 1] Retreived from: <http://opennet.net/research/profiles/jordan>.

[24] ESCWA. Regional profile of the information society in western Asia. [Internet]. 2007. [Cited 2013Apr 24]. Retrieved from: <http://www.escwa.un.org/information/pubdetails.asp>.

[25] ESCWA. Regional profile of the information society in western Asia. [Internet]. 2011. [Cited 2013 Apr 24.] <http://www.escwa.un.org/information/pubdetails.asp>.

[26] Privacy International. Surveillance Monitor 2007 -International country rankings; 2007. <https://www.privacyinternational.org/reports/surveillance-monitor-2007-international-country-rankings>.

[27] Molla A. Licker PS. Perceived e-readiness factors in e-commerce adoption: an empirical investigation in a developing country. Int J Electron Commerce 2005;10(1):83−110.

Network and Infrastructure Security

Theory Reviews of the Field

A Survey of Quantum Key Distribution (QKD) Technologies

Jeffrey D. Morris[1], Michael R. Grimaila[1], Douglas D. Hodson[1], David Jacques[1], and Gerald Baumgartner[2]

[1]*United States Air Force Institute of Technology, Wright-Patterson AFB, OH, USA*
[2]*Laboratory for Telecommunications Sciences, College Park, MD, USA*

INFORMATION IN THIS CHAPTER

- Defining Quantum Key Distribution
- Reviewing Quantum Key Distribution architectures
- Exploring Quantum Key Distribution networks
- Identifying the key technologies for future Quantum Key Distribution research
- Viewing a Quantum Key Distribution usage scenario

Cryptography

Cryptography, the practice and study of techniques for securing communications between two authorized parties in the presence of one or more unauthorized third parties, is the centerpiece of a centuries-old battle between code maker and code breaker [1]. Historically, government and military applications chiefly used cryptography, but today almost everyone is dependent on cryptography to provide security services including confidentiality, integrity, authentication, authorization, and non-repudiation [2].

The strength of commonly used cryptographic algorithms relies on computational security, which means the algorithm is secure if there is a negligible chance of discovering the key in a "reasonable" amount of time using current computational technology [3]. As computational technology progresses, adversaries may be able to acquire enough computational power to decode encrypted messages in a "reasonable" amount of time. In fact, recent developments in quantum computing technology (including supporting algorithms) have placed certain classes of commonly used asymmetric cryptographic algorithms (e.g., those that rely on the difficulty of factoring large numbers into their constituent primes, such as the Rivest, Shamir, and Adleman (RSA) algorithm), at risk [4,1]. The resulting loss of security in commonly used asymmetric public key cryptographic algorithms will likely increase the usage of symmetric cryptographic systems and intensify the need for secure and efficient key distribution.

Quantum key distribution

The genesis of Quantum Key Distribution (QKD) can be traced back to Stephen Wiesner, who developed the idea of quantum conjugate coding in the late 1960s [5]. As a student at Columbia University, he described two applications for quantum coding: a method for creating fraud-proof banking notes (quantum money) and a method for broadcasting multiple messages in such a way that reading one of the messages destroys the others (quantum multiplexing). Wiesner's quantum multiplexing uses photons polarized in conjugate bases as "qubits" to pass information. In this manner, if the receiver measures the photons in the correct polarization basis, he or she receives a correct result with high likelihood. However, if the receiver measures the photons in the wrong (conjugate) basis, the measured result is random, and due to the measurement, all information about the original basis is destroyed.

In 1984, Charles Bennett and Gilles Brassard proposed the first QKD protocol, BB84, for secure key exchange based on Wiesner's ideas [6]. The goal of the system is to provide perfect secrecy during key distribution. Using the BB84 protocol, a sender and receiver "grow" an unconditionally secure secret key by leveraging properties of quantum mechanics in the form of polarized photons that are transmitted from the sender to the receiver. Because of the quantum properties of photons, any operations performed on photons in transit would irrevocably alter their state, which would be detectable by the receiver. Additionally, as stated by the no-cloning theorem, no photon copies can be produced for the purpose of operating on the copies without affecting the original photons.

As in any communications system, errors may be introduced from a wide variety of sources. In the security analysis of QKD systems, all errors are attributed to a hypothetical adversary (Eve) who is attempting to eavesdrop on the key distribution communications. If the errors are below a defined threshold, the two parties involved in the key exchange can distill an unconditionally secure key even in the presence of an adversary. Otherwise, the key exchange is aborted. When a QKD-generated unconditionally secure key is combined with the one-time pad (an unconditionally secure classical symmetric cryptographic algorithm), the result is an unconditionally secure cryptographic system.

Since the BB84 protocol was first proposed, there have been many QKD-related protocols and architectural and technological developments that make implementing a QKD system more practical and commercially viable. In 2001, ID Quantique SA offered and sold the first commercially available QKD system [7]. Today, QKD systems are available globally from sellers in Europe (ID Quantique, http://www.idquantique.com/; SeQureNet, http://www.sequrenet.com/), Australia (Quintessence Labs, http://qlabsusa.com/), North America (MagiQ, http://www.magiqtech.com/MagiQ/Home.html), and Asia (Quantum Communication Technology Co., Ltd., http://www.quantum-info.com).

QKD is suitable for use in any key distribution application that has high security requirements. Existing documented applications include financial transactions and electoral communications [8,9], but there are numerous potential applications in law enforcement, government, and military applications. The commercial systems typically use QKD as a means to produce shared secret keys for use in bulk symmetric encryption algorithms, such as the Advanced Encryption Standard (AES), instead of using the unconditionally secure one-time pad. In this case, the QKD-generated key is used to update the encryption key frequently (e.g., once a minute) greatly reducing the required QKD key generation rate which is inversely related to the distance between the QKD systems. While it is not unconditionally secure, users in the commercial domain consider this an improvement when compared with updating the key less frequently (e.g., daily or monthly).

Quantum key distribution systems

In this section, we present a historical survey of the development of QKD systems and their architectures. We also present research that is focused on developing QKD networks that can broaden the application domains of QKD.

QKD system architectures
The first QKD system: BB84

The first QKD system was a research platform built in 1989 by Bennett and Brassard to produce a physical realization of their QKD theory [10]. This system, built at IBM's Thomas J. Watson research center, was the first system to deal with the issues posed by non-ideal hardware as opposed to the perfect hardware envisioned in QKD theory. The system used a weak-coherent light source to generate light that was focused by a lens, passed through filters, and then polarization modulated using Pockels cells. At the receiver, the entering light first passed through a Pockels cell, selecting the polarization measurement basis, then went to a prism to split the light into two paths leading to photomultiplier tubes that counted the number of photons in each of the two polarization states belonging to the selected measurement basis. The distance between the transmitters and receiver was an air-gap of roughly 30 cm. The platform used the BB84 protocol for key generation and showed that QKD could be implemented using standard, non-ideal components [10].

Los alamos: QKD leaves the laboratory

In 1996, Richard Hughes of Los Alamos Laboratories led a team that built a QKD system using 14 km of underground optical fibers [11]. Hughes' system used the B92 protocol [12] instead of BB84—the B92 protocol requires that the system be able to generate two quantum states rather than four. At the transmitter (Alice), the system used a 1300 nm laser source and an attenuator to produce weak, coherent pulses. These pulses were then directed to a 50:50 fiber coupler that formed the input to an unbalanced Mach-Zehnder Interferometer (MZI) that split the incoming photon packet into two photon packets. In the MZI, the photons that traveled along the long arm of the interferometer were phase modulated relative to the photons that traveled along the short arm of the interferometer. The pulse-to-pulse randomly selected relative phase encoding provided the bit and basis value used for key exchange. At the output of the MZI, the two time-separated photon packets were injected into the 14 km fiber leading to the receiver.

At the receiver (Bob), the two incoming photon packets entered another unbalanced MZI identical to the one at the transmitter. The phase modulator in the long arm of Bob's MZI was used to select the measurement basis. At the output of the MZI, the photon packet that passed through both the long arm of Alice's MZI and the short arm of Bob's MZI interfered with the photon packet that passed through the short arm of Alice's MZI and the long arm of Bob's MZI. The results of this interference were measured using a time-gated single-photon Avalanche Photo Diode (APD) detector.

Plug and play: QKD made easier

In 1996, Muller et al. created a hardware-protocol system, based on Faraday mirrors, between the cities of Nyon and Geneva [13]. This system is notable for automatically compensating for birefringence and polarization-dependent losses in the transmission fiber. This system attached easily to existing telecommunication fibers with no need for adjustment of the QKD systems, leading to the name "plug and play." This system has heralded the beginning of QKD transitioning from the domain of the physics laboratory to existing infrastructure.

The key to overcoming the effects of birefringence in the "plug and play" architecture is the use of Faraday mirrors. In this architecture, Bob generates two classical level light pulses that he sends to Alice. Alice reflects the two pulses using a Faraday mirror (which rotates the polarization of the incoming light so that the reflected light is orthogonally polarized to the incoming light), phase modulates one of the two pulses relative to the other, and attenuates both pulses to the single-photon level. The fact that the single-photon light pulses returning to Bob have a polarization orthogonal to what they had when they traveled to Alice undoes any birefringence effects the pulses experienced when traveling to Alice.

Damien Stucki and his teams used variations of the "plug and play" architecture to connect Geneva and Lausanne [14], a distance of 67 km, over regular telecom fiber using the BB84 protocol.

First entanglement-based system: EPR and Bell's theorem

In 2004, a team from the University of Geneva proposed and built a system utilizing Ekert's E91 QKD protocol based on quantum entanglement and Bell's theorem. This protocol uses Bohm's version of the Einstein-Podolsky-Rosen (EPR) experiment and Bell's theorem to test for eavesdropping [15]. This system was one of the first to demonstrate the use of entanglement in QKD. The team's goal was to demonstrate a system using violations of Bell's inequalities as the foundation for secure key exchange.

This system uses time-bin entangled qubits created from a laser pulse sent through an unbalanced Michelson interferometer (short and long leg), then through a type 1 Lithium Triborate (LBO) nonlinear crystal, where spontaneous parametric down conversion creates a pair of entangled photons. The photons pass through the transmission channel to both Alice and Bob, who perform projective measurements using the same type of unbalanced interferometer. Here, a significant difference from other QKD systems is that the photon source is not at either Alice's or Bob's location, but at a third location. By placing the emitter between Alice and Bob, the system is able to exchange keys at twice the distance of a conventional system with the same loss.

By placing the photons in separate time-bins with two different phases and using the Clauser-Horne-Shimony-Holt (CHSH) Bell inequality, an upper bound for correlations can be determined. By scanning the phases, one of the CHSH parameters can be inferred and the correlation coefficients of the CHSH inequality determined. These coefficient values prove a violation of the CHSH inequality. Nicholas Gisin proved in 2002 that when the Bell inequality is violated, the entangled photons can be used in QKD [16].

Continuous variable QKD: short-ranged but fast and secure

The first Continuous Variable QKD (CV-QKD) system debuted in the European SEcure COmmunication based on Quantum Cryptography (SECOQC) network, with the prototype built expressly for the project. Timothy Ralph first described the CV-QKD protocol in 1999, with several variations proposed by Cerf, Assche, Lutkenhaus, and Grosshans. These protocols use squeezed Gaussian states of light that have classical intensity levels to carry information, rather than discrete single photon states [17–20].

This system encodes information in the amplitude and phase of the classical light level beam and produces high rates of key generation over a short distance (such as a metropolitan network), as it is not as sensitive to individual photon loss as the discrete-variable protocols. Originally, it was not suitable over long distances because the higher noise ratios in longer fibers created errors in the quadratures of pulses, interfering in the homodyne detection, but improvements in post-processing have increased the transmission range. The protocol is resistant against general and collective eavesdropping attacks, and has a security proof for coherent attacks as well. These security proofs show it is more secure than some other types of QKD systems against attacks that exploit the non-ideal hardware flaws of QKD systems [21].

QKD networks

Photon loss between the transmitter and receiver due to attenuation in the optical fiber connecting the transmitter with the receiver, coupled with dark counts at the receiver's detectors, dramatically limits the maximum effective range of QKD compared to classical optical telecommunications. However, even with these range limitations, researchers have implemented small-scale QKD networks to demonstrate its potential. The next section describes some of these networks.

DARPA network: introducing layers

In 2002, the Defense Advanced Research Projects Agency (DARPA) built a QKD system to explore networks that had multiple Alice and Bob system pairs rather than a single system [22]. The system integrated QKD-based key generation, traditional Ethernet encryption, and key management to secure a virtual private network (VPN) that was compatible with existing telecommunication infrastructure.

This system is notable for demonstrating QKD using existing security technology and introducing the idea of "trusted relays." This relay system extends the range of a QKD network but introduces the concerns of adequately securing the relays.

SECOQC Network: mixing and matching with nodes

From 2004 to 2008, the SECOQC project operated in Europe to design and set up a network of QKD systems to show the uses of QKD [23]. The network consisted of a collection of point-to-point systems including: three plug and play systems by ID Quantique SA; a one-way weak-pulse system from Toshiba Research in the UK; a Coherent One-way System (COW) by GAP Optique-ID Quantique SA-Austrian Institute of Technology (AIT); an entangled photon system from the University of Vienna and the AIT; a continuous variables (CV-QKD) system by Centre National de la Recherche Scientifique (CNRS), THALES Research and Technology and Université Libre de

Bruxelles; and a free-space link by the Ludwig Maximillians University. The average link length was between 20 km and 30 km, and the longest link was 83 km.

The project created a QKD trusted-repeater network, much like a connected graph, where each vertex is a QKD node and the edges are the QKD communication channels. Each link retransmits key material along the link, so the key hops from link to link. Keys move forward using an algorithm secured with QKD key material to the next node, and the process is repeated until the key reaches its destination. This creates a "trusted repeater" system, where each node is secured to prevent tampering and attack. The network stripped each QKD system of its key distillation functions and set each one to access only the quantum channel. This reduced redundancy between the systems and moved the key management to upper layers of the network [23]. This architecture extends the DARPA network in both number of nodes and the key transmission maximum distance.

SwissQuantum network: simplifying QKD integration

The SwissQuantum network connected three nodes, two in the center of Geneva and one at the European Organization for Nuclear Research (CERN), with a maximum length of 17.1 km, using ID Quantique SA id5100 commercial servers, and ran between March, 2009 and January, 2011. The servers used the BB84 and SARG04 protocols to generate a shared secret key for standard Ethernet network encryptors across a 10 Gbps channel. This network introduced the concept of layers to QKD networks [24].

Adding a mediation layer between the QKD layer and the secure layer allows integration of QKD devices into an existing telecommunication network. The focus of the research was on integration of QKD and the simplification of the plug and play architecture. This network extended the ideas of SECOQC by making it easier to add QKD to an existing network without specially adapting the QKD systems.

Tokyo network: a high-speed network

Much like the SECOQC network, a consortium of schools, industry, and government organizations created a trusted-node QKD network in Tokyo in 2010 to explore the use of many different types of QKD working together [25]. The Tokyo network created a secure environment to demonstrate secure television conferencing, secure mobile phones, and stable long-term operation at high speeds.

Nine organizations from the EU and Japan employed multiple links to demonstrate QKD technologies such as several decoy-state BB84 systems, a Differential Phase-Shift (DPS) QKD demonstrator, an entanglement system, and ID Quantique's commercial QKD system [25]. The network consisted of six links, with a maximum link distance of 90 km. The network was designed as a three-layer architecture using trusted nodes: a QKD node, a key management layer, and a communication layer. The key management layer is notable for passing secret keys between nodes that do not have a quantum channel by using the unconditionally secure one-time pad cryptographic algorithm.

The future of QKD

The short-term future of QKD lies in creating and extending quantum networks. Until the maximum fiber range of QKD hardware increases significantly, long-range QKD communications depends on some form of multi-node networks. These types of networks, while increasing the range and usability of QKD, increase the security concerns of the telecommunications provider. Using a trusted node within a network increases the security overhead and increases the possibility of corruption or hijacking of the quantum channel. Two promising areas of research may help to overcome these types of security issues.

Quantum repeaters

A workable long-range QKD network needs a method of passing qubits from one network segment to the next without destroying the quantum particle. Recall, an observer cannot clone the state of a quantum particle (i.e., the no-cloning theorem) with perfect fidelity. The process of trying to clone a quantum state introduces unavoidable noise in the output, so the copied states generated by the cloning process are not identical to the input state. Hence, the quantum information carriers cannot be copied (amplified) as is typical in classical communication systems.

For a quantum "repeater" to work, the device would need some way of storing the quantum state of incoming quantum particles for a brief time so they can be forwarded to another QKD system. Quantum entanglement, quantum teleportation, and quantum memory are potential tools for building a quantum repeater. Quantum entanglement and teleportation would allow a device to receive a quantum particle from a sender, and then entangle that photon with another photon in the device, which will be sent to a receiver [26]. This idea is the basis of the Quantum Repeaters for Long Distance Fibre-Based Quantum Communication program (QuReP) (http://quantumrepeaters.eu), a project funded by Switzerland, Sweden, France, and Germany. This multiyear project started in 2010 and is scheduled to finish in 2013.

Quantum memory

Quantum memory is a technology needed in order to build a practical quantum repeater. Quantum memory allows a quantum state to be stored for some amount of time before it is read and used. Current research centers on leveraging the properties of rare-earth doped crystals as the basis for holding and emitting the quantum state. This memory stores a copy of the input state, destroying the input state during the process, and can output a perfect copy of the stored input state with high efficiency (>90%). During the output process, the quantum state of the memory is changed, losing the information about the state it emitted. Additional research centers on increasing the emission efficiencies and increasing the number of simultaneous stored states [27].

Continued research using spin-wave storage in the rare-earth doped crystals and experiments in matter-matter entanglement has led to Pr:YSO and Eu:YSO rare-earth crystals that absorb a quantum state and emit that state with high certainty over a multi-minute time frame [28,29]. Improvements in high-speed photon detectors, single photon or pure-state emitters, and the interfaces between disparate technologies may allow these memory crystals to realize quantum repeaters within the next decade.

Free-space QKD: satellites

With technology advancing terrestrial QKD, advances in free-space QKD are being made. Bennett and Brassard originally demonstrated free-space QKD in their first device, but only over a gap of

30 cm. Various experiments, including some of the networks discussed earlier in this article, used a free-space component and pushed the boundaries for QKD. Improvements in lasers, optical tracking and emitting systems, and computers and software have allowed the free-space QKD distance to far exceed that of terrestrial QKD [30−34].

Free-space QKD, with maximum distances over 140 km, has been demonstrated by an experiment in the Canary Islands of La Palma and Tenerife in 2007 [33]. This experiment showed that QKD could communicate through an atmosphere path length much longer than that between a ground station and a low earth orbit satellite. The experiment used a variation of the original BB84 protocol and used telescopes for tracking and receiving. This experiment showed that, using free-space QKD, a link from ground to an orbiting satellite could establish a secret key between any two ground stations, easing the key distribution problem and potentially secure ground-to-satellite communications.

Chinese researchers are working with free-space experiments with the intention of creating an Earth-to-satellite QKD link. In 2010, one group demonstrated a QKD system using a ground station and a balloon-based transmitter. They developed the optics and tracking systems necessary to deal with high relative angular motion, random motion of the platforms, and atmospheric turbulence that would be found in a ground-to-satellite system [35]. Furthering this research, another group in China recently reported reflecting a beam of photons off an orbiting German satellite that is covered with retro-reflectors. These reflected enough of the single photons back to a receiving telescope to meet the standards of a QKD channel [36]. Nicolas Gisin wrote in 2010 that he would not be surprised if Chinese researchers are the first to demonstrate a QKD link between Earth and a satellite [26].

Device independent QKD (DI-QKD)

QKD provides a way of increasing communications security, but it relies on several assumptions: (i) Alice and Bob use truly random number generators, (ii) Alice and Bob prepare and measure the quantum states exactly as required by the QKD protocol, (iii) Alice and Bob can accurately bound the information that an eavesdropper gains about the key by all methods, and (iv) Alice and Bob use a privacy amplification algorithm that eliminates all of the eavesdropper information about the final key. A major advance in combating this information leakage to the eavesdropper is a relatively new protocol known as Device-Independent QKD (DI-QKD). This QKD protocol makes no assumptions about the hardware used by Alice, Bob, and Eve and goes so far as to assume that Alice and Bob may have no knowledge about how their hardware works. The only requirements are that Alice and Bob randomly select their measurement basis and Eve cannot influence this random selection or know its results until after she can no longer act on the quantum states, and that Eve does not know the results of Alice's and Bob's measurements [37].

The DI-QKD protocol uses a form of Artur Ekert's 1991 entanglement-based protocol proposed by Acin, Massar, and Pironio and uses CHSH inequalities to provide security [38]. It handles the problem that real-life implementations differ from the ideal design. It also makes testing of components easier and covers the scenario where the quantum devices are not trusted [39]. The protocol has been proven secure against collective attacks as long as there is no leakage of classical information from Alice and Bob [37]. Several protocols and experiments have been suggested to take advantage of DI-QKD, including using heralded qubit amplification, extending the range and key rate of normal QKD [40], and one that is valid against most general attacks and based on any arbitrary Bell inequalities, not just those based on CHSH inequalities [41]. Unfortunately, DI-QKD requires high-efficiency near-perfect detectors and provides relatively low key rates due to the need for the near-perfect detections.

Measurement device independent QKD (MDI-QKD)

Though DI-QKD provides increased security for non-ideal devices, there is still a major flaw in today's implementations: that of the "detector loophole." The "loophole" is that not all entangled photons are detected, there is always loss in a quantum channel, each detector has finite detection efficiency and is potentially susceptible to side-channel attacks. All of these factors disturb the Bell's inequality tests and affect protocols based on such tests, ultimately limiting the key rate and reducing security [40].

A method has been proposed to eliminate all detector side-channel information, thus avoiding the problems with the "detector loophole." Measurement Device Independent QKD (MDI-QKD) portends to double the transmission distance for normal QKD with comparable key rates. MDI-QKD works by assuming that Alice and Bob have near-perfect state preparation of their photons and can send them to an untrusted relay called Charlie, who performs Bell state measurements that project the incoming photons into a Bell state [42]. Note that Charlie can be untrusted or even under the control of Eve.

The MDI-QKD protocol tolerates high losses for communication of up to 200 km, assuming Charlie is placed in the middle. Unlike the DI-QKD, this protocol doesn't require the use of Bell's inequalities and can be used for any QKD system, as long as Alice and Bob have near-perfect state preparation as in phase or polarization-based systems [43].

A military QKD usage scenario

How could the QKD benefit be used in a military environment? Imagine a crisis affecting the United States in the near future. The president enters his command center, receiving information from around the globe carried by satellites and telecommunication circuits. As decisions flow from the center, the secret instructions are carried by regular telecommunications circuits to the Pentagon and have been encrypted by QKD devices providing key material to fast network encryption devices. These devices change their large-bit keys several times a second, making it virtually impossible for cyber adversaries to decrypt the traffic.

Once at the Pentagon, these decisions are coordinated with contingency plans, then orders are generated to forces around the globe. Once the orders and plans are ready, the information is sent to satellites in orbit, again using QKD-secured circuits. Not only are the ground-to-space links hard to intercept, the data is encrypted using the same large-bit network encryptors. The signals are then sent from space to ground stations using the same type of encrypted circuits. On the ground, adversaries may listen in on the space-to-ground communications, but with the encryption key changing so fast, it is impossible to decrypt the data. As the distance for QKD links increases, many more communication circuits could be secured by such systems. The unconditionally secure nature of QKD-generated key material makes it attractive for high security requirements often found in the military domain.

CONCLUSION

QKD provides significant security advantages when compared with conventional key distribution. First, due to the laws of quantum mechanics, an eavesdropper cannot copy the quantum bits used in the key exchange. Second, increases in computing power do not help an adversary, as a QKD-generated key is unconditionally secure. Third, QKD allows the sender and receiver to know if there is an eavesdropper listening in on the key exchange. Fourth, the security of QKD security rests on the foundations of quantum mechanics. As long as an eavesdropper has not discovered new laws of physics, the security premise of QKD holds true. This contrasts with traditional key distribution protocols, which rely on computational security to secure the key [44].

As QKD technology matures, the architecture of systems will change. Since quantum states randomly selected from any two or more non-orthogonal quantum bases can be used to encode information for a QKD system, there are many ways to implement such a system. Current research focuses on new types of QKD, such DI-QKD and MDI-QKD, which provide methods to overcome the security limitations of existing hardware. As interest in QKD continues to grow and commercial QKD systems become more common, so will the research efforts focused upon improving the quality of emitters, detectors, and fiber to enable QKD to perform over greater distances and at higher key rates.

Disclaimer

The views expressed in this chapter are those of the authors and do not reflect the official policy or position of the United States Air Force, the Department of Defense, or the US Government.

Acknowledgments

This work was supported by the Laboratory for Telecommunications Sciences [grant number 5713400-301-6448].

References

[1] Singh S. The code book: the secret history of codes and code-breaking. 17th ed. London: Fourth Estate; 1999.

[2] Barker EB, Barker WC, Lee A. NIST special publication 800-21 guideline for implementing cryptography in the federal government NIST. [Internet]. 2005. Retrieved from: <http://csrc.nist.gov/publications/nistpubs/800-21-1/sp800-21-1_Dec2005.pdf>.

[3] Schneier B. In: Sutherland P, editor. Applied cryptography: protocols, algorithms, and source code in C. 18th ed. New York: John Wiley & Sons, Inc.; 1995.

[4] Loepp S, Wootters WK. Protecting information: from classical error correction to quantum cryptography. 1st ed. New York: Cambridge University Press; 2006.

[5] Wiesner S. Conjugate coding. ACM SIGACT News 1983;15(1):78−88.

[6] Bennett CH, Brassard G. Quantum cryptography: Public key distribution and coin tossing. Paper presented at the Proceedings of IEEE International Conference on Computers, Systems and Signal Processing, 175. Retrieved from: < http://www.cs.ucsb.edu/~chong/290N-W06/BB84.pdf >.

[7]   ID Quantique SA. Cerberis quantum key distribution (qkd) server. [Internet]. 2011a. Retrieved from: <http://www.idquantique.com/network-encryption/products/cerberisquantum-key-distribution.html>.

[8]   ID Quantique SA. Redefining Security Geneva government secure data transfer for elections. [Internet]. 2011b. Retrieved from: < http://www.idquantique.com/images/stories/PDF/cerberis-encryptor/user-case-gva-gov.pdf > .

[9]   Weier H. (European quantum key distribution network. [Internet]. 2011. Ludwig-Maximilians-Universität München. European Quantum Key Distribution Network. Retrieved from: <http://edoc.ub.uni-muenchen.de/13320/1/Weier_Henning.pdf>.

[10] Bennett CH, Brassard G, Ekert AK. Quantum cryptography. Sci Am 1992;1:50−7.

[11] Hughes RJ, Luther GG, Morgan GL, Peterson CG, Simmons C. Quantum cryptography over underground optical fibers. Lect Notes Comput Sci 1996;1109:329−42.

[12] Bennett CH. Quantum cryptography using any two nonorthogonal states. Phys Rev Lett 1992;68 (21):3121−4. Retrieved from: <http://www.infoamerica.org/documentos_pdf/bennett1.pdf>.

[13] Muller A, Herzog T, Huttner B, Zbinden H, Gisin N. "Plug and play" systems for quantum cryptography. Appl Phys Lett 1997;70(7):793−5. Retrieved from: <http://arxiv.org/pdf/quant-ph/9611042>.

[14] Stucki D, Gisin N, Guinnard O, Ribordy G, Zbinden H. Quantum key distribution over 67 km with a plug&play system. New J Phys 2002;4:41−8. Retrieved from: <http://arxiv.org/pdf/quantph/0203118>.

[15] Ekert AK. Quantum cryptography based on Bell's theorem. Phys Rev Lett 1991;67(6):661−3.

[16] Gisin N, Ribordy G, Tittel W, Zbinden H. Quantum cryptography. Rev Mod Phys 2002;74(1):145−95. Retrieved from: <http://arxiv.org/pdf/quantph/0101098>.

[17] Cerf NJ, Lévy M, Van Assche G. Quantum distribution of gaussian keys using squeezed states. Phys Review A 2001;63(5): 052311-1. Retrieved from: < http://dx.doi.org/10.1103/PhysRevA.63.052311>.

[18] Grosshans F, Grangier P. Reverse reconciliation protocols for quantum cryptography with continuous variables. [Internet]. 2002. Paper presented at the Proceedings of the Sixth Internationl Conference on Quantum Communications, Measurement, and Computing (QCMC'02). Retrieved from: < http://arxiv.org/pdf/quant-ph/0204127.pdf > .

[19] Grosshans F, Van Assche G, Wenger J, Brouri R, Cerf NJ, Grangier P. Quantum key distribution using gaussian-modulated coherent states. Nature 2003;421. Retrieved from: <http://arxiv.org/pdf/quant-ph/0312016>.

[20] Silberhorn C, Ralph TC, Lütkenhaus N, Leuchs G. Continuous variable quantum cryptography: beating the 3 dB loss limit. Phys Rev Lett 2002;89(16). Retrieved from: < http://dx.doi.org/10.1103/PhysRevLett.89.167901 >

[21] Fossier S, Diamanti E, Debuisschert T, Villing A, Tualle-Brouri R, Grangier P. Field test of a continuous-variable quantum key distribution prototype. New J Phys 2009;11(4):045023-04538. Retrieved from: <http://arxiv.org/pdf/0812.3292>.

[22] Elliott C, Pearson DS, Troxel G. Quantum cryptography in practice. [Internet]. Paper presented at the Proceedings of the 2003 Conference on Applications, Technologies, Architectures, and Protocols for Computer Communications; 2003; Karlsruhe, Germany. p. 227−238. Retrieved from: <http://arxiv.org/pdf/quant-ph/0307049>.

[23] Peev M, Pacher C, Alléaume R, Barreiro C, Bouda J, Boxleitner W, et al. The SECOQC quantum key distribution network in Vienna. New J Phys 2009;11(7):075001. Retrieved from: <http://stacks.iop.org/1367-2630/11/i = 7/a = 075001>.

[24] Stucki D, Legré M, Buntschu F, Clausen B, Felber N, Gisin N, et al. Long-term performance of the SwissQuantum quantum key distribution network in a field environment. New J Phys 2011;13:1−18. Retrieved from: <http://www.gap-optic.unige.ch/wiki/_media/publications:bib:stucki2011a.pdf>.

[25] Sasaki M, Fujiwara M, Ishizuka H, Klaus W, Wakui K, Takeoka M, et al. Field test of quantum key distribution in the Tokyo QKD network. Opt Express 2011;19(11):10387−409. Retrieved from: <http://arxiv.org/pdf/1103.3566>.

[26] Gisin N, Thew RT. Quantum communication technology. Electron Lett 2010;46(14):965−7. Retrieved from: <http://quantumrepeaters.eu/images/attachments/Gisin10.pdf>.

[27] Afzelius M, Simon C, De Riedmatten H, Gisin N. Multimode quantum memory based on atomic frequency combs. Phys Rev A 2009;79(5):052329. Retrieved from: <http://arxiv.org/pdf/0805.4164.pdf>.

[28] Clausen C, Usmani I, Bussieres F, Sangouard N, Afzelius M, de Riedmatten H, et al. Quantum storage of photonic entanglement in a crystal. Nature 2011;469(7331):508–11. Retrieved from: <http://arxiv.org/pdf/1009.0489.pdf>.

[29] Simon C, De Riedmatten H, Afzelius M, Sangouard N, Zbinden H, Gisin N. Quantum repeaters with photon pair sources and multimode memories. Phys Rev Lett 2007;98(19):190503. Retrieved from: <http://arxiv.org/pdf/quant-ph/0701239.pdf>.

[30] Buttler WT, Hughes RJ, Kwiat PG, Luther GG, Morgan GL, Nordholt JE, et al. Free-space quantum key distribution. ArXiv Preprint Quant-ph/9801006. [Internet]. 1998. Retrieved from <http://arxiv.org/pdf/quant-ph/9801006.pdf>.

[31] Hughes RJ, Nordholt JE, Derkacs D, Peterson CG. Practical free-space quantum key distribution over 10 km in daylight and at night. New J Phys 2002;4(1):43. Retrieved from: <http://arxiv.org/ftp/quant-ph/papers/0206/0206092.pdf>.

[32] Jacobs BC, Franson JD. Quantum cryptography in free space. Opt Lett 1996;21(22):1854–6.

[33] Schmitt-Manderbach T, Weier H, Fürst M, Ursin R, Tiefenbacher F, Scheidl T, et al. Experimental demonstration of free-space decoy-state quantum key distribution over 144 km. Phys Rev Lett 2007;98(1):010504. Retrieved from: <http://www.univie.ac.at/qfp/publications3/pdffiles/2007-02.pdf>.

[34] Weier H, Schmitt-Manderbach T, Regner N, Kurtsiefer C, Weinfurter H. Free space quantum key distribution: towards a real life application. Fortschritte Der Physik 2006;54(8–10):840–5. Retrieved from: <http://arxiv.org/pdf/1204.5330>.

[35] Wang J, Yang B, Liao S, Zhang L, Shen Q, Hu X, et al. Direct and full-scale experimental verifications towards ground-satellite quantum key distribution. Nat Photonics 2013;7(5):387–93.

[36] Yin J, Cao Y, Liu S, Pan G, Wang J, Yang T, et al. Experimental single-photon transmission from satellite to earth. Unpublished manuscript. [Internet]. 2013 [retrieved 2013 July 5]. Retrieved from: <http://arxiv.org/pdf/1306.0672v1.pdf>.

[37] Acin A, Brunner N, Gisin N, Massar S, Pironio S, Scarani V. Device-independent security of quantum cryptography against collective attacks. Phys Rev Lett 2007;98(23):230501. Retrieved from: <http://arxiv.org/pdf/quant-ph/0702152>.

[38] Acin A, Massar S, Pironio S. Efficient quantum key distribution secure against no-signalling eavesdroppers. New J Phys 2006;8(8):126. Retrieved from: <http://arxiv.org/pdf/quant-ph/0605246>.

[39] Pironio S, Acin A, Brunner N, Gisin N, Massar S, Scarani V. Device-independent quantum key distribution secure against collective attacks. New J Phys 2009;11(4):045021. Retrieved from: <http://arxiv.org/pdf/0903.4460.pdf>.

[40] Gisin N, Pironio S, Sangouard N. Proposal for implementing device-independent quantum key distribution based on a heralded qubit amplifier. Phys Rev Lett 2010;105(7): 070501. Retrieved from: <http://arxiv.org/pdf/1003.0635.pdf>

[41] Masanes L, Pironio S, Acín A. Secure device-independent quantum key distribution with causally independent measurement devices. Nat Commun 2011;2:238. Retrieved from: <http://arxiv.org/pdf/1009.1567.pdf>.

[42] Lo H, Curty M, Qi B. Measurement-device-independent quantum key distribution. Phys Rev Lett 2012;108(13):130503. Retrieved from: <http://arxiv.org/pdf/1109.1473.pdf>.

[43] Tamaki K, Lo H, Fung CF, Qi B. Phase encoding schemes for measurement-device-independent quantum key distribution with basis-dependent flaw. Phys Rev A 2012;85(4):042307. Retrieved from: <http://arxiv.org/pdf/1111.3413.pdf>.

[44] Scarani V, Bechmann-Pasquinucci H, Cerf NJ, Dušek M, Lütkenhaus N, Peev M. The security of practical quantum key distribution. Rev Mod Phys 2009;81(3):1301. Retrieved from: <http://arxiv.org/pdf/0802.4155>.

Advances in Self-Security of Agent-Based Intrusion Detection Systems

10

Falkner Moraes, Zair Abdelouahab, Denivaldo Lopes, Emerson Oliveira, Cenidalva Teixeira,
Sofiane Labidi, and Ariel Teles

Federal University of Maranhão, São Luís, MA, Brazil

INFORMATION IN THIS CHAPTER

- Defining Intrusion detection systems (IDSs) based on agents
- Emergent Issues in Security for IDSs
- Towards the development of a Framework for Self-Security, Self-Reliability and Self-Integrity
- Identification of areas for further research

INTRODUCTION

Over the years, computer systems have evolved successfully from mere monolithic computing devices supporting static applications to large networks of distributed computing. These systems are becoming exposed to malicious interactions and are subject to a number of threats to their safety, requiring the development of mechanisms to provide security services. IDSs (Intrusion Detection Systems) are largely used to protect networks against threats like hackers and other malicious individuals or software. Currently, IDSs are created using software agents [1−5]. However, IDSs are constantly subjected to attacks with the aim to remove network protection, steal information, and then erase the footprints of the hackers. The goal of our research is to propose a framework for self-security, self-reliability of message exchange, self-reliability of components, and self-integrity of agent-based IDSs. This research is part of the project IDS-NIDIA (Network Intrusion Detection System Based on Intelligent Agents) [1]. NIDIA proposes a real-time intrusion detection system, capable of monitoring a network through an intelligent agent society, in order to detect unauthorized access of external entities (such as hackers) or even malicious individuals within the organization. However, these components must have the ability to ensure their own safety during their execution. The proposed framework is implemented as an extension of IDS-NIDIA in order to fill security gaps.

This chapter is structured as follows: In the "Overview" section, an overview of IDSs, multi-agent systems, and IDS-NIDIA is presented. In "Framework for Self-Security, Self-Reliability, and Self-Integrity of Agent-Based IDSs," the proposed framework for securing the execution of IDSs is shown; for example, security of configuration information, authentication and authorization, key and timestamp management, and message persistence. "Prototyping and Extending IDS-NIDIA" outlines the prototype of our solution. "Tests" illustrates the tests. "Related Works" presents related works. The "Conclusion" reflects on the results obtained with this solution.

Overview

This section describes the concepts related to multi-agent systems, agent-based IDS, IDS-NIDIA, and MOM (Message-Oriented Middleware).

A software agent is an autonomous entity that can interact with its environment. Software agents are implemented through software and can react with other entities such as humans, machines, and other agents in various environments, across multiple platforms. They are applicable in various ways, for example, in teaching-learning, industry, simulation, virtual reality, services, and computer networks [3,4,6]. Multi-agent systems consist of multiple agents that interact and work together to achieve a particular set of tasks or goals.

An IDS is a system able to monitor a network traffic searching suspicious activities by issuing a warning to the system or the network administrator. It previews all activities within and outside the network, identifying suspicious patterns that might indicate an attack by an intruder trying to break or compromise a system [2]. The use of agents in IDS software design provides the introduction of agent technologies characteristics. An agent-based IDS is a set of autonomous components working together in cooperation. Since the attacks change dynamically, the signatures also change. Therefore, these agents have the ability to learn new signatures or detect abnormal traffic caused by new attacks. Among major projects of agent-based IDSs are CAMNEP (an intrusion detection system for high-speed networks) [2], CIDS (Cougaar-Based Intrusion Detection System) [3], MIDS (Multi-Level and Multi-Agent Intrusion Detection System) [4], IDS-NIDIA [1], and others [7,8].

IDS-NIDIA [1] aims to present a system model for detecting intrusion in real time based on an intelligent agent society capable of detecting new attacks by a neural network. IDS-NIDIA is inspired by the CIDF [9] logical model, having agents with the task of generating events (sensors agents), mechanisms for data analysis (monitoring and security evaluation agents), history storage mechanisms (databases), and a module for carrying out countermeasures (countermeasure agents).

The general objectives of IDS-NIDIA project are: generate rates of suspected attack through information analysis collected from host logs and network traffic, take countermeasures based on achieved rates, and learn from the information obtained upgrading their knowledge databases.

The IDS-NIDIA model [1] is based on detection by anomaly and abuse to ensure greater system robustness. This choice is made because the majority of attacks can be coded in order to capture and record variants of activities that exploit the same vulnerabilities. Figure 10.1 shows the IDS-NIDIA architecture. It consists of six layers, and each layer contains a set of activities. The activities are performed through a society of agent behaviors that compose the layer. It is also through these agents that the layers communicate with each other, exchanging information to perform different activities.

The Monitoring Layer is responsible for capturing the occurrence of events in logs and network traffic and provides the same data for the rest of the system. The System Monitoring Agents (SMA) are located in this layer and are divided into two categories: Network Sensor Agents

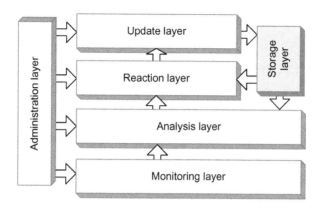

FIGURE 10.1

IDS-NIDIA architecture.

(NSA), which capture packets of the network, and Host Sensor Agents (HSA), which collect information from a host and provide them for examination.

The Analysis Layer has the task of examining the received events from the Monitoring Layer. In this layer, the events are collected and formatted in order to identify real attack patterns. The following knowledge databases are used as part of the analysis: the Intruder and Intrusion Pattern Database (IIDB), the Incident Damage Assessment and Forensic Database (DFDB), and the Strategies Database (STDB). In this layer, the System Evaluation Agents (SEA) analyze and provide a suspicion degree about the events that were previously formatted.

The Reaction Layer is responsible for taking countermeasures if a security incident is confirmed. In this layer, the System Controller Agents (SCA) carry out countermeasures in accordance with the Strategies (STDB) and Actions (RADB) databases.

The Update Layer is responsible for maintaining updates to all databases. In this layer, System Update Agents (SUA) have the responsibility to maintain the integrity and consistency of information stored and are the only ones able to change these databases.

The Administration Layer is composed of the Main Controller Agents (MCA), which are responsible for the administration and integrity of all system agents.

The Storage Layer keeps persistent information for all layers. All of the databases used by the IDS-NIDIA are contained here.

Among security problems encountered in the IDS-NIDIA, the ones that stand out are: open access to IDS resources, for example, the access to the key provider (XMKS server) is not controlled; lack of a validity control system for keys used in the encoding communication messages; no guarantee of message delivery between the agents if a receiver agent fails; and lack of a protection mechanism of information configuration necessary to promote the communication and configuration of the system. Our proposed framework fills these gaps in IDS-NIDIA.

MOM (Message-Oriented Middleware) [10] can be seen as a natural extension of the communication paradigms in the lower layers of the OSI model. Unlike the RPC (Remote Procedure Call) and the OOM (Object-Oriented Model), the MOM is a form of asynchronous communication; that is, there is non-blocking waiting from the sender to the receiver during message exchange. If the messaging service offers persistence and reliability, then the receiver does not need to be active and running when the message is sent. The messages are generally not typed, and their internal structures are the application's responsibility. Some MOM examples that stand out include IBM's WebSphere MQ [11], the TIBCO Rendezvous [12], and the messaging provider OpenJMS of Sun Microsystems [13].

Framework for self-security, self-reliability and self-integrity of agent-based IDSs

The proposed framework is a solution for providing self-security, self-reliability, and self-integrity for agent-based IDSs. Figure 10.2 presents the proposed framework, which consists of:

- Self-security: provides a security mechanism for agent-based IDSs
- Self-reliability of message exchange: provides reliability of message exchange between agents

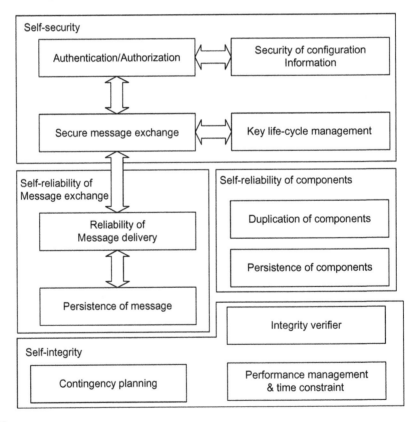

FIGURE 10.2

The proposed framework for self-security, self-reliability, and self-integrity.

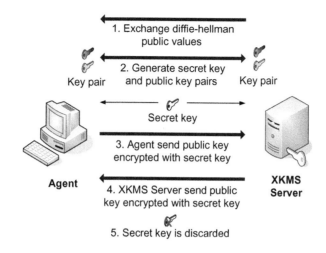

1. Exchange diffie-hellman
   public values

Key pair   2. Generate secret key   Key pair
            and public key pairs

Secret key

3. Agent send public key
   encrypted with secret key

Agent   4. XKMS Server send public   **XKMS**
             key encrypted with secret key   **Server**

5. Secret key is discarded

FIGURE 10.3

Model for registering public keys in the XKMS Server.

- Self-reliability of components: provides duplication and persistence of components (agents are cloned and their states are saved in a persistent memory)
- Self-integrity: analyzes integrity, performance, and time constraint of the agents and provides a contingency plan if the IDS is corrupted due to an attack

Self-security

Self-security takes care of the security of configuration information, authentication/authorization, secure message exchange, and key life cycle management. Configuration information is a crucial element in all security mechanisms that are physically distributed. In an IDS based on agents, communication can be made through encrypted messages. For this purpose, all agents that constitute the system must register their public keys in a repository such as the XKMS Server[1] [14]. The proposed model contains specific security measures for registering these keys in the XKMS Server. The security measure adopted employs a shared and temporary key called secret key that allows the encryption and decryption of messages used to register public keys between the agents and the XKMS Server. This secret key is unique, so it is different for each agent that performs this registry.

Figure 10.3 illustrates the process for registering a public key in the XKMS Server. The registry process begins when an agent and an XKMS Server agree and generate the same secret key, using the Diffie-Hellman algorithm [15]. Afterward, the agent starts its activities and separately generates its public and private key pair. A public key is encrypted using the secret key and the result is sent to the XKMS Server. Once the XKMS Server receives this encrypted message, it decrypts the message using the secret key, recovers the public key, and stores it in its PKI database. Then the XKMS Server sends an answer to the agent containing its public key in an encrypted message using the secret key. Once the agent receives this last message, it decrypts this message using the secret

[1]XKMS Server is a server that implements some functionality specified in the XML Key Management Specification.

key and recovers the public key of the XKMS Server. When the public key exchange between an agent and the XKMS Server finishes, the server discards the secret key.

Another security measure proposed in this chapter is the use of cryptography for securing the configuration information of the XKMS Server. This information includes the parameters that are the static inputs for the MAC address of the server and the parameters of the Diffie-Hellman algorithm that are used to generate the secret key. This information is stored in a file because this avoids a man-in-the-middle attack [16] and prevents an intruder from interfering in the communication or successfully deluding the XKMS Server and any agent that is registering or locating a public key. The parameters contained in the file are encrypted, and the agents have static inputs for the MAC address of the XKMS Server. The configuration information stored in this file represents a barrier to possible attacks. The way this configuration file can be accessed is defined by the network administrator, for example, using Secure File Transfer Protocol (SFTP) or shared directories. In order to use this file, an agent must obtain the public key that is the pair of the private key used to encrypt the file. This public key is owned only by the XKMS Server. It is provided after the authentication and authorization process (presented in the next subsection). Note that this model consists of two parts: (1) the parameters of Diffie-Hellman are stored in an encrypted file, and (2) the public key needed to decrypt the file is obtained only after authentication and authorization of an agent in the XKMS Server.

In some IDSs, the configuration information is stored in a static document containing data that can seriously compromise the system in the event that it is captured, analyzed, and decrypted by intruders. The proposed solution is a protection model based on a dynamic generation of the configuration information and its storage in an encrypted file (XML document) that can be accessed in many ways, such as SFTP.

For this purpose, when the XKMS Server is started, the following procedures are performed: a public and private key pair is created specifically for this solution, called XKMS Server "configuration keys"; a file is generated at runtime; and its content is encrypted using the private key. The access to this file is done by agents, for example, through the SFTP protocol, and the reading is executed through the public key provided by the XKMS Server. This public key is distributed to agents that are authenticated and authorized by the XKMS Server.

Authentication/authorization and secure message exchange

The proposed solution is based on a robust mechanism of authentication and authorization of agents to ensure the security of the message exchange. The aim is to allow only the agents of the IDS to have access to the functionalities of the XKMS Server. As seen in Figure 10.3, the XKMS Server provides the elements for a secure communication channel. Before an agent can register its public key in the XKMS Server, the former must authenticate itself and obtain the authorization needed to access the latter. Figure 10.4 presents the steps for authentication and access control in the XKMS Server.

The process presented in Figure 10.4 has the following steps for authentication and authorization: An agent and the XKMS server exchange the certificates in order to activate the secure connection through SSL (Secure Socket Layer). Using the secure connection based on SSL, the agent sends its username and password to access the XKMS Server. The XKMS Server verifies the username and password and provides the public key needed to decrypt the configuration file that contains the parameters of the Diffie-Hellman algorithm. The agent uses this public key to decrypt the

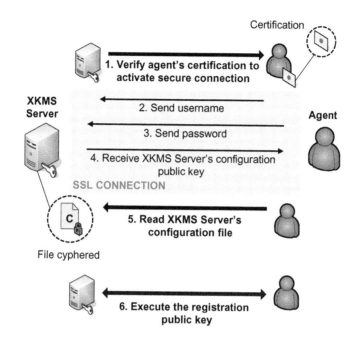

FIGURE 10.4

Schema of authentication and access control to key registration.

configuration file, obtaining the parameters to use the Diffie-Hellman algorithm. The agent and the XKMS Server use the Diffie-Hellman algorithm to exchange their public keys to secure the communication between agents.

Once an agent has obtained the public key of the XKMS Server and registered its public key, the messages are encrypted with the corresponding private key and decrypted by other agents using the public key of the sender. In our proposed framework, the messages are encrypted using XML-Encryption, XML-Signature, and Diffie-Hellman specifications, as presented in [15].

Key life cycle management

Cryptography is considered a critical element of any security system. Key management is directly related to the measures made to define a good design of a cryptographic system. These measures include the creation, exchange, storage, protection, utilization, verification, and renovation of keys. An IDS can profit from the XKMS Server for managing keys. The proposed solution is based on a model similar to PKI (Public Key Infrastructure), developed as an adaptation of XKMS. The role of the XKMS Server is to receive requests to find keys and return suitable answers. Figure 10.5 illustrates the XKMS Server functionality.

The XKMS Server designed for an IDS is based on a key management model that meets requirements of generation, lookup, exchange, storage, protection, utilization, and key verifications, but it does not have a mechanism that defines a key deadline and its consequent substitution done

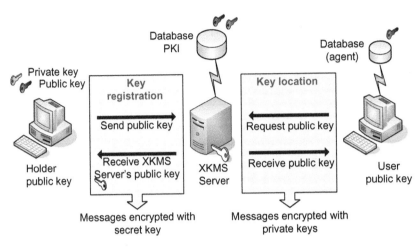

FIGURE 10.5

XKMS Server: key registration and lookup.

by agents [17]. The key renewal is an important security feature, because it protects the system by avoiding encrypted messages with corrupted public keys.

The proposed solution is based on a security model where all the keys stored in the XKMS Server will have a lifetime defined by the server through the use of digital statements called "time-stamp." Figure 10.6 shows how an entity (i.e., an agent) manages the lifetime of public keys. When an agent begins the process of generating a key pair, the system generates a timestamp that represents the creation date of the public key. This timestamp is then sent to the XKMS Server, which calculates the time that the public key is available for other agents in the system. This deadline defines the expiration time of a public key, which is then returned to the owner of the corresponding key. Once the deadline is over, a new generation and registration of a public key should proceed. The agent identifier, deadline, and public key are stored in the server's PKI database.

When an agent aims to establish a secure communication with another agent, it must acquire the public key from the XKMS Server. This key and deadline (i.e., expiration timestamp) are stored in the agent's database. For each message sent, an agent (sender) verifies the validity of the other agent's (receiver's) key. If the key is available and the validity date is correct, then the communication proceeds. Otherwise, the agent requests the new public key to the XKMS server. There are cases where a key is verified by the sender with a correct validity date. The sender uses this key to encrypt a message that is read by a receiver later, when the validity date has already expired (i.e., the deadline is over), generating a failure in the validity date verification. Generally, this problem happens when there is a possible surcharge in the network and this causes a large time interval between the verification of the key validity by the sender and a reading of encrypted message with this key by the receiver. In the meantime, the receiver has changed its public key in the XKMS Server. Thus, the receiver refuses the message, launches a failure alert to the sender, and requests a new message encrypted with the current public key with a new validity date.

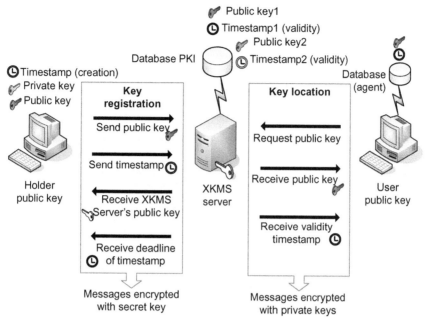

FIGURE 10.6

XKMS Server functioning with a timestamp solution.

Self-reliability of message exchange

Reliability of Message Delivery: Self-reliability takes care of message delivery and message persistence. In an agent-based IDS, the focus of reliability of message consists of ensuring the delivery of messages exchanged between agents. In addition, it is important to ensure that messages are delivered in the sequence in which they are sent. In our framework, we adopt the WS-ReliableMessage specification [18] for guaranteeing reliable messages with four types of delivery policies: AtMostOnce, AtLeastOnce, ExactlyOnce, and InOrder.

Message Persistence: Persistent messages are messages written in logs and data file queues through the use of managers. If a queue manager is restarted after a failure, it recovers messages from the recorded data and makes them available to their destinations (receivers). The aim is to enhance the security and integrity of messages that are sent when a failure occurs in any component of the system. Figure 10.7 (a) shows how the communication is achieved between a sender agent and a receiver agent inside the proposed model. Figure 10.7 (b) illustrates the proposed solution for message persistence.

Self-reliability of components

In agent-based IDS, components are agents that are cloned (i.e., duplicated) or saved in a persistent memory. Our approach to establishing self-reliability is presented in Figure 10.8 and is an extension of the proposal presented in [6].

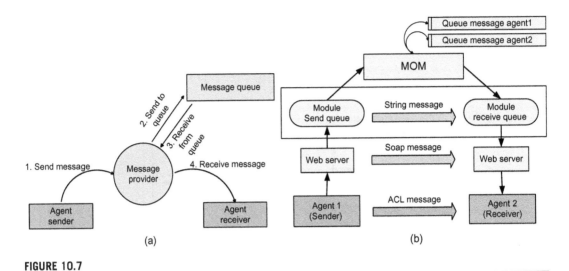

FIGURE 10.7

(a) The proposed model (b) Details of the model

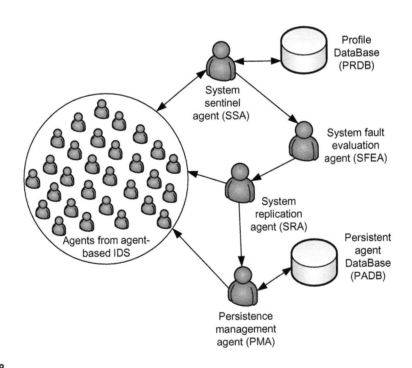

FIGURE 10.8

Self-reliability of components (agents).

The mechanism for self-reliability is composed of:

- System Sentinel Agent (SSA): This type of agent is installed in each host. It is responsible for monitoring the resources in the host (e.g., CPU time-slice, free memory, and network load) and other agents that compose the IDS. The monitoring information is passed to SFEA in order to process it.
- Profile DataBase (PRDB): This component stores the profiles of each agent and of their clones.
- System Fault Evaluation Agent (SFEA): This component determines if another agent or a host has a failure and invokes the SRA.
- System Replication Agent (SRA): This component activates one clone if an agent fails. If no clones are available for any reason, SFEA invokes the SRA.
- Persistent Management Agent (PMA): This component restores an agent saved in a persistent memory. The states of agents are saved in specific checkpoints, so that an agent is resumed from the last checkpoint.
- Persistent Agent DataBase (PADB): This component stores agents saved in a persistent memory.

Self-integrity

Self-integrity takes care of integrity verification, contingency planning, performance management, and time constraint.

Integrity verification aims to ensure that an agent is performing the activities that are designated to it and that an agent is not corrupted (i.e., the code is not modified). Each agent is designed to perform activities and capabilities that are attributed to it. A capability describes the activities that an agent can do. Thus the behavior of an agent is monitored and confronted to its capabilities. If an agent tries to perform an activity that is not part of its capabilities, then an exception is raised and an attack may be happening.

An agent can be captured and modified by a malicious person in order to compromise the functionalities of the IDS and hide the footprints of an attack. The solution provided in our framework to avoid this occurring, and to identify if an agent has been modified, is described as follows:

- After compilation, a hash value is calculated and stored in a secure database for each agent. For example, this hash value can be calculated using an MD5 algorithm.
- The agent code is encrypted using RSA algorithm. Before loading the agent code, it is decrypted.
- Before executing the agent code, the hash value for this code is calculated and compared to the value stored in the secure database.

Integrity verification is dependent on platform implementation. For example, if an agent-based IDS is implemented in Java, then the source code of an agent is written in bytecodes that are vulnerable to reverse engineering. For this reason, the agent code must be encrypted and a hash value associated to it. On the one hand, Java is vulnerable to reverse engineering; on the other hand, it provides facilities to manipulate the agent code, such as the class loader. The latter can be customized to decrypt the code, calculate the hash value, and compare it to the hash value stored in the secure database, and if the hash values match, then the code is loaded in memory to be executed. Figure 10.9 illustrates the steps for integrity verification.

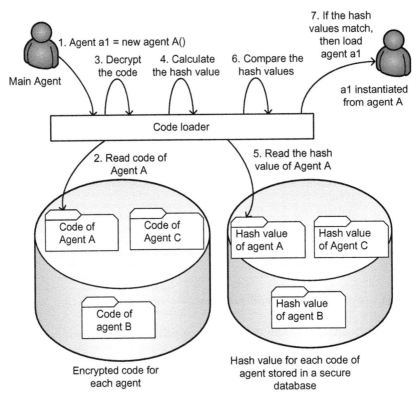

FIGURE 10.9

Self-integrity verification for agent-based IDS.

Contingency planning provides a standard action if the IDS is compromised after an attack. If an attack to the IDS is successful, then the agents that are compromised must not continue executing or performing actions. For this purpose, some standard actions are provided, such as blocking the messages sent to/from a compromised agent, canceling the public keys of these agents, denying their accesses to the XKMS Server, and sending an alert for the network administrator.

An efficient IDS must be able to capture packages and host information, analyze them in order to find threats, and perform countermeasures before these threats can produce damages. Thus performance and time constraint are important non-functional requirements for IDS.

Recently, thanks to the gigabits networks, the amount of data that can be analyzed in a short time by an IDS has increased. In our proposed framework, each agent must finalize actions before a deadline, or else a low performance alert is launched and a load balancing can take place. Another important measure is to install the monitoring and analysis layers in the same dedicated machine with a robust configuration, that is, a machine with many cores and large memory space.

However, this solution is not sufficient because periods of low performance can happen, and an attack can cause damage in the interim. An ideal solution for performance and time constraint in

IDSs should be conceived, designed, and implemented according to a real-time operating system in order to support a real-time process. However, real-time operating systems are not common in networks. In the near future, perhaps extensions of Linux for real-time can be used for this purpose.

Prototyping and extending IDS-NIDIA

The implementation of our framework is an extension of the IDS-NIDIA. We use the following elements in its development: Java, JADE [18] agents platform, and Systinet Server [19], to provide SOAP and WS-Reliable Messaging; Trust Service Integration Kit (TSIK) [7] for programming the specifications for XKMS, XML-Encryption and XML-Signature; and OpenJMS [14] for implementing the MOM infrastructure.

The prototype implements our proposed secure and reliable message exchange and uses extra resources for meeting the requirements of enhanced key management, persistent messages, and protection of configuration information. These proposals include new libraries and the creation of software packages that have classes with specific functionalities for each requirement in order to secure IDS like IDS-NIDIA. To include these proposals as an extension and adaptation of IDS-NIDIA, existing source code containing classes were modified through the introduction of new attributes and methods and the adaptation of existing methods.

Tests

To proceed with testing and analysis of the results obtained with the proposed solution applied to IDS-NIDIA, some tools were used to visualize the behavior of agents. These are: the development environment Eclipse for Java, the agent Sniffer of JADE, the sniffer Wireshark used to capture data packet transmitted in the network, and OpenMS.

Figure 10.10 shows the sequence of messages exchanged between two agents (sender and receiver) and the XKMS Server after successful authentication. The sequence shows two registry operations with key XKMS Server and a key request operation for secure messaging.

Figure 10.11 shows packets of messages exchanged for creating the secure channel and authentication of agents. The XKMS Server is identified by the IP 192.168.0.146 and communicates with the agent using TCP (Transmission Control Protocol), SSLv2 (Secure Sockets Layer - v 2), TLSv1 (Transport Layer Security - v 1), and port 443. The agent is identified by the IP 192.198.0.176 and communicates with the XKMS Server using the same protocols used in the server and port 50268.

Figure 10.12 illustrates the key management mechanism used for defining the validity lifetime of the public keys stored in the XKMS Server. It shows the creation date of the key owner (receiver) being received by the XKMS Server and the expiration date calculated and sent to the agent owner of the key.

Figure 10.13 shows the persistence mechanism for handling messages that are sent to the MOM queue for treatment; later these are received by the agents.

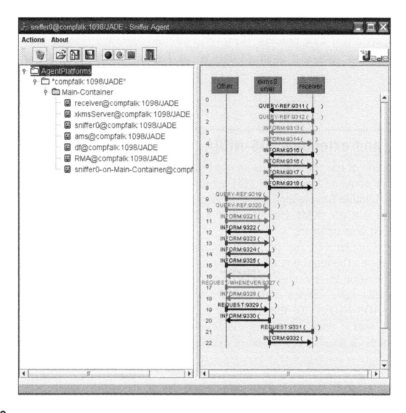

FIGURE 10.10

Exchange of messages: registration and lookup.

Related works

Recent research has been developed for enhancing the self-security in agent based-IDS [16,17,20,21].

Emerson Oliveria et al. [17] provide a set of security services based on XML specification and Web services for providing security and reliability of messages exchanged between agents. Tieyan Li et al. [20] propose resistant mobile agent architecture in order to avoid DoS attacks to IDS. In this approach, critical components of the IDS are protected through backup mechanism of agents and some mechanism for hiding the internal structure of the system. For this last purpose, a group of agent acts as a proxy for hiding the critical components of the IDS. A group of agents called "buddy" is created in order to protect the proxy agents and disseminate the service of the main directory. This approach also provides analysis of attack patterns in order to detect and correct the points of failure in the IDS. A mechanism of honeypot is implemented in order to simulate the system, giving to an intruder the illusion that his attack is successful.

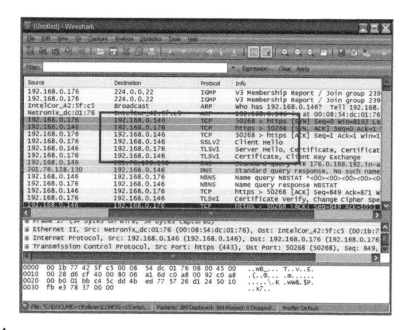

FIGURE 10.11

Message package used in the creation of the secure channel.

FIGURE 10.12

Keys lifetime.

Zhu Shu-ren and Li Wei-qin [21] provide an approach for self-protection of agent that uses the analysis of a Network Intrusion Detection System (NIDS) and adopt security policies as package filtering, process control, secure communication, validity of message, and cooperative agents. The authors claim that their approach does not impact on the performance of the network because NDS is implemented inside the kernel of the operating system.

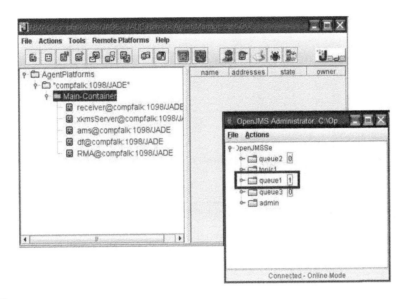

FIGURE 10.13

Representation of messages stored in the MOM queue.

The solutions proposed in the literature for self-security of agent based-IDS covers only a few aspects of self-security. In our proposal, we provide a framework that covers several aspects for securing the agents that constitute the agent based-IDS, namely, authentication/authorization, security of configuration information, secure message exchange, key life cycle management, reliability of message delivery, persistence of message, reliability of components, integrity verification, contingency planning, and performance and time constraint.

CONCLUSION

Security is an important issue in all networks. Some techniques, methodologies, and tools are deployed for securing networks that provide security barriers against threats. On the one hand, security policies, firewalls, and antivirus are security barriers used to prevent attacks from threats, avoiding damages. On the other hand, when threats traverse the security barriers, an IDS must detect the threats and provide a countermeasure before relevant damage can take place. A threat can be directed to attack IDSs in order to disable their functionalities of detection and countermeasure, and to erase the attacker's footprints.

In general, IDSs are conceived, designed, and implemented having only the security provided by the subjacent operating system, such as account privileges for creating, editing, or erasing configuration files or for starting, stopping, or killing processes. In actual context, this measure is not enough to ensure security to IDS. For example, a threat can intercept, modify, or break the flow of messages between the elements of the IDS; control elements of the IDS to hide its presence; or disable or open security barriers such as firewalls. (In general, IDSs can control firewalls to close or open ports.) A threat can attack the IDS and then execute its aims without being perceived.

In order to fill the security gaps in the conception, design, and implementation of agent-based IDS, we have proposed a framework that secures main elements such as communication, components (i.e., agents), and configuration files. In addition, if the barriers to secure IDS are traversed, then a contingency plan can be executed in order to avoid significant damages to the system or network. The framework is based on open standards such as XML and Web service specifications. Moreover, it introduces some techniques, algorithms, and agents for providing security to agent-based IDSs. This framework defines changes in the conception of agent-based IDSs in order to ensure the integrity of agents before executing them. Our approach promotes the use of ACL messages that are signed, encrypted, and enveloped in SOAP messages that are transmitted using MOM. The message delivery is assured because the framework is based on WS-ReliableMessage specification and message persistence. We enhance the encryption of the message through a schema for key life cycle management. In this schema, public and private keys have a limited duration and are renewed in order to avoid being compromised.

The proposed framework is implemented as an extension of IDS-NIDIA in order to demonstrate that an agent-based IDS can acquire self-protection. The model of IDS-NIDIA is modified in order to introduce new classes, attributes, and methods for introducing self-protection. Some code fragments illustrated, such as the modifications, are implemented. Some tests illustrate the behavior of the IDS-NIDIA and the role of self-protection in runtime.

In the literature, little research has addressed self-protection for agent-based IDSs. In this chapter, we have presented a framework that covers important security gaps in agent-based IDSs. Despite the approaches presented in [16,20−23], our framework is not platform dependent and is not specific to IDS-NIDIA. In fact, this proposed framework can be ported in other agent-based IDSs because it is based on standard specifications and well-known technologies and libraries (e.g., WS-ReliableMessage, XML-Enc, XML-Sig, and OpenJMS).

As part of our future research work, we intend to extend and apply the proposed framework to other security tools such as antivirus and firewalls. Afterward, we intend to apply the proposed framework as a service infrastructure for supporting the transparent and secure interaction between different security tools in order to promote a unified threat management based on open source tools such as Clamav, iptables, and IDS-NIDIA. We also need to create test cases to evaluate the performance impact from the additional load generated by the implementation of the framework.

Acknowledgments

The authors would like to thank CAPES, CNPq, and FAPEMA for supporting this research work.

References

[1] Silva M, Lopes D, Abdelouahab Z. A remote IDS based on multi-agent systems, Web services and MDA. In: IEEE International Conference on Software Engineering Advances; 2006.

[2] Rehak M, Pechoucek M, Bar-Tos K, Grill M, Celeda P, Krmicek V. CAMNEP: an intrusion detection system for high-speed networks. Progress in Informatics 2008;5:65−74 (JPN).

[3] Dasgupta D, Gonzalez F, Yallapu K, Gomez J, Yarramsettii R. CIDS: an agent-based intrusion detection system. Computers & Security 2005;24(5):387−98.

[4] Briffaut J. MIDS: Multi-level and multi-agent intrusion detection system. In: First International Workshop on Privacy and Security in Agent-based Collaborative Environments. Japan Hakodate; 2006.

[5] Hegazy IM, Faheem HM, al-Arif T, Ahmed T. Evaluating how well agent-based IDS perform. IEEE Potentials 2005;24(2):27−30.

[6] Siqueira L, Abdelouahab Z. A fault tolerance mechanism for network intrusion detection system based on intelligent agents (NIDIA). The IEEE International Workshop on Collaborative Computing, Integration, and Assurance; 2006. p. 49−54

[7] Vyavhare A, Bhosale V, Sawant M, Girkar F. Survey on a co-operative multi-agent based wireless intrusion detection systems using MIB. Advances in Intelligent Systems and Computing 2012;167:873−81.

[8] Eid HF, Darwish A, Hassanien AE, Kim TH. Intelligent hybrid anomaly network intrusion detection system. Communications in Computer and Information Science 2012;265:209−18.

[9] Staniford-Chen S. Common intrusion detection framework (CDIF). Computer Emergency Response Team (Coordination Center); 1999.

[10] Menascé DA. MOM vs. RPC: Communication models for distributed applications. Internet Computing, IEEE 2005;9(2):90−3.

[11] IBM WebSphere MQ. [Internet]. Available from: <http://www-01.ibm.com/software/integration/wmq/>; [accessed 27.01.12].

[12] TIBCO Rendezvous. [Internet]. Available from: <http://www.tibco.com/software/messaging/rendezvous/default.jsp>; [accessed 27.03.11].

[13] OpenJMS. [Internet]. Available from: <http://OpenJMS.sourceforge.net>; [accessed 10.02.12].

[14] XKMS. XML key management specification (XKMS). [Internet]. Available from: <http://www.w3.org/TR/xkms/>; [accessed 25.04.11].

[15] Diffie-Hellman. Diffie-Hellman key agreement method RFC 2631. [Internet]. Available from: <http://tools.ietf.org/html/ rfc2631>; [accessed 07.03.12].

[16] Oyegoke E, Thyfonas T, Blyth A. Exploring vulnerabilities of agent-based IDS: The need for agent self-defence. Proceedings of the First European Conference on Computer Network Defence School of Computing. Springer: London; 2006.

[17] Oliveira E, Abdelouahab Z, Lopes D. Security on MASs with XML security specifications. In: International Workshop on Network Based Information Systems; 2006; Krakow. For IEEE Computer Society; 2006.

[18] Davis D, Karmarkar A, Pilz G, Winkler S, Yalçinalp Ü. Web services reliable messaging (WS-ReliableMessaging) - wsrm-1.1-spec-cd-04; 2006.

[19] VeriSign. VeriSign home page. [Internet]. Available from: <http://www.verisign.com>; [accessed 10.10.12].

[20] Li T, Chew WM, Lam KY. Defending against distributed denial of service attacks using resistant mobile agent architecture. In: International Parallel and Distributed Processing Symposium: IPDPS 2002. Workshops; 2002.

[21] Shu-Ren Z, Li WQ. Design and implementation of self-protection agent for network-based intrusion detection system. Journal of Central South University of Technology 2003;10:1.

[22] Nguyen Vu QA, Canal R, Gaudou B, Hassas S, Armetta F. TrustSets: Using trust to detect deceitful agents in a distributed information collecting system. Journal of Ambient Intelligence and Humanized Computing 2012;3(4):251−63.

[23] Yang H, Wang D, Chen C. Research on network self-protection system model and its security event correlation engine. Advances in Intelligent and Soft Computing 2012;162:773−80.

Further reading

Systinet. Systinet Server for Java 6.5.3. API; 2006.

JADE, Java Agent DEvelopment framework. [Internet]. Available from: <http://jade.tilab.com>; [accessed 10.01.10].

Secure Communication in Fiber-Optic Networks

11

Ben Wu, Bhavin J. Shastri, and Paul R. Prucnal

Princeton University, Princeton, NJ, USA

INFORMATION IN THIS CHAPTER

* Confidentiality
* Privacy and optical steganography
* Availability

INTRODUCTION

Optical networks form the backbone of the Internet and are an integral constituent of the physical layer of these networks. Since the physical layer forms the bottom layer in the open systems interconnection (OSI) model [1], the performance and security of the physical layer and especially optical networks have a critical influence on the six layers above it. For example, the channel capacity of the optical network determines the resources available for encryption processes in the upper layer. The security approach in upper layers is limited by both the processing speed of electronic devices and the capacity availability in the optical network. Fundamental improvements can be achieved for the entire network by increasing the optical network's performance in terms of channel capacity, data rate, and processing speed. Furthermore, the security of the optical network has an impact on the security of the entire communication system. Since it is inherently risky to build a security system on top of a physical infrastructure that is already under threat [2], defending against threats to the optical network also benefits the security of the upper layer.

Optical network security can be effectively protected by fiber-based methods, including all-optical signal processing [3–5], optical key distribution [6–8], optical steganography [9–11], and optical chaos-based communication [12–14]. Fiber-based devices do not radiate an electromagnetic signature and are immune to electromagnetic interference, so the adversary can neither eavesdrop from the leaked information to free space nor jam the fiber channel with electromagnetic waves. Another motivation for securing the network based on optical approaches is that fiber-based devices

173

have low latency and high processing speed; thus, the network is protected without compromising its transmission speed. Moreover, studies in the optical layer security aim at increasing the capacity of the fiber network instead of consuming the available capacity of the fiber-optic network. For example, optical steganography demonstrates that noise in the public channel can also be used as a stealth channel for private data transmission [11]. Optical key distribution develops a separate channel with higher security level to carry the key information for data encryption [6].

In this chapter, we classify optical fiber security techniques by the threat they can address. In the section titled "Confidentiality" we discuss confidentiality of data communications and summarize the application of optical encryption and optical code-division multiple access (CDMA) in protecting the confidentiality. We also analyze an optical key distribution method for the encryption and decryption process. In the section titled "Privacy and Optical Steganography" we describe different approaches to optical steganography and analyze its functions in transmitting private data without being detected. In the section titled "Availability" we examine methods for assuring network availability, including anti-jamming and optical chaos-based communication. Throughout the chapter, we briefly describe the experimental schemes used and compare the different physical techniques. We also analyze the application and relation of each technique to the various threats that exist in the network.

Confidentiality

Data confidentiality ensures that confidential data is not disclosed to an unauthorized user in the network [15]. In an optical fiber network, the eavesdropper may receive residual crosstalk from an adjacent channel [16] or by physically tapping the optical fiber [17]. Optical encryption and optical coding can effectively protect the confidentiality of the physical layer network and satisfy the high speed requirements of modern networks. As fiber-based devices do not generate electromagnetic radiation, optical encryption and coding processes are immune to attacks based on the electromagnetic signature of the signal. In this section, we first provide examples of optical encryption and analyze its applications in secure communication. Next, we briefly summarize an optical CDMA technique. Lastly, we describe the key distribution methods for the encryption and coding.

Optical encryption

Encryption protects data transmission by encrypting the original data into cipher text. Without knowing the key for the encryption process, the eavesdropper cannot recover the data. Optical encryption has been widely studied in literature [3,4,18−22]. Compared with electronic circuits, optical processing and transmission devices have lower latency and higher speed. Another motivation for optical encryption is that fiber-based devices do not generate an electromagnetic signature. The signal in the fiber neither radiates an electromagnetic signal nor is it jammed by external electromagnetic interference. Although, compared to electronic encryption, optical encryption has limited functionality, it still plays an important role in areas that require both strong security and fast processing speed. For example, optical encryption could be especially important in the area of high-frequency trading.

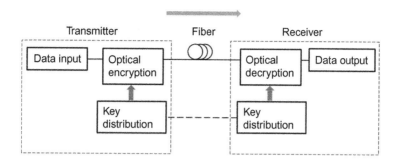

FIGURE 11.1

Schematic diagram for optical encryption.

Optical encryption includes the encryption and decryption process together with the key distribution between the transmitter and receiver (Figure 11.1). In this section, we discuss the encryption and decryption process; the key distribution method is summarized in the section titled "Optical Key Distribution." Optical exclusive OR (XOR) logic operation has been widely studied to achieve optical encryption and decryption. The optical XOR gate can be integrated into a conventional optical CDMA system and improve the overall security performance [18].

Various techniques have been developed and experimentally demonstrated to achieve the XOR operation. Chan et al. employed four-wave mixing (FWM) in a semiconductor optical amplifier (SOA) to achieve an XOR gate operating up to 20Gb/s [4]. Fok et al. investigated polarization sensitivity of an XOR gate based on FWM in a highly nonlinear fiber [19]. Other techniques, including cross polarization modulation [20], cross gain modulation [21], and cross-phase modulation [22], have also been studied to achieve optical XOR operation. These optical XOR operation methods successfully achieve all-optical data encryption. The XOR-encrypted data is protected from detection without compromising the speed for data transmission.

Optical CDMA

Optical CDMA protects data confidentiality by using a code pattern to represent "0" and "1" bits [23–28]. Multiple users with different (orthogonal) codes can share the same channel to transmit data simultaneously. Optical CDMA can be divided into two categories: coherent optical CDMA and incoherent optical CDMA. A typical coherent optical CDMA system uses spectral-phase encoding, which gives different phase shifts to the coherent spectral components at the transmitter. To decode the signal, conjugate phase shifts are used at the receiver. A typical incoherent optical CDMA scheme is called wavelength-hopping time-spreading (WHTS). WHTS uses incoherent pulses on different wavelengths to represent a code sequence (Figure 11.2). Within each code sequence, each pulse has a different delay and occupies a different time chip in each bit. The receiver for a desired code sequence compensates for the delays of the different pulses to form an autocorrelation peak (ACP). Applying the same delay compensation to the other undesired code sequences forms a cross-correlation function, and due to the orthogonal nature of the codes, this results in multiple-access interference (MAI). To improve the signal-to-noise (SNR) ratio, an optical thresholder can be used to suppress the MAI [29].

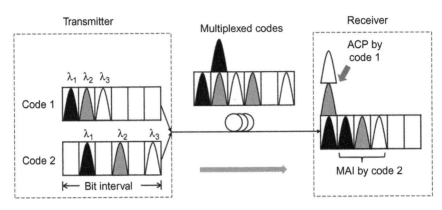

FIGURE 11.2

Schematic diagram for wavelength-hopping time-spreading optical CDMA (ACP: autocorrelation peak; MAI: multiple-access interference).

In an optical CDMA network, multiple users have their multiplexed codes overlapped, so without knowing the code used by a particular user, the eavesdropper can neither separate the pulses within each code nor recover the autocorrelation peak. However, for a point-to-point link with only one pair of transmitters and receivers, the data security may be vulnerable to attack [30]. To secure point-to-point links, Wang et al. propose a method to divide the original data stream into multiple data streams and then generate multiplexed signals. The experiment results indicate that the system is robust against various types of attack models [31].

Optical key distribution

Although the optical encryption and optical coding can effectively protect the confidentiality of the physical layer, the key for the encryption and decryption process should be distributed in a secure way between the authorized users. The key can be transmitted at a lower rate than the encrypted data but requires a higher security level. Quantum key distribution can effectively protect the encryption process by encoding the key information on the quantum states of a single photon. In 1984, Bennett and Brassard proposed using non-orthogonal polarization states of photons to transmit digital information [32]. This is now known as the BB84 protocol. After it was experimentally demonstrated in 1992 [33], different approaches have been used to achieve key exchange [6,7,34].

One important property for quantum key distribution is that it can indicate the existence of an eavesdropper trying to receive any information about the key. This is because of the unique property of quantum mechanics, in which the measurement of a certain parameter in a system also disturbs this parameter. Although the quantum channel provides a high security level to the key distribution, the requirement of single photon transmission and detection leads to difficulty in practically realizing the system. The transmission range and data rate is limited by the noise and attenuation in the single photon transmission channel. To achieve a longer range and higher data rate, classic quantum distribution also has been studied [8,35]. Scheuer et al. use a large fiber laser to exchange the key so that each user can compare the received signal with his or her own key to obtain the key generated by the other user. Compared to quantum key distribution, this system allows longer ranges and a higher key-establishing rate [8].

Privacy and optical steganography

Privacy ensures individual control of what information may be received or collected and to whom the information may be transmitted or disclosed [15]. Although data encryption can protect the original data in a signal channel from being received by the eavesdropper, it cannot protect the existence of the channel from being detected. In some instances, the system is already under threat if the adversary knows the existence of a private channel. The aim of optical steganography in a fiber communication network is to hide signals in the existing public channels so that the eavesdropper can neither receive the signals nor detect the existence of the hidden channel [9,36−39]. The hidden channel, which carries the stealth signals, is designed in such a way that no one, apart from the intended recipient, can detect the existence of the signal in either the time domain or the spectral domain. To bury the stealth channel in the noise that already exists in the system, the power of the stealth signal is typically 10 dB−20 dB lower than the public channel [11].

Optical steganography was first proposed and experimentally demonstrated by Wu et al. [9]. The basic approach in optical steganography is to temporally stretch a short optical pulse through chromatic dispersion. Without using the right dispersion compensation at the receiver, the stretched signal is buried in the system noise of the public channel. In the spectral domain, because the spectral width of the optical pulse is on the order of several nanometers, which is much wider than the public channel spectrum, the optical spectrum of the stealth channel merges into the background noise of the public channel.

Optical steganography has been experimentally demonstrated to be compatible with public channels with various modulation formats, including return-to-zero (NRZ) on-off-keying (OOK) [40], non-return-to-zero (RZ) OOK [41], OOK optical CDMA [42], and differential (quadrature) phase-shift keying (DPSK/DQPSK) [43]. To further improve the privacy of the stealth channel, a temporal phase mask is designed to provide additional phase shift to the stretched stealth data (Figure 11.3) [44]. Each stealth data bit is covered by a 16-chip phase mask. To demodulate the data, both the dispersion and the phase mask need to be matched between the transmitter and receiver.

Recently, another approach for optical steganography was proposed to carry the stealth signal in the system noise [11] (Figure 11.4). Instead of stretching the optical pulse to mimic the noise, this method directly employs the amplified spontaneous emission (ASE) noise from amplifiers that are conventionally used to boost the signal in the fiber channel. The ASE noise from erbium-doped fiber amplifiers (EDFA) is the most prevalent noise in fiber communication systems. Since the ASE noise carrying the stealth signal has identical optical spectral properties to the ASE noise that originally existed in the system, an eavesdropper cannot differentiate whether it is signal ASE or noise ASE in the spectral domain. In the time domain, the short coherence length properties of the ASE noise provide a large key space between the transmitter and receiver. Phase modulation is used on the stealth channel at the transmitter. To demodulate the signal at the receiver, the optical

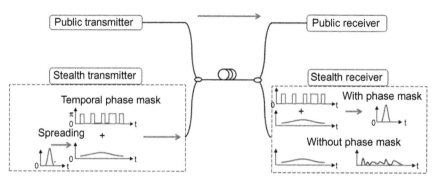

FIGURE 11.3

Schematic diagram for temporal phase modulation on spread stealth pulses.

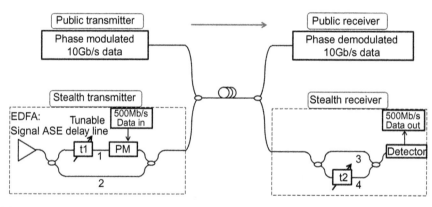

FIGURE 11.4

Schematic diagram for optical steganography based on amplified spontaneous emission noise (EDFA: erbium-doped fiber amplifier; ASE: amplified spontaneous emission; PM: phase modulator).

path length difference between the transmitter and the receiver has to be matched to be within the coherence length of the ASE noise, which is extremely short and nearly impossible to determine. If an eavesdropper tries to steal the private signal without information about the delay length difference, only noise with constant power is received. The optical path length difference at the transmitter is designed to be over 10^4 times longer than the coherence length of ASE and is deliberately changed in a dynamic fashion, so that, even if an unintended receiver finds the length difference using a quick scanning technique, it cannot follow the rapid changes of the delay length.

In the experiment, the coherence length of ASE noise is measured to be 372 μm or 1.24 ps in terms of optical delay, and the optical path length difference between path 1 and 2 at the transmitter is 6 m (Figure 11.4). The eavesdropper needs to search for a 372 μm length in a 6 m space to find the matching condition. To make acquisition even more difficult, this delay can be changed dynamically. The bit error rate (BER) measurement of the channel shows that a low BER can only be achieved at the receiver when the unknown delay is properly tuned within the coherence length of ASE noise. If the matching condition is not satisfied, the BER is so large that it cannot be measured. To further increase the key space, dispersion is used as another key parameter between the transmitter and the receiver [45]. Since the keys for the delay length and the dispersion are mutually orthogonal, the expansion to two dimensions increases the key space geometrically. Using dispersion as another key in an ASE system also benefits from the wide spectrum of ASE noise. The wide optical spectrum of the ASE noise makes the signal nosier with relatively smaller dispersion, so besides the delay length, the dispersion also must be matched between the transmitter and receiver to demodulate the data.

In addition to protecting the privacy of data transmission, a hidden channel in the public network can also be applied to other security techniques for countering other possible threats. For example, the stealth channel can be used to transmit information having a high security level requirement, such as the key distribution for the encrypted public channel. The stealth channel can also be used to carry the users' information about the public channel, so the receiver can identify whether the information in the public channel comes from an authorized user.

Availability
Jamming and anti-jamming

"Availability" is an aspect of security that ensures that a network service is not denied to authorized users. One possible threat to network availability is to jam a signal channel with strong noise. Optical steganography based on ASE noise, discussed in the last section, can effectively protect the availability when the signal is carried by ASE, which covers the entire transmission band (known as the "C band") for fiber optic communications [11]. This increases the difficulty of carrying out malicious jamming, and even if the adversary could jam the entire C band, there would be no bandwidth left for its own data communication. Another potential solution to ensure availability uses waveband conversion. In this scheme, multiple wavebands are used for communication. If the current waveband gets jammed, the data channel can be either up-converted or down-converted to a new waveband range. Waveband conversion can be implemented with a periodically-poled lithium niobate ($LiNbO_3$) material, resulting in a low power penalty and BER [46].

Optical chaos-based communications

Chaos-based communications provide an approach for transmitting confidential data with a high level of robustness [13]. The broadband chaotic signal not only enhances the robustness of the data transmission to a narrow band interference or malicious jamming, it can also be used to jam the communication of adversaries. In contrast to optical steganography, which aims to reduce the amplitude of the stealth signal to as small as possible, the strategy of chaos-based communications is to mask the confidential data with much stronger chaos. The generation of the chaos is based on the input signal, so only the receiver that has knowledge on how the chaos is generated can reproduce the chaos and cancel it to recover the signal.

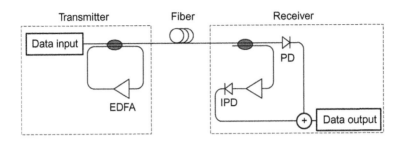

FIGURE 11.5

Schematic diagram for optical chaos communication (PD: photodiode; IPD: sign-inversing photodiode).

Chaos-based communications have been demonstrated in electronic circuits at bandwidths of tens of kilohertz; the low latency property in the fiber network enables the possibility of optical chaos communications with higher data rates [12,47]. Argyris et al. have demonstrated optical chaos-based communications with data rates higher than 1 Gb/s and bit-error rates lower than 10^{-7} [13]. In their experiment, the optical chaos-covered signal was transmitted over a 120 km distance in a commercial optical network over the metropolitan area of Athens, Greece. In an optical chaos communications system, the optical chaos is generated by fiber loops and an EDFA [14,48]. At the transmitter, the original data is coupled into the fiber loop and amplified by the EDFA (Figure 11.5). While the amplified signal is circulated and coupled back to the transmission line each time it goes through the coupler, the original signal in the transmission line is covered by a sequence of amplified signals, each having a time delay τ. The value of τ depends on the length of the fiber loop. At the receiver, the chaos-masked signal is split by another fiber coupler, and one of them goes through an open loop to regenerate the chaos. The EDFA at the receiver must be matched with the one at the transmitter. A pair of photodiodes and a sign-inverting photodiode is used to receive the chaos-masked signal and regenerated chaos. By summing the photocurrent from the two photodiodes, the chaos generated at the receiver and chaos from the transmitter is cancelled, so the signal is recovered. Besides providing confidentiality to the network, chaos-based communications also brings a high level of robustness to data transmission. By spreading the narrowband signal into a wideband signal, chaos-based communication can both create desired jamming and avoid malicious jamming.

Summary

In this chapter, we summarize the optical fiber-based techniques for protecting network security from potential threats. Optical encryption—specifically, optical XOR logic gates—is discussed. Because optical processing has low latency and is immune to electromagnetic interference, optical encryption is especially important in areas that require a high level of security without compromising the processing speed. Optical code division multiple access techniques and their application to defending the threat against data confidentiality are summarized. We also discuss methods for improving the security of point-to-point links. Both classic and quantum key distribution in the fiber channel are discussed. Optical steganography techniques for protecting the privacy of networks are discussed. A recently developed optical steganography method is also introduced. Instead of mimicking the noise in the system, this novel method uses the noise itself to carry the data. Optical steganography based on ASE noise also has potential applications to protect the availability of the network. The technique of waveband conversion and its applications on anti-jamming and assurance of channel availability are discussed. Finally, schemes for chaos-based communication are described. Chaos-based communication can be used to either enhance the robustness of a desired data transmission or to jam an unwanted channel. Although a variety of approaches have been proposed and demonstrated to protect multiple threats in the physical layer of an optical network, much work remains to further develop and apply these results.

References

[1] Zimmermann H. OSI reference model-the ISO model of architecture for open systems interconnection. IEEE T Commun 1980;28(4):425−32.

[2] Fok MP, Wang Z, Deng Y, Prucnal PR. Optical layer security in fiber-optic networks. IEEE T Inf Foren 2011;6(3):725−36.

[3] Vahala K, Paiella R, Hunziker G. Ultrafast WDM Logic. IEEE J Sel Toptics Quantum Electron 1997;3(2):698−701.

[4] Chan K, Chan CK, Chen LK, Tong F. Demonstration of 20-Gb/s all-optical XOR gate by four-wave mixing in semiconductor optical amplifier with RZ-DPSK modulated inputs. IEEE Photon Technol Lett 2004;16(3):897−9.

[5] Wang Z, Fok MP, Prucnal PR. Physical encoding in optical layer security. J Cyber Secur Mobility 2012:83−100.

[6] Rosenberg D, Harrington JW, Rice PR, Hiskett PA, Peterson CG, Hughes RJ, et al. Long-distance decoy-state quantum key distribution in optical fiber. Phys Rev Lett 2007;98:010503-1-010503-4.

[7] Hadfield RH, Habif JL, Schlafer J, Schwall RE, Nam SW. Quantum key distribution at 1550 nm with twin superconducting single-photon detectors. Appl Phys Lett 2006;89:241129-1-241129-3.

[8] Scheuer J, Yariv A. Giant fiber lasers: a new paradigm for secure key distribution. Phys Rev Lett 2006;97:140502-1-140502-4.

[9] Wu BB, Narimanov EE. A method for secure communications over a public fiber-optical network. Opt Express 2006;14(9):3738−51.

[10] Fok MP, Prucnal PR. A compact and low-latency scheme for optical steganography using chirped fiber Bragg grating. Electron Lett 2009;45(3):179−80.

[11] Wu B, Wang Z, Tian Y, Fok MP, Shastri BJ, Kanoff DR, et al. Optical steganography based on amplified spontaneous emission noise. Opt Express 2013;21(2):2065−71.

[12] VanWiggeren GD, Roy R. Communication with chaotic lasers. Sci 1998;279(20):1198−200.

[13] Argris A, Syvridis D, Larger L, Lodi VA, Colet P, Fischer I, et al. Chaos-based communications at high bit rates using commercial fibre-optic links. Nat 2006;438(17):343−6.

[14] Yang L, Zhang L, Yang R, Yang L, Yue B, Yang P. Chaotic dynamics of erbium-doped fiber laser with nonlinear optical loop mirror. Opt Commun 2012;285:143−8.

[15] Stallings W. Cryptography and network security principles and practice. Pearson; 2011. p. 9−14 [Chapter 1].

[16] Furdek M, Skorin-Kapov N, Bosiljevac M, Sipus Z. Analysis of crosstalk in optical couplers and associated vulnerabilities. Proc 33rd Int Convention (MIPRO) 2010:461−6.

[17] Shaneman K, Gray S. Optical network security: Technical analysis of fiber tapping mechanisms and methods for detection & prevention. In: Proc IEEE Military Communications Conf (MOLCOM); 2004. p. 711–6.

[18] Fok MP, Prucnal PR. All-optical encryption based on interleaved waveband switching modulation for optical network security. Opt Lett 2009;34(9):1315–7.

[19] Fok MP, Prucnal PR. Polarization effect on optical XOR performance based on four wave mixing. IEEE Photon Technol Lett 2010;22(15):1096–8.

[20] Soto H, Erasme D, Guekos G. 5-Gb/s XOR optical gate based on cross-polarization modulation in semiconductor optical amplifier. IEEE Photon Technol Lett 2001;13(4):335–7.

[21] Kim JH, Jhon YM, Byun YT, Lee S, Woo DH, Im SH. All optical XOR gate using semiconductor optical amplifier without additional input beam. IEEE Photon Technol Lett 2002;14(10):1436–8.

[22] Jinno M, Matsuoto T. Ultrafast all-optical logic operation in a nonlinear Sagnac interferometer with two control beams. Opt Lett 1991;16(4):220–2.

[23] Prucnal PR. Optical code division multiple access: Fundamentals and applications. Taylor & Francis; 2006.

[24] Prucnal PR, Santoro MA, Fan TR. Spread spectrum fiber-optic local area network using optical processing. J Lightwave Technol 1986;4(5):547–54.

[25] Weiner AM, Heritage JP, Salehi JA. Encoding and decoding of femtosecond pulse. Opt Lett 1988;13(4):300–2.

[26] Brès CS, Huang Y-K, Glesk I, Prucnal PR. Scalable asynchronous incoherent optical CDMA [Invited]. J Opt Netw 2007;6(6):599–615.

[27] Goldberg S, Menendez R, nd Prucnal P. Towards a cryptanalysis of spectral-phase encoded optical CDMA with phase-scrambling. In: Proc Optical Fiber Communication, OThJ7; 2007.

[28] Wang Z, Chang J, Prucnal PR. Theoretical analysis and experimental investigation on the security performance of incoherent optical CDMA Code. J Lightw Technol 2010;28(12):1761–9.

[29] Kravtsov K, Prucnal PR, Bubnov MM. Simple nonlinear interferometer-based all-optical thresholder and its applications for optical CDMA. Opt Express 2007;15(20):13114–22.

[30] Jiang Z, Leaird DE, Weiner AM. Experimental investigation of security issues in O-CDMA. J Lightw Technol 2006;24(11):4228–34.

[31] Wang Z, Xu L, Chang J, Wang T, Prucnal PR. Secure optical transmission in a point-to-point link with encrypted CDMA codes. IEEE Photonics Technol. Lett 2010;22(19):1410–2.

[32] Bennett CH, Brassard G. Quantum cryptography: Public key distribution and coin tossing. In: Proc IEEE International Conference on Computers, Systems, and Signal Processing; 1984. p. 175–9.

[33] Bennett CH, Bessette F, Brassard G, Salvail L, Smolin J. Experimental quantum cryptography. J. Cryptology 1992;5(1):3–28.

[34] Gordon KJ, Fernandez V, Townsend PD, Buller GS. A short wavelength gigahertz clocked fiber-optic quantum key distribution system. IEEE J Quantum Electron 2004;40(7):900–8.

[35] Zadok A, Scheuer J, Sendowski J, Yariv A. Secure key generation using an ultra-long fiber laser: Transient analysis and exeperiment. Opt Express 2008;16(21):16680–90.

[36] Prucnal PR, Fok MP, Kravtsov K, Wang Z. Optical steganography for data hiding in optical networks. In: Proc the 16th Int Conf Digital Signal Processing (DSP), T3B.4; 2009.

[37] Wu BB, Prucnal PR, Narimanov EE. Secure transmission over an existing public WDM lightwave network. IEEE Photon Technol Lett 2006;18(17):1870–2.

[38] Wu BB, Narimanov EE. Analysis of stealth communications over a public fiber-optical network. Opt Expres 2007;15(2):289–301.

[39] Hong X, Wang D, Xu L, He S. Demonstration of optical steganography transmission using temporal phase coded optical signals with spectral notch filtering. Opt Express 2010;18(12):12415–20.

[40] Wu BB, Agrawal A, Glesk I, Narimanov E, Etemad S, Prucnal P. Steganographic fiber-optic transmission using coherent spectral-phase-encoded optical CDMA. In: Proc CLEO/QELS, CFF5; 2008.

[41] Kravtsov K, Wu BB, Glesk I, Prucnal PR, Narimanov E. Stealth transmission over a WDM network with detection based on an alloptical thresholder. In: Proc IEEE/LEOS Annual Meeting; 2007. p. 480–1.

[42] Huang Y-K, Wu BB, Glesk I, Narimanov EE, Wang T, Prucnal PR. Combining cryptographic and steganographic security with self-wrapped optical code division multiplexing techniques. Electron Lett 2007;43(25):1449–51.

[43] Wang Z, Prucnal PR. Optical steganography over a public DPSK channel with asynchronous detection. IEEE Photon Technol Lett 2011;23(1):48–50.

[44] Wang Z, Fok MP, Xu L, Chang J, Prucnal PR. Improving the privacy of optical steganography with temporal phase masks. Opt Express 2010;18(6):6079–88.

[45] Wu B, Wang Z, Shastri BJ, Tian Y, Prucnal PR. Two dimensional encrypted optical steganography based on amplified spontaneous emission noise. In: Proc CLEO/QELS, AF1H; 2013.

[46] Wang Z, Chowdhury A, Prucnal PR. Optical CDMA code wavelength conversion using PPLN to improve transmission security. IEEE Photon Technol Lett 2009;21(6):383–5.

[47] Strogatz SH. Nonlinear dynamics and chaos with applications to physics, biology chemistry and engineering. Westview; 2000. p. 335–39 [Chapter 9].

[48] Abarbanel HDI, Kennel MB, Buhl M, Lewis CT. Chaotic dynamics in erbium-doped fiber ring lasers. Phys Rev A 1999;60(3):2360–74.

Methods

Advanced Security Network Metrics

12

Ivan Homoliak, Maros Barabas, Petr Chmelar, Michal Drozd, and Petr Hanacek

Brno University of Technology, Brno, Czech Republic

INFORMATION IN THIS CHAPTER

- Method description
- Metrics definition
- Experiments description
- Result of experiments

INTRODUCTION

There is considerable interest in developing novel detection methods based on new metrics that describe network flow to identify connection characteristics, for example, to permit early identification of emerging security incidents, rapid detection of infections within internal networks, and instantaneous prevention of forming attacks. Buffer overflows continue to be one of the most common vulnerabilities prevalent today, especially in undetected and most dangerous "zero-day" attacks. This has motivated researchers to create more or less sophisticated defenses addressing this threat. The first line of defense is based on memory randomization (ASR), which makes the attack harder to accomplish, but unfortunately it is still possible to offset the current process address. The second line of defense is based on automated signature generation techniques that generate filters to block network traffic similar to an attack payload signature. Unfortunately, polymorphic attacks can evade these signatures, and hence subsequent research has focused on behavioral signatures that favor the development of several data mining methods defining sets of network metrics that describe the attack vector by its behavioral features. These methods use either the existing NetFlow standard or network traffic packets. Several earlier research studies left NetFlow to create its own set of network metrics, which provided more information and context in analyzed connections.

Recognizing the importance of the quality of network metrics for successful detection, our approach proposes a new set of metrics with a high detection and low false positive ratio. It is expected that detection algorithms based on these new network behavioral metrics will outperform existing methods and will be applicable to a wider range of intrusion detection and prevention systems.

Our primary goal is to create a network-based system for online defense against zero-day buffer overflow attacks in the production environment. We described the reduction of attack types to buffer overflow in a previous article [1]. The secondary goal of this research is (a) to design the architecture of a detection framework that will enhance the overall network security level with the ability to learn new attack behaviors without human intervention by using expert knowledge from honeypot (or similar) systems; and (b) to find the most suitable set of metrics for describing attack behaviors in network traffic and significantly increasing the detection rate and lowering the false positive rate.

In our previous article [1] we proposed a framework architecture that could be used for the detection of various network threats. The paper presented a novel Automated Intrusion Prevention System (AIPS) that uses honeypot systems for the detection of new attacks and automatic generation of behavioral signatures based on network flow metrics. We have successfully experimented with the architecture of the AIPS system and have defined 112 metrics (recently updated to 167), divided into five categories according to type. These metrics are used to describe properties of a detected attack, based not on the fingerprint of a common signature but on its behavior.

In this chapter we define the method used for generating network behavioral signatures from a set of network security metrics, Advanced Security Network Metrics (ASNM), consisting of 167 metrics enhancing the ability of detecting potential attacks from network traffic.

Related work

Since 1999, the KDD'99 [2] dataset, based on the DARPA'98 IDS evaluation program, has been used for evaluating new intrusion detection methods based on analyzing network traffic. The training dataset consists of approximately 4.9 million single connection vectors, each labeled either normal or attack, containing 41 features per connection record. This dataset is criticized [3] mainly because it does not seem to be similar to traffic in real networks, and also for its attack taxonomies and performance issues. As a result, many researchers have proposed new measures to overcome these deficiencies.

The DARPA IDS evaluation dataset [4] was created for training and testing intrusion detectors. However, in the dataset, all the traffic was generated by software that is not publicly available, so it is not possible to determine the accuracy of the background traffic used in the evaluation. Also, evaluation criteria do not account for the system resources used, ease of use, or what type of system it is.

The 2005 Moore sets of data [5] are intended to aid in the assessment of classification work. A number of data sets are described; each data set consists of a number of objects, and each object is described by a set of features (also referred to as discriminators). Leveraged by a quantity of hand-classified data, each object within each data set represents a single flow of TCP packets between client and server. Features of each object consist of (application-centrist) classification derived elsewhere plus a number of features derived as input to probabilistic classification techniques.

In the classification, applications with similar dynamics are put into the same class. A naive Bayesian classificator is used in the algorithm in which the Bayes formula is used to calculate the posterior probability of a testing sample and selects the largest probability class as the classification result. Approximately 200 features of a network flow are used to train the model, and a kernel-based function is used to estimate the distribution function [6]. The total accuracy is about 95 percent in the dimension of a flow number being correctly classified and 84 percent in the dimension of the flow size.

In our research, classifying IP traffic is crucial, and it is important to include general classification techniques for classifying network attacks. A survey paper [7] reviewed the state of the art work in machine learning IP traffic classification between 2004 and 2007. This paper proposed four categories of machine learning classification techniques: clustering approach, supervised learning, hybrid, and comparisons with related work approaches. Each category was reviewed according to a number of requirements divided between offline and real-time classification.

Auld et al., based on a Bayesian method introduced in [6], proposed the Bayesian Neutral Network method [8]. Compared with the Bayesian method, it increased the classification correct rate to 99 percent on data from a single site for two days, eight months apart.

In [9], a novel probabilistic approach was proposed that uses the Markov chain for probabilistic modeling of abnormal events in network systems. The performance of this approach was evaluated through a set of experiments using the above-mentioned DARPA 2000 data set. The proposed approach achieves high detection performance while representing a level of attacks in stages.

None of these approaches can be used in a real-time evaluation of network traffic due to performance issues or a high false positive ratio. Only a little research has been done on creating new network metrics for the behavioral description of network attacks as a way of raising the classification accuracy, which makes this area still attractive for researchers.

Method description

In this section we provide the abstract description of a method used for extracting network connections and generating attack signatures.

Principle of the method

The method of our approach is based on the extraction of various types of properties from each analyzed TCP connection. We suppose having all packets set P. The identification of each packet is represented by its index i. A packet p_i can be expressed as a tuple:

$p_i = (id; ips; ipd; ps; pd; t; size; ethsrc; ethdst; ps; pd; tcpsum; tcpseq; tcpack; tcpoff; tcpflags; tcpwin; tcpurp; iplen; ipoff ; ipttl; ipp; ipsum; iptos)$.

Symbols used in the packet tuple are described in Table 12.1.

TCP connection c is represented by tuple $c = (ips; ipd; ps; pd; ts; te; idsyn; idsynack; idack; idfinack; Ps; Pd)$. The symbols used in the tuple is briefly described in Table 12.2.

The source part of the TCP connection is the one with the initiation of the connection, and the destination part is the opposite part of the connection.

The set of all packets can also be interpreted as a set of all TCP connections C. The minimum packets count, which is necessary to identify the TCP connection, is three packets, which are used to establish a TCP connection according to TCP specifications. These three or more packets must contain the same IP addresses (ip_s, ip_d), ports (p_s, p_d) and fields tcp_{seq}, tcp_{ack} corresponding to a three-way handshake specification stated in RFC 793.[1]

---

[1]URL: http://www.ietf.org/rfc/rfc793.txt, page 30

Table 12.1 Symbols Used in the Packet Tuple

Symbol	Meaning
$id \in \aleph_0$	Id of the packet
$ip_s \in \{0, \dots, 2^{32} - 1\}$	Source IP address of the packet
$ip_d \in \{0, \dots, 2^{32} - 1\}$	Destination IP address of the packet
$p_s \in \{0, \dots, 2^{16} - 1\}$	Source port of the packet
$p_d \in \{0, \dots, 2^{16} - 1\}$	Destination port of the packet
$t \in \mathscr{R}^+$	Timestamp of the packet capture
$size \in \aleph$	Size in Bytes of the whole Ethernet frame which wraps the IP packet
$eth_{src} \in \{0, \dots, 2^{48} - 1\}$	Source MAC address of the Ethernet frame
$eth_{dst} \in \{0, \dots, 2^{48} - 1\}$	Destination MAC address of the Ethernet frame
$tcp_{sum} \in \{0, \dots, 2^{16} - 1\}$	TCP Checksum of the header
$tcp_{seq} \in \{0, \dots, 2^{32} - 1\}$	TCP sequence number of the packet
$tcp_{ack} \in \{0, \dots, 2^{32} - 1\}$	TCP acknowledgment number of the packet
$tcp_{off} \in \{0, \dots, 2^8 - 1\}$	TCP offset and reserved fields together
$tcp_{flags} \in \{0, \dots, 2^8 - 1\}$	TCP control bits
$tcp_{win} \in \{0, \dots, 2^{16} - 1\}$	TCP window
$tcp_{urp} \in \{0, \dots, 2^{16} - 1\}$	TCP urgent pointer
$ip_{len} \in \{0, \dots, 2^{16} - 1\}$	Size in Bytes of the whole IP packet with IP header
$ip_{off} \in \{0, \dots, 2^{13} - 1\}$	IP offset
$ip_{ttl} \in \{0, \dots, 2^8 - 1\}$	IP time to live
$ip_p \in \{0, \dots, 2^8 - 1\}$	IP protocol
$ip_{sum} \in \{0, \dots, 2^{16} - 1\}$	IP checksum of the header
$ip_{tos} \in \{0, \dots, 2^8 - 1\}$	IP type of service

Then we define a sliding window of length τ and a set of TCP connections W_j that are delimited by the sliding window:

$$W_j \subseteq C, W_j = \{c_k\},$$

$$c_k[t_s] > c_j[t_s] - \frac{\tau}{2},$$

$$c_k[t_e] > c_j[t_s] + \frac{\tau}{2}.$$

The next fact about each TCP connection c_j is an unambiguous association of c_j to the particular sliding window W_j. We can interpret the start time t_s of the TCP connection c_k as a center of the

Table 12.2 Symbols Used in the TCP Connection Tuple

Symbol	Meaning
$ip_s \in \{0, \ldots, 2^{32} - 1\}$	Source IP address of the TCP connection
$ip_d \in \{0, \ldots, 2^{32} - 1\}$	Destination IP address of the TCP connection
$p_s \in \{0, \ldots, 2^{16} - 1\}$	Source port of the TCP connection
$p_d \in \{0, \ldots, 2^{16} - 1\}$	Destination port of the TCP connection
$t \in \mathscr{R}^+$	Timestamp of the connection start
$t \in \mathscr{R}^+$	Timestamp of the connection end
$id_{syn} \in I$	Id of the first packet which contains SYN flag of TCP 3WH
$id_{synack} \in I$	Id of the first packet which contains SYN, ACK flags of TCP 3WH
$id_{ack} \in I$	Id of the last packet which contains ACK flag
$id_{finack} \in I$	Id of the packet p_i which contains FIN, ACK flags
$P_s \subset P$	Source packet set of the TCP connection
$P_d \subset P$	Destination packet set of the TCP connection

sliding window W_j. We can also denote that a shift of the sliding window $\Delta(W_j)$ is always defined by start time differences of two consecutive TCP connections in C:

$$\Delta(W_j) = c_{j+1}[t_s] - c_j[t_s],$$

$$j \in \{1, \ldots, |C| - 1\}.$$

Next we define the context of the TCP connection, which is a set of all connections in a particular sliding window W_k without an analyzed TCP connection c_k:

$$K_k = \{c_1, \ldots, c_n\} = \{W_k / c_k\}.$$

The defined terms are shown in figure Figure 12.1. In this figure the x axis displays time, while along the y axis, TCP connections are shown in their order of occurrence. Packets are represented by small squares, and TCP connections are represented by rectangular boundaries around particular packets. A bold line and font highlights the analyzed TCP connection c_k, which has an associated sliding window W_k and context K_k. TCP connections that are part of the sliding window W_k are drawn using a full-line boundary, and TCP connections that are not part of this sliding window are drawn using a dashed-line boundary.

Metrics extraction

Having identified all TCP connections set C in a set of all packets P, next we extract metrics for each TCP connection from a set C in the order of their beginnings. It should be noted that real data stream conditions are simplified by set notation for the sake of this discussion.

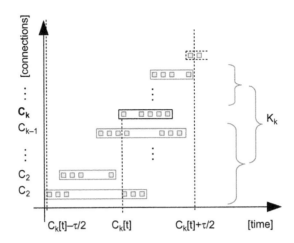

FIGURE 12.1

Sliding window and context of the first analyzed TCP connection c_k.

The metrics extraction process is defined as an advanced process of signature computation from all packets of analyzed TCP connection and its context. We define metric m as a tuple consisting of natural or real numbers or an enumerated set of finite symbolic literals:

$$m = (e_0, \ldots, e_n), n \in \aleph_0,$$
$$e_i \in \aleph | e_i \in \mathcal{R} | e_i \in \Gamma^+, i \in \{0, \ldots, n\},$$
$$\Gamma = \{a - z, A - Z, 0 - 9\}.$$

The input of the metrics extraction process is sliding window set W_k, TCP connection c_k with meta-information of its associated packets. The output of the process is the set of all extracted metrics $M_k = \{m_1^k, m_2^k, \ldots, m_D^k\}$, where D is the number of all defined metrics and m_i^k for $i \in \{1, \ldots, D\}$ contains a tuple of values specific for analyzed input TCP connection c_k and its sliding window set W_k.

Functions for metrics extraction

Metrics for the particular connection c_k are extracted by several functions with very similar input, which in all cases includes an analyzed TCP connection c_k. The other part of the input may be, in some cases, context K_k of the TCP connection c_k.

There are exactly 30 functions used for metrics extraction, and 7 of them use the context of the TCP connection. Some functions return more than one metric when these can be directly extracted. Other functions are parameterized by various parameters as a direction of the TCP connection, order and type of polynomial, thresholds of the data size or packet count, etc.

One metric extraction function f declaration has the following form:

$$m^k = f_{extr}(c_k, K_k),$$

Table 12.3 Distribution of Metrics	
Metric	Count
Statistical	50
Dynamic	32
Localization	8
Distributed	34
Behavioral	43

where m^k is the set of values of one defined metric m for input TCP connection c_k. K_k is the context of input TCP connection. The function f_{extr} can be parameterized by additional arguments in many cases (as we mention above).

Metrics definition

All metrics were defined by properties, process, and behavior of network attacks or legitimate TCP connections. By using these metrics we have a higher probability of identifying an attack. For the best relevant signature of the TCP connections we use 167 metrics as signature. These 167 metrics are, in many cases, the result of reasonable parameterization of base metrics functions. Since writint our previous article [1] we have slightly changed the categorization of the set of all metrics and have also defined several new metrics with emphasis on the behavior of a TCP connection. Our metrics sets are depicted in Table 12.3 with a number of them in each category. We decided to name the categories of metrics according to their principles, not according to static data representation. Vector and polynomial metrics from our previous article [1] were arranged into behavioral and distributed metrics categories. The list of all metrics with regard to the categorization is introduced in a master's thesis [10].

Statistical metrics

In the statistical category of our proposed metrics, statistic properties of TCP connections are identified. All packets of the TCP connection were considered in order to determine count, mode, median, mean, standard deviation, and ratios of some header fields of packets or the packets themselves. This category of metrics partially uses a time representation of packet occurrences contrary to the dynamic category definition. Therefore, it includes particularly dynamic properties of the analyzed TCP connection, but without any of its context. Most of the metrics in this category also distinguish inbound and outbound packets of analyzed TCP connection. In total, 50 statistical metrics are defined (50 features).

Dynamic metrics

Dynamic metrics were defined in order to examine dynamic properties of the analyzed TCP connection and transfer channel such as speed or error rate. These properties can be real or simulated. Fourteen of the metrics consider the context of an analyzed TCP connection. The difference between some of the statistic and dynamic metrics from a dynamic view can be demonstrated in two instances of the same TCP connection, which performs the same packet transfers, but in different context conditions and with different packet retransmissions and attempts to start or finish the TCP connection. Thirty-two dynamic metrics were defined in total (32 features). Many of them distinguish between inbound and outbound directions of the packets and consider statistic properties of the packets and their sizes as mentioned in the section on statistical metrics.

Localization metrics

The principal character of the localization metrics category is that it contains static properties of the TCP connection. These properties represent the localization of participating machines and their ports used for communication. In some metrics, localization is expressed indirectly by a flag that distinguishes whether participating machines lie in a local network or not. Metrics included in this category do not consider the context of the analyzed TCP connection, but they distinguish the analyzed TCP connection's direction. We defined eight localization metrics (eight features).

Distributed metrics

One characteristic property of distributed metrics category is the fact that they distribute packets or their lengths to a fixed number of intervals per unit time specified by a logarithmic scale (1 s, 4 s, 8 s, 32 s, and 64 s). A logarithmic scale of fixed time intervals was proposed for better performance of used classification methods. Another principal property of this category is vector representation. All of these metrics are supposed to work in the context of an analyzed TCP connection. Altogether, we defined 34 metrics (480 features) in this category. These are the result of parameterization of two functions, which accept as their parameters unit time, threshold, direction, and the context of an analyzed TCP connection.

Behavioral metrics

Behavioral metrics are based on a description of the properties directly associated with TCP connection behavior. Examples include legal or illegal connection closing, the number of flows at defined time intervals, and polynomial approximation of the length of packets in a time domain or in an index of occurrence domain. Since writing our previous article [1] we have proposed new behavioral metrics:

- Count of mutual TCP flows of participating nodes before an analyzed TCP connection bounded by a specified time interval. The context of an analyzed TCP connection is considered.
- Count of new TCP flows after starting an analyzed TCP connection. This also works in the context of an analyzed TCP connection.

- Coefficients of Fourier series in a trigonometric representation with distinguished direction of an analyzed TCP connection.
- Standard deviation of time intervals between TCP connections on the same ports and the same IP addresses.
- Standard deviation of time intervals between TCP connections on the same IP addresses.
- Normalized products of the analyzed communication with $1,\ldots,n$ Gaussian curves with regard to direction.

We defined 43 behavioral metrics (308 features). Most of them use the direction of the analyzed TCP connection, and six of them consider the context.

Description of experiments

The performance of our behavioral metrics was evaluated in comparison with discriminators suggested by [5]. The authors of that paper considered only TCP connections to perform extraction of discriminators the same way we did, so there are equivalent conditions for performance comparison between our suggested metrics and the discriminators suggested in the above-mentioned work. There were 248 discriminators defined, including all items of vector types. Unlike their approach, we considered the entire particular vector metric as one. In their work, each TCP flow is described by three modes according to packet transmissions: idle, interactive, and bulk. Many discriminators use these three modes as their input. The authors did not mention any explicit categorization of defined discriminators. The only possible categorization follows implicitly from a direction of the TCP flow. We performed a similar analysis of discriminators and metrics definition. We discovered that approximately 20 percent of discriminators' definitions were principally similar to or the same as in the metrics case. Unique properties of discriminators' definitions include, for example, the use of quartiles for a statistical analysis, analysis of selective acknowledgment of TCP, a number of window probe indications, pushed or duplicate packets, and so on.

A dataset CDX 2009 was used for these experiments, which was generated by Sangster et al. in [11]. This dataset is available from URL [12]. It contains data captured by NSA, data captured outside the West Point network border (in TCP dump format), and snort intrusion prevention log as relevant sources for our experiments.

The CDX 2009 dataset was created during the network warfare competition, in which one of the goals was to generate a labeled dataset. By "labeled dataset," the authors meant TCP dump traces of all simulated communications and snort log with information about occurrences of intrusions. The network infrastructure contained four servers with four vulnerable services (one per server). These services, with IP addresses of their hosted servers, are described in Table 12.4. Two types of IP addresses are shown in this table:

- internal IP addresses — corresponding to snort log, and
- external IP addresses — corresponding to a TCP dump network captured outside the West Point network border.

This fact has to be considered in the process of matching snort log entries with a TCP dump capture.

Table 12.4 List of CDX 2009 Vulnerable Servers

Service	OS	Internal IP	External IP
Postfix Email	FreeBSD	7.204.241.161	10.1.60.25
Apache Web Server	Fedora 10	154.241.88.201	10.1.60.187
OpenFire Chat	FreeBSD	180.242.137.181	10.1.60.73
BIND DNS	FreeBSD	65.190.233.37	10.1.60.5

We noticed that specific versions of services described in [11] were not announced. Since this fact was not crucial for our research, it was of no concern to us.

We discovered that the snort log can be associated only with data capture outside the West Point network border and only with significant timestamp differences—approximately 930 days. We did not find any association between the snort log and data capture performed by the National Security Agency. We focused only on buffer overflow attacks found in a log from snort IDS, and a match with the packets contained in the West Point network border capture was performed. Buffer overflow attacks were performed only on two services: Postfix Email and Apache Web Server. An example of the buffer overflow snort log entry follows:

```
[**] [124:4:1] (smtp) Attempted specific command
    buffer overflow: HELO, 2320 chars [**]
    [Priority: 3]
    11/09-14:22:25.794792
    10.2.195.251:2792 -> 7.204.241.161:25
    TCP TTL:240 TOS:0×10 ID:0 IpLen:20 DgmLen:2360
    ***AP*** Seq: 0×68750738 Ack: 0×24941B59
Win: 0xFDC0 TcpLen: 20.
```

We used IP addresses (5th row), ports (5th row), time of occurrence (4th row), and TCP sequence and acknowledgment numbers (7th row) as information to match the snort log entries with particular TCP connections identified in TCP dump traces.

Despite all efforts, exactly 44 buffer overflow attacks were matched out of all 65, and these identified attacks were used as expert knowledge for the data mining process. To correctly match snort entries, it was necessary to remap IP addresses of the internal to external network, because a snort detection was realized in the internal network and TCP dump data capture contains entries from outside the IP address space.

The content of buffer overflow attacks, which were matched with data capture, were in only two TCP dump files: *2009-04-21-07-47-35.dmp*, *2009-04-21-07-47-35.dmp2*. Due to the enormous count of all packets (approximately four million) in all dump files, only two files were considered. These contained 1,538,182 packets. We also noticed that network data density increased at the time the attacks were performed. Consequently, we made another reduction of packets, which filtered enough of the temporal neighborhood of the attack occurrences. As a result, 204,953 packets were used for the next phases of our experiments.

The whole process of metrics and discriminators extraction with data mining comparison is illustrated in Figure 12.2.

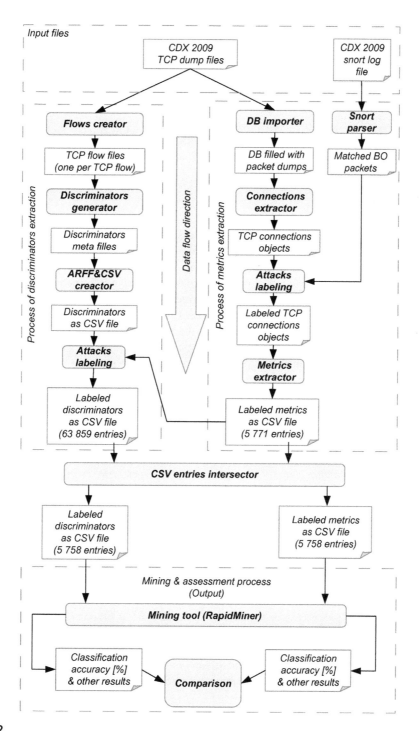

FIGURE 12.2

The process of metrics extraction and assessment.

Four segments and data flow direction from top to bottom are depicted in the figure. White boxes represent data as input or output of some processes and filled ovals represent working components that perform some action. A working component takes input data and outputs output data. The upper segment represents the input of the whole experiment process and includes input data files *CDX 2009 TCP dump files* and *CDX 2009 snort log file*. The *CDX 2009 TCP dump files* are the mutual input of both extraction processes. The input of expert knowledge (*CDX 2009 snort log file*) is directly provided to the metrics extraction process and is indirectly bounded to extracted discriminators after the end of metrics extraction process. The right segment contains the metrics extraction process with expert knowledge processing, and the left segment contains phases of discriminators extraction.

Metrics extraction process

In Figure 12.2, an all packets set *P* is represented by the input of *CDX 2009 TCP dump files*, which are imported into the database by a *DB importer* component. Next, an active component *Connection extractor* performs the identification of all TCP connections set *C* in all packet set *P*. The extraction of TCP connections is followed by expert knowledge information processing, which means matching extracted TCP connections with parsed snort log information. If a match occurrs, the TCP connection is labeled as an attack by the *Attacks labeling* component. Then metrics extraction is performed for each TCP connection in *C* by the *Metrics extractor* component; the result of this step are metrics values for each TCP connection object in CSV file. It should be noted that the metrics extraction process is independent of expert knowledge information.

Discriminators extraction process

The input of the discriminators extraction process is the same for the metrics extraction process. The component *Flows creator* performs the identification of TCP connections with the netdude tool[2] and creates a TCP dump file for each identified TCP connection. These TCP dump files are used as input for *Discriminator generator* component, which performs extraction of discriminators for each identified TCP connection. This component performs an operation equivalent to that performed by the *Metrics extractor* component during metrics extraction. It generates discriminators meta files, which contain intermediate results of discriminators values. These meta files are processed and joined by the *ARFF&CSV creator* component into a CSV file. After this step, the attack TCP connections are labeled by the *Attack labeling* component.

Mining and assessment process

The mining and assessment process is depicted in the lower part of Figure 12.2. Before this process takes place, it is necessary to make an intersection between output CSV files of metrics and discriminators extraction processes; this is performed by the *CSV entries intersector* component. At the output of this step there are metrics and discriminators of the same TCP connections objects, so there are equivalent conditions for the data mining process. Two intersected CSV files with equal

---

[2]URL: http://netdude.sourceforge.net/

numbers of entries are used as the input of the *Mining tool* component, and output consists of classification accuracy and other results suitable for comparison.

It should be noted that we found 5,771 TCP connections by our TCP connections extractor and 63,859 TCP connections by the TCP demultiplexer from netdude framework used in discriminators extraction. This is because we consider only established TCP connections, since only an established TCP connection can perform a buffer overflow attack. The intersection of metrics and discriminators outputs contained 5,758 objects and 44 of them represented attacks. This intersection was used in the data mining process and, therefore, these outputs were adjusted according to the same conditions applied to both metrics and discriminators outputs with the same TCP connections entries. Thirteen established TCP connections were not found by the TCP demultiplexer. The discriminators extraction was performed using a source code available from the author's website.[3] The whole process of discriminators extraction itself was not described in [5], so we deduced it from a source code and README instructions. It was also necessary to debug some of the functionality of provided tools. During the preparation for discriminators extraction, there were some compatibility issues caused by old versions of dependencies. We finally used Linux Fedora 4 as the most suitable operating system for the operation.

Results of experiments

We analyzed the joined outputs of metrics and discriminators extraction processes by the RapidMiner tool.[4] Our training model used the Naive Bayes classificator kernel. A stratified sampling with five-cross fold validation for every experiment was performed. A feature selection component was used that tries to select the most relevant attributes for final model generation. We focused only on the accuracy evaluation of particular metrics and discriminators. Our experiments were adjusted for maximal classification accuracy of input data. The best results were merged from both input CSV files. In Figure 12.3 the best metrics and discriminators (over 99.43% overall accuracy) are shown, sorted by the overall accuracy.

The names of discriminators consist of a number and label defined in [5]. The names of metrics are defined in [10].

The names of polynomial approximation metrics consist of five parts: polynomial metric label, method of approximation (indexes or time), order of polynomial, direction, and coefficient index. Fourier coefficient metrics' names consist of the Fourier coefficient metric label, the goniometric representation, the angle or the module, the direction, and the coefficient index. Gaussian products metrics' names are a compound of the Gaussian metric label, the number of Gaussian curves, the direction and the product index (e.g., *PolynomIndexes5OrdOut [1]*).

We can see that the best classification accuracy for the metrics sets was achieved by several polynomial approximation metrics. In most of these cases we achieved better results by the output direction, but we were also able to achieve interesting results with the input direction. A good performance was also achieved by Gaussian curves approximation and Fourier coefficients. The

---

[3]URL: http://www.cl.cam.ac.uk/research/srg/netos/nprobe/data/papers/sigmetrics/index.html
[4]URL: http://rapid-i.com/content/view/181/190/lang,en/

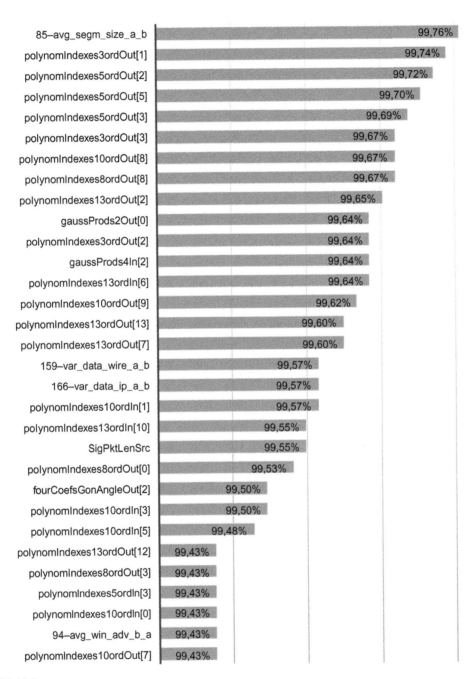

FIGURE 12.3

List of metrics sorted by overall accuracy (over 99.43%).

relevance in the case of standard deviation of packet length in the output direction (*sigPktLenSrc*) is also presented.

In the set of discriminators, the best results were achieved by an average segment size discriminator in the direction from client to server (*avg_segm_size_a_b*). It could be caused by the fact that the exploit's payload contains a huge amount of data necessary to perform application buffer overflow and that these data are segmented. Another distinguished discriminator is the variance of bytes count in Ethernet or IP datagram in the destination direction (*var_data_wire_ab* and *var_data_ip_a_b*). This discriminator is equivalent to the average standard deviation metric of packet length in the output direction and brings nearly equivalent results. Also, the average window advertisement in the input direction (*avg_win_adv_b_a*) holds relevant information potentially useful in the process of classification.

We have successfully increased the detection rate by 0.9 percent from the previous state-of-the-art classification method (99.0%) by extending the set of network metrics used for classification.

CONCLUSION

In this chapter, we focus on defining the process of extraction metrics from separated connections of captured network traffic and consequently focus attention on the experiments that proved the concept of a designed metrics set. In the experiments described we achieved 99.9 percent accuracy of detecting buffer overflow attacks by combining an existing proposed metrics set with our solution.

Accuracy is highly dependent on training samples parsed from captured network traffic. The training and testing samples may be biased towards a certain class of traffic. For example, valid communication (according to the separation into valid and attack connections) represents a large majority of the samples in the testing dataset [6] (approximately 99.24%). The reason for the high classification capability of fewer metrics is that classification of buffer overflow attacks was highly predictable due to the size of data in fragmented packets, which caused the overflow, and the nature of valid communication with a small number of fragmented packets.

Our future work focuses on extending the metrics set to achieve better results in the detection of buffer overflow attacks. We plan to perform more experiments with actual metric sets. The efficiency of the current detection method was tested only on a small number of attacks. In the near future, we plan to create a public detection set that will challenge the development of detection algorithms in order to detect unknown attacks.

References

[1] Barabas M, Drozd M, Hanacek P. Behavioral signature generation using shadow honeypot. In: World Academy of Science, Engineering and Technology; 2012.
[2] Stolfo S, Wei F, Lee W, Prodromidis A, Chan P. KDD cup knowledge discovery and data mining competition; 1999.

[3] Stolfo SJ, Fan W, Lee W, Prodromidis A, Chan PK. Cost-based modeling for fraud and intrusion detection: Results from the JAM project. In DISCEX'00: DARPA Information Survivability Conference and Exposition; 2000; Proceedings. 2000.

[4] Thomas C, Sharma V, Balakrishnan N. Usefulness of DARPA dataset for intrusion detection system evaluation. In: SPIE Defense and Security Symposium; 2008.

[5] Moore AW, Zuev D, Crogan M. Discriminators for use in flow-based classification; 2005.

[6] Moore AW, Zuev D. Internet traffic classification using Bayesian analysis techniques. In: ACM SIGMETRICS Performance Evaluation Review; 2005.

[7] Nguyen TT, Armitage G. A survey of techniques for Internet traffic classification using machine learning. Communications Surveys & Tutorials, IEEE 2008;10(4):56−76.

[8] Auld T, Moore AW, Gull SF. Bayesian neural networks for Internet traffic classification. IEEE Trans Neural Networks 2007;18(1):223−39.

[9] Shin S, Lee S, Kim H, Kim S. advanced probabilistic approach for network intrusion forecasting and detection. Expert Systems with Applications; 2012.

[10] Homoliak I. Metrics for intrusion detection in network traffic; 2011.

[11] Sangster B, O'Connor T, Cook T, Fanelli R, Dean E, Adams WJ, et al. Toward instrumenting network warfare competitions to generate labeled datasets. In CSET'09: Proc of the 2nd Workshop on Cyber Security Experimentation and Test; 2009.

[12] Toward instrumenting network warfare competitions to generate labeled datasets. [Internet]. Available from: https://www.itoc.usma.edu/research/dataset.

Designing Trustworthy Software Systems Using the NFR Approach

13

Nary Subramanian[1], Steven Drager[2], and William McKeever[2]

[1]*University of Texas at Tyler, Tyler, TX, USA*
[2]*US Air Force Research Lab, Rome, NY, USA*

INFORMATION IN THIS CHAPTER

- Trustworthy software systems
- Case study: Phoenix System
- Understanding the NFR Approach
- Applying the NFR Approach for trustworthy software design

INTRODUCTION

The National Institute of Standards and Technology defines trustworthy information systems as reliable, usable, interoperable, and secure [1]. Trustworthy systems are essential for critical operations and are expected to deliver when they are most needed. There are environments in military, government, and civil domains where trustworthiness is an essential property. Examples include missile deployment control systems, the tax submission system of the federal government, and nuclear safety control systems. Improving software trustworthiness is considered the most important goal in cybersecurity by 2015 [2], and trustworthiness in cyberspace is a national priority in the United States [3]. Trustworthiness is also an important emerging requirement for software systems deployed by the US Air Force.

Trustworthiness has been defined differently by different sources, based on their approach to determining trust in a system. For example, in [4], trustworthiness is defined as the degree of confidence that the system meets its requirements; [5] defines trustworthiness as a level of confidence in using software engineering techniques to reduce failure rates and enhance testing, reviews, and inspections; and in [6, p. 114], a trusted computer system is defined as a system that employs sufficient hardware and software integrity measures to allow its use for processing simultaneously a range of sensitive or classified information. Another definition of trustworthiness [7] includes correctness, safety, availability, reliability, performance, security, and privacy. A discussion of software trustworthiness among stakeholders often invokes numerous non-functional attributes like reliability, safety, usability, portability, and maintainability, which together ensure non-interference with the normal operation of the system.

However, there seems to be a lack of systematic processes for developing trustworthy systems. For example, [8] proposes a technique to develop a trustworthy operating system for software applications, and [9] proposes a trustworthy computing platform for a voting application; however, each follows its own approach to develop those specific target systems. While trustworthy systems evaluation criteria have been proposed [6], these criteria are oriented mostly toward incorporating security requirements into systems being developed. A trustworthiness model for open-source software has been proposed in [10] wherein factors that impact trustworthiness in a product are identified and then evaluated for the extent to which the factors have been achieved. A process for improving trustworthiness has been suggested in [11] with the belief that a trustworthy process improves trustworthiness in the product.

In this chapter we employ the goal-oriented framework called the NFR Approach [12] for engineering trustworthy software systems. The NFR Approach, where NFR stands for "non-functional requirements," treats trustworthiness as a goal to be achieved during the process of software development. NFRs are global characteristics of systems such as flexibility, security, and performance, and they synergistically or conflictingly interact with each other. The NFR Approach is well suited to reason about these NFRs and their interactions. The NFR Approach adapts the NFR Framework [13] to ensure that the system being developed satisfies the goals for which the system is being developed during the process of system development. The NFR Approach uses a structure called the Softgoal Interdependency Graph (SIG) to analyze and reason about trustworthiness. The SIG captures the definition(s) for trustworthiness, depicts design elements as softgoals, and records design rationale. The SIG also provides a platform for arriving at consensus among alternate definitions of trustworthiness from stakeholders and for qualitatively evaluating the extent of trustworthiness in a design; it also maintains an archive of design decisions. The NFR Approach has been used to develop adaptable [14], testable [15], and maintainable [16] systems, and we extend it to develop trustworthy software systems.

It is widely accepted that NFRs such as trustworthiness must be incorporated into designs from the earliest stages so that the final system is trustworthy. Since software architecture [17,18] is the first step in developing a software system after requirements have been elicited, the software architecture should itself be trustworthy for the final system to be trustworthy. In this chapter we develop trustworthy software architecture for the Phoenix system [19] used by the US Air Force. The Phoenix system is a middleware system developed by the air force for use in tactical and enterprise systems. Phoenix belongs to the class of message-oriented middleware and provides transparent message transport facilities over multiple operating systems and network protocols. Applications can communicate with Phoenix using well-defined interfaces and exchange real-time data. Phoenix operates using a producer-consumer paradigm and uses a store-and-forward technique for increased reliability of message transport over any unreliable communication links. The code base of Phoenix is over 100,000 lines of code and consists of fifteen subsystems.

During the process of architecture design, multiple views for the software architecture [20] are developed, including component and connector view, detailed structural view, logical deployment view, physical deployment view, and use-case scenarios. These views follow from the functional and non-functional requirements for the Phoenix system, where the functional requirements specify what is to be done, and non-functional requirements specify the characteristics of the software system such as reliability, maintainability, and flexibility. In this chapter we re-engineer trustworthy designs for the Phoenix system using the NFR Approach. This chapter is a significant extension of the presentation in [21]; detailed discussion of our results is included in this chapter.

The remainder of the chapter is organized into four sections and a summary, as follows: the first section describes the NFR Approach briefly; the second section describes four use-case scenarios that exemplify the lack of trustworthiness in the current Phoenix system; the third applies the NFR Approach to design the trustworthy Phoenix system. The fourth section discusses validation and lessons learned, and the summary concludes the paper and provides directions for future work.

The NFR approach

The NFR Approach is a goal-oriented approach that can be applied to determine the extent to which objectives are achieved by a process or product [22]. NFR stands for "non-functional requirements," which represent properties of a system such as reliability, maintainability, and flexibility, and could equally well represent functional objectives and constraints for a system. In this chapter we apply the NFR Approach to design a trustworthy software system by evaluating whether a specific design element satisfied trustworthy requirements for the system. The NFR Approach uses a well-defined ontology for this purpose that includes NFR softgoals, operationalizing softgoals, claim softgoals, contributions, and propagation rules; each of these elements is described briefly below (details may be seen in [13]). Furthermore, the NFR Approach uses the concept of satisficing, a term borrowed from economics, which indicates satisfaction within limits instead of absolute satisfaction, since absolute satisfaction of NFRs is usually difficult.

NFR softgoals represent NFRs and their decompositions. Elements that have physical equivalents (process or product elements) are represented by operationalizing softgoals and their decompositions. Each softgoal is named using the convention

$$Type[Topic1, Topic2, \ldots]$$

where *Type* is the name of the softgoal and *Topic* (could be zero or more) is the context where the softgoal is used; *Topic* is optional for a softgoal; for a claim softgoal, which is a softgoal capturing a design decision, the name may be the justification itself.

Following decompositions of either the NFR softgoals or the operationalizing softgoals are possible:

1. AND decomposition is used when each child softgoal of the decomposition has to be satisficed for the parent softgoal to be satisficed, but the denial of even one child softgoal is sufficient to deny the parent;
2. OR decomposition is used when satisficing of even one child satisfices the parent, but all children need to be denied for the parent to be denied; and
3. EQUAL decomposition has only one child for a parent and propagates the satisficing or the denial of the child to the parent.

Contributions (MAKE, HELP, HURT, and BREAK) are made by operationalizing softgoals to the NFR softgoals. Reasons for contributions are captured by claim softgoals, and claim softgoals may form a chain of evidence where one claim satisfices another, which in turn satisfices another, and so on. Each of the four types of contributions has a specific semantic significance: MAKE contribution refers to a strongly positive degree of satisficing of the objectives (represented by NFR softgoals) by artifacts (represented by operationalizing softgoals) under consideration, HELP contribution refers to a positive degree of satisficing, HURT contribution refers to a negative degree of satisficing, and BREAK contribution refers to a strongly negative degree of satisficing. Due to these contributions, some of the softgoals acquire labels that capture the extent to which a softgoal is satisficed: satisficed, weakly satisficed, weakly denied (or weakly not satisficed), denied (or not satisficed), or unknown (indicated by an absence of any label attribute). Moreover, high priority softgoals, decompositions, and contributions may be indicated using the criticality symbol. The graph that captures the softgoals, their decompositions, and the contributions is called the Softgoal Interdependency Graph (SIG). A partial ontology of the NFR Approach is shown in Figure 13.1.

Propagation rules propagate labels from child softgoal to the parent across decompositions, from operationalizing softgoals to NFR softgoals across contributions, and from claim softgoals to contributions; propagation rules aid in the rationalization process of the NFR Approach. In a SIG represented graphically, the NFR softgoals and their decompositions are shown at the top of the figure, the operationalizing softgoals and their decompositions are shown at the bottom of the figure, while the contributions between the operationalizing softgoals and the NFR softgoals are shown in the middle. Therefore, contributions are usually received by the leaf NFR softgoals that are at the bottom of the NFR softgoal decomposition hierarchy. While detailed propagation rules may be seen in [13], a simplified list is provided here:

R1. A satisficed label is propagated as satisficed by a MAKE contribution, as weakly satisficed by a HELP contribution, as weakly denied by a HURT contribution, and as denied by a BREAK contribution.

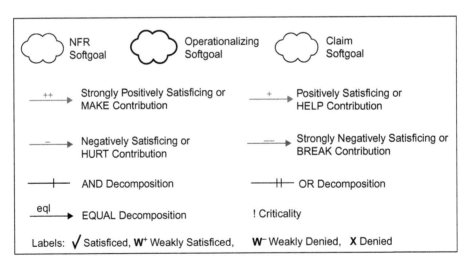

FIGURE 13.1

Partial ontology of the NFR Approach.

R2. A denied label is propagated as denied by a MAKE contribution, as weakly denied by a HELP contribution, as weakly satisficed by a HURT contribution, and as satisficed by a BREAK contribution.

R3. If most of the contributions propagated to an NFR softgoal are satisficed, then that NFR softgoal is considered satisficed.

R4. If most of the contributions propagated to an NFR softgoal are denied, then that NFR softgoal is considered denied.

R5. In the case of priority softgoals, or when there is a tie between positive and negative contributions, the system architect or the developer can take the decision based on, or a variation of, R3 and R4.

R6. In the case of an AND-decomposition, if all the child softgoals are satisficed, then the parent NFR softgoal is satisficed; else the parent softgoal is denied.

R7. In the case of an OR-decompostion, if at least one child softgoal is satisficed then, the parent NFR softgoal is satisficed; else the parent softgoal is denied.

R8. In the case of EQUAL-decomposition (only one child) the parent is satisficed if the child is satisficed, and the parent is denied if the child is denied.

Upon applying these propagation rules, if the root NFR softgoals are satisficed, then the goals for the domain of interest have been met, to a large extent. In this chapter, the root NFR softgoals are related to trustworthiness, and therefore the SIG helps determine the extent to which a particular design is trustworthy.

The NFR Approach requires the following interleaving tasks, which are iterative:

1. *Develop NFR goals and their decompositions*: In this task, the trustworthiness softgoal is decomposed into its constituent NFR softgoals; this decomposition captures the trustworthiness requirements for a system as viewed by a particular group of stakeholders. These decompositions may be developed from scratch or may be extensions of existing decompositions.

2. *Develop operationalizing goals and their decompositions:* In this task, we develop operationalizing softgoals and their decompositions. In this chapter, operationalizing softgoals correspond to architectural models since we are focusing on developing architectural models.[1] This task consists of two subtasks: the development of architectural models and the development of operationalizing softgoal hierarchy corresponding to the architectural models. Each individual model may form its own operationalizing softgoal decomposition hierarchy. These models may be developed from scratch or may use existing catalogs as a starting point.

3. *Develop goal tradeoffs and rationale*: In this task, we determine contributions between operationalizing softgoals (task 2) and the NFR softgoals (task 1) and the rationale for the contributions are captured by claim softgoals; synergies and conflicts between different NFR softgoals are captured by the contributions, and tradeoffs (manifested by changes to contributions) that take place are captured by corresponding changes to rationale. This historical record-keeping also helps back-tracking, if required.

---

[1]The NFR Approach supports any level of realization: strategic level, conceptual level, system level, requirements level, architectural design level, detailed design level, code level, and so on; however, in this chapter we develop architectural models and therefore we refer to architectural model development in task 2.

4. *Develop goal criticalities*: In this task, we assign priorities to softgoals—some softgoals (NFR softgoals, operationalizing softgoals, and claim softgoals) may be more important for the stakeholders involved and they are indicated as critical softgoals.
5. *Evaluation and analysis*: In this task, the propagation rules of the NFR Approach are applied to determine whether the architectural models satisfy the requirements (represented by NFR softgoal decomposition hierarchy) and to what extent, that is, strongly positive, positive, negative, or strongly negative; if positively satisficed, then those architectural models satisfy the requirements and if negatively satisficed, then there is scope for improvement.

The Phoenix system and trustworthiness deficit

In this section we describe the lack of trustworthiness in the current Phoenix system. The Phoenix system is a middleware, and as such, it serves as a transparent transport layer for its users. Publishers and subscribers send messages to each other over the Phoenix system. Figure 13.2 shows four use-case scenarios for the Phoenix system as it exists now.

(A)
1. Subscriber registers with Phoenix for a specific service.
2. Phoenix searches its repository for Publishers of the service.
3. If a Publisher is found, Phoenix Connects the Subscriber to the Publisher.
4. Publisher and Subscriber communicate with each other using plain text.
5. Phoenix logs the information.

Pub-Sub Connection Using Plain Text

(B)
1. Publisher sends 100M data to the Subscriber.
2. Phoenix gets the data and tries to transmit to the Subscriber.
3. Phoenix crashes.
4. Audit log is incomplete.
5. Message transfer is incomplete.

Pub-Sub Connection not Scalable

(C)
1. Subscriber is communicating with Publisher through Phoenix.
2. The Subscriber's link to Phoenix is broken.
3. Phoenix informs the Publisher that the Subscriber is not communicating.
4. Phoenix waits for the Subscriber to return on that connection.
5. The connection is never dropped.

Connections Never Dropped

(D)
1. Phoenix logs transactions in its repository.
2. Adversary is able to spoof the repository to read its contents.
3. Adversary is able to modify repository.
4. Message history has been corrupted.
5. Audits do not yield useful information.

Repository Can be Corrupted

FIGURE 13.2

Use-case scenarios for the current Phoenix system.

As can be seen in Figure 13.2 (a), the use-case scenario describes the lack of confidentiality in the current Phoenix system since messages are sent in plain-text. In Figure 13.2 (b), the scenario describes the lack of availability of the system when large messages are sent between the publisher and the subscriber—the system simply crashes. Likewise, the scenario of Figure 13.2 (c) describes how accumulation of non-dropped connections can also make the system available after a period of time. The scenario of Figure 13.2 (d) describes how the lack of sufficient authentication and authorization can reduce the integrity of the data in the Phoenix system due to an attack. For these and other reasons, Phoenix is not considered trustworthy enough for use in future applications that have more stringent trustworthy requirements. In subsequent sections we elicit these trustworthy requirements, analyze the shortcomings using the NFR Approach, and suggest modifications to the Phoenix system for the new environment.

Application of the NFR approach for designing a trustworthy Phoenix system

In this section, we describe the application of the five tasks of the NFR Approach for generating trustworthy designs for the Phoenix system. To obtain trustworthiness requirements, we interviewed stakeholders—users who plan to use the Phoenix system in a trustworthy environment. As mentioned earlier, trustworthiness, being an NFR, can have multiple definitions and each stakeholder can have a different definition for trustworthiness; we apply the five tasks of the NFR Approach to one definition and discuss how the NFR Approach can be used for building consensus among stakeholders. In order to automate the evaluation process, we used the StarUML tool [23] for developing the SIGs. This tool is free to use and comes with a toolset for capturing all aspects of a SIG; moreover, all propagation rules are built into StarUML, which makes its use for the evaluation and analysis task convenient.

Develop NFR softgoals and their decompositions

The upper part of the SIG of Figure 13.3 (indicated by a rounded rectangle marked "Task 1") shows the definition of trustworthiness from the viewpoint of one stakeholder. This part of the SIG contains the NFR softgoal decomposition hierarchy for the softgoal Trustworthiness[Phoenix], which represents trustworthiness of the Phoenix system. As mentioned earlier, this softgoal's type is Trustworthiness and the topic to which this softgoal applies is Phoenix. This softgoal is AND-decomposed into five child sub-softgoals: Trustworthiness[Phoenix, Hardware], Trustworthiness [Phoenix, Workers], Trustworthiness[Phoenix, Information], Trustworthiness[Phoenix, Software], and Performance [Phoenix, Environment], wherein the four components of a system [20,24[2]] (hardware, workers, information, and software) have been included. Performance has also been included, as required by the stakeholder. That this decomposition is an AND-decomposition is indicated by a

---

[2]On page 8 of [24] we find: "[Trust] properly can and should be applied to hardware/software combinations; to communication networks; to overall systems; to application programs; to individual components of a system; to information processes whether automated, manual, or both; to procedures whether automated or manual; and, particularly, it should be applied to people."

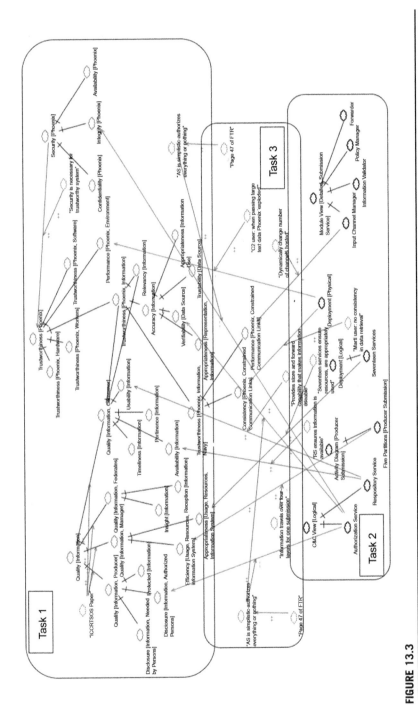

FIGURE 13.3

Softgoal interdependency graph for applying the NFR Approach.

single cross on the line connecting the child (or sub-)softgoals to the parent softgoal, Trustworthiness [Phoenix]. In the "Task 1" rectangle in Figure 13.3, on the left, the NFR softgoal Quality [Information] is AND-decomposed into Quality [Information, Producer], Quality [Information, Manager], Quality [Information, Federates], and Quality [Information, Consumer]; this decomposition is based on [25], which is indicated as "ICCRTS05 Paper" in the accompanying claim softgoal (the cloud-shaped figure with a dashed border). This decomposition captures the fact that quality of information is based on quality of information supplied by the producer, quality of information supplied to the manager, quality of information supplied to federates (partners), and quality of information supplied to consumers.

According to the stakeholder, the information produced in a trustworthy Phoenix system will be disclosed to those who need it and to those who are authorized; moreover, producers assume information is protected. These requirements are captured in the SIG by the AND-decomposition of the NFR softgoal Quality [Information, Producer] into the child softgoals of Disclosure [Information, Needed by Persons], Disclosure [Information, Authorized Persons], and Protected [Information]. In a similar manner we AND-decomposed Quality [Information, Manager] into child softgoals Efficiency [Usage, Resources, Information System] and Appropriateness [Usage, Resources, Information System]. Quality [Information, Federates] was AND-decomposed into Insight [Information] and Reception [Information]. Quality [Information, Consumer] is AND-decomposed into Timeliness [Information], Availability [Information], Pertinence [Information], Usability [Information], and Trustworthiness [Phoenix, Information].

As per the stakeholder needs, the NFR softgoal Trustworthiness [Phoenix, Information] is AND-decomposed into five child softgoals: Trustworthiness [Phoenix, Information, Navy], Accuracy [Information], and Relevancy [Information], where the softgoal Trustworthiness [Phoenix, Information, Navy] indicates the fact that trustworthiness of the Phoenix system's information processing capabilities is important for the navy (who will use the Phoenix middleware). This softgoal Trustworthiness [Phoenix, Information, Navy] is further AND-decomposed into Consistency [Phoenix, Constrained Communication Links] and Performance [Phoenix, Constrained Communication Links] which refer to, respectively, the information processing capabilities over constrained communication links. Finally, the softgoal Accuracy [Information] is AND-decomposed into four child softgoals: Appropriateness [Representation, Information], Verifiability [Data Source], Trustability [Data Source], and Appropriateness [Information Use].

Finally, on the top right, we have Security [Phoenix] being AND-decomposed into the CIA triad [26]: Confidentiality [Phoenix], Integrity [Phoenix], and Availability [Phoenix].

Develop operationalizing softgoals and their decompositions

This task has two sub-tasks: development of architectural models and creation of operationalizing softgoal hierarchy based on these models. The architectural models may be created from scratch or may use existing catalogs as the basis. We used existing models as the starting point. The models we started with are given in Figure 13.4 and include the Component and Connection (C&C View), the Activity Diagram for one scenario (Produce Submission scenario), the logical and physical deployment architectures, and the module view for one service (the Submission Service).-

We then converted these models into operationalizing softgoals, as indicated in the bottom part of Figure 13.3, within the rounded rectangular box marked "Task 2." These five models are

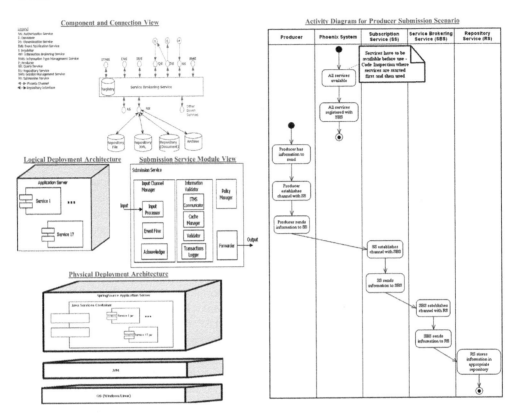

FIGURE 13.4

Initial architectural models for the Phoenix system.

captured by the operationalizing softgoals C&C View [Logical] representing the component and connection view, Activity Diagram [Producer Submission] representing the activity diagram for the producer submission scenario, Deployment [Logical] for the logical deployment architecture, Deployment [Physical] for the physical deployment architecture, and Module View [Detailed Submission Service] for the submission service module view (which is a detailed view of this service). Many of these softgoals have been further decomposed: C&C View [Logical] is AND-decomposed into Authorization Service and Repository Service operationalizing softgoals,[3] Activity Diagram [Producer Submission] is decomposed into Five Partitions [Producer Submission], Deployment [Logical] is decomposed into Seventeen Services, and Module View

---

[3]In the Component and Connection View diagram, there are several components and connections besides these two components—we should be able to decompose the C&C View [Logical] operationalizing softgoal into all its constituent softgoals—however, during subsequent tasks, the two softgoals included in the decomposition were sufficient to explain the use of the NFR Approach and therefore the other constituents are not shown. This policy is used when decomposing other operationalizing softgoals in this section.

[Detailed Submission Service] is decomposed into four operationalizing child softgoals: Input Channel Manager, Information Validator, Policy Manager, and Forwarder. This completes task 2.

Develop goal tradeoffs and rationale

During the process of SIG development we determine the contributions between softgoals—specifically, the contributions that operationalizing softgoals make to the NFR softgoals. The reasons (or rationale) for these contributions are captured by claim softgoals. This task is shown in Figure 13.3 within the rounded rectangle named "Task 3." Table 13.1 lists these contributions and their rationale.

As can be seen in Table 13.1, rows 1 through 10 list the contributions by operationalizing softgoals to NFR softgoals; row 11 describes a contribution between two NFR softgoals. Likewise, contributions may be between operationalizing softgoals, between claim softgoals (as shown in Figure 13.3 corresponding to rows 1, 2, and 3 of Table 13.1), between claim softgoals and contributions themselves (this is shown in Figure 13.3 for all claim softgoals), and between claim softgoals and decompositions (as shown in Figure 13.3 by the claim softgoal "ICCRTS05 Paper" [25] at the top left). In this manner, contributions help capture conflicts and synergies between NFRs—for example, Efficiency [Usage, Resources, Information System] receives a BREAK contribution while Appropriateness [Usage, Resources, Information System] receives a MAKE contribution from two different architectural models; therefore, the parent softgoal Quality [Information, Manager] sees conflicting contributions propagated to itself. Synergies occur similarly, though they are usually easier to handle.

Developing goal criticalities

In practice, not all requirements need be equally important; for example, security may be considered more important for a trusted system by some stakeholders [7]. Likewise, some architectural models may be more important for design since, for example, they are part of the enterprise architecture. The NFR Approach provides facilities to indicate certain NFR softgoals, operationalizing softgoals, claim softgoals, decompositions, and contributions as being higher priority; subsequently, during the evaluation phase, appropriate propagation rules may be used for these critical elements. In this discussion we assume all elements are of the same priority so that we may focus more on the process of the NFR Approach without getting too deep into its nuances.

Evaluation and analysis

During this task, two sub-tasks are performed: evaluation and analysis. During the evaluation task, we apply the propagation rules to determine if the softgoals of interest were satisficed or denied. During the analysis task, we analyze the reasons for satisficing or denial and determine improvement opportunities.

Table 13.2 lists the application of propagation rules to a few key softgoals in the SIG of Figure 13.3. Some of the rows from Table 13.1 appear in Table 13.2, and the latter applies the propagation rules to obtain labels propagated to the destination or parent softgoal. The rows in Table 13.2 are relatively easy to follow: for example, in row 1, the child softgoal Authorization Service makes a BREAK contribution to the parent softgoal Verifiability [Data Source] (which is indicated by row 2 of Table 13.1); therefore, by the propagation rule, R1, since the child softgoal is satisficed, the parent softgoal is denied. In a similar manner, other rows of Table 13.2 may be read.

Table 13.1 List of Contributions in SIG of Figure 13.3 and Their Rationale

Number	Source Softgoal of the Contribution	Destination Softgoal of the Contribution	Contribution Type	Rationale	Source of Rationale
1	Authorization Service	Disclosure [Information, Authorized Persons]	BREAK	"AS (Authorization Service) is simplistic-authorizes everything or nothing"	"Page 47 of FTR (Final Technical Report)"
2	Authorization Service	Verifiability [Data Source]	BREAK	same as above	same as above
3	Authorization Service	Integrity [Phoenix]	BREAK	same as above	same as above
4	Repository Service	Availability [Information]	MAKE	"RS (Repository Service) ensures information is available"	Developer of Phoenix
5	Repository Service	Usability [Information]	MAKE	"Provides store and forward capability that makes information usable"	Developer of Phoenix
6	Five Partitions [Producer Submission]	Efficiency [Usage, Resources, Information System]	BREAK	"Information travels over four layers for one submission"	Developer of Phoenix
7	Seventeen Services	Appropriateness [Usage, Resources, Information System]	MAKE	"Seventeen services ensure resources are appropriately used"	Developer of Phoenix
8	Deployment [Physical]	Consistency [Phoenix, Constrained Communication Links]	BREAK	"Marti users no consistency in data retrieval"	A user of Phoenix
9	Deployment [Physical]	Performance [Phoenix, Environment]	BREAK	"C2 user: when passing large text data Phoenix "exploded""	A user of Phoenix
10	Input Channel Manager	Performance [Phoenix, Constrained Communication Links]	MAKE	"Dynamically change number of channels hosted"	Developer of Phoenix
11	Security [Phoenix]	Trustworthy [Phoenix]	MAKE	"Security is necessary for trustworthy system"	Stakeholder in trustworthy Phoenix project

Table 13.2 Application of Propagation Rules of the NFR Approach

No.	Child (Source) Softgoal (s)	Child Label	Contribution/ Decomposition Type	Parent (Destination) Softgoal	Row No. in Table 13.1	Propagation Rule Applied	Parent Label
1	Authorization Service	Satisficed	BREAK	Verifiability [Data Source]	2	R1	Denied
2	Authorization Service	Satisficed	BREAK	Integrity [Phoenix]	3	R1	Denied
3	Five Partitions [Producer Submission]	Satisficed	HURT	Efficiency [Usage, Resources, Information System]	6	R1	Weakly Denied
4	Seventeen Services	Satisficed	MAKE	Appropriateness [Usage, Resources, Information System]	7	R1	Satisficed
5	Deployment [Physical]	Satisficed	HURT	Consistency [Phoenix, Constrained Communication Links]	8	R1	Weakly Denied
6	Deployment [Physical]	Satisficed	HURT	Performance [Phoenix, Environment]	9	R1	Weakly Denied
7	Verifiability [Data Source]	Denied	AND	Accuracy [Information]	—	R6	Denied
8	Consistency [Phoenix, Constrained Communication Links]	Weakly Denied	AND	Trustworthiness [Phoenix, Information, Navy]	—	R6	Denied
9		Denied, Denied	AND		—	R6	Denied

(Continued)

Table 13.2 (Continued)

No.	Child (Source) Softgoal (s)	Child Label	Contribution/ Decomposition Type	Parent (Destination) Softgoal	Row No. in Table 13.1	Propagation Rule Applied	Parent Label
	Trustworthiness [Phoenix, Information, Navy], Accuracy [Information]			Trustworthiness [Phoenix, Information]			
10	Trustworthiness [Phoenix, Information]	Denied	AND	Quality [Information, Consumer]	—	R6	Denied
11	Integrity [Phoenix]	Denied	AND	Security [Phoenix]	—	R6	Denied
12	Security [Phoenix]	Denied	MAKE	Trustworthiness [Phoenix]	11	R2	Denied
13	Trustworthiness [Phoenix, Information], Performance [Phoenix, Environment]	Weakly Denied, Denied	AND	Trustworthiness [Phoenix]	—	R6	Denied
14	Efficiency [Usage, Resources, Information System], Appropriateness [Usage, Resources, Information System]	Weakly Denied, Satisficed	AND	Quality [Information, Manager]	—	R6	Denied
15	Quality [Information, Manager], Quality [Information, Consumer]	Denied, Denied	AND	Quality [Information]	—	R6	Denied

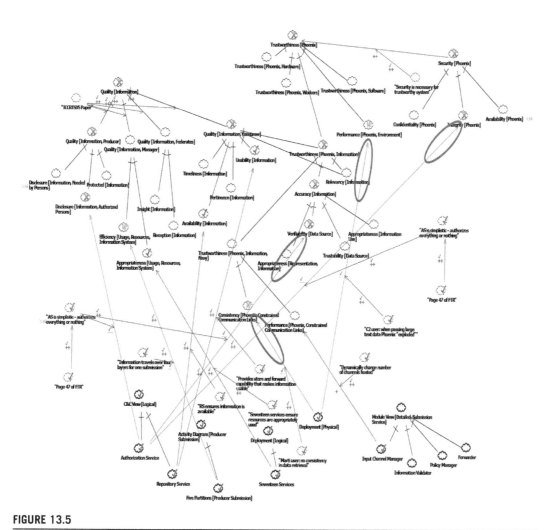

FIGURE 13.5

SIG for evaluation and analysis task of the NFR Approach.

From this table we find that the three root NFR softgoals are all denied: that is, the NFR softgoals Quality [Information], Security [Phoenix], and Trustworthiness [Phoenix] are all denied, which means that the architectural models of Figure 13.4 do not satisfy trustworthiness requirements.

Figure 13.5 shows the SIG of Figure 13.4 updated with propagated labels. This figure was generated using the StarUML [23] tool which automatically propagates the labels. In Table 13.2 and in Figure 13.5, we have assumed the operationalizing softgoals to be satisfied in order to apply the propagation rules; this is because these softgoals represent architectural models that exist. If, in the future, we were to find that some of these models are not correct, then we can modify the labels of those softgoals accordingly and then apply the propagation rules; however, historical record is preserved by the SIGs.

Table 13.3 Architectural Modifications to Improve Trustworthiness Satisficing

No.	Contribution to be Improved	Possible Techniques for Improvement	Explanation	Reference
1	Verifiability of Data Source by Authorization Service	Passwords, Biometrics, Kerberos	Passwords help verify data source by comparing a stored hashed version of the password with the one provided by the data source; biometrics provide similar facility, while Kerberos provides an extended authentication scheme.	[26]
2	Integrity of System by Authorization Service	Access Control Lists, Feedback Control	Ensuring that only sources with authorized access control access Phoenix will improve integrity; also feedback control for frequently checking for errors will help improve integrity.	[26,27]
3	Consistency over Constrained Communication Links by Physical Deployment	Neighborhood Group Data Caching	This technique pre-fetches data in the neighborhood of the requested data and stores this data locally; this way, even if the link is constrained, data throughput consistency can be achieved.	[28]
4	Performance by Physical Deployment	Increased Bandwidth, Higher Processing Power, Larger Buffers	Compression algorithms together with adaptive radio protocols can help in increasing the baud rate; higher processing power provided by newer microprocessors with redundant cores can help; larger memory based on flash can help improve performance, as well.	[29]

During the analysis sub-task, we identify reasons for poor trustworthiness. As can be observed from Table 13.2 and Figure 13.5, the poor satisficing of the softgoal Trustworthiness [Phoenix] results from the negative contributions (HURT or BREAK) indicated by oval shapes, corresponding to rows 1, 2, 5, and 6 of Table 13.2. What are the reasons for these negative contributions? The rationale in Table 13.1, corresponding to rows 2, 3, 8, and 9, respectively, guides us in improving these contributions. Considering row 1 of Table 13.2, the poor contribution (BREAK) by the Authorization Service to the softgoal Verifiability of Data Source is due to the simplistic nature of the Authorization Service (row 2 of Table 13.1); from the published literature, a few of the techniques to improve verifiability include use of passwords, biometrics, and Kerberos protocol [26]. Therefore, if the Authorization Service is enhanced with these techniques, then its contribution to verifiability of data source will be improved, which will help move the system toward improved trustworthiness. In a similar manner, we identified techniques that will improve these four contributions; they are documented in Table 13.3.

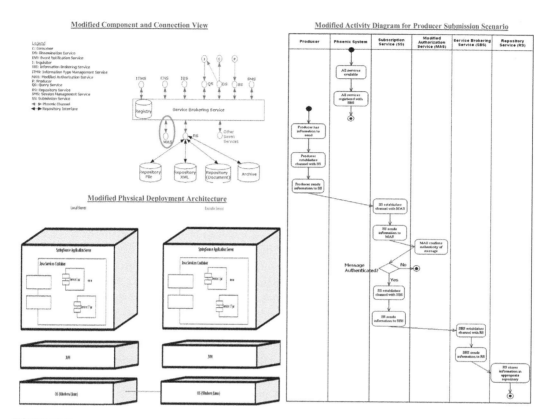

FIGURE 13.6

Updated architectural models for the Phoenix system.

The modified architectural models are shown in Figure 13.6. The updated component in the Component and Connector view is called the Modified Authorization Service (MAS) that has the modifications in rows 1 and 2 of Table 13.3. The modified Activity Diagram shows the use of MAS for authentication during the submission scenario. The physical deployment has two servers, one local and the other remote; the local server caches data locally so that benefits in row 3 of Table 13.3 are realized. Besides, the duplicated servers allow improved integrity by performing data checks between themselves, as mentioned in row 4 of Table 13.3.

Validation and lessons learned

The architectural modifications for improved trustworthiness were validated by three of the original Phoenix development engineers. We presented the modified designs along with a questionnaire that required them to evaluate the artifacts by comparing them with the system documents for Phoenix (which we did not have access to) in the spirit of the Delphi technique [30]. Developers answered the questionnaires independently of each other without having recourse to answers provided by others. The developers were provided the updated architectural models and a modified version of Table 13.3 as part of their questionnaire; their responses are tabulated in Table 13.4.

The development engineers were in agreement that techniques such as passwords, biometrics, and Kerberos will help the Authorization Service component satisfy the requirement for Verifiability of Data Source; one of them pointed out that two-factor authorization will also be a preferred technique. Likewise, the techniques identified from catalogs for improving integrity of the Phoenix system, namely, access control lists and feedback control, were also perceived by the engineers as helpful to achieve the goal; however, it was felt that integrity can still be impacted by bypassing Authorization Service and attacking other components of the system directly. In row 3 of Table 13.4, the technique neighborhood group data caching in a deployed physical system was expected to improve consistency over constrained communication links. However, synchronization of fetched data with that of the central store was important so that data viewed by users were not stale; a differential data pre-fetching (where only differences were obtained from the central store) was felt to be more useful, and this technique is planned for incorporation in a future version of the Phoenix system. In row 4 of Table 13.4, the common techniques of increasing bandwidth/processing power/buffers in a deployed physical system were expected to improve performance of the system; however, it was pointed out that scalability of such an increase is not linear in general and incurs costs of time and effort to realize improved performance. Row 5 of Table 13.4 was a control row. It was used to ensure that engineers were actually focusing on the questionnaire; the technique "noncryption" was a made-up word for plain text transmission, and all three engineers were unanimous in their opinion that this will not improve security.

Table 13.4 conveys the point that recommendations from the NFR Approach are largely acceptable to the industry practitioners from a trustworthy system development standpoint. An interesting observation is the comment in row 3 of Table 1.4: the feature identified as important using the NFR Approach has been under consideration by the development team for some time, but we arrived at this point using the systematic process of the NFR Approach, while the development team identified this issue from user feedback. The suggestions from the SIG analysis could be used to improve the trustworthiness of the system being designed with a high confidence that these suggestions will find acceptance from the designer community.

An important aspect of the NFR Approach is that it helps build consensus among stakeholders: we obtained three differing definitions of trustworthiness from stakeholders. Figure 13.7 shows another definition for trustworthiness from a different stakeholder—trustworthiness includes reliability and dependability attributes. The oval shapes in Figure 13.7 are the constraints imposed on a design to satisfy certain trustworthiness requirements. The architectural models of Figure 13.6 may not satisfy all the requirements in Figure 13.7; however, the NFR Approach provides a mechanism to reason about the "gaps," if any. For example, one constraint (oval shape) is that all messages be encrypted to satisfice the NFR softgoal Security [Messages]. However, the connector Phoenix Channel in Figure 13.6 does not encrypt messages and therefore, after applying the propagation rules of the NFR Approach, we find the models of Figure 13.6 are not trustworthy by this definition (Figure 13.7), either. Therefore, if an Augmented Phoenix Channel connector is used in the updated models of Figure 13.6, then these updated models will satisfy to some extent the definition in

Table 13.4 Summary of Developers' Responses to Questionnaire for Design Validation

No.	Goal	Design Element Considered	Possible Techniques for Goal Achievement	Will the technique achieve the goal?	Comments
1	Verifiability of Data Source	Authorization Service	Passwords, Biometrics, Kerberos	All three said "Yes," and they concurred on the fact that these techniques will achieve the goal to a large extent.	It was pointed out that multi-factor authorization will be a useful technique to consider in the field, especially when devices could be lost.
2	Integrity of Phoenix System	Authorization Service	Access Control Lists, Feedback Control	All three said "Yes," and they concurred on the fact that these techniques will achieve the goal to a medium extent.	These techniques help but are not enough, because other services can still be cyber-attacked by bypassing authorization service.
3	Consistency over Constrained Communication Links	Physically Deployed Phoenix System	Neighborhood Group Data Caching	Two developers said "Yes," to a medium extent; the third developer said maybe.	There is the question of liveliness and staleness of info; if info is stale it is of no use; also there should be sync between partitioned data. If pre-fetching loads the network, it is not useful. *This feature has already been planned for a future version of Phoenix.*
4	Performance	Physical Deployed Phoenix System	Increased Bandwidth, Higher Processing Power, Larger Buffers	All three said "Yes," and they concurred on the fact that these techniques will achieve the goal to a medium to high extent.	Scalability plateaus after some processors are added; to increase the plateau level, more time and effort need to be expended.
5	Security	Communication	Noncryption	All three said "No."	This entry was used for control purposes.

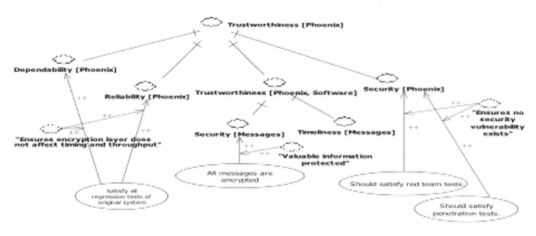

FIGURE 13.7

Definition of trustworthiness from another stakeholder.

Figure 13.7 besides meeting all requirements in Figure 13.3. This way, consensus between definitions may be reached using the NFR Approach.

As mentioned in the introduction, the SIG captures trustworthiness definitions, architectural or design elements, and the design rationale in the form of claim softgoals. The propagation rules help qualitatively evaluate the extent to which designs satisfy trustworthiness requirements, and the historical record of design decisions are captured by different versions of the SIG. If any change occurs to the SIG due to requirements changes, design changes, or rationale changes, the resulting change to trustworthiness can be quickly recomputed; therefore, impact analysis can be performed. Also, "what if" scenarios can be studied by deliberate changes to the SIG and by analyzing the resulting impact on trustworthiness.

One aspect that we did not discuss is the process of converting interview notes into a SIG, such as in Figure 13.3 and Figure 13.6. We have discussed this aspect in another paper [31]; however, this process involves creating elements of SIG from interview notes and is a predominantly manual process. There does not seem to be a one-to-one correspondence between a given interview note and the SIG developed; however, based on our experience, the results of the reasoning process seem to be highly synchronous between different SIGs generated from an interview note. Therefore, we believe that the NFR Approach's process is repeatable across projects and organizations.

Certain aspects of the NFR Approach have not been described here; for example, the propagation rules in the section "The NFR Approach" are simplified versions (as mentioned earlier). For example, rule R6 assumes if even one child softgoal is not satisficed in an AND-decomposition, then the parent softgoal is denied. However, what if, as we observe in Table 13.2, rows 8 and 14, one of the child softgoals is weakly denied? The NFR Approach actually defines rules that allow the parent to the weakly denied instead of denied, but we have assumed simpler rules in this chapter to convey the spirit of the NFR Approach without overwhelming the reader with details. Another aspect of the NFR approach not discussed here is the fact that claim softgoals can have labels as well, which allows claims (or rationales) to change with time and their impact(s) to be quickly reflected in the SIG.

SUMMARY

Trustworthiness is an important emerging requirement for software systems deployed by the US Air Force. While NIST [1] has defined trustworthiness to be reliable, usable, interoperable, and secure, there seems to be no uniformity in the definition of this requirement within the Air Force. Moreover, there seems to be no systematic method to develop trustworthy systems. In this chapter, we employ the goal-oriented framework called the NFR Approach [12,13] for engineering trustworthy software systems. The NFR Approach treats trustworthiness as a goal to be achieved during the process of software development. Since software architecture is the first step in the development of a solution, we employ the NFR Approach to develop a trustworthy architecture for a software system. The software system considered for validation is the Phoenix system [19] used by the US Air Force; the Phoenix system is a middleware system developed by the Air Force for use in tactical and enterprise systems. We applied the NFR Approach, developed trustworthy architectural models for the Phoenix system, and validated the models by having them evaluated by Phoenix's engineers. The results are encouraging, with many design updates for improved trustworthiness being approved by developers as being not only feasible but actually useful for a trustworthy Phoenix system.

In the future we plan to partially automate this process by incorporating natural language processing to identify elements of SIGs from interview notes, which should speed up the process considerably. Furthermore, integrating natural language processing with tools available for handling NFR approach, for example, StarUML [23], will enable automating the processing of knowledge recovery from users. However, we believe that the NFR Approach provides a systematic technique for developing trustworthy software systems.

Acknowledgments

This research was sponsored by Air Force Research Laboratory/Information Directorate, Rome, New York, USA. In the summers of 2011 and 2012, the authors spent many months on this project, and we thank several engineers at the lab for their help, including Mark Lindermann, James Hanna, Vaughn Combs, James Milligan, Chris Schuck, Tim Blocher, Dawn Nelson, Mark Mowers, and Brian Lipa. We also thank the reviewers of the initial version of this chapter for their valuable suggestions and comments.

References

[1] [Internet]. Retrieved from: www.nist.gov/itl/tis/index.cfm [accessed 22.05.12].

[2] Software 2015: A national software strategy to ensure U. S. security and competitiveness. Report of 2nd National Software Summit. [Internet]. Retrieved from: <www.cnsoftware.org/NSS2>; 2005 [accessed 06.06.12].

[3] Trustworthy cyberspace: Strategic plan for the federal cybersecurity research and development program. Executive Office of the President, National Science and Technology Council; 2011 Dec.

[4] Parnas DL, van Schouwen AJ, Kwan SP. Evaluation of safety-critical software. Communications of ACM 1990;33(6):636−48.

[5]   Amoroso E, Taylor C, Watson J, Weiss J. A process-oriented methodology for assessing and improving software trustworthiness. Proceedings of the 2nd ACM Conference On Computer and Communication Security; 1994. p. 39–50.

[6]   DoD 5200.28-STD. Department of Defense standard: Department of Defense trusted computer system evaluation criteria. [Internet]. Retrieved from: <csrc.nist.gov/publications/history/dod85.pdf>; 1985 [accessed 22.05.12].

[7]   Hasselbring W, Reussner R. Toward trustworthy software systems. IEEE Computer 2006;39(4):91–2.

[8]   Garfinkel T, Rosenblum M, Boneh D. Flexible OS support and applications for trusted computing. [Internet]. Retrieved from: <suif.stanford.edu/papers/trusted-hotos03.pdf>; [Accessed 22.05.12].

[9]   Fink RA, Sherman AT. Combining end-to-end voting with trustworthy computing for greater privacy, trust, accessibility, and usability. [Internet]. Retrieved from: <csrc.nist.gov/groups/ST/e2evoting/documents/papers/SHERMAN_trustworthye2e-NISTrevised9-25-09a.pdf>; [accessed 22.05.12].

[10] Taibi D. Defining an open source software trustworthiness model. Proceedings of 3rd International Doctoral Symposium on Emperical Software Engineering; 2008.

[11] Yang Y, Wang Q, Li M. Process trustworthiness as a capability indicator for measuring and improving software trustworthiness. ICSP '09 Proceedings of the International Conference on Software Process: Trustworthy Software Development Processes; 2009. p. 389–401.

[12] Subramanian N, Chung L. Software architecture adaptability: An NFR approach. Proceedings of the International Workshop on Principles of Software Evolution (IWPSE 2001). Vienna: ACM Press; 2001. p. 52–61.

[13] Chung L, Nixon BA, Yu E, Mylopoulos J. Non-functional requirements in software engineering. Boston: Kluwer Academic Publishers; 2000.

[14] Chung L, Subramanian N. Adaptable architecture generation of embedded systems. Journal of Systems and Software. 2004;71(3):271–95.

[15] Chung L, Subramanian N. Testable and adaptable architectures for embedded systems. University of Texas at Dallas Technical Report No. UTDCS-22-01; 2001 Nov.

[16] Subramanian N, Puerzer R, Chung L. A comparative evaluation of maintainability: A study of engineering department's website maintainability. Proceedings of the International Conference on Software Maintenance; 2005 Sep; Budapest, IEEE Computer Society, Hungary. p. 669–672.

[17] Shaw M, Garlan D. Software architecture: Perspectives on an emerging discipline. Prentice Hall; 1996.

[18] Bass L, Clements P, Kazman R. Software architecture in practice. SEI Series in Software Engineering. 2nd ed. Addison-Wesley; 2003.

[19] Combs VT, Hillman RG, Muccio MT, McKeel RW. Joint battlespace infosphere: Information management within a C2 enterprise. 10th International Command and Control Research and Technology Symposium: 2005.

[20] Eeles P, Cripps P. The process of software architecting. Upper Saddle River, NJ: Addison-Wesley; 2010.

[21] Subramanian N, Drager S, McKeever W. Engineering a trustworthy software system using the NFR approach. Presented at the Systems & Software Technology Conference; Salt Lake City, UT. 2012 Apr.

[22] Chung L, Supakkul S, Subramanian N, Garrido JL, Noguera M, Hurtado MV, et al. Goal-oriented software architecting. In: Avgeriou P, et al., editors. Relating Software Requirements and Architectures. Springer; 2011. p. 91–109.

[23] [Internet]. Retrieved from: http://staruml.sourceforge.net/en/modules.php; [accessed 11.10.11].

[24] Ware WH. Perspectives on trusted computer systems. Rand Library Collection; 1988 Sep. p. 7478.

[25] Linderman M, et. al. A reference model for information management to support coalition information sharing needs. 10th International Command and Control Research and Technology Symposium. Verginia; 2005 Oct.

[26] Stallings W, Brown L. Computer security: Principles and practice. 2nd ed. Prentice Hall; 2011.

[27] Mandke VV, Nayar MK. Information integrity: A structure for its definition. In: Strong DM, Kahn BK, editors. Proceedings of the 1997 Conference on Information Quality; MIT, Cambridge, MA, 1997.

[28] Shanmugavadivu K, Madheswaran M. Caching technique for improving data retrieval performance in mobile ad hoc networks. International Journal of Computer Science and Information Technologies 2010;1(4):249–55.

[29] Hennessy JL, Patterson DA. Computer architecture: A quantitative approach. 5th ed. Morgan Kaufmann Publication; 2011.

[30] Hsu C-C, Sandford BA. The delphi technique: making sense of consensus. Journal of Practical Assessment, Research, and Evaluation 2007 Aug;12:10 ISSN: 1531-7714.

[31] Subramanian N, Drager S, McKeever W. Eliciting software design from interviews using the NFR approach. Submitted for publication.

Analyzing the Ergodic Secrecy Rates of Cooperative Amplify-and-Forward Relay Networks over Generalized Fading Channels

14

Annamalai Annamalai, Abiodun Olaluwe, and Eyidayo Adebola

Prairie View A&M University, Prairie View, TX, USA

INFORMATION IN THIS CHAPTER

- Improving wireless physical layer security using cooperative relays
- Ergodic secrecy rates of cooperative amplify-and-forward relay networks

INTRODUCTION

The purpose of secure communications is to enable the legitimate destination node to successfully recover the source information, while keeping the eavesdroppers (wire-tappers) ignorant of this information as much as possible. In recent years, the issues of privacy and security concerns have taken on an increasingly important role in the design of tactical wireless networks owing to the broadcast nature of wireless transmissions and to growing proliferations of wireless sensors in military and homeland security applications.

Traditionally, security is viewed as an independent feature addressed above the physical layer, and all widely used cryptographic protocols (e.g., RSA and AES) are designed and implemented assuming the physical layer has already been established and provides an error-free link. In contrast with this paradigm, there exist both theoretical and practical contributions that support the potential of physical layer security ideas to significantly strengthen the security of wireless communication systems. This line of work was pioneered by Wyner, who introduced the wire-tap

227

channel and established the possibility of creating perfectly secure communication links without relying on private (secret) keys [1]. But the impact of the seminal articles by Wyner and later by Csiszár and Körner [2] was limited in the 1980s, partly because practical wire-tap codes were not available then, but mostly because a strictly positive secrecy capacity in the classical wire-tap channel setup requires the legitimate receiver to have some advantage over the attacker in terms of channel quality. Almost at the same time, Diffie and Hellman [3] published the basic principles of public-key cryptography, which was to be adopted by nearly all contemporary security schemes.

Recently there has been a renewed interest in information-theoretic security (i.e., perfect secrecy), arguably due to the work of Maurer [4], who proved that even when the legitimate users (say Alice and Bob) have a worse channel than the eavesdropper (say Eve), it is possible for them to generate a secret key through public communication over an insecure yet authenticated channel. The advent of wireless communications, which is particularly susceptible to eavesdropping owing to the broadcast nature of the transmission medium, has also motivated a closer analysis of the secrecy potential of wireless networks. For instance, fading wire-tap channels were studied in [5–7] (also see references therein) while multiple-antenna wire-tap channels were investigated in [8,9] and references therein.

However, practical implementation issues associated with packing a large number of antenna elements on tiny (i.e., small form-factor) sensor/communication nodes suggest that cooperative relaying strategies may be simpler and perhaps more appropriate for improving the achievable secrecy rate in wireless sensor and ad-hoc networks. In this emerging wireless communication paradigm, a relay node may either amplify what it receives (in case of amplify-and-forward relaying protocol) or digitally decodes and re-encodes the source information (in case of decode-and-forward relaying protocol) before re-transmitting it to the destination node. Other variations of cooperative relaying strategies include opportunistic, incremental, variable-gain, and fixed-gain (either blind or semi-blind) relaying that are implemented based on the availability of channel side information (CSI) and the number of active participating nodes for information relaying. The cooperative relaying architecture also offers a modular and flexible solution to meet a prescribed design objective (e.g., secrecy rate, data rate, error rate, energy constraint, etc.) by enabling the source node to tap into the available resources of local neighboring nodes to increase its throughput, range, reliability, and covertness. However, theoretical contributions on the achievable ergodic secrecy rates of cooperative relay networks are rather limited (e.g., [10–13] and [26]). Therefore, development of a unified analytical framework for computing the ergodic secrecy rates of cooperative secure wireless communications in a myriad of fading environments is of both theoretical and practical interest. This is because it allows one to gain a better understanding as to how much the fundamental limit of secure communication rate can be improved by exploiting/mitigating channel effects via node cooperation as well as to study the impact of channel fading statistics (e.g., fade distribution, locations of the relays and the eavesdroppers) on the achievable ergodic secrecy rates. To the best of our knowledge, the ergodic secrecy rates of cooperative relay networks in generalized fading environments have not been studied previously. This might be attributed to the analytical difficulties associated with computing the statistical expectation of the logarithmic function with respect to the random variable that characterizes the fading channel, as well as finding the exact probability density function (PDF) of the end-to-end signal-to-noise ratio (SNR) for the amplify-and-forward cooperative relaying protocol.

Secure cooperative wireless communications
Improving wireless physical layer security using cooperative relays in a Gaussian channel

Suppose a source node S is transmitting information to the destination node D through an amplify-and-forward variable-gain relay R in the presence of an eavesdropper E as depicted in Figure 14.1.

Given the distances d_{SD}, d_{SR}, and d_{SE}, we may compute d_{RD} and d_{RE} via the cosine rule as $d_{RD} = \sqrt{d_{SD}^2 + d_{SR}^2 - 2d_{SD}d_{SR}\cos(\alpha)}$ and $d_{RE} = \sqrt{d_{SE}^2 + d_{SR}^2 - 2d_{SE}d_{SR}\cos(\theta + \alpha)}$. These distances will be utilized in the calculations of the mean link SNRs in a fading channel. The two angles shown in Figure 14.1 are also important to investigate the impact of relay/eavesdropper locations on the achievable secrecy rate.

It can be shown (in the context of information-theoretic wireless physical layer security) that mutual information between the source-destination and the source-eavesdropper links with cooperative amplify-and-forward (CAF) variable-gain relay in a Gaussian (non-fading) channel are given by (1) and (2), respectively:

$$I_{SD}^{(AF)} = \frac{1}{2}\log_2\left(1 + P_S|h_{SD}|^2 + \frac{P_S|h_{SR}|^2 P_R|h_{RD}|^2}{1 + P_S|h_{SR}|^2 + P_R|h_{RD}|^2}\right) \tag{1}$$

$$I_{SE}^{(AF)} = \frac{1}{2}\log_2\left(1 + P_S|h_{SE}|^2 + \frac{P_S|h_{SR}|^2 P_R|h_{RE}|^2}{1 + P_S|h_{SR}|^2 + P_R|h_{RE}|^2}\right) \tag{2}$$

where h_{ij} denotes the channel gain of link i-j while P_S and P_R or P_{R_i} correspond to the transmit power during the first phase and the second phase of cooperation, respectively. Hence the secrecy rate in the Gaussian channel with receiver-only channel state information is given by the difference

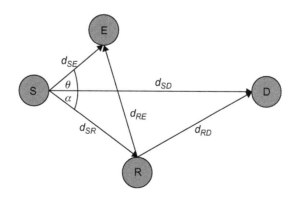

FIGURE 14.1

Wyner wire-tap channel with a single cooperative amplify-and-forward relay.

between the mutual information between the source (Alice) and the legitimate receiver (Bob) $I_{SD}^{(AF)}$ and the source (Alice) and the eavesdropper (Eve) $I_{SE}^{(AF)}$:

$$R_S^{(AF)} = I_{SD}^{(AF)} - I_{SE}^{(AF)} = \frac{1}{2}\log_2 \left(\frac{1 + P_S|h_{SD}|^2 + \dfrac{P_S|h_{SR}|^2 P_R|h_{RD}|^2}{1 + P_S|h_{SR}|^2 + P_R|h_{RD}|^2}}{1 + P_S|h_{SE}|^2 + \dfrac{P_S|h_{SR}|^2 P_R|h_{RE}|^2}{1 + P_S|h_{SR}|^2 + P_R|h_{RE}|^2}} \right) \tag{3}$$

It is therefore evident that in a non-fading channel, there will be a positive secrecy rate if the condition (4) is satisfied:

$$\frac{P_R|h_{SR}|^2 \left(P_S|h_{SR}|^2 + 1 \right) \left(|h_{RD}|^2 - |h_{RE}|^2 \right)}{\left(1 + P_S|h_{SR}|^2 + P_R|h_{RD}|^2 \right) \left(1 + P_S|h_{SR}|^2 + P_R|h_{RE}|^2 \right)} > |h_{SE}|^2 - |h_{SD}|^2 \tag{4}$$

This result is interesting in that it might be possible to achieve a positive secrecy rate even when the channel quality between the Alice and Eve (i.e., eavesdropper channel) is better than Alice and Bob (i.e., main channel) by proper selection of the position of cooperative relay and the power allocation. The link between the source-relay provides an additional avenue to transmit secure information while the link between the relay and the legitimate destination node compensates the secret information loss at the source. But the secrecy rate is zero when $h_{SD} < h_{SE}$ without cooperative relay.

If there are multiple J eavesdroppers, then the secrecy rate may be calculated as

$$R_S^{(AF)} = \min\left\{ I_{SD} - I_{SE}^{(j)} \right\}, \; j = 1, 2, ..., J \tag{5}$$

This is portrayed in the second expression in (3). It is also important to note that our study and network architecture is different from [13] since we do not assume that the source first transmits locally to a set of "trusted" cooperative relay nodes, which then convey the source information to the destination securely by finding suboptimal weights at the relays that maximize the secrecy rate under total power constraint. Moreover, their analysis does not take into account the deleterious effects of multipath fading. Similarly, the analysis and the results in [26] were restricted to a Gaussian (non-fading) channel.

Ergodic secrecy rates of cooperative amplify-and-forward relay networks

To the best of our knowledge, the ergodic secrecy rates of cooperative amplify-and-forward relay networks in generalized fading environments have not been studied previously. This might be attributed to the analytical difficulties associated with finding the exact PDF of the end-to-end SNR for the amplify-and-forward relaying protocol, as well as the evaluation of the statistical expectation of a logarithmic function with respect to the random variables that characterizes the fading channel.

In a recent work [14,15], we discovered an exponential-type integral representation for $\ln \gamma$, $\gamma > 0$, in which the conditional fading SNR appears only in the exponent (i.e., thus facilitates the task of statistical averaging with respect to the PDF of SNR) and presented a novel moment generating function-(MGF) based analytical framework for calculating the ergodic capacities of cooperative relay networks under three distinct source-adaptive transmission policies in a myriad of fading environments. Details of the derivation of this exponential-type integral representation of the logarithmic function are provided in the appendix for completeness.

To facilitate the statistical averaging of (3) over the independent but non-identically distributed (i.n.d) fading SNR random variables, $\gamma_{ab} = P_a|h_{ab}|^2$, we first re-write (3) (given N = 1 and J = 1) as:

$$R_S^{(AF)} = \frac{1}{2}\left[\log_2\left(1 + \gamma_{SD} + \frac{\gamma_{SR}\gamma_{RD}}{1 + \gamma_{SR} + \gamma_{RD}}\right) - \log_2\left(1 + \gamma_{SE} + \frac{\gamma_{SR}\gamma_{RE}}{1 + \gamma_{SR} + \gamma_{RE}}\right)\right] \tag{6}$$

Substituting $\log_2(1 + \gamma) = \frac{1}{\ln 2}\ln(1 + \gamma)$ in (6) and then invoking the exponential-type integral representation for logarithmic function (A.5), it is quite straightforward to show that the ergodic secrecy rate is given by

$$\overline{R}_S^{(AF)} = \frac{1}{2\ln 2}\left\{\int_0^\infty \frac{e^{-x}}{x}\left[\int_0^\infty (1 - e^{-x\gamma})f_{\gamma_L}(\gamma)d\gamma\right]dx - \int_0^\infty \frac{e^{-x}}{x}\left[\int_0^\infty (1 - e^{-x\gamma})f_{\gamma_E}(\gamma)d\gamma\right]dx\right\}$$

$$= \frac{1}{2\ln 2}\left\{\int_0^\infty \frac{e^{-x}}{x}\left[1 - \phi_{\gamma_L}(x)\right]dx - \int_0^\infty \frac{e^{-x}}{x}\left[1 - \phi_{\gamma_E}(x)\right]dx\right\} \tag{7}$$

where $\phi_{\gamma_L}(s)$ and $\phi_{\gamma_E}(s)$ correspond to the MGF of $\gamma_L = \gamma_{SD} + \frac{\gamma_{SR}\gamma_{RD}}{1 + \gamma_{SR} + \gamma_{RD}}$ and $\gamma_E = \gamma_{SE} + \frac{\gamma_{SR}\gamma_{RE}}{1 + \gamma_{SR} + \gamma_{RE}}$ random variables, respectively (i.e., Laplace transform of their respective PDF of the end-to-end SNRs $f_\gamma(\gamma)$). But the evaluation of the exact MGFs of γ_L and γ_E are known to be very cumbersome and an exact expression (but very complicated formula) is available only for the special cases of i.n.d Nakagami-m fading channels with positive integer fading severity indices (obviously, the special case of Rayleigh fading can be treated by setting the fading severity parameter m to unity). In [16,17], we have also found a highly accurate and efficient closed-form expression to approximate MGF of SNR for a dual-hop CAF relayed path in generalized fading environments. This solution is directly relevant and can be leveraged in this work for estimating the ergodic secrecy rates of cooperative secure communications in a myriad of fading environments. Mimicking the developments in [16,17], we obtain simple closed-form approximations for $\phi_{\gamma_L}(s)$ and $\phi_{\gamma_E}(s)$ in a generalized fading environment with i.n.d. fading statistics corresponding to the distinct (spatially distributed) wireless links:

$$\phi_{\gamma_L}(s) \approx \phi_{\gamma_{SD}}(s)\left[\phi_{\gamma_{SR}}(s) + \phi_{\gamma_{RD}}(s) - \phi_{\gamma_{SR}}(s)\phi_{\gamma_{RD}}(s)\right] \tag{8}$$

$$\phi_{\gamma_E}(s) \approx \phi_{\gamma_{SE}}(s)\left[\phi_{\gamma_{SR}}(s) + \phi_{\gamma_{RE}}(s) - \phi_{\gamma_{SR}}(s)\phi_{\gamma_{RE}}(s)\right] \tag{9}$$

The MGF expressions shown above are very attractive, as they only require the knowledge of MGF of individual links in closed-form, which is readily available in the literature (e.g., [21] and [25 Table 3, p. 28]).

Computational results

In this section, selected numerical results are provided to demonstrate the efficacy of our analytical framework for assessing the ergodic secrecy rates of cooperative wireless communications in a generalized fading environment. Assuming a simple path-loss model, we can show that the mean received SNR of the wireless link i-j is given by

$$\Omega_{ij} = c \left| \frac{d_{ij}}{d_{SD}} \right|^{-n} W_i \frac{E_b}{N_0}, \quad i \in \{S, R\}, \ j \in \{D, E\} \tag{10}$$

where n denotes the path-loss exponent, c is a constant (arbitrarily chosen to be $c = 0.01$ in our case, unless stated otherwise), $W_i = P_i/(P_S + P_R)$ corresponds to the transmit power ratio such that $W_S + W_R = 1$, and $W_S E_b/N_0$ represents the transmit energy per bit over the noise spectral density ratio at the source node.

All the figures were generated using (7), (8), and (9), and we have also arbitrarily chosen $d_{SD} = 100$, $d_{SE} = d_{SR} = 50$ with the two angles set to be $\theta = 60^\circ$ and $\alpha = 18^\circ$ (unless stated otherwise). In the instances where we investigate the effects of dissimilar fade distributions and/or mean signal strengths of the different links of the Wyner's wire-tap channels, we have arbitrarily assumed (without any loss of generality) the fading parameters summarized in Table 14.1 for each of the distinct links identified in Figure 14.1. In Figure 14.2 we have assumed all links to be Rayleigh faded, while in Figure 14.3, Figure 14.5, and Figure 14.9 we have assumed Nakagami-m faded links.

Unless stated otherwise, the format 1 structure of the η-μ distribution is used [24]. Hence, the acceptable range of values of η is $0 < \eta < \infty$ where η is the scattered-wave power ratio between the quadrature and in-phase components of each multipath cluster, while h and H are given as $h = \frac{2 + \eta^{-1} + \eta}{4}$ and $H = \frac{\eta^{-1} - \eta}{4}$ respectively, and m denotes the Nakagami-m fading index. For the generalized η-μ distribution, we have arbitrarily selected the fading severity parameters as $\eta = 0.5$ and $\mu_\eta = 1$. Moreover, the default κ-μ fading parameters are defined as $\mu_\kappa = 0.5$ and $\kappa = 2$, while Ω_{ij} denotes the link mean SNR, which can be calculated with the aid of (10). In the following subsections we investigate the effects of different factors of both the channel and system parameters on the achievable secrecy rates of cooperative secure wireless communications.

Table 14.1 Fading Distributions for Different Links in a Cooperative Relay Network and Their Corresponding MGFs of Fading SNR

Wireless Link	Fading Channel	MGF of SNR
Source–Eavesdroppe Source–Relay	Nakagami-m	$\left(\dfrac{m}{m + s\Omega_{ij}} \right)^m$
Source–Destination Relay–Eavesdropper	Generalized $\eta - \mu$ [24]	$\left(\dfrac{4\mu_\eta^2 h}{\left(2(h-H)\mu_\eta + s\Omega_{ij} \right) \left(2(h+H)\mu_\eta + s\Omega_{ij} \right)} \right)^{\mu_\eta}$
Relay–Destination	Generalized $\kappa - \mu$ [24]	$\left(\dfrac{\mu_\kappa(1+\kappa)}{\mu_\kappa(1+\kappa) + s\Omega_{ij}} \right)^{\mu_\kappa} \exp\left(-\dfrac{s\Omega_s \mu_\kappa \kappa}{\mu_\kappa(1+\kappa) + s\Omega_{ij}} \right)$

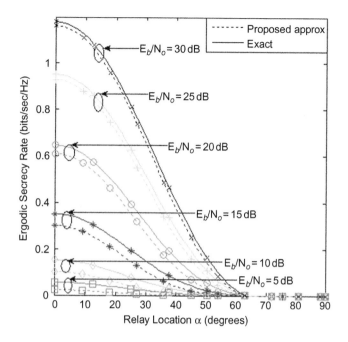

FIGURE 14.2

Ergodic secrecy rate of a CAF relay network (as illustrated in Figure 14.1) in Rayleigh fading plotted as a function of the relay location for several different values and equal power allocation during the two transmission phases (i.e., $W_S = W_R = 0.5$ and $\theta = 60°$).

Tightness of the approximation for the MGF of SNR

In Figure 14.2 we show a comparison of the ergodic secrecy rate predicted using our proposed approximate MGF shown in (8) and (9) versus the exact expression for the half harmonic mean SNR of a two-hop relayed path given in [22, Eq. (52)] or [23, Eq. (5) and Table 1] for Rayleigh fading. It is apparent that our simple closed-form MGF formula can yield very accurate predictions of the ergodic secrecy rate over a wide range of E_b/N_0 values. The result is very encouraging in the sense that we may now use our closed-form MGF expressions (8)–(9) with a high confidence to predict the ergodic secrecy rate of CAF relay networks in a myriad of fading environments, especially for many practical settings and fading environments where a computationally stable expression for the MGF of half harmonic mean SNR is not available.

Effects of fade distributions

In Figure 14.3, the ergodic secrecy rates of the CAF relay network illustrated in Figure 14.1 were calculated as a function of the relay node location in two different Nakagami-m channels. We found that the ergodic secrecy rate is greater in channels that experience less severe fading (i.e., higher

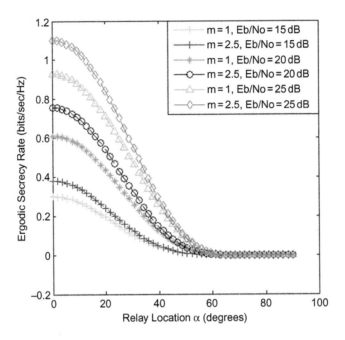

FIGURE 14.3

Impact of the fade distribution (i.e., fading severity parameter) on the ergodic secrecy rate of a CAF relay network when (i.e., $W_S = W_R = 0.5$ and $\theta = 60°$).

values of the fading severity parameter m), especially when the locations of the eavesdropper and the cooperative relay nodes are fixed. It is also evident from Figure 14.2 and Figure 14.3 that an appropriate choice of the relay location could maximize the ergodic secrecy rate for a specified location of the eavesdropper node. Thus, we believe that further research in this direction might lead to some good design guidelines/principles for the selection of relay nodes that maximizes the ergodic secrecy rate metric. It is also important to highlight that this optimization metric represents a new paradigm to the cooperative wireless communication design by taking into account the physical layer security considerations in the formation of a cooperative wireless network. It is also fundamentally different from the prior works on CAF relay network optimization that were focused on maximizing the ergodic and/or outage capacity metrics.

In order to buttress this effect, we also consider two additional scenarios as presented in Table 14.2; the resulting curves are plotted in Figure 14.4.

Figure 14.4 shows how different combinations of path fade distributions affect the ergodic secrecy rate of a CAF relay network when E_b/N_o is fixed (i.e., the mean signal strengths are fixed and only fading severity parameters are altered for Case 1 and Case 2). It is observed that when the critical paths do not experience severe fading, the ergodic secrecy rate maximizes at a higher value transmit power allocation W_S than when the critical paths experience deep fades. Also, the ergodic secrecy rate dwindles faster when the channel experiences more severe fading. It is also good to note the shifting effect of this impact on the curves in the light of effect of the constituent

Table 14.2 Paths' Fading Distributions and their Fading Indices

Path(s)	Fading Distribution	Fading Indices	
		Case 1	Case 2
Source–Eavesdropper	Nakagami-m	$m = 1$	$m = 1$
Source–Destination	$\eta - \mu$	$\eta = 0.9, \mu_\eta = 1$	$\eta = 0.9, \mu_\eta = 1$
Source–Relay	Nakagami-m	$m = 2.5$	$m = 4$
Relay–Destination	$\kappa - \mu$	$\kappa = 2, \mu_k = 0.5$	$\kappa = 3, \mu_k = 2.5$
Relay–Eavesdropper	$\eta - \mu$	$\eta = 0.5, \mu_\eta = 1$	$\eta = 5, \mu_\eta = 1$

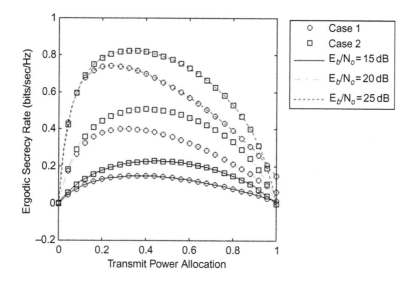

FIGURE 14.4

Ergodic secrecy rate of a CAF relay network versus transmit power allocation in two different fading environments (with $\theta = 60°$, and $\alpha = 18°$).

components of equation (7). The second integral has a lower value at initial values of the allocated power, which makes the secrecy rate to climax early enough, but its value increases drastically as power allocation during the first transmission phase increases, forcing the secrecy rate to decline with it. It can be adjudged also that the fading conditions of the link between the relay-destination and relay-eavesdropper during the second phase of the transmission can affect the achievable secrecy rate.

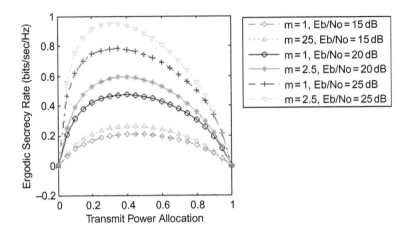

FIGURE 14.5

Ergodic secrecy rate of a CAF relay network (depicted in Figure 14.1 with $\theta = 60°$ and $\alpha = 18°$) plotted as a function of transmit power allocation W_S for several different E_b/N_0 values and Nakagami-m fading severity parameters.

Effects of transmit power allocation in distinct transmission phases

Our proposed MGF-based analytical framework for ergodic secrecy rate analysis can be readily used to facilitate an investigation of the optimal power allocation strategy that maximizes the ergodic secrecy rate of the CAF relay network depicted in Figure 14.1. Figure 14.5 depicts that there exists an optimal transmit power allocation during the two different transmission phases, which maximizes the ergodic secrecy rate. The optimal power allocation depends on a few factors, including the distance ratios between the source, relay, destination, and eavesdropper nodes as well as the channel fading statistics of the spatially distributed wireless links. However, we observed that the optimal power allocation does not appear to be very sensitive to the variations in the fading severity parameters when all the links have an identical fading severity index.

In Figure 14.6, we have plotted the secrecy rate against the transmit power allocation when distinct wireless links are assumed to undergo different fading according to Table 14.1. The secrecy rate is calculated at different Nakagami-m indices for the source and eavesdropper, source and relay links, while other links are fixed at their default values. It is noticed that there is an increase in secrecy rates with increased transmit power allocation, but the secrecy rate decreases after an optimum transmit power allocation is exceeded. It is also observed that an increase in E_b/N_0 results in a corresponding increase in the ergodic secrecy rate. Comparison between Figure 14.5 and Figure 14.6 also reveals that the values of fading severity parameters of the source-eavesdropper and source-relay links have a noticeable impact on the achievable secrecy rate, although the optimal power allocation ratio seems to be less susceptible to these variations. This in turn suggests that coarse side information of the distance ratios between the source, relay, destination, and the

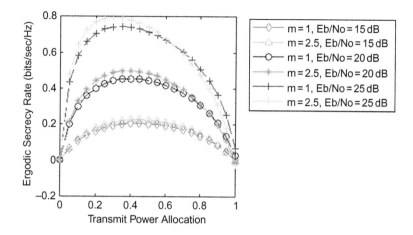

FIGURE 14.6

Ergodic secrecy rate of a CAF relay network plotted as a function of transmit power allocation W_S when $\theta = 60°$ and $\alpha = 18°$ for several different E_b/N_0 values and non-identical fading parameters.

eavesdropper nodes are probably sufficient to develop a simple rule of thumb for the "optimal power allocation" policy.

Effects of dissimilar mean signal strengths

The mean strengths of the signals received by the eavesdropper and the relay are characterized by the angles θ and α and also the distances d_{SE} and d_{SR}. Hence an array of plots is presented in Figure 14.7 (a–d) to capture nicely how the ergodic secrecy rate varies in accordance with these four parameters. To generate these plots, we have assumed the channel fading parameters for various links as summarized in Table 14.1 and equal power allocation during the two transmission phases. As expected, the ergodic secrecy rate decreases with increasing value of the angle α while an increase in any of the parameters θ, d_{SE}, or d_{SR} improves the ergodic secrecy rate. It is evident from Figure 14.7 (a) and Figure 14.7 (b) that the ergodic secrecy rate climaxes as α is closer to zero and plummets afterward, while this metric increases with a larger value of θ. This is anticipated, as both the distances d_{RE} and d_{RD} increase with a larger value of θ and α, respectively. For instance, the distance d_{SR} is shortest when $\alpha = 0$, which coincidentally forms the shortest route path to the destination node. Moreover, in order to ensure positive secrecy we must choose the relay location at an angle below a certain value which, from Figure 14.7 (a), can be deduced to be approximately 60°. Figure 14.7 (b) and Figure 14.7 (c) also indicate that there would not be any secrecy if the eavesdropper is within a certain distance range and/or angle to the source node, irrespective of the transmit signal energy. Figure 14.7 (d) reveals the possibility of achieving a higher secrecy rate by increasing the relay distance coupled with increasing the transmit SNR if the relay angle is fixed. It is also important to note that secure communication is only possible when the secrecy rate is positive (i.e., negative ergodic secrecy rate in these plots simply indicates that the

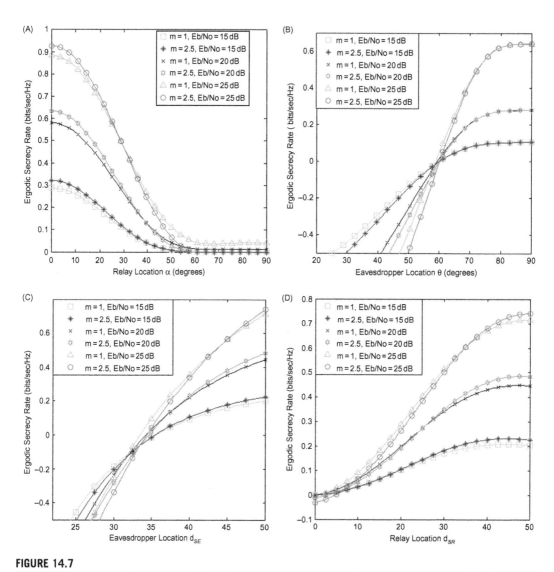

FIGURE 14.7

(a) Ergodic secrecy rate versus relay location angle α; (b) Ergodic secrecy rate versus eavesdropper location angle θ (with $\alpha = 60°$); (c) Ergodic secrecy rate versus d_{SE}; (d) Ergodic secrecy rate versus d_{SR}.

eavesdropper node has a "better" channel condition compared to the legitimate destination node, and thus secure wireless communication is not viable). Figure 14.7 (b) and Figure 14.7 (c) also suggest that the eavesdropper node is disadvantaged when its position is at angle $\theta \geq 60°$ or when the distance $d_{SE} \geq 35$ (under the assumptions of the network topology considered herein). These parameters could also be a precursor to determining the threshold distance and/or angle at which to position or select the cooperating relay node in order to achieve a positive secrecy rate.

Effects of increasing number of cooperative relays

In the presence of multiple cooperating relays, the secrecy rate can be expressed as in (11) (instead of equation (6)):

$$
R_S^{(AF)} = I_{SD}^{(AF)} - I_{SE}^{(AF)} = \frac{1}{(N+1)} \log_2 \left(\frac{1 + P_S|h_{SD}|^2 + \sum\limits_{k=1}^{N} \left\{ \dfrac{P_S|h_{SR_k}|^2 P_{R_k}|h_{R_kD}|^2}{1 + P_S|h_{SR_k}|^2 + P_{R_k}|h_{R_kD}|^2} \right\}}{1 + P_S|h_{SE}|^2 + \sum\limits_{k=1}^{N} \left\{ \dfrac{P_S|h_{SR_k}|^2 P_{R_k}|h_{R_kE}|^2}{1 + P_S|h_{SR_k}|^2 + P_{R_k}|h_{R_kE}|^2} \right\}} \right) \tag{11}
$$

where N denotes the number of cooperating relays. Without any loss of generality, we assume that the fading parameters for various links are distributed according to Table 14.1 with $m = 1$ for the links that are subject to Nakagami-m fading, while the source-relay distances and the relay location angles are assumed to be $d_{SR_1} = d_{SR_2} = d_{SR_3} = 50$, $\alpha_1 = 72°$, $\alpha_2 = 23°$, $\alpha_3 = 6°$. Moreover, we arbitrarily assume an equal transmit power allocation strategy $W_s = W_k = 1/(N+1)$ such that $W_S + \sum\limits_{k=1}^{N} W_k = 1$, where W_S corresponds to the transmit power allocation ratio during the first phase of cooperative transmission while W_1, W_2, and W_3 denote power allocation ratios corresponding to the multiple cooperative relays during the second phase of transmission. It is evident from Figure 14.8 that the ergodic secrecy rate improves with increase in the angle θ subtended by the eavesdropper as well as in the presence of

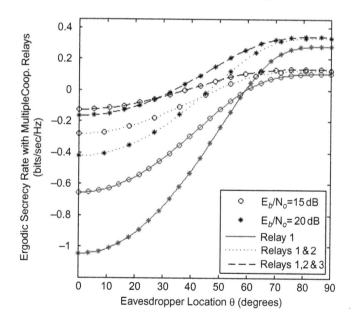

FIGURE 14.8

Ergodic secrecy rate of a CAF network with multiple cooperative relays plotted as a function of the eavesdropper position angle.

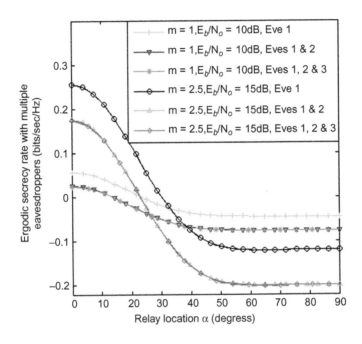

FIGURE 14.9

Ergodic secrecy rate of a CAF relay network (depicted in Figure 14.1 with multiple eavesdroppers at angles $\theta_1 = 51°$ (Eve1), $\theta_2 = 60°$ (Eve2), and $\theta_3 = 80°$ (Eve3)) plotted as a function of the relay location angle in a Nakagami-m environment and equal transmit power allocation policy ($W_S = W_R = 0.5$).

multiple cooperative relays, subject to the prescribed transmit power allocation ratios during the distinct transmission phases. It is interesting to note that a positive secrecy rate is not achievable below a certain value of θ while increasing the mean SNR of the links does have a significant positive impact on the achievable ergodic secrecy rate.

Effects of increasing number of eavesdroppers

Figure 14.9 depicts the effects of varying the number of eavesdroppers where all the distinct channels are assumed to experience Nakagami-m fading. It can be observed that the ergodic secrecy rate reduces with the increasing number of eavesdroppers. This trend is expected as the ergodic secrecy rate is dictated by the "best" source-eavesdropper channel (see equation (5)). For example, there is a reduction in the secrecy rate from approximately 0.25 bits/sec/Hz to 0.15 bits/sec/Hz for $m = 2.5$ and $\alpha = 0°$ when the number of eavesdropper is increased from one to three.

CONCLUSION

In this chapter, we have demonstrated that cooperative relays can be exploited to enhance the wireless physical layer security of the classical Wyner wire-tap channel. We have also presented a unified analytical framework based on the MGF method to approximate the ergodic secrecy rates of cooperative amplify-and-forward variable-gain relay networks in a myriad of fading environments. Since the cooperative relaying architecture offers a flexible and a modular approach for increasing the ergodic secrecy rates (i.e., using physical layer security approaches) at a low cost but without requiring an antenna array, it is an attractive proposition for providing a "more secure" wireless communication (i.e., prevents eavesdropping) in wireless sensor networks without (or with only limited) upper layer data encryption. These results may be exploited to develop policies and/ or algorithms for secure wireless communications.

It is also critically important to be able to accurately estimate the ergodic secrecy rates for other variations of the node-cooperation strategies (e.g., fixed-gain versus variable gain relays, "opportunistic" relaying, and decode-and-forward protocols) and these are recommended for future research. Further research and development of asymptotic closed-form approximations for the ergodic secrecy rates of cooperative relay networks are also highly desirable for system-level optimization. A comprehensive study on the impact of path correlations on the achievable ergodic secrecy rates of both non-cooperative and cooperative wireless networks are also of significant theoretical and practical interest, and is highlighted here to motivate further research in this direction.

Appendix

In this appendix, we outline the derivation of an "exponential-type" integral representation for the logarithmic function $\ln \gamma$ when $\gamma > 0$. Such a representation will facilitate the statistical averaging problem that is typically encountered in the average capacity analysis over fading channels, and therefore leads to a unified approach for calculating the ergodic capacity of cooperative amplify-and-forward relay networks in a myriad of fading environments. Utilizing [19, eq. (1.512.2)], we have

$$\ln\gamma = 2 \sum_{\substack{k=1 \\ k \ odd}}^{\infty} \frac{1}{k}\left(\frac{\gamma-1}{\gamma+1}\right)^k = 2 \sum_{\substack{k=1 \\ k \ odd}}^{\infty} \frac{1}{k}(y)^k, \quad \gamma > 0 \tag{A.1}$$

where $y = \frac{\gamma-1}{\gamma+1}$. Substituting $y^k = \frac{1}{\Gamma(k)}\int_0^{\infty} x^{k-1}e^{-x/y} \, dx$ [19, eq. (3.381.4)] into (A.1), we obtain

$$\ln\gamma = 2 \sum_{\substack{k=1 \\ k \ odd}}^{\infty} \frac{1}{k}\left(\frac{1}{\Gamma(k)}\int_0^{\infty} x^{k-1}e^{-x/y}\right) dx = 2\int_0^{\infty} e^{-x/y}\left(\sum_{\substack{k=1 \\ k \ odd}}^{\infty} \frac{1}{k!}x^{k-1}\right) dx \tag{A.2}$$

Recognizing that $\frac{1}{x}shx = \frac{e^x - e^{-x}}{2x} = \sum_{k=1}^{\infty} \frac{1}{k!}x^{k-1}$ [19, eq. (1.411.2)], (A.2) can be re-stated as

$$\ln \gamma = \int_0^{\infty} \frac{1}{x}(e^x - e^{-x}) e^{-x\left(\frac{\gamma+1}{\gamma-1}\right)} dx \tag{A.3}$$

Finally, using variable substitution $x = z(\gamma - 1)$, $dz = \frac{dx}{\gamma - 1}$, we arrive at (A.4) after some routine algebraic manipulations:

$$\ln\gamma = \int_0^\infty \frac{1}{z} \left[\overset{\leftarrow}{} e^{-2z} - e^{-2z\gamma} \right] dz, \gamma > 0 \tag{A.4}$$

It is also obvious from (A.4) that

$$\ln(1 + \gamma) = \int_0^\infty \frac{e^{-2z}}{z} \left[\overset{\rightarrow}{} 1 - e^{-2z\gamma} \right] dz = \int_0^\infty \frac{e^{-x}}{x} \left[\overset{\rightarrow}{} 1 - e^{-x\gamma} \right] dx, \; \gamma > -1 \tag{A.5}$$

Incidentally, the second term in (A.5) is identical to [18, eq. (6)]. However, it should be emphasized that in Lemma 1 of [18, eq. (6)], the author indicated that his representation for (A.5) is valid only for $\gamma > 0$ instead of $\gamma > -1$ (from our derivation). In fact, if one starts the derivation with the power series for $\ln \gamma$ shown in [19, eq. (1.512.3)] (which was used in [18]), then the representation in (A.4) would be valid for any $\gamma \geq 0.5$. In this case, the resulting expression [18, eq. (6)] cannot be used for the ergodic capacity analysis of the optimal power and rate adaptation (OPRA) policy. Perhaps for this reason, [20] had abandoned the approach in [18] and attempted to develop yet another MGF-based method based on the E_i-transform to unify the analysis of ergodic capacities of CAF relay networks with different source adaptive transmission policies over generalized fading channels.

References

[1] Wyner AD. The wire-tap channel. Bell Syst Tech Journal 1975;54(8):1355−67.

[2] Csiszár I, Körner J. Broadcast channels with confidential messages. IEEE Trans Inf Theory 1978;IT-24 (3):339−48.

[3] Diffie W, Hellman M. New directions in cryptography. IEEE Trans Inf Theory 1976;IT-22(6):644−54.

[4] Maurer U. Secret key agreement by public discussion from common information. IEEE Trans Inf Theory 1993;39(3):733−42.

[5] Bloch M, Barros J, Rodrigues MRD, McLaughlin SW. Wireless information theoretic security. IEEE Trans Inf Theory 2008;54(6):2515−34.

[6] Gopala PK, Lai L, El Gamal H. On the secrecy capacity of fading channels. IEEE Trans Inf Theory 2008;54(10):4687−98.

[7] Liang Y, Poor V, Shamai S. Secure communication over fading channels. IEEE Trans Inf Theory 2008;54(6):2470−92.

[8] Khisti A, Wornell G. The MIMOME channel. Proc 45th Annual Allerton Conference on Communication, Control and Computing; 2007; Monticello.

[9] Oggier F, Hassibi B. The secrecy capacity of the MIMO wiretap channel. Proc IEEE International Symposium on Information Theory. Toronto; 2008 Jul. p. 524−28. Also appeared in IEEE Trans Information Theory 2011;57(8):4961-72.

[10] Tekin E, Yener A. The general Gaussian multiple access and two-way wire-tap channels: Achievable rates and cooperative jamming. IEEE Trans Inf Theory 2008;54(6):2735−51.

[11] Lai L, El Gamal H. The relay-eavesdropper channel: Cooperation for secrecy. IEEE Trans Info Theory 2008;54(9):4005−19.

[12] Tang X, Liu R, Spasojevic P, Poor HV. The Gaussian wiretap channel with a helping interferer. Toronto, Ontario, Canada: Proc IEEE ISIT; 2008 Jul.

[13] Dong L, Han Z, Petropulu A, Poor V. Improving wireless physical layer security via cooperating relays. IEEE Trans Signal Processing 2010;58(3):1875−88.

[14] Modi B, Annamalai A, Olabiyi O, Palat RC. Ergodic capacity analysis of cooperative amplify-and-forward relay networks over Rice and Nakagami fading channels. International Journal of Wireless & Mobile Networks 2012;4(1):97−116.

[15] Modi B, Olabiyi O, Annamalai A, Palat RC. Ergodic capacity analysis of cooperative amplify-and-forward relay networks over generalized fading channels with limited channel side-information. Wiley Journal on Wireless Communications and Mobile Computing; Published Online: August 1, 2013; DOI: 10.1002/wcm.2407.

[16] Olabiyi O, Annamalai A. ASER analysis of cooperative non-regenerative relay systems over generalized fading channels. Proc 20th International Conference on Computer Communication and Networks; 2011 Aug; Maui. Also appeared in the International Journal of Computer Networks & Communications. 2012;4(6):1−20.

[17] Olabiyi O, Annamalai A. Efficient symbol error rate analysis of cooperative non-regenerative relay systems over generalized fading channels. International Journal of Wireless & Mobile Networks 2012;4(1):1−20.

[18] Hamdi KA. Capacity of MRC on correlated Rician fading channels. IEEE Trans Communications 2008;56:708−11.

[19] Gradshteyn I, Ryzhik I. Table of integrals, series and products. Academic Press; 1995.

[20] Renzo M, Graziosi F, Santucci F. Channel capacity over generalized fading channels: A novel MGF-based approach for performance analysis and design of wireless communication systems. IEEE Trans Veh Technol 2010;59(1):127−49.

[21] Simon MK, Alouini MS. Digital communication over fading channels. 2nd ed. John Wiley & Sons; 2005.

[22] Anghel P, Kaveh M. Exact symbol error probability of a cooperative network in a Rayleigh-fading environment. IEEE Trans Wireless Communications 2004;3(9):1416−21.

[23] Di Renzo M, Graziosi F, Santucci F. A unified framework for performance analysis of CSI-assisted cooperative communications over fading channels. IEEE Trans Communications 2009;57:2551−7.

[24] Yacoub MD. The κ-μ distribution and the η-μ distribution. IEEE Antennas Propag Mag 2007;49:68−81.

[25] Annamalai A, Adebola E, Olabiyi O. Further Results on the Dirac delta approximation and the moment generating function techniques for error probability analysis in fading channels. International Journal of Computer Networks & Communications 2013;5:1.

[26] Zhang P, Yuan J, Chen J, Wang J, Yang J. Analyzing amplify-and-forward and decode-and-forward cooperative strategies in Wyner's channel model. Proc IEEE Wireless Communications and Networking Conference; 2009.

Algebraic Approaches to a Network-Type Private Information Retrieval

15

Vladimir B. Balakirsky[†] and Anahit R. Ghazaryan

State University of Aerospace Instrumentation, St-Petersburg, Russia

INFORMATION IN THIS CHAPTER

- Information retrieval
- Privacy
- How to form the query
- How to encode the database
- How to decode replicas

INTRODUCTION

Private information retrieval schemes are cryptographic protocols designed to safeguard the privacy of database users. They allow clients to retrieve records from public databases while completely hiding the identity of the retrieved records from database owners [1]. One of the earliest references for problems of this sort belongs to Rivest et al. [2]. Formalization of the private retrieval problem, which was studied by many authors, belongs to Chor et al. [3] and a number of surveys are available on the Internet. If the database is owned by one server and information-theoretic privacy is required, then there is no better solution than the trivial one when the server transmits the whole database to the user. However, if constraints on the privacy of the retrieval are relaxed, there are algorithms based on the use of computationally hard problems that have to be solved by the server to discover the data and the use of the so-called one-way hash functions. An implementation of these algorithms is usually time-consuming for the database user. Solutions to the multi-server private information retrieval problem are based on the encoding of the content of the database, as shown by Chor et al. [3]. In particular, Woodruff-Yekhanin [4] proposed solutions that are based on algebraic encoding.

We use the ideas of the Woodruff-Yekhanin scheme and present a simple algebraic solution to a variant of the multi-server private information retrieval problem. Moreover, the database

[†]Deceased

user in our scheme can be split between the user-sender, who sends the query to the servers, and the user-receiver, who decodes the retrieved bit. This network-type organization of information retrieval brings additional possibilities. As the server, which makes the decision associated with the corresponding bits, does not emit energy, its location cannot be discovered. Furthermore, the query is randomized by the user-sender, but parameters of the randomization should not be delivered to the user-receiver, which decodes the retrieved bit without knowledge of the query.

The chapter is organized as follows: In the first section we describe the data processing scheme and discuss its constraints and complexities. In the second section we present algorithmic aspects of the approach, while we discuss their algebraic background in the third sections. Possible extensions of the setup are briefly discussed in the concluding section.

The data processing scheme and statement of the problem
Description of the data processing scheme

We will consider the data processing scheme containing the user-sender, the user-receiver, and L servers. Each server has a binary vector, $x = (x_0, ..., x_{K-1}) \in \{0, 1\}^K$, which is interpreted as content of the database. The user-sender chooses an index, $i \in \{0, ..., K-1\}$. The user-receiver wants to know the bit x_i, while servers have to be ignorant about the index i.

We fix an integer m and assume that $L = \phi(m)$, where $\phi(m) \approx (2^m - 2)/m$ is the function specified later, which is determined by the structure of the m-ary extension of the Galois field $GF(2)$, and design a scheme parameterized by the integers w, n, chosen in such a way that $w = L - 1$, $n = 2w$ and $n!/(w!(n - w)!) = K$. The user-sender sends a query $(S_1, ..., S_L)$ formed as a list of L binary $m \times n$ matrices, where the matrix S_l is constructed by application of a deterministic function of i and a randomly chosen binary matrix $C \in \{0, 1\}^{m \times n}$, that is, $S_l = S_l(i, C) \in \{0, 1\}^{m \times n}$ for all $l = 1, ...L$. The l-th server computes the replica, expressed as a binary column vector r_l of length m by application of a deterministic function of the query and the vector x, that is, $r_l = r_l(x, S_l) \in \{0, 1\}^{m \times 1}$ for all $l = 1, ..., L$. The scheme is constructed in such a way that the value of i and the binary vector of length mL, obtained by the concatenation of replicas $r_1, ..., r_L$, allows the user-receiver to decode bit x_i.

Constraints on parameters and complexities of the data processing scheme

The communication complexity of the scheme is defined as the total number of bits transmitted over the channels user-sender → servers → user-receiver. As mLn and mL are lengths of the query and the replicas, the communication complexity can be expressed as Comp $= mLn + mL$. We are also interested in the quantity $c = \text{Comp}/(\log K + 1)$, since $\log K$ is the number of bits needed to specify the index i when no constraints on privacy of the retrieval are included. The computational complexity is understood as the total number of arithmetic operations performed by the user-sender, the servers, and the user-receiver. As it will follow from the description of the scheme, all operations are reduced to multiplications of binary matrices and their number is linear in n.

The approximation $n!/(n/2!)^2 \approx 2^n$ and the approximation to the function $\phi(m)$, given above, bring $n, L, w \approx \log K$ and $m \approx \log \log K$. Therefore, Comp $\approx c^* \log K$, where $c^* = (\log \log K) \log K$. The numerical illustration of the line

$$m \to (L, n) \to \lg K \to c$$

where we do not use the approximations, is as follows:

$4 \to (3,4) \to 0.8 \to 17$
$6 \to (9,16) \to 4.1 \to 63$
$8 \to (30,58) \to 16.5 \to 63$
$10 \to (99,196) \to 57.8 \to 1011$

Algorithmic description of the solution
The *(n, w)*-Encoding of indices and polynomial representation of the database

We assume that $n!/(w!(n-w)!) = K$ and introduce J as the set of column-vectors whose components, denoted by $j_0, ..., j_{w-1}$, belong to the set $\{0, ..., n-1\}$ and $j_{\tau+1} \geq j_\tau + 1$ for all $\tau = 0, ..., w-2$. Let us construct a one-to-one mapping $k \in \{0, ..., K-1\} \to j(k) \in J$, which will be referred to as the (n, w)-encoding. This can be done by the following lexicographic algorithm: (1) Set $j_\tau(0) = \tau$ for all $\tau = 0, ..., w-1$, output the vector $j(0)$ having components $0, ..., w-1$ and the set $J(0) = \{0, ..., w-1\}$. (2). For all $k = 1, ..., K-1$, find the minimum index $\lambda \in \{0, ..., w-1\}$ such that $j_{\lambda+1}(k-1) > j_\lambda(k-1) + 1$, where $j_w(k-1) = n-2$, and set $j_\tau(k)$ equal to τ, $j_\tau(k-1) + 1$, $j_\tau(k-1)$ if $\tau < \lambda, \tau = \lambda, \tau > \lambda$, respectively. Output the vector $j(k)$ having components $j_0(k), ..., j_{w-1}(k)$ and the set $J(k) = \{j_0(k), ..., j_{w-1}(k)\}$.

Let $GF(2^m)$ be the m-ary extension of the Galois field $GF(2)$ constructed using a primitive polynomial $g(\gamma)$ of degree m and let $\alpha \in GF(2^m)$ be the primitive element defined as the root of the polynomial $g(\gamma)$; that is, $g(\alpha) = 0$. As each element $\beta \in GF(2^m)$ can be uniquely expressed by a linear combination of the elements $\alpha^0, ..., \alpha^{m-1}$, components $\text{bin}_0(\beta), ..., \text{bin}_{m-1}(\beta) \in \{0, 1\}$ of the column-vector $\text{bin}(\beta)$, which specifies the binary representation of the element β, are determined by the equality

$$\beta = \text{bin}_0(\beta)\alpha^0 + ... + \text{bin}_{m-1}(\beta)\alpha^{m-1}$$

Moreover, $b = \text{bin}(\beta)$ implies $\beta = \text{bin}^{-1}(b)$ and vice versa for all $\beta \in GF(2^m)$ and $b \in \{0, 1\}^m$. For any vector $Z = (z_0, ..., z_{n-1}) \in GF(2^m)$, let

$$F_x(Z) = x_k \, \text{bin}(f(Z|0)) + ... + x_{n-1}\text{bin}(f(Z|x_{n-1}))$$

where $f(Z|k) = \prod_{j \in J(k)} z_j$.

Encoding the algorithm

Let the encoding algorithm be organized on the basis of L binary matrices $A_1, ..., A_L \in \{0, 1\}^{m \times m}$. We also introduce the $m \times n$ binary matrix $U(i) = (u_0(i), ..., u_{n-1}(i))$, where the vector $u_j(i) \in \{0, 1\}^{m \times 1}$ is constructed in such a way that the 0-th component is equal to 1 or 0, if $j \in J(i)$ or

$j \notin J(i)$, respectively. All other components of the vector $u_j(i)$ are 0s. Let the encoding be defined as L dependent transformations

$$S_l(i, C) = U(i) \oplus A_l C$$

for all $l = 1, ..., L$.

Constructing the *l*-th replica to the query

Let the l-th server run the following algorithm: (1) Represent the matrix S_l by the vector $Z_l = (\mathrm{bin}^{-1}(s_{l,0}), ..., \mathrm{bin}^{-1}(s_{l,n-1})) \in GF(2^m)$. (2) Compute $R_l = F_x(Z_l)$ and transmit the binary column-vector $r_l = \mathrm{bin}(R_l) \in \{0, 1\}^{m \times 1}$ to the user-receiver.

Decoding of the bit x_i by the user-receiver

The user-receiver uses the received replicas and the binary matrix $D \in \{0, 1\}^{m \times mL}$, determined by the primitive polynomial $g(\gamma)$, and runs the following algorithm: (1) Construct the binary column-vector r of length mL by concatenating column-vectors $r_1, ..., r_L$. (2) Compute the binary column-vector $Dr \in \{0, 1\}^{m \times 1}$ and output the decision $x_i = 0$ if Dr is the all-zero vector and $x_i = 1$ otherwise.

Implementing the data processing algorithms

The testing program contains the subroutines:

Construct_query: $(i, C) \rightarrow (S_1, ..., S_L)$
Form_replica: $(x, S_l) \rightarrow r_l$
Decode_bit: $(i, r_1, ..., r_L) \rightarrow x_i$

and it should be organized according to a certain scenario of generating the index i, the matrix C, and the vector x. The subroutines above use the matrices $A_1, ..., A_L$ and D determined by the primitive polynomial $g(\gamma)$.

In the following numerical illustration, we assume that $m = 4$ and use the hex-decimal notation for binary vectors.

Suppose that $g(\gamma) = 1 + \gamma + \gamma^4$ is the primitive polynomial, which is used to construct $GF(2^4)$. Then the elements of $GF(2^4)$ are determined by the vector

$$(\mathrm{bin}(0), \mathrm{bin}(\alpha^0), \mathrm{bin}(\alpha^1), ..., \mathrm{bin}(\alpha^{14}) = (0, 8, 4, 2, 1, C, 6, 3, D, A, 5, E, 7, F, B, 9)$$

We set $(L, w, n) = (3, 2, 4)$ and consider the retrieval of a bit in the binary vector x of length $K = 4!/(2!)^2 = 6$. If the (4,2)-encoding is organized according to the lexicographic algorithm, then

$$(J(0), ..., J(5)) = (\{0, 1\}, \{0, 2\}, \{0, 3\}, \{1, 2\}, \{1, 3\}, \{2, 3\})$$

In particular, if $i = 2$, then $J(i) = \{1, 2\}$ and $U(i) = (0,8,8,0)$. The columns of the $m \times m$ matrices A_1, A_2, A_3 are defined as binary representations of four powers of the elements $\alpha^1, \alpha^3, \alpha^7$, that is,

$$A_1 = (4, 2, 1, C), \quad A_2 = (1, 3, 5, F), \quad A_3 = (D, 9, 3, B)$$

Suppose that $C = (5, 3, 9, 4)$. Then

$$A_1C = (E, 3, 8, 2), \quad A_2C = (C, 6, E, 3), \quad A_3C = (2, A, 6, 9)$$

and

$$S_1 = U(2) \oplus A_1C = (E, B, 0, 2), \quad S_2 = U(2) \oplus A_2C = (C, E, 6, 3)$$

The 4×4 matrices S_1, S_2, S_3 are transmitted to the first server, the second server, and the third server, respectively. Having received the matrix S_l, the l-th server forms the vector $Z_l = \text{bin}^{-1}(S_l)$, $l = 1, 2, 3$. Thus,

$$Z_1 = (\alpha^{10}, \alpha^{13}, 0, \alpha^2), \quad Z_2 = (\alpha^4, \alpha^{10}, \alpha^5, \alpha^6), \quad Z_3 = (\alpha^2, \alpha^2, \alpha^{10}, \alpha^{14})$$

Let $x = 10001$. As $J(0) = \{0, 1\}$, $J(5) = \{2, 3\}$, we write $F_x(Z) = z_0 z_1 + z_2 z_3$. Therefore,

$$R_1 = \alpha^{10} \cdot \alpha^{13} + 0 \cdot \alpha^2 = \alpha^8 + 0 \qquad r_1 = \text{bin}(R_1) = \text{bin}(\alpha^8) \oplus \text{bin}(0) = A$$

$$R_2 = \alpha^4 \cdot \alpha^{10} + \alpha^5 \cdot \alpha^6 = \alpha^{14} + \alpha^{11} \qquad r_2 = \text{bin}(R_2) = \text{bin}(\alpha^{14}) \oplus \text{bin}(\alpha^{11}) = E$$

$$R_3 = \alpha^2 \cdot \alpha^2 + \alpha^{10} \cdot \alpha^{14} = \alpha^4 + \alpha^9 \qquad r_3 = \text{bin}(\alpha^4) \oplus \text{bin}(\alpha^9) = 9$$

The l-th server sends the vector r_l to the user-receiver, who concatenates the received vectors r_1, r_2, r_3 and constructs the column-vector $r \in \{0, 1\}^{12 \times 1}$. The product of the matrix

$$D = (8, 4, 2, 1, A, 3, D, 1, A, B, 7, 4)$$

by the vector r is equal to the all-zero column-vector of length 4. Therefore, the user-receiver decides that $x_2 = 0$. Rules for constructing the decoding matrix D will be specified in the next section.

Algebraic description of the solution
Cyclotomic classes of $GF(2^m)$ having the maximum size m

Let $h = (h_1, ..., h_{\phi(m)})$ be the vector of the maximum length $\phi(m)$ whose components $h_1 < ... < h_{\phi(m)}$ belong to the set $\{1, ..., 2^m - 2\}$ and satisfy the condition $|Cl(h_l)| = m$, where $Cl_l = \cup_{d=0}^{m-1}(2^d h_l, \text{mod}(2^m - 1))$. Under additional constraint that h_l is the minimum element of the set $Cl_l(h_l)$, the vector h is uniquely determined, and it is known as the vector specifying leaders of cyclotomic classes or chords of size m. We also denote $\alpha_l = \alpha^{h_l}$ and $g_l(\gamma) = \prod_{e \in Cl(h_l)}(\gamma + \alpha^e)$ for all $l = 1, ..., L = \phi(m)$. Notice that all coefficients of the polynomial $g_l(\gamma)$ belong to $GF(2)$. For example, if $m = 4$, then $L = 3$, $h = (1, 3, 7)$ and $(\alpha_1, \alpha_2, \alpha_3) = (\alpha^1, \alpha^3, \alpha^7)$.

Assigning the encoding matrices

For all $\gamma \in GF(2^m)$, let us introduce the matrix $A(\gamma) = (\gamma^1, ..., \gamma^m)$ and let $A_l = \text{bin} A(\alpha^l)$ for all $l = 1, ..., L$. For example, if $m = 4$ and $g(\gamma) = 1 + \gamma + \gamma^4$, then

$$(A_1, A_2, A_3) = (\text{bin}(A(\alpha^1)), \ \text{bin}(A(\alpha^3)), \ \text{bin}(A(\alpha^7)))$$

For a binary column-vector c_j having components $c_{0,j}, ..., c_{m-1,j}$, let

$$s_j(\gamma) = u_j(i) + A(\gamma)c_j = u_j(i) + c_{0,j}\gamma^1 + ... + c_{m-1,j}\gamma^{d+1}$$

where $u_j(i) = \alpha^0$ if $j \in J(i)$ and $u_j(i) = 0$ if $j \notin J(i)$. One can easily see that $s_{l,j} = \text{bin}(s_j(\alpha_l))$, $l = 1, ..., L$, are binary representations of the values of the polynomial $s_j(\gamma)$ at $\gamma = \alpha^1, ..., \alpha^L$. We also denote $s(\gamma) = (s_0(\gamma), ..., s_{n-1}(\gamma))$.

Representing the algorithm for constructing the bit x_i as finding the solution to the two-hypotheses testing problem

Notice that $r(\gamma) = \Psi_x(s(\gamma)|i)$ if $x_i = 0$ and $r(\gamma) = \Psi_x(s(\gamma)|i) + f(s(\gamma)|i)$ if $x_1 = 1$, where $\Psi_x(s(\gamma)|i) = \sum_{k \neq i: x_k=1} f(s(\gamma)|k)$ is the polynomial of degree at most mw having the 0-th coefficient equal to 0. The 0-th coefficient of the polynomial $f(s(\gamma)|i)$ is equal to 1. We force the user-receiver to solve the problem of constructing the bit x on the basis of the values $r(\alpha_1), ..., r(\alpha_L)$, which is formulated as finding the solution to the two-hypotheses testing problem: $\text{Hyp}_0: x_i = 0; \text{Hyp}_0': x_i \neq 0$. The scheme should be designed in such a way that this problem has a unique solution in the following sense. Suppose that the system consisting of L equations $\psi(\alpha_1) = r(\alpha_1), ..., \psi(\alpha_L) = r(\alpha_L)$ uniquely specifies the 0-th coefficient of the polynomial $\psi(\gamma)$ of degree at most mw. The user-receiver outputs this coefficient as bit x_i.

Let us extend the notation of the previous subsection and denote

$$A^{(w)}(\gamma) = (\gamma^1, ..., \gamma^{mw}) \in (GF(2^m))^{mw}$$

$$\text{bin}(A^{(w)}(\gamma)) = (\text{bin}(\gamma^1), ..., \text{bin}(\gamma^{mw})) \in \{0, 1\}^{m \times mw}$$

We also introduce θ as the vector of length w whose components are different and belong to the set $\{1, ..., L\}$. As $w = L - 1$, the possible vector is $\theta = (2, ..., L)$. Let $A_\theta \in (GF(2^m))^{w \times mw}$ and $\text{bin}(A_\theta) \in \{0, 1\}^{mw \times mw}$ be the matrices constructed by the row concatenation of the matrices $A^{(w)}(\alpha_{\theta_1}), ..., A^{(w)}(\alpha_{\theta_w})$ and $\text{bin}(A^{(w)}(\alpha_{\theta_1})), ..., \text{bin}((A^{(w)}(\alpha_{\theta_w}))$, respectively.

Consider the system of linear equations $A_\theta^{(w)} \psi = r_\theta$ or, equivalently, the system

$$\text{bin}(A_\theta^{(w)}) \, \psi = \text{bin}(r_\theta)$$

where $\psi \in \{0, 1\}^{mw}$ is a binary column-vector of length mw. These systems have a unique solution for ψ or, equivalently, the $mw \times mw$ matrix $\text{bin}(A_\theta^{(w)})$ has rank mw, because there does not exist a polynomial of γ having the degree at most mw and the 0-th coefficient equal to 0, which is divisible by the product $g_{\theta_1}(\gamma)...g_{\theta_w}(\gamma)$. Let us denote the solution by ψ_θ and let $j^* = \{1, ..., L\}\setminus\{\theta_1, ..., \theta_w\}$. Construct the vector $\text{bin}(A^{(w)}(\alpha_{j^*}))\psi_\theta$ and notice that

$$\text{bin}(A^{(w)}(\alpha_{j^*}))\psi_\theta = \text{bin}(r(\alpha_{j^*})) \Rightarrow x_i = 0$$

$$\text{bin}(A^{(w)}(\alpha_{j^*}))\psi_\theta = \text{bin}(r(\alpha_{j^*})) \Rightarrow x_i \neq 0$$

Therefore, if $\theta = (2, ..., L)$, then the matrix D, which is used by the user-receiver, can be constructed by the concatenation of the binary identity $m \times m$ matrix and the product of the matrix bin $(A^{(w)}(\alpha_1))$ by the inverse matrix for the matrix $\text{bin}(A_{(2,...,L)}^{(w)})$.

CONCLUSION

Implementation of the proposed simple data processing scheme, where all operations are reduced to matrix multiplications, can meet practical difficulties, as we require many servers to have the identical database, and all servers should simultaneously carry out any update of the database. However, our algorithms are prepared for extensions and used in the situation when the setup with the user-sender, L servers, and the user-receiver is modified. Here we mention a few extensions:

1. There is a one-server scheme and the server, having received the query, forms the replicas from which he knows the bit transmitted to the user-receiver (actually, the decoding can be assigned to the server in this case). In other words, there is some information leakage in the retrieval. However, if the database contains approximately equal numbers of 0s and 1s, then the knowledge that the index i belongs to the subset of cardinality $\approx K/2$ does not seem to be essential. The problem is to find the encoding algorithm, which does not allow further reduction of the ambiguity about the index i by analyzing the query. Algebraic approaches, described for the L-server scheme, can be used to attack this problem.
2. Some of replicas in the scheme with L servers can be incorrect. The case appears when some servers do not update the content of the database. This situation leads to the problem of decoding bit x_i when at least L' replicas are generated by servers having identical databases.
3. The user-receiver wants to know whether a certain fragment of the database coincides with the fixed vector or not. In particular, the user-receiver can be interested in the solution to the problem when the fixed vector is the all-zero vector. A more efficient solution than asking the server(s) about all bits of the fragment can be found in this case.

We believe that the investigations in the directions above should start with the understanding of the approaches for the setup that is presented in this chapter.

Summary

In this chapter, we present simple algebraic solutions to some multi-server private information retrieval problems. Approaches are general, and they are useful for the development of other private information retrieval schemes.

References

[1] Yekhanin S. A locally decodable codes and private information retrieval schemes. Foundations and Trends in Theoretical Computer Science 2011;7(1):1−117.
[2] Rivest R, Adelman L, Dertouzos M. On database and privacy homomorphism. Foundations of Secure Computation 1978:168−77.

[3] Chor B, Goldreich O, Kushilevitz E, Sudan M. Private information retrieval. Proceedings of the thirty sixth Annual Foundations of Computer Science; 1995. p. 41–50. Also in Journal of the ACM 1998;45: 965–81.

[4] Woodruff D, Yekhanin S. A geometric approach to information-theoretic private retrieval. Proceedings of the twentieth IEEE Computational Complexity Conference 2005:275–84.

Using Event Reasoning for Trajectory Tracking

16

Jianbing Ma
Bournemouth University, Bournemouth, UK

INFORMATION IN THIS CHAPTER

- Event model
- Scenario adapts
- Event functions and inference rules
- Experiments

INTRODUCTION

During the past decade, there has been massive investment in CCTV technology in the UK. Currently, there are approximately four million CCTV cameras operationally deployed. Despite this, the impact on anti-social and criminal behavior has been minimal. Although most incidents, also called events, are captured on video, there is no response because very little of the data is actively analyzed in real time. Consequently, CCTV operates in a passive mode, simply collecting enormous volumes of video data. For this technology to be effective, CCTV has to become active by alerting security analysts in real time so that they can stop or prevent the undesirable behavior. Such a quantum leap in capability will greatly increase the likelihood of offenders being caught, a major factor in crime prevention.

To ensure in-time reaction for intelligent surveillance [1,2], one fundamental task to utilize CCTV videos is to track the trajectory of any subject of interest (e.g., [3,4], etc.). This trajectory knowledge is very powerful as an input to future reasoning, but even on its own it would allow us to augment traditional CCTV monitoring displays. For example, rather than just present a human operator with a live CCTV image of a subject, we could also augment the live feed with a series of key timestamped frames taken at other points in the facility.

Example

Consider a subject with the intent of leaving a suitcase with an explosive device in a crowded airport space and leaving before detonation. The CCTV operator is shown a live video feed of the subject exiting the airport through a recognized exit at time T. However, using our trajectory tracking, the live feed can also be supplemented with earlier footage of the subject entering the airport at time T - 4 minutes. Conceivably, the operator might also be shown a representation or map of the route taken by the subject through the space. Crucially, by comparing the images, the operator observes that the subject entered with a suitcase (from the archived frames) but left with no baggage (from the live frames). This could warrant an alert.

This example shows that the short-term historical details are extremely valuable to the human operator by putting a live feed into a wider context.

Key to the success of subject tracking is subject reacquisition [5]. That is, when we have detected a subject, we should be able to know who it is by retrieving from our subject database on past records. Currently, common approaches for subject acquisition are face recognition and clothing color signature classification, etc.

We should notice that in some testing scenarios, these methods can behave well, but they are facing major challenges in real application.

Face recognition can give a pretty precise result for cooperative subjects (that is, a subject looks at the camera for a few seconds with the face clearly exposed) within a small subject database. When the size of the subject database increases, there will be a considerable decline in the precision of face recognition, since the possibility that subjects with similar face features increases. This problem can be alleviated by improving face recognition algorithms. Clothing color signature method only applies when we assume that the subject does not change clothes while in the environment. Most importantly, pure video analytic approaches can be hard to apply or the results can be not enough to obtain a clear trajectory when there are not enough cameras or when some cameras have been tampered with.

While video analytics alone are not sufficient to obtain a clear trajectory, we are aware that there is usually more information that can be used in tracking, for example, (identity) card reading results, topological information about the environment, etc. These kinds of dynamic information (e.g., video analytics, card reading results, etc.) and background information (e.g., it takes a person 30 seconds to walk from location A to location B) can be combined by event reasoning [6,7] techniques.

The aim of this chapter is to successfully determine a subject's passage through a series of monitored spaces, given the following scenario. Some spaces (called zones) have sensors capable of making observations about the physical location of a subject at a given time and observing key appearance signatures of a subject at a given time (facial features, clothing color, etc.). Some zones have no sensors. We have domain knowledge regarding the topology of connecting zones and we have expected time-of-flight information for subjects moving between zones. Access to some zones is protected by access control hardware. It should be noticed that this chapter focuses more on augmenting trajectory information by using background information than on computing accurate paths by some trajectory tracking efforts, such as in [8,9], etc.

To this end, in this chapter, event reasoning techniques are introduced to integrate information from various sources, for example, video analytics, card reading results, domain knowledge, etc.

The main idea is to use inference rules to infer the passage of a subject when there is not enough dynamic information. Another focus of this chapter is how to obtain a precise identity of a subject.[1] That is, when a subject is detected by a camera, how to classify it as one of a subject already in our database, since a camera can only detect a subject, not recognize a subject. Here the detector is a combination of the camera and the video analytics, while the recognition results follow the reasoning process.

In the literature, event reasoning systems have been proposed for dealing with event composition in many areas, such as those discussed in [10–13], etc. This chapter extends frameworks proposed in [10,11] to allow event functions. We also have simplification settings with respect to the frameworks in [10,11], especially for rule definitions. Subsequently, in the "Event Model" section, we introduce our event model. In the section titled "Scenario Adapts," we adapt event settings with respect to the application practice. "Event Functions and Inference Rules" shows event functions and rules used in the application. Experimental results are provided in the "Experiments" section. In the summary, we conclude the chapter.

Event model

In this section, we introduce an event reasoning model that is a variant of the event reasoning framework proposed in [10,11] to adapt our scenario.

Event definition

In this chapter, we distinguish two kinds of events: *observable events* and *domain events*. An observable event is an occurrence that is instantaneous (event duration is 0, i.e., takes place at a specific point in time) and atomic (it happens or not). The atomic requirement does not exclude uncertainty. For instance, when there is a person entering a building who can be Bob or Chris based on face profiling, then whether it is Bob or Chris who enters the building is an example of uncertainty. But Bob (resp. Chris) is entering the building is an atomic event that either occurs completely or does not occur at all. To represent uncertainty encountered during event detection, in the following, we distinguish an observation (with uncertainty) from possible events associated with the observation (because of the uncertainty). This can be illustrated by the above example: an observation is that a person is entering the building and the possible observable events are Bob is entering the building and Chris is entering the building. An observation says that something happened, but the subject being observed is not completely certain yet, so we have multiple observable events listing who that subject might be.

This event definition is particularly suitable for surveillance, where the objects being monitored are not complete clear to the observer.

---

[1]It is called "subject reacquisition" in the video analysis community. In this chapter, subject determined by inference is somehow beyond this meaning. But for simplicity, we will still call it subject reacquisition.

Event representation

A concrete event definition in this special application is defined as follows:

occT:	the point in time that an event occurred
location:	the 3-D location that an event occurred
pID:	the classified person ID of that event
iID:	the information source ID that reports that event

This format is specially designed for our subject tracking scanario. Here a subject is the human entity detected in the event. We don't know who it is, so we should determine the subject's identity by *subject reacquisition* (SR). However, SR techniques usually cannot provide us precise classification results; instead, it yields several possible candidates. As in this application, our dynamic information comes from either face recognition, clothing color recognition, pure localization, or card reading; iID hence can be one of the following values: *{face, color, loc, card}*. In addition, we will introduce a kind of inferred event, which also follows this definition, but its iID is *infer*.

Formally, we define an event e as: $e = (occT, location, pID, iID)$.

Event cluster

Any two events with the same occT location, and iID are from the set of possible events related to a single observation. For example, $e1 = (20{:}01{:}00, 13.5/12.5/0, Bob, face)$ and $e2 = (20{:}01{:}00, 13{:}5/12.5/0, Chris, face)$ are two possible events from a single observation. To represent these, *event cluster*, denoted as *EC*, is introduced, which is a set of events that have the same occT, location, and iID, but with different pID values. Events e1 and e2 above form an event cluster for the observed fact that a subject is entering the building at 20:01:00 at location 13.5/12.5/0.

An event is always attached to a probability, and we use p(e) to denote the probability of e.

For an event e in event cluster EC, we use notations like e.occT to denote the time of occurrence of e, etc. By abuse of notations, we also write EC.occT to denote the time of occurrence of any event in EC, etc., since all the events in EC share the same values on these attributes.

Probabilities for events in an event cluster EC should satisfy the normalization condition: $\forall_{e \in EC} p(e) = 1$. That is, EC does contain an event that really occurred. For example, for the two events, e1 and e2, introduced above, a possible probability function p can be $p(e1) = 0.85$ and $p(e2) = 0.15$.

An event cluster hence gives a full description of an observed fact with uncertainty from the perspective of one source.

Event functions

Event functions are functions applied on events to get required results. For instance, a simple but useful function EC(e, e′) is a boolean function that determines whether two events e and e′ are in the same event cluster.

$$EC(e, e') = (e.occT = e'.occT \wedge e.location = e'.location \wedge e.iID = e'.iID)$$

Some event functions are generic to any application (e.g., EC(e, e′)) while some event functions may only be proposed for special applications. To our knowledge, the notion of event functions has not been proposed by any event reasoning frameworks in the literature.

Event inference

Event inference is expressed as a set of rules that are used to represent the relationships between events. An inference rule R is formatted as:

If cond1
and cond2
and cond3
...
then action1

Conditions can be evaluated by known information of current events and other assertions about the environment/situation. If all conditions are evaluated as true, then action1 can be taken, which usually sets values for some events or raises alerts, etc.. An example of the rule is as follows:

If e1.occT = e2.occT
and e1.location $\neq$ e2.location
and e1.pID = e2.pID
and e1.iID = infer
and e2.iID = infer,
then RaiseAlert

The conditions of this rule are that, at the same time but in different locations, there are two inferred events indicating that two subjects are the same person. Obviously this is impossible, so if all these conditions hold, an alert should be raised to the monitor.

Scenario adapts

In this section, we introduce the details of dynamic events generated in this scenario, including face or clothing color recognition events, localization events, and card reading events.

Video sensor observations generate observation events, and in the application these observations have the following primary attributes:

- A timestamp
- A face signature
- A color signature
- A localization (in the image plane)

Face recognition, color histogram matching, and localization algorithms generate the following secondary attributes:

- An n-best list of face matches
- An n-best list of color histogram matches
- A localization (in the real world)

Here, an n-best list of matches means that a subject is being classified as several candidate persons, with associated probabilities derived by video analytic algorithms (namely face recognition algorithm, color matching algorithm, etc.). For instance, a subject can be classified as: Bob with probability 0.65, Chris with probability 0.2, and David with probability 0.15. Note that either an n-best list of face matches or an n-best list of color matches generates an event cluster.

Overall, we find that these resulted events by algorithms can be described by our event definition given previously. That is, we have occT , location (real world), pID (each taken from the n-best lists), and iID (face or color), which perfectly matches our event definition. In addition, these events are attached with probabilities.

In practice, for the sake of computational efficiency, we cannot afford always recording facial or clothing color information and applying corresponding algorithms. Hence, most of the time, we only apply localization sensing that records only the location of a subject. The ratio of facial/color recognition events and pure localization events are about 1:5 to 1:10, etc. A localization event has the following primary attributes:

- A timestamp
- A localization (in the image plane)

A localization event can generate the following secondary attributes:

- An n-best list of matches (using the closest facial or clothing matching results)
- A localization (in the real world)

Since the ratio of facial/color recognition events and pure localization events are about 1:5 to 1:10, etc., we can always find a nearest facial/color recognition event cluster with the same subject ID. As there can be two closest event clusters (i.e., one for face recognition and the other for clothing color), we select the event cluster that contains a greatest probability. After obtaining the closest n-best matches, the localization events form an event cluster. For example, if the two nearest event clusters are: $e1 = (20{:}01{:}00, 13.5/12.5/0,$ Bob, face) with probability 0.85, $e2 = (20{:}01{:}00, 13.5/12.5/0,$ Chris, face) with probability 0.15, and $e'1 = (20{:}01{:}00, 13.5/12.5/0,$ Bob, color) with probability 0.55, $e'2 = (20{:}01{:}00, 13.5/12.5/0,$ David, color) with probability 0.45, then the localization event cluster will take the face matching results as its n-best list of matches for the events in the event cluster.

Access control events, or card reading events, have the following attributes:

- A timestamp
- A unique card identity reference
- A location (of the access control panel)

Secondary attributes of this event are:

- A user identity (name of the card owner)
- Other employee details; however, we should ignore these in this case for clarity.

For a card reading event, we will set its subject ID sID to a special value, ANY, which matches any subject ID. Therefore, we also have the required occT, location, sID, pID, and iID values. The probability is 1.

Environment topological information, or more generally, background information (also called domain knowledge), is seen mostly about the expected time-of-flight information for subjects moving between zones; that is, the time a person took to go from one zone to another. For instance, a person cannot appear within zone A and then appear in zone B within 10 seconds. But if the 10 s is changed to 10–20 seconds, then it could be possible; if the time-of-flight is 20–40 seconds, it is highly possible; if the time is greater than 40 seconds, it is possible, etc. Empirical probabilities for such information can be found by tests. However, we will use simple settings that in some special range of time-of-flight, the certainty is 1 instead of probabilities.

Assumptions

Our ultimate objective aims at complicated environments. However, initially, we will begin with simple scenarios with simplification assumptions. Complexity can be incrementally increased. This process clarifies our objective. Some initial assumptions are listed below:

- Only one subject shall be considered (no occlusions, etc.).
- The subject will be cooperative at key points (i.e., look into the camera for a few frames).
- The subject will not change clothing for the duration of the scenarios.
- The subject swiping the access card can be assumed to be the registered owner of the card (i.e., not stolen or cloned).

Event functions and inference rules

In this section, we introduce the event functions and inference rules used in this application.

First, we define some useful event functions. The next event with the same classified person is defined as:

$$Next(e) = e1 : e1.iID \neq infer \wedge e.occT < e1.occT \wedge e.pID = e1.pID \wedge /\exists e2:$$

$$e.occT < e2.occT < e1.occT \wedge e.pID = e2.pID.$$

Here recall that "infer" is the iID of an inferred event.

Given the Next(e) function, similarly, a Prev(e) function that obtains the very previous event of e with the same subject can be defined as:

$$Prev(e) = e1 : e = Next(e1).$$

Note that Prev(e) only defines for dynamic events. It is not defined for inferred events.

We also define a local function Neighbor(e, e′) to judge whether e and e′ are neighbors with respect to space and time.

$$Neighbor(e, e') = (abs(e.occT - e'.occT) < 0.1 \ sec \wedge dis(e.location, e'.location) < 0:5m$$

Here, *dis* is a measure of distance between two locations.

The following function judges whether e is the very last event that appears on ground floor. That is, any event exactly next to it is not on ground floor.

$$GroundLast(e) = (e.location.z = GROUNDFloor \wedge /\exists e'(e' = next(e) \wedge e'.location.z = GROUNDFloor))$$

Here GROUNDFloor is a predefined application constant. Note that this function is a special one for this application.

Another important event function is to create an event.

$$Create(occT, location, pID, iID, x) = (e : e = (occT, location, pID, iID) \ and \ p(e) = x)$$

Note that only inferred events can be created. Based on the dynamic (video, card information, etc.) information and background information, we can set up rules to infer which person it is.

First, we list rules for inferring a *KnownSubjectAcquired* event, which is a special kind of event used for indicating the most possible candidate of a subject. The iID value of a KnownSubjectAcquired event $e = (occT, location, pID, iID)$ is set to *infer*. Also note KnownSubjectAcquired events are not attached to an event cluster.

Rules for inferring KnownSubjectAcquired events are listed as follows:

- *If e1.iID $\neq$ infer and p(e1) > 0.5 and $/ \exists e2$ (EC(e1; e2) $\wedge p(e1) - p(e2) < 0.3$) , then Create (e1.occT, e1.location, e1.pID, infer, p(e1)).*
- *If e1.iID $=$ card, then Create(e1.occT, e1.location, e1.pID, infer, 1).*
- *If e1.iID $=$ infer and e2.iID $\neq$ infer and Neighbor(e1,e2) and e1.pID $=$ e2.pID and e2.pID > 0.5, then Create(e2.occT, e2.location, e2.pID, infer, p(e2)).*
- *If e1.iID $=$ infer and e2.iID $=$ infer and Neighbor(e1,e2) and e1.pID $\neq$ e2.pID and p(e1) $> p(e2)$ and $\exists e3((e3 = Prev(e1) \vee e3 = Next(e1)) \wedge e3.occT = e2.occT \wedge e3.location = e2.location)$, then e2. pID $=$ e1.pID, p(e2) $= p(e1)$.*

Note that rule 1 implies that if a dynamic event has an associated probability of at least 0.65, then it must satisfy conditions of rule 1. Rule 2 takes advantage of no-stolen and no-clone assumption of cards. Rule 3 indicates that if some subject has been reacquired, then the subject in the neighbor event is also him/her. This rule makes use of the one-subject-at-a-time assumption and is shown satisfied, in most cases. Also, it is proved very useful and powerful in reasoning. Rule 4 is used to resolve inconsistency. That is, if two neighbor events provide different classifications, then the more reliable one should be respected.

There are also rules for inferring KnownSubjectAcquired events that use background knowledge. For instance, we use event reasoning rules to judge whether a person takes a lift or goes from the stairway when he is found at the first floor.

- *If e1.iID $\neq$ infer and dis(e1.location, LIFTLocation) < 1 m and e1.pID $=$ e2.pID and e1. location.z $=$ GROUNDFloor and e2.location.z $=$ FIRSTFloor and $0 < e2.occT - e1.$ occT < 5 sec, then Create((e1.occT $+$ e2.occT)/2, INLIFT, e2.pID, infer, 1). If e1.iID $\neq$ infer and GroundLast(e1) and e1.pID $=$ e2.pID and e1.location.z $=$ (GROUNDFloor and e2.location.z $=$ FIRSTFloor and e2.occT $-$ e1.occT > 10 sec, then Create ((e1.occT $+$ e2. occT)/2, INSTAIR, e2.pID, infer, 1).*
- *If e1.iID$\neq$infer and GroundLast(e1) and e1.pID $=$ e2.pID and e1.location.z $=$ GROUNDFloor and e2.location.z $=$ FIRSTFloor and $8 < e2.occT - e1.occT <= 10$ sec and dis(e1.location, STAIRLocation) < 1 m, then Create ((e1.occT $+$ e2.occT)/2, INSTAIR, e2.pID, infer, 1).*
- *If e1.iID $\neq$ infer and e1.iID $\neq$ infer and e1.pID $=$ e2.pID and dis(e1.location, WCLocation) < 1 m and dis(e2.location,WCLocation) < 1 m and e2.occT $-$ e1.occT > 60 sec and e2 $=$ next(e1), then Create((e1.occT $+$ e2.occT)/2, INWC, e2.pID, infer, 1).*

Here *LIFTLocation, FIRSTFloor, INLIFT, WCLocation* and *INWC* are predefined application constants. The first rule says if a subject first appears on the ground floor and then is detected at the first floor within five seconds, then the subject must have taken a lift. The second and third rule indicate how to judge whether the subject uses the stairway to go to the first floor. The last rule tells that if a subject goes to and leaves the WC (the lavatory) for one minute and does not appear anywhere during that period, then the subject must be in the WC. In addition, similar rules can be set up for subjects who go down from the first floor, etc.

There can be many such rules using topological and time-of-flight information of the environment.

There are also rules for inferring inconsistencies between events. Usually, an inconsistency indicates a potential system failing and warranting investigation. An example rule is:

*If e1.iID = infer and e2.iID = infer and e1.pID = e2.pID and dis(e1.location; e2.location) > 10 * abs(e1.occT − e2.occT), then RaiseAlert.*

Here *RaiseAlert* is a system function to alert the monitor, or it just acts as a report of system failure.

A trajectory can be set up by tracing KnownSubjectAcquired events, which provides more information than video analytic results.

The system architecture is shown in Figure 16.1.

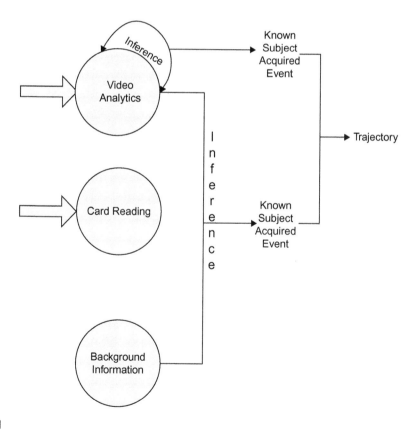

FIGURE 16.1

Using event reasoning for trajectory.

Experiments

We demonstrate our system by the following scenario, showing that we can infer trajectories of subjects even if we do not have clear images in some zones. This experiment scenario shows that our method can be used to enhance security.

Consider: five subjects sequentially enter a building, with their faces (as our cooperative subject assumption) detected, analyzed, and recognized (with a high certainty). They move in, with only their clothing color signature being detected (with a medium or low certainty). After some time, they are detected on the first floor. They swipe their cards and go to their offices, which are captured by cameras in the corridors. They go to the WC occasionally. Finally, they leave the building.

Video analytics only provide clear information when the subjects are cooperatively looking at the cameras, and card reading can only prove the identity of the card owner at the moment of card swiping. However, even for cooperative subjects, sometimes video analytic algorithms make wrong classifications. Figures 16.2, 16.3, and 16.4 show some video dynamic information on face recognition and clothing color signature.

In this experiment, we compare the clear information provided by dynamic information only, and by our event reasoning systems.

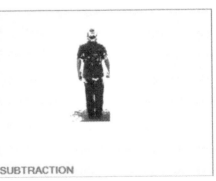

FIGURE 16.2

Video analytic results.

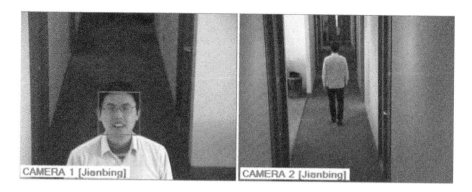

FIGURE 16.3

Video analytic results.

For this experiment, the performance is characterized by the true positive rate: $T_{PR} = N/N_{PR}$, where N_{PR} is the number of pieces of clear information in which the subject has been correctly classified and N is the total number of pieces of clear information in which the subject is classified.

We applied the methods on the scenario previously proposed. The comparison results are presented in Table 16.1.

The generated dynamic events include 5 card reading events, 10 face recognition events at the ground floor, 5 face recognition events at the first floor, and 20 clothing color recognition events, of which there are 8 mis-classifications. The generated 348 pieces of clear information include 40 dynamic events, 280 localization events (ratio 1:7), 10 subject going up events, 10 subject going down events, and 8 WC events, in which the mis-classification events are due to the original video mis-classification. But some mis-classifications are fixed by rule 4 proposed in the above section.

From Table 16.1, we can see that an event reasoning system provides much more clear information about the trajectory of the subject. It is not surprising because, with event reasoning, we can provide clear information for localization events and other tracking events when there are no cameras (e.g., the subject is in WC, etc.). We can also see that the event reasoning system gives an increase of approximately 11 percent in TPR compared to that provided by dynamic information only. This is because the mis-classification of cooperative subjects can be corrected by neighbor classifications.

FIGURE 16.4

Video analytic results.

Table 16.1 Comparison of T_{PR} for Dynamic Information Only and for Event Reasoning System			
Methods	**N**	**N_{PR}**	**T_{PR} (%)**
Dynamic	40	32	80
Event Reasoning	348	316	91

Summary

In this chapter, we propos an event reasoning system which can help to track the trajectory of subjects. We set up rules to infer which subject is seen based on uncertain video analytic results. We also infer the position of subjects when there is no camera data by using topological information of environments. This framework has been evaluated by a simulated experiment, which shows a better performance than using video analytic results only.

We find that the advantage of using event reasoning in these scenarios are two-fold:

- Event reasoning helps to determine which subject is tracked when we have uncertain video analytic results.
- Event reasoning helps to determine the route the subject passes when we have no video analytic results.

For future work, we want to extend this event reasoning model to include the expression of incomplete information using probability theory (induced from combining knowledge bases [14,15]) or Dempster-Shafer theory [16–19]. Also, we need to consider cases where a combination of some uncertain results can provide more certain results. In addition, we will gradually loosen our assumptions to allow multiple subjects to appear at the same time, allow non-cooperative subjects, allow unreliable card information, etc. Furthermore, situation calculus [20,21] can be used to keep a record of the events. Belief revision [22–27] and merging [28–31] techniques for uncertain input can also be considered in our framework.

Acknowledgments

This research work is sponsored by the EU Project: 251617 (the INFER project) and EPSRC projects EP/D070864/1 and EP/G034303/1 (the CSIT project).

References

[1] Liu W, Miller P, Ma J, Yan W. Challenges of distributed intelligent surveillance system with heterogenous information. In: Procs of QRASA. CA: Pasadena; 2009. p. 69–74.
[2] Miller P, Liu W, Fowler F, Zhou H, Shen J, Ma J, et al. Intelligent sensor information system for public transport: To safely go ... In: Procs of AVSS; 2010.
[3] Jiang X, Motai Y, Zhu X. Predictive fuzzy logic controller for trajectory tracking of a mobile robot. In: Procs of IEEE Mid-Summer Workshop on Soft Computing in Industrial Applications; 2005.
[4] Klancar G, Skrjanc I. Predictive trajectory tracking control for mobile robots. In: Proc of Power Electronics and Motion Control Conference; 2006. p. 373–78.
[5] Ma J, Liu W, Miller P. An improvement of subject reacquisition by reasoning and revision. In: Procs of SUM; 2013.
[6] Ma J, Liu W, Miller P. Evidential fusion for gender profiling. In: Procs of SUM; 2012. p. 514–24.
[7] Ma J, Liu W, Miller P. An evidential improvement for gender profiling. In: Procs of Belief Functions; 2012. p. 29–36.
[8] Corban E, Johnson E, Calise A. A six degree-of-freedom adaptive flight control architecture for trajectory following. In: AIAA Guidance, Navigation, and Control Conference and Exhibit; 2002. AIAA-2002-4776.
[9] Ahmed M, Subbarao K. Nonlinear 3-d trajectory guidance for unmanned aerial vehicles. In: Procs of Control Automation Robotics Vision (ICARCV); 2010. p. 1923–7.
[10] Wasserkrug S, Gal A, Etzion O. Inference of security hazards from event composition based on incomplete or uncertain information. IEEE Transactions on Knowledge and Data Engineering 2008;20 (8):1111–4.

[11] Ma J, Liu W, Miller P, Yan W. Event composition with imperfect information for bus surveillance. Procs of AVSS. IEEE Press; 2009. p. 382–7.

[12] Ma J, Liu W, Miller P. Event modelling and reasoning with uncertain information for distributed sensor networks. Procs of SUM. Springer; 2010. p. 236–49.

[13] Han S, Koo B, Hutter A, Shet VD, Stechele W. Subjective logic based hybrid approach to conditional evidence fusion for forensic visual surveillance. In: Proc AVSS'10; 2010. p. 337–44.

[14] Ma J, Liu W, Hunter A. Inducing probability distributions from knowledge bases with (in)dependence relations. In: Procs of AAAI; 2010. p. 339–44.

[15] Ma J. Qualitative approach to Bayesian networks with multiple causes. IEEE Transactions on Systems, Man, and Cybernetics 2012;42(2 Pt A):382–91.

[16] Ma J, Liu W, Dubois D, Prade H. Revision rules in the theory of evidence. In: Procs of ICTAI; 2010. p. 295–302.

[17] Ma J, Liu W, Dubois D, Prade H. Bridging Jeffrey's rule, AGM revision and Dempster conditioning in the theory of evidence. Int J Artif Intell Tools 2011;20(4):691–720.

[18] Ma J, Liu W, Miller P. A characteristic function approach to inconsistency measures for knowledge bases. In: Procs of SUM; 2012. p. 473–85.

[19] Ma J. Measuring divergences among mass functions. In: Procs of ICAI; 2013.

[20] Ma J, Liu W, Miller P. Belief change with noisy sensing in the situation calculus. In: Procs of UAI; 2011.

[21] Ma J, Liu W, Miller P. Handling sequential observations in intelligent surveillance. In: Proceedings of SUM; 2011. p. 547–60.

[22] Ma J, Liu W. A general model for epistemic state revision using plausibility measures. In: Procs of ECAI; 2008. p. 356–360.

[23] Ma J, Liu W. Modeling belief change on epistemic states. In: Procs of FLAIRS; 2009.

[24] Ma J, Liu W. A framework for managing uncertain inputs: An axiomization of rewarding. Int J Approx Reasoning 2011;52(7):917–34.

[25] Ma J, Liu W, Benferhat S. A belief revision framework for revising epistemic states with partial epistemic states. In: Procs of AAAI; 2010. p. 333–8.

[26] Ma J, Benferhat S, Liu W. Revising partial pre-orders with partial pre-orders. A unit-based revision framework; 2012.

[27] Ma J, Benferhat S, Liu W. Revision over partial pre-orders: A postulational study. In: Procs of SUM; 2012. p. 219–32.

[28] Ma J, Liu W, Hunter A. The non-Archimedean polynomials and merging of stratified knowledge bases. In: Procs of ECSQARU; 2009. p. 408–20.

[29] Ma J, Liu W, Hunter A. Modeling and reasoning with qualitative comparative clinical knowledge. Int J Intell Syst 2011;26(1):25–46.

[30] Ma J, Liu W, Hunter A, Zhang W. An XML based framework for merging incomplete and inconsistent statistical information from clinical trials. In: Soft Computing in XML Data Management; LNAI; 2010. p. 259–90.

[31] Ma J, Liu W, Hunter A, Zhang W. Performing meta-analysis with incomplete statistical information in clinical trials. BMC Med Res Methodol 2008;8(1):56.

Resource-Efficient Multi-Source Authentication Utilizing Split-Join One-Way Key Chain

17

Seonho Choi[1], Kun Sun[2], and Hyeonsang Eom[3]

[1]Bowie State University, Bowie, MD, USA
[2]George Mason University, Fairfax, VA, USA
[3]Seoul National University, Seoul, Korea

INFORMATION IN THIS CHAPTER

- Emerging Issues in Multi-source Authentication for Multicast and Broadcast
- Towards the resource-efficient Multi-source Multicast Authentication protocol
- Application of the protocol to wireless ad hoc networks

INTRODUCTION

In wireless ad hoc networks, most of the authentication protocols assume a single source of trust. For example, in a wireless sensor network (WSN), it is typically assumed there is one trustworthy base station and it is the only source of the trust. However, in the presence of multiple trust sources (called source group in this chapter), it becomes difficult to design resource- (or energy-) efficient authentication protocols utilizing multiple trust sources at the same time. Some traditional authentication approaches may be extended and used for this purpose. However, the communication overhead, for example, may increase significantly proportional to the number of trust sources. In this chapter, we propose a new scheme named Multi-Source Authentication utilizing Split-Join One-Way Key Chain (SOKC). In this new technique, the communication overhead is small and constant, and the memory requirement at the verifier node is also small. The source node needs to store n keys, where n represents the key chain length, which may be a reasonable requirement considering that the trust sources usually have more resources compared to other regular node(s) in the network (e.g., as in sensor network).

Our technique utilizes a delayed key disclosure mechanism as in TESLA and uTESLA approaches [1,2], and also extends the one-way key chain technique to achieve the goals of minimal communication overhead and minimal storage requirements at the verifier nodes.

Our SOKC scheme may be applied to both unicast and multicast/broadcast authentication services. But the application of our scheme would be simpler for unicast cases, and for most of the cases, broadcast authentication services are more important, since conveying the information from the trustworthy source to other nodes may be more critical compared to the communication between non-trustworthy nodes. For example, several routing protocols were proposed based on periodic broadcasting (e.g., flooding) of routing (or beacon) messages. These include TinyOS beaconing [3], directed diffusion and its multi-path variants [4], etc. Also, several location discovery schemes have been proposed that utilize broadcasting capabilities to estimate node locations [1]. Even though more advanced broadcast techniques may be utilized in the network, simple flooding may be preferred or required due to the simplicity or instability of network connections. Our proposed approach may be applied in both cases. Hence, we will focus on developing and applying the SOKC scheme for the multicast/broadcast services.

This SOKC scheme may be applied for various authentication problems. However, to show its applicability, we chose two authentication problems. For example, in wireless ad hoc networks, some attacks exploit the fact that it is hard to authenticate the actual path (or number of hops) data packets traversed—especially the attacks against the broadcast services. Sinkhole and wormhole attacks belong to this attack category [3]. With the multi-source authentication capabilities, each node would be able to detect and cope with such attacks. A new path authentication technique may be developed by utilizing our multi-source SOKC scheme. For example, the source group keys may be duplicated and randomly distributed across the network, so that the verifier nodes may be able check whether a packet has really passed through a certain number of source group nodes along the routing path from the claimed origination point.

The SOKC scheme may also be applied to WSNs with multiple base stations. It is typically assumed that a WSN has only one base station. However, there may exist several drawbacks. Degraded reliability may be a problem due to a single point of failure. The latency may be an issue if the number of hops in the delivery paths become large, which may cause the reduced lifetime of the sensor nodes and, thus, the entire sensor network. The deployment of multiple base stations were proposed to overcome these limitations [5−7]. However, in the presence of multiple base stations, it would be more difficult to provide robust authentication services since it would be required to tolerate compromise of multiple base stations as well as sensor nodes. If we assume that the base stations can communicate with each other directly using a separate channel, then our SOKC-based approach may be used in providing multi-source broadcast authentication services. It is also assumed that all the base stations need to participate in authenticating the broadcast messages to provide increased security levels. If we consider the importance of the broadcast messages in WSNs, this would be a valid assumption.

Related works

Several security mechanisms for authentication and secure routing protocols in a wireless ad hoc network are based on public key cryptography [8,9]. However, until now, the public key cryptography has still been too expensive for the resource-constrained mobile nodes. Secure routing protocols based on symmetric key cryptography have been proposed (e.g., [10,11]). SEAD [10] is a distance vector routing protocol based on DSDV. The basic idea is to use one-way hash chains to authenticate the metrics and the sequence number of a routing table. The destination node can authenticate the source node; however, it cannot authenticate the intermediate nodes along the path from the source node to the destination node. Ariadne [11] uses a per-hop hashing technique and source routing techniques to prevent route misbehaviors. However, it requires a precise time synchronization among all the nodes, which is usually difficult to achieve in the mobile networks. Moreover, the communication overhead may increase significantly when including all the identifiers and corresponding MACs for all the nodes along the path.

Authenticating broadcast (or multicast) traffic in wireless ad hoc networks is also a difficult problem, since the traditional approaches like digital signatures may not be adequate due to the heavy resource requirements. TESLA and μTESLA approaches [2,12] were proposed as viable solutions to the authentication problem in such networks. μTESLA utilizes the delayed key disclosure and one-way key chain techniques. First, the packet is broadcast with a calculated keyed Message Authentication Codes attached along with the original data portion, and only after sufficient time is elapsed for all the nodes in the network to receive it will the corresponding key be disclosed to the network nodes for authentication of the previously sent data and MAC. TESLA and μTESLA requires loose time synchronization among the network nodes.

Researchers have proposed several mechanisms to prevent the false data injection attacks. Przydatek, Song, and Perrig propose SIA [13], a secure information aggregation scheme for sensor networks that addresses the issue of false data injection using statistical techniques and interactive proofs, ensuring that the aggregated result reported by the aggregation node is a good approximation to the true value, even if a small number of sensor nodes and the aggregation node may have been compromised. SIA focuses on the accuracy of query results reported from the base station, whereas our scheme focuses on the authenticity of the reports from sensor nodes and provides a means to filter out any injected false data as early as possible. Both schemes can be combined to make the network more robust to false data injection attacks.

SEF [14] is a statistical en-route filtering mechanism to detect and drop false reports during the forwarding process. Authenticating event reports requires that nodes share certain security information; however, attackers can obtain such information by compromising a single node. To prevent any single compromised node from breaking down the entire system, SEF carefully limits the amount of security information assigned to each node and relies on the collective decisions of multiple sensors for false report detection. First, SEF divides a global key pool into multiple partitions and carefully assigns a certain number of keys from one partition to an individual node. Given that any single node knows only a limited amount of the system secret, compromising one or a small number of nodes cannot disable the overall network from detecting bogus reports. Second, by assuming that the same event can be detected by multiple sensors, in SEF each of the detecting sensors generates a keyed message authentication code (MAC) and multiple MACs are attached to the event report. As the report is forwarded, each node along the way verifies the correctness of the MACs probabilistically and drops those with invalid MACs. Finally, the sink verifies the correctness of each MAC and eliminates remaining false reports that elude en-route filtering. Compared to the statistical solution provided by SEF, our solution can provide a more resource-efficient path authentication, but it cannot handle the broadcast authentication.

Zhu et al. [15] present an interleaved hop-by-hop authentication scheme for addressing the false data injection attack launched by the compromised nodes. The scheme guarantees that the base station will detect any injected false data packets when no more than a certain number t nodes are compromised. To defend against false data injection attacks, at least $t + 1$ sensor nodes have to agree upon a report before it is sent to the base station. t is a security threshold based on the security requirements of the application under consideration and the network node density. Further, it provides an upper bound for the number of hops that a false data packet could be forwarded before it is detected and dropped, given that there are up to t colluding compromised nodes. In other words, it also attempts to filter out false data packets injected into the network by compromised nodes before they reach the base station, thus saving the energy for relaying them. Zhu et al. [15] offers the most similar work to our proposed scheme, but their approach cannot handle the broadcast authentication. Our solution approach utilizes a new SOKC technique, along with the delayed key disclosure, to achieve a much smaller communication overhead.

Methodology
Assumptions

We refer to the minimum number of hops necessary for a packet to reach from any node located at one extreme edge of the network to another node located at the opposite extreme, as the *diameter* of the ad hoc network. Packets may be lost or corrupted in transmission on the network. A node receiving a corrupted packet can detect the error and discard the packet. Nodes within the ad hoc network may move at any time without notice, and may even move continuously, but we assume that the speed with which nodes move is moderate with respect to the packet transmission latency and wireless transmission range of the particular underlying network hardware in use. We assume that nodes may be able to enable a *promiscuous* receive mode on their wireless network interface hardware, causing the hardware to deliver every received packet to the network driver software without filtering based on the link-layer destination address. Even though this feature is not required, by utilizing this feature, the performance of our scheme may be enhanced, especially when the mobility level is high in the network.

The local clocks of the nodes are assumed to be (at least) loosely synchronized, with a maximum time synchronization error Δ. Various time synchronization techniques were proposed for wireless ad hoc networks, and any of them may be utilized to achieve this requirement. Similar assumptions were made in the broadcast authentication schemes such as TESLA, μTESLA, etc. [2,12].

Also, the time line is assumed to be divided into block periods, as in TESLA and μTESLA approaches [2,12]. In each block period, one packet may be sent out for broadcasting by any valid broadcast originator (which may be determined by the application). A delayed key disclosure mechanism is adapted and incorporated in our scheme. Each broadcast packet contains the message, the authentication-related information, and the key information that is disclosed for the previously sent out message. The key disclosure delay is denoted as d block periods. These can be seen in Figure 17.1.

We assume that there is one source and one or more recipients that are involved in each session (one or more data packets are delivered in each session). That is, our authentication approach may be used for both unicast and multicast/broadcast communications. However, we will focus on developing protocols for broadcast services, as mentioned before. The packets are transmitted along a multi-hop delivery path to the receiver(s). The delivery path is determined by a routing protocol used in the network. Many routing protocols were proposed for wireless ad hoc networks, and any of them with reasonable route change rates (due to mobility) may be utilized in the network.

Finally, it is assumed that the number of different source group keys in one source group (which is denoted as m) is an odd number.

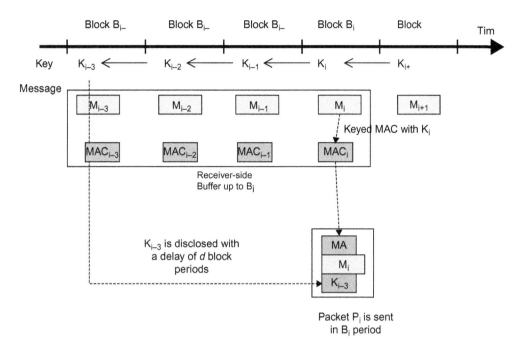

FIGURE 17.1

A μTESLA technique [2,12] is shown with a key disclosure delay of $d = 3$ block periods. Note that keys are disclosed later, while the message and MAC portions are disclosed in the corresponding block.

Overview of the protocol

The protocol carries out the following three processes to provide the multi-source authentication. In this scheme it is assumed that the number of source group keys, m, is an odd number.

1. **Offline SOKC generation (Figure 17.2):** SOKC is generated offline by utilizing the source seed (Z_0), source keys (a_i), one-way hash operation, and the bitwise EXOR operation. Source nodes with a secret source key a_i will be equipped with a chain of keys that are obtained from the intermediate keys, Y_j ($1 \leq j \leq n-1$), by applying the EXOR operation with a_i. The keys generated in this process are denoted as $SOKC^i = \{K_{n-1}^i, ... K_2^i, K_1^i\}$.

   The intermediate keys that are generated in this process are named as Y_j and Z_j, which will be explained in more detail in a later section.

2. **Semi-encrypted key pre-distribution (Figure 17.3):** When the original sender node (this may or may not be one of the source group nodes) has some message to send, it will first send a packet that has the following field:
   - random nonce R_j of k bits. This would be used to prevent the disclosure of the next key (Y_j) in the SOKC that is needed for the next round of validation.

   Once this field is filled with a random number generated by the original source and the packet is sent out, the first source group node from a_i (this may be the same as the original sender node)

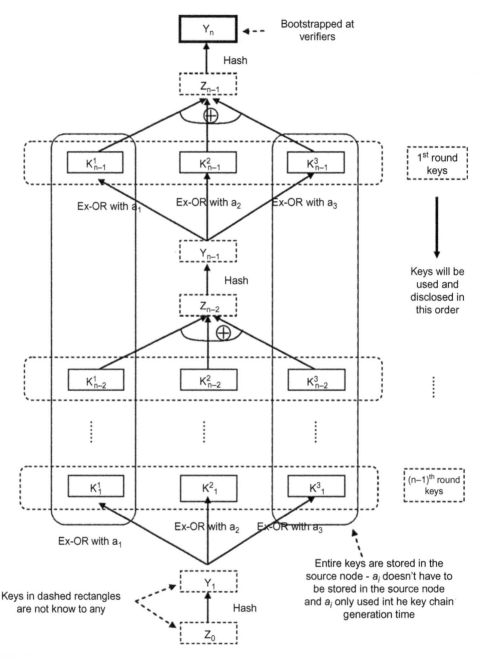

FIGURE 17.2

SOKC generation: The entire key chain is generated offline and only the keys in the solid rectangles are stored in the nodes. The keys, K_j^i, are stored in the i-th source node(s). Y_n is bootstrapped in each verifier node. The intermediate keys and even the secret source keys, a_i, are not stored in any node in the network.

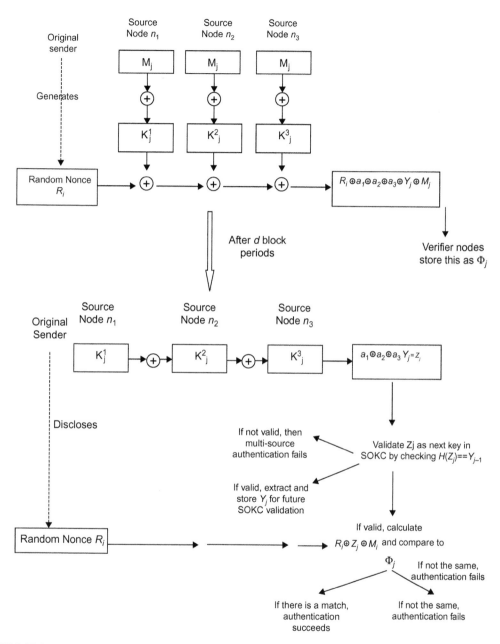

FIGURE 17.3

Semi-encrypted key pre-distribution and a delayed key disclosure along with the verifications at verifier nodes.

will apply EXOR operation with this random number to its next key in the $SOKC^i \oplus$ its Message and forward the packet to the next node in the delivery path. The next source group nodes with different source keys will carry out the same process: get the value from this field and apply the EXOR operation to it. But this process is done only once for each source key a_j, $1 \leq j \leq m$. In other words, if there are multiple source group nodes with the same source key in the delivery path, only the first one will carry out this process. When the packet finishes traversing all the source group nodes with m different source keys, then the verifier nodes in the remaining path will have the following value in the packet field:

$$\Phi_j = R_j \oplus a_1 \oplus a_2 \oplus a_3 \oplus Y_j \oplus M_j$$

M_j stands for the message in the j-th packet. This value will be stored in the verifier nodes for later authentication purposes. Verifiers may store the other field values, such as the actual message (M_j), depending upon the scheme.

3. Delayed key disclosure with verification (Figure 17.3): After the key disclosure delay (d block periods), the original sender of R_j will start the key disclosure process by including the following fields in the packet:
   - Disclose the actual random nonce used d block period before (R_j)—the original sender will initialize this field to all 0s.
   - Key disclosure field for accommodating the $SOKC^j$ keys from the m source group nodes (they will be EXORed and this field requires only k bits).

Each group source node will apply the EXOR operation between the next key in $SOKC^i$ and the value from the key disclosure field mentioned above, and store back the result into the key disclosure field again. After the packet traverses all of the m source group nodes with different source keys, the packet will contain the following value in its key disclosure field:

$$a_1 \oplus a_2 \oplus a_3 \oplus Y_j = Z_j$$

Once the packet reaches a verifier node, and if the packet is claimed to have traversed m different source group nodes, then the verifier node will carry out a sequence of steps. First, it will extract the intermediate key, Z_j, from the key disclosure field, and check whether this intermediate key is really from the authentic SOKC by applying the one-way hash operation and comparing the result to the already stored Y_{j+1}. If they don't match, then the key disclosure packet is discarded, and the already stored message M_j will not be authenticated. If they match, then the verifier extracts the intermediate key, Y_j, by multiplying $a_1 \oplus a_2 \oplus a_3$ to Z_j, and stores it as Y_j as a newly disclosed authentic SOKC key to be used in the next round of authentication.

Then the verifier will check the following condition to compare to the already stored Φ_j:

$$R_j \oplus a_1 \oplus a_2 \oplus a_3 \oplus Y_j \oplus M_j = \Phi_j$$

If the equality holds, then the previously (in TESLA) stored R_j and M_j are validated.

Basic scheme

Notations

The following are defined for our authentication process:

- Source group: A group of nodes equipped with SOKCs generated from m different source keys, a_i where $1 \leq i \leq m$, are distributed among N_{src} number of source nodes ($m \leq N_{src}$). It is assumed that m is an odd number in this scheme. The source nodes may or may not be located in close proximity, and some source nodes may have the same source key if $m < N_{src}$. The source key size is denoted as k bits.

- Verifier group: N_{vrf} nodes (e.g., multicast group members or all the nodes in the broadcast case) are equipped with verification information for authenticating a packet's traversing of at least m source nodes with different a_i in the routing path. That is, a verifier node has the ability to verify that the packet passed through all the source group nodes with m different source keys.

Information kept in the source group node and the verifier group node is as follows:

- Source node from a_i keeps the following items:
  - Split-Join One-Way Key Chain from a_i : $SOKC^i = \{K^i_{n-1}, ...K^i_2, K^i_1\}$
  - public source key sum $a = a_1 \oplus a_2 \oplus \cdots \oplus a_m$
  - cryptographic one-way hash function
- Verifier node keeps the following items:
  - public source key sum $a_1 \oplus a_2 \oplus \cdots \oplus a_m$
  - last key, Y_n, in the SOKC
  - cryptographic one-way hash function

SOKC Generation with m *source keys,* a$_i$, $1 \le i \le m$ *(Figure 17.2)*

The process of SOKC generation is assumed to be carried out offline before the network launch time. The possible issues that may arise in developing online SOKC generation is addressed in the proposed research section later. For the offline case, the detailed algorithm is shown in Figure 17.2 and the detailed steps are as follows:

1. Apply a cryptographic hash function to Z_0 to generate Y_1, which is also k-bit long.
2. That is, $Y_1 = H(Z_0)$.
3. Calculate a key QUOTE K^i_1 in the chain by applying the EXOR operation with a secret source key a_i, $K^i_1 = a_i \oplus Y_1$.
4. Calculate $Z_1 = a \oplus Y_1 = (a_1 \oplus a_2 \oplus \cdots \oplus a_m) \oplus Y_1$.
5. Apply a cryptographic hash function to Z_1 to generate Y_2. That is, $Y_2 = H(Z_1)$.
6. Calculate the second key K^i_2 in the chain, $K^i_2 = a_i \oplus Y_2$.
7. Calculate $Z_2 = a \oplus Y_2 = (a_1 \oplus a_2 \oplus \cdots \oplus a_m) \oplus Y_2$.
8. Repeat steps 4 through 6 until key K^i_{n-1} is obtained.

The one-way key chain at the source is now obtained as $SOKC^i = \{K^i_{n-1}, ...K^i_2, K^i_1\}$. The keys in this $SOKC^i$ are bootstrapped in the source group nodes. These keys are used in reverse order starting from K^i_{n-1}. The last key, Y_n, in the entire $SOKC$ is assumed to be bootstrapped at each verifier node.

Packet format

The j-th packet, $1 \le j < n$, has the following packet format consisting of five fields:

1. SRC index bits
2. Semi-Encrypted Key (Φ_j) pre-distribution; k bits
3. Nonce (R_{j-d}) disclosure; k bits
4. SOKC key (for $a \oplus Y_{j-d}$) disclosure; k bits
5. Message (M_i)

SRC index bits are used for showing which source group nodes the packet has been traversed. For example, if its i-th bit is set to 1, then it means that the packet is claiming that it has already traversed a node with the source key a_i, and if its i-th bit is 0, then it means that the packet has not traversed any such node. If another source node with the same a_i receives the packet whose i-th SRC index bit is set to 1, then it will forward the packet without modifying any of the fields, even though it can repeat the process without any adverse effect; but it will waste resource if it does.

The other three fields following the SRC index bits field will be used in the semi-encrypted key pre-distribution and the delayed key disclosure with verification processes. Note that the nonce disclosure and SOKC key disclosure fields will disclose the values that were previously used in the $(j-d)$-th block period.

After the key disclosure delay (i.e., d block periods), another packet needs to be sent by the original sender; it would contain the following fields:

1. SRC index bits
2. Semi-Encrypted Key (Φ_{j+d}) pre-distribution; k bits
3. Nonce (R_j) disclosure; k bits
4. SOKC key (for $a \oplus Y_j$) disclosure; k bits
5. Message (M_i)

Semi-encrypted key pre-distribution at the source node with a source key a_i $(1 \leq i \leq m)$

Again, the purpose of the semi-encrypted key pre-distribution is to let source group nodes reveal their SOKC keys in a semi-encrypted form by applying the EXOR operation to the random nonce (R_j) sent out by the original sender of the packet. Let's assume that a j-th packet is sent out by the original sender. The process is shown in Figure 17.3 and the detailed steps are described as follows:

1. Original sender generates a random nonce (R_j) and insert it into the semi-encrypted key pre-distribution field in the packet before sending it.
2. Each source group node from a source key, a_i, in the delivery path will carry out the following:
    a. If the SRC index bit (whose index value is i) is equal to 1, then go to step 3.
    b. Extract the value in the semi-encrypted key pre-distribution field (let it be denoted as x).
    c. Extract M_j from the packet.
    d. Calculate $M_j \oplus K_j^i \oplus x$ and store this as a new value in the semi-encrypted key pre-distribution field of the packet.
    e. Set the SRC index bit (whose index value is i) as 1.
3. Each verifier node will perform the following step:
    a. If all of the m bits are set to 1 in the SRC index bits field, then the node will extract the value of the semi-encrypted key pre-distribution field, and store it as Φ_j to be used at the future verification time (after d block periods).
4. Forward the packet if it is needed.

Delayed key disclosure and verification after the key disclosure delay

Because the actual SOKC keys are disclosed after the delay (d block periods), the verifications of the keys and messages that were included in the j-th packet may be carried out when the nodes receive/process a packet in the $(j+d)$-th block period. So, we disclose the j-th keys from the

SOKCs in the $(j + d)$-th packet, and the verifications will be carried out by the verifier nodes upon the receipt of the $(j + d)$-th packet. This process is depicted in Figure 17.3, and the detailed steps are described as follows:

1. Original sender discloses the nonce (R_j) by including in the $(j + d)$-th packet's nonce disclosure field.
2. Each source group node from a source key, a_i, in the delivery path will carry out the following:
   a. If the SRC index bit (whose index value is i) is equal to 1, then go to step 3.
   b. Extract the value from the SOKC key disclosure field (let it be denoted as y).
   c. Calculate $K_j^i \oplus y$ and store this as a new value into the SOKC key disclosure field of the packet.
   d. Set the SRC index bit (whose index value is i) as 1.
3. Each verifier node will perform the following steps:
   a. If all of the m bits are set to 1 in the SRC index bits field, then the node will perform the following steps:
     i. Extract the value of the SOKC key disclosure field (let it be denoted as z).
     ii. Check whether $H(z) = Y_{j+1}$
       a) If not, then the key validation for SOKC fails, discards the packet and exit from the algorithm.
       b) If the equality holds, then store $a_1 \oplus \cdots \oplus a_m \oplus z$ as a valid Y_j for future SOKC validation.
         A. Calculate $R_j \oplus z \oplus M_j = R_j \oplus a_1 \oplus a_2 \oplus a_3 \oplus Y_j \oplus M_j$ and compare this to Φ_j that were extracted and stored in the previously received j-th packet.
           i. If they are the same, then the multi-source authentication succeeds for M_j.
           ii. If they don't match, then the multi-source authentication fails for M_j.
4. Forward the packet if it is needed.

Resource requirements

The resource requirements at a source group node from a_i are:

- $n \times k$ bits are needed for storing the SOKC keys.

  The resource requirements at a verifier node are:

- k bits: for storing the SOKC validation key Y_n
- $d \times k$ bits: for storing Φ_j in, at most, d consecutive block periods
- $2k$ bits: for temporarily storing Z_j and $a_1 \oplus a_2 \oplus a_3 \oplus Y_j = Z_j$

  Hence, the total memory requirement at a verifier node is $(d + 3) \times k$ bits.

  The communication overhead required at each packet (purely needed for our scheme) consists of the following:

- m bits: for SRC index bits
- $3k$ bits: for semi-encrypted key pre-distribution field, nonce disclosure field, SOKC key disclosure field

  Hence, the total overhead is $m + 3k$ bits for each packet.

CONCLUSION

We present a new resource-efficient multi-source authentication scheme with Split-Join One-Way Key Chain (SOKC). In this new technique, the communication overhead is small and constant, and the memory requirement at the verifier node is also minimal. This technique may be effectively used for wireless ad hoc networks when there exist multiple trust sources to be utilized at the same time. For example, wireless sensor networks with multiple base stations may utilize this technique to provide enhanced security by incorporating multiple trust sources.

Acknowledgments

This work was supported by the US Army Research Office (ARO) grant W911NF-12-1-0060.

References

[1] Park S, Bhatia A, Youn J-H. Hop-count based location discovery in ad hoc sensor networks. In: Proceeding (424) Wireless Networks and Emerging Technologies; 2004.

[2] Perrig A, Canetti R, Song D, Tygar D. Efficient and secure source authentication for multicast. In: Proceedings of Network and Distributed System Security Symposium; 2001.

[3] Karlof C, Wagner D. Secure routing in wireless sensor networks: Attacks and countermeasures. In: Proceedings of the First IEEE International Workshop on Sensor Network Protocols and Applications; 2003 May.

[4] di Pietro R, Mancini LV, Law YW, Etalle S, Havinga PA. Directed diffusion-based secure multicast scheme for wireless sensor networks. First International Workshop on Wireless Security and Privacy (WiSPr'03).

[5] Deng J, Han R, Mishra S. Enhancing base station security in wireless sensor networks. Technical Report CU-CS-951-03. University of Colorado; 2003 Apr.

[6] Gandham S, Dawande M, Prakash R, Venkatesan S. Energy efficient schemes for wireless sensor networks with multiple mobile base stations. IEEE Globecom '03 2004:377−81.

[7] Ramamurthy Y, Xue B. A key management protocol for wireless sensor networks with multiple base stations. ICC'08: Proceedings of the IEEE International Conference on Communications. Beijing, China; 2008. p. 1625−9.

[8] Hubaux J, Buttyan L, Capkun S. The quest for security in mobile ad hoc networks. In: Proceedings of the ACM Symposium on Mobile Ad Hoc Networking and Computing (MobiHOC 2001); 2001.

[9] Zhou L, Haas Z. Securing ad hoc networks. IEEE Network Magazine 1999;13(6).

[10] Hu Y-C, Johnson DB, Perrig A. SEAD: Secure efficient distance vector routing for mobile wireless ad hoc networks. WMCSA 2002. Proceedings of the fourth IEEE Workshop on Mobile Computing Systems and Applications 2002 Jun:3−13.

[11] Hu Y-C, Perrig A, Johnson D. Ariadne: a secure on-demand routing protocol for ad hoc networks. Wireless Networks Journal 2005;11:1.

[12] Liu D, Ning P. Multi-level u-TESLA: A broadcast authentication system for distributed sensor networks. Submitted for journal publication. Also available as Technical Report, TR-2003-08; North Carolina State University, Department of Computer Science; 2003 Mar.

[13] Przydatek B, Song D, Perrig A. SIA: Secure information aggregation in sensor networks. In: Proc of ACM sensys; 2003.

[14] Ye F, Luo H, Lu S. Statistical en-route filtering of injected false data in sensor networks. IEEE J Sel Areas Commun 2005;23:4.

[15] Zhu S, Setial S, Jajodia S. An interleaved hop-by-hop authentication scheme for filtering of injected false data in sensor networks.

Real-time Network Intrusion Detection Using Hadoop-Based Bayesian Classifier

18

Sanjai Veetil and Qigang Gao
Dalhousie University, Halifax, NS, Canada

INFORMATION IN THIS CHAPTER

- Introduction
- Overview on Hadoop based technologies
- Survey of Intrusion Detection Systems
- Hadoop-based real-time Intrusion Detection: System architecture
- Practical application scenario and system evaluation
- Summary

INTRODUCTION

There are many real-world examples of large-scale intrusions that had wreaked havoc, causing far-reaching damage. The attack on the Sony PlayStation Network (PSN) created ripples of fear among several technology giants [1]. The reason was simple—the Distributed Denial of Service (DDOS) attack left Sony struggling to revive its online gaming service, which in turn caused a huge loss (in millions of dollars) for Sony. Furthermore, credit card information of thousands of PSN users were stolen. Sony had to opt for an expensive security measure to prevent attacks in the future. Sony's misfortune was an invaluable lesson for security experts across the globe. Another tech giant, Twitter, became the latest victim of an intrusion, wherein the Associated Press (AP) Twitter account was hacked. The AP tweets were then used for sharing links that directed users to malicious sites and for propagating false rumors [2]. This attack questioned the credibility of Twitter's security measures. In [3], the author has listed several infamous hack attacks. The year 1999 witnessed the shocking case of a successful hack that penetrated the military network belonging to the US Department of Defense. The attack's impact was so far-reaching that NASA had to shut down their network as an immediate measure to curtail the attack. In 2008, a hacker group allegedly took down the Church of Scientology's official website using DDOS. Therefore, we can infer that the attacks have become technologically advanced and often difficult to detect. The demand is urgent and tremendous for a cost-effective system that can efficiently detect such attacks in real time.

In this article, we present a system to tackle the following research questions:

- How do we deal with the challenges of real-time intrusion detection on large volume stream data?
- Could we build a distributed, scalable, and fault-tolerant intrusion detection system?
- Are Hadoop and HStreaming viable platforms for building an intrusion detection system?
- Is a Hadoop-based Naive Bayes classifier faster than a standalone Naive Bayes?
- Could we build an efficient intrusion detection system using a heterogeneous/homogeneous cluster comprising obsolete hardware?

Overview on Hadoop based technologies

This section gives a brief description of all the prominent technologies that were used to implement the proposed solution.

Apache Hadoop

Apache Hadoop is an open-source distributed computing framework based on Java API [4]. Hadoop allows developers to process big data in parallel by using batch-processed jobs. The two core components of Hadoop are MapReduce and the Hadoop Distributed File System (HDFS) [5]. The MapReduce component is responsible for submission of jobs and making parallel processing of big data possible. The HDFS component is a unique file system used by Hadoop for storing and managing big data. Only those classes belonging to Hadoop's API can read/write into the HDFS system, while the rest of the OS components are oblivious to its existence. The jobs that run in parallel on the Hadoop cluster read the input file and write out the output file into the HDFS.

Figure 18.1 shows the typical architecture of a Hadoop multi-node cluster that consists of a single master and multiple slave machines. There are two master processes known as the Namenode and Jobtracker that run as daemon processes on the master machine. Each slave machine runs the Datanode daemon and the Tasktracker daemon. The Namenode daemon manages Hadoop's Distributed File System (DFS) and supervises the datanode daemons on the slave machines. The Jobtracker daemon on the master accepts the submitted MapReduce job and assigns it to any of the tasktracker daemons on the slave machines. The slave daemons periodically send heartbeats that comprise the information pertaining to the data blocks they store and their available slots of executing the tasks. The job may be assigned to multiple tasktrackers, depending on the size of the input data. In certain cases, the master machine also runs the slave daemon processes so that it may also run the jobs [5]. In typical real-case scenarios, the high-end machine is configured as the master, hence making it run both the slave and master daemons improves its utilization. Optionally, a daemon process known as the Secondary Namenode is run on a separate machine that backs up all the necessary files used to recover a failed Namenode.

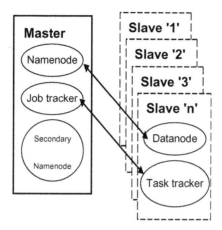

FIGURE 18.1

The Hadoop Master-Slave cluster architecture.

MapReduce

Hadoop's MapReduce programming model focuses on processing big data in parallel. This is achieved by harnessing the processors of multiple machines on either a heterogeneous or a homogeneous cluster. A typical MapReduce job mainly consists three phases; namely, the map phase, shuffle phase, and the reduce phase [5]. The map phase is invoked for each record contained in the input file read from the HDFS. To make each record unique, Hadoop prefixes each record with an offset, which is usually a random number. The output from the map phases are key-value pairs wherein the key from several map phases may be identical. The mappers write their output to memory buffers. Overflowing data is spilled to the disk. Too much spilling implies heavy I/O operations that severely affect performance. Practically, the mappers perform a portion of the sorting operation. A shuffle-and-sort phase follows the map phase and sorts the output from the map phase based on the key. The reduce phase is invoked as soon as the shuffle-and-sort phase generates a stream of sorted key-value pairs. Each reduce phase is invoked for each unique key and its corresponding values. The result of the reduce phases are written onto HDFS. It is worth noting that the map and reduce phases are invoked in sequence. There may be multiple map phases and reduce phases that run in parallel, based on the size of the input file.

Hadoop Distributed File System (HDFS)

The HDFS is a special file system that is exclusive to MapReduce jobs [5]. The HDFS acts like a storage for big data, which can be loaded from the local file system by using a CLI utility that ships in with any Apache Hadoop distribution. The main feature of HDFS is that it facilitates the partitioning of the big data contained within HDFS to multiple machines. The basic unit of the big data resident on HDFS is a block, which is comparatively larger than that of the local file system. This approach ensures that the cost of seeking these blocks is minimal. The Namenode is the core component and is responsible for maintaining metadata about all files contained on the HDFS and for distributing a large file to multiple datanodes on the cluster.

Apache Hive

Apache Hive is a petabyte datawarehouse that can house big data [6]. It even has an SQL-like language called HivQL for performing database-related operations on the big data loaded into tables. Apache Hive relies on the HDFS for storing its data, which can comprise tables, views, and files that are loaded into external tables.

In [6], the author states the features of Apache Hive as follows:

- Support for ETL operations
- HiveQL: an SQL-like query language that can perform data definition and data manipulation operations
- Query execution in the form of MapReduce job
- Hive Web interface, which allows access to Hive objects and performs query execution

HStreaming API

The HStreaming API is a Java library that is built on top of the native Hadoop library; hence, the native MapReduce programs can be easily ported to the HStreaming API [7]. As a result, these streaming MapReduce jobs run continuously unless they are manually terminated or aborted. Hadoop is a distributed computing framework and is best suited for situations where slow batch-processed jobs need to be speed-boosted with the help of Hadoop's parallel processing ability. Although Apache Hadoop has all the bells and whistles, it still lacks the capability to process big data in real time. The HStreaming API helps Hadoop achieve this by providing the developers with a set of handy Java classes that allow MapReduce jobs to read from a live stream of data.

To make the streaming possible, HStreaming utilizes "stream endpoints," one each for the input and the output. The user defines these stream endpoints as TCP/HTTP/UDP-based URLs. These URLs are spawned by using a CLI-based tool called streamgen [7], which ships with the HStreaming API. Figure 18.2 shows a streaming MapReduce job. Hence, with the power of real-time analytics offered by the HStreaming API, MapReduce jobs can now process big data in real time.

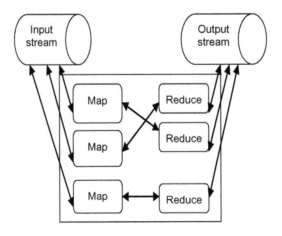

FIGURE 18.2

A high-level depiction of a streaming MapReduce job.

Survey of Intrusion Detection Systems

Intrusion detection is the process of monitoring the events occurring in a computer system or network and analyzing them for signs of *intrusions,* defined as attempts to compromise the confidentiality, integrity, and availability, or to bypass the security mechanisms, of a computer or network [8, p. 5].

With the increase in dependency on networks for carrying out day-to-day businesses, the reliability, security, and availability of such networks are of utmost importance for administrators. Networks have become an indispensable part of business, and a severe downtime of a network could only mean loss, sometimes to the tune of millions of dollars. Intrusion Detection Systems (IDS) address the security concerns of these networks and can operate in four configurations.

Based on [8], IDSes are differentiated based on the following features:

- The source of information used as input for intrusion detection (e.g. Web server log files, network traffic data, etc).
- The target, which is monitored by the IDS. The target can be an entire network (NIDS) or a single host (HIDS).
- The data mining technique (e.g. anomaly detection, signature-based intrusion detection) used to deduce whether an intrusion has occurred or not.
- Reaction to threats/intrusions detected at the target.

Host Intrusion Detection System

As mentioned above, HIDSes focus on monitoring and detecting intrusions at a single host. Network administrators have to carefully analyze the pros and cons of installing a commercial IDS on a target host, since it is costly in terms of licensing fee and maintenance. Typically, in large corporations, a single high-end machine, designated as a powerful Web server that caters to millions of requests/transactions per day, is an ideal candidate for installing an HIDS. It is highly likely that this Web server becomes the target for hackers. The HIDS is configured to monitor the target machine's Network Interface Card (NIC), which connects it to the rest of the network. The traffic data (and optionally, the log files) generated by the target machine are monitored by the HIDS.

Network Intrusion Detection System

An HIDS will not suffice if we want to detect intrusions at multiple targets that jointly function as an indispensible asset for day-to-day business. This scenario is apt for a Network-based Intrusion Detection System, which acts like a second line of defense next to a firewall. A traditional NIDS will have a distributed architecture, which relies on processes running on the target machine to report on any suspicious activity related to the network traffic. These processes generally report to a central process that acts as the core management component for the IDS. An NIDS monitors the exchange of communication between internal hosts to detect threats within the network. This component can be used to configure the IDS for generating alerts for specific intrusions, for selecting the mode of alerting the administrator, and for performing in-depth analysis of alert log files. In [9], the author states that the NIDS cannot operate in switched, encrypted, or high-speed networks. A prime example of an NIDS is Snort [10], a packet sniffer that employs sensors on multiple target machines to monitor and detect intrusions.

Misuse-based Intrusion Detection System

This system is also known as the signature-based approach for detecting intrusions. The misuse-based detection approach employs a data mining algorithm that can be trained with data that is labeled with known attack types. The efficiency of this system relies on the comprehensiveness of the training data that must contain instances of all possible known attacks. Furthermore, a misuse-based detection system produces very few false positives when compared to an anomaly-based IDS. The Naive Bayes, Decision Tree, and Support Vector Machines (SVM) algorithms are examples of data mining algorithms, which are incorporated into a misuse-based IDS. All of these algorithms have their own advantages and disadvantages, so their selection is based on the purpose and requirements. A shortcoming of the misuse-based IDS is that it cannot detect newer/unknown forms of attacks.

Anomaly-based Intrusion Detection System

Anomaly-based IDSes also rely on data mining algorithms for creating models representing "normal" behavior. This model is used as a reference for detecting any "deviation" from it. Any kind of deviation or abnormal pattern is labeled as a attack. Hence, anomaly-based IDSes are capable of detecting even newer/unknown attacks. However, such systems are known to generate a high number of false positives wherein a legitimate traffic is labeled as an attack. This leads to many false alerts and often the alert logs grow exponentially, hence making it difficult to perform an alert log analysis. To make matters worse, the administrator has to carefully distinguish between legitimate and illegitimate traffic based on experience.

Common attack types

The Denial-of-Service (DOS) and Probe attacks are major forms of attack, while the User-to-Root (U2R) and Remote-to-Local (R2L) attacks are minor forms of attack. In case of a DOS attack, the hacker prevents the legitimate user from accessing a service (e.g., online multiplayer games). The hacker bombards the main server with packets until it goes down. Probe attacks are most common. Hackers use probe attacks to gain a better understanding of their targets. A plethora of tools is freely available on the Internet to probe remote hosts. A U2R attack is a situation in which the attacker has already gained access to the target machine and is attempting to gain root/super user privileges. These attacks often involve brute-force techniques to crack the root/super user's password. A common practice to prevent such attacks is to use strong passwords for all accounts. An R2L attack is a case where the hacker is attempting to gain access into the target machine by using any of the accounts that are available on the target machine. Usually, logging into the guest account is attempted before trying rest of the accounts. The user accounts that are currently used on a remote machine can be determined using nmap. Figure 18.3 gives examples of each attack category.

A Javascript-based visualization API: D3

D3 is JavaScript library that visualizes data using a variety of visual metaphors, such as bar charts, pie charts, and scatter plots [11]. Visualization aids the user to assimilate the information quickly. In the case of NIDS, the network traffic data is often huge, so it is an ideal candidate for visualization. The visualizations are accessed via the front-end Web interface through which the network administrator can assess the situation of the network.

Attack	Examples of attacks/tools
DOS	Ping of death, neptune attack, land attack, smurf attack, teardrop attack, back
Probe	ipsweep, portsweep
U2R	Buffer overflow, load module (Solaris OS program), Perl, root kits
R2L	ftpwrite, jack the ripper (password cracking software), IMAP, mutlihop attack, phf attack, warezmaster, warezclient, spy

FIGURE 18.3

Examples of network intrusions for each attack category.

Ganglia: a cluster monitor

Monitoring a cluster is an important task for the network administrator. The administrator has to take the necessary actions in case of any failure within the cluster. It is tedious to monitor the nodes on a cluster using a CLI-based tool (e.g., Nmap); hence, we need a GUI-based tool that monitors the cluster's health in real time. Ganglia is a Web-based GUI tool that monitors the cluster by using two daemon processes called gmetad and gmond [12]. The gmetad daemon is a central process that requests information from the gmond process. The gmetad process runs on a single machine, while the gmond process runs on all the nodes that constitute the cluster. The authors in [12] state that Ganglia can easily monitor a cluster composed of 100 nodes. However, Ganglia has to be improved to make it efficient in monitoring more than 100 nodes.

Naive Bayes algorithm

The Naive Bayes algorithm makes use of the Bayes rule for defining the Naive Bayes Class (NBC). The authors have discussed this in [13].

Bayes rule

The Bayes rule uses a hypothesis's prior probability to compute its corresponding probability. A hypothesis is a mere fact that does not have any scientific verification. Let "D" be a given data and "h" denote the hypothesis; then the Bayes rule is given by equation (1).

$$P(h|D) = \frac{P(D|h)P(h)}{P(D)} \tag{1}$$

P(h|D) is the posterior probability, which represents the probability that the hypothesis "h" occurs given that the data "D" has occurred. P(D|h) is defined as the conditional probability that gives the probability of data "D," provided the hypothesis "h" has occurred. P(D) is the probability that the data "D" occurs, while P(h) is the probability that the hypothesis "h" occurs. While constructing a model, we need to consider a set of hypotheses, say, "H," which is the superset of a hypothesis "h" that has the highest probability for a given data "D." This hypothesis "h" is known as the Maximum Posterior (MAP) hypothesis. By applying Bayes rules described in equation (1), we can compute the posterior probability of all hypotheses and then select the MAP from among them. By substituting for P(h|D) in the below equation and ignoring P(h), the final equation we arrive at is shown in equation (2).

$$
\begin{aligned}
h_{map} &= \operatorname{argmax}_h \in_H P(h|D) \\
&= \operatorname{argmax}_h \in_H \frac{P(h|D)P(h)}{P(D)} \\
&= \operatorname{argmax}_h \in_H P(D|h)\,P(h) \\
&= \operatorname{argmax}_h \in_H P(D|h)\,P(h)
\end{aligned}
\tag{2}
$$

Naive Bayes classifier

The Naive Bayes classifier is a simple classifier that is based on the Bayes rule. The classifier relies on supervised learning for being trained for classification. As part of this classifier, certain assumptions are considered. These assumptions state that there is a strong independence between the features (in the dataset) and that each attribute's probability is independent of the others' [13]. Despite this rather unrealistic assumption, the Naive Bayes classifier has impressive accuracy. The classifier is used to determine the probability given in equation (3).

$$
\operatorname{argmax}_{ci} \in c \frac{P(A_1=a_1 \ldots A_k=a_k | C=ci)\,P(C=ci)}{P(A_1=a_1 \ldots A_k=a_k)}
\tag{3}
$$

The formula given in equation (3) refers to $P(C = ci|A1 = a1, \ldots Ak = ak)$. To understand the above equation, consider a dataset with a set of "k" attributes ranging from "A1" to "Ak." Each of these attributes has a set of values. The attribute for which there are no values available becomes the class C. The aim of the NBC is to determine the value of class C for any given instance of the dataset. The probability, which is computed for a given instance, is given by equation (4). The value of C, which maximizes this probability, is used to label the given instance.

$$
\operatorname{argmax}_{ci} \in c = P(C=ci) \sum_{i=1}^{k} P(A_i = a_i | C=ci)
\tag{4}
$$

In a real-world scenario, a learner/model is generated by using an extensive training dataset that contains the label for the target class (learning phase). This model is then used to label unclassified data instances (prediction phase).

Other related work

In [14], the authors have illustrated the advantage of using a layered approach for detecting intrusions using an NB classifier. This approach involves selecting specific features for classifying a particular class/target value. The attacks (i.e., classes) were segregated into four groups. Then, for classifying the labels for each group, only the relevant features were selected for generating the model. With their experiments, they proved that the NB classifier was better than the Decision tree in terms of accuracy. However, they have not discussed the actual implementation of their proposed IDS. Their solution is implemented using WEKA 3.6—a machine-learning tool, which does not employ distributed computing. In [15], the authors have implemented a counter-based and an access pattern-based method to detect DDOS attacks. However, they have used native Hadoop API, which does not support real-time processing capability. Hence, the detection happens in offline mode. In [16], a real-time IDS has been proposed using an ensemble-based adaptive learning configuration along with a feature selection algorithm. Additionally, the system utilizes sensors, detectors, and a data warehouse as part of the architecture. The authors have not provided experimental results of their architecture and their system does not operate in a distributed manner. Moreover, the authors do not state the scalability and fault tolerance of their system.

Snort is an NIDS, which relies on a signature-based detection technique [10]. Although Snort has been lauded as a better alternative to commercial IDSes, it is known to fill up the disk with large alert/log files [17]. Snort requires a single powerful machine that has no fault tolerance. This means that if the machine on which Snort resides goes down, then the intrusions can go unnoticed. Snort depends on sensors to receive information about remote nodes. These sensors run on each of the nodes that need to be monitored. Ultimately, these sensors increase traffic and directly affect other high priority network applications/services. In [18], the authors have presented an NIDS called Bro, which contends with Snort. Like Snort, Bro does not feature fault tolerance.

Hadoop-based real-time Intrusion Detection: System architecture

The amount of data generated by network traffic is considerably huge. Although current hardware offers a great array of storage options for such large data, the processing paradigm used by most software cannot handle this huge data. Distributed computing is a promising domain. In fact, it is distributed computing that is the most apt and economical solution when compared to a single piece of hardware, with ultra-high configuration doing all the data crunching with multiple threads. Typically, distributed computing relies on the availability of a cluster, which consists of multiple machines that share responsibilities (rather than a single dedicated powerful server machine). A master-client relationship is generally adopted wherein a single machine acts as a master that supervises the rest of the "slave" machines. Several software frameworks are available that help developers to implement their solutions with the power of distributed computing—Apache Hadoop is one such solution.

Only the KDD '99 intrusion detection dataset [19] was used to evaluate the system. The dataset contains the instances of attacks, which are given in Figure 18.3. We used Apache Hive to preprocess the training data. This task involves the use of HiveQL to replace missing values with a default value, to replace highly distributed values with nominal values, and to remove duplicate records. The setup of the cluster consists of eight machines, of which one acts as the Hadoop master as well as a slave, while the rest of the machines act as slaves. The cluster is heterogeneous, meaning that each machine has a different hardware configuration; some of them are even obsolete when compared to present-day desktop machines. The master alone has 6GB of RAM with four processor cores, while two machines have 3GB of RAM and two cores each. The rest of the machines have just 1GB of RAM with a single core. All of the machines have at least 50GB of hard disk space dedicated to the HDFS. Each machine ran the Ubuntu Lucid (10.04) operating system. One aim of our study was to determine whether we could rely on obsolete hardware for building a critical system such as an NIDS.

A typical example of big data generated in real time is the network traffic data captured using packet sniffers. A MapReduce job is used to implement a Naive Bayes learner that uses pre-recorded network traffic data as the training data and consequently generates the model in the form of a text file. This is known as the learning phase. Snort is used to capture network traffic in tcpdump format. This tcpdump (raw) data is then converted to CSV format by using a Command Line Interface- (CLI) based tool called tshark. This CSV file is then streamed to a TCP/UDP-based URL called the "In" stream, using HStreaming's StreamGen. After that, another MapReduce job is triggered that loads the model into memory and uses it to classify connections that are read from the "In" stream. The MapReduce job classifies/labels each record as either an attack or a normal connection, then writes them to the "Out" stream (another TCP/UDP-based URL). This is known as the prediction phase. The solution also consists of a Web interface through which the administrator can initiate the learning phase to generate the Naive Bayes classifier, and trigger the prediction phase using live traffic data. Visualizations such as pie charts and bar charts are available to the administrator for quickly assessing the status of the network. Using HIDS on each of these multiple targets is not a cost-effective way of ensuring security, although there are advantages. The best possible solution is to employ an NIDS that is installed on a host, which acts like the single point of access for multiple targets. Typically, a machine that acts like a gateway/firewall can be used to host the NIDS. The firewall has access to the packets that flow through the network and not just to itself. Hence, the NIDS can detect attacks by monitoring all the packets that flow through the firewall and detect any kind of suspicious activity by using either the misuse-based or the anomaly-based approach for intrusion detection. The proposed architecture is given in Figure 18.4.

As the prediction phase is running continuously in real-time, a standalone Java-based program called streamreader reads the labeled records from the "Out" stream and writes them to a file on the file system. A bash shell script reads this file and generates statistical data that is used as input for the bar charts and pie charts (see Figure 18.5). Only the statistics are mailed to the administrator, which avoids spamming the mailbox with an alert of each detected attack. Ganglia is used to monitor the cluster's performance.

The pie chart gives the distribution of real-time threats that were detected by the system. The user needs to tap on the "Refresh Data" button to update the chart.

Practical application scenario and system evaluation

This section discusses the practical application scenario of our system and its experimental evaluation.

Experimental evaluation

To demonstrate the capability of the system, we devised a real-world setup of a heterogeneous cluster composed of nine machines (including the gateway). The setup of our cluster is depicted in Figure 18.6.

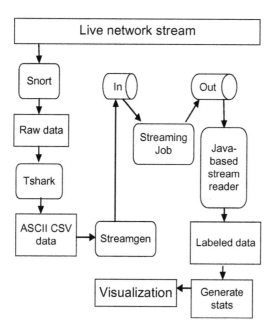

FIGURE 18.4

System architecture.

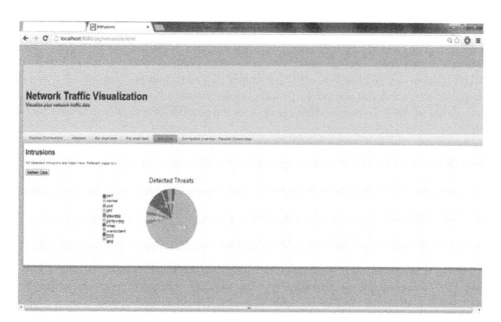

FIGURE 18.5

Visualization of detected threats.

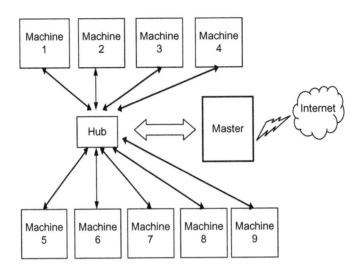

FIGURE 18.6

The heterogeneous cluster setup.

Our cluster setup is similar to that of small internal LANs that are maintained by many organizations such as companies, schools, and universities.

We performed experimental analysis in multiple phases. In the first phase of our experiment, we wanted to compare the performance of our heterogeneous cluster composed of obsolete hardware with a homogeneous cluster. Each node on the homogeneous cluster has an Intel Xeon X3350 processor with 2.66 GHz speed, four cores, 4GB RAM, three 1 TB Seagate ES.2 hard drives, and an Intel PRO/1000 e1000e Ethernet card. We ran our Hadoop-based NBC on both clusters with the 10% KDD training set described in [19] that consisted of all features. Additionally, we ran the training phase with a reduced number of features, as discussed in [19]. The result of the first phase is shown in Figure 18.7. Normally, Hadoop decides the number of mappers to spawn for a given MR job.

From Figure 18.7, we can infer that the heterogeneous cluster is slower than the homogeneous cluster by an average of 68.5 seconds (approximately one minute). The mappers and reducers on the heterogeneous cluster frequently complained of a Java heap space (out of memory) error. We anticipated this error, owing to the size of our training data and the very limited RAM available on the obsolete nodes. The OS on the nodes utilize at least 300MB of the RAM; hence, the space available for the Java Virtual Machine (JVM) is very limited for processing large data in-memory. The number of DFS blocks in the input file controls the number of mappers that are assigned for the job.

In newer versions of Hadoop, the parameter called *dfs.blocksize* is used to define the DFS block size. We have to optimally set this parameter so that the number of mappers assigned to the MapReduce job is more than sufficient. Spawning a large number of mappers creates a significant overhead and affects the overall performance. In the case of our experiments, we found that only one mapper was spawned for all the jobs. We used the homogeneous cluster as our test bed for rest

Cluster \ Features	Heterogeneous cluster training time (seconds)	Homogeneous cluster training time (seconds)
All features	115 (1 Mapper, 13 Reducers)	38 (1 Mapper, 13 Reducers)
Reduced features [25]	88 (1 Mapper, 13 Reducers)	28 (1 Mapper, 13 Reducers)

FIGURE 18.7

Training speeds on heterogeneous and homogeneous clusters.

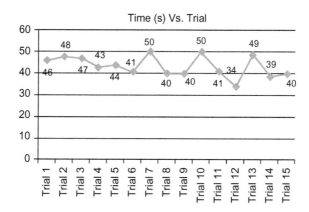

FIGURE 18.8

The completion time for each trial.

of the experimental phases; we inferred that it is faster than the heterogeneous cluster. In the second phase, we conducted several trials of running our Hadoop-based Naive Bayes classifier on the homogenous cluster to determine whether we could achieve further speed boost. The result of the trials is given in Figure 18.8.

We tried to performance-tune Hadoop by varying the Hadoop-based parameters mentioned in [5]. Along with tuning Hadoop, we tuned our MapReduce job, as well. The performance tuning configurations we defined for the trial runs is shown in Figure 18.9.

The various combinations of the configurations distinguish the trial runs. The details of each trial are shown in Figure 18.10. Each trial consisted of a single mapper.

We can rest assured that it was in trial run 12 that we achieved the fastest performance, as seen in Figure 18.10. The number of reducers for a job can be programmatically set using Hadoop's built-in classes and methods. We controlled the number of reducers to determine if we could make the job run faster than the standalone Naive Bayes. From Figure 18.10, we can infer that the job that used 13 reducers was the fastest.

In the third phase, we compared the training speed of our Hadoop-based classifier with a standalone non-Hadoop-based Naive Bayes classifier and two other improved algorithms (presented in [13]); namely, an adaptive Bayesian algorithm and an improved self-adaptive Bayesian algorithm. The 10% KDD training set mentioned in [19] was used in this phase. The result is seen in Figure 18.12.

Clearly, the Hadoop-based Naive Bayes algorithm is faster than the standalone Naive Bayes by 8.9 seconds (a 20 percent decrease in time). However, the Hadoop-based Naive Bayes is not as fast as the adaptive and self-adaptive Bayesian algorithms. Further speed boost can be achieved only if we adopt any of these faster algorithms. These algorithms are computationally more efficient than the Naive Bayes algorithm. We believe that the available memory on the nodes is a major downfall for large data processing. We anticipate an increase in speed by upgrading the RAM on the nodes

No.	Performance Configuration
C1	Change reducer output pair data type to String
C2	Declare variables inside class body instead of the Map and Reduce methods.
C3	Set *mapred.reduce.slowstart.completed.maps* to 0.0, so that the reducers do notwait until mappers complete.
C4	Increase *io.sort.mb*to avoid spilling of records to disk (increases I/O)
C5	Increase *io.sort.factor* so that the streams are sent to reducer before merging them
C6	Compress map output by setting *mapred.compress.map.output* to true (Saves time when data is sent to reducer)
C7	Compress reduce output by setting *mapred.compress.reduce.output* to true (Saves time when data is written to HDFS)
C8	Enable speculative execution by setting *mapred.map/reduce.tasks.speculative.execution* to true. Clones map/reduce tasks if they run slow.
C9	Change the map output key data type to string.
C10	Increase number of threads that copy map output to reducer by increasing *mapred.reduce.parallel.copies* from 5 to 8

FIGURE 18.9

Performance tuning configurations.

Trial no.	No. of Reducers	Performance Configurations used
1	5	C1
2	5	C1, C2
3	1	C1, C2
4	1	C1, C2, C3
5	1	C1, C2, C3, C4, C5, C10
6	10	C1, C2, C3, C4, C5, C10
7	20	C1, C2, C3, C4, C5, C10
8	12	C1, C2, C3, C4, C5, C10
9	12	C1, C2, C3, C4, C5, C8, C10
10	15	C1, C2, C3, C4,C5, C8, C9, C10
11	15	C2, C3, C4, C5, C8, C9, C10
12	13	C1, C2, C3, C4, C5, C6, C8, C9, C10
13	13	C2, C3, C4, C5, C8, C9, C10
14	13	C2, C3, C4, C5, C6, C8, C9, C10
15	14	C2, C3, C4, C5, C6, C7, C8, C9, C10

FIGURE 18.10

Details of trial runs and their respective configurations.

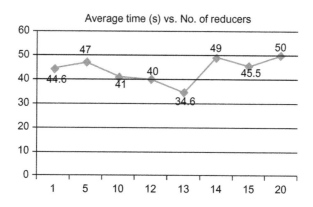

FIGURE 18.11

The completion times for varying numbers of reducers.

to at least 16GB. Delays caused by the Hadoop framework can also affect the overall performance of the job. As seen from the trial runs, we need to optimize the execution of the MapReduce job by checking for improvements by varying the number of reducers. The cluster performance was monitored using Ganglia while the MapReduce jobs (training) were running. Figure 18.13 shows the

Algorithm	Training speed (seconds)
Naive Bayes	42.9
Hadoop-based Naive Bayes	34
Adaptive Bayesian	24.6
Self Adaptive Bayesian	28.4

FIGURE 18.12

Training speed comparison of Hadoop-based Naive Bayes algorithm with non-Hadoop-based Naive Bayes algorithms.

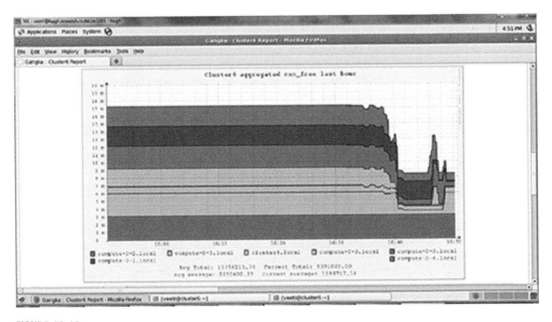

FIGURE 18.13

A stacked graph showing the aggregated free memory for the homogeneous cluster.

available free memory on the homogeneous cluster while the Hadoop-based Naive Bayes algorithm generated the learning model. During most of the trials, the nodes used swap space to carry out the processing.

In the fourth phase, we conducted four trials in which the streaming job classified the unlabeled KDD '99 testing dataset. The aim of this experiment is to determine the number of records classified per minute. From the trials shown in Figure 18.14, we were able to deduce that the streaming Naive Bayes classifier can classify an average of 434 records per minute (i.e., seven records per second, approximately). We ran Snort on a standalone machine to sniff for packets for 49 seconds. Snort was able to capture about 527 packets. This means that Snort captures 11 packets per second. We estimate that there would be a delay of a few seconds when tshark [20] converts the binary data generated by Snort into a CSV file (see Figure 18.4). Hence, we concluded that the performance of our streaming Naive Bayes classifier is acceptable in real-world scenarios.

In the final phase, we found that our Hadoop-based NBC has a detection rate of 90 percent. We had not used live traffic data for testing the classifier, since we did not simulate attacks in our cluster. Hence, to determine the efficiency of our classifier, we used the labeled and unlabeled KDD testing data.

Practical application

The experimental evaluation has proven that our system has realistic performance in terms of speed and efficiency. Our research does not focus on preparing the dataset for training the classifier; instead, it presents a novel design architecture for an intrusion detection system. Data preparation is a much broader research area. We did not want to reinvent the wheel so, for practical use, we propose to make use of the approach discussed in [21] to extract the relevant features from the real-time raw packet data generated by tcpdump. We would like to point out that this approach is feasible for our system since it uses Snort, which also generates the packet data in tcpdump format.

Trial runs	No. of records classified per minute
Trial 1	534
Trial 2	345
Trial 3	368
Trial 4	491

FIGURE 18.14

Classification speed of the Hadoop-based Naive Bayes classifier.

As Snort generates the tcpdump file, tshark [20] converts the binary packet data into a CSV file. An example for the single-line command that translates the binary packet data into a CSV file is as follows:

```
snort-l /log-b
# Start tshark to convert tcpdump data to ASCII
tshark-F text-E header = y separator = ","-T fields-e tcp.ack-e tcp.port-e frame.color-
ing_rule.name-e ip.checksum_good-e frame.len-e ip.src-e ip.dst-e tcp.port-e udp.port
```

Note that the fields extracted from the packets are determined by the technique presented in [21].

Once we determine the features that are useful for intrusion detection, we can utilize more elaborate and realistic network traces, such as the ISCX dataset presented in [23]. The ISCX dataset consists of network traces representing connections that are normal or a type of attack. The network traces can be used for training the Hadoop-based algorithm and generating the knowledge model. This knowledge model can then be used to label each packet-related record as "normal" or as "attack." Alternatively, we envision that NetFlow data can be used to train our model. A practical system that uses NetFlow data for detecting intrusions has been discussed in [23]. However, to train our Hadoop-based classifier, we require labeled NetFlow records.

SUMMARY

Our Hadoop-based Naive Bayes Classifier is faster than the standalone Naive Bayes Classifier. There is scope for further increase in performance by upgrading hardware and performing software optimizations. We have learned that a homogeneous cluster performs better than a heterogeneous cluster. The choice of hardware is of utmost importance while setting up a cluster for running MapReduce jobs. In the case of our system, we succeeded in building a fault-tolerant, scalable, and reliable architecture for detecting intrusions in real time. As part of our future work, we intend to port our code to the Storm API [24], which shares similar features with Hadoop, such as fault tolerance, reliability, and distributed processing. Storm API provides real-time processing capabilities like that of HStreaming. Moreover, Storm is open source; hence, it is more economical than HStreaming, which requires a fee for the full edition. The choice of the Naive Bayes algorithm for our system is worthwhile, yet other performance-oriented algorithms can be used, as well. Our approach is not directed at improving classification accuracy or detection rate. Instead, we focused on designing an architecture that has the advantages of the Hadoop framework with real-time processing capabilities thanks to the HStreaming API. We believe that our Web-based visualizations would help security analysts stay abreast of intrusions and network traffic.

References

[1] Hosaka T. Thousands of PlayStation network accounts targeted by massive attack. Sony Hack. [Internet]. 2011 Oct. Retrieved from: <http://www.informationweek.com/security/attacks/twitter-battles-syrian-hackers/240153424>; 2011.

[2]   Schwartz M. Twitter battles Syrian hackers. [Internet]. Retrieved from: <http://www.thedailybeast.com/articles/2010/12/11/hackers-10-most-famous-attacks-worms-and-ddos-takedowns.html>; 2013.

[3]   Ries B. Most famous attacks, worms, and DDos takedowns. [Internet]. Retrieved from: http://www.thedailybeast.com/articles/2010/12/11/hackers-10-most-famous-attacks-worms-and-ddos-takedowns.html; 2010.

[4]   Welcome to Apache™ Hadoop®! The Apache Software Foundation. [Internet]. Retrieved from: <http://hadoop.apache.org/>; 2013 [accessed 03.06.13].

[5]   White T. Hadoop: The definitive guide. Web. 1st ed. O'Reilly Media, Inc.; 2009.

[6]   Mujummdar P. Home-Apache Hive-Apache Software Foundation. [Internet]. Retrieved from: <https://cwiki.apache.org/confluence/display/Hive/Home>; 2013.

[7]   Release 1.1.b2. (2011, December 20). HStreaming Developer Guide, pp. 6−9.

[8]   Bace R, Mell P. NIST special publication on intrusion detection systems. Booz Allen Hamilton Inc. McLean VA 2001.

[9]   Innella P. The evolution of intrusion detection systems | Symantec connect community. Symantec. [Internet]. Retrieved from: <http://www.symantec.com/connect/articles/evolution-intrusion-detection-systems>; 2001.

[10] Roesch M. Snort-lightweight intrusion detection for networks. In: Proceedings of the 13th USENIX Conference on System Administration; 1999. p. 229−238.

[11] Bostock M. D3. js: Data-driven documents. 2011.

[12] Massie ML, Chun BN, Culler DE. The ganglia distributed monitoring system: Design, implementation, and experience. Parallel Computing 2004;30(7):817−40.

[13] Farid D, Rahman M. Anomaly network intrusion detection based on improved self adaptive Bayesian algorithm. Journal Of Computers 2010;5(1):23−31. doi:10.4304/jcp.5.1.23−31.

[14] Sharma N, Mukherjee S. Layered approach for intrusion detection using naïve Bayes classifier. Proceedings of the International Conference on Advances in Computing, Communications and Informatics 2012;639−44 ACM.

[15] Lee Y, Lee Y Detecting DDoS attacks with Hadoop. In: Proceedings of The ACM CoNEXT Student Workshop ACM; 2011. p. 7.

[16] Lee W, Stolfo SJ, Chan PK, Eskin E, Fan W, Miller M, et al. Real time data mining-based intrusion detection. In: DARPA Information Survivability Conference & Exposition II, 2001. DISCEX'01. Proceedings IEEE. 2001;1:89−100.

[17] May C, Baker M, Gabbard D, Good T, Grimes G, Holmgren M, et al. Advanced information assurance handbook (No. CMU/SEI-2004-HB-001). Carnegie-Mellon Univ Pittsburgh Pa Software Engineering Inst; 2004.

[18] Paxson V. Bro: a system for detecting network intruders in real-time. Computer Networks 1999;31(23):2435−63.

[19] Olusola AA, Oladele AS, Abosede DO. Analysis of KDD'99 intrusion detection dataset for selection of relevance features. In: Proceedings of the World Congress on Engineering and Computer Science. 2010;1:20−22.

[20] tshark-The Wireshark network analyzer 1.10.0. [Internet]. Retrieved from: <http://www.wireshark.org/docs/man-pages/tshark.html>; [accessed 10.07.13].

[21] Esposito M, Mazzariello C, Oliviero F, Romano SP, Sansone C. Evaluating pattern recognition techniques in intrusion detection systems. In: PRIS; 2005. p. 144−153.

[22] Shiravi A, Shiravi H, Tavallaee M, Ghorbani AA. Toward developing a systematic approach to generate benchmark datasets for intrusion detection. Computers & Security 2012;31(3):357−74.

[23] Ahamad T, Aljumah A, Ahmad Y. Detecting cyber attacks at data dribble. Network and Complex Systems 2012;2(5):1−7.

[24] Leibiusky J, Eisbruch G, Simonassi D. Getting started with storm. O'Reilly Media, Inc.; 2012.

Optimum Countermeasure Portfolio Selection: A Knapsack Approach

19

Maryam Shahpasand and Sayed Alireza Hashemi Golpayegani
Amirkabir University of Technology (Tehran Polytechnic), Tehran, Iran

INFORMATION IN THIS CHAPTER

- Knapsack problem
- Optimal security countermeasure selection issues
- A binary knapsack approach using dynamic programming
- Application in a practical case

INTRODUCTION

As a result of the extension of information technology into all aspects of business, information security became one of the most important issues in all types of organizations. The vast usage of information systems and computer networks in organizations has provided them with immense benefit. Yet alongside the benefits they offer, these systems can be faced with many new threats that can interrupt, spy upon, or take personal advantage of them. Even the best systems are not completely impervious, since there are always a way to target and penetrate the system's weaknesses. These weaknesses are known as vulnerabilities. "How to find these vulnerabilities?" "How to identify the threats that could exploit these vulnerabilities?" and "How to formulate the best plan to confront the threats and not to let them become serious attacks?" are the questions for which organizations seek answers.

All of these questions can be answered through the task of risk management [1]. This task includes several subtasks and concepts like risk assessment, which tries to answer the first two questions, and risk mitigation, which is looking for the answer to the last question. In risk assessment, organizations look at threat list and the probability and severity of occurrences and related costs if these threats lead to attacks. Risk mitigation implements the appropriate countermeasure for each asset the organization owns to save them from probable loss. How are these tasks accomplished? For organizations with lots of information assets, such as personal computers, network components, data bases, and so on, these tasks become very complicated.

To face this issue appropriately, major organizations like the National Institute of Standards and Technology (INST) [2],, the International Organization for Standards (ISO) [3], and the Australian/New Zealand Standard (AS/NZS 4360) [4] have defined systematic frameworks as standards, in which they classify most of the information attacks that have occurred and introduce best plans and related technologies in order to prevent probable loss. Each plan and its related technology are defined as a countermeasure. However, considering and implementing all proposed countermeasures defined by these standards is not feasible for business in all types and sizes.

In this regard, many researchers have proposed frameworks and tools to simplify this task. In order to assess the information risk and decide on mitigation strategies with respect to the aforementioned standards, [5] proposed a system called OCTAVE, which utilizes qualitative information to assess risk. CRAMM (CCTA Risk Analysis and Management Method), an ISO-based method, was established in 1985 by the Central Computing and Telecommunications Agency (CCTA) of the United Kingdom, tried to manage information risk in three stages as detailed in [6]. The European Union conducted an information security project in 2001 that led to CORAS, an approach that utilizes UML and XML technologies and combinations of standards and best practices to provide a complete and reliable tool for risk management [7]. However, these approaches are still complicated and general, so there remains a need for more agile frameworks. Moreover, how to answer the third question above and choose the optimal countermeasure portfolio should be the primary focus.

Getting serious about developing a best countermeasure portfolio, GAO/AMID [8] proposed a risk assessment matrix that represents risk level by assessing a threat's severity and the probability of occurrence in a qualitative way. [9] tried to develop a checklist in table form that enables IT experts to plan a coverage strategy. [10] used defense trees and conditional preference networks (CP-nets) to select sets of countermeasures. [11] applied a Multi-Objective Tabu Search (MOTS) algorithm to find the best solution for choosing a countermeasure portfolio on a limited budget. Following [12], a paper on mitigating information security risks within the available budget, [13] tried to develop a knapsack-based algorithm to get to the best subset of countermeasures. However, the author defined control groups and a scoring system in order to calculate countermeasure effectiveness that does not fit all organizations. As a result, IT experts have to decide whether to use this grouping and scoring system as well. [14] conducted a quantitative data set based on the threat set reported on the IT security forum EndpointSecurity.org [15], and proposed a model to find the optimal solution out of all the possible countermeasure options, with respect to a given limited budget. [16] proposed a mixed-integer programming model, similar to Rakes et al.'s, taking advantage of two popular concepts, Value at Risk and Conditional Value at Risk, to make the expert decisions more risk-aversive.

The present research was inspired by [14]'s work. Following their risk modeling approach, I propose a knapsack-based approach that tries to solve a similar model and results in the same optimal solution, which is discussed in the following sections.

The rest of the chapter is organized as follows: The knapsack problem as a NP-hard problem and the best solution for small search spaces is discussed in the next section. In the section after that, a description of a countermeasure selection problem in IT security planning is presented. The subsequent section describes the simple knapsack-based solution and the pseudo code. Numerical examples and some computational results are illustrated in the final section, which is followed by a conclusion.

The Knapsack problem and a dynamic programming solution

The knapsack problem is a problem in combinatorial optimization: given a set of items, each with a weight and a value, determine the number of each item to include in a collection so that the total weight is less than or equal to a given limit and the total value is as large as possible. It derives its name from the problem faced by someone who is constrained by a fixed-size knapsack and must fill it with the most valuable items [17]. The most famous knapsack problem is the binary (0−1) knapsack problem, where the decision maker is allowed to pick (1) or not to pick (0) the item, in other words, the items are not dividable.

The problem can be formulated as follows:

Let there be n items, x_1 to x_n where x_i has the v_i value and weight w_i. The maximum weight the knapsack can carry is W. It is common to assume that all values and weights are non-negative. To simplify the representation, it is also assumed that the items are listed in increasing order of weight.

$$Maximum \sum_{i=1}^{n} v_i * x_i \tag{1}$$

$$s.t. \sum_{i=1}^{n} w_i * x_i \leq W \quad x_i \in \{0, 1\} \tag{2}$$

Many algorithms have been proposed to arrive at the optimal subset of items [18]. A simple dynamic programming algorithm with polynomial time complexity for a small search space was proposed in [19]. Dynamic programming algorithms try to solve complex problems by dividing them into smaller sub-problems. A matrix is used to store the answers to sub problems, and the final answer is found after the matrix is filled.

To illustrate, assume $w_1, w_2, \ldots, w_n$ are strictly positive integers. Define $m[i, w]$ to be the maximum value that can be attained when the weight is less than or equal to w using items up to i. The definition of $m[i, w]$ is then as follows:

- $m[i, w] = m[i - 1, w]$ if $w_i > w$ (the new item is more than the current weight limit)
- $m[i, w] = \max(m[i - 1, w], m[i - 1, w - wi] + v_i)$ if $w_i \leq w$

The solution can then be found by calculating $m[i, w]$. The pseudo code is shown in Figure 19.1

The algorithm takes *value* and *weight* arrays, *number of items*, and *knapsack capacity* as inputs. From line 6 to line 8, the first row of m matrix is set with value "0," which means that when no items are picked, no value is gained. Lines 9 to 17 repeat for all items (filling m matrix rows, with index i in each iteration) so that at the last cell ($m[i, w]$) will get the maximum value. Following iterations for the loop that starts at line 10, the algorithm considers the situation that we have j unit(s) capacity in our knapsack and will return the maximum value that can be taken. This solution will therefore run in $O(nW)$ time and $O(nW)$ space. Additionally, if we use only a 1-dimensional array $m[w]$ to store the current optimal values and pass over this array $i + 1$ times, rewriting from $m[w]$ to $m[1]$ every time, we get the same result for only $O(W)$ space.

There are many practical applications for the binary knapsack theory. For example, assume that n projects are available to an investor; each one will cause a specific profit and will cost w_j money

```
1    // Input:
2    // Values (stored in array v)
3    // Weights (stored in array w)
4    // Number of distinct items (n)
5    // Knapsack capacity (W)
6    for w from 0 to W do
7      m[0, w] := 0
8    end for
9    for i from 1 to n do
10     for j from 0 to W do
11       if j >= w[i] then
12         m[i, j] := max(m[i-1, j], m[i-1, j-w[i]] + v[i])
13       else
14         m[i, j] := m[i-1, j]
15       end if
16     end for
17   end for
```

FIGURE 19.1

Dynamic programming solution pseudo code for the binary knapsack problem.

unit to invest in j^{th} project. The investor has limited capital for this investment. The optimal investment plane would result by mapping this problem as a binary knapsack problem and solving it [20]. Another common application is for cutting stock problems. For example, paper factories produce huge rolls of paper that are not fit to customer order at the first place, so they have to slice these rolls into smaller rolls. The value of the smaller rolls depends on the selling price. Fiber optic cable manufacturers are faced with a similar problem; they must decide how to cut lengths of cable to satisfy customer orders while extracting the greatest value from each length of cable. The knapsack idea also applies to solving problems that warehouses or distribution centers (DC) have with space. The main concern among DCs is filling customer orders as fast as possible. On the other hand, they have limited warehouse space for holding their inventories [21]. All of the above problems can be modeled as knapsack problems and solved by the dynamic programming algorithm in a reasonable time.

The dynamic programming algorithm discussed in this section, not only runs in polynomial time complexity but also provides a definite solution. For this reason, this theory is used in our proposed approach to get to the optimal solution for our problem, A described in next section.

Problem description

In this section, the algorithm and its inputs and variables are illustrated, using the notation shown in Table 19.1:

Defined $I = \{1, \ldots m\}$, the set of m threats and $J = \{1, \ldots n\}$ the set of n countermeasures. Denote by $Prop(i,j)$ the proportion of threat i that will survive if countermeasure j is implemented and, respectively, $(1 - Prop(i,j))$ the proportion of this threat that will successfully be blocked. We are looking for maximum block by choosing the optimal countermeasure portfolio. This will cost equal to summation of countermeasures' cost, which belong to this portfolio, which is denoted by

Table 19.1 Notation
Indices
I = threat, $i \in I = \{1, \ldots, m\}$ J = countermeasure, $j \in J = \{1, \ldots, n\}$ K = chosen countermeasure, $k \in K, K \subseteq J = \{1, \ldots, n\}$
Input parameters
$Loss(i)$ = cost of a successful attack episode of threat i B = available budget for countermeasures implementation $Cost(j)$ = cost of countermeasure j implementation $Freq(i)$ = frequency of threat i per year $Prop(i,j)$ = proportion of threat i that survives if countermeasure j is implemented $\in [0, 1]$
Variable
$y(j)$ 1, if countermeasure j is implemented, otherwise 0 $Proportion(i,k)$ total blocked proportion of threat i if countermeasure k is implemented, $Proportion(i,k) \in [0, 1]$ $Control$ Effectiveness of countermeasure j in case of implementing countermeasures $Effectiveness(j)$ $k \in K$ (amount of money that is saved from all attacks' loss, if this countermeasure has been implemented)

$Cost(j)$. By $Freq(i)$, we mean the frequency of threat i that occurs each year and $Loss(i)$, the financial cost imposed by each occurrence of threat i.

We now want to determine the optimal subset of possible solutions. For this purpose, an effectiveness score is assigned to each countermeasure. To describe the effectiveness of each countermeasure, we look for other countermeasures' state of implementation and then calculate the following formula in algorithm:

Let $Proportion(i,k) \in [0, 1]$ be the total blocked proportion of threat i if countermeasure k is implemented, considering other countermeasures' state, calculate as:

$$Proportion(i,k)$$

$$= (1 - Prop(i,k)) \, \Pi j \in K \, Prop(i,j) * y(j) \tag{3}$$

For countermeasure effectiveness we have:

$$ControlEffectiveness(j)$$

$$= \Sigma i \in I \, (Freq(i) * Loss(i) * Proportion(i,k)) \tag{4}$$

Our objective function to determine the maximum countermeasure effectiveness is as follows:

$$Max \sum j \in J \ ControlEffectiveness(j) * y(j) \qquad (5)$$

$$s.t. \sum j \in J \ cost(j) * y(j) <= Budget \qquad (6)$$

To illustrate how these variables work, assume we have the following data for $Prop(i,j)$, $Loss(i)$ and $Freq(i)$:

	Count. #1	Count. #2	Count. #3	Loss	Frequency per year
Threat #1	0.01	1	0.2	24$	200
Threat #2	0.03	0.8	0.6	50$	122
Decision about countermeasure implementation, $y(j) \in \{0,1\}$, $K = \{1\}$	1	0	?		

Calculating the blocked proportion of threats 1 and 2 for countermeasure ($k = 3$) and its effectiveness, we have:

$$Proportion(1, 3) = (1 - 0.2) * (0.01 * 1) = 0.008$$
$$Proportion(2, 3) = (1 - 0.6) * (0.03 * 1) = 0.012$$
$$ControlEffectiveness(3) = (200 * 24 * 0.008) + (122 * 50 * 0.012) = 111.6\$$$

To illustrate the logic behind this formula, consider the above example, in case of implementation of first countermeasures, that the number of occurrences of first threat, if countermeasure #3 is implemented, would not be 40(0.2 * 200) any more, since the first countermeasure blocked 198(0.99 * 200) of its occurrences. As a result, countermeasure # 3 will only block 0.008((1 − 0.2) * 0.01) of its occurrences. Having each countermeasure's cost, it is feasible to find the optimal subset of countermeasures whose total cost does not exceed the budget limits.

As shown, in each step of making the decision about remained countermeasures, we must have the decision that was made about the previous countermeasures (K). This may seem like a limitation, but by applying the dynamic programming solution to resolve the binary knapsack problem, it becomes a less complex problem for which a definite solution can be found.

The proposed binary knapsack-based approach and its dynamic programming algorithm

In this section, we introduce our proposed binary knapsack−based approach and its dynamic programming algorithm. This approach begins with the first countermeasure and calculating its effectiveness, in case it is going to be implemented and no other countermeasures have been decided on ($K = \{1\}$). This action takes place at the first *if* condition (line 11 in Figure 19.1). In order to record the decision about the countermeasures, it's enough to insert a matrix with

```
1    // Input:
2    // Values (stored in array v)
3    // Weights (stored in array w)
4    // Number of distinct items (n)
5    // Knapsack capacity (W)
6    for w from 0 to W do
7      m[0, w] := 0
8    end for
9    for b from 0 to 2*(W+1) do
10     for i from 1 to m do
11         Selection[b,i] := 0
12   //this is a matrix that save the decision for all states about current and previous items
13       end for
14   end for
15   for i from 1 to n do
16     Selection[1:(W+1),all] := Selection[((W+1)+1):2*(W+1),all]
17     Selection[(W+1)+1 : (2*(W+1)),all] := 0
18     for j from 0 to W do
19       if j >= w[i] then
20         m[i, j] := max(m[i-1, j], m[i-1, j-w[i]] + v[i])
21         if (m[i-1, j-w[i]] + v[i]> m[i-1, j])
22             Selection[(W+1)+j, all] := Selection[j- w[i],all]
23             Selection[(W+1)+j, i] :=1
24         else
25             Selection[(W+1)+j, all] := Selection[j, all]
26         end if
27       else
28         m[i, j] := m[i-1, j]
29         Selection[(W+1)+j, all] := Selection[j, all]
30       end if
31     end for
32   end for
```

FIGURE 19.2

Pseudo code for using a matrix about decision for items.

"$2 * (budget + 1)$" rows and "number of items" columns. This is simple, as shown in Figure 19.2. The last row in this matrix shows the final decision, which corresponds to $m[m, Budget]$, which contains the maximum effectiveness.

The pseudo code for the proposed algorithm is shown in Figure 19.3. In this algorithm, the decision about implementing countermeasures is in $Selection[W + 1, all]$. As a result we can calculate current countermeasure effectiveness with respect to other chosen countermeasures' state of selection. We discuss the logic behind the algorithm and its structure in the following.

Assume $Cost_1, Cost_2, \ldots, Cost_m$, are strictly positive integers corresponding to each countermeasure implementation cost. Define $m[j, money]$, to be the maximum effectiveness that can be attained with cost less than or equal to $money$ using countermeasures up to j. This can be defined as follows:

- $m[j, money] = m[j - 1, money]$ if $Cost_j > money$ (implementation cost of the new countermeasure is more than the current budget limit)
- $m[j, money] = \max\left(m[j - 1, money], m\left[j - 1, money - Cost_j\right] + Effectiveness_j\right)$ if $Cost_j \leq money$

```
1   // Input:
2   // Costs (stored in array Cost)
3   // Number of countermeasures (n)
4   // cost of a successful attack episode of threat i (stored in array loss)
5   // Number of threats (m)
6   // limited budget (Budget)
7   //Proportion of threat i that survive if countermeasure j is implemented (stored in matrix
8   //prop[i,j])
9
10  Temp:= 1
11
12  for money from 0 to Budget do
13    m[0, money] := 0
14  end for
15
16  for b from 0 to 2*(Budget+1) do
17     for j from 1 to n do
18         Selection[b,j] := 0
19     end for
20  end for
21
22  for j from 1 to n do
23
24    Selection [1:( Budget+1),all] := Selection[((Budget +1)+1):2*( Budget+1),all]
25    Selection[(Budget+1)+1 : (2*( Budget+1)),all] := 0
26
27    for money from 0 to Budget do
28
29      if   (money >= cost[j]) then
30
31        for i from 1 to m do
32
33              effectiveness[j] := ((1-prop[i,j])* Produt(prop[i,k], where
34              Selection[money-cost[j], k]= = 1 )* temp) *loss[i]* Freq[i]
35        end for
36
37        m[j, money] := max(m[j-1, money], m[j-1, money-cost[j]] + effectiveness [j])
38
39        if (m[j-1, money - cost [i]] + effectiveness [j]> m[j-1, money])
40           Selection[( Budget+1)+ money, all] := Selection[money - cost [j],all]
41           Selection[( Budget+1)+ money, j] :=1
42        else
43           Selection[( Budget+1)+ money, all] := Selection[money, all]
44        end if
45
46      else
47         m[j, money] := m[j-1, money]
48         Selection[( Budget+1)+ money, all] := Selection[money, all]
49      end if
50
51    end for
52
53  end for
```

FIGURE 19.3

Pseudo code for our proposed binary knapsack algorithm.

If adding j^{th} countermeasure in this step would cause the maximum, change *Selection* [(*Budget* + 1) + *money*, *j*] form 0 to 1

The *Effectiveness*$_j$ can be calculated as described in previous section, and the maximum effectiveness can then be found in $m[m, Budget]$. Countermeasures are selected where the corresponding indexes have the value "1" in the last row of *Selection*[] matrix.

The algorithm takes the number of countermeasures and their related cost of implementation, the number of threats and their cost of a successful attack, *Prop*[] matrix that contains the survival proportion of each attack episode for each countermeasure and available budget as inputs. *Temp* variable at line 10 is set with value "1" to prevent any wrong calculation in the equation in line 33. The *for* loop in lines 16 to 20 makes the *Selection*[] matrix with initial values "0". From the 22nd line, the algorithm starts to make a decision about each countermeasure implementation. In lines 24 and 25, *Selection*[] matrix changes its upper half rows, which is about $j - 1^{th}$ status for each money(0 to budget), with its bottom half, which is about j^{th} status for each money (0 to budget), and puts "0" for all bottom half rows, in order to put the decision about $j + 1^{th}$ countermeasure in each step for money value (0 to budget) in the *for* loop that starts at line 27. This exchange happens for each iteration on *j* index. This is necessary, since we want to calculate the effectiveness of the jth countermeasure, and this value is related to other countermeasures that are selected for implementation by this step. This value is calculated in lines 31 to 35, based on Eq. (3) and Eq. (4). The rest of *for* loop started at line 27 follows the simple steps in the algorithm in Figure 19.1.

To understand how this algorithm works, two shots of algorithm operations using a simple example are shown in Figure 19.4.

As can be seen in Figure 19.4, in each step in the *for* loop on index *j*, the *Selection*[] matrix changes to keep the last decision about countermeasure 1 to Countermeasure #j − 1. A computational example with reliable and practical data is discussed in the next section.

Computational example and comparison

In this section, a computational example is presented to show the proposed binary knapsack−based approach and its related dynamic programming algorithm results. The parameters used for the example problem can be seen in Table 19.2.

The above data set is the same one presented in [14], which was conducted based on a threat set reported on the IT security forum EndpointSecurity.org [15]. This 8∗8 matrix is a tabulation representation of the survival proportion of each threat for each countermeasure. The diagonal cells where $i = j$, represent the primary relationship between threats and countermeasures, that is, the related countermeasure is specifically designed to prevent the related threat. However, other cells where $i \neq j$, which is less than one, indicate countermeasures that prevent their primary threat as well as other threats.

Briefly describing the [14] model, we show that we can provide the same results in an algorithmic approach. The comparison is shown in Table 19.3. In [14], the authors defined the

Inputs:

Countermeasures (j)

Threat (i)	1	2	3	Freq	Loss
1	0.01	0.5	1	200	$5K
2	1	0.04	1	50	$2K
3	1	1	0.01	100	$7K
Cost	$4K	$3K	$8K		

$m[]$ matrix: money = 8 ⟶ Budget

j=2	0	1	2	3	4	5	6	7	8
0	0	0	0	0	0	0	0	0	0
1	0	0	0	0	990	990	990	990	990
2	0	0	0	596	990	990	990	1091	1091
3									

Selection[] matrix: (money = 8, j = 2)

Cells in m matrix	Decision about countermeasure implementation		
1,0	0	0	0
1,1	0	0	0
1,2	0	0	0
1,3	0	0	0
1,4	1	0	0
1,5	1	0	0
1,6	1	0	0
1,7	1	0	0
1,8	1	0	0
2,0	0	0	0
2,1	0	0	0
2,2	0	0	0
2,3	0	1	0
2,4	1	0	0
2,5	1	0	0
2,6	1	0	0
2,7	1	1	0
2,8	1	1	0

money:8 => money:0

j:2 => j:3

Selection[] matrix: (money = 0, j = 3)

Cells in m matrix	Decision about countermeasure implementation		
2,0	0	0	0
2,1	0	0	0
2,2	0	0	0
2,3	0	1	0
2,4	1	0	0
2,5	1	0	0
2,6	1	0	0
2,7	1	1	0
2,8	1	1	0
3,0	0	0	0
3,1	0	0	0
3,2	0	0	0
3,3	0	0	0
3,4	0	0	0
3,5	0	0	0
3,6	0	0	0
3,7	0	0	0
3,8	0	0	0

FIGURE 19.4

Snapshots of algorithm operations on *Selection[]* and *m[]* matrix transition from (money = 8, j = 2) to (money = 0, j = 3).

problem input parameters as we defined them in the preceding section. They defined their model as follows:

- *Prop(i)*, the probability of threat *i* to occur:

$$Prop(i) = \prod_{j \in J} Prop(i,j) * y(j) \tag{7}$$

- Related Risk:

$$Risk = \sum_{i \in I}(Freq(i) * Loss(i) * Prop(i)) \tag{8}$$

- The objective function, whose minimum amount is desired:

$$Min \sum_{i \in I}(Freq(i) * Loss(i) * Prop(i)) \tag{9}$$

$$s.t. \sum_{j \in J}(cost(j) * y(i)) \leq Budget \tag{10}$$

Table 19.2 Quantitative Data About Current Risk and Countermeasures Effectiveness [14]

		Countermeasures (j)								Fereq	Loss
		1	2	3	4	5	6	7	8		
	1	0.01	0.5	1	1	1	1	1	1	200	$24K
	2	1	0.04	1	1	0.6	1	1	1	50	$122K
	3	1	1	0.01	0.8	1	0.8	0.9	1	100	$350K
Threats (i)	4	1	1	1	0.25	1	0.8	0.9	0.8	50	$5K
	5	1	0.5	1	0.8	0.02	0.8	0.9	1	50	$250K
	6	1	0.6	1	1	1	0.1	0.6	1	300	$20K
	7	1	0.5	1	1	1	0.5	0.15	1	100	$20K
	8	1	1	1	1	1	1	1	0.2	0.01	$20000K
	Cost	$40K	$28K	$80K	$24K	$70K	$50K	$40K	$80K		

Table 19.3 Comparison Between [14] and Our Results

Budget	(Rakes, Deane and Rees 2012) Optimal Countermeasure Portfolio	Our Proposed Approach Optimal Countermeasure Portfolio	Effectiveness (and Risk) (1000$)
80	3	3	34,650 (Risk = 32,200)
108	2,3	2,3	52,556 (Risk = 14,294)
132	2,3,4	2,3,4	54,063 (Risk = 12,787)
148	2,3,7	2,3,7	55,531 (Risk = 11,319)
158	2,3,6	2,3,6	57,666 Risk = 9,184)
178	2,3,5	2,3,5	58,778 (Risk = 8,071)
182	2,3,4,6	2,3,4,6	58,872 (Risk = 7,978)
198	1,2,4,6	1,2,3,6*	60.042 (Risk = 6,808)
222	1,2,3,4,6	1,2,3,4,6	61,248 (Risk = 5,602)
228	2,3,5,6	2,3,5,6	62,663 (Risk = 4,186)
252	2,3,4,5,6	2,3,4,5,6	62,889 (Risk = 3,960)
268	1,2,3,5,6	1,2,3,5,6	65,039 (Risk = 1,810)
292	1,2,3,4,5,6	1,2,3,4,5,6	65,295 (Risk = 1,584)
320	1,2,3,5,6,7	1,2,3,5,6,7	65,666 (Risk = 1,183)
332	1,2,3,4,5,6,7	1,2,3,4,5,6,7	65,870 (Risk = 9,80)
412	1,2,3,4,5,6,7,8	1,2,3,4,5,6,7,8	66,039 (Risk = 811)

*countermeasure #3 is as effective as countermeasure #4, as a result they can be in the optimal portfolio interchangeably, as the related Risk is the same.

This is almost the same model we have utilized in this paper, except that they tried to minimize the risk, while in contrast, we were looking for maximum effectiveness. In concept these are the same, but our definition of problem led us to knapsack problem modeling. In addition, the strength of our approach is that it takes advantage of a dynamic programming algorithm, which does not need any extra variables or linearization. For linearization and solving the non-linear formula in Eq. (7), [14] proposed an integer programming model that finds the optimum solution using multilevel variables in this order. As an example to support this claim, we have defined one level variable for our decision variable $y(j)$, which gets 1 if the countermeasure j is in the optimum portfolio and 0 if it is not. However, in [14], a two-level variable y_{jl} is presented as the decision variable. y_{jl} is defined as binary variable that is 1 if the jth countermeasure is implemented in the lth level. There are two levels of implementation for each countermeasure: 1 if it is implemented, 0 if it is not. This means that countermeasure j is selected for implementation if $y_{jl} = 1$ and $y_{j0} = 0$, otherwise $y_{jl} = 0$ and $y_{j0} = 1$. Four multilevel variables are defined in [14] in order to solve the integer programming model. The authors state that without this added level, the linearity of the formulation would not be possible.

As shown in Table 19.3, the proposed binary knapsack−based approach results in the same portfolio as in [14], by using an algorithmic solution in dynamic programming. In other words, using a dynamic programming method that breaks the problem into sub-problems yielded a systematic process for decision-making and arriving at a reliable solution.

This approach is being pursued in a software development company categorized as an SME (small or medium-sized enterprise). Pre-conditions for establishing the proposed model are as follows, according to priority:

1. Identifying a list of all information assets in place (in digital and physical form)
2. Gathering a list of threats against information assets (using standards guidelines)
3. Estimating the frequency of each threat's occurrence per year ($Freq(i)$), the cost (loss) of each successful attack episode on each asset ($Loss(i)$) (following [22] guidelines)
4. Gathering a list of advised countermeasures against threats (using standards guidelines)
5. Estimating each countermeasure's power of blocking probable attacks and normalizing them between 0 and 1 ($Prop(i,j)$), and estimating the cost of implementation for each one ($cost(j)$)

Having these inputs and the *Budget* for firming up security as desired by the organization's leaders, the proposed approach can be followed to arrive at the best decision. One important feature of this approach is that as the dynamic programming algorithm runs, the most effective solution it comes up with may even be under budget. For example, the budget may be $1,000 but the most effective portfolio costs $800.

CONCLUSION

Making a risk-based decision about a collection of countermeasures having various degrees of effectiveness is a complicated task that affects the continuity of business in organizations. As a result, IT security planners are always looking for a way to conduct a systematic analysis in order to make sure their final decision is the best one.

Despite the many existing frameworks and models in this regard, decision-making in this area remains confusing and complicated. All the countermeasures presented in standards or guidelines are not always effective for a given organization. Some security controls even cost more than the loss they are supposed to prevent. In this chapter, we propose a binary knapsack—based approach for choosing the best countermeasures for IT security, following recent research by [14]. Inspired by their reasoning and risk-based model to find the optimal countermeasure portfolio, a new approach is proposed that results in the same solution in different situations, using their input parameters.

A brief road map for employing the proposed algorithm is explained in the previous section. After assessing the resident risk on assets and estimating security control effectiveness, the most preventive portfolio of countermeasures can be chosen for implementation.

References

[1] Bornman WG. Information security risk management: A holistic framework [dissertation submitted for MS]; Rand Afrikaans University; 2004.

[2] Stoneburner G, Goguen A, Feringa A. Risk management guide for informationtechnology systems. NIST Special Publication; 2002. p. 800—30.

[3] ISO/IEC 27005. Information security risk management. International Standard Organization; 2008.

[4] AS/NZS. Risk management. Australian/New Zealand Standard. 3rd ed; 2004.

[5] Albert C, Dorofee A. Introduction to the OCTAVE approach. Carnegie Mellon Software Engineering Institute; 2003. p. 4—16.

[6] Yazar Z. A qualitative risk analysis and management tool—CRAMM. SANS InfoSec Reading Room White Paper; 2002.

[7] Lund MS, Solhaug B, Stølen K. Model-driven risk analysis: The CORAS approach. Springer; 2011.

[8] US Government Accountability Office. Information security risk assessment: Practices of leading organizations. United States General Accounting Office; 1999.

[9] Egan M. The executive guide to information security. Indianapolis: Symantec Press; 2005.

[10] Bistarelli S, Fioravanti F, Peretti P. Using cp-nets as a guide for countermeasure selection. ACM Symposium on Applied Computing. Seoul; 2007.

[11] Viduto V, Maple C, Huang W, López-Peréz D. A novel risk assessment and optimisation model for a multi-objective network security countermeasure selection problem. Decision Support Systems 2012;53(3):599—610.

[12] Lenstra A, Voss T. Information security risk assessment, aggregation, and mitigation. Lect Notes Comput Sci 2004:391—401.

[13] Altena JA. ISO/IEC 27002 baseline selection. Nijmegen: Radboud Universiteit Nijmegen; 2012.

[14] Rakes TR, Deane JK, Rees LP. IT security planning under uncertainty for high-impact events. Omega: International Journal of Management Science; 2012. p. 79—88.

[15] Security breaches and the cost of downtime. Endpoint security. [Internet]. Available from: http://www. endpointsecurity.org/Documents/Security_Breaches_and_the_Cost_of_Downtime.pdf.

[16] Sawik T. Selection of optimal countermeasure portfolio in IT security planning. Elsevier; 2013.

[17] Kellerer H, Pferschy U, Pisinger D. Knapsack problems; 2004.

[18] Martello S, Toth P. Knapsack problems: Algorithms and computer interpretations; 1990.

[19] Andonov R, Poirriez V, Rajopadhye S. Unbounded knapsack problem: Dynamic programming revisited. Eur J Oper Res 2000;123(2):168—81. http://dx.doi.org/10.1016/S0377-2217(99)00265-9.

[20] Pisinger D. Algorithms for knapsack problems [Ph.D. thesis]. Copenhagen, Denmark: Dept of Computer Science; University of Copenhagen; 1995.

[21] Bartholdi III JJ. The knapsack problem. In: Building Intuition. Springer; 2008. p. 19−31.

[22] Sonnenreich W, Albanese J, Stout B. Return on security investment (rosi)-a practical quantitative model. J Res Practice Inf Technol. 2006:45−56.

CSRF and Big Data: Rethinking Cross-Site Request Forgery in Light of Big Data

20

Maria Angel Marquez-Andrade, Hamzeh Roumani, and Natalija Vlajic

York University, Toronto, ON, Canada

INFORMATION IN THIS CHAPTER

- Cross-site request forgery
- Big Data integrity
- Browser security
- Same origin policy
- Document Object Model
- CSRF defenses
- HTTP origin header
- Vulnerabilities in social media and networking sites
- Web/URL scanning tools

INTRODUCTION

Big Data has become one of the most buzzed-about topics in today's business world. It is widely believed that the wealth of information buried in Big Data carries an enormous potential and is key to achieving a competitive advantage (i.e., superior productivity and higher profits) in the new digital age. According to [1], a retailer using Big Data to the fullest has the potential to increase its operating margin by more than 60 percent. Moreover, according to [2], the worldwide market for Big Data is expected to grow to a $16.9 billion industry by 2015.

Social and media sites are considered to be the biggest generators of Big Data. For example, it is estimated that on any given day, Facebook processes 500 terabytes of data, Twitter processes over 400 million tweets, and YouTube users upload 48 hours of new video every minute [3]. The sheer volume and availability of this data, however, does not translate into the same amount of intelligible or useful information. This is because, in its raw, unprocessed form, Big Data is known to comprise lots of noise. Thus, effective mining of Big Data requires that an appropriate level of pre-processing be applied.

Noise, however, is not the only challenge when it comes to the mining of Big Data. Another critical yet often overlooked issue is that of Big Data integrity and accuracy. This is especially true for data collected from social and media sites. In the past, these sites have often fallen victim to various forms of security attacks and social-engineering ploys. As an inherent consequence, the integrity of data stored at and/or collected out of these sites has also frequently suffered.

Cross-Site Request Forgery is a type of malicious exploit of a website in which unauthorized commands get executed simply by virtue of being transmitted via the browser of a previously successfully authenticated/authorized user. Clearly, when utilized on a larger scale (e.g., affecting hundreds or thousands of user), unauthorized commands that get falsely attributed to legitimate users can have a profound effect on the integrity of the data being stored/collected at the site targeted by a CSRF attack. If the victim site happens to be any of the popular social or media domains, it is easy to see how CSRF can be used as a deliberate (or accidental) tool against the integrity of Big Data.

In our work, we have looked at several major social and media sites and examined the current state of their CSRF defense. We have discovered that, even though it has been more than a decade since CSRF was first identified, many of these sites (including YouTube, LinkedIn, and Wikipedia) still remain vulnerable to some easily exploitable forms of CSRF. We have also learned that these particular forms of CSRF exploits are not recognizable as dangerous, even by some of the leading URL scanning tools (i.e., they successfully pass the safety checks). In addition, we have looked at the three leading Web browsers and the mechanisms that they employ in order to facilitate the global defense against CSRF. Our findings show that each browser type employs a slightly different set of anti-CSRF measures. We have also discovered that some of the developer tools in Chrome and Firefox might unintentionally serve as an aid to CSRF.

The content of this paper is organized as follows: In the section titled "SOP and CSRF," we give an overview of CSRF in relation to the Same Origin Policy (SOP)—the key browser-side mechanism against CSRF and XSS. In the section titled "Motivation and Related Work," we describe the motivation for our work and give an overview of the related literature. In the section titled "Defenses against CSRF: Server and Browser Sides," we discuss the importance of both the browser and the server side defense against CSRF, and also present some of our findings on this topic. In the section titled "Experimental Results: CSRF in Social Media and Networking Sites," we describe our experimental framework and provide a summary of our main findings concerning the CSRF vulnerabilities in YouTube, LinkedIn, Dailymotion, and Wikipedia. In the section titled "Analysis of Test Framework with Popular Web/URL Scanning Tools," we present the safety scan scores for our experimental/attack framework as provided by Jsunpack and Wepawet. Finally, in the section titled "Conclusions and Future Work," we make our concluding remarks and outline the future work.

SOP and CSRF

Many modern Web applications rely on browser state data such as certificates, cookies, and authorization headers to authenticate users and consequently provide them with services that handle their private data [4]. These applications send pages containing several elements to the user's Web browser, which it subsequently organizes as a document. At any given time, several such documents may coexist within the browser (in separate frames, tabs, or windows), and hence, a mechanism is needed to control inter-document access and protect each document's private data. The

Same Origin Policy (SOP), implemented by most Web browsers, prevents elements in one document from reading or modifying the data in another, unless the two documents have originated from the same Web application. Specifically, each document is tagged by its origin, which is defined as the (domain, port, protocol) tuple of the sending Web application. This organization can be observed with the DOM Inspector Firefox add-on, as shown in Figure 20.1[5].

In the example depicted in Figure 20.1, the document from huffingtonpost.ca contains an iframe with id "ttwttrHubFrame", and that iframe fetches a page from platform.twitter.com. This is, thus, an example of a Web page comprising two documents, and since they have different origins, elements in the huffingtonpost.ca document should not get access to elements in the iframe (i.e., platform.twitter.com document) and vice versa.

Note that SOP does not prevent documents from making cross-origin requests (e.g., to populate an iframe, include a script, or fetch an image from a different origin). Instead, SOP only blocks access to the response of that request. This property of SOP is precisely what Cross-Site Request Forgery (CSRF) aims to exploit. Namely, a typical CSRF attack involves a user who is logged into a legitimate site S in one document and is visiting the attacker's site in another document, in a different tab, for example. If the attacker's site makes a cross-site request to S, the browser will not only allow such a request, it will also attach the login or cookie credentials of the victim user to it. In effect, the attacker can impersonate the victim-user by making the victim-user's browser perform authenticated requests without the victim-user's explicit knowledge.

To illustrate the above, let us assume that search engine S allows users to make search queries with a simple GET request, such as www.S.com/search?q=Toronto to search for "Toronto." Assume also

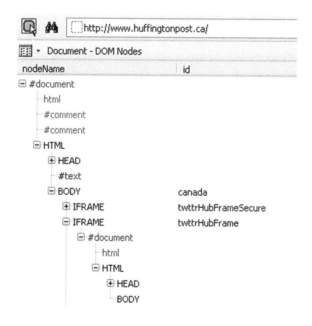

FIGURE 20.1

Organization of huffingtonpost.ca as depicted by DOM Inspector.

that S allows users to sign up for accounts so it can keep track of their queries. The account feature also enables users to see their search histories and enables S to deliver user-targeted ads and collect aggregate statistics about popular searches. In a CSRF scenario involving S, we envision the user being logged into S in one tab and subsequently visiting the attacker's page in a second tab. We also envision the attacker's page containing an image or an auto-submitted form that submits a search request for "York" to S: www.S.com/search?q = York. (The request can be made covert so that the user does not notice it being sent and/or its respective reply being received.) Since such an action does not violate the SOP policy, the browser will allow the request to be sent and will also attach the user's authentication data to it. When the response arrives, the browser will correctly prevent the attacker's page from accessing it, as per SOP, but this is irrelevant because the damage has already been done: (1) the "York" search will be added to the user's history, and (2) if the same attack is repeated in large numbers, "York" can become a popular trendy search word even though no user has consciously searched for it. Moreover, S will start sending ads about "York" to all affected users.

Luring the user to visit the attacker's page while logged in to a legitimate site can be achieved through a variety of attack vectors such as cross-site scripting (XSS), SQL injection, or social engineering (e.g., clicking a link in an email). For certain legitimate sites, such as Facebook or Google, the success rate of CSRF is high because most users are logged in to them at all times.

CSRF has traditionally targeted use cases involving financial transactions (e.g., the attacker's page issues a money transfer request to the user's online baking site) or identity theft (e.g., the attacker's page issues a password change request). Lately, however, the focus has shifted to "softer" targets such as posting a "Like," adding a new contact, or inserting a phone number in someone's dial log. At first glance, these may seem to be harmless or mere mischiefs, but in the context of Big Data, the implications are far more serious. In a world where major marketing decisions are based on the number of "Likes," and where the importance of events is based on what is trending on Twitter, these petty mischiefs aggregate a tectonic impact. To better appreciate the connection between CSRF and Big Data, let us analyze the impact of the attack in the above example, in which a search for "York" was forged. Three victims are involved here:

- The end user: Since the user repeatedly searches for "York" (or so it seems), it will be assumed that the user may have an interest in "York" or an association with it. If this (incorrect) observation is shared with security/law enforcement agencies or insurance companies, then it may affect the profile that these parties create for the user.
- The website's revenue: Data collected at the site will indicate that this user is interested in "York"; hence, ads related to "York" will be embedded in all pages sent to this user. Since this apparent interest is false, the user will not click on these ads and the advertising site will have wasted a marketing opportunity.
- The website's Big Data integrity: Analytics at the site, which track frequent searches by distinct IP addresses, will indicate that "York" is a very popular subject because many users are looking it up. This can occur, for example, if the attack vector involves a mass email containing a link with "York" as its query (with a large number of recipients, chances are high that some will click on the link while logged into S). The integrity of the data collected out of the site will thus suffer.

Of these three victims, the last is often overlooked and has the potential, in our view, of inflicting the most wide-spread damage.

Motivation and related work
Prevalence of CSRF

Statistics on Web application attacks, such as the one published in April 2013 by the cloud hosting company FireHost, reveal that CSRF is one of the most prevalent attacks. Moreover, the volume of such attacks has increased 132 percent since 2012 [6]. In recent years, some of the most popular sites have also been victims of CSRF attacks.

In August 2012, a CSRF vulnerability was found in Facebook's new feature, the App Center, where users can manage and download applications for Facebook. The attack consists of forging a request to download a specific application. Consequently, an attacker can force victims to download an application of the attacker's choosing. The vulnerability exists because the request required for downloading a Facebook application is a simple POST request with an anti-CSRF token, which cannot be forged but that the App Center Web application does not validate! Hence, even though the token may not appear in the request, the server will accept it. A proof-o-concept-attack page was published by the discoverer of the vulnerability once he reported it to Facebook, and in return he was awarded USD $5000 for the discovery. The attack page contains a form which sends a POST request to www.facebook.com/connect/uiserver.php. The form input fields contain several static parameters such as the ID of the application being requested. The form is auto-submitted via the onload event in the body tag [7]. The attack would succeed if the user visiting the attack page has already authenticated in Facebook, which would make the browser attach the user's Facebook credentials to the forged request.

More recently, in January, 2013, a CSRF vulnerability was found in LinkedIn, a social networking site for professionals, with over 175 million users. The vulnerability resided in LinkedIn's Add Connections functionality, which is one of the most important functionalities in the site, since the visibility of a profile depends mainly on the number of connections it has. This functionality includes a Send Invitation option, which allows a user to send an invitation to other users to become part of the first user's network. The user receiving the invitation is only required to accept the invitation in order to be added into the sending user's network. The attack consists of forging the Send Invitation request to force a user to send an invitation to the attacker. This enables the attacker to be added to the user's network, thus increasing the attacker's visibility. The Send Invitation request consists of a POST request with four parameters: the email of the user being invited, an invitation message, a CSRF token, and a sourceAlias token. The vulnerability exists because the CSRF token is not validated by the LinkedIn Web application. Additionally, the Web application processes POST and GET requests identically, thereby making it easier to forge the request covertly. The discoverer gave the following example as a proof of concept for the attack [8]:

1. The attacker creates a page (csrf-exploit.html) containing this image tag: <img src = "http://www.linkedin.com/fetch/manual-invite-create?emailAddresses=&subject=" width = 0 height=0>.
2. A user authenticated to LinkedIn visits csrf-exploit.html.
3. The attacker receives the invitation from the user and accepts it.
4. The user is now added to the attacker's contacts.

The success of this attack also affects the user, as the attacker can now view information only visible to the user's contacts.

Previously published work on CSRF

W Zeller and EW Felten, 2008 [9]

In the paper [9], the authors present four CSRF vulnerabilities discovered in popular websites, as well as recommendations for server-side defenses and a client-side plugin to protect against CSRF. The first vulnerability was found in 2007 in The New York Times website (nytimes.com), a major news site and US newspaper that allows users to recommend articles to other users through an "Email This" tool. The tool sends an email to the recipient of the recommendation, specifying the email of the authenticated user who recommended the article. Hence, a request could be forged to covertly force a user to send a recommendation to the attacker and thus reveal the user's email address. The second attack discussed was a much more serious vulnerability in ING Direct, which permitted opening new accounts and transferring funds from a user's account. The site did not implement any protection against CSRF, hence all the requests required to perform the previously mentioned actions could be forged covertly as a series of GET and POST requests using JavaScript. At that time, YouTube, a video-sharing website, did not implement any CSRF defenses either, so vulnerabilities in almost all features in the site were discovered.

In addition to identifying the above-mentioned vulnerabilities, [9] also provides the following recommendations to protect against CSRF at the server side:

1. Restrict the use of GET requests to actions with no persistent side effects in order to reduce the possible attack variations and covertness.
2. Add a pseudo-random value to all POST requests site-wide. This value should be unrelated to the user's account so that it can be conferred even before authentication.

The authors of [9] have also developed a plugin for the Code Igniter framework, which validates pseudo-random values in POST requests and appends pseudo-random values to function calls requesting form tags as well as AJAX requests.

Regarding the client side (browser side), a Firefox extension was developed that restricts HTTP requests, allowing all GET requests and blocking all cross-origin POST requests to sites not implementing Adobe's cross-domain policy [9].

A Barth, C Jackson, and JC Mitchell, 2008 [4]

The work presented in paper [4] studies some known forms of CSRF vulnerabilities, analyzes current defenses, and proposes an implementation of a browser defense. The authors introduce login CSRF attacks, which consist of forging a login request to a victim site with the attacker's credentials and sending the request from the user's browser. The impact of the attack depends on the data managed by the application. One of the attacks they describe is an attack to a search engine that logs user queries, indicating that the attacker would have access to the victims' queries since the victim would be navigating with the attacker's account [4].

The authors experiment with the Referer header as an alternative CSRF defense. The results indicate that the Referer header is mostly suppressed by the network and not the browser, and that it is more likely to be suppressed in cross-site requests than in same-origin requests. Thus, they propose analyzing the Referer header of requests sent through HTTPS to spot CSRF attacks, since the network cannot suppress headers of HTTPS requests. The Referer header, however, exposes the path and querystring of the referring document and thus represents a privacy concern. Consequently, the authors propose adding an Origin header instead—which includes only the scheme, host, and port of the referring document—to all POST requests. To implement their scheme, the authors created a patch for WebKit and an extension for Firefox, as well as a server-side Web application firewall in ModSecurity [4].

R Shaikh, 2013 [10]

In this most recent paper on CSRF [10], the author describes how most client-side CSRF defenses are based on either anomaly or signature detection schemes, and as such, are too restrictive or not scalable. With the assumption that pseudo-random values in requests do not provide sufficient protection, the author proceeds to describe a solution employing a variation of Bayesian Belief Networks, a graphical probability model that aims to predict whether the current request constitutes a CSRF. In this model, the probability of a request being a CSRF is measured based on the characteristics of previously monitored requests. The model is implemented through a browser plugin that monitors and collects requests and proceeds to suppress authentication data from suspected CSRF requests. Figure 20.2 illustrates the screening process for each request according to the proposed algorithm [10].

Motivation for our work

The term CSRF was coined 12 years ago [11]; since then, numerous countermeasures have been identified both on the server and browser sides, as well as in the HTTP protocol itself. It is therefore surprising, and frustrating, that despite all this effort, today CSRF remains in the OWASP's

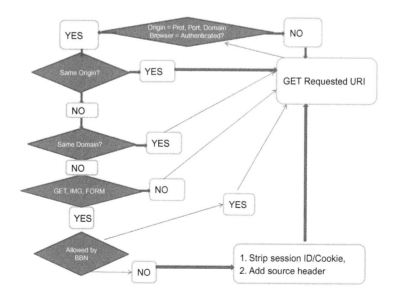

FIGURE 20.2

High level diagram of proposed CSRF detection algorithm [10].

Top 10 2013 vulnerabilities [12] and the fourth most prevalent vulnerability discovered by WhiteHat Security in 2012 [13].

Moreover, it seems that, primarily, sites that hold sensitive data, such as banks, are implementing CSRF countermeasures. This is alarming in the context of a Big Data world, as decisions are increasingly being based on mining insensitive data, such as number of views, number of follows, or browsing history, which are easy CSRF targets. Furthermore, an increasing number of websites—most notably sites such as Reddit, Tumblr and Pinterest, where the re-post functionality is essential—are basing their value on the fact that their content is appraised by users. Consequently, CSRF is a prevalent vulnerability that threats to perturb the data that gives trend and structure to Web application use.

The choice of CSRF protection also impacts the efficiency of gathering user data. For instance, users, as well as the developers of Pinterest, are often confused by anti-CSRF token errors. The error message presented in Figure 20.3 proceeds from the Django implementation of CSRF protection, as further discussed in the next section [15].

Defenses against CSRF: Server and browser Sides
Existing Anti-CSRF mechanisms in the web

As suggested in [4], the validation of HTTP Referer is the simplest CSRF defense. This defense, however, requires that the browser attaches the header to each request and the Web application or server firewall analyzes its value. It also has several drawbacks, such as being suppressed by the network and introducing privacy concerns, as mentioned earlier.

Using the origin HTTP header overcomes the privacy concerns of the Referer header. Nevertheless, since HTTP origin does not contain the path of the requesting document (only the host), it restricts validation to complete domains. For instance, a site wanting to accept requests only from example.com/private/ cannot differentiate between it and requests from example.com/forum/. Furthermore, the origin header is not added to requests such as links in anchor tags or script window navigation such as "window.open" [14].

Introducing pseudo-random numbers/tokens in POST requests is a widely used CSRF defense. The defense consists of making the Web application/server produce a token tied to the user's

FIGURE 20.3

Pinterest's response to a request with an invalid anti-CSRF token.

session and appending this token to the page sent to the browser. Once in the browser, the document will decide when to add the token to POST requests. Subsequently, the Web application/ server will validate the token and either allow or block the request. It might be somewhat challenging to implement this solution from scratch, as evidenced by the Facebook and LinkedIn CSRF vulnerabilities discussed in the section titled "SOP and CSRF." Furthermore, tokens can only be added to POST requests, since they should not be visible from the querystring; thus, only POST requests can be protected [14].

Server-side modifications

CSRF token protection is included in the standard development packages of modern Web development platforms such as ASP.NET, Django and Ruby on Rails. These frameworks append tokens to HTML output and validate tokens in received POST requests. Developers can choose which pages or their elements will submit the token. The use of these frameworks, however, may also confuse developers—as in the Pinterest example from the section titled "Motivation for Our Work"—which may also lead to developers making cross-site requests that include the token and thus reveal it to other domains [14].

Browser-side modifications

Most browser-side solutions are browser extensions (similar to the ones described in the section titled "Previous Published Work on CSRF"), whereby the extension screens HTTP requests to either block or strip authentication data from a specific class of requests.

Request Rodeo is a proxy that runs parallel to the browser, intercepting requests and responses to label them according to origin and subsequently strips their authentication data if they do not adhere to the configured policy. It is similar to the server-side solution, but occurs in the browser-side machine. Since the solution requires traffic to go through a process of modification, the implementation of this solution can introduce significant latency [14].

Our findings and observations

The following summarizes our findings and observations:

1. AJAX accompanied by Origin header: Through our work on CSRF, it has been observed that, in the executed tests, AJAX requests are always accompanied by an origin header in both Google Chrome and Mozilla Firefox requests. Internet Explorer (IE), however, has its own preferences regarding which requests should include the origin header. There is only partial support for the origin header on IE 8 and 9 and full support in IE 10, as discussed in [16].
2. The SOP is enforced, but developer tools leak headers; Firefox and Chrome have built-in developer tools that allow users to observe the response headers from a cross-site request. Even though the body of the request is not revealed, the rest of the headers are shown, as seen in Figure 20.4.

Response Headers	Δ240ms
X-YouTube-Other-Cookies:	VISITOR_INFO1_LIVE=Avdq4BUdCXg
X-XSS-Protection:	1; mode=block
x-frame-options:	SAMEORIGIN
X-Content-Type-Options:	nosniff
Server:	gwiseguy/2.0
Expires:	Tue, 27 Apr 1971 19:44:06 EST
Date:	Tue, 09 Jul 2013 03:02:21 GMT
Content-Type:	video/x-flv
Content-Length:	0
Cache-Control:	no-cache

FIGURE 20.4

Response headers shown by Firefox's built-in developer's tool.

Experiment results: CSRF in social media and networking sites

We conducted several tests consisting of uploading test pages containing cross-site requests to popular sites, which attempt to impersonate the user who loaded the test page and has previously been successfully authenticated by the target website.

Description of the test framework

Table 20.1 gives a description of each test page we created. The tests can be found at http://www.cse.yorku.ca/~mma/tests/. As YouTube was the first site we tested, a few of the presented test pages apply only to YouTube and have a Y in their test number.

The tests were carried out by authenticating the victim user to the target site in one tab and subsequently requesting the attack page in another tab, as shown in Figure 20.5.

If the attack page is indicated as covert, then it carries out the attack in the background and displays an innocent page. Otherwise, the user is aware of a new request for the target site, since the user will get to see the respective response in clear sight.

YouTube results

YouTube is a major video-sharing site. Our objective on YouTube was to generate a GET request for a specific video and thus impact the user's watch history—a YouTube feature that logs the authenticated user's viewed videos. The generation of a watch history element is linked to the generation of a view, or hit count, in a video. Thus, if a user generates a view, the video is added to the user's history. YouTube has three different APIs to give access to its videos. If the video is watched in YouTube, then the link communicates to www.youtube.com/watch. If the video is embedded in a site, then the HTML5 code communicates to www.youtube.com/embed (the embed API). If the video is embedded as a flash file, then the resource is from www.youtube.com/v (old YouTube embed code). The results from our tests indicate that, if the embed API is used, then the

Table 20.1 CSRF Test Pages

Test #	Covert	Test Name	Description
1	yes	Image tag	The HTML image tag generates a GET request to the target in src.
1.1	yes	Image object	An image object is created and appended to the file. A GET request is sent to the object src.
2	maybe	Form GET request	A form is automatically submitted to the target with the GET method using JavaScript. An attempt for covertness is made by opening a new window to the test page to hide the target's response.
3	maybe	Form POST request	Same as Test 2 but with POST.
4	yes	Iframe src =	An iframe with src = target.
6y	yes	Iframe src = embed API + autoplay	An iframe with src pointing to YouTube's embed API + querystring, indicating autoplay.
9	yes	GET XMLHttpRequest	AJAX that creates a GET request for the target.
10y	yes	Old YouTube embed code	YouTube embed code, before HTML5, consists of an embed tag + object tag linking to a flash video. (This code is supplied by YouTube).
10	yes	Embed tag	An embed tag with src = target.
11	yes	CSS background URL	CSS code that states that the background image of the page resides at the target.
12	yes	CSS bg URL in external stylesheet	Same as 11, but the CSS code is in an external file.
13	no	PDF with JS launchURL	Blank PDF file with JavaScript that generates a GET request for the target through the launchURL method.
15	no	Flash SWF with JS getURL	Flash movie with JavaScript that generates a GET request with the getURL method.

FIGURE 20.5

Screenshot of Dailymotion test in Chrome browser.

view count increases only if the user clicks on the video to play it. Responses with autoplay do not count as views.

As observed in Table 20.2, only our non-covert CSRF attacks on YouTube where successful. There are, however, mechanisms through which the visible manifestations of our successful CSRF attacks could be made less obvious, thereby reducing the likelihood that the exploits get detected (i.e., the overall effectiveness of the attacks are increased).

LinkedIn results

LinkedIn is a social networking site focused on creating a network of business partners and colleagues for the purpose of career advancement. Its users are encouraged to constantly visit the site to create bigger networks, update their profiles, and observe who has commented on or viewed their profiles. The tests generate a simple GET request for the user's profile at http://www.linkedin.com/in/(username). If the attack is successful, then the attacker sees the victim added to the list of users who have viewed the attacker's profile, as depicted in Figure 20.6. The results of the tests are shown in Table 20.3.

On this occasion, there were two successful covert attacks, tests 9 and 10, in Firefox and Chrome, respectively. Using these attacks, an attacker can easily boost his or her view rating by forging victim views.

Wikipedia results

Wikipedia is a free online encyclopedia built by volunteers who can either have a user account or be anonymous. Having an account gives users access to more functionality such as creating a

Table 20.2 YouTube Results

Test #	Test Name	Browser		
		FF	GC	IE
1	Image tag	✗	✗	✗
1.1	Image object	✗	✗	✗
2	Form GET request	✓	✓	✓
3	Form POST request	✗	✗	✗
4	Iframe src =	✗	✗	✗
6y	Iframe src = embed API + autoplay	✗	✗	✗
9	GET XMLHttpRequest	✗	✗	✗
10y	Old YouTube embed code	✗	✗	✗
11	CSS background URL	✗	✗	✗
12	CSS bg URL in external stylesheet	✗	✗	✗
13	PDF with JS launchURL	✗	✗	✓
15	Flash SWF with JS getURL	✓	✓	✗

FF is Firefox, IE is Internet Explorer, GC is Google Chrome.
✓ indicates that the requested video was added to the watch history.
✗ indicates that there was no change in the watch history.

FIGURE 20.6

Screenshot of LinkedIn profile stats after CSRF.

Table 20.3 LinkedIn Results

		Browser		
Test #	Test Name	FF	GC	IE
1	Image tag	✗	✗	✗
2	Form GET request	✓	✓	✓
3	Form POST request	✓	✓	✓
4	Iframe src =	✗	–	–
9	GET XMLHttpRequest	✓	–	✗
10	Embed tag	✗	✓	–
11	CSS background URL	✗	✗	✗
13	PDF with JS launchURL	✗	✗	✓
15	Flash SWF with JS getURL	✓	✓	✗

FF is Firefox, IE is Internet Explorer, GC is Google Chrome.
✓ indicates that the victim was added to the list of users who viewed the attacker's profile.
✗ indicates that there was no change in the list of users who viewed the attacker's profile.

Watchlist, which allows them to follow the modifications that have recently been made to a specific article. We found a CSRF vulnerability that exists if several users use the same browser in a device (i.e., the browser on a computer in a cybercafé). The request for adding a new item in the Watchlist is a POST request to http://en.wikipedia.org/w/api.php. The body of this request contains the following parameters:

> "action = watch&format = json&title = Love&uselang
>   = en&token = aecc0da89c011dce98583d4a4f529b06%2B%5C"

The token attribute protects the request by linking it to the user's browser state. Once the user logs out, however, if the next user logs in the same browser, the token will still be valid for this new user for about a day. Subsequently, we attempted to get the same result by forging the request as a GET request. Wikipedia does not accept this request as GET and responds with the following error header: MediaWiki-API-Error: mustbeposted, so the test was carried out with a POST XMLHttpRequest. The test script consisted of the following lines:

```
xmlhttp.withCredentials = true;
xmlhttp.open("POST","http://en.wikipedia.org/w/api.php",true);
xmlhttp.setRequestHeader("Content-type", "application/x-www-form-urlencoded");
xmlhttp.send
("action = watch&format = json&title = Love&uselang = en&token = 274660c0fdf3a8b10f91-
a415f2e5c8b3%2B%5C");
```

The attack has to be carried out in several steps:

1. The attacker makes a request to add an article to their Watchlist and logs the request made by the browser.
2. The attacker extracts the parameters in the request body and adds them to the test script in the "xmlhttp.send" method.
3. The attacker logs out and the victim logs into Wikipedia employing the same browser.
4. The victim visits the test page.

Once the victim loads the test page, the new item will be added to their Watchlist. Step 1 will generate a request, as shown at the top of Figure 20.7 (where user Secma is the attacker), and Step 4 will generate a request, shown at the bottom (where user Secdrma is the victim).

We can observe that none of the authentication data (cookies) match. Therefore, the token is most likely tied to the initial sections of the values of the cookies, which do match. If the attack is successful, then the attacker will be able to add articles to the victim's Watchlists and make them appear as more relevant than they really are.

Dailymotion results

Dailymotion is a video-sharing site whose users are predominantly interested in video blogging and artistic content creation. It has a global Alexa rank of #83, ranking it near sites such as CNN and Netflix [17]. As with many other video-sharing sites, Dailymotion provides authenticated users with the capability to post comments on videos. We found a CSRF vulnerability in this function, which requires a POST request, as the one shown in Figure 20.8.

Forging the request was done with a JavaScript POST XMLHttpRequest sent to http://www.dailymotion.com/pageitem/comment/post/?request = %2Fvideo%2Fxzfw9p_(name of video), including the following string in the body of the request:

"form_name = dm_pageitem_comment_post&comment = funny"

The attack was successful in both Chrome and Firefox Web browsers. Internet Explorer, however, did not allow the attack for reasons possibly related to its Platform of Privacy Preferences, as

```
POST http://en.wikipedia.org/w/api.php HTTP/1.1
Host: en.wikipedia.org
Accept: application/json, text/javascript, */*; q=0.01
X-Requested-With: XMLHttpRequest
Referer: http://en.wikipedia.org/wiki/Love
Content-Length: 91
Cookie: centralnotice_bucket=1-4.2;
enwiki_session=f136b50e7fdf440fde739d26965e2d78;
enwikiUserName=Secma; centralauth_LoggedOut=20130615185323;
enwikiLoggedOut=20130615185323; centralauth_User=Secma;
centralauth_Session=7ab13a4c68b6e9ab36bf3df4ef2701cc;
enwikiUserID=19165777

action=watch&format=json&title=Love&uselang=en&token=71ae65c09d7d
d7aac683c768d148d2d7%2B%5C
```

```
POST http://en.wikipedia.org/w/api.php HTTP/1.1
Host: en.wikipedia.org
Accept:text/html,application/xhtml+xml;q=0.9,*/*;q=0.8
Referer: ***.com/Testwikipedia.html
Content-Length: 91
Origin: http://drtest.site11.com
Cookie: centralnotice_bucket=1-4.2;
enwiki_session=c78bc3b634f26a3789fc898de6fb98c0;
enwikiUserName=Secdrma; centralauth_LoggedOut=20130615185733;
enwikiLoggedOut=20130615185733; centralauth_User=Secdrma;
centralauth_Session=13cad15ed4c82c605768a3697bb86ed3;
enwikiUserID=19178890

action=watch&format=json&title=Love&uselang=en&token=71ae65c09d7d
d7aac683c768d148d2d7%2B%5C
```

FIGURE 20.7

Requests made to Wikipedia. At *top* is a legitimate request made by the attacker to add an article to Watchlist. At *bottom* is a forged request with the victim's credentials.

```
POST
http://www.dailymotion.com/pageitem/comment/post/?request=%2Fvideo%2Fxz
fw9p__(name of video) HTTP/1.1
Host: www.dailymotion.com
Content-Length: 48
Origin: (attack site).com
User-Agent: Mozilla/5.0 (Windows NT 5.1) AppleWebKit/537.36 (KHTML,
like Gecko) Chrome/27.0.1453.110 Safari/537.36
Content-type: application/x-www-form-urlencoded
Referer: (attack site).com/Testdailymotion.html
Accept-Encoding: gzip,deflate,sdch
Accept-Language: en;q=0.8,en-US;q=0.6
Cookie: (user's cookie)

form_name=dm_pageitem_comment_post&comment=funny
```

FIGURE 20.8

A POST request made to Dailymotion requesting the addition of a comment consisting of the string "funny".

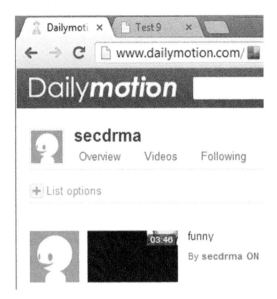

FIGURE 20.9

Screenshot of a modified user's comment tab after a CSRF attack.

mentioned in [9]. If the attack succeeds, then the comment appears at the bottom of the video and in the victim's comment history, as shown in Figure 20.9, where user secdrma is the victim.

This attack impersonates a user and deforms the appraisal of the website's content. Thus, it is an important vulnerability that requires the prompt implementation of CSRF protection.

Analysis of test framework with popular Web/URL scanning tools

URL scanning tools are Web applications that work like a sandbox: they run the documents received from a specific URL in their own browsers and provide an analysis report of the activities carried out by the received documents. They use signatures and anomaly detection similar to the defenses mentioned in the section titled "Motivation and Related Work" to analyze static and running code. Subsequently, they return an appraisal of the level of danger of the document activities. In this work, we make use of two URL scanners: Wepawet [18] and Jsunpack [19].

Scores of test pages

Table 20.4 shows the URL scanner scores.

We observed that the majority of our test/decoy pages were categorized as "benign" by both Wepawet and Jsunpack, which was both interesting and quite concerning, from the perspective of global CSRF defense. The only pages that were labeled as suspicious, and only by Jsunpack, were the LinkedIn and Dailymotion tests. This was because the requests embedded in these pages were

Table 20.4 URL Scanner Scores

Test #	Test Name	Wepawet	Jsunpack
1	Image tag	benign	benign
Source	http://www.cse.yorku.ca/~mma/tests/Test1h.html http://www.cse.yorku.ca/~mma/tests/Test1i.html		
Target	http://www.youtube.com/watch?v=tBIUEwtNi5w http://www.linkedin.com/in/secma		
1.1	Image object	benign	benign
Source	http://www.cse.yorku.ca/~mma/tests/Test1-1h.html		
Target	http://www.Youtube.com/watch?v=tBIUEwtNi5w		
2	Form GET request	benign	benign
Source	http://www.cse.yorku.ca/~mma/tests/Test2h.html		
	http://www.cse.yorku.ca/~mma/tests/Test2i.html		
Target	http://www.Youtube.com/watch?v=tBIUEwtNi5w		
	http://www.linkedin.com/in/secma		
3	Form POST request	benign	benign
Source	http://www.cse.yorku.ca/~mma/tests/Test3.html		
	http://www.cse.yorku.ca/~mma/tests/Test3i.html		
Target	http://www.Youtube.com/watch?v=tBIUEwtNi5w		
	http://www.linkedin.com/in/secma		
4	Iframe src =	benign	benign
Source	http://www.cse.yorku.ca/~mma/tests/Test4h.html		
Target	http://www.youtube.com/watch?v=tBIUEwtNi5w		
4 (LinkedIn)	Iframe src =	benign	suspicious
Source	http://www.cse.yorku.ca/~mma/tests/Test4i.html		
Target	http://www.linkedin.com/in/secma		
6y	Iframe src = embed API + autoplay	benign	benign
Source	http://www.cse.yorku.ca/~mma/tests/Test6h.html		
Target	http://www.youtube.com/embed/tBIUEwtNi5w?autoplay=1		
9	GET XMLHttpRequest	benign	benign
Source	http://www.cse.yorku.ca/~mma/tests/Test99.html		
Target	http://www.youtube.com/watch?v=tBIUEwtNi5w		
9 (LinkedIn)	GET XMLHttpRequest	benign	suspicious
Source	http://www.cse.yorku.ca/~mma/tests/Test9i.html		
Target	http://www.linkedin.com/in/secma		
10y	Old YouTube embed code	benign	benign
Source	http://www.cse.yorku.ca/~mma/tests/Test10.htm		
Target	http://www.youtube.com/v/tBIUEwtNi5w?version=3& hl=en_US		
10	Embed tag	error	suspicious
Source	http://www.cse.yorku.ca/~mma/tests/Test10i.htm		
Target	http://www.linkedin.com/in/secma		

(Continued)

Table 20.4 (Continued)

Test #	Test Name	Wepawet	Jsunpack
11	CSS background URL	benign	benign
Source	http://www.cse.yorku.ca/~mma/tests/Test11.html		
	http://www.cse.yorku.ca/~mma/tests/Test11i.html		
Target	http://www.youtube.com/watch?v=tBlUEwtNi5w		
	http://www.linkedin.com/in/secma		
12	CSS bg URL in external stylesheet	benign	benign
Source	http://www.cse.yorku.ca/~mma/tests/Test12.htm		
Target	http://www.youtube.com/embed/tBlUEwtNi5w		
13	PDF with JS launchURL	benign	benign
Source	http://www.cse.yorku.ca/~mma/tests/Test13h.pdf		
	http://www.cse.yorku.ca/~mma/tests/Test13i.pdf		
Target	http://www.youtube.com/watch?v=tBlUEwtNi5w		
	http://www.linkedin.com/in/secma		
15	Flash SWF with JS getURL	benign	benign
Source	http://www.cse.yorku.ca/~mma/tests/Test15h.swf		
Target	http://www.youtube.com/watch?v=tBlUEwtNi5w		
15 (LinkedIn)	Flash SWF with JS getURL	benign	suspicious
Source	http://www.cse.yorku.ca/~mma/tests/Test15i.swf		
Target	http://www.linkedin.com/in/secma		
–	Test Wikipedia	benign	benign
Source	http://www.cse.yorku.ca/~mma/tests/Testwikipedia.html		
Target	http://en.wikipedia.org/w/api.php		
–	Test Dailymotion	benign	suspicious
Source	http://www.cse.yorku.ca/~mma/tests/Testdailymotion.html		
Target	http://www.dailymotion.com/pageitem/comment/post/?request=%2Fvideo%2Fxzfw9p_(name of video)		

made in the background, which made the processing time longer than what Jsunpack expected from its analysis.

CONCLUSIONS AND FUTURE WORK

Many Web applications remain very vulnerable to CSRF. Moreover, most of the ones that do implement some type of CSRF protection do so on a function-by-function basis rather than as a site-wide endeavor. In other words, certain functionalities are deemed "important" and are thus protected while others are left vulnerable. Determining what is important and worth protecting is based on each site's risk assessment model, which likely focuses on protecting the site's users. But as the hypothetical use case of the section titled "SOP and CSRF" illustrates, the user is not the only victim of CSRF. In the context of Big Data, the most wide-spread impact of CSRF is the integrity of the conclusions drawn from aggregating a large number of noisy and/or potentially corrupted pieces of data.

The fact that not all browsers support the new origin header complicates things for developers and reduces their options for implementing pan-browser countermeasures against CSRF. Also, the presence of add-ons may make browsers vulnerable to leaking information between domains.

As mentioned in the section titled "Defenses against CSRF: Server and Browser Sides", browser add-ons may become attack vectors if they are not properly isolated from other elements in the browser. Analyzing their implementation is part of a future work on measuring the extent of protection against CSRF attacks.

References

[1] McKinsey Global Institute. Big data: The next frontier for innovation, competition and productivity. [Internet]. Available at: http://www.mckinsey.com/insights/business_technology/big_data_the_next_frontier_for_innovation; 2011.

[2] International Data Corporation (IDC). Worldwide big data technology and services 2012−2015. [Internet]. Available at: http://www.idc.com/getdoc.jsp?containerId = prUS23355112; 2012.

[3] Jim Yu, The importance of big data, integrity & security in enterprise SEO. [Internet]. Available at: <http://searchengineland.com/the-importance-of-big-data-integrity-and-security-enterprise-seo-143066>; 2013.

[4] Barth A, Jackson C, Mitchell JC. Robust defenses for cross-site request forgery. In: Proceedings of the 15th ACM conference on computer and communications security. ACM; 2008. p. 75−88.

[5] Addons.mozilla.org. DOM inspector. [Internet]. Available at: <https://addons.mozilla.org/en-us/firefox/addon/dom-inspector-6622/>; [accessed 06.13].

[6] Firehost.com. Dangerous cross-site request forgery attacks up 132 percent since Q1 2012. [Internet]. Available at: <http://www.firehost.com/company/newsroom/web-application-attack-report-first-quarter-2013>; 2013 [accessed 06.13].

[7] E Hacking News [EHN]-Latest IT security news. AMol NAik earned $5000 after finding CSRF vulnerability in Facebook. Hacker News. [Internet]. Available at: <http://www.ehackingnews.com/2012/08/amol-find-csrf-vulnerability-in-facebook.html>; 2012 [accessed 06.13].

[8] Internet Security Auditors. Advisories [Internet]. Available at: <http://www.isecauditors.com/advisories-2013#2013-001>; 2013 [accessed 06.13].

[9] Zeller W, Felten EW. Cross-site request forgeries: Exploitation and prevention. NY Times (Print) 2008:1−13.

[10] Shaikh R. Defending cross site reference forgery (CSRF) attacks on contemporary web applications using a Bayesian predictive model. [Internet] 1. Available at SSRN: <http://ssrn.com/abstract=2226954 or http://dx.doi.org/10.2139/ssrn.2226954>; 2013.

[11] Burns J. Cross site request forgery. An introduction to a common web application weakness. Information Security Partners 2005.

[12] Owasp.org. Top 10 -Top 10−OWASP. [Internet]. Available at: <https://www.owasp.org/index.php/Top_10_2013-Top_10>; 2013 [accessed 06.13].

[13] Whitehat Security. Website security statistics report. [Internet]. .Available through: Whitehat Security. Available at: <https://www.whitehatsec.com/assets/WPstatsReport_052013.pdf>; [accessed 06.13].

[14] Czeskis A, Moshchuk A, Kohno T, Wang HJ. Lightweight server support for browser-based CSRF protection. In: Proceedings of the 22nd International Conference on World Wide Web. International World Wide Web Conferences Steering Committee; 2013. p. 273−284.

[15] Stackoverflow.com. iphone-CSRF verfication failed. Request aborted error with Pinterest in iOS-Stack Overflow. [Internet]. Available at: <http://stackoverflow.com/questions/14966016/csrf-verfication-failed-request-aborted-error-with-pinterest-in-ios>; [accessed 06.13]

[16] Blogs.msdn.com. CORS for XHR in IE10-IEBlog-site home. MSDN Blog. [Internet]. Available at: <http://blogs.msdn.com/b/ie/archive/2012/02/09/cors-for-xhr-in-ie10.aspx>; 2013 [accessed 06.13].

[17] Alexa.com. Dailymotion.com site info. [Internet]. Available at: <http://www.alexa.com/siteinfo/daily-motion.com>; [accessed 06.13].

[18] Wepawet.iseclab.org. Wepawet » Home. [Internet]. Available at: <http://wepawet.iseclab.org/>; [accessed 06.13]

[19] Jsunpack.jeek.org. jsunpack-a generic JavaScript unpacker. [Internet]. Available at: <http://jsunpack.jeek.org/>; [accessed 06.13]

Security through Emulation-Based Processor Diversification

21

Héctor Marco, Ismael Ripoll, David de Andrés, and Juan Carlos Ruiz

Universitat Politècnica de València, Valencia, Spain

INFORMATION IN THIS CHAPTER

- Systems and Data Security
- Information Systems Applications (including Internet)
- Software diversification
- Information Systems and Communication Service

INTRODUCTION

Computer systems are under constant threat by hackers who attempt to seize unauthorized control for malicious ends. Memory errors have been around for over 30 years and, despite research and development efforts carried out by academia and industry, they are still included in the CWE SANS top 25 list of the most dangerous software errors [1]. Classically, they were exploited pursuing the remote injection of binary code into the target application's memory and then diverting the control flow to the injected code. Today, memory error exploitation has evolved toward code-reuse attacks, where no malicious code is injected and legitimate code is reused for malicious purposes [2]. Interested readers can find in [3] a detailed analysis of the past, present, and future of memory errors. As authors conclude, memory errors "still represent a threat undermining the security of our systems."

Various approaches have been proposed and developed so far to eradicate or mitigate memory errors and their exploitation. The use of safe languages [4] may be the most effective approach, since it removes memory error vulnerabilities entirely. The idea consists in imposing stronger memory models on programming languages in order to increase their safety. Other effective strategies for fighting against memory errors rely on bounds checkers [5], which audit programs execution for out-of-bounds accesses; deploy countermeasures to prevent overwriting memory locations [6]; detect code injections at early stages [7]; and prevent attackers from finding, using, or executing injected code [8]. Commonly, these techniques rely on keeping secret key information required by attackers to break the system protection. Notably, all of them cause protected systems or applications to crash in the case of memory errors. Although not perfect, those solutions have shown their usefulness in greatly reducing the success of attackers. This is why they are nowadays incorporated in most computer systems [9].

The decision to abort an application to hinder an attack can, however, be questionable, especially in the context of critical networking business services. The cost of one hour of downtime for an airline reservation center is about $89,000, for eBay is about $225,000 and in the case of a credit card authorization that cost grows to $6,450,000 [10]. To deal with this unavailability problem, modern server-oriented architectures commonly make use of process-based abstractions as error containment regions [11]. As a result, and despite the crash of a concrete process serving a particular request, the server may continue processing ongoing and new requests.

Another pending issue in existing crash-based protection techniques relates to their inability to keep the confidentiality of the secret key information in the presence of brute force attacks. Depending on the protection technique and the internal architecture of the targeted application, the number of tries or guesses to find the secret varies. For instance, it takes around 216 seconds to bypass the Address Space Layout Randomization mechanism included in an Apache server running on Linux [12]. Unfortunately, this is a too short time to enable system administrators to deploy any effective countermeasure.

To address the problem of brute force attacks, one PaX developers group recommendation relies on combining existing protection techniques with a "crash detection and reaction mechanism" [13]. This approach could be applied to any protection technique that causes the attacked process to crash (wrong guess of the secret key information), thus becoming detectable. As already mentioned, nowadays, very limited actions are usually taken when brute force attacks are detected: either the service is shut down, with subsequent economic cost, or it keeps running and an alert is issued to administrators, who may not be able to intervene fast enough to prevent a successful intrusion.

Diversification is an approach with high potential to build effective defenses against attacks in general and brute force attacks against Web servers in particular. Applied to systems development, diversification can be seen as a system (or application) with at least two variants plus a decider that monitors results from the variants' execution in order to make decisions affecting their execution [14]. These variants are different versions of the same application (coming from different designs and/or implementations) that, although different, behave as expected from their specifications, that they provide the same service as perceived by users. However, differences existing among variants lead them to exhibit dissimilar sets of vulnerabilities, and thus different degrees of sensitivity against accidental and malicious faults.

The proposal presented in this chapter builds on the principle that the exploitation of memory errors relies on highly specific processor characteristics, so the same procedure rarely works on different hardware architectures. Obviously, diversifying the hardware also means diversifying the considered software. Software diversification, that is, the production of server variants, can be achieved using off-the-shelf cross-compilation suites, whereas hardware diversification relies on the emulation of different processor architectures. In this way, some vulnerabilities that manifest on a given architecture could be removed just by changing the execution platform to another architecture where existing software faults no longer constitute a vulnerability. Basically, a variant replacement policy is deployed upon detecting a process crash issued from memory errors. This approach can be seamlessly combined with existing protection techniques to complement a highly secure mechanism against memory error exploitation.

The key contributions of this chapter are:

1. Proposing a multi-architecture variant system running on a single platform and taking advantage of improvements in emulation support,
2. Employing off-the-shelf cross-compilation *toolchains* as a diversification technique,
3. Offering a novel recovery strategy, after an attack attempt, that maintains service continuity while invalidating brute force attacks and prevents the manifestation of accidental faults, and
4. Demonstrating through two case studies the effectiveness and portability of the technique, as well as the low implementation cost because it involves reuse of already existing tools.

The rest of this chapter describes in detail this proposal. The section titled "Background and Challenges" provides the background required to understand the problem tackled by this solution. The section "Proposed Security Approach" details the approach, whereas the section titled "A Case Study: Web Server" reports all practical aspects related to its deployment onto a real Web server running on two different platforms. Results issued from the evaluation of the developed prototypes are presented in the section "Experimentation and Results" and discussed in "Discussion." The chapter closes with the section "Conclusions and Future Work."

Background and challenges

This section describes the vulnerabilities that commonly lead to memory errors, the already existing mechanisms developed to cope with this problem, and the attacks that could bypass those mechanisms and successfully exploit existing vulnerabilities in the context of networking servers. Finally, identifying the common characteristics of presented vulnerabilities and attacks paves the way to defining a new architecture for memory error prevention. Figure 21.1 maps the concepts introduced in this section against the well-known AVI (Attack + Vulnerability → Intrusion) model [15].

Memory errors

Memory errors usually derive from the exploitation of vulnerabilities (depicted as holes in a wall in Figure 21.1) existing in a given application due to software faults introduced during the software's implementation. The most common software faults leading to memory errors are off-by-one, integer, and buffer overflow.

Off-by-one vulnerabilities [16] write one byte outside the bounds of allocated memory. They are often related to iterative loops iterating one time too many or common string functions incorrectly terminating strings. For instance, the bug reported by Frank Bussed [17] in the libpng library allowed remote attackers to cause an application crash via a crafted PNG image that triggered an out-of-bounds read during the copy of an error-message data.

Integer vulnerabilities [18] are usually caused by an integer exceeding its maximum or minimum boundary value. They can be used to bypass size checks or cause buffers to be allocated a size too small to contain the data copied into them. A recent bug discovered on the libpng library did not properly handle certain malformed PNG images [19]. It allowed remote attackers to

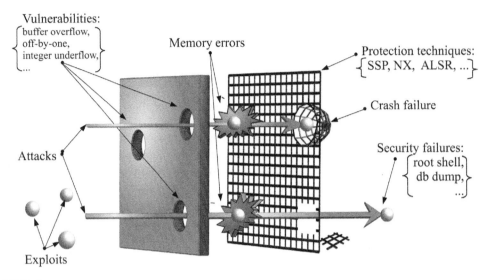

FIGURE 21.1

Mapping memory errors to the AVI model.

overwrite memory with an arbitrary amount of data and possibly have other unspecified impact, via a crafted PNG image. Vendors affected included Apple, Debian GNU/Linux, Fedora, Gentoo, Google, Novell, Ubuntu, and SUSE.

Buffer overflows [20] are caused by overrunning the buffer's boundary while writing data into a buffer. This allows attackers to overwrite data that controls the program execution path and hijack the program to execute the attacker's code instead of the process code. A recent stack-based buffer overflow example involved the cbtls_verify function in FreeRADIUS, causing server crashes and possibly executing arbitrary code via a long "not after" timestamp in a client certificate [21].

Over the past decade, different techniques have been developed to prevent attacks from successfully exploiting these vulnerabilities, thus reducing their chance of causing memory errors.

Protection mechanisms

The most effective protection techniques commonly used nowadays to fight against memory errors, represented as a grid in Figure 21.1, are Address-Space Layout Randomization, Stack-Smashing Protection, Non-Executable Bit, and Instruction Set Randomization.

Address-Space Layout Randomization (ASLR)[13]. Whenever a new process is loaded in the main memory, the operating system loads different areas of the process (code, data, heap, stack, etc.) at random positions in the process's virtual memory space. Attacks that rely on precisely knowing the absolute address of a library function, like ret2libc or the already injected shellcode, are very likely to crash the process, thus preventing a successful intrusion.

Stack-Smashing Protection (SSP) [22]. A random value, commonly known as canary, is placed on the stack just below the saved registers from the function prologue. That value is checked at the end of the function, before returning, and the program aborts if the stored canary does not match its initial value. Any attempt to overwrite the saved return address on the stack will also overwrite the canary and lead to a process crash to stop the intrusion.

Non-Executable Bit (NX) or "W⊕X"[6]. The memory areas (pages) of the process not containing code are marked as non-executable, so they cannot be written. On the other hand, those areas containing data are marked as just writeable, so they cannot be executed. Processors must provide hardware support to check for this policy when fetching instructions from the main memory. Even if an attacker successfully injects code into a writeable (not executable) memory region, any attempt to execute this code would lead to a process crash.

Instruction Set Randomization (ISR)[23]. ISR randomly modifies the instructions (code) of the process so they must be properly decoded before being effectively executed by the processor. Successful binary code injection attacks will crash the process, as decoding the injected code will not render the correct instructions. ISR is less commonly used than the preceding three techniques.

Despite the high protection provided by these techniques, their effectiveness is greatly reduced in the case of networking servers. Typically, the implementation of these servers is crash resilient (see crash failure in Figure 21.1), which increases the availability of the provided service. However, this also makes servers very sensitive to brute force attacks (note the grid hole leading to security failures in Figure 21.1). The next section focuses on this problem.

Networking server weaknesses

Traditionally, networking server architectures [24] are available in two main flavors: thread-based and process-based.

Multi-threaded architectures associate incoming connections with separate lightweight threads. Those threads share the same space address and thus also the same global variables and state. These architectures require small amounts of memory and provide fast inter-thread communication and response time, making them suitable for high performance servers. However, memory errors on one thread may corrupt the memory of any other thread, resulting in compromised threads accessing sensitive data from the rest of threads.

Multi-process architectures are well-suited for the compartmentalization philosophy promoted in security manuals. Incoming connections are handled by separate child processes, which are *forked* (created) by making an exact copy of the memory segments of the parent process in a separate address space (see Figure 21.2). Although performance suffers the effects of larger memory footprints and heavyweight structures, these architectures are more suitable for, and typically used in, highly secure servers [24].

Nevertheless, the common operation of multi-process servers makes them vulnerable to different attacks. Since all the children have the same secrets (ASLR offset, canary value, etc.) as the father, a brute force attack can be created.

ASLR provides little benefit for 32-bits systems, as there are only 8 random bits for *mmapped* areas, and the secret can be guessed by brute force in a matter of minutes [12].

Applications protected with SSP are vulnerable to buffer overflows in the heap, functions overwrites, and brute force attacks [25]. The most dangerous vulnerabilities are those allowing a "byte for byte" brute force attack, which will compromise the system with 1024 attempts (32-bit machine), like the latest pre-auth ProFTPd bug [26].

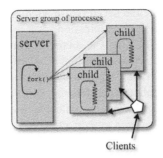

FIGURE 21.2

Multi-process model for server architectures.

The NX technique is easily bypassed by overwriting the return address on the call stack, so instead of returning into code located within the stack, it returns into a memory area occupied by a dynamic library [27]. Typically, the libc shared library is used, as it is always linked to the program and provides useful calls to an attacker (like system("/bin/sh") to get a shell).

ISR, like SPP, is vulnerable to brute force attacks, and also to attacks that only modify the contents of variables in the stack or the heap that cause control flow change or logical operation of the program [23].

Although several techniques have been proposed so far to prevent the successful exploitation of memory errors, the truth is that all these mechanisms can be bypassed one way or another. The following section discusses how to complement these mechanisms with an approach to improve their resilience against brute force attacks.

Proposed security approach

The core idea of the proposed security appraoch consists of having the same application compiled for different processors and replacing the executable process when an error is detected. Each variant is executed in sequential order on the same host by a fast processor emulator. In the case of a malicious attack, since code execution is highly processor dependent, changing the processor that runs the application greatly hinders the attack's success. The proposed architecture has the following elements:

1. A set of cross-compiler suites for creating the set of variants
2. A set of emulators for running the variants
3. An error detection mechanism, which triggers the variant replacement
4. A recovery strategy that selects the variant that will be used once an error has been detected

Creation of variants

Many diversification techniques are based on compiler or linker customizations for the automatic generation of variants [28]. Although it eliminates the need to manually rewrite the source code for diversification, deploying the required customizations on different compilers/linkers or introducing new modifications is costly and prone to introducing new errors.

The proposed approach (see Figure 21.3) uses already existing cross-compilers to generate variants, one for each target architecture, in an easy and effective way. Cross-compiler toolchains provide the set of utilities (compiler, linker, support libraries, and debugger) required to build binary code for a platform other than the one running the toolchain. For instance, the GNU cross-compiling platform toolchain is a highly portable widespread suite that is able to generate code for almost all of the 32-bit and 64-bit existing processors.

Just by compiling the application source code for different target processors, the particular architecture of each processor provide variants with different (i) *endianness* and *instruction sets*, so raw data and machine code injected by attackers are differently interpreted; (ii) *register sets*, thus changing the stack layout (on non-orthogonal architectures); (iii) *data and code alignments*, so unaligned instructions and word data type raise an exception; (iv) *address layouts*, which result in different positions for functions and main data structures according to the resulting code size and data layout; and (v) *compiler optimizations*, some generic and some processor specific, resulting in register allocation, instruction reordering, or function reordering.

Furthermore, most applications use the services provided by one or more libraries, which are linked during the compilation process. For instance, the standard C library provides the interface to the operating system (system calls), basic algorithms (string manipulation, math function, sorting, etc.), types definition, and so on. Since several implementations of the C library exist for achieving different goals, such as license issues, small memory footprint, better portability, or multi-thread support, by linking variants with different libraries it is possible to (i) get a higher degree of diversification among them, and (ii) get rid of specific software faults that are not present in some libraries.

This form of binary diversification preserves the semantic behavior of each variant. It is easy to implement because it uses widely available and tested software, and it offers a strong differentiation between resulting binaries.

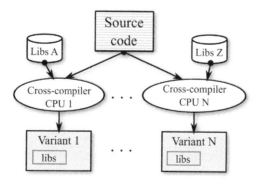

FIGURE 21.3

Variant generation.

Execution of variants

In order to run, variants require a proper execution environment, including the operating system API, system calls convention, processor instruction set, and the executable file format. The native variant—the one compiled for the physical processor and operating system hosting the server—runs on the native execution environment. However, as the rest of variants have been built for different processors, it is necessary to create a virtual execution environment to run them all.

Nowadays, there are two different virtualization solutions (see Figures 21.4a and 21.4b) to build a complete execution environment: (i) platform emulation, where the emulator provides a virtual hardware to execute the guest operating system managing the guest application, and (ii) user-mode

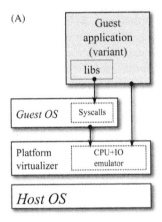

FIGURE 21.4A

Platform approach to virtualization.

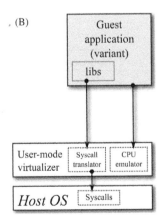

FIGURE 21.4B

User-mode approach to virtualization.

emulation, where the emulator provides both processor virtualization and operating system services, translating guest system calls into host system calls that are forwarded to the host operating system.

User-mode emulation is the less common form of emulation but offers better performance, since the operating system code is directly executed by the host processor. The emulator loads the guest executable code in its process memory space. The guest executable code is then dynamically translated into host native code, and the system calls are emulated (converted from guest format to host and back). Conceptually, user-mode emulation is very close to the Java Run-time Environment (JRE), which is a software emulator for running the Java Virtual Machine Specification. The main difference between user-mode emulation and JRE is that the former emulates real processors and real operating systems, while the latter emulates the Java Virtual Machine Specification.

Because of these advantages, the proposed security approach promotes the use of user-mode emulation to create the execution environment required for each variant. Variants should be compiled for the same operating system as the host machine is running (or a compatible one).

Memory error detection

The proposed approach relies on existing protection mechanisms (SSP, ASLR, etc.) to crash the compromised process. A monitor is in charge of detecting these crash-related events and triggering the established variants replacement strategy according to the defined security policy.

Notably, although those techniques were initially developed to deal with malicious faults, they also provide good coverage for accidental faults, like wild pointers. Accordingly, accidental activation of software faults leading to memory errors will also crash the process, giving the system a chance to deal with them.

Precisely diagnosing whether the problem is related to an accidental or a malicious fault and its precise origin (kind of attack), in order to define a more specific reaction, is still an issue for further research.

Variants replacement strategy

The widely used multi-process architecture of networking servers provides an ideal scenario for deploying different security policies for variant replacement upon detection of memory errors. The proposed policy consists of three successive stages (see Figure 21.5):

1. High performance service
2. Fault avoidance
3. Confusing the attacker

Stage 1: High performance service

Initially, the service is provided by the native variant, directly running on the host computer, and is thus free of any overhead due to virtualisation. Upon detecting a process crash, the system enters into a fault avoidance mode.

Stage 2: Fault avoidance

In the second stage, the system assumes that an attack, or an accidental software fault, exists that could cause another crash on another child. To try to hinder or even prevent the successful exploitation of the memory error, the next variant to be executed is selected among those with more

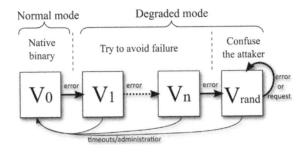

FIGURE 21.5

Variant replacements policy.

architectural differences with respect to the previously selected one. For instance, a buffer overflow by one byte is likely to cause an error on the i386 architecture but not on the SPARC one, due to the different ways the processor registers are managed; the Apache chunked-encoding was exploitable on 32-bit processors but not on 64-bit Unix platforms [29]; and a busybox integer overflow [30] only affected big endian systems.

After changing the variant, the service runs in a performance degraded mode due to the processor emulation overhead. This performance penalty also runs against attackers by slowing down the attacks, which administrators valuable time to fix the problem. If no new crashes occur during a given period, the system can automatically revert to the native mode to increase its performance, or it could require an explicit command from the system administrator to do so. If there are new process crashes, the system keeps changing from one variant to another until all of them have been tried. When no new variants are available, the system assumes it is under a brute force attack and the fault manifests on all variants, which requires a more aggressive replacement policy.

Stage 3: Confuse the attacker
The third stage is focused on confusing a possible attacker to reduce as much as possible the information that could be retrieved from unsuccessful exploitation attempts. If variant replacement is sequential, although difficult and time-consuming, expert attackers might finally guess the processor architecture of some variants and could develop exploits to compromise the system. Accordingly, the proposed policy relies on randomly selecting the next variant to be executed, which makes construction of a brute force attack more difficult. The policy to revert to native mode is the same as in the second stage.

Obviously, different policies should be defined according to the particular needs and resources available for each server, such as existing variants, and diagnosis and detection capabilities, so they vary from one case to another. Since each request is redirected to a different variant independently, whether they crash or not, *brute force attacks are no longer possible.*

A case study: Web server

As a proof of concept to show the feasibility and portability of the proposed approach, two hardware platforms have been chosen for case studies: an HTTP server running on a PC and a smartphone. The first hardware platform, selected as representative of a common platform for Web servers, consists of a PC running an Ubuntu 12.04.1 LTS operating system. The PC is equipped with an x86_64 Intel Core i3-370 M CPU, clocked at 2.4 GHz and 3072 MB RAM. The second target platform, selected to show the portability of the proposed approach even on devices with limited resources, is a Samsung Galaxy S smartphone running the Android 2.3.6 operating system. The smartphone is equipped with a 1 GHz ARM Cortex A8 processor with 512 MB RAM and a PowerVR SGX 540 GPU.

The busybox-httpd application [31] has been selected to provide the required networking service. It is a complex, full-featured application widely used on many platforms, including smartphones, routers, and media players, running a variety of POSIX environments like Linux, Android, and FreeBSD. The busybox application consists of a single executable file that can be customized to provide a subset of over 200 utilities specified in the Single Unix Specification (SIS) plus many others that a user would expect to see on a Linux system, including the HTTPD Web server considered for this case study.

The following sections describe in detail the particular instantiation of all the elements required to deploy the proposed approach, including variants created using cross-compilation, the processor emulation support, the detection mechanism, the recovery strategy deployed for variant replacement procedure, and the security policy. The following implementation has been seamlessly applied to both hardware platforms with minor changes. An overview of the prototype developed for the smartphone is depicted in Figure 21.6.

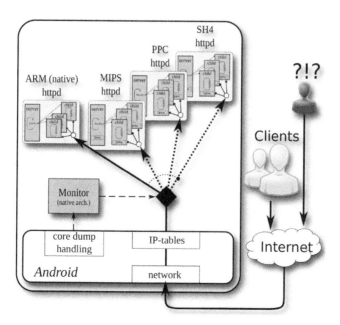

FIGURE 21.6

System prototype overview for the smartphone.

Building cross-compilers

To build the binary images (HTTPD variants) for each target architecture, a cross-compiling tool-chain suite is required for each of them. One possibility is to download pre-compiled versions from different projects or providers, but these would not be flexible enough to achieve the desired level of diversification. Another possibility is to build the required toolchain suites from the source code of each element (compiler, linker, library, and debugger) to get greater controllability when creating variants.

Although building a toolchain is quite tricky due to the strong dependence among elements, thanks to the buildroot project (http://buildroot.net) it is possible to build (and customize) the GNU toolchain very easily. Buildroot uses the same source code configuration tools as the Linux kernel, commonly known as *menuconfig*, which presents a simple menu interface (see Figure 21.7) that guides the user to configure code features while avoiding conflicting or incompatible options.

Buildroot V2012.05 was selected for this case study, and, according to the target architectures, generation parameters were customized to build the required cross-compilers as follows: (i) according to the host operating system the selected *kernel headers* were "Linux 3.2.x kernel headers"; (ii) the considered *target architecture* included the native ones, "x86_64" and "ARM," as well as others with very different architectures, like "SPARC," "i386," "SH4," "MIPS," and "PowerPC"; (iii) the *uClibc C* library version was "uClibc 0.9.32.x"; and (iv) the selected version of the processor emulator does not support "Native POSIX Threading (NPTL)" for all architectures, the "linuxthreads (stable/old)" *Thread library implementation* was used. The remaining options were configured to be as similar as possible to each other in order to perform an accurate comparative analysis.

Qemu emulator

Qemu [32] is a generic, open source, and fast machine emulator and virtualizer that uses a portable dynamic translator for various target CPU architectures. As an example of its high quality and popularity, it is the base of the Android emulator currently distributed in the Android SDK.

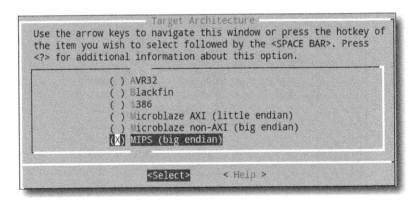

FIGURE 21.7

Buildroot configuration menu interface.

Besides the standard CPU emulation mode, Qemu implements the user-mode emulation, capable of running a single program (process) in a complete virtualized environment, that constitutes the core of the proposed approach as described in the subsection "Execution of Variants." User-mode emulation is not limited to statically compiled binaries, but can also load dynamic libraries, thereby enabling the direct execution (emulation) of most existing applications.

Combining the user-mode emulation with the Linux capability to run arbitrary executables (called binfmt_misc), it is possible to run a guest binary executable (variant) as if it were a native one. Note that it is the operating system kernel, and not a module of the command interpreter or another user application, that interprets the executable format. In fact, all variants (regardless of the target processor) use the same operating system and can access the same directory hierarchy and network interfaces. With this form of emulation, it is not necessary to set up a complete virtual platform, and variants are transparently and efficiently executed as if they were native processes.

Detecting crashes

The *core dump* facility of Linux (also available on many operating systems) was selected as a suitable tool for detecting the abnormal termination of variants. Core dumps are triggered by different signals (see Table 21.1). Since Linux 2.6. the operating system infrastructure for dumping process core images (/proc/sys/kernel/core_pattern file) provides facilities to send the core image to a crash reporter program along with command-line information about the crashed process.

Although core dumps provide lots of useful information for diagnosing and debugging programming errors, the proposed approach only requires notification that the process has crashed, regardless of its cause (as previously mentioned, this could be an enhancement requiring further research). The *core_pattern* file has been configured (see Code 1) to call a tiny shell script *log_crashes.sh* (see Code 2), whenever any process of the system crashes. This script will receive the PID of the crashed process (%p), the triggering signal (%s), the executable filename name (%e), and the time of dump (%t). It will append a single line containing the received information into a file named */var/log/m/crashes.log.*

```
echo "|/var/log/m/log_crashes.sh %p %s %e %t" >/proc/sys/kernel/core_pattern
```

Table 21.1 Signals Leading to Core Dump

Signal	Description
SIGQUIT	Quit from keyboard
SIGILL	Illegal Instruction
SIGABRT	Abort signal from abort(3)
SIGFPE	Floating point exception
SIGSEGV	Invalid memory reference
SIGBUS	Bus error (bad memory access)
SIGTRAP	Trace/breakpoint trap
SIGXCPU	CPU time limit exceeded
SIGXFSZ	File size limit exceeded
SIGIOT	IOT trap. A synonym for SIGABRT

Code 1 Command for configuring *core_pattern*

```bash
#!/bin/bash
pid = $1
signal = $2
ex_name = $3
time = $4
fcrash = "/var/log/m/crashes.log"
echo "[$pid] [$signal] [$ex_name] [$time]" >> $fcrash
```

Code 2 Saving core dump information into *crashes.log*

The Linux *inotify* mechanism, which provides an efficient file system events monitoring service, has been used to monitor when new entries are written in the *crashes.log* file. This makes it possible to read new entries from the file and consider only those caused by variants processes without overhead. Note that the monitor is compiled for the native architecture and will be blocked (inactive) until a new entry is written.

As the monitor is a critical component of this approach, it has been designed to be simple and small, with the aim of minimizing the probability of introducing design or software faults. Another requisite was to isolate the monitor from the application so attackers cannot know of the monitor's presence and use a communication channel to interfere with it.

Contrary to other protection solutions, the monitor does not act as a barrier between clients/ attackers and servers, and it does not add new code or features that attackers could exploit. The kernel facilities used to handle core files enable the immediate detection of crashed variants, without modifications of either the variants' code or their configuration. The fact that it is a one-way communication channel with a very limited and simple interface makes it extremely difficult to successfully attack the monitor through this channel.

Alternating among variants

Once the crash has been detected, the current variant is replaced by another one according to the established replacement policy. The straightforward solution would be to stop (kill) all the processes (in the case of a multi-process server) of the current variant and start up the next one. However, this solution presents two important drawbacks: (i) the failure of a single server process serving a particular client is propagated to the rest of processes, so all ongoing connections are affected by the failure; and (ii) the service is unavailable until the next variant is up and running.

A less drastic solution can be implemented using kernel firewall facilities, known as *iptables*, which allow a system administrator to customize the tables provided by the Linux kernel firewall and the chains and rules it stores. Using *iptables*, the active connections are preserved for the server processes that are working properly, while new connections (clients) are redirected to the newly selected variant, thus solving any μ-*denial-of-service* (μ-*DOS*) or temporary service unavailability problem.

Following this approach, all variants are created and started as if they were the actual server. Each variant is configured to listen for connections on different ports (other than the external server port), which are blocked using *iptables* to prevent external connections from directly accessing variants. The internal firewall is then configured to redirect incoming connections from the service port to the active port of the current variant. When a process of the current variant crashes, the policy of the recovery strategy is applied to decide which will be the next variant, and the service port is redirected to the next variant port. A sample *iptables* rule implementing this approach is shown in Code 3.

Following the isolation design principle of the monitor, the variant selection procedure implemented using the *iptables* facility is an indirect mechanism that takes advantage of the kernel IP routing tables. Variants are not aware of the presence of the monitor, and they are not modified in any way. In this case, there is no communication channel that attackers could exploit to reach the monitor through variants.

```
iptables -A PREROUTING -t nat -p tcp --dport [service-port] -j
REDIRECT --to-ports [variant-port]
```

Code 3 Firewall configuration to change the active variant

In this prototype, all variants are simultaneously launched when the service is started. More advanced replacement and recovery policies enabled by the kernel firewall facility are discussed in the "Discussion" section VI.

Experimentation and results

In order to assess the effectiveness of the proposed approach, the prototypes considered in the case study were exposed to a number of exploitable vulnerabilities leading to memory errors. The results show the importance of properly selecting hardware architectures to prevent the further exploitation of existing vulnerabilities, either because software faults no longer lead to memory errors or because brute force attacks get confused. Finally, the temporal and spatial overhead induced by the solution is analyzed.

Fault Manifestation

The exploitation of software faults leading to memory errors may manifest differently according to the variant being executed due to its particular processor architecture. To illustrate this, a buffer overflow fault was injected into the busybox HTTPD web server (see Code 4") whereas, for the sake of clarity, off-by-one and integer underflow faults were manually injected into a standalone program (see Code 5).

```
static int get_line(void) {
int count = 0;
char c;
char buffer[256]; // Injected code

    ...

    ...
strcpy(buffer, iobuf); // Injected code
```

```
return count;
}
```

Code 4 Buffer overflow fault injected in busybox-httpd

The code injected into the *httpd.c* file, in the function get_line(void) (see Code 4"), constitutes a typical buffer overflow, similar to the one found in Oracle 9 [33]. The URL of the HTTP request is copied into the added buffer, but since there is no length check, long URLs overflow the buffer and cause a memory error. HTTP requests of increasing URL lengths were tested for each variant. Table 21.2 lists the minimum length required to crash the process. The results show that the SPARC architecture is, by far, the most robust against that particular fault, so it could be a good choice for preventing problems derived from buffer overflows.

```
void offByOne(char*arg) {
char buffer[128];
if(strlen(arg)>128) {
  printf("Overflow\n");
  exit(0);
}
strcpy(buffer, arg);
}
void intUnderflow(unsigned int len, char*src){
  unsigned int size;
  size = len-2;
  char*comment = (char*) malloc (size + 1);
  memcpy (comment, src, size);
}
```

Code 5 Standalone code for off-by-one and integer underflow faults

The *offByOne()* function from Code 5 line 1, inspired by one affecting an FTP server in [34], includes an offset-by-one software fault, since arguments with a length of 128 will cause the *strcpy()* function to overflow the buffer by just one byte (the appended '\0' char). Table 21.2 lists how this

Table 21.2 Manifestation of Exploitation Attempts on Different Software Faults

Variant	Off-by-one -O2 flag	Integer Underflow -O0 flag	Buffer Overflow	bytes to crash
x86_64	Crash	No crash	Crash	68
i386	Crash	No crash	Crash	250
ARM	Crash	No crash	No crash	62
MIPSEL	No crash	Crash	No crash	258
SPARC	No crash	No crash	Crash	1234
SH4	Crash	Crash	Crash	50
PPC	No crash	No crash	Crash	70

fault manifests for two different variants created for each considered architecture: one with the commonly used -O2 optimization flag, and the other with no optimizations (-O0). SPARC is again the most robust architecture, as the fault does not crash the process regardless of the selected optimization flags, whereas the SH4 architecture always crashes. The negative influence of compiler optimizations that, in general, produce less robust variants is worth noting.

The integer underflow software fault was tested using a real-world vulnerability [35] in a JPEG processing code. The code of the faulty *intUnderflow()* function is shown in Code 5 line 10. When 1 is passed as the first parameter, the size variable has the value -1, which is interpreted as a large positive value (0xFFffFFff) in the third parameter of the *memcpy()* function (line 14), on a 32-bit architecture. This incorrect value is then used to perform a memory copy into the buffer reserved by the previous *malloc()*. The behavior of a *malloc()* request for zero bytes is implementation dependent (some implementations return NULL, while others return a pointer to the heap area). As shown in Table 21.2, only the ARM and MIPSEL variants prevent the process from crashing.

Protection against attacks

The basic idea behind brute force attacks is to make continuous requests, trying all the possible values of the unknown secret (a memory address or a random value, for instance), until the right value is found. On a system equipped with ASLR, NX, and stack protector techniques, the typical steps taken to build an attack are:

1. Find out the offset to the canary on the stack. It can be estimated accurately from the application image (which we assume the attacker has), but often the offset is verified by testing sequentially the position of the canary.
2. Find out the value of the canary (using brute force against the target).
3. Build the Return Oriented Programming (ROP) sequence (based on the ELF). For simplicity's sake, we assume the ROP gadgets are from the libc.
4. Find the entry point for the ROP (using brute force against the target).

Depending on the kind of error, all of these steps may not be required. For example, a memory error in the data segment can be exploited without knowing the canary.

The final exploit string must have the correct values of all these elements: canary value and off-set, and ROP sequence and entry point. The parts of the exploit not known by the attacker can be obtained using brute force, building a partial exploit using the values already known and testing only the values that are missing. Any incorrect value in the exploit (or a partial exploit string) is detected by the protection mechanisms, and the application is crashed. Since the protection mechanisms are applied sequentially, the attacker builds a partial exploit that affects only one of these protections. One the protection is bypassed, the next one can be addressed.

Our solution prevents exploits from being built this way because the following assumptions no longer hold:

- The active server target is not always the same, so a fault cannot be unequivocally interpreted as an incorrect value guess. For instance, variants may crash not only due to a wrong guess but also due to different memory layouts (invalid offsets) or endianness (invalid instruction/data format).
- Some software faults may not manifest in certain variants (as previously discussed), which exploits interpret as a successful guess.

- Once an emulated variant is active, the performance of the server is degraded due to the emulation overhead, which plays against the attacker by increasing the time required to guess the secret, similar to the GRKERNSEC_BRUTE [36] option.

In [12], the authors show how ASLR can be bypassed using a brute force attack to find out the correct address for a *return-to-libc*. The proposed exploit succeeded in just 216 seconds on average. However, using our technique, the current variant is replaced when the monitor detects a crash. In a variant with a different stack layout (the offset of the return address) the attacker will be overwriting the wrong one, so the return address is not overwritten with the guessed value and the exploit can never succeed.

The most dangerous way to bypass the SSP mechanism is the "byte for byte" approach, whereas the most generic procedure is a generic brute force attack [37]. In the first case, if attackers may overwrite individual bytes of the canary (secret), at the most $256\frac{wordsize}{8}$ tries (1024 attempts for a 32-bits machine) are required to guess the right value, which takes just a few seconds. For generic brute force attacks, exploits need to try all the possible values of the secret (2^{32} attempts at most for a 32-bits secret), returning the first one that does not cause a crash. This kind of attack cannot succeed on the proposed architecture. After a variant is replaced, the address being overwritten by the attacker is not that belonging to the canary. If the process does not crash, *the exploit will wrongly assume that the secret has been accurate guessed* ; if it crashes (which is not related to wrong guesses), *the exploit will keep erroneously discarding possible values*. From this point on, the next steps of the exploit are completely useless.

Spatial and temporal cost

In spite of the great security benefits provided by the proposed approach, there is also a price to be paid in terms of spatial and temporal overhead due to the execution of multiple virtual environments.

Spatial overhead refers to the amount of main memory consumed at run time for each variant when it is interpreted by the processor emulator (Qemu). This total amount of memory has three different components: (i) the size of the executable image of the variant, which depends on the libraries selected for building the toolchain, the compiler optimization flags, and the code density of the related architecture; (ii) the size of Qemu's memory translation cache, where application code is dynamically translated from guest to host architecture; and (iii) the memory required by Qemu itself. Note that the native variants have no memory overhead, since they are executed as if the proposed approach were not used.

The memory consumed by each variant has been estimated according to the set of pages unique to a process (Unique Set Size, or USS), which has been measured with the smem(8) tool. As both Qemu and variants are statically compiled, there is no shared memory other than the pages shared between father and children processes (all pages copied to children are marked as copy-on-write). Table 21.3 summarizes the average USS memory for each variant. The total memory used in the proposed implementation is the memory used by all running variants. By default all variants are launched, but more conservative solutions are possible in which only the active and next variant are ready (i.e., launched).

Table 21.3 Spatial and Temporal Overhead of the Web Server

Variant	Memory (kB)		Latency (ms)		Throughput (KB/s)			
	PC	Phone	PC	Phone	PC	Phone		
Native	x86_64	36	—	0.18	—	6290	—	
	i386	32	—	0.26	—	4502	—	
	ARM	—	32	—	9.8	—	120	
Qemu	x86_64	408	400	2.23	55	529	21	
	i386	416	336	2.35	52	503	22	
	ARM	364	328	2.95	54	401	21	
	MIPSEL	364	308	3.22	60	368	19	
	PPC	404	346	8.02	118	147	10	
	SH4	428	356	4.96	77	239	15	
	SPARC	504	436	3.20	72	370	16	

The temporal overhead is introduced by the emulation support provided by Qemu when executing non-native variants. In the absence of crashes, the native variant is executed without any temporal overhead. This overhead has been estimated by means of the Apache HTTP server benchmarking tool, which was configured to perform 100 simultaneous requests for a total of 5,000 requests. Table 21.3 summarizes the average latency and throughput (from the user viewpoint) obtained by the considered HTTPD Web server when running the benchmark for each variant. Notably, requests on the PC were made locally, which could be considered the best possible scenario, whereas requests on the smartphone were made remotely, thus incurring all the delays related to wireless networks, which could be considered the worst possible scenario. The time required for the monitor to detect a process crash and configure the firewall was on the order of a few microseconds and considered negligible, so it is not included in the table, where latency is expressed in milliseconds.

Discussion

Successfully exploiting a memory error is not an easy task for anyone to achieve. However, due to the proliferation of popular websites that act as repositories for existing exploits, even inexpert hackers have a chance to succeed. According to their knowledge and available resources, three basic types of attackers can be considered: script kiddies, black hat hackers, and Advanced Persistent Threat (APT) groups.

Most attacks come from script kiddies or *skiddies*, who are non-expert users who simply download and use existing exploits. These exploits are usually highly customized to target a specific vulnerability on a given architecture. Thus, unless the exploit succeeds on the very first try (quite unlikely, but there is always a chance), replacing the variant under attack will prevent this kind of user from successfully exploiting the memory error.

The knowledge and experience required to exploit a software fault is mastered by only a few. Due to the complexity and the time required, black hat hackers usually specialize in a given platform (operating system and architecture). It is rare to find hackers able to target multi-architecture platforms like the one proposed in this chapter. Bypassing the proposed solution would require developing a meta-exploit, targeting multiple architectures, that could extract some valuable information from the running variant. As long as the next variant is randomly selected, it is unlikely that brute force attacks could succeed.

Finally, APT groups are sets of people with the capability, knowledge, and resources as well as the intent to persistently and effectively break the security of a specific target. With the proposed plan, even these groups will be highly delayed in achieving a successful attack, not only by the complexity involved in developing a suitable exploit but also due to the temporal overhead caused by the emulation process, which greatly delays the attack. This delay gives administrators enough time to react and deploy the required countermeasures.

Following this line of thought, this technique should not be used as a stand-alone mechanism but shall be integrated into the server's security policy. Whenever the server switches to a degraded mode (a non-native variant is active), administrators should be notified to deploy the most suitable countermeasures.

Typically, successful brute force attacks are launched by compromising a set of Internet-connected computers (*zombies*) that collaborate in the exploitation attempt (*botnet*). Distributed attacks are one of the most difficult kinds of attacks to handle with common firewalls because the request come from a variety of sources. Since the proposed solution does not take into account the source address of the attackers, it is equally effective whether it is facing a single node or multiple botnet attacks.

Although the primary source of diversification is the use of cross-development tools, it is also possible to create variants for native architectures using different compilation flags. It might even be interesting to create some variants from former versions of the code. Considering that newer code is more likely to have bugs than older and more tested versions, using old versions of the code is a good solution when the focus prioritizes security over functionality.

Another possible improvement consists in adapting the policy for variant replacement according to a diagnosis of the particular kind of attack and the exploited vulnerability. In this way the most suitable architecture to deal with each exploitation attempt could be selected from the variant pool.

Likewise, a simple improvement to decrease the spatial overhead could be to keep only two variants launched: the current and next.

CONCLUSIONS AND FUTURE WORK

Nowadays, memory errors continue to rank among the top dangerous software errors despite many research efforts by both academia and industry. Although existing protection mechanisms constitute a formidable barrier to the successful exploitation of memory errors by common hackers, these mechanisms do not constitute an impassable obstacle to more capable and resourceful opponents, like black hat hackers and APT groups.

Due to the nature of the protection mechanisms, most attacks are thwarted at the cost of causing a server crash. The administrator can configure the service to either stop it at once, with related economical losses, or keep it running, with an increasing likelihood of successful attacks. The work presented in this chapter, which relies on diversification, complements existing protection mechanisms with a detection and reaction approach that offer administrators a third possibility, less drastic and dangerous, for hindering and even preventing the successful exploitation of memory errors while preserving continuity of service.

Based on the fact that software faults leading to memory errors are highly dependent on the hardware architecture (processor), our technique uses processor diversification as an effective protection against most kind of attacks and accidental faults. Attacks designed to target a specific processor will not succeed. The only alternative for attackers is to build meta-exploits for all available target architectures, greatly hindering the possibility of a real attack. Even if such a meta-exploit were available, applying a replacement policy in which the next variant is randomly selected would prevent attackers from obtaining useful information to bypass existing mechanisms. The processor diversification required for this policy can be done efficiently due to current advances in processor emulation techniques.

Contrary to most automatic diversification techniques, which customize the compiler or even the resulting executable binary, the use of cross-toolchains provides a simple and powerful means of software diversification, with the added benefit of using widely used and tested tools without having to modify them. Combining this with the underlying hardware diversification, existing software faults will manifest differently among variants and may not manifest at all in some of them.

The feasibility and portability of this secure approach has been proven by deploying a HTTP Web server in two very different scenarios: a personal computer and a smartphone. The results show that common attacks against existing protection mechanisms are effectively handled at the cost of degrading the service performance due to the processor emulator overhead. The service degradation, usually considered an undesired side-effect, in fact plays against attackers, since it delays brute force attacks, thus giving administrators time to react while still providing service.

The powerful capabilities of the proposed approach open up a wide range of possibilities for further research. Some of these are: (i) a deep study of different hardware architectures with regard to how memory errors manifest in order to characterize their robustness against exploitation attempts; (ii) a careful diagnosis of an attack in process, which could be invaluable in selecting the most suitable hardware architecture to hinder that attack or even prevent it; and (iii) research into tailoring the variant replacement policy to fit the needs of particular services or scenarios.

Acknowledgments

This work has been supported by Spanish MICINN grant TIN2009-14205-C04-02 and MEC TIN2012-38308-C02-01.

References

[1] CWE/SANS. (2011) Top 25 most dangerous software errors. [Online]. Available: http://cwe.mitre.org/top25.

[2] Tran M, Etheridge M, Bletsch T, Jiang X, Freeh V, Ning P. On the expressiveness of return-into-libc attacks. In RAID'11: Proceedings of the 14th International Conference on Recent Advances in Intrusion

Detection;Berlin, Heidelberg: Springer-Verlag. p. 121−141. [Internet]. Available from: <http://dx.doi.org/10.1007/978-3-642-23644-0_7>; 2011.

[3] van der Veen V, dutt Sharma N, Cavallaro L, Bos H. Memory errors: The past, the present, and the future. In RAID: Proceedings of the 15th International Symposium on Research in Attacks Intrusions and Defenses; 2012.

[4] Wichmann BA. Requirements for programming languages in safety and security software standards. Comput Stand Interfaces 1992;14(5-6):433−41. Available from: < http://dx.doi.org/10.1016/0920-5489 (92)90009-3 >

[5] Brünink M, Süßkraut M, Fetzer C. Boundless memory allocations for memory safety and high availability. In DSN. Proceedings of The 41st Annual IEEE/IFIP International Conference on Dependable Systems and Networks. Los Alamitos, CA, USA: IEEE Computer Society; 2011Proceedings of The 41st Annual IEEE/IFIP International Conference on Dependable Systems and Networks. Los Alamitos, CA, USA: IEEE Computer Society; 2011. p. 13−24

[6] Paulson LD. New chips stop buffer overflow attacks. Computer 2004;37(10):28−30.

[7] Snow KZ, Krishnan S, Monrose F, Provos N. Shellos: Enabling fast detection and forensic analysis of code injection attacks. In USENIX Security Symposium. USENIX Association. [Internet]. Available from: <http://dblp.uni-trier.de/db/conf/uss/uss2011.html#SnowKMP11>; 2011.

[8] Salamat B, Jackson T, Wagner G, Wimmer C, Franz M. Runtime defense against code injection attacks using replicated execution. IEEE Transactions on Dependable and Secure Computing 2011;8:588−601.

[9] Riley R, Jiang X, Xu D. An architectural approach to preventing code injection attacks. IEEE Trans Dependable Secur Comput 2010;7(4):351−65. Available from: http://dx.doi.org/10.1109/TDSC.2010.1

[10] Patterson DA. A simple way to estimate the cost of downtime. In LISA: Proceedings of the 16th USENIX Conference on System Administration; Berkeley, CA, USA. USENIX Association; 2002. p. 185−188. [Internet]. Available from: <http://dl.acm.org/citation.cfm?id = 1050517.1050538>; 2002.

[11] Chapin J, Rosenblum M, Devine S, Lahiri T, Teodosiu D, Gupta A Hive: fault containment for shared-memory multiprocessors. SIGOPS Oper Syst Rev. 1995 Dec;29(5):12-25. [Internet]. Available from: http://doi.acm.org/10.1145/224057.224059.

[12] Shacham H, Page M, Pfaff B, Goh E-J, Modadugu N, Boneh D. On the effectiveness of address-space randomization. In CCS '04: Proceedings of the 11th ACM Conference on Computer and communications security; New York, NY, USA; ACM. p. 298−307. [Internet]. Available from: <http://doi.acm.org/10.1145/1030083.1030124>; 2004.

[13] Pax Team. PaX address space layout randomization (ASLR). [Internet]. Available from: <http://pax.grsecurity.net/docs/aslr.txt>; 2003.

[14] Laprie J-C, Béounes C, Kanoun K. Definition and analysis of hardware- and software-fault-tolerant architectures. Computer 1990;23(7):39−51 [Internet]. Available from: < http://dx.doi.org/10.1109/ 2.56851 >

[15] Verissimo PE, Neves NF, Cachin C, Poritz J, Powell D, Deswarte I, et al. Intrusion tolerant middleware: The road to automatic security. IEEE Security and Privacy 2006;4(4):5−62.

[16] Koziol J., Litchfield D., Aitel D., et al. The shellcoder's handbook: Discovering and exploiting security holes. Wiley Publishing Inc; 2006.

[17] NIST. Vulnerability summary for CVE-2011-2501. [Internet]. Available from: <http://web.nvd.nist.gov/view/vuln/detail?vulnId = CVE-2011-2501>; 2011.

[18] Brumley D, Chiueh T-C, Johnson R, Lin H, Song D. Rich: Automatically protecting against integer-based vulnerabilities. In: Symp on Network and Distributed Systems Security; 2007.

[19] NIST. Vulnerabilitysummary for CVE-2011-3026. [Internet]. Available from: <http://web.nvd.nist.gov/view/vuln/detail?vulnId = CVE-2011-3026>; 2012.

[20] One A. Smashing the stack for fun and profit. Phrack 1996;7:49.

[21] NIST. Vulnerability summary for CVE-2012-3547. [Internet]. 2012 Nov. Available from: < http://web. nvd.nist.gov/view/vuln/detail?vulnId = CVE-2012-3547>; 2012.

[22] Cowan C, Pu C, Maier D, Hintongif H, Walpole J, Bakke P, et al. Stackguard: Automatic adaptive detection and prevention of buffer-overflow attacks. Proc of the 7th USENIX Security Symposium 1998 Jan;63−78.

[23] Kc GS, Keromytis AD, Prevelakis V. Countering code injection attacks with instruction-set randomization. In CCS '03: Proceedings of the 10th ACM Conference on Computer and Communications Security; 2003; New York, NY, USA; ACM. p. 272-280. [Internet]. Available from: <http://doi.acm. org/10.1145/948109.948146>.

[24] Erb B Concurrent programming for scalable web architectures. [diploma thesis]; Institute of Distributed Systems: Ulm University; . [Internet]. Available: <http://www.benjamin-erb.de/thesis>; 2012.

[25] Bulba, Kil3r. Bypassing stackguard and stackshield. Phrack. 56; 2002.

[26] NIST. Vulnerability summary for CVE-2010-3867. [Internet]. 2011 Sep. Available from: <http://web. nvd.nist.gov/view/vuln/detail?vulnId = CVE-2010-3867>; 2011.

[27] Nergal. The advanced return-into-lib(c) exploits: PaX case study. Phrack; 58; 2001.

[28] Salamat B, Jackson T, Wagner G, Wimmer C, Franz M. Run-time defense against code injection attacks using replicated execution. IEEE Trans Dependable Sec Comput 2011;8(4):588−601.

[29] CERT. Advisory CA-2002-17 Apache Web server chunk handling vulnerability. [Internet]. Available from: <http://www.cert.org/advisories/CA-2002-17.html>; 2002.

[30] Glaser T Busybox: integer overflow in expression on big endian. [Internet]. Available from: <http:// bugs.debian.org/cgi-bin/bugreport.cgi?bug=635370.>; 2011

[31] Perens B Busybox. [Internet]. Available from: <http://www.busybox.net>; 1996.

[32] Bellard F. Qemu, a fast and portable dynamic translator. In: USENIX Annual Technical Conference, FREENIX Track. USENIX; 2005. p. 41−46.

[33] CERT. Advisory CA-2002-08 Multiple vulnerabilities in Oracle servers. [Internet]. Available from: <http://www.cert.org/advisories/CA-2002-08.html>; 2002.

[34] NIST. WFTPD Pro server denial of service. [Internet]. Available from: <http://web.nvd.nist.gov/view/ vuln/detail?vulnId = CVE-2004-0342>; 2004.

[35] MS Bulletin. Buffer overrun in JPEG processing (GDI+) could allow code execution. [Internet]. Available from: <http://technet.microsoft.com/en-us/security/bulletin/ms04-028>; 2004.

[36] Grsecurity kernel patches. [Internet]. Available from: <http://grsecurity.net/>; 2013.

[37] Zabrocki A. Scraps of notes on remote stack overflow exploitation. Phrack 2010;13:63.

On the Use of Unsupervised Techniques for Fraud Detection in VoIP Networks

22

Yacine Rebahi[1], Tran Quang Thanh[1], Roman Busse[1], and Pascal Lorenz[2]

[1]*Fraunhofer Institute for Open Communication Systems (FOKUS), Berlin, Germany*
[2]*University of Haute Alsace, Colmar, France*

INFORMATION IN THIS CHAPTER

- VoIP
- Fraud
- Signatures
- NN-SOM
- Unsupervised learning

INTRODUCTION

Various definitions of fraud are reflected in the literature. However, fraud can simply be seen as any activity that leads to obtaining financial advantage or causing loss by implicit or explicit deception. In traditional telecommunication networks, fraud is already a threat depriving telecom operators of huge amounts of money every year. With the migration from circuit-switched networks to packet-switched networks, this situation can be expected to worsen. This is mainly due to the lack of strong built-in security mechanisms and the use of open standards in IP-based networks. Based on a 2011 survey, the Communication Fraud Control Association (CFCA) reports that telecom fraud costs businesses more than $40 billion every year [1].

Unfortunately, the problem of detecting fraud in telecom in general and in Voice over IP (VoIP) in particular is very difficult. Supervised classification techniques can be useful if a training sample of data with fraud labels is obtained. A training sample is required in standard supervised techniques to help the system learn the fraud cases. In reality, it is costly and sometimes impossible to obtain a training sample with unambiguous fraud labels [2].

In telecommunication, Call Data Records (CDRs) are the type of data usually used for fraud investigation. Unfortunately, CDRs are not enough, and the fraud management expert needs to look into the customer's data (service subscription, number of persons using the service, etc.) as well. On the other hand, the use of CDRs is not straightforward. The expert has to prepare the CDRs data, which means: separating business accounts from residences accounts; identifying which accounts can be reached from outside and which ones cannot (similar to private IP addresses); and identifying non-real accounts which are just accounts used to test whether the VoIP components are alive or not. The testing accounts usually generate huge traffic, which can lead to confusion. From these comments, it is clear that building an effective training sample requires deep knowledge in VoIP and a lot of time. In addition, even if such a sample is produced, it can be subject to classification errors that will affect the developed model. Moreover, to avoid to be detected, fraudsters frequently change their behavior, which can certainly reduce the effectiveness of the supervised developed model.

For these reasons, we believe that building a Fraud Management System (FMS) based only on expert knowledge and supervised techniques is not effective enough. We also believe that unsupervised techniques that do not require knowledge of fraud labels for a subset of data can be applied to VoIP fraud detection, and that the corresponding results can complement the results obtained with supervised models. This approach is being explored in the SUNSHINE [3] project.

This chapter is organized as follows: The next section provides the background needed for understanding the subsequent sections. It includes an overview of VoIP, a taxonomy of VoIP fraud, and an overview of the state of the art. The subsequent section explains our design of the signature-based technique, including aspects such as dealing with data fluctuation, comparison between short-term and long-term signatures, and signature initialization and update. In the final section, we discuss the performance and effectiveness of the proposed technique.

Background
Voice over IP (VoIP) technologies

VoIP is a set of technologies enabling voice calls to be carried over the Internet. Distinguishing it from the traditional telephone system—the Public Switched Telephone Network (PSTN) —what drives the use of the VoIP technology is the very low cost and free voice calls, as well as VoIP's ability to converge with other technologies, in particular, presence and instant messaging, which in turn can result in new services and applications.

A number of protocols can be employed to provide VoIP communication services; however, the Session Initiation Protocol (SIP) [4] has rapidly gained widespread acceptance as the signaling protocol of choice for fixed and mobile Internet multimedia and telephone services. SIP is an application-layer control protocol that allows users to create, modify, and terminate sessions with one or more participants. It can be used to create two-party, multiparty, and multicast sessions that include Internet telephone calls, multimedia distribution, and multimedia conferences.

In SIP (see Figure 22.1), a user is identified through an SIP-URI in the form of user@domain. This address can be resolved to a SIP proxy that is responsible for the user's domain. To identify the actual location of the user in terms of an IP address, the user needs to register his or her IP address at the SIP registrar responsible for his or her domain. Thereby, when inviting a user, the caller sends his or her invitation to the SIP proxy responsible for the user's domain, which checks in the registrar's database the location of the user and forwards the invitation to the callee. The callee can either accept or reject the invitation. The session initiation is finalized by the caller's acknowledging the reception of the callee's answer. During this message exchange, the caller and

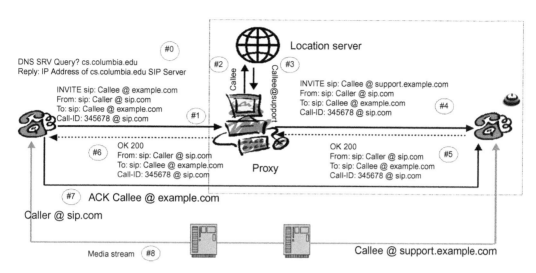

FIGURE 22.1

SIP basic operation.

callee exchange the addresses where they would like to receive the media and indicate what kind of media they can accept. After the session has been established, the end systems can exchange data directly without involving the SIP proxy.

Call data records

Every time a call is placed on a telecommunication network, descriptive information about the call is saved as a Call Data Record (CDR). Millions of CDRs are generated and stored every day. In addition, at minimum, each Call Data Record has to include the originating and terminating phone numbers, the date and time of the call, and the duration of the call. The CDRs might also include other kinds of data that are not necessary but are useful for billing, for instance, the identifier of the telephone exchange writing the record, a sequence number identifying the record, the result of the call (whether it was answered, busy, etc.), the route by which the call entered the exchange, any fault condition encountered, and any features used during the call, such as call waiting. An example of CDRs made available by a VoIP provider and used for testing (see the final section for more details) include the fields: Time (the start time of call); SIP Response Code: 2xx, 3xx, 4xx, 5xx or 6xx; SIP Method: INVITE (mainly); User-name (From URI); To URI; To-Tag; From-Tag; User-Agent; Source IP; RPID (Remote Party ID); and Duration.

VoIP Fraud detection taxonomy

Fraud can be classified in different ways according to the point of view from which the related activities are observed. However, the categorization generally cited in the literature is the following:

- Subscription fraud: Someone sets up an account or service, often using false identity details, without the intention of paying. The account is usually used for selling calls or intensive personal use.
- Superimposed fraud: Someone illegally obtains resources from legitimate users by gaining access to their phone accounts. This kind of fraud can be detected by the appearance of unknown calls on the bill of the compromised account. Scenarios involving this kind of fraud include mobile phone cloning, breaking into a PBX system, etc.

Based on what we have discussed in this section, we would like to add to the subscription fraud category activities in which the service usage does not match the subscription type, a type of fraud that can cause a substantial damage to VoIP providers. For instance, some customers subscribe to a residential service, which is usually cheaper than a business service, and use it for business purposes.

Another example is where the customer chooses to uses the customer's own PBX and then uses this PBX as a dialer for call center purposes. A dialing system in a call center dials more calls than the number of employed agents, usually at a ratio of one call and half or two calls per agent. This means that for 100 agents logged on, the system will place 150 (or 200) outbound calls. Then the dialing system will monitor each call and determine its outcome. From the 150 (or 200) calls made, the system will discard busy calls, calls with no answers, calls ending at answering machines, and calls with invalid numbers. If a call is apparently being answered by a person, it will be passed through to an agent. On the infrastructure side, this service abuse appears as a Denial of Service (DoS) attack, affecting the VoIP provider's network and reducing its capacity. The seriousness of this situation depends on the capacity of the SIP trunk and how often the operation is repeated.

Another kind of abuse, which does not fit the subscription type, is when the customer uses the provider infrastructure to build a subscriber database that can be sold to marketing companies. For instance, some customers look for operational mobile accounts by trying to connect to them without establishing the calls. They determine whether the targeted mobile accounts are operational or not based on the provisioning response messages.

The fraud cases just described are based not on theoretical brainstorming but on real observations reported by several VoIP providers. Unfortunately, the VoIP provider cannot know the device that is installed on the customer's premises or the purpose for which it is being used. Moreover, the VoIP provider who has hundreds of thousands of customers cannot easily check the installations related to all these accounts.

Related work

The diversity of fraud activities in telecommunication in general and in VoIP in particular has made the detection of such misbehaviors a difficult task. Most of the telecom operators and VoIP providers currently rely on simple rule-based systems for reviewing customers' activities. The rule-based system defines fraud patterns as rules [5]. The rules might consist of one or more conditions. If all the conditions are met, an alarm is produced. These rules are usually developed as a result of investigations of past fraudulent activities. In addition, they tend to be very basic, consisting of simple threshold conditions on some features of the service subscription.

To the best of our knowledge, the use of more sophisticated technologies in telecom fraud detection is still in a research phase [5−8]. This is mainly because the new technologies are based on data mining and pattern recognition, which often require skills that the operators and VoIP providers do not have. As the convergence between telecom networks and the Internet continues (under the name of VoIP or Next Generation Networks [NGN]) and a lot of telecom services are being replaced by similar IP-based services, applying data mining techniques to the IPDRs data when investigating fraud may become more attractive. An IP Detail Record (IPDR) [9] provides information about Internet Protocol(IP)-based service usage and other activities. It targets emerging services such as VoIP, CableLabs DOCSIS, WLAN access services, and streaming media services. The use of IPDRs in fraud detection was investigated by [10] (and also [11] in the context of rule-based systems), suggesting a high-level model for NGN fraud detection. Unfortunately, the use of IPDRs is very limited, and most VoIP providers still rely on traditional CDRs. This has led us to stick to the use of CDRs for our fraud activity investigations.

Data mining falls into two categories: supervised and unsupervised learning. The former makes use of extensive training using labeled data classes of both fraudulent and non-fraudulent cases. This training data is used to develop a model for discovering new cases that can be classified as legitimate or fraudulent. The use of supervised techniques was not an option for us due to the difficulty of obtaining training data and other reasons discussed earlier in the introduction.

Contrary to the supervised methods, unsupervised techniques can be used even when we are not certain which transactions in the database are fraudulent and which are legal. These techniques are based on "profile/signature" [6] or "normal behavior" ([7,8]), in which the past behavior of the user is collected in order to build a profile used to predict the user's future behavior. Since this profile describes the user's habitual service usage pattern of the user ("normal behavior"), any significant deviation from this profile is reported because it might hide fraudulent activity. A signature is a statistical description or a set of features that captures the user's typical behavior, namely, the average number of calls, times of the calls, areas where the calls are made, number of calls during work hours), and number of calls at night [8].

This chapter discusses the development of a signature-based technique for VoIP fraud detection. Although signatures or profiles (in other words. anomaly detection) have been extensively discussed in the literature in the context of intrusion detection [12−14], the use of this technique in telecommunication is still limited [6−8]. In addition, the current use of this method in telecom fraud detection does not take into account several aspects. including the business plans of the VoIP providers. What it has been discussed in the literature ([6,8]) is the generation of one profile with different types of features. Unfortunately, evaluating such approaches is not easy task in the absence of sufficient detail (in the literature, enough detail is provided about how the proposed techniques were developed). We also believe that such anapproach leads to performance problems, especially as the signature gets bigger. We also believe that using global metrics for comparison (such as the Hellinger distance [15]) leads to loss of information about individual features. This means it is difficult to know which feature led to the misbehavior.

Our work uses the z-score model [16] for each feature of the signature, as it shows the impact of this feature on the entire signature. In addition, and contrary to the solutions already proposed in the literature, we use various profiles instead of a single complex one, as it is easier to manipulate them separately. (The profile discussed in this chapter is related to user calls. We have also developed another one related to used IP addresses and their geolocation).

When computing the signature, we account for data fluctuation in the use of service, which varies from one day to another including periods of inactivity in which the subscriber did not use the service. Our solution also investigates how the signatures can be initialized and updated, based on the related specification.

Signature-based fraud detection

In this section, we describe how we implement a subscriber's signature. In short, it is defined as a set of the following features:

- Total number of calls per period of time, dividing the day to four intervals
  - night 00 am−06 am
  - morning 06 am−12 am
  - afternoon 12 pm−06 pm
  - evening 06 pm−00 am
- Number of calls to premium numbers
- Number of calls to international destinations
- Number of calls to mobile destinations
- Mean and standard deviation for the above features

The number of calls to premium, international, and mobile destinations are also divided into four intervals similar to the ones mentioned for "Total number of calls." These features were chosen because they usually reflect calls that are relatively expensive, which makes them possible targets for fraudsters.

Activities per day

The signature features implemented are the ones described above. If we take, for instance, the number of calls for the period of time 06am−12am, this value is computed on a daily basis. Table 22.1 shows a simple example where the long-term signature is calculated over 10 days, and the values reflect the number of calls within the mentioned period of time.

This example reflects normal usage for a given user. The value 70 (on day 7) is an example of how usage data might fluctuate.

Dealing with data fluctuation

In our work, the statistical metrics used to describe the service usage of a given user are the mean and the standard deviation. One problem with using the mean is that it often does not show the typical behavior. Data fluctuation can severely affect the signature computation. To mitigate its impact on the

Table 22.1 Example of 10-Days of Call Activity

Day1	Day2	Day3	Day4	Day5	Day6	Day7	Day8	Day9	Day10
20	30	0	16	25	0	70	23	0	17

signature, we divided the week into groups of days, the time into several time slots, and the call duration into several smaller time windows. However, this might not be sufficient. To clarify this issue, let us consider Table 22.1: if one value (like the 70 on Day 7) in the user activity is very far from the rest of the data, then the mean will be strongly affected by that value. Such values are called outliers.

An alternative measure, resistant to outliers, is the trimmed mean, which is the mean after getting rid of the smallest and biggest values of the list describing the activity. In our case, we removed 5 percent of the values from both ends of the list. To compute the trimmed mean, we needed to sort the list into an increasing order. From Table 22.1 we got the following sequence:

$$0;\ 0;\ 0;\ 16;\ 17;\ 20;\ 23;\ 25;\ 30;\ 70$$

Another issue is the existence of periods of inactivity (reflected by the 0 values), which can also affect the computation of the mean. Fraud is usually perpetrated for profit purposes, reflected in excessive use of the service through a fraudulent subscription or fraudulent activities using a legitimate account. As inactivity means no losses, considering the periods of inactivity in computing the mean does not yield any valuable information for fraud detection. As a consequence, we only need to compute the mean for the values of the list that are different from 0.

$$16;\ 17;\ 20;\ 23;\ 25;\ 30;\ 70$$

Five percent of the length of this sequence is 0:35. By rounding this value to 1, we remove the first and the last values of this list. In this case, the mean and the standard deviation are as follows:

$$\text{Mean} = (17 + 20 + 23 + 25 + 30)/5 = 23$$

$$\text{Standard deviation (std)} = 4.95$$

Comparison of long-term and short-term signatures

In order to compare the user's historical and current behaviors, we need a distance metric. In our case, the current behavior (the short-term signature) is computed every day. The values obtained for the short-term signature features, described above, can be compared to the means of the values of the same features of the user's historical behavior (the long-term signature). If these values do not belong to the confidence intervals related to the computed means, the user's activity appears suspicious and an alarm is sent. This comparison technique is also called the z-score test in the literature [16].

The confidence interval is reflected by the value "$\alpha * std_i$" where α is a real number greater than 1 that can be tuned based on the testing activities, while (std_i) denotes the standard deviation related to the ith feature of the long-term signature. This solution can be extended to instances where the short-term signature counts more than one day. In this case, we do not compare the related values to the means of the same features belonging to the long-term signature; rather, we compare the means related to the same features in the long-term and short-term signatures.

Signature initialization

New users might also be fraudsters. This means they have to be monitored right after they start using the service. To build a reliable profile for a user, we need to observe the person's behavior for some time (a week, a month, etc.). However, this does not apply to users who have just signed up for the service. Typical subscription fraud behavior is the excessive usage of an account or a subscription in a very short time interval, which enables the fraudster to escape the detection.

It turns out that signature initialization is an important step in detecting and preventing subscription fraud. However, signature initialization is a challenging task due to the very limited data about new subscribers.

Dealing with a new subscriber relies on the signature technique that we have already discussed, in which the user's service usage is mainly described by the mean and the related standard deviation. In addition, the signature is updated on a per-day basis. As a consequence, a new subscriber can be observed over two days; if no fraudulent activity is found, requiring interruption of the service, the new user is assigned a signature in the manner discussed earlier. In general, the mean and the standard deviation for each feature can be computed over two days but not over one day. However, it is also possible to monitor the new user over one day (instead of two days); however, this requires some changes in the implemented signature itself.

Observing the new subscriber for the first two days involves looking particularly for whether this subscriber

- has made at least one international call (or a premium call) with a duration greater than a predefined threshold, or
- has made a call to a destination on the black list. (We assume that the VoIP provider maintains a list of phone numbers or account IDs of subscribers who have committed fraud.)

A subscriber who engages in either of these activities is labeled as suspicious and is monitored closely during the mentioned two days.

Signature update

As the user's activities are tracked on a daily basis, updating the user's signature is straightforward. The values related to the first day in the long-term signature are discarded, and the values generated by the short-term signature are considered in the calculation of the long-term signature being updated. This is achieved as described in the beginning of this section. For instance, the earlier example, yielded the following:

$$\text{Mean} = (17 + 20 + 23 + 25 + 30)/5 = 23$$

$$\text{Standard deviation (std)} = 4.95$$

The same user's activities during days 11 and 12 are shown by the values in Table 22.2.

If we assume that the confidence interval has a length of $2*\text{std} = 9.9$, we can note that $(24-23) = 1 < 9.9$; this means that the value for Day11 is not an outlier. Updating the signature in

Table 22.2 Example of Recent Activities: Normal Case	
Day11	**Day12**
24	35

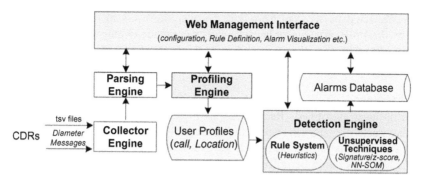

FIGURE 22.2

Testbed Architecture.

this case works as before: we sort the values from Day2 to Day11, remove the inactivity periods, and compute the trimmed mean. This yields:

$$\text{Mean} = (17 + 23 + 24 + 25 + 30)/5 = 23.8$$

$$\text{Standard deviation (std)} = 4.66$$

If we assume that the confidence interval has a length of $2.\text{std} = 9.32$, we can note that $35 - 23.8 = 11.2 > 9.32$; this means the value for Day12 is an outlier.

Experiments

To handle the testing activities, a testbed was set up (see Figure 22.2). This testbed is a part of the Fraud Management System being developed as a part of the SUNSHINE project [3]. Some of the components of the testbed are discussed in this section.

Data used for testing

To test our algorithms, we used real-life data provided by a VoIP provider. The data consisted of three months of CDRs dating from the January 1, 2011 to the end of March 2011. The data belonged to 4,825 subscribers, who generated almost 31 million CDRs during these three months. The CDRs were provided in a tsv file, which required the development of a parser module, using parallel processes, to parse the information in the file and store it in a relational database within a reasonable period of time.

Known fraudulent cases

The VoIP provider offered a list of 17 accounts that seemed to be compromised and from which fraudulent activities were committed during this three-month period. Most of the fraudulent activities were detected by the VoIP provider because the users in question exceeded a virtual threshold set by the VoIP provider, or because calls were made to unusual destinations. Other scam activities were detected (by chance) while checking the logs of some network monitoring components.

Call center behavior

As mentioned in the section titled "Background," call center activities can be considered a kind of fraud when these activities do not respect the subscription agreement. Unfortunately, VoIP providers do not have a means to deal with such an issue. This fact pushed us to investigate how the unsupervised techniques could be utilized to detect such activities. The first step in this direction was to define some heuristics to classify the data into potential call centers and non-call centers. The heuristics we used related to the total number of calls, the success rate, and the IP addresses' geolocation, as discussed later in the chapter. Other filtering criteria could be considered, such as the number of calls made during nights and on weekends. These numbers should be very small, as call centers are businesses, so they are often not active during these times—although this is not always true, since the VoIP provider might have business with other countries on other continents which requires taking into account the time offset between these countries. We used the following heuristics for classification:

- The total number of calls made from a given account is greater than 100 per day, and this happened at least three times during the three months.
- The call success rate is less than 60 percent.
- For a given account the geolocation does not change (in other words, the IP addresses used by this account remain in the same network). To achieve this, the IP geolocation database from MaxMind [17] was integrated into our system.

These criteria allowed us to generate a list of 69 potential call centers, representing 1.43 percent of the accounts used in the tests. This sounds reasonable because the scam-related data is usually a small portion of all the data. The heuristics were defined with the help of the VoIP provider. The list of potential call centers was also reviewed by the VoIP provider. who confirmed that the subscription accounts figuring on this list were call centers.

Signature-based technique testing

Before assessing the signature-based technique, it is worth mentioning that we cannot be certain, based only on statistical analysis, that fraud has been committed. Unsupervised techniques, in particular, profiling and clustering, should be regarded as a means for producing warnings of cases that need deeper investigation.

The signature-based technique was evaluated against two categories: known fraud cases and the call center behavior. To test its performance, we built for each user a short-term signature representing his or her daily activities as discussed in the preceding section. The short-term signatures were collected on a 30-day basis to generate long-term signatures (see the preceding section). In other words, the first long-term signature started on January 1 and ended on January 30. Then, a comparison was made with the short-term signature reflecting the activities on January 31. After that, the long-term signature was updated, and a comparison with February 1 was made. This occurred until we reached March 31. In all, we ended up with 60 long-term signatures and 60 comparisons.

Technically, it is possible to have shorter or longer long-term signatures. However, short long-term signatures (duration of one or two weeks) lose information that could be valuable for describing the subscriber's behavior. Longer long-term signatures (duration of more than one month) are better at describing subscriber behavior, as our tests confirmed. However according to German law, keeping personal information about subscribers for more than one month is forbidden.

When developing a signature for 30 days without distinguishing between weekdays and weekends, the assumption is that the user's behavior is the same for all the days within this period of time. However, this might not always be realistic, especially since user behavior could change in terms of call volume and duration. To take into consideration this possibility, the signature was divided into two sub-signatures, one for weekdays and the other one for weekends. The comparison in this case was achieved by looking at whether the short-term signature reflected activities for a weekday or a weekend day, and then comparing it with the appropriate sub-signature. Unfortunately, the obtained results did not show any improvement, which can be simply explained by the fact that in this case we computed signatures for fewer days (22 days for the weekday signature and 8 days for the weekend signature).

It is worth mentioning that the z-score test usually applies to normal distributions. Therefore, the comparison between the long-term signatures and the short-term signatures was not performed on the original data, which does not follow a normal distribution, but on transformed data. To handle the transformation, we explored two commonly used transformations (logarithm function-$\ln(x + 1)$, square root function is $-\sqrt{x}$), and found that the logarithm transformation was better, especially in producing fewer alarms.

The comparison was performed on a feature basis. This means that one comparison between a long-term and a short-term signature leads to a number of alarms between 0 and the number of features considered in the signature (20 features in this case). Here are two different ways of counting and integrating the alarms:

- **Option one:** Whenever a feature presents a misbehavior, it is counted as an alarm. This means a signature can generate a number of alarms less than or equal to the number of feature misbehaviors detected in the comparison. This also depends on the features chosen for comparison. The VoIP provider might select features that ,when abused, have greater impact on its business, for example, premium and international calls, as they are usually expensive. The provider can also select features related to calls made during the night, if fraud is expected to be committed during that time.
- **Option two:** In contrast to the previous option, all the alarms generated during a comparison for one account are considered one alarm. This is sufficient to trigger a deeper investigation of that account. This scenario has the advantage of reducing the number of alarms; however, it leaves the fraud details related to the features to the fraud management expert, who needs to investigate the case more deeply.

Both options were tested in our framework; however, for simplicity, we focus on the second option in this chapter. The distribution of alarms with respect to the type of call is depicted in Figure 22.3. The figure shows that almost half of the numbers that generated alarms are related to

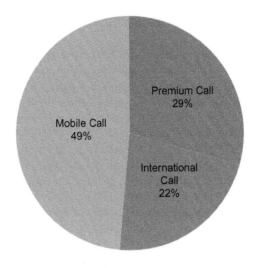

FIGURE 22.3

Alarm distribution with respect to call type.

Table 22.3 Signature Testing Results

Total Number of Accounts	Set A	Set B
4825	2413	2412
Known fraud cases	Set A	Set B
17	11	6
16 (detected-94.18%)	10 (90.90%)	6 (100%)
Call center behavior	Set A	Set B
69	33	36
64 (detected-92.75%)	31 (93.93%)	33 (91.66%)

the mobile call type, suggesting that the VoIP provider should monitor more closely that type of call.

Now, let us check how effective is the signature based technique in detecting the known fraud cases and the call center behavior discussed previously. Detection here means that such cases have generated at least one alarm during the 3 months period.

To handle the testing, the three-months of data were divided into two data sets, A and B, using a 50-50 random sample split, which also led to some proportions (for both sets) of the known fraud cases and call center behavior that were not known beforehand. Then, the signature-based technique was applied to both sets (A and B), and the results were matched against the fraudulent account proportions in both sets. A similar approach was introduced in [2] to evaluate the stability of the algorithm, which is stable if the obtained results do not depend on the data. The splitting technique can be handled in two ways: either apply the algorithm to both sets separately and then compare the obtained results, or apply the algorithm to set B using the results obtained when applying the algorithm to set A. Both ways were investigated in our work. To test the signature-based technique, we applied it separately to sets A and B; however, to assess the NN-SOM technique (discussed later in the chapter), we used the results obtained from the set A as training data for testing the NN-SOM on set B. The testing results are depicted in Table 22.3 and show the stability of the technique as well as a very good performance. The detection rate in all cases is above 90 percent, and the success rates related of sets A and B are very close to each other.

Performance and effectiveness

A general question frequently asked about unsupervised classifications techniques is how to assess the reasonableness of the obtained results and by which standards [2]. One method is to create a list of potential suspicious accounts and ask the VoIP provider to assess each of these accounts in terms of its functionality and the criteria used for filtering. For instance, some accounts are used by the VoIP provider to test the status of the network components, so one should expect a huge amount of calls generated by these accounts with a weak rate of call success, as the provider is often interested in whether these components react or not, so there is no need to establish the calls.

This behavior (huge number of calls with weak success rate) is typical call center behavior, and the accounts for testing cannot be separated from the potential call centers without the provider's help. Unfortunately, this method requires time and resources, especially if the list is long. In our work, we used this method as a first assessment, and the results are presented in the preceding sections.

Another method is to compare the signature-based technique with other unsupervised or supervised methods [2]. In our research, we also compared our work to the Neural Network Self Organizing Map (NN-SOM) technique [18]. A neural network can be seen as an adaptive machine that is able to store experimental knowledge and make it available for use [19]. There are two types of architecture for Neural Networks:

- Supervised training algorithms: Here, in the learning phase, the network learns the desired output for a given input or pattern. The besy-known architecture for supervised neural networks is the Multi-Level Perceptron (MLP) [20]. The MLP is employed for pattern recognition problems.
- Unsupervised training algorithms: In this case, in the learning phase, the network learns without specifying desired output. Self-Organizing Maps (SOM) are popular unsupervised training

Table 22.4 NN-SOM Testing Results

Total Number of Accounts	Set A	Set B
4825	2413	2412
Known fraud cases	Set A	Set B
17	11	6
15 (detected–88.23%)	10 (90.90%)	5 (83.33%)
Call center behavior	Set A	Set B
69	33	36
63 (detected-91.30%)	32 (96.96%)	31 (86.11%)

algorithms; an SOM tries to find a topological mapping from the input space to clusters. SOMs are employed for classification problems.

The testing activities related to NN-SOM were based on modified software provided by T.E.I. of Mesolonghi ([21]). This software is, in its turn, based on the Encog Neural Network Framework ([18]). In this chapter, we present just the results obtained from NN-SOM. The NN-SOM technique was first applied to set A, and then the results obtained were used as input for the testing phase of the NN-SOM. The results depicted in Table 22.4 show a very good performance of the NN-SOM algorithm, although the signature-based technique exceeds it slightly. In fact, looking further at the results of both techniques, we found that at least 88 percent of the fraud activities discussed in this paper were detected by both techniques. This rate is more than reasonable for unsupervised techniques [2].

CONCLUSION

In this chapter, we investigate the use of signature-based techniques in VoIP fraud detection. We explain that the supervised techniques and the system experts, in spite of their importance, need not be the only means for fraud detection. Unsupervised methods are another means for data classification, and they do not require training cases to produce results. Signature-based techniques belong to the unsupervised category and have been addressed within this work. We discuss in detail the generation of the signatures, and their initialization, update, and comparison. In addition, we describe how the prototype was implemented and tested. The reasonableness of the obtained results is also assessed.

References

[1] Humbug Labs. Communications fraud control association (CFCA) report; 2011.

[2] Ai J, Golden L, Brockett L. Assessing consumer fraud risk in insurance claims: An unsupervised learning technique using discrete and continuous predictor variables. North American Actuarial Journal. Hawaii, USA; 13(4).

[3] The Sunshine project. [Internet]. 20XX Mon(th) [accessed on 20XX Mon(th)]. Available from: <http://www.sunshineproject.net/index.html>.

[4] Rosenberg J, Schulzrinne H, Camarillo G, Johnston A, Peterson J, Sparks R, et al. RFC 3261-SIP: Session Initiation Protocol; 2002.

[5] Verrelst H, Lerouge E, Moreau Y, Vandewalle J, Störmann C, Burge P. A rule based and neural network system for fraud detection in mobile communications. [Internet]. Available from: <http://ftp.cordis.europa.eu/pub/ist/docs/ka4/10396.pdf;2003>.

[6] Ferreira P, Alves R, Belo O, Cortesão L. Establishing fraud detection patterns based on signatures. Proceedings of the 6th Industrial Conference on Data Mining. Berlin, Heidelberg: Springer-Verlag; 2006.

[7] Hilas CS, Sahalos JN. User profiling for fraud detection in telecommunications networks. Proceedings of 5th International Conference Technology and Automation ICTA05; 2005; Greece. p. 382−387.

[8] Cortes C, Pregibon D. Signature based methods for data streams. Data Mining and Knowledge Discovery Journal, 5. Springer; 2001167−182

[9] Internet protocol detail record (ipdr). [Internet]. Available from: <http://www.tmforum.org/InternetProtocolDetail/4501/home.html>.

[10] Bihina Bella MA, Olivier MS, Elo JHP. A fraud detection model for next-generation networks. [Internet]. Available from: <http://mo.co.za/open/ngnfms.pdf>.

[11] Mcgibney J, Hearne S. An approach to rules based fraud management in emerging converged neworks. [Internet]. Available from: <http://eprints.wit.ie/619/1/2003> itsrs mcgibney hearne final.pdf.

[12] Ashman H, Pannell G. Anomaly detection over user profiles for intrusion detection. Proceedings of the 8th Information Security Mangement Conference, Australia; 2010.

[13] Dickerson JE, Dickerson JA. Fuzzy network profiling for intrusion detection. In NAFIPS: Proceedings of the 19th International Conference of the North American, Fuzzy Information Processing Society; 2000.

[14] Buennemeyer TK, Nelson TM, Clagett LM, Dunning JP, Marchany RC, Tront JG. Mobile device profiling and intrusion detection using smart batteries. In: Proceedings of the 41st Annual Hawaii International Conference on System Sciences. 2008 Jan7-10;296.

[15] The Hellinger distance. [Internet]. Available from: <http://www.encyclopediaofmath.org/index.php/Hellinger_distance>.

[16] The z-score. [Internet]. Available from: <http://wise.cgu.edu/sdtmod/reviewz.asp>.

[17] MaxMind Geolocation. [Internet]. Available from: <http://www.maxmind.com>.

[18] Neural network framework. [Internet]. Available from: <http://www.heatonresearch.com/encog>.

[19] Boukerche A, Notare MSMA. Neural fraud detection in mobile phone operations. Workshops on parallel and distributed processing. Proceedings of the 15th IPDPS. 2000;1800:636-644.

[20] Multilayer Perceptrons (MLP). [Internet]. Available from: <http://deeplearning.net/tutorial/mlp.html>.

[21] Technological Education Institute of Mesolonghi (T.E.I.). [Internet]. Available from: <http://www.teimes.gr/wwwen/>.

Mobile and Cloud Computing

Reviews of the Field

Emerging Security Challenges in Cloud Computing, from Infrastructure-Based Security to Proposed Provisioned Cloud Infrastructure

23

Mohammad Reza Movahedisefat[1], Seyyed Mohammad Reza Farshchi[2], and Davud Mohammadpur[3]

[1]*Amirkabir University of Technology (Tehran Polytechinc), Tehran, Iran*
[2]*Ferdowsi University of Mashhad, Mashhad, Iran*
[3]*University of Zanjan, Zanjan, Iran*

INFORMATION IN THIS CHAPTER

- Security challenges
- Cloud computing
- Infrastructure-based security
- Cloud infrastructure

INTRODUCTION

In cloud environments, one of the most pervasive and fundamental challenges for organizations in demonstrating policy compliance is proving that the physical and virtual infrastructure of the cloud can be trusted—particularly when those infrastructure components are owned and managed by external service providers.

For many business functions commonly run in the cloud—hosting websites and wikis, for example—it's often sufficient to have a cloud provider vouch for the security of the underlying infrastructure. For business-critical processes and sensitive data, however, third-party attestations usually aren't enough. In such cases, it's absolutely essential for organizations to be able to verify for themselves that the underlying cloud infrastructure is secure.

The next frontier in cloud security and compliance will be to create transparency at the bottom-most layers of the cloud by developing the standards, tools, and linkages to monitor and prove that the cloud's physical and virtual machines are actually performing as they should. Verifying what's happening at the foundational levels of the cloud is important for the simple reason that, if organizations can't trust the safety of their computing infrastructure, the security of all the data, software, and services running on top of that infrastructure falls into doubt. There's currently no easy way for organizations to monitor actual conditions and operating states within the hardware, hypervisors, and virtual machines comprising their clouds. At those depths, we go dark.

Cloud providers and the IT community are already preparing to address this problem. Groups of technology companies have banded together to develop a new, interoperable, and highly secure computing infrastructure for the cloud based on a "hardware root of trust," which provides tamper-proof measurements of every physical and virtual component in the entire computing stack, including the hypervisor. Members of the IT community are exploring ways to use these measurements to improve visibility, control, and compliance in the cloud.

They're collaborating on a conceptual IT framework to integrate the secure measurements provided by a hardware root of trust into adjoining hypervisors and virtualization management software. The resulting infrastructure stack would be tied into data analysis tools and a governance, risk, and compliance (GRC) console, which would contextualize conditions in the cloud's hardware and virtualization layers to present a reliable assessment of an organization's overall security and compliance posture. This type of integrated hardware-software framework would make the lowest levels of the cloud's infrastructure as inspectable, analyzable, and reportable for compliance as the cloud's top-most application services layer.

As we mentioned above, many communities have already adopted the "cloud," a flexible computational platform allowing scalability and a service-based provision model.

Unfortunately, there are currently significant limitations when using a cloud infrastructure to perform security-critical computations and/or store sensitive data. Specifically, at the moment, there is no way to guarantee the trustworthiness of a Virtual Machine (VM) in terms of its origin and identity and the trustworthiness of the data uploaded and managed by the Elastic Block Storage or the Simple Storage Service (S3). These limitations made us to propose a macro-level solution for identified common infrastructure security requirements and design a hybrid model for on-demand infrastructure services provisioning.

Because of these limitations, public cloud computing uptake by business-critical communities is limited. A number of communities whose emerging information models appear otherwise well-suited to cloud computing are forced to either avoid the pay-per-use model of service provision or deploy a private cloud infrastructure. Deploying a private cloud is rarely a desirable solution. It requires an extended time frame and significant investment in hardware, management, and software resources. These limitations also apply to the deployment of a private cloud based on open source software because, while licensing costs are eliminated, the bulk of the investment in hardware and support resources is still required.

This chapter presents recent results of the ongoing research on developing an architecture and a framework for dynamically provisioned security services as part of the provisioned on-demand cloud-based infrastructure services. It shows that the proposed model, with a number of emerged patterns, can be applied to the infrastructure aspect of cloud computing as a proposed shared security approach in a system development life cycle focusing on the plan-build-run scope. Some of this information was adopted from *Cloud Security and Privacy* [1].

Background

The current cloud security model is based on the assumption that the user/customer can trust the cloud service provider (CSP). However, such an approach addresses only the first part of the problem and does not scale well with the potential need to combine cloud-based services from multiple providers when building complex infrastructures.

Cloud providers are investing significant efforts and costs into making their own infrastructures secure and achieving compliance with the existing industry security services management standards (e.g., Amazon Cloud recently achieved the Payment Card Industry Data Security Standard [PCI DSS] compliance certification and Microsoft Azure Cloud claims compliance with ISO27001 security standards). However, overall security of cloud-based applications and services will depend on two other factors: security services implementation in user applications and binding between virtualized services and cloud virtualization platforms. Advanced security services and fine-grained access control cannot be achieved without deeper integration with the cloud virtualization platform and incumbent security services, which, in its turn, can be achieved with open and well-defined cloud IaaS platform architectures.

Infrastructure security
The network level

When looking at the network level of infrastructure security, it is important to distinguish between public clouds and private clouds. With private clouds, there are no new attacks, vulnerabilities, or changes in risk specific to this topology that information security personnel need to consider. Although an organization's IT architecture may change with the implementation of a private cloud, its current network topology will probably not change significantly. If there is a private extranet in place (e.g., for premium customers or strategic partners), for practical purposes, the organization probably has the network topology for a private cloud already in place. The security considerations in place today apply to a private cloud infrastructure, too. And the security tools in place (or should be in place) are also necessary for a private cloud and operate in the same way. Figure 23.1 shows the topological similarities between a secure extranet and a private cloud.

However, if an organization chooses to use public cloud services, changing security requirements will require changes to its network topology. The organization must address how its existing network topology interacts with its cloud provider's network topology. There are four significant risk factors in this use case [2,3]:

- Ensuring the confidentiality and integrity of the organization's data-in-transit to and from its public cloud provider
- Ensuring proper access control (authentication, authorization, and auditing) to whatever resources the organization is using as its public cloud provider
- Ensuring the availability of the Internet-facing resources in a public cloud that are being used by the organization or have been assigned to the organization by its public cloud providers
- Replacing the established model of network zones and tiers with domains

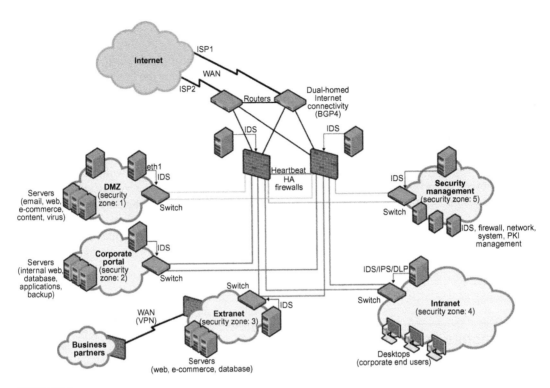

FIGURE 23.1

Topological similarities between a secure extranet and a private cloud.

Ensuring data confidentiality and integrity

Some resources and data previously confined to a private network are now exposed to the Internet and to a shared public network belonging to a third-party cloud provider.

An example of problems associated with this first risk factor is an Amazon Web Services (AWS) security vulnerability reported in December 2008. In a blog post, the author detailed a flaw in the digital signature algorithm used when "... making Query (aka REST) requests to Amazon SimpleDB, to Amazon Elastic Compute Cloud (EC2), or to Amazon Simple Queue Service (SQS) over HTTP." Although use of HTTPS (instead of HTTP) would have mitigated the integrity risk, users not using HTTPS (but using HTTP) did face an increased risk that their data could have been altered in transit without their knowledge.

Network-level mitigation

Given the factors discussed in the preceding sections, what can be done to mitigate these increased risk factors? First, note that network-level risks exist regardless of what aspects of "cloud computing" services are being used (e.g., software-as-a-service, platform-as-a-service, or infrastructure-as-a-service). The primary determination of risk level is therefore not which IaaS is being used, but rather whether an organization intends to use or is using a public, private, or hybrid cloud. Although some IaaS clouds offer virtual network zoning, they may not match an internal private cloud environment that performs stateful inspection and other network security measures.

If an organization is large enough to afford the resources of a private cloud, its risks will decrease—assuming the organization has a true private cloud that is internal to its network. In some cases, a private cloud located at a cloud provider's facility can help meet security requirements but will depend on the provider capabilities and maturity.

An organization can reduce its confidentiality risks by using encryption; specifically by using validated implementations of cryptography for data-in-transit. Secure digital signatures make it much more difficult, if not impossible, for someone to tamper with the data, and this ensures data integrity.

Availability problems at the network level are far more difficult to mitigate with cloud computing—unless the organization is using a private cloud that is internal to its network topology. Even if the private cloud is a private (i.e., non-shared) external network at a cloud provider's facility, an increased risk is faced at the network level. A public cloud faces even greater risk. But let's keep some perspective here—greater than what?

Even large enterprises with significant resources face considerable challenges at the network level of infrastructure security. Are the risks associated with cloud computing actually higher than the risks enterprises are facing today? Consider existing private and public extranets, and take into account partner connections when making such a comparison. For large enterprises without significant resources, or for small to medium-size businesses (SMBs) [4,5,6], is the risk of using public clouds (assuming that such enterprises lack the resources necessary for private clouds) really higher than the risks inherent in their current infrastructures? In many cases, the answer is probably no—there is not a higher level of risk.

The host level

When reviewing host security and assessing risks, an organization should consider the context of cloud services delivery models (SaaS, PaaS, and IaaS) and deployment models (public, private, and hybrid). Although there are no known new threats to hosts that are specific to cloud computing, some virtualization security threats—such as VM escape, system configuration drift, and insider threats by way of weak access control to the hypervisor—carry into the public cloud computing environment. The dynamic nature (elasticity) of cloud computing can bring new operational challenges from a security management perspective. The operational model motivates rapid provisioning and fleeting instances of VMs. Managing vulnerabilities and patches is therefore much harder than just running a scan, as the rate of change is much higher than in a traditional data center.

In addition, the fact that the clouds harness the power of thousands of compute nodes, combined with the homogeneity of the operating system employed by hosts, means the threats can be amplified quickly and easily—call it the "velocity of attack" factor in the cloud. More importantly, one should understand the trust boundary and the responsibilities that falls on one's shoulders to secure the host infrastructure that one manages. And one should compare the same with providers' responsibilities in securing the part of the host infrastructure the CSP manages.

Cloud service models

Cloud computing enables hardware and software to be delivered as services, where the term "service" is used to reflect the fact that they are provided on demand and are paid on a usage basis—the more you use the more you pay. Draw an analogy with a restaurant. A restaurant provides a food and drinks service. If we would like to eat at a restaurant, we don't buy it, we just use it as we require. The more we eat, the more we pay. Cloud computing provides computing facilities in the same way as restaurants provide food: when we need computing facilities, we use them from the cloud. The more we use, the more we pay. When we stop using them, we stop paying.

Although the above analogy is a great simplification, the core idea holds. Since computing is many things, cloud computing has a lot of things to deliver as a service. This is where the SPI model helps organize things. Let's consider these in turn.

Software as a Service: These software products are typically end user applications delivered on demand over a network on a pay-per-use basis. The software requires no client installation, just a browser and network connectivity. An example of SaaS is Microsoft Office365. Until its launch, if a user required, say, Word, they would have to purchase it, install it, back up files, etc. With Office365, Word can be acquired for a small monthly fee, with no client installation. The files are automatically backed up, software upgrades are automatically received, and the software can be accessed from anywhere. If users decides they no longer want to use Word , they stop paying the monthly fee. It is that simple.

Platform as a Service: These types of platforms are used by software development companies to run their software products. Software products need physical servers to run on, along with database software and often Web servers, too. These comprise the platform that the application runs on. Building a platform is a time-consuming task, and it needs to be continually monitored and updated. PaaS provides all of the platform-out-of-the-box enabling software applications for the platform and will execute them with no requirement for administration of the lower level components.

Infrastructure as a Service: This covers a wide range of features, from individual servers to private networks, disk drives, and various long-term storage devices, as well as email servers, domain name servers, and messaging systems. All of these can be provisioned on demand and often include software license fees for operating systems and associated software installed on the servers. Organizations can build a complete computing infrastructure using IaaS on demand.

All of the services provided by cloud computing fit into one of the three delivery models above. End users typically use SaaS, software development teams use PaaS, and IT departments whose responsibility is the infrastructure use IaaS. There is much more to cloud computing, including aspects such as automatic scaling and security, for example. As a starting point, categorizing the delivery models helps to explain that all aspects of computing are covered; these cloud services are potentially useful for everybody involved in, or using, IT.

SaaS and PaaS host security

In general, CSPs do not publicly share information related to their host platforms, host operating systems, and the processes that are in place to secure the hosts, since hackers can exploit that information when they are trying to intrude into the cloud service. Hence, in the context of SaaS (e.g., Salesforce.com, Workday.com) or PaaS (e.g., Google App Engine, Salesforce.com's Force. com) cloud services, host security is opaque to customers and the responsibility of securing the hosts is relegated to the CSP. To get assurance from the CSP on the security hygiene of its hosts, one should ask the vendor to share information under a Non-Disclosure Agreement (NDA) or simply demand that the CSP share the information via a controls assessment framework such as SysTrust or ISO 27002. From a controls assurance perspective, the CSP has to ensure that appropriate preventive and detective controls are in place and will have to ensure the same via a third-party assessment or ISO 27002-type assessment framework.

Since virtualization is a key enabling technology that improves host hardware utilization, among other benefits, it is common for CSPs to employ virtualization platforms, including Xen and VMware hypervisors, in their host computing platform architecture. One should understand how the provider is using virtualization technology and the provider's process for securing the virtualization layer.

Both the PaaS and SaaS platforms abstract and hide the host operating system from end users with a host abstraction layer. One key difference between PaaS and SaaS is the accessibility of the abstraction layer that hides the operating system services the applications consume. In the case of SaaS, the abstraction layer is not visible to users and is available only to the developers and the CSP's operations staff, whereas PaaS users are given indirect access to the host abstraction layer in the form of a PaaS application programming interface (API) that, in turn, interacts with the host abstraction layer. In short, if you are a SaaS or a PaaS customer, you are relying on the CSP to provide a secure host platform on which the SaaS or PaaS application is developed and deployed by the CSP and you, respectively.

In summary, host security responsibilities in SaaS and PaaS services are transferred to the CSP. The fact that a customer does not have to worry about protecting hosts from host-based security threats is a major benefit from a security management and cost standpoint. However, the customer still owns the risk of managing information hosted in the cloud services. It's the user's responsibility to get the appropriate level of assurance regarding how the CSP manages host security hygiene.

Virtual server security

Customers of IaaS have full access to the virtualized guest VMs that are hosted and isolated from each other by hypervisor technology. Hence, customers are responsible for securing, and ongoing security management of, the guest VM. A public IaaS, such as Amazon's Elastic Compute Cloud (EC^2), offers a Web services API to perform management functions such as provisioning, decommissioning, and replication of virtual servers on the IaaS platform. These system management functions, when orchestrated appropriately, can provide elasticity for resources to grow or shrink in line with workload demand. The dynamic life cycle of virtual servers can result in complexity if the process to manage the virtual servers is not automated with proper procedures. From an attack surface perspective, the virtual server (Windows, Solaris, or Linux) may be accessible to anyone on the Internet, so sufficient network access mitigation steps should be taken to restrict access to virtual instances. Typically, the CSP blocks all port access to virtual servers and recommends that customers use port 22 (Secure Shell or SSH) to administer virtual server instances. The cloud management API adds another layer of attack surface and must be included in the scope of securing virtual servers in the public cloud. Some of the new host security threats in the public IaaS include:

- Stealing keys used to access and manage hosts (e.g., SSH private keys)
- Attacking unpatched, vulnerable services listening on standard ports (e.g., FTP, NetBIOS,
- SSH)
- Hijacking accounts that are not properly secured (i.e., weak or no passwords for standard
- accounts)
- Attacking systems that are not properly secured by host firewalls
- Deploying Trojans embedded in the software component in the VM or within the VM image (the OS) itself

Securing virtual servers

The simplicity of self-provisioning new virtual servers on an IaaS platform creates a risk that insecure virtual servers will be created. Secure-by-default configuration needs to be ensured by following or exceeding available industry baselines.

Securing the virtual server in the cloud requires strong operational security procedures coupled with automation of procedures. Here are some recommendations:

- Use a secure-by-default configuration. Harden the image and use a standard hardened image for instantiating VMs (the guest OS) in a public cloud. A best practice for cloud-based applications is to build custom VM images that have only the capabilities and services necessary to support the application stack. Limiting the capabilities of the underlying application stack not only limits the host's overall attack surface, but also greatly reduces the number of patches needed to keep that application stack secure.
- Track the inventory of VM images and OS versions that are prepared for cloud hosting. The IaaS provider provides some of these VM images. When a virtual image from the IaaS provider is used, it should undergo the same level of security verification and hardening for hosts within the enterprise. The best alternative is to provide your own image that conforms to the same security standards as internal trusted hosts.
- Protect the integrity of the hardened image from unauthorized access.
- Safeguard the private keys required to access hosts in the public cloud.
- In general, isolate the decryption keys from the cloud where the data is hosted—unless they are necessary for decryption, and then only for the duration of an actual decryption activity. If an application requires a key to encrypt and decrypt for continuous data processing, it may not be possible to protect the key since it will be collocated with the application.
- Include no authentication credentials in your virtualized images except for a key to decrypt the file system key.
- Do not allow password-based authentication for shell access.
- Require passwords for sudo or role-based access (e.g., Solaris, SELinux).
- Run a host firewall and open only the minimum ports necessary to support the services on an instance.
- Run only the required services and turn off the unused services (e.g., turn off FTP, print services, network file services, and database services if they are not required).
- Install a host-based IDS such as OSSEC or Samhain.

- Enable system auditing and event logging, and log the security events to a dedicated log server. Isolate the log server with higher security protection, including access controls.

The application level

Application or software security should be a critical element of an organization's security program. Most enterprises with information security programs have yet to institute an application security program to address this realm. Designing and implementing applications targeted for deployment on a cloud platform will require that existing application security programs re-evaluate current practices and standards. The application security spectrum ranges from stand-alone single-user applications to sophisticated multi-user e-commerce applications used by millions of users. Web applications such as content management systems (CMSs), wikis, portals, bulletin boards, and discussion forums are used by small and large organizations. A large number of organizations also develop and maintain custom-built Web applications for their businesses using various Web frameworks (PHP, .NET, J2EE, Ruby on Rails, Python, etc.). According to SANS, until 2007, few criminals attacked vulnerable websites because other attack vectors were more likely to lead to an advantage in unauthorized economic or information access. Increasingly, however, advances in cross-site scripting (XSS) and other attacks have demonstrated that criminals looking for financial gain can exploit vulnerabilities resulting from Web programming errors as new ways to penetrate important organizations. In this section, we limit our discussion to Web application security: Web applications in the cloud accessed by users with standard Internet browsers such as Firefox, Internet Explorer, or Safari, from any computer connected to the Internet.

Since the browser has emerged as the end user client for accessing in-cloud applications, it is important for application security programs to include browser security into the scope of application security. Together they determine the strength of end-to-end cloud security that helps protect the confidentiality, integrity, and availability of the information processed by cloud services.

Application-level security threats

According to SANS, Web application vulnerabilities in open source as well as custom-built applications accounted for almost half the total number of vulnerabilities discovered between November, 2006 and October, 2007. The existing threats exploit well-known application vulnerabilities (e.g., the OWASP Top 10), including cross-site scripting (XSS), SQL injection, malicious file execution, and other vulnerabilities resulting from programming errors and design flaws. Armed with knowledge and tools, hackers are constantly scanning Web applications (accessible from the Internet) for application vulnerabilities. They are then exploiting the vulnerabilities they discover for various illegal activities including financial fraud, intellectual property theft, converting trusted websites into malicious servers serving client-side exploits, and phishing scams. All Web frameworks and all types of Web applications are at risk of Web application security defects, ranging from insufficient validation to application logic errors.

It has been a common practice to use a combination of perimeter security controls and network- and host-based access controls to protect Web applications deployed in a tightly controlled environment, including corporate intranets and private clouds, from external hackers. Web applications built and deployed in a public cloud platform will be subjected to a high threat level, attacked, and potentially exploited by hackers to support fraudulent and illegal activities. In that threat model, Web applications deployed in a public cloud (the SPI model) must be designed for an Internet

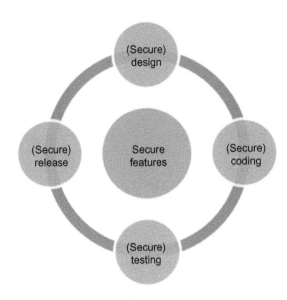

FIGURE 23.2

Software development life cycle.

threat model, and security must be embedded into the Software Development Life Cycle (SDLC); see Figure 23.2.

SaaS Application security

The SaaS model dictates that the provider manages the entire suite of applications delivered to users. Therefore, SaaS providers are largely responsible for securing the applications and components they offer to customers. Customers are usually responsible for operational security functions, including user and access management as supported by the provider. It is a common practice for prospective customers, usually under an NDA, to request information related to the provider's security practices. This information should encompass design, architecture, development, black- and white-box application security testing, and release management.

Some customers go to the extent of hiring independent security vendors to perform penetration testing (black-box security testing) of SaaS applications (with consent from the provider) to gain assurance independently. However, penetration testing can be costly and not all providers agree to this type of verification.

Extra attention needs to be paid to the authentication and access control features offered by SaaS CSPs. Usually that is the only security control available to manage risk to information. Most services, including those from Salesforce.com and Google, offer a Web-based administration user interface tool to manage authentication and access control of the application. Some SaaS applications, such as Google Apps, have built-in features that end users can invoke to assign read and write privileges to other users. However, the privilege management features may not be advanced, fine-grained access and could have weaknesses that may not conform to a organization's access control standard. One example that captures this issue is the mechanism that Google Docs employs in handling images embedded in documents, as well as access privileges to older versions of a document. Evidently, embedded images stored in Google Docs are not protected in the same way that a document is protected with sharing controls. That means if a user has shared a document containing embedded images, the other person will always be able to view those images even after the first user has stopped sharing the document. A blogger discovered this access control quirk and brought it to Google's attention. Although Google has acknowledged the issue, its response conveys that it believes those concerns do not pose a significant security risk to its users.

Another incident related to Google Docs was a privacy glitch that inappropriately shared access to a small fraction (Google claims 0.05 percent of the documents were affected) of word processing and presentation documents stored on its Google Apps cloud service. Though the documents were shared only with the people with whom the Google Docs users had already shared documents, rather than with the world at large, the problem illustrates the need to evaluate and understand cloud-specific access control mechanisms.

Cloud customers should try to understand cloud-specific access control mechanisms— including support for strong authentication and privilege management based on user roles and functions—and take the steps necessary to protect information hosted in the cloud. Additional controls should be implemented to manage privileged access to the SaaS administration tool and enforce segregation of duties to protect the application from insider threats. In line with security standard practices, customers should implement a strong password policy—one that forces users to choose strong passwords when authenticating to an application.

It is a common practice for SaaS providers to commingle their customer data (structured and unstructured) in a single virtual data store and rely on data tagging to enforce isolation between customer data. In that multi-tenant data store model, where encryption may not be feasible due to key management and other design barriers, data is tagged and stored with a unique customer identifier. This unique data tag makes it possible for the business logic embedded in the application layer to enforce isolation between customers when the data is processed. It is conceivable that the application layer enforcing this isolation could become vulnerable during software upgrades by the CSP. Hence, customers should understand the virtual data store architecture and the preventive mechanisms the SaaS providers use to guarantee the compartmentalization and isolation required in a virtual multi-tenant environment.

Established SaaS providers, such as Salesforce.com, Microsoft, and Google, are known to invest in software security and practice security assurance as part of their SDLC. However, given that there is no industry standard to assess software security, it is almost impossible to benchmark providers against a baseline.

PaaS Application security

PaaS vendors broadly fall into the following two major categories:

- Software vendors (e.g., Bungee, Etelos, GigaSpaces, Eucalyptus)
- CSPs (e.g., Google App Engine, Salesforce.com's Force.com, Microsoft Azure, Intuit QuickBase)

Organizations evaluating a private cloud may utilize PaaS software to build a solution for internal consumption. Currently, no major public clouds are known to be using commercial off-the-shelf or open source PaaS software such as Eucalyptus (Eucalyptus does offer a limited experimental pilot cloud for developers at Eucalyptus.com, however). Therefore, given the nascent stage of PaaS deployment, we will not discuss software security of standalone PaaS software in this chapter. Nonetheless, it is recommended that organizations evaluating PaaS software perform a risk assessment and apply the software security standard similar to acquiring any enterprise software.

By definition, a PaaS cloud (public or private) offers an integrated environment to design, develop, test, deploy, and support custom applications developed in the language the platform supports. PaaS application security encompasses two software layers:

- Security of the PaaS platform itself (i.e., runtime engine)
- Security of customer applications deployed on a PaaS platform

Generally speaking, PaaS CSPs (e.g., Google, Microsoft, and Force.com) are responsible for securing the platform software stack that includes the runtime engine that runs the customer applications. Since PaaS applications may use third-party applications, components, or Web services, the third-party application provider may be responsible for securing their services.

Hence, customers should understand the dependency of their application on all services and assess risks pertaining to third-party service providers. Until now, CSPs have been reluctant to share information pertaining to platform security, using the argument that such security information could provide an advantage for hackers. However, enterprise customers should demand transparency from CSPs and seek information necessary to perform risk assessment and on-going security management.

IaaS Application security

IaaS cloud providers (e.g., Amazon EC2, GoGrid, and Joyent) treat the applications on customer virtual instances as a black box, and therefore are completely agnostic to the operations and management of the customer's applications. The entire stack—customer applications, runtime application platform (Java, .NET, PHP, Ruby on Rails, etc.), and so on—runs on the customer's virtual servers and is deployed and managed by customers. To that end, customers have full responsibility for securing their applications deployed in the IaaS cloud.

Hence, customers should not expect any application security assistance from CSPs other than basic guidance and features related to firewall policy that may affect the application's communications with other applications, users, or services within or outside the cloud.

Web applications deployed in a public cloud must be designed for an Internet threat model and embedded with standard security countermeasures against common Web vulnerabilities (e.g., the OWASP Top 10). In adherence with common security development practices, they should also be periodically tested for vulnerabilities, and most importantly, security should be embedded into the SDLC. Customers are solely responsible for keeping their applications and runtime platform patched to protect the system from malware and hackers scanning for vulnerabilities to gain unauthorized access to their data in the cloud. It is highly recommended that applications be designed and implemented with a "least-privileged" runtime model (e.g., configure the application to run using a lower privileged account).

Developers writing applications for IaaS clouds must implement their own features to handle authentication and authorization. In line with enterprise identity management practices, cloud applications should be designed to leverage delegated authentication service features supported by an enterprise Identity Provider (e.g., OpenSSO, Oracle IAM, IBM, CA) or a third-party identity service provider (e.g., Ping Identity, Simplified, TriCipher). Any custom implementations of Authentication, Authorization, and Accounting (AAA) features can become a weak link if they are not properly implemented, and they should be avoided when possible.

In summary, the architecture for IaaS-hosted applications closely resembles enterprise Web applications with an n-tier distributed architecture. In an enterprise, distributed applications run with many controls in place to secure the host and the network connecting the distributed hosts.

Different cloud security approaches

Comparable controls do not exist by default in an IaaS platform and must be added through a network, user access, or as application-level controls. Customers of IaaS clouds are responsible for all aspects of their application security and should take the steps necessary to protect their application to address application-level threats in a multi-tenant and hostile Internet environment.

As mentioned in the previous section, the Cloud Security Alliance (CSA) was formed with the aim of promoting the use of best practices for providing security assurance within cloud computing. In this section, we learn from Robert Temple, director and chief architect of security platform for BT Innovate and Design, about security concerns as they relate to three different types of cloud services.

Are there any significant differences when approaching security between the three cloud service models, SaaS, PaaS and IaaS?

Different kinds of cloud computing services expose different entry points into the cloud provider and offer to the customer different types of service management operations. In turn, these create different attack surfaces, severity, and effects of exploits, as well as different probabilities of a security breach.

From resilience and availability, multi-tenancy and data co-mingling, cloud provider lock-in, control of data location, protection of data at rest in the cloud, and compliance to regulations and law about privacy, data protection, cross-border data movement, auditing, etc., there are too many to list in this chapter, but here's a quick snapshot about what customers should make themselves aware:

SaaS customers should understand if their applications have been secured to establish best practice guidance, such as that from the Open Web Application Security Project (OWASP), and ensure that application level security controls have been implemented (for example, application-aware firewalling and intrusion prevention systems).

IaaS customers should understand how resource sharing occurs within their cloud provider—if they require significant scaling-up of provision at the same time as other users of the same cloud, it may risk breaching the capacity of the cloud provider, and therefore affect availability. Also, customers should be aware if their cloud provider's technology architecture uses new and unproven methods for failover and verify what they use for disaster recovery, and customers should understand how their cloud provider deletes "old" data, particularly on the cessation of a contract.

For the PaaS in particular, a cloud provider's patch management policies and procedures have significant security impact, so the customer should ensure that the patching policy is documented.

Provisioned access control infrastructure (DACI)

Developing a consistent framework for dynamically provisioned security services requires deep analysis of all underlying processes and interactions. Many processes typically used in traditional security services need to be abstracted, decomposed, and formalized. First of all, it is related to security services setup, configuration, and security context management that, in many present solutions/frameworks, is provided manually, during the service installation or configured out-of-band.

The general security framework for on-demand provisioned infrastructure services should address two general aspects: (1) supporting secure operation of the provisioning infrastructure, which is typically provided by the providers' authentication and authorization infrastructure (AAI) supported also by federated identity management services (FIdM), and (2) provisioning a dynamic access control infrastructure as part of the provisioned on-demand virtual infrastructure. The first task is primarily focused on the security context exchanged between involved services, resources, and access control services. The virtualized DACI must be bootstrapped to the provisioned on-demand group-oriented virtual infrastructure (VI), the virtual infrastructure provider (VIP), and the virtual infrastructure operator (VIO). Such security bootstrapping can be done at the deployment stage.

Virtual access control infrastructure setup and operation is based on the above-mentioned DSA that will link the VI dynamic trust anchor(s) with the main actors and/or entities participating in the VI provisioning: VIP and the requestor or target user organization (if they are different). As discussed above, the creation of such a dynamic security association (DSA) for the given VI can be done during the reservation and deployment stage.

The reservation stage will allow the distribution of the initial provisioning session context and collection of the security context (e.g., public key certificates) from all participating infrastructure components. The deployment stage can securely distribute either shared cryptographic keys or another type of security credential that will allow validation of information exchange and application of access control to VI users, actors, and services.

CONCLUSION

The primary focus of this chapter is the security infrastructure for cloud-based infrastructure services provisioned on demand that in fact should be a part of the overall cloud infrastructure provisioned on demand. The proposed solutions should allow moving current enterprise security infrastructure—that currently requires large amounts of manual configuration and setup—to a fully functional virtualized infrastructure service.

In this chapter, we looked at network-, host-, and application-level security and the issues surrounding each level with specific regard to cloud computing. At the network level, although there are definitely security challenges with cloud computing, none of those challenges are caused specifically by cloud computing. All of the network-level security challenges associated with cloud computing are instead exacerbated by cloud computing—not specifically caused by it. Likewise, security issues at the host level, such as an increased need for host perimeter security (as opposed to organizational entity perimeter security) and secured virtualized environments, are exacerbated by cloud computing but not specifically caused by it. And the same holds true for the application level. Certainly, there is an increased need for secure software development life cycles due to the public-facing nature of (public) cloud applications, and the need to ensure that APIs have been thoroughly tested for security, but those application-level security requirements are again exacerbated by cloud computing and are not specifically caused by it. Therefore, the issues of infrastructure security and cloud computing are about understanding which party provides which aspects of security (i.e., does the customer provide them or does the CSP provide them?)—in other words, defining trust boundaries.

References

[1] Mather T, Kumaraswamy S. Cloud security and privacy. O'Reilly; 2009.
[2] NIST SP 800-145. The NIST definition of cloud computing. [Internet]. [Accessed on 2012 Jan 29]. http://csrc.nist.gov/publications/ nistpubs/800-145/SP800-145.pdf.
[3] Demchenko Y, Mavrin A, de Laat C. Defining generic architecture for cloud infrastructure as a service provisioning model. In: Proceedings CLOSER2011 Conference; 2011 May 7–9; Nordwijk, Netherlands. SciTePress; 2011. ISBN 978-989-8425-52-2.
[4] Demchenko Y, van der Ham J, Ghijsen M, Cristea M, Yakovenko V, de Laat. C. On-demand provisioning of cloud and grid based infrastructure services for collaborative projects and groups. CTS 2011: Proceedings of the 2011 International Conference on Collaboration Technologies and Systems; 2011 May 23–27; Philadelphia, PA, USA.
[5] Demchenko Y, de Laat C, Lopez DR, Garcia-Espin JA. Security services lifecycle management in on-demand infrastructure services provisioning. In: Proceedings of the IEEE Second International Conference on Cloud Computing Technology and Science. Indianapolis, IN, USA; 2010. p. 644–650.
[6] Demchenko Y, Ngo C, de Laat C, Wlodarczyk T, Rong C, Ziegler W. Security infrastructure for on-demand provisioned cloud infrastructure services. CloudCom2011: Proceedings of the 3rd IEEE Conference on Cloud Computing Technologies and Science; Nov 29-Dec 1; Athens, Greece. ISBN 978-0-7695-4622-3;2011.

Methods

Detection of Intent-Based Vulnerabilities in Android Applications

24

Sébastien Salva[1] and Stassia R. Zafimiharisoa[2]
[1]*University of Auvergne, Clermont-Ferrand,France*
[2]*Blaise Pascal University, Clermont-Ferrand, France*

INFORMATION IN THIS CHAPTER

- Security testing
- Android applications
- Intent mechanism
- Automatic testing

INTRODUCTION

Many recent security reports and research papers show that mobile device operating systems and applications are suffering from a high rate of security attacks. They are rapidly becoming attractive targets for attackers due to significant advances in both hardware and operating systems, which also tend to open new security vulnerabilities. The Android platform is often cited in these reports [1,2]. Android was indeed created with openness in mind and offers a lot of flexibility and features to develop applications. On the other hand, some of these features, if incautiously used, can also lead to security breaches that can be exploited by malicious applications. Many important security flaws are based on the intent system of Android, which is a message-passing mechanism employed to share data among applications and components of an application.

Android applications consist of components that are tied together with intents. These interactions among components are by default highly controlled: components within an application are sandboxed by Android, and other applications may access such components only if they have the required permissions. Some papers and tools have already been proposed to check the validity of these permissions [3]. But even with the right ones, applications can be still vulnerable to malicious intents if incorrectly designed. This chapter focuses on data vulnerabilities that may result from components called *ContentProviders*. Data can be stored in an Android mobile device by various options; for example, in raw files or SQLite databases. The ContentProvider component represents a more elegant interface thatmakes data available to applications. The ContentProvider access is more restricted (no intent) and requires permissions. Without permission (the default mode), data cannot be directly read by external applications. Considering this case, data can still be exposed by the components that have a full access to ContentProviders; that is, those composed with ContentProviders inside the same application. These components can be attacked by malicious intents [4], composed of incorrect data or attacks, that are indirectly forwarded to ContentProviders. As a result, data may be exported or modified. This work tackles this issue by proposing a model-based testing method that automatically generates test cases from intent-based vulnerabilities.

Our method takes intent-based vulnerabilities formally expressed with *vulnerability patterns*. These are specialised ioSTS (input output Symbolic Transition Systems [5]) that formally exhibit vulnerable and non-vulnerable behaviors and help define test verdicts without ambiguity. From vulnerability patterns, our method performs both the automatic test case generation and execution. The originality of our approach comes from the generation of partial specifications, from Android applications, built with algorithms that reflect a part of the Android documentation [6]. The benefits of using them are manifold: they determine the nature of each component (type, links to other components) and describe the functional behavior that should be observed from components after receiving intents. They also avoid giving false positive verdicts (false alarms), because each component is exclusively experimented with test cases generated from its specification. In particular, since the chapter is dealing with data vulnerabilities, test cases shall be constructed from the components that are composed with ContentProviders. Secondly, these specifications help refine test results with special verdicts that notify when a component is not compliant to its specification.

Afterward, we introduce the evaluation of the tool *APSET* (Android aPplications SEcurity Testing), which implements this method. The test results on some popular applications of the Android Market[1] show that this tool is effective in detecting vulnerability flaws within a reasonable time delay.

The chapter is structured as follows: "Comparison to Related Work" compares our approach with related work. We briefly recall some definitions of the ioSTS model in "Model Definition and Notations," and vulnerability patterns are defined in "Vulnerability Modeling." The testing methodology is described in "Security Testing Methodology." We give some tests results in "Implementation and Experimentation," and end the chapter with a "Conclusion."

Comparison to related work

Several works and tools dealing with Android security have been recently proposed in the literature. Below, we compare our approach with some of them.

Some works focus on privilege problems in Android applications. For instance, the tool *Stowaway* was developed to detect over-privilege [3]. It statically analyzes application codes and compares the maximum set of permissions needed for an application with the set of permissions actually requested. This approach offers a different point of view from our work, since we assume that permissions are correctly set. Amalfitano et al. proposed a GUI crawling-based testing technique of Android applications

---

[1]http://play.google.com

[7] that is a kind of random testing technique based on a crawler simulating real user events on the user interface and automatically infers a GUI model. The source code is instrumented to detect defects. This tool can be applied on small size applications to detect crashes only. In contrast, our method can detect a larger set of vulnerabilities since it takes vulnerability scenarios on not only Activities, but also on Services and ContentProviders. However, we do not consider sequences of Activities.

The analysis of the Android IPC mechanism was also studied in [4]. Chin et al. described the permission system vulnerabilities that applications may exploit to perform unauthorized actions. The vulnerability patterns considered in our method can be directly extracted from this work. The same authors also proposed the tool Comdroid, which analyzes Manifest files and application source codes to detect weak permissions and potential intent-based vulnerabilities. Nevertheless, the tool provides a high rate of false negatives (about 75 percent), since it warns users on potential issues but does not verify the existence of attacks. Actually, our tool APSET completes Comdroid, since it tests vulnerability issues on running applications. Another way to reduce intent-based vulnerabilities is to modify the Android platform. In this context, Kantola et al. proposed to alter the heuristics that Android uses to determine the eligible senders and recipients of messages [8]. Intents are passed through filters to detect those unintentionally sent to third-party applications. It is manifest that all attacks are not blocked by these filters, so security testing is still required here. Furthermore, ContentProviders and the management of personal data are not considered.

Other studies deal with the security of pre-installed Android applications and show that target applications receiving oriented intents can re-delegate wrong permissions [9,10]. Some tools have been developed to detect the receipt of wrong permissions by means of malicious intents. In our work, we consider vulnerability patterns to model more general threats based on availability, integrity, or authorization, etc. Permissions can be taken into consideration in APSET with the appropriate vulnerability patterns. Jing et al. introduced a model-based conformance testing framework for the Android platform [11]. As in our approach, partial specifications are constructed from Manifest files. Test cases are generated from these specifications to check whether intent-based properties hold. This approach lacks scalabilit,y though, since the set of properties provided in the paper is based on the intent functioning and cannot be modified. Our work can take as input a larger set of vulnerability patterns.

Model definition and notations

After discussion with the Android developers of the Openium company, we chose the input/output Symbolic Transition Systems (ioSTS) model [5] to express vulnerabilities, since it is flexible enough to describe a large set of intent-based vulnerabilities and is still user-friendly enough to represent vulnerabilities that do not require obligation, permission, and related concepts. An ioSTS is a kind of automata model that is extended with two sets of variables: internal variables to store data and parameters to enrich the actions. Transitions carry actions, guards, and assignments over variables. The action set is separated with inputs beginning by ? to express actions expected by the system, and with outputs beginning by ! to express actions produced by the system. An ioSTS does not have states, but locations.

Below, we give the definition of an ioSTS extension, called ioSTS suspension, that also expresses quiescence; that is, the authorized deadlocks observed from a location. For an ioSTS $\mathscr{S}$, quiescence is modeled by a new action, $!\delta$, and an augmented ioSTS denoted $\mathscr{S}^{\delta}$, which are obtained by adding a self-loop labeled by $!\delta$ for each location where no output action may be observed.

DEFINITION 1

Definition 1 (ioSTS suspension): A deterministic *ioSTS suspension* $\mathscr{S}^{\delta}$ is a tuple $<L, l0, V, V0, I, \Lambda, \rightarrow>$, where:

- L is the finite set of locations, $l0$ the initial location
- V is the finite set of internal variables, I is the finite set of parameters. We denote D_v the domain in which a variable v takes values. The internal variables are initialized with the assignment $V0$, which is assumed to be unique
- Λ is the finite set of symbolic actions $a(p)$, with $p = (p_1, \ldots, p_k)$ a finite list of parameters in $I^k (k \in \mathbb{N})$. p is assumed unique. $\Lambda = \Lambda^I \cup \Lambda^O \cup \{!\delta\}$: Λ^I represents the set of input actions, Λ^O the set of output actions
- $\rightarrow$ is the finite transition set. A transition $(l_i, l_j, a(p), G, A)$, from the location $l_i \in L$ to $l_j \in L$, also denoted $l_i \xrightarrow{a(p), G, A} l_j$, is labeled by an action $a(p) \in \Lambda$. G is a guard over $p \cup V \cup T(p \cup V)$ that restricts the firing of the transition. T is a set of functions returning Boolean values only (a.k.a. predicates) over $(p \cup V)$. Internal variables are updated with the assignment function A of the form $(x := A_x)(x \in V)$; A_x is an expression over $p \cup V \cup T(p \cup V)$
- for any location $l \in L$ and for all pair of transitions $(l, l_1, a(p), G_1, A_1)$, $(l, l_2, a(p), G_2, A_2)$ labeled by the same action, $G_1 \wedge G_2$ is unsatisfiable.

An ioSTS is also associated to an ioLTS (Input/Output Labeled Transition System) to formulate its semantics. In short, ioLTS semantics correspond to valued automata without symbolic variables, which are often infinite. The semantics of an ioSTS $\mathscr{S} = <L, l0, V, V0, I, \Lambda, \rightarrow>$ is the ioLTS $[\![\mathscr{S}]\!] = <Q, q0, \Sigma, \rightarrow>$ composed of valued states in $Q = L \times D_v$, $q0 = (l_0, V0)$ is the initial one, Σ is the set of valued symbols and $\rightarrow$ is the transition relation. The ioLTS semantics definition can be found in [5].

Runs and traces of an ioSTS, which are typically action sequences observed while testing, are defined from its semantics:

DEFINITION 2

Definition 2 (Runs and traces): For an ioSTS $\mathscr{S} = <L, l0, V, V0, I, \Lambda, \rightarrow>$, interpreted by its ioLTS semantics $[\![\mathscr{S}]\!] = <Q, q0, \Sigma, \rightarrow>$, a run $q0\alpha_0 \ldots q_{n-1}\alpha_n$ is an alternate sequence of states and valued actions of $[\![\mathscr{S}]\!]$. It follows that a trace of a run r is defined as the projection $proj_{\Sigma}(r)$ on actions. $Traces_F(\mathscr{S}) = Traces_F([\![\mathscr{S}]\!])$ is the set of traces of all runs finished by states in $F \times D_v$.

Below, we recall the definitions of some classic operations on ioSTS. The same operations can also be applied on the underlying ioLTS semantics. An ioSTS can be completed on its output set to express its incorrect behavior with new transitions to the sink location Fail, guarded by the negation of the union of guards of the same output action on outgoing transitions:

DEFINITION 3

Definition 3 (Output completion): The output completion of a deterministic ioSTS $\mathcal{S} = <L, l0, V, V0, I, \Lambda, \rightarrow>$ gives the ioSTS $\mathcal{S}^! = <L \cup \{Fail\}, l0, V, V0, I, \Lambda, \rightarrow \cup \{(l, Fail, (a(p), G = \bigwedge_{(l,l',a(p),G_1,A_1)\in\rightarrow} \neg G, A = (x := x)_{x \in V}) | l \in L, a(p) \in \Lambda^O\}>$.

DEFINITION 4

Definition 4 (ioSTS product $\times$): The product of the ioSTS $\mathcal{S}_1$ with the ioSTS $\mathcal{S}_2$, denoted $\mathcal{S}_1 \times \mathcal{S}_2$, is the ioSTS $\mathcal{P} = <L_\mathcal{P}, l0_\mathcal{P}, V_\mathcal{P}, V0_\mathcal{P}, I_\mathcal{P}, \Lambda_\mathcal{P}, \rightarrow_\mathcal{P}>$ such that $V_\mathcal{P} = V_1 \cup V_2$, $V0_\mathcal{P} = V0_1 \wedge V0_2$, $I_\mathcal{P} = I_1 \cup I_2$, $L_\mathcal{P} = L_1 \times L_2$, $l0_\mathcal{P} = (l0_1, l0_2)$, $\Lambda_\mathcal{P} = \Lambda_1 \cup \Lambda_2$. The transition set $\rightarrow_\mathcal{P}$ is the smallest set satisfying the following inference rules:

$$l_1 \xrightarrow{a(p),G_1,A_1} l_2 \in \rightarrow_{\mathcal{S}_1}, l_1' \xrightarrow{a(p),G_2,A_2} l_2' \in \rightarrow_{\mathcal{S}_2} \vdash (l_1, l_1') \xrightarrow{a(p),G_1 \wedge G_2, A_1 \cup A_2} (l_2, l_2') \in \rightarrow_\mathcal{P} \quad (1)$$

$$l_1 \xrightarrow{a(p),G_1,A_1} l_2 \in \rightarrow_{\mathcal{S}_1}, a(p) \notin \Lambda_2, l_1' \in L_2 \vdash (l_1, l_1') \xrightarrow{a(p),G_1,A_1 \cup \{x:=x\}_{x \in V_2}} (l_2, l_1') \in \rightarrow_\mathcal{P}, \quad (2)$$

(and symmetrically, $a(p) \notin \Lambda_1$, $l_1 \in L_1$.)

The parallel composition of two ioSTS is a specialized product that illustrates the shared behavior of the two original ioSTS that are compatible:

DEFINITION 5

Definition 5 (Compatible ioSTS): An ioSTS $\mathcal{S}_1 = <L_1, l0_1, V_1, V0_1, I_1, \Lambda_1, \rightarrow_1>$ is compatible with $\mathcal{S}_2 = <L_2, l0_2, V_2, V0_2, I_2, \Lambda_2, \rightarrow_2>$ iff $V_1 \cap V_2 = \emptyset$, $\Lambda_1^I = \Lambda_2^I$, $\Lambda_1^O = \Lambda_2^O$ and $I_1 = I_2$.

DEFINITION 6

Definition 6 (Parallel composition $\|$): The parallel composition of two compatible ioSTS $\mathcal{S}_1$ and $\mathcal{S}_2$, denoted $\mathcal{S}_1 \| \mathcal{S}_2$, is the ioSTS $\mathcal{P} = <L_\mathcal{P}, l0_\mathcal{P}, V_\mathcal{P}, V0_\mathcal{P}, I_\mathcal{P}, \Lambda_\mathcal{P}, \rightarrow_\mathcal{P}>$ such that $V_\mathcal{P} = V_1 \cup V_2$, $V0_\mathcal{P} = V0_1 \wedge V0_2$, $I_\mathcal{P} = I_1 \cup I_2$, $L_\mathcal{P} = L_1 \times L_2$, $l0_\mathcal{P} = (l0_1, l0_2)$, $\Lambda_\mathcal{P} = \Lambda_1 \cup \Lambda_2$. The transition set $\rightarrow_\mathcal{P}$ is the smallest set satisfying only the first rule of Definition 4.

Vulnerability modeling

A vulnerability pattern, denoted $\mathcal{V}$, is a specialized ioSTS suspension composed of two distinct final locations *Vul, NVul*, which aim to recognize the vulnerability status over component executions. Intuitively, runs of a vulnerability pattern, starting from the initial location and ended by *Vul*, describe the presence of the vulnerability. By deduction, runs ended by *NVul* show the absence of the vulnerability. $\mathcal{V}$ is also output-complete to recognize a status, whatever the actions observed while testing.

Naturally, a vulnerability pattern $\mathcal{V}$ has to be equipped with actions also employed for describing Android components. We denote AuthAct$_t$ the set that gathers all these actions for components having the type *t*. Transition guards can also be composed of specific predicates to ease their writing. In this chapter, we consider some predicates such as *in*, which stands for a Boolean function returning true if a parameter list belongs to a given value set. In the same way, we consider several value sets to categorize malicious values and attacks: *RV* is a set of values known for relieving bugs enriched with random values. *Inj* is a set gathering XML and SQL injections constructed from database table URIs found in the tested Android application. *URI* is a set of randomly constructed URIs completed with the URIs found in the tested Android application.

DEFINITION 7

Definition 7 (Vulnerability pattern): A vulnerability pattern is a deterministic and output-complete ioSTS suspension $\mathcal{V}$ such that the sink locations of $L_{\mathcal{V}}$ belong to $\{Vul, NVul\}$. *type*($\mathcal{V}$) is the component (or component composition) type targeted by $\mathcal{V}$. The action set is $\Lambda_{\mathcal{V}} = \text{AuthAct}_{type}$ where *type* is equal to *type*($\mathcal{V}$).

It remains to populate vulnerability patterns with concrete actions having a real signification in accordance with the Android documentation. In this chapter, we focus on the detection of data vulnerabilities based on the intent mechanism. The components that may play a role with these vulnerabilities are:

- Activities, the most common components that display user interfaces used to interact with an application
- Services, which represent long tasks executed in the background
- ContentProviders, which are dedicated to the management of data stored in a smartphone. Without permission (the default mode), data cannot be directly accessed by external applications.

In this context, a Vulnerability pattern $\mathcal{V}$ is then composed of actions of a component *Comp* (Activity or Service), composed with a ContentProvider. Consequently, $\Lambda_{\mathcal{V}} = \text{AuthAct}_{Comp \times ContentProvider} = \text{AuthAct}_{Comp} \cup \text{AuthAct}_{ContentProvider}$. For readability, we only consider Activities here.

Activities display screens to let users interact with programs. We denote *!Display(A)* the action modeling the display of a screen for the Activity *A*. Activities may also throw exceptions that we group into two categories: those raised by the Android system on account of the crash of a component and the other ones. This difference can be observed while testing with our framework. This is modeled with the actions *!SystemExp* and *!ComponentExp*, respectively. Components are joined together with intents, denoted *intent(Cp, a,d, c, t, ed)*, with *Cp* the called component, *a* an action which has to be performed, *d* a data expressed as a URI, *c* a component category, *t* a type that specifies the MIME type of the intent data, and finally, *ed*, which represents additional (extra) data [6]. Intent actions have different purposes; that is, the action VIEW is called to display something and the action PICK is called to choose an item and to return its URI to the calling component. Hence, in reference to the Android documentation [6], the action set, denoted *ACT*, is divided into two categories: the set ACT_r gathers the actions requiring the receipt of a response and ACT_{nr} gathers the other actions. We also denote *C* the set of predefined Android categories and *T* the set of types. Finally, one can deduce that $AuthAct_{Activity}$ is the set *{?intent(Cp,a,d,c,t,ed), !Display(A), !δ, !SystemExp, !ComponentExp}*. ContentProviders are components that receive SQL-oriented requests (no intents) denoted *!call(Cp, request, tableURI)* and eventually return responses denoted *!callResp (Cp, resp)*. Consequently, $AuthAct_{ContentProvider}$ is the set *{!call(Cp, request, tableURI), !callResp(Cp, resp), !δ, !ComponentExp, !SystemExp}*. These action sets can be completed, if required.

Figure 24.1 illustrates a straightforward example of a vulnerability pattern related to data integrity. It aims to check whether an Activity, called with an intent composed of malicious data, cannot alter the content of a database table managed by a ContentProvider. Intents are constructed with data and extra data composed of malformed URIs or String values known for relieving bugs or XML/SQL injections. If the called component crashes, it is considered as vulnerable. Once the intent is performed, the ContentProvider is called with the *query* function of the Android SDK to retrieve all the data stored in a table whose URI is given by the variable *tableURI*. If the result set is not composed of incorrect data given in the intent, then the component is not vulnerable. Otherwise, it is vulnerable. The label *!** is a shortcut notation for all valued output actions that are not explicitly labeled by other transitions.

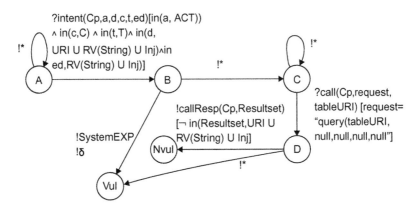

FIGURE 24.1

Vulnerability pattern example.

Assuming a vulnerability pattern $\mathscr{V}$, the vulnerability status of an ioSTS $\mathscr{S}$ compatible with $\mathscr{V}$ can be stated when its suspension traces are also the suspension traces of $\mathscr{V}$ recognised by the locations *Vul* or *NVul*:

DEFINITION 8

Definition 8 (Vulnerability status of an ioSTS): Let $\mathscr{S}$ be an ioSTS and $\mathscr{V}$ be a vulnerability pattern such that $\mathscr{S}^{\delta}$ is compatible with $\mathscr{V}$. We define the vulnerability status of $\mathscr{S}$ (and of its underlying ioLTS semantics $[\![\mathscr{S}]\!]$) over $\mathscr{V}$ with:

- $\mathscr{S}$ is not vulnerable to $\mathscr{V}$, denoted $\mathscr{S} \models \mathscr{V}$ if $Traces(\mathscr{S}^{\delta}) \subseteq Traces_{NVul}(\mathscr{V})$
- $\mathscr{S}$ is vulnerable to $\mathscr{V}$, denoted $\mathscr{S} \not\models \mathscr{V}$ if $Traces(\mathscr{S}^{\delta}) \cap Traces_{Vul}(\mathscr{V}) \neq \varnothing$

Security testing methodology

Initially, a component under test (*CUT*) is regarded as a black box whose interfaces are all that are known. However, one usually assumes the following test hypotheses to carry out the test case execution:

- The functional behavior of the component under test can be modeled by an ioLTS *CUT*. *CUT* is unknown (and potentially nondeterministic). *CUT* is assumed input-enabled (it accepts any of its input actions from any of its states); CUT^{δ} denotes its ioLTS suspension.
- To dialog with *CUT*, one assumes that *CUT* is a composition of an Activity or a Service with a ContentProvider whose type is equal to $type(\mathscr{V})$, and that it is compatible with $\mathscr{V}$.

Since *CUT* is assumed modeled by an ioLTS, Definition 8 exhibits that the vulnerability status of *CUT* against a vulnerability pattern $\mathscr{V}$ can be determined with the *CUT* traces. These are constructed by testing *CUT* with test cases. Our method generates them by the following steps, illustrated in Figure 24.2: we assume having a set of vulnerability patterns modeled with ioSTS suspensions. From an unpacked Android application, we begin extracting a partial class diagram that lists the components and the associations between them. We keep only the components composed with ContentProviders here. From the Android configuration file called *Manifest*, an ioSTS suspension is generated for each component. It partially describes the intent-based normal functioning of a component combined with a ContentProvider. Models, called vulnerability properties, are then derived from the composition of vulnerability patterns with specifications. Test cases are obtained by concretizing vulnerability properties to obtain executable test cases. These steps are detailed below.

Model generation

Android applications gather a lot of information that can be exploited to produce partial specifications. For this method, we generate the following structures and models:

1. First, the tools *dextojar*[2] and *apktool*[3] are successively called to produce a .jar package and to extract the application configuration file, named *Manifest*. The latter declares the components

---

[2]https://code.google.com/p/dex2jar/
[3]https://code.google.com/p/android-apktool/

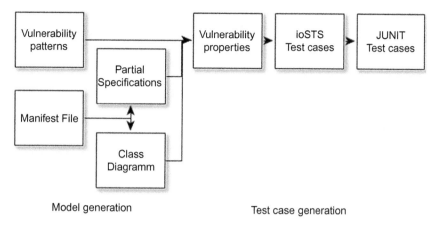

FIGURE 24.2

Test case generation.

participating in the application and the kinds of intents accepted by them. From the .jar package, a class diagram, depicting Android components of the application and their types, is initially computed. The component methods and attribute names are recovered by applying reverse engineering based on Java reflection. This class diagram also gives some information about the relationships between components. This step particularly gives the Activities or Services composed with ContentProviders: $L_C = \{ct_i \times cp_j\}$ is the set gathering the combinations of a component ct_i with a ContentProvider cp_j.

2. An ioSTS suspension $\mathscr{S}_{ct_i \times cp_j} = (\mathscr{S}_{ct_i} \times \mathscr{S}_{cp_j})'$ is generated for each item of L_C such that $type(\{ct_i \times cp_j\})$, for example, Activity $\times$ ContentProvider, is also the type of the vulnerability pattern $\mathscr{V}$. $\mathscr{S}_{cp_j}$ is an ioSTS suspension modeling the call of the ContentProvider cp_j, derived from a generic ioSTS where only the ContentProvider name and the variable tableURI are updated from the information found in the Manifest file. Naturally, this specification is written in accordance with the set $AuthAct_{\text{ContentProvider}}$. $\mathscr{S}_{ct_i}$ is the ioSTS suspension of the component ct_i constructed by means of the intent filters listed in the Manifest file of the Android project. An intent filter, $IntentFilter(act,cat,data,type)$, declares a type of intent accepted by the component. For readability, we present a simplified version of the algorithm dedicated to Activities only in Algorithm 24.1. Initially, the action set of $\Lambda_{\mathscr{S}_{ct_i}}$ is set to $AuthAct_{\text{Activity}}$. Then Algorithm 24.1 produces the ioSTS suspension $\mathscr{S}_{ct_i}$ from intent filters and, with respect to the intent functioning, described in the Android documentation. It covers each intent filter and adds one transition carrying an intent followed by two transitions labeled by output actions (lines 7−15). Depending on the action type read in the intent filter, the guard of a transition equipped by an output action is completed to reflect the fact that a response may be received or not. For instance, an action in ACT_r (line 9) implies both the display of a screen and the receipt of a response. If the action of the intent filter is unknown (lines 13 and 14), no guard is formulated on the output action (a response may be received or not). Finally, the product $\mathscr{S}_{ct_i} \times \mathscr{S}_{cp_j}$ is completed on the output action set to also describe its incorrect behavior, modeled with new

---

Algorithm 1: Component specification Generation

---

input : Manifest file MF

output: Partial specifications S_{ct_i}

1 **foreach** *component* ct_i *in* MF **do**

2     $it := 0$;

3   S_{ct_i} is the ioSTS specification of ct_i ;

4     $\Lambda_{S_{ct_i}} = AuthAct_{type(ct_i)}$;

5   Add $l0_{S_{ct_i}} \xrightarrow{!\delta} S_{ct_i} l0_{S_{ct_i}}$ to $\rightarrow_{S_{ct_i}}$;

6   **if** *type of* ct_i $==$ *Activity* **then**

7   **foreach** *IntentFilter(act,cat,data,type) of* ct_i *in* MF **do**

8             $it := it + 1$;

9   **if** $act \in ACT_r$ **then**

10   Add $l0_{S_{ct_i}} \xrightarrow{?evt_1^{(1)}} S_{ct_i} (l_{it,1})$
$$\xrightarrow{!di_1^{(2)}, [ct_i.resp \neq Null]} l0_{S_{ct_i}} \text{ to } \rightarrow_{S_{ct_i}}$$

11   **else if** $act \in ACT_{nr}$ **then**

12   Add $l0_{S_{ct_i}} \xrightarrow{?evt_1^{(1)}} S_{ct_i} (l_{it,1})$
$$\xrightarrow{!di_1^{(2)}, [ct_i.resp = Null]} l0_{S_{ct_i}} \text{ to } \rightarrow_{S_{ct_i}}$$

13   **else**

14   Add $l0_{S_{ct_i}} \xrightarrow{?evt_1^{(1)}} S_{ct_i} (l_{it,1}) \xrightarrow{!di_1^{(2)}} l0_{S_{ct_i}}$
to $\rightarrow_{S_{ct_i}}$

15   Add $(l_{it,1}) \xrightarrow{!ComponentExp} S_{ct_i} l0_{S_{ct_i}}$ to $\rightarrow_{S_{ct_i}}$;

16 (1) $?intent(Cp, a, d, c, t, ed)[Cp = ct_i \wedge a = act \wedge d = data \wedge c = cat \wedge t = type], A = (x := x)_{x \in VS_{ct_i}}$

17 (2) $!Display(Activity\ a)[Cp = ct_i], A = (x := x)_{x \in VS_{ct_i}}$

ALGORITHM 24.1

Activity specification generation algorithm.

transitions to a *Fail* location. The *Fail* location shall be particularly useful to refine the test verdict by helping to recognize correct and incorrect behaviors of an Android component with respect to its specification. For the Service components, the specification generation algorithm is similar. These algorithms were evaluated by the Android developers of the Openium company to check their soundness and relevance.

Figure 24.3 illustrates a specification example that stems from the product of one Activity with the ContentProvider Contacts. This composition accepts intents composed of the action *PICK* and data whose URI corresponds to the contact list stored in the device. It returns responses (probably a chosen contact). This composition also accepts requests to the ContentProvider Contacts. The incorrect behavior is expressed with transitions to *Fail*.

Test case selection

Test cases are extracted from the compositions of vulnerability patterns with specifications. Given a vulnerability pattern $\mathcal{V}$ compatible with a specification $\mathcal{S}_{ct_i \times cp_j}$, the composition $\mathcal{V}\mathcal{P}_{ct_i \times cp_j} = (\mathcal{V} \| \mathcal{S}_{ct_i \times cp_j})$ is called a vulnerability property of $\mathcal{S}_{ct_i \times cp_j}$. It represents the vulnerable and non-vulnerable behaviors that can be observed from $ct_i \times cp_j$. Furthermore, the parallel composition $\mathcal{V} \| \mathcal{S}_{ct_i \times cp_j}$ produces new locations and, in particular, new final verdict locations:

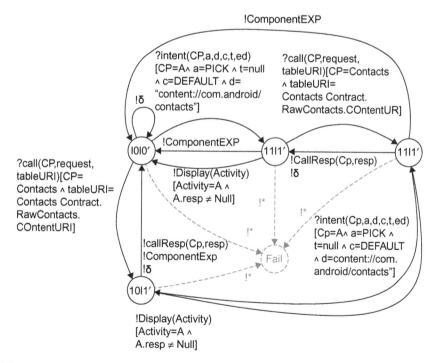

FIGURE 24.3

A specification example.

DEFINITION 9

Definition 9 (Verdict location sets): Let $\mathscr{V}$ be a vulnerability pattern and $\mathscr{S}_{ct_i \times cp_j}$ a specification compatible with $\mathscr{V}$. The vulnerability property $\mathscr{V}\mathscr{P}_{ct_i \times cp_j} = (\mathscr{V} \| \mathscr{S}_{ct_i \times cp_j})$ is composed of new locations recognizing vulnerability status:

1. **$NVUL = NVul \times L_{\mathscr{S}_{ct_i \times cp_j}}$. $NVUL/FAIL = (NVul, Fail)$** is a special verdict location recognizing incorrect behavior with respect to the specification $\mathscr{S}_{ct_i \times cp_j}$ and not vulnerable behaviors with respect to $\mathscr{V}$.
2. **$VUL = Vul \times L_{\mathscr{S}_{ct_i \times cp_j}}$. $VUL/FAIL = (Vul, Fail)$** aims to recognize incorrect behavior with respect to $\mathscr{S}_{ct_i \times cp_j}$ and vulnerable behavior with respect to $\mathscr{V}$.
3. **$FAIL = L_v \times Fail$** recognizes incorrect behavior with respect to $\mathscr{S}_{ct_i \times cp_j}$.

Test cases are achieved with Algorithm 24.2, which performs two main steps. Firstly, it splits a vulnerability property $\mathscr{V}\mathscr{P}_{ct_i \times cp_j}$ into several ioSTS. Intuitively, from a location l having k transitions carrying an input action, for example, an intent, k new test cases are constructed to test CUT with the k input actions and so on for each location l having transitions labeled by input actions (lines 1−4). Then, a set of valuation tuples is computed from the undefined parameter list of each input action (line 5). For instance, intents are composed of several variables whose domains are given in guards. These ones have to be concretized before testing; that is, each undefined parameter is assigned to a value. Instead of using a Cartesian product to construct a tuple of valuations, we adopted a *Pairwise* technique [13]. This technique strongly reduces the coverage of variable domains by constructing discrete combinations for pairs of parameters only. The set of valuation tuples is constructed with the *Pairwise* procedure, which takes the list of undefined parameters and the transition guard to find the domain of each parameter. In the second step (lines 6−13), input actions are concretized. Given a transition t and its set of valuation tuples $P(t)$, this step constructs a new test case for each tuple $pv = (p_1 = v_1, ..., p_n = v_n)$ by replacing the guard G with $G \wedge pv$ if $G \wedge pv$ is satisfiable. Finally, if the resulting ioSTS suspension tc has verdict locations, then tc is added in the test case set TC. Steps 1 and 2 are iteratively applied until each combination of valuation tuples and each combination of transitions carrying input actions are covered. Since the algorithm may produce a large test case set, depending on the number of tuples of valuations given by the *Pairwise* function, the algorithm also ends when the test case set TC reaches a cardinality of $tcnb$ (lines 17 and 18).

A test case example, derived from the specification of Figure 24.3 and the vulnerability pattern of Figure 24.1, is depicted in Figure 24.4. It calls the Activity A with intents whose extra data parameter is composed of an SQL injection. Then, the data managed by the ContentProvider Contacts must not have been modified. Otherwise, the component is vulnerable. If it crashes, it is vulnerable as well.

A test case constructed, with Algorithm 24.2, from a vulnerability property $\mathscr{V}\mathscr{P}_{ct_i \times cp_j}$, produces traces that belong to the trace set of $\mathscr{V}\mathscr{P}_{ct_i \times cp_j}$. In other words, the test selection algorithm does not add new traces leading to verdict locations. Indeed, a test case is composed of paths of a vulnerability property, starting from its initial location. Each guard G' of a test case transition carrying an input action stems from a guard G completed with a tuple of valuations such that, if G' is satisfied, then G is also satisfied. This is captured by the following proposition:

Algorithm 2: Test case generation

---

input : A vulnerability property $\mathcal{VP}_{ct_i \times cp_j}$, $tcnb$ the maximal number of test cases

output: Test case set TC

1 **begin** 1. input action choice
2   **foreach** *location l having outgoing transitions carrying input actions* **do**
3   Choose a transition $t = l \xrightarrow{?a(p),G,A} \mathcal{VP}_{ct_i \times cp_j} l_2$;
4   remove the other transitions labelled by input actions;
5          $P(t) = Pairwise(p_1, ..., p_n, G)$ with $(p_1, ..., p_n) \subseteq p$ the list of undefined parameters;

6 **begin** 2. input concretisation
7   **foreach** $t = l \xrightarrow{?a(p),G,A} \mathcal{VP}_{ct_i \times cp_j} l_2$ **do**
8   Choose a valuation tuple $pv = (p_1 = v_1, ..., p_n = v_n)$ in $P(t)$;
9   **if** $G \wedge pv$ *is satisfiable* **then**
10   Replace G by $G \wedge pv$ in t;
11   **else**
12   Choose another valuation tuple in $P(t)$;
13   tc is the resulting ioSTS suspension;

14 **begin** 3.
15   **if** tc *has reachable verdict locations* **then**
16          $TC := TC \cup \{tc\}$;
17   **if** $Card(TC) \geq tcnb$ **then**
18   STOP;
19   Repeat 1. and 2. until each combination of transitions carrying input actions and each combination of valuation tuples are covered;

ALGORITHM 24.2

Test case generation.

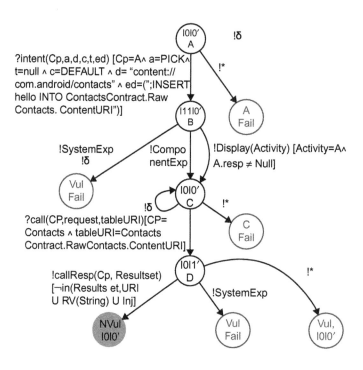

FIGURE 24.4

A test case example.

PROPOSITION 10

Proposition 10: Let $\mathscr{V}\mathscr{P}_{ct_i \times cp_j} = (\mathscr{V} \| \mathscr{S}_{ct_i \times cp_j})$ be a vulnerability property. *TC* is the test case set generated from $\mathscr{V}\mathscr{P}_{ct_i \times cp_j}$ with Algorithm 24.2. We have: $\forall tc \in TC, Traces(tc) \subseteq Traces(\mathscr{V} \| \mathscr{S}_{ct_i \times cp_j})$.

Test case execution definition

The test case execution is defined by the parallel composition of the test cases with the implementation under test *CUT*:

PROPOSITION 11

Proposition 11 (Test case execution): Let *TC* be a test case set obtained from the vulnerability pattern $\mathscr{V}$ and the specification $\mathscr{S}_{ct_i \times cp_j}$. *CUT* is the ioLTS of the component under testing, assumed compatible with $\mathscr{V}$. For all test cases $tc \in TC$, the execution of *tc* on *CUT* is defined by the parallel composition $tc \| CUT^\delta$.

The above proposition leads to the test verdict of a component under test against a vulnerability pattern $\mathscr{V}$. Intuitively, it refers to the vulnerability status definition, completed by the detection of incorrect behavior described in the specification with the verdict locations *VUL/FAIL* and *NVUL/FAIL*. An inconclusive verdict is also defined when a *FAIL* verdict location is reached after a test case execution. This verdict means that incorrect actions or data were received. To avoid false positive results, the test is stopped without completely executing the scenario given in the vulnerability pattern.

DEFINITION 13

Definition 13 (Test verdict): We take back the notations of Proposition 11. The execution of the test case set *TC* on *CUT* yields one of the following verdicts:

1. *CUT* is vulnerable to $\mathscr{V}$ if $\exists tc \in TC, tc \| CUT^{\delta}$ produces a trace σ such that $\sigma \in Traces_{VUL}(tc)$. If σ is a trace of $Traces_{VUL/FAIL}(tc)$, then *CUT* is not compliant with $\mathscr{S}_{ct_i \times cp_j}$.
2. *CUT* is not vulnerable to $\mathscr{V}$ if $\forall tc \in TC, tc \| CUT^{\delta}$ produces a trace σ such that $\sigma \in Traces_{NVUL}(tc)$. However, if σ is a trace of $Traces_{NVUL/FAIL}(tc)$ then *CUT* is not compliant with $\mathscr{S}_{ct_i \times cp_j}$.
3. *CUT* has an unknown status (inconclusive verdict) with $\mathscr{V}$ if $\exists tc \in TC, tc \| CUT^{\delta}$ produces a trace σ such that $\sigma \in Traces_{FAIL}(tc)$.

Implementation and experimentation
Methodology implementation

The above security testing method has been implemented in a prototype tool called *APSET* (Android aPplications SEcurity Testing), publicly available in a Github repository.[4] As presented in "Security Testing Methodology," it takes as inputs vulnerability patterns written in dot format[5] and an Android application. IoSTS test cases are converted into JUNIT test cases in order to be executed with a test runner (set of control methods to run tests). Any action or predicate defined in the previous sections has its corresponding function coded in the tool. For instance, the action *!Display(A)* is coded by the function Display() returning true if a screen is displayed. This link between actions and Java code eases to the development of final test cases, which actually call Java sections of code that can be executed. In short, JUNIT test cases are constructed as follows: input actions representing component calls are converted into Java code composed of parameter values given by guards. Output actions are translated into Java code and JUNIT assertions composed of verdicts. The actions *!ComponentExp* and *!SystemExp* are converted into try/catch statements.

Afterward, JUNIT test cases can be executed on Android emulators or devices by means of the test execution framework depicted in Figure 24.5. This framework is composed of the Android testing execution tool provided by Google, an enriched framework with the tool PolideaInstrumentation,[6] to yield XML reports.

---

[4]https://github.com/statops/apset.git
[5]http://www.graphviz.org/
[6]www.polidea.pl/

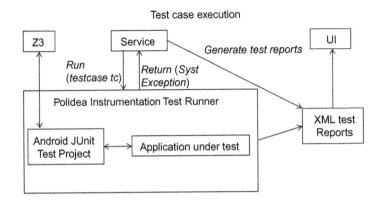

FIGURE 24.5

Test case execution.

Test cases are executed on Android devices or emulators by an Android Service component, which returns an XML report directly displayed on the device. (External computers are not required during this step.) The test runner starts *CUT* and iteratively executes JUNIT test cases in separate processes.

This procedure is required to catch the exceptions raised by the Android system when a component crashes. Once all the test cases are executed, the XML report gathers all the assertion results. In particular, the VUL, VUL/FAIL messages exhibit the detection of a vulnerability issue.

The following example illustrates part of an XML report expressing the crash of a component. We obtain a VUL/FAIL message inside a failure XML block. Hence, the verdict is *VUL/FAIL*.

```
<test suite errors = "0" failures = "1"
name = "packagename.test.Intent.ContactActivityTest"
package = "packagename.test.Intent" tests = "1" time = "0.15"
timestamp = "2013-02-13T10:05:02">
<testcase classname = "packagename.test.Intent.ContactActivityTest" name = "test1"
time = "0.15">
<failure> VUL/FAIL
INSTRUMENTATION RESULT: shortMsg = java.lang.NullPointerException
INSTRUMENTATION RESULT:longMsg = java.lang.NullPointerException INSTRUMENTATION CODE: 0
</failure></testcase>
</testsuite>
```

The guard solving, used in Algorithm 24.2 and in the test execution framework, is performed with the SMT (Satisfiability Modulo Theories) solver Z3[7] that we have chosen, since it allows a direct use of arithmetic formulae. However, it does not support String variables. So, we extended the Z3 expression language with new predicates, and in particular with String-based predicates

---

[7]http://z3.codeplex.com/

(e.g., *in, streq, contains*). A predicate stands for a function over ioSTS internal variables and parameters that return Boolean values.

Experimentation

We randomly chose 50 popular applications in Google Play Store and 20 applications provided by the Openium company. Among these, we kept the 25 applications composed of ContentProviders, (18 applications of the Android Market and 7 developed by Openium, app 1 up to app 13). We tested them with three vulnerability patterns: $\mathscr{V}1$ corresponds to the vulnerability pattern taken as an example in the paper. $\mathscr{V}2$ checks whether an Activity called with intents composed of malicious data cannot change the structure of a database managed by a ContentProvider (modification of attribute names, removal of tables, etc.). $\mathscr{V}3$ checks that incorrect data, already stored in a database, are not displayed by an Activity after having called it with intents.

Our tool APSET detected a total of 22 vulnerable applications using only these three vulnerability patterns. Figure 24.6 illustrates the obtained test results. This chart shows the number of test cases executed per application and the number of *VUL* verdicts. Some application test results revealed a high number of *VUL* verdicts, for example, *smspopup* with 94 failures. These do not necessarily reflect the number of security defects, though. Several *VUL* verdicts can arise from the same flaw in the source code.

Analyzing XML reports can help developers localize these defects by identifying the incriminated components, the raised exceptions, or the actions performed. Figure 24.7 depicts the percentage of applications vulnerable to the vulnerability patterns $\mathscr{V}1$, $\mathscr{V}2$, and $\mathscr{V}3$. Eighty-eight percent of the applications are vulnerable to $\mathscr{V}1$, $\mathscr{V}2$, or both, and hence are not protected against SQL injections. Seventy-two percent of the applications display incorrect data on user interfaces ($\mathscr{V}3$) without checking for consistency.

Thereafter, we manually analyzed the test reports and codes of six applications. The test results are depicted in Table 24.1. It respectively illustrates the number of tested components, the number of issues detected with each vulnerability pattern, and the total number of test cases providing a vulnerable verdict. For instance, with app5, 102 test cases were generated and 17 showed vulnerability issues. Ten test cases showed that app5 is vulnerable to $\mathscr{V}1$. More precisely, we noticed that one test case showed that personal data can be modified by using malicious intents. App5 crashed with the other test cases, probably because of the bad handling of malicious intents by the components. Two test cases revealed that the structure of the database can be modified ($\mathscr{V}2$). By analysing the app5 source codes, we actually detected that no ContentProvider methods were protected against malicious SQL requests. Finally, five test cases revealed the display of incorrect data stored in the database ($\mathscr{V}3$). This means that the database content is directly displayed into the user interface without validation.

Thirty-nine test cases revealed vulnerability issues with the application *Google Maps*. Twenty-eight vulnerabilities were detected with $\mathscr{V}1$: three test cases showed that databases can be updated or modified with incorrect data through the component *Maps-Activity*. One test case revealed the same flaw for the component *ResolverActivity*. As a consequence, one can conclude that *Google Maps* is vulnerable to some SQL injections and has integrity issues. The other failed test cases concern *MapsActivity* crashes. With $\mathscr{V}3$, the 11 detected defects also correspond to component crashes. For *Youtube*, we obtained three vulnerability issues corresponding to component crashes, with the

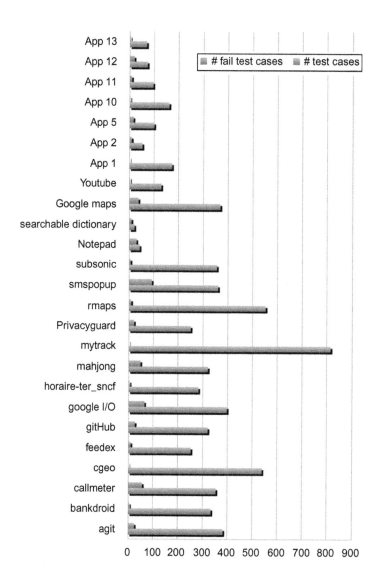

FIGURE 24.6

Test results on 25 applications.

exception *NullPointerException*. No more serious vulnerabilities were detected. Table 24.1 also gives the average test case execution time, measured with a mid-2011 computer with a CPU of 2.1Ghz Core i5. The execution time is included between some milliseconds up to some seconds, depending of the number of components and the code of the tested components. These results are coherent with other available Android application testing tools [12]. These results, combined with the number of vulnerability issues detected on real applications, tend to show that our tool is effective and leads to substantial improvement in security vulnerability detection.

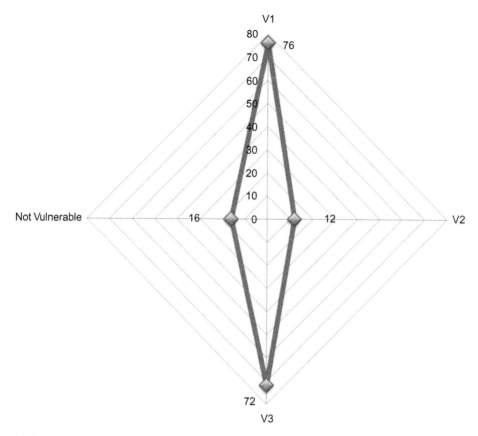

FIGURE 24.7

Percentage of vulnerable applications/vulnerability pattern.

Table 24.1 Experimentation Results

Applications		Test Results				
Name	#component	✓1	✓2	✓3	#vul/#testcases	Time
app5	15	10	2	5	17/102	2,3
NotePad	5	27	0	4	31/44	0.004
Searchable Dictionary	3	10	0	3	13/22	1,02
Google Maps	38	28	0	11	39/370	1,7
YouTube	12	3	0	0	31/131	3,21
Callmeter	27	31	4	22	57/355	1,56

CONCLUSION

In this chapter, we present a security testing method for Android applications that aims at detecting data vulnerabilities based on the intent mechanism. The originality of this work resides in the automatic generation of partial specifications, used to generate test cases. These enrich the test verdict with the verdicts *NVUL/FAIL* and *VUL/FAIL*, pointing out that the component under testing does not comply with the recommendations provided in the Android documentation.

They also avoid false positive verdicts, since each component is exclusively tested by means of the vulnerability patterns that share behavior with the component specification. We tested our approach on 25 randomly chosen Android applications. Our tool reported that 22 applications have defects that can be exploited by attackers to crash applications, to extract personal data, or to modify them.

This experimentation firstly showed that our tool *APSET* is effective. The *APSET* effectiveness could be yet improved by using more vulnerability patterns or, eventually, by generating more test cases per pattern. In comparison to other intent-based testing tools [4,8], *APSET* is scalable, since existing vulnerability patterns can be modified or new vulnerability patterns can be proposed to meet the testing requirements. Value sets considered for testing, for example, the SQL injection set Inj and the set of predicates used in guards, can be updated, as well. Nevertheless, *APSET* is only based on the intent mechanism. Consequently, it cannot test any kind of vulnerability. For instance, attacks carried out by sequences of user actions performed on the application interface cannot be applied with our tool. *APSET* does not consider the component type *BroadcastReceiver*, either. This component type is vulnerable to malicious intents, though. These drawbacks could be explored in future works.

Acknowledgments

This work was undertaken in collaboration with the Openium company.[8] Thanks for their valuable feedback and advice on this work.

References

[1] IT business: Android security. [Internet]. Retrieved from: http://www.itbusinessedge.com/cm/blogs/weinschenk/google-must-deal-with-android-security-problems-quickly/?cs=49291>; 2012 Jun [accessed 02.13].

[2] Shabtai A, Fledel Y, Kanonov U, Elovici Y, Dolev S. Google Android: A state-of-the-art review of security mechanisms. CoRR; 2009.

[3] Felt AP, Chin E, Hanna S, Song D, Wagner D. Android permissions demystified. In: Proceedings of the eighteenth ACM Conference on Computer and Communications Security; 2011. p. 627–38.

[4] Chin E, Felt AP, Greenwood K, Wagner D. Analyzing inter-application communication in Android. Proc of the nineth International Conference on Mobile Systems Applictaions and Services; 2011.

---

[8]http://www.openium.fr

[5] Frantzen L, Tretmans J, Willemse T. Test generation based on symbolic specifications. FATES 2004; 2005. p. 1−17.

[6] Android developer. [Internet]. Retrieved from: http://developer.android.com/index.html; 2013 [accessed 02.13].

[7] Amalfitano D, Fasolin A, Tramontana P. A gui crawling-based technique for Android mobile application testing. ICSTW: IEEE Fourth International Conference on Software Testing, Verification and Validation Workshops; 2011. p. 252−61.

[8] Kantola D, Chin E, He W, Wagner D. Reducing attack surfaces for intra-application communication in Android. Proceedings of the second ACM workshop on security and privacy in smartphones and mobile devices; 2012. p. 69−80.

[9] Zhong J, Huang J, Liang B. Android permission redelegation detection and test case generation. In: Computer Science Service System (CSSS). 2012 International Conference; 2012. p. 871−74.

[10] Grace M, Zhou Y, Wang Z, Jiang X. Systematic detection of capability leaks in stock Android smart-phones. In: Proceedings of the nineteenth Network and Distributed System Security Symposium (NDSS); 2012.

[11] Jing Y, Ahn G-J, Hu H. Model-based conformance testing for Android. Proceedings of the 7th International Workshop on Security (IWSEC); 2012. p. 1−18.

[12] Benli S, Habash A, Herrmann A, Loftis T, Simmonds D. A comparative evaluation of unit testing techniques. Proceedings of the 2012 Ninth International Conference on Information Technology; 2012. p. 263−8.

[13] Cohen MB, Gibbons PB, Mugridge WB, Colbourn CJ. Constructing test suites for interaction testing. In: Proc of the twenty fifth International Conference on Software Engineering; 2003. p. 38−48.

PART 4

Cyber Crime and Cyber Terrorism

Theory

A Quick Perspective on the Current State in Cybersecurity

25

Diogo A.B. Fernandes, Liliana F.B. Soares, João V. Gomes, Mário M. Freire, and Pedro R.M. Inácio

University of Beira Interior, Covilhã, Portugal

INFORMATION IN THIS CHAPTER

- Cybersecurity
- Cyber-criminality
- Cyber-warfare
- Malware
- Phishing
- Spam
- Vulnerabilities

INTRODUCTION

This section starts by defining cybersecurity and information security terms, focusing on the latter, and then shedding light on the contributions this chapter makes. The clipping method used for this chapter is then described, and the chapter's organization is outlined in the end.

The scope of cybersecurity

The terms "cybersecurity" and "information security" are sometimes used interchangeably. They overlap in meaning, but they also differ in key aspects [1]. "Security" refers to protecting resources from threats that exploit vulnerabilities. The distinction between "information" and "cyber" points to information versus technology. Non-technological elements, like people, fall within the information security. Non-information assets, like a hard drive or an Ethernet link, are part of the cybersecurity.

Cybersecurity involves the cyberspace itself and its users, along with their personal, ethical, societal, and national capacity and interests. The Internet-enabled cyberspace, however, is a place full of dispute—an open battleground. Copyright infringement, intellectual property theft, censorship, privacy breach, digital surveillance, and cyberwarfare all contribute to these disputes [2]. The drama apart, the reality is that computer security is not generally prioritized, leaving systems wide open to threats. Meanwhile, security vendors, often accused of spreading fear, uncertainty, and doubt (FUD) to drum up business, tend to skew their reports according to the companies' best interests [3]. But the threats are real and the consequences can be severe, as proven by history. Therefore, it is worthwhile to periodically survey the current state of cybersecurity by analyzing incidents, cases, and trends.

Contributions

This chapter's purpose is to provide a quick perspective on the current state of the international arena of cybersecurity. Its contribution is threefold: First, some concepts important in this field are introduced and practical examples are provided. Second, key incidents of the past as well as recent events are discussed in order to understand how cybersecurity has evolved through the time. Third, the chapter discusses several current hot topics in the cyber-world. We have gathered an extensive set of security resources and used them for this chapter. The chapter does not consider solutions but rather points out unresolved issues.

Clipping method

The work presented in this chapter is the result of daily efforts performed throughout the first half of 2013. On a daily basis, we searched for relevant cybersecurity discussions in the following places: the blogs of major vendors like Symantec, Kaspersky, and F-Secure; news feeds from various sites, online magazines and journals; security documents of research laboratories; scientific articles; blogs and tweets of security experts; vulnerabilities databases; and search engines. This resulted in a set of articles, news clips, reports, and other documents from which we extracted the more interesting ones, analyzed their credibility, veracity, and theoretical groundings to include them in the chapter. Every day, chosen items were rendered in a list organized after the structure of this chapter in order to classify each source. The study presented in this chapter distinguishes itself for its methodical analysis and discussion of the state-of-the-art on cybersecurity. Due to space constraints, we do not include every reference compiled, citing only the most important ones.

Organization

The remainder of this chapter is structured as follows: The next section introduces key concepts in the cybersecurity field. Then, focus is put on malware and phishing, describing what stems from them while also discussing botnets, spam, and spear-phishing. The discussion then shifts to a description of vulnerabilities and data breaches, while providing remarkable examples for each. Toward the end, the chapter sheds light on the current state of cyberspace through the lens of three profile threats. The final section reflects on the main lessons learned.

Understanding the scope of cybersecurity

The prefix "cyber" originated in the 1990s, but only recently has it been combined with "security" [4] and given proper attention as a field. As security awareness has improved, protocols and applications have started to include an "s" for "secure" in acronyms like "HTTPS." This section focuses on security enforcement in enterprise environments, who are the stakeholders of the cyberspace, and how they operate in it.

Network perimeter

Since the 1990s, the openness of networks has gradually increased, opening doors for applications like email and websites, while the perimeter trust has gradually narrowed down, creating an attack spectrum spanning several vectors [5]. To reduce the exposure gap, networks are enclosed within various layers of security controls, whose purpose is preventing, detecting, and mitigating intrusions and other activities of similar nature. Such perimeters are traditionally composed of firewalls, intrusion prevention/detection systems, sensors and traffic analyzers, proxies and reverse proxies, load balancers, and anti-* solutions.[1]

Security controls are set up to log events according to the syslog standard for a centralized point that is part of the Security Information and Event Management (SIEM) process. Security logs can be extremely huge data sets, with on the order of millions or even billions of rows. When processed by SIEM devices, the resulting information gives a picture of the network's health status—a holistic view of the egress and ingress traffic points and systems. Front-end platforms analyze those events, correlate them, track patterns, and trigger pre-set alarms for a monitoring team typically placed within a Security Operations Center (SOC)—a Computer Emergency Response Team (CERT).

The advent of "big data" has caused quite a commotion, and the industry has started to work out solutions. Thus, the SIEM process could surely benefit from such technology that would optimize log processing and event correlation at a large scale.

Responding to cybersecurity incidents

Responding to cybersecurity incidents involves internal procedures defined by the company's policy. The de facto framework for incident response involves five steps: preparation, identification, mitigation, eradication, and recuperation. The preparation phase consists of knowing the network, systems, applications, and the SOC infrastructure beforehand. The remaining four steps define the response flow for real-time incident response. The incident is first detected and identified. Then it is mitigated, that is, contained, to at least diminish its impact. Eradication involves eliminating possible compromised artifacts, like patching vulnerabilities or purging malware, which supports the idea that a capacity for deep technical forensic investigation is required in the cybersecurity field. Finally, targeted systems are recovered and restored to their normal operation. In the majority of the simplest cases, the last two steps might not even be executed. Afterward, the lessons learned should be used to optimize the infrastructure and improve incident response in the future.

Sometimes Internet protocol (IP) addresses get included in known international blocking lists (e.g., the Spam and Open Relay Blocking System [SORBS]) for participating in spam or phishing campaigns. To delist IP addresses, CERTs have to cooperate with those cyber-authorities and provide evidence of eradication. CERTs also collaborate with other security teams around the world, thereby creating a white hat network of cyber-warriors that fight malefactors.

The most straightforward way to mitigate an incident is to block the source IP address or addresses. Blackhole Access Control Lists (ACLs) or drop rules are among the common techniques used. But these approaches can be problematic under Distributed Denial of Service (DDoS) conditions. It can be time-consuming to block lots of IP addresses, and both ACLs and rules put

---

[1]Anti-* is used in terms like "anti-spam," "anti-virus," and "anti-phishing."

processing constraints on routers and firewalls. Moreover, many security controls are still stateful nowadays and rely on deep packet inspection and signature databases. However, both enterprise networks and the Internet are now lively, dynamic places, where many kinds of traffic originate from countless discrete devices, decreasing the effectiveness of such approaches. For example, the probability of anti-viruses correctly matching signatures with malware is roughly 30 to 50 percent [6].

Dynamic environments

Both the Internet and corporate networks are changing and becoming more dynamic environments, and security controls have to keep up with the changes. Cloud computing and Bring Your Own Device (BYOD) are gaining ground, but they also raise several security questions. How can company policy be enforced on outsourced infrastructures or on employee devices? They can move from one Wi-Fi hotspot to another and to telecommunications networks (e.g., 4 G) seamlessly, and can carry malware while accessing the enterprise's applications. Security controls lack the monitoring capability to address this situation, and end-point protection still needs development on this regard as well. Cisco [7] believes that people-to-machine, people-to-people, and machine-to-machine connections will dictate and play a key role in the future. Clearly, to maintain the traditional holistic perspective while overseeing evolving network components in long term, it is necessary to recognize these key issues and adapt cybersecurity accordingly.

Threat profiles

In the context of cybersecurity, three threat profiles are considered: the hacktivist, the cyber-criminal, and the nation-state. Each of these profiles is enough to categorize cyber-threats in terms of personality, habits, motives, methods, and dedication. The hacktivist is the sort of a threat that can be dangerous within a very short time-frame. It is also normally easy to guess when and where attacks are going to hit, because they are often publicized ahead of time to show off and gather supporters. The cyber-criminal, in contrast, is more keen, looking over his or her shoulder, as it were, constantly. This profile is characterized by a meticulous and methodical approach that aims to make profit at any cost on the underground. The nation-state profile is intrinsically linked to Advanced Persistent Threats (APTs) and state-sponsored threats. Hacktivists tend to engage in crisis, whereas nation-states mean to disable target abilities for cyber-warfare. Cyber-espionage lies somewhere in the gray area between these three, as it can be conducted by an entity with any profile, individual or group.

Malware, the infectious disease, and phishing, the fraud

Early computer viruses, dating from the late 1980s and early 1990s were written for the pure challenge of it. Some would show simple animations over and over, while others showed just text. The Joshi virus, for example, would ask for user input only on its writer's birthday. The early Linux and Windows viruses would only spread via disks. Today, viruses are dynamically carried on data files for various systems—Windows, Mac, and Linux—and purposes. The following sections provide an overview of what malware masterminds and phishers have been up to lately.

Malware trends

The continual search for profit is the reason for new surges of trojans mainly targeting the finance sector. Beta Bot evolved from an HTTP bot to a banking malware [8]. Shipped with an embedded rootkit, it offers a kill switch for other malware and is capable of stealing home banking credentials by capturing HTTP requests. VSkimmer steals credit card information from card readers plugged into machines running Windows [9]. With thousands of infected machines, the Kangoo botnet targets home banking theft [10]. In Brazil, a homemade browser tricks a home banking website into not needing a security plugin by disguising itself as a mobile browser [11] while, in fact, it is stealing user credentials.

It is more convenient to control a victim computer than to provoke damage. However, McAfee [12] believes that destructive malware and ransomware on mobile devices will make a comeback. Indeed, in August of 2012, the Saudi Arabian oil company Aramco had thousands of machines down for a week [13]—caused by the Shamoon malware. These types of attacks can be troubling because they impact the real world. In this case, oil prices could increase. More recently, a time-bomb wiped out several computer hard drives of Korean financial institutions and TV broadcasters [14]. Other cases of Master Boot Record (MBR) wiping [15] have been reported, but with ransomware functionality too. Ransomware locks victim computers and encrypts data, asking for payment in order to undo the lock. Fees are demanded in the name of policing authorities, like the Federal Bureau of Investigation (FBI) [16]. Moreover, Reveton, a well-known ransomware strain, has been updated with a password purloining function [17].

Malware writers are focusing their efforts on new platforms. Smartphones, and consequently the BYOD paradigm, along with social networks and Mac machines, are making strides in the technology scene, but they also give rise to new arenas for malware development. On top of that, consumers are less aware of security risks on these environments, making them especially phishable. In 2012, a 2577 percent Android malware growth was recorded [7], with hundreds of new malicious samples per day and thousands already estimated for 2013 [18,19]. Most are profit-motivated and do not connect to Command-and-Control (CnC) servers, but the noteworthy ones do so, making mobile botnets little different than traditional ones.

Mobile malware focuses on toll fraud (premium-rate Short Message Service [SMS] messages), ad jacking, and bank fraud by capturing mobile Transaction Authentication Numbers (TANs) [19,20]. They disseminate via drive-by downloads or malvertising, or even disguising themselves as legitimate applications on official stores like Google Play Store and Apple App Store. A noteworthy malware with multiple advanced functionalities has been uncovered [21]. Obad, as it was dubbed, is able to send premium-rated SMS messages, download and install other malware onto the device or send it further via Bluetooth, and remotely issue console commands on Android devices. Of more concern is the fact that the user cannot delete it without root access once it acquires administrative privileges by exploiting a flaw in the operating system.

Regarding social networks, the Dorkbot malware spreads through Facebook internal chat, hopping from one friend to another. It circulates in many countries and is capable of stealing personal information and spying on user activities [22]. Another malware [23] posts malicious links on Facebook, while a surge [24] tweets malicious links onto Twitter. Furthermore, signs of malware are beginning to show up on Macs. The best example is the popular Flashback trojan, which exploited a vulnerability in Java. Recently found, the spyware Kumar dumps and uploads screenshots to CnC servers [25]. The most interesting aspect of this evildoer is that it was signed with a valid Apple Developer ID.

In general, cyber-criminals develop mainstream functionalities to reinforce malware but also to avoid detection and slip past anti-viruses. Recent anti-virtual machine, anti-debugging, and anti-sandbox techniques have been used by malware to evade detection because those isolated environments are used to analyze malware [26]. For example, a malware can ascertain if infected machines have mouse movements or not, the latter being evidence of dormant systems devoid of user interaction. These techniques are also particularly of concern for cloud computing. Truly, it is a game of cat and mouse between the white hat and dark hat communities. Malware, the infectious digital disease, will not fade away in the near future. When new technologies come along, malware can be expected to follow them into unexpected places [27]. This is the case of the Internet of Everything (IoE) [7], where IP-enabled devices connected to the Internet, like TVs and cars, can run existing operating systems similar to Android.

Botnets

Botnets are a network of computer bots infected with malware controlled by a CnC infrastructure, or mothership. Botmasters issue commands from CnC servers to bots. Malware can be written for virtually anything. In some cases, Remote Administration Tools (RATs) (e.g., the Travnet botnet [28]) allow complete control over the machines, being suitable for APTs. Botnets are mostly known and perceived (negatively) in this way.

Botnet defenses

There have been successful shutdowns of botnets (e.g., Waledac, Kelihos, more recently Citadel [29] and ZeuS, although ZeuS variants are reemerging strong [30]). But Peer-to-Peer (P2P) botnets (e.g., ZeroAccess and Sality) are more resilient to sinkholing because the absence of a central server makes it harder to redirect bots and to estimate population through upwards crawling discovery (bots restrict who they add to their peering lists, including injected sensors) [31]. P2P botnets have been growing at a fast pace ever since the advent of their forefathers, like Storm and Waledac. For example, the MultiBanker botnet recently added Jabber P2P communication [32].

Although rare, some botnets borrow the fast-flux feature from the Domain Name Service (DNS) to hide proxies, CnC servers, or even phishing and drive-by malware websites. This feature rapidly swaps in and out DNS records with small time-to-live values, meaning that an array of IP addresses are hidden behind the Fully Qualified Domain Name (FQDN) for a single fast-flux mode. The double fast-flux mode changes both A and NS records of a domain. Furthermore, botnets can use a deterministic Random Domain Name Generator (RDNG) to hinder sinkholing. For this to work, botmasters must register the domains before they are generated. A RDNG is a basic algorithm. If understood, it may be possible to sinkhole bot traffic by anticipating the domain's registration, pointing DNS records to controlled sinkhole servers. However, some malware might include blacklists of known vendor subnets to prevent this. In such a case, it is more effective to set up a proxy or use the same fast-flux technique. To make things worse, CnC servers can be spread throughout various nations, thus crossing jurisdictional bounds and creating legal issues. In addition, the emergence of cloud computing has made it easy to acquire on-demand servers. That, combined with bulletproof hosting and the botnet defenses described above, makes hunting CnC servers a tricky and challenging task.

Carna botnet

A recent anonymous study [33] showed how to use a botnet for added scientific value. An Internet census of the entire Internet Protocol version 4 (IPv4) address space was presented, aiming at collecting network statistics. But to achieve that in practical time, the researcher used the so-called Carna botnet, composed of thousands of insecure embedded devices reachable from the Internet, rather than being behind a firewall or Network Address Translation (NAT). Simple `telnet` login combinations (e.g., root:root or passwordless) on routers from vendors like Cisco and Juniper were sufficient to install a small binary—a worrying industry-wide phenomenon. On one hand, the study changes the widespread notion of botnets as evil. On the other, the way it was collated is highly illegal in most countries and may fall under Articles 2 and 5 of the Cybercrime Convention [34]. The author confessed good intentions and omitted the source of the study, and thus the legal consequences in this matter cannot be determined.

Wordpress botnet

Recently, cyber-criminals have explored the popular blogging platform WordPress to build a large botnet with potentially over 90,000 nodes in a couple of days [35]. This achievement was possible because most WordPress-based websites have a default username "admin" with weak passwords like "123456," so cracking them by brute force was easy.

Bitcoin botnets

Although quite new, bitcoin is already a popular digital currency. After its value increased to over $100, what followed was not surprising. Malware for mining bitcoins was spotted—a form of currency theft. First, a malicious campaign on Skype pointed towards malware going after bitcoin wallets [36]. Then, bitcoins were directly targeted [37]. A dropper would download the mining payload from a file hosting service. Generating bitcoins is based on complicated mathematics processing. Because of this, the malware is easily detected by checking Central Processing Unit (CPU) usage. Another malware was discovered [38] that receives CnC commands but uses a legitimate mining application.

Good old DDoS

DDoS attacks are making a comeback as actively as they once were. Prolexic reported [39] a steep increase of 718 percent on bandwidth-related attacks, moving from 5.9 Gbps in Q4 2012 to 48.25 Gbps in Q1 2013. These findings, together with the 32.4 Mpps statistic, make blackholing mitigation techniques nonviable. In March 2013, Spamhaus was under the fiercest DDoS attack ever. The attack caused quite a commotion in the media and the industry. CloudFlare diluted an impressive bombardment of 300 Gbps [40] against Spamhaus—a mark that became iconic. Such a high bit rate was attained through DNS reflection and amplification by querying open DNS resolvers around the world with small-sized `ANY` questions. In return, large-sized responses would be redirected to the target spoofed IP address.

Phishing and spam

Email spam is undoubtedly one of the greatest cyber-weapons. Good mass mail, such as newsletters, is characterized as non-spam (also known as ham). Mass mail carrying malicious attachments or images with Uniform Resource Locators (URLs) or text URLs pointing to malware or phishing servers is characterized as spam. Tricky social engineering methods fool email readers into opening such attachments or clicking on those URLs. Some 91 percent of targeted attacks involve spear-phishing emails, 94 percent of which have malicious email attachments [41]. Spam numbers have been decreasing for the past few years, but an increase was witnessed in early 2013: 97.4 billion spam emails and 973 million malware emails were sent worldwide each day, almost double the number tallied at the end of the previous year [42].

Email is a main tool for businesses but also a doorway for infiltrating corporate networks. Because software can remain unpatched for some time, some vulnerabilities can still be exploited by malware spammed years later. Malicious binaries are usually encapsulated within files of vulnerable programs or zip archives. They are not directly attached to messages because email gateways and spam filters usually block such attempts. For example, Gmail does not allow attachment of any executable file, compressed or not.

Year-round spam is about spoofed brands, mostly pharmaceuticals [7]. The *Kelihos* botnet was used for that purpose, sending enormous spam waves without regard for spam filters [43]. This is an old technique to maximize email throughput: if 99.99 percent gets blocked, the 0.01 percent that is not blocked still accounts for many emails. Spammers also take advantage of real-life events for improving their effectiveness, such as the tax season or a gadget launch, or unexpected events like the pope's election. The recent Boston Marathon bombing [44] is a perfect example. Moreover, malware and phishing websites are usually set up on generic Top-Level Domains (TLDs) or on domains belonging to countries where cybersecurity laws are not stringent [45].

Beyond common email spam, SMS spam has become more frequent due to the increase in mobile devices. SMS messages are combined with phishing scams, such as promotional lures or advanced fee frauds. A particular spam campaign in Europe [46] has been active for several months with profit intents. Social networks, namely, Facebook, are also targeted for credentials theft [47] or credit card information [48]. Twitter widely uses short URLs because of space constraints. Fake Twitter profiles spam tweets or direct messages with long URLs hidden behind shorter services [49]. PayPal phishing scams were also on the rise during the initial months of 2013 [42].

Another spam profit-oriented technique consists of increasing the value of pre-bought penny stocks that are typically traded at low prices. Pump-and-dump spam advertises cheap targeted shares with a twist: also spamming that the company is on the verge of success. Unsuspecting individuals buy a portion of shares, and stock values rise momentarily. Then the spammers sell their stocks at higher prices. This technique has not been used for a while, but it is now making a massive comeback [42,50].

In general, phishing targets popular user platforms, and massive spam volumes are returning. Because spam mail with attachments tend to stand out among legitimate mail, spam filters are more likely to block it. While spam with attachments accounts for only 3 percent of all spam [7], spam with URLs is on the rise [51].

Vulnerabilities: The long exploitable holes

Vulnerabilities are a headache for system administrators. Upgrading a vulnerable operating system in a production environment is not straightforward because it may be supporting critical services or applications. Even so, patching must be considered carefully before committing to it. Vulnerabilities were the real story of 2012 reported Cluley at Sophos [3]. Indeed, mobile vulnerabilities are increasing [52]. Humans are not error-free, and software holes keep re-emerging. The following sections discuss vulnerabilities management, zero-days, and noteworthy vulnerable software.

Vulnerabilities management

In the security field, vulnerabilities are formally and officially described through a Common Vulnerabilities and Exposures (CVE) identifier [53], which has been a baseline index for evaluating tools and resources online since 1999. The National Vulnerability Database (NVD) contains a total of over 50,000 records of vulnerabilities. The NVD is the responsibility of the National Institute of Standards and Technology (NIST), while MITRE is its main CVE Numbering Authority (CNA). CVE management is nevertheless a collaboration among several vendors, third-party coordinators, and researchers. Other initiatives, like the Open Source Vulnerability Database (OSVDB), which was created in 2002 for the security community, already contains over 90,000 entries. This initiative clearly shows that some want vulnerability management to be in the hands of the community rather than a few people selected by the government.

Zero-day vulnerabilities

In the realm of vulnerabilities, zero-days are particularly important and can be alarming when exploited in the wild. A zero-day vulnerability is one unknown to the vendor and is most likely spotted when being exploited in the wild by malware. A watering hole campaign targeting older versions of Microsoft Internet Explorer [54] exploited the use-after-free zero-day identified as CVE-2012-4792. If fake objects could be allocated in the heap via heap spraying, the browser would call a function of a previously freed object, which would point to an attacker-controlled shellcode. Since then, many other exploits of the same vulnerabilities in Internet Explorer were discovered; these were eventually patched in the cumulative update MS13-037 on a patch Tuesday [55]. On the same day, Adobe also corrected many flaws for Flash. In total, 11 zero-days have been identified when these programs, along with Adobe Reader and Oracle Java [56], were exploited. This is quite a high number.

Noteworthy vulnerable software

When discussing vulnerabilities, various exploits and subsequent attacks come to mind. Typically, the intent of a front-end hole exploit is to gain access to back-end system servers, notably, databases. Popular attack vectors include Structured Query Language Injection (SQLi) and Cross-Site Scripting (XSS), and others with broken authentication and session management schemes [57]. Popular software is often the most scrutinized, and it is not surprising that flaws were found in them. The Web has become a streamlined attack vector, and thus holes in Web applications, browsers, plugins, and other sorts of software are critical for malware and hackers. Adobe Flash and Reader are among the top three most vulnerable, along with Java [52]. For the latter, a patch [58] addressing 50 vulnerabilities successively found in early 2013 was issued. Amaong browsers, Apple Safari, Google Chrome, and Mozilla Firefox rank as the top three most vulnerable.

Parallels Plesk Panel was recently found to be vulnerable to remote code execution. An exploit for spawning a shell was quickly disclosed. Not surprisingly, an Internet Relay Chat (IRC) botnet exploiting this vulnerability was found [59]. Although it was shut down, other botnets may appear. Also worrisome are long-standing vulnerabilities that are not patched. For example, Schneider Electric took 18 months to patch some product holes [60].

Data breach: A faulty containment

Cybersecurity is about protecting systems, but incident response is also about containment and eradication. In the case of data breaches, cybersecurity professionals should respond accordingly and make the necessary system modifications to prevent further breaches. This section discusses data breaches from three standpoints: cyber-attacks, unintentional data leakage, and whistleblowers. Current trends are discussed at the end.

Cyber-attacks

Cyber-attacks in the realm of data breach come from external entities, and such breaches occurred in the first half of 2013. Evernote issued a service-wide password reset for 50 million users after experiencing a network breach that potentially leaked usernames, emails, and encrypted passwords [61]. Twitter [62] did the same when 250,000 users' data got compromised. Drupal also experienced this [63]. In particular, and quite different from other attacks, a hacker was able to penetrate a military database containing sensitive information [64]. A cyber-attack originating from China and targeting *The New York Times* lasted four months [65]. The network was breached, and so was data used to access employees' computers. This attack might be related to the Chinese APT recently uncovered by Mandiant [66]. The case of Mat Honan [67] is also worth mentioning. Some culprit was able to telephonically extract little pieces of sensitive data from Amazon and Apple support, and then wipe out all of Honan's Apple devices, revealing a data breach at a smaller but no less dangerous scale.

Unintentional data leakage

Human error and system glitches drive nearly two-thirds of data breaches, according to a recent survey [68]. In 2013, privacy breaches of the Health Insurance Portability and Accountability Act (HIPAA) were common. A hospital employee accidentally uploaded over 1,000 patients' personal information onto the hospital public website [69]. The leak was only detected some two months later. An incident at a health center affected almost 1,700 patients after a workstation infected with malware copied health records off premises. Finally, unattended or lost hardware can also lead to data leakage. This was the case with over 14,000 students' social security numbers lost on a portable hard drive that sat on a college computer for two days.

Whistleblowers

The possibility of an insider turning rogue is always present. Malicious insiders, inside persons, informants, and whistleblowers are all capable of leaking data to the outside. These types of data breach often involve more sensitive types of data that are under a national security umbrella.

In fact, the government industry ranks first in data breach [70]. The most polemic case in late years is the one of Julian Assange, founder of WikiLeaks. WikiLeaks exposes large sets of secret information provided by anonymous sources. More recently, a former National Security Agency (NSA) employee, Edward Snowden, leaked the so-called NSA PRISM project [71], which has been causing quite a sensation. Snowden now finds himself in the same boat as Assange, searching refuge and political asylum. Schneier [72], a field expert, supports the need for whistleblowers in order to protect people from the abuse of power.

Trends

According to Verizon, in 2012, 98 percent of data breaches were originated by external agents, mainly through some form of hacking—a number that has been continuously growing [73]. Another relevant figure is the 61 percent of breaches caused by a combination of hacking and malware, both mainly going after credentials and cards data. But theft or loss accounted for 36 percent of all data breaches in 2013, surpassing hacking, according to Symantec [74]. Breaches in the healthcare sector rose in 2012 [70,73] , and so far the trend continues [74]. A good omen for cybersecurity in terms of data breaches is their cost, which has been on a downward trajectory for two years [68]. It has been steadily falling because organizations have acknowledged breaches and improved incident response and systems protection.

Cyber-war, the latest war front

Cyberspace has become the fifth domain of war, along with land, sea, air, and outer space [75]. In the vain hope of avoiding protests that use the Internet, some nations decide to prevent access to it. Culture, censorship, religion, and politics all play key roles in this decision. The Great Firewall of China blocks social networks like Facebook and YouTube, and even Google. In North Korea, the Internet is available only to a handful of people, mostly government and military personnel. Such utter control shapes user surfing habits in those countries and restricts them greatly, if not totally.

Similarly, cyber-war introduces complications concerning the scope of laws of war, such as applying lawful combatancy to cyber-warriors [76]. Lately, several nations have been involved in disputes over cyberspace. From our analysis, the United States, China, Israel, Syria, South Korea, India, and Norway have either been victims or perpetrators of some sort of cyber-war. Attacks shifting to critical sectors like energy [77] or oil [13,78] production were also witnessed. This section takes up the topic of underground cyber-criminality and then focuses on the current state od cyber-war and hacktivism. The section ends with an overview of developments by governments with regard to cybersecurity and cyber-warfare.

The underground cyber-crime industry

Cyber-crime was once an activity of isolated individuals, but the underground is now crowded with organized criminal gangs. It is as if the classical gangsters and crime lords, who once counterfeited and smuggled drugs, now make malware, sell it, and perform strategic cyber-attacks in exchange for money. A new crime class has emerged, and nation-states must fight back this threat as well.

In the underground, cyber-crime is democratized. Malware, spam, and phishing campaigns aim at pocketing millions for their masterminds, and each gang member has a specific expertise: one writes the malware, another the spear-phishing email, another prepares the spam botnet, and so on. Like any other economy, the underground markets competitive solutions. Crime packs or exploit packs agglomerate onto a single software numerous functionalities for commanding a botnet or exploiting zero-days. Whoever is the quickest to implement exploits might as well win the day. Famous crime packs include BlackHole, ProPack and Sakura [79]. For example, the death of Margaret Thatcher was hastily used as a spam technique on BlackHole [80].

Cyber-criminals sell their solutions and services. Trend Micro provided [81] valuable insight into the Russian crimeware marketplace, which is one of the most dangerous in Eastern Europe. A pay-as-you-go business model is used, meaning that customers pay only for what it is used. Additionally, DDoS-as-a-Service (DDoSaaS) has been gaining popularity [82]. On top of that, products and services are sold cheap, while creating a multi-billion-dollar Cybercrime-as-a-Service (CaaS) economy [52]. When the *ZeuS* source code leaked in 2011, an open-source criminal project of one of the most prolific malwares ever was released. After that, variants started to show up on mobile devices [83] and on social networks as well [84].

Notably, an underground forum devoted to smuggling stolen credit card data was recently disabled in Vietnam [85]. It had already facilitated over $200 million worth of card fraud relating to over one million credit cards. Various worldwide agencies, including the FBI, jointly accomplished this deed—a good sign for international cooperation against cyber-crime. Nevertheless, it is predicted [27] that it is going to take time to fully address global cyber-crime effectively.

Advanced persistent threats

During the 1980s, PC revolution hackers were mostly teenagers, playing around with code, computers, and networks. They thought trespassing in neighbors' computers was something quite different from trespassing on neighbors' properties. But system administrators did not take such actions lightly, and saw them as vandals and criminals [86,87]. A pioneer incident of cyber-espionage related by Stoll [88] in the late 1980s confirms precisely this. He was able to trace the source of an attacker through the maze of telephone circuitry to an overseas country after 10 months, but only after struggling with three-letter agencies in the United States. None of them were willing to cooperate fully, either domestically or abroad. In the end, a German hacker who had been persistently active in cyber-espionage for almost two years, was discovered and sentenced for his crimes, including selling stolen data to the KGB.

Today, the goal of cyber-espionage is no different, except that its significance, technology, and methods have changed. A targeted attack consists of three phases [89]: intelligence gathering, threat modeling, and the attack itself. In the first half of 2013, four APT campaigns of note were uncovered by major security players.

Mandiant indicted a Chinese military unit that had been engaged in extensive cyber-espionage since 2004 [66]. This APT developed its own assault tools and malware, used hundreds of CnC servers and domains, and perpetrated several spear-phishing campaigns for stealing hundreds of terabytes from 141 countries, spanning 20 major industries. The news was acknowledged by the information security community, which started to search for signs of this APT. Tensions between China and other countries have followed, and since then, China has been under several attacks.

Operation Red October, as it was dubbed by Kaspersky [90], has been active for at least since 2007, targeting government and military sites in several countries. Interestingly, this botnet infrastructure uses a second layer of proxy servers before contacting the real CnC servers. Another APT campaign, dating back to 2005, has also been uncovered by Kaspersky [91]. A surveillance malware named *NetTraveler* is related to the *Travnet* botnet. Although its source has not been disclosed, perhaps due to insufficient evidence, the modus operandi of the group resembles that of the Chinese group. Various industries are targeted by both, and the attack vectors are similar. Greater *NetTraveler* activity has been observed in the past few years on high-profile victims.

Norman unveiled the Hangover group [92], an APT emanating from India. This APT attacked various countries and industries for some years, during which over 700 malware samples and hundreds of FQDNs were collected and analyzed. It was also discovered that the Hangover group was selling services on the underground, but preferred to install previously unknown backdoors on customer computers [93]. This APT has been linked with the Mac backdoor malware mentioned earlier.

Hacktivism

Hacktivism is an act of political, religious, or patriotic protest conceived by non-state groups driven by the desire to correct what they see as wrongful laws and corrupt governments. Notorious groups include LulzSec and Anonymous. Key members of the former have been arrested, and the group is now believed to be extinct, while the latter is globally spread. Hacktivists take actions against targeted computer infrastructures usually using popular, free tools, some considered "script kiddie" tools, to launch Denial of Service (DoS) attacks (e.g., the Low Orbit Ion Cannon [LOIC]), hack websites and put up defacement pages [94,95] or URL redirection, or even leak sensitive data [95]. Some tools are capable of automated cyber-attacks. Marketing stunts are used to gather a cyber-militia empowered by a common vision. Normally, hacktivism targets oppressed nations like Syria and Israel, in the name of stepping up for the oppressed people. In this case, ethical hacking seeks quality of life and world improvement.

Although hacktivists attacks are publicized beforehand, their outcome may or not be successful. For example, the operations dubbed #OpIsrael and #OpUSA (hashtags for "operation Israel," set, up to protest the Israeli policy toward the Palestinians, and for "operation USA," mounted to protest American foreign policy) had an overall low attack impact [96,97]. Sometimes sensitive attack information leaked onto paste sites (e.g., Pastebin) can be used by CERTs to prevent an attack. Still, the DDoS attacks experienced by US banks in late 2012 and early 2013 were strong, lowering their available bandwidth [98]. This corroborates the DDoS trend discussed earlier. Operations named #OpInnocence and #OpPedoHunt aim at stopping child abuse [99], while #OpGTMO opposes the Guantanamo Bay detention camp [100]. Interestingly enough, hackers gained access to the Twitter account of the Associated Press to post false information of explosions at the White House [101]. This momentarily sent the United States stock market into freefall.

Governments

The Stuxnet worm was a big government stone dropped into a lake. Specifically infecting uranium production equipment in nuclear-empowered nations is a clear sign of government peeking, but it was likely an illegal act of force [102]. It is unclear whether Iran, which was attacked with Stuxnet, has the right to strike back under the Geneva Convention—after all, cyber-war is a form of war if certain conditions are met [103]. This is, unfortunately, the tip of the iceberg. Stuxnet is an instance of a large malware saga that includes Duqu, Flame, and Gauss [104]. These mainly target Middle Eastern countries, pack numerous functionalities, and only run under specific conditions, but little is yet known about their true goals. The mysteriousness surrounding this saga raises suspicions pointing toward nation-state threats. Other high-profile attacks have been quite common. For example, compromised websites belonging to governments have been found to host malware [105,106].

Given the current state of cybersecurity, nations and enterprises are building response infrastructures and teaming up to meet the challenge. For example, in the United States and in Australia, General Electric is building cybersecurity centers [107] although the Australian state will be in charge of its new center [108]. Both are expected to open in late 2013. The Pentagon is assembling 13 teams capable of offensive cyber-operations and governed by a response framework giving them clear hacking authority [109]. In fact, the Commission on the Theft of American Intellectual Property [110] says that US companies should hack back at cyber-thieves. While the *Tallinn Manual on the International Law Applicable to Cyber Warfare* attempts to resolve the legal disputes of cyber-warfare, it controversially advises the approval of physical retaliation if data is destroyed or death is proved [111]. It also suggests that engagements be one-on-one in order to reduce collateral damage. A new bill currently being worked out on the United States aims to curb foreign threats [112]. In Spain, a bill draft authorizes the police to install malware on computers without the owners' knowledge [113]. Perhaps more concerning is the controversial NSA PRISM spy program [71]. Probably the first of its kind, it supposedly mines data from lawful backdoors on major Internet players like Google, Skype, and Facebook.

The industry is investing in cybersecurity to monitor domestic and foreign threats. One way to do this is by installing backdoors on targets. FinFisher is an industrial spy software capable of that. Indeed, a commercial surveillance software marketed through law enforcement channels for spying on dissidents is gaining recognition among governments, particularly under repressive regimes. Some of its samples have been extensively analyzed [114]. The HackingTeam provides a remote control solution for governments or agencies only. Essentially, it creates a spy botnet that can monitor targets on a variety of platforms, including mobile operating systems.

Lessons learned

Decades ago, cybersecurity was a minor topic. Once a thing of real spies, today, espionage can be conducted a common computer and at a great physical distance, but with a small communications latency. The cyberspace landscape has changed into a battlefield, shifting cybersecurity perceptions, maturing cyber-warfare, and concerning spearheaded nation-states. The welfare of computers, networks, the Internet, its users, and data is becoming a priority. Yet one thing Stoll noted years ago is still true today: security is a human problem; it cannot be solved by technical solutions alone. This means that security controls must adapt accordingly, but the mentality, awareness, and wisdom of the cyberspace stakeholders also has to be changed.

Our analysis shows that cyber-attacks and enterprise incidents routinely made headlines. This field morphs constantly, and because of that security professionals must respond at the same pace. It is a widespread opinion that hacktivism and cyber-espionage will continue to increase. Hacktivists do break the law and thereby are punishable. But are they the real concern for the future of cybersecurity, or are they more of a sensationalist stunt? The spotlight shines on them often, but the more severe threats and financial or data loss come from organized crime groups headquartered in Russia, Ukraine, China, or Brazil, and from state-sponsored APTs. Cyber-war is partially hype at the moment. So far it has not caused loss of life, and thus other threats currently outweigh cyber-warfare. Still, it is clear that nations are taking action and shaping the world of cyber-war. The United States is one of the pioneers in the field. It is of interest for the rest of the world to take action in the light of cybersecurity and create interchangeable guidelines to cooperatively and efficiently respond to incidents and cyber-engagements. The highest caliber of international cooperation to fight back against cyber-crime is needed. This includes agencies, teams, and lawful support.

The cyber-war hysteria will eventually fade away, and time will tell who becomes essential in the field. Nothing suggests that cyber-war is equivalent to nation-state conflicts, and thus it is entirely possible to envision a many-to-many engagement. Virtually anybody can participate, from individual hacktivists to companies to governments, including the latter possibly contracting cyber-criminals. It is also possible for cyber-threats to devolve into physical engagement.

Meanwhile, there is the need to monitor traffic at the Internet scale while maintaining user privacy; to monitor perimeter traffic at the enterprise scale; to keep analyzing malware, shut down botnets and pursue underground cyber-criminals—to exert oneself against cyber-threats. Digital surveillance provokes chilling thoughts, nonetheless.

References

[1] von Solms R, van Niekerk J. From information security to cyber security. Computers & Security 2013;38:97−102.

[2] Berson TA, Denning DE. Cyber Warfare. IEEE Secur Privacy 2011;9(5):13−5.

[3] Mansfield-Devine S. Security review: the past year. Computer Fraud & Security 2013;1:5−11.

[4] Kurbalija J. An introduction to internet governance. 5th ed. Diplo Foundation; 2012.

[5] Amoroso E. From the enterprise perimeter to a mobility-enabled secure cloud. IEEE Secur Privacy 2013;11(1):23−31.

[6] Websense. Threat Report. [Internet]. Available from: https://www.websense.com/content/websense-2013-threat-report.aspx; 2013.

[7] Cisco. 2013 Cisco Annual Security Report. [Internet]. Available from: http://www.cisco.com/en/US/prod/vpndevc/annual_security_report.html; 2013.

[8] Kessem LS. New commercial Trojan. #INTH3WILD: Meet beta bot. RSA Blog. Available from: <https://blogs.rsa.com/new-commercial-trojan-inth3wild-meet-beta-bot/>; 2013 [accessed Jun. 2013].

[9] Shah C. Skimmer botnet targets credit card payment terminals. McAfee Labs. Available from: <http://blogs.mcafee.com/mcafee-labs/vskimmer-botnet-targets-credit-card-payment-terminals>; 2013 [accessed Apr. 2013].

[10] Paganini P. Group-IB exclusive details on Kangoo botnet that hit Australian banks. Security Affairs Blog. Available from: <http://securityaffairs.co/wordpress/14444/cyber-crime/from-group-ib-kangoo-botnet-against-australian-banks.html>; 2013 [accessed May 2013].

[11] Romera R. Homemade browser targeting Banco do Brasil Users. TrendLabs Blog. Available from: <http://blog.trendmicro.com/trendlabs-security-intelligence/homemade-browser-targeting-banco-do-brasil-users/>; 2013 [accessed May 2013].

[12] McAfee. Threats Predictions. [Internet]. Available from: <http://www.mcafee.com/us/resources/reports/rp-threat-predictions-2013.pdf>; 2013.

[13] Reuters. Aramco says cyberattack was aimed at production. The New York Times. Available from: <http://www.nytimes.com/2012/12/10/business/global/saudi-aramco-says-hackers-took-aim-at-its-production.html?_r=0>; 2012 [accessed Jan. 2013].

[14] Yang K. Digital attack on Korean networks: WIPERS, time-bombs and Roman soldiers. Fortinet Blog. Available from: <http://blog.fortinet.com/digital-attack-on-korean-networks-wipers-time-bombs-and-roman-soldiers/>; 2013 [accessed Mar. 2013].

[15] Bermejo L. Backdoor wipes MBR, locks screen. TrendLabs Blog. Available from: <http://blog.trendmicro.com/trendlabs-security-intelligence/backdoor-wipes-mbr-locks-screen/>; 2013 [accessed Jun. 2013].

[16] Melick R. Recent spike in FBI ransomware striking worldwide. Webroot Blog. Available from: <http://www.webroot.com/blog/2013/05/23/recent-spike-in-fbi-ransomware-striking-worldwide/>; 2013 [accessed May 2013].

[17] Donohue B. Reveton ransomware adds password purloining function. Threatpost. Available from: <https://threatpost.com/reveton-ransomeware-adds-password-purloining-function>; 2013 [accessed May 2013].

[18] Apvrille A. 1,000 malicious Android samples per day. Fortinet Blog. Available from: <http://blog.fortinet.com/1-000-malicious-Android-samples-per-day/>; 2013 [accessed May 2013].

[19] F-Secure. Mobile threat report Q1 2013. [Internet]. Available from: <http://www.f-secure.com/static/doc/labs_global/Research/Mobile_Threat_Report_Q1_2013.pdf>; 2013.

[20] Lookout. State of Mobile Security. [Internet]. Available from: <https://www.lookout.com/resources/reports/state-of-mobile-security-2012>; 2012.

[21] Unuchek R. The most sophisticated android trojan. Securelist Blog. Available from: <https://www.securelist.com/en/blog/8106/The_most_sophisticated_Android_Trojan>; 2013 [accessed Jun. 2013].

[22] Stanescu B. Dorkbot malware infects facebook users: spies browser activities and grabs data. Bitdefender Labs. Available from: <http://www.hotforsecurity.com/blog/dorkbot-malware-infects-facebook-users-spies-browser-activities-and-grabs-data-6165.html>; 2013 [accessed May 2013].

[23] Wanve U. Turkish 'delete virus' targets facebook users. McAfee Labs. Available from: <http://blogs.mcafee.com/mcafee-labs/turkish-delete-virus-targets-facebook-users>; 2013 [accessed Apr. 2013].

[24] Tamir D. Twitter malware: spreading more than just ideas. Trusteer Blog. Available from: <https://www.trusteer.com/blog/twitter-malware-spreading-more-than-just-ideas>; 2013 [accessed Apr. 2013].

[25] Boutin J-I. Operation hangover: more links to the oslo freedom forum incident. ESET Blog. Available from: <http://www.welivesecurity.com/2013/06/05/operation-hangover-more-links-to-the-oslo-freedom-forum-incident/>; 2013 [accessed Jun. 2013].

[26] Ortega A. Your malware shall not fool us with those anti analysis tricks. AlienVault Labs. Available from: <http://www.alienvault.com/open-threat-exchange/blog/your-malware-shall-not-fool-us-with-those-anti-analysis-tricks>; 2012 [accessed Jan. 2013].

[27] Genes R. Trend micro predictions for 2013 and beyond: threats to business, the digital lifestyle, and the cloud. TrendLabs Blog. Available from: <http://blog.trendmicro.com/trendlabs-security-intelligence/predictions-for-2013/>; 2012 [accessed Jan. 2013].

[28] Wanve U. Travnet botnet controls victims with remote admin tool. McAfee Labs. Available from: <http://blogs.mcafee.com/mcafee-labs/travnet-botnet-controls-victims-with-remote-admin-tool>; 2013 [accessed May 2013].

[29] Smith B. Microsoft, financial services and others join forces to combat massive cybercrime ring. Microsoft News Center. Available from: <https://www.microsoft.com/en-us/news/press/2013/jun13/06-05dcupr.aspx>; 2013 [accessed Jun. 2013].

[30] Yaneza J. ZeuS/ZBOT malware shapes up in 2013. TrendLabs Blog. Available from: <http://blog.trendmicro.com/trendlabs-security-intelligence/zeuszbot-malware-shapes-up-in-2013/>; 2013 [accessed May 2013].

[31] Rossow C, Andriesse D, Werner T, StoneGross B, Plohmann D, Dietrich C J, et al. SoK: P2PWNED-Modeling and evaluating the resilience of peer-to-peer botnets. In: Proc of the 34th IEEE Symp on Security and Privacy; 2013; San Francisco, CA, USA. IEEE Computer Society, p. 1–15.

[32]   News on multibanker, features now a Jabber P2P functionality. Kleissner & Associates SRO. Blog; 2013.

[33]   Internet Census 2012: Port scanning /0 using insecure embedded devices. [Internet]. Available from: http://internetcensus2012.bitbucket.org/paper.html; 2012.

[34]   Valerie. Lawful botnet and Internet census: When law is not the case? [Internet]. Available from: <http://www.diplointernetgovernance.org/profiles/blogs/lawful-botnet-and-internet-census-when-law-is-not-the-case>; 2012

[35]   Liska A. Wordpress botnet explodes over weekend. Symantec Blog. Available from: <http://www.symantec.com/connect/blogs/wordpress-botnet-explodes-over-weekend>; 2013 [accessed Apr. 2013].

[36]   Bestuzhev D. An avalanche in skype. Securelist Blog. Available from: <https://www.securelist.com/en/blog/208194206/An_avalanche_in_Skype>; 2013 [accessed Apr. 2013].

[37]   Bestuzhev D. Skypemageddon by bitcoining. Securelist Blog. Available from: <https://www.securelist.com/en/blog/208194210/>; 2013 [accessed Apr. 2013].

[38]   Shah H. Delving deeply into a bitcoin botnet. McAfee Labs. Available from: <http://blogs.mcafee.com/mcafee-labs/delving-deeply-into-a-bitcoin-botnet>; 2013 [accessed May 2013].

[39]   Prolexic. Prolexic quarterly global DDoS attack report Q1 2013. [Internet]. Available from: <https://www.prolexic.com/knowledge-center-ddos-attack-report-2013-q1.html>; 2013.

[40]   Prince M. The DDoS that almost broke the internet. CloudFlare. Available from: <http://blog.cloudflare.com/the-ddos-that-almost-broke-the-internet>; 2013 [accessed Mar. 2013].

[41]   Trend Micro. Spear-phishing email: Most favored APT attack bait. [Internet]. Available from: <http://www.trendmicro.com/cloud-content/us/pdfs/security-intelligence/white-papers/wp-spear-phishing-email-most-favored-apt-attack-bait.pdf>

[42]   Commtouch. Internet threat trend report: April 2013. [Internet]. Available from: <http://www.commtouch.com/uploads/2013/04/Commtouch-Internet-Threats-Trend-Report-2013-April.pdf>; 2012.

[43]   Schultz J. Massive canadian pharmacy spam campaign. Cisco Blog 2013.

[44]   Williams C. Massive spam and malware campaign following the Boston tragedy. Cisco Blog. Available from: <http://blogs.cisco.com/security/massive-spam-and-malware-campaign-following-the-boston-tragedy/>; 2013 [accessed Apr. 2013].

[45]   Anti-Phishing Working Group. Global phishing survey: Trends and domains name use in 2 H 2012. [Internet]. Available from: <http://docs.apwg.org/reports/APWG_GlobalPhishingSurvey_2H2012.pdf>; 2013.

[46]   SMS phishing leads to an advance fee spam scam across Europe. Infosecurity Magazine. Available from: <http://www.infosecurity-magazine.com/view/32319/sms-phishing-leads-to-an-advance-fee-spam-scam-across-europe/>; 2013 [accessed May 2013].

[47]   White D, Christensen B. Facebook 'fan page verification program' phishing scam. Hoax-Slayer Blog. Available from: <http://www.hoax-slayer.com/fan-page-verification-scam.shtml>; 2013 [accessed May 2013].

[48]   Melgarejo AJ. Malware phishes with fake facebook security check page. TrendLabs Blog. Available from: <http://blog.trendmicro.com/trendlabs-security-intelligence/malware-phishes-with-fake-facebook-security-check-page/>; 2013 [accessed Apr. 2013].

[49]   Diaz V. Is digital marketing the new spam? Securelist Blog. Available from: <https://www.securelist.com/en/blog/208194237/Is_digital_marketing_the_new_spam>; 2013 [accessed Apr. 2013].

[50]   Muralidharan A. Increase in pump and dump stock spam. Symantec Blog. Available from: <http://www.symantec.com/connect/blogs/increase-pump-and-dump-stock-spam>; 2013 [accessed May 2013].

[51]   Patil S. Rise in URL spam. Symantec Blog. Available from: <http://www.symantec.com/connect/blogs/rise-url-spam>; 2013 [accessed May 2013].

[52]   Symantec. Internet security threat report 2013. [Internet]. Available from: <https://www.symantec.com/security_response/publications/threatreport.jsp>; 2013.

[53]   MITRE. CVE website. [Internet]. Available from: <https://cve.mitre.org/>; 2013.

[54] Symantec Security Response. Internet Explorer zero-day used in watering hole attack: Q&A. Symantec Blog. Available from: <http://www.symantec.com/connect/blogs/internet-explorer-zero-day-used-watering-hole-attack-qa>; 2012 [accessed Jan. 2013].

[55] Krebs B. Microsoft, adobe push critical security updates. KrebsOnSecurity Blog. Available from: <https://krebsonsecurity.com/2013/05/microsoft-adobe-push-critical-security-updates-2/>; 2013 [accessed May 2013].

[56] Symantec. First quarter zero-day vulnerabilities. Symantec Blog. Available from: <http://www.symantec.com/connect/blogs/2013-first-quarter-zero-day-vulnerabilities>; 2013 [accessed Apr. 2013].

[57] OWASP. The ten most critical Web application security risks. [Internet]. 2013. Available from:https://www.owasp.org/index.php/Top_10_; 2013.

[58] Oracle. Oracle Java SE critical patch update advisory. [Internet]. Apr. Available from: <http://www.oracle.com/technetwork/topics/security/javacpuapr2013-1928497.html>; 2013.

[59] RepoCERT. Botnet using Plesk vulnerability and takedown. Seclists Website. Available from: <http://seclists.org/fulldisclosure/2013/Jun/36>; 2013 [accessed Jun. 2013].

[60] Fisher D. Schneider patches 18-month-old SCADA bugs. Threatpost. Available from: <https://threatpost.com/schneider-patches-18-month-old-scada-bugs>; 2013 [accessed Jun. 2013].

[61] Engberg D. Service-wide Password Reset. Evernote Blog. Available from: <https://evernote.com/corp/news/password_reset.php>; 2013 [accessed May 2013].

[62] Lord B. Keeping our users secure. Twitter Blog. Available from: <https://blog.twitter.com/2013/keeping-our-users-secure>; 2013 [accessed Feb. 2013].

[63] Ross H. Reset your drupal.org password. Drupal Forum. Available from: <https://drupal.org/news/130529SecurityUpdate>; 2013 [accessed Jun. 2013].

[64] Zetter K. Hacker breached U.S. army database containing sensitive information on dams. Wired. Available from: <http://www.wired.com/threatlevel/2013/05/hacker-breached-dam-database/>; 2013 [accessed Jan. 2013].

[65] Perlroth N. Hackers in china attacked the Times for last 4 months. The New York Times. Available from: <http://www.nytimes.com/2013/01/31/technology/chinese-hackers-infiltrate-new-york-times-computers.html>; 2013 [accessed Feb. 2013].

[66] Mandiant. APT1: Exposing one of China's cyber espionage units. [Internet]/ Apr. Available from: <http://intelreport.mandiant.com/Mandiant_APT1_Report.pdf>; 2013.

[67] Honan M. How Apple and Amazon security flaws led to my epic hacking. Wired. Available from: <http://www.wired.com/gadgetlab/2012/08/apple-amazon-mat-honan-hacking/>; 2012 [accessed Jan. 2013].

[68] Ponemon Institute. 2013 cost of data breach study: Global analysis. Symantec Website. Available from: <http://www.symantec.com/about/news/resources/press_kits/detail.jsp?pkid=ponemon-2013>; 2013 [accessed May 2013].

[69] Sun News. Hospital discloses privacy breach. Sun News. Available from: <http://news.sonomaportal.com/2013/05/24/hospital-discloses-privacy-breach/>; 2013 [accessed May 2013].

[70] Check Point. Check point 2013 security report. [Internet]. Available from: <https://www.checkpoint.com/campaigns/security-report/>; 2013.

[71] Barton Gellman AB, Miller G. Edward Snowden comes forward as source of NSA leaks. The Washington Post. Available from: <http://articles.washingtonpost.com/2013-06-09/politics/39856642_1_extradition-nsa-leaks-disclosures>; 2013 [accessed Jun. 2013].

[72] Schneier B. Government secrets and the need for whistle-blowers. Schneier on Security Blog. Available from: <https://www.schneier.com/blog/archives/2013/06/government_secr.html>; 2013 [accessed Jun. 2013].

[73] Verizon. 2012 data breach investigations report. [Internet]. Available from: <http://www.verizonenterprise.com/DBIR/2012/>; 2012.

[74] Symantec. Symantec intelligence report. [Internet]. Available from : <http://www.symantec.com/connect/blogs/symantec-intelligence-report-may-2013>; 2013.

[75] Taddeo M. An analysis for a just cyber warfare. In CYCON: 4th International Conference on Cyber Conflict; 2012; Tallinn, Estonia. p. 1–10.

[76] Watts S. The notion of combatancy in cyber warfare. In CYCON: 4th Int Conf on Cyber Conflict; 2012; Tallinn, Estonia. p. 1–15.

[77] ICS-CERT. Monthly Monitor. [Internet]. Available from: <https://ics-cert.us-cert.gov/sites/default/files/ICS-CERT_Monitor_Jan-Mar2013.pdf>; 2013.

[78] Shauk Z. Rise in URL spam. Symantec Blogs. Available from: <http://www.symantec.com/connect/blogs/rise-url-spam>; 2013 [accessed May 2013].

[79] McAfee. McAfee threats report-fourth quarter 2012. [Internet]. 2013. Availabe from: <http://www.mcafee.com/us/resources/reports/rp-quarterly-threat-q4-2012.pdf.>

[80] Coronado C. Blackhole exploit kit leverages Margaret Thatcher's death. Trend Micro. Available from: <http://about-threats.trendmicro.com/us/spam/460/Blackhole+Exploit+Kit+Leverages+Margaret+Thatchers+Death>; 2013 [accessed Apr. 2013].

[81] Trend Micro. Russian underground 101. [Internet]. 2012. Available from: <http://www.trendmicro.com/cloud-content/us/pdfs/security-intelligence/white-papers/wp-russian-underground-101.pdf.>

[82] Musthaler L. DDoS-as-a-service? You betcha! It's cheap, it's easy, and it's available to anyone. Security Bistro. Available from: <http://www.securitybistro.com/?p=4121>; 2012 [accessed Jan. 2013].

[83] Trustwave. 2013 global security report. [Internet]. Available from: <https://www2.trustwave.com/2013GSR.html>; 2013.

[84] Schwartz M.J. Zeus bank malware surges on Facebook. InformationWeek. Available from: <http://www.informationweek.com/security/attacks/zeus-bank-malware-surges-on-facebook/240156156>; 2013 [accessed Jun. 2013].

[85] Eleven arrests as global investigation dismantles criminal web forum. SOCA Website. Available from: <http://www.soca.gov.uk/news/552-eleven-arrests-as-global-investigation-dismantles-criminal-web-forum>; 2013 [accessed Jun. 2013].

[86] Stoll C. Stalking the wily hacker. Commun ACM 1988;31(5):484–97.

[87] Thompson K. Reflections on trusting trust. Commun ACM 1984;27(8):761–3.

[88] Stoll C. The cuckoo's egg: Tracking a spy through the maze of computer espionage. New York, NY: Doubleday; 1989.

[89] Sood A, Enbody R. Targeted cyberattacks: A superset of advanced persistent threats. IEEE Secur Privacy 2013;11(1):54–61.

[90] GReAT. "Red October" diplomatic cyber attacks investigation. Securelist Blog. Available from: <http://www.securelist.com/en/analysis/204792262/Red_October_Diplomatic_Cyber_Attacks_Investigation>; 2013 [accessed Jan. 2013].

[91] Kaspersky Lab. The NetTraveler. [Internet]. 2013. Available from: <http://www.securelist.com/en/downloads/vlpdfs/kaspersky-the-net-traveler-part1-final.pdf.>

[92] Norman. Operation hangover: Norman unveiling an Indian cyberattack infrastructure. [Internet]. 2013. Available from: <http://enterprise.norman.com/resources/files/Unveiling_an_Indian_Cyberattack_Infrastructure.pdf.>

[93] Fagerland S. The hangover report. Norman Blog. Available from: <http://blogs.norman.com/2013/security-research/the-hangover-report>; 2013 [accessed May 2013].

[94] Kovacs E. 20 Chinese government sites defaced by anonymous Algeria hacker Charaf Anons. Softpedia. Available from: <http://news.softpedia.com/news/28-Chinese-Government-Sites-Defaced-by-Anonymous-Algeria-Hacker-Charaf-Anons-339986.shtml>; 2013 [accessed Mar. 2013].

[95] Kredo A. Anonymous-linked groups hack Israeli websites, release personal data. Washington Free Beacon. Available from: <http://freebeacon.com/the-cyber-front/>; 2013 [accessed Mar. 2013].

[96] Lake E. Why #OpIsrael was an #OpFail. The Daily Beast. Available from: <http://www.thedailybeast.com/articles/2013/04/08/why-opisrael-was-an-opfail.html>; 2013 [accessed Apr. 2013].

[97] Schultz J. The effects of #OpUSA. Cisco Blog. Available from: <http://blogs.cisco.com/security/the-effects-of-opusa/>; 2013 [accessed May 2013].

[98] Rudger A. Understanding the impact of Web attacks-The user perspective. Keynote Blog. Available from: <http://blogs.keynote.com/the_watch/2013/04/understanding-the-impact-of-web-attacks-the-user-perspective.html>; 2013 [accessed Apr. 2013].

[99] Bigs. Anonymous leaked massive pedophile d0x in response to child s*x rings. Cyberwarzone. Available from: <http://cyberwarzone.com/anonymous-leaked-massive-pedophile-d0x-response-child-sx-rings>; 2013 [accessed Mar. 2013].

[100] Heller J. Guantanamo Bay shuts off wi-fi after Anonymous threatens #OpGTMO attack on prison camp. International Business Times. Available from: <http://www.ibtimes.com/guantanamo-bay-shuts-wi-fi-after-anonymous-threatens-opgtmo-attack-prison-camp-1273041>; 2013 [accessed May 2013].

[101] Moore H, Roberts DAP. Twitter hack causes panic on Wall Street and sends Dow plunging. The Guardian. Available from: <http://www.theguardian.com/business/2013/apr/23/ap-tweet-hack-wall-street-freefall>; 2013 [accessed Apr. 2013].

[102] Zetter K. Legal experts: Stuxnet attack on Iran was illegal 'act of force'. Wired. Available from: <http://www.wired.com/threatlevel/2013/03/stuxnet-act-of-force/>; 2013 [accessed Mar. 2013].

[103] Gossels J. Cyber war, this is not. SCMagazine. Available from: <http://www.scmagazine.com/cyber-war-this-is-not/article/284430/>; 2013 [accessed Apr. 2013].

[104] Kaspersky Lab. Gauss: Nation-state cyber-surveillance meets banking Trojan. SecureList Blog. Available from: <http://www.securelist.com/en/blog/208193767/Gauss_Nation_state_cyber_surveillance_meets_banking_Trojan>; 2012 [accessed Jan. 2013].

[105] Santos R. BANKER malware hosted in compromised Brazilian government sites. TrendLabs Blog. Available from: <http://blog.trendmicro.com/trendlabs-security-intelligence/banker-malware-hosted-in-compromised-brazilian-government-sites/>; 2013 [accessed May 2013].

[106] To D. Compromised US government webpage used zero-day exploit. TrendLabs Blog. Available from: <http://blog.trendmicro.com/trendlabs-security-intelligence/compromised-us-government-webpage-used-zero-day-exploit/>; 2013 [accessed May 2013].

[107] General Electric. GE information security technology center. [Internet]. 2013. Available from: http://www.ge.com/careers/ge-information-security-technology-center.

[108] Benitez J. Australia's new cyber security center will be 'fully operational by late 2013.. NATOSource News Blog. Available from: <http://www.atlanticcouncil.org/blogs/natosource/australias-new-cyber-security-center-will-be-fully-operational-by-late-2013>; 2013 [accessed Jan. 2013].

[109] Brito H. Pentagon creating "rules of engagement" for responding to advanced attackers. Mandiant M-Unition. Available from: <https://www.mandiant.com/blog/pentagon-creating-rules-engagement-responding-advanced-attackers/>; 2013 [accessed Apr. 2013].

[110] Commission on the theft of American intellectual property. The Report of the Commission on the Theft of American Intellectual Property. [Internet]. Available from: <http://ipcommission.org/report/IP_Commission_Report_052213.pdf>; 2013.

[111] Colon M. 2 minutes on: The rule of war. SCMagazine. Available from: <http://www.scmagazine.com/2-minutes-on-the-rule-of-war/article/288854/>; 2013 [accessed May 2013].

[112] Kerr D. US government to propose bill targeting foreign hackers. CNET. Available from: <http://news.cnet.com/8301-1009_3-57587942-83/u.s-government-to-propose-bill-targeting-foreign-hackers/>; 2013 [accessed Jun. 2013].

[113] Rial N. Spanish police might use Trojans to spy computers. New Europe. Available from: <http://www.neurope.eu/article/spanish-police-might-use-trojans-spy-computers>; 2013 [accessed Jun. 2013].

[114] Marquis-Boire M, Marczak B, Guarnieri C, Scott-Railton J. The Commercialization of Digital Spying. [Internet]. Available from: <https://citizenlab.org/storage/finfisher/final/fortheireyesonly.pdf>; 2013.

A Paradigm Shift in Cyberspace Security

26

Mihai Horia Zaharia

"Gheorghe Asachi" Technical University, Iaşi, România

INFORMATION IN THIS CHAPTER

- Computer aided decision support
- Intelligent agents
- Information security
- Information retrieval
- Data mining

INTRODUCTION

The term "cyberspace" was introduced into the science fiction community by William Gibson, [1], but with a different meaning than the current one. Today the term usually refers to the common space created by any combination of hardware and software that is at the base of the Internet and offers support for any facility offered to the user. The various faces of cyberspace are similar to the main directions of Internet application development, which are: networked media and search systems, cloud computing, Internet services, trustworthy computing, and the "future Internet."

Cyberspace consists of hardware, operating systems, communication networks, and applications. There is a supplementary layer composed of the frameworks that allow the execution of applications. When an application is developed, the security aspect of the application may be analyzed at each stage of design and also at the interfaces between layers or tiers. In fact, a security architecture design overlaps with the main design of the application, involving a system security plan, some control specifications, security documentation, and assessment of evidence. All of these are needed for a proper life cycle of the secured application, beginning from the first tests and finishing with long-term maintenance [2]. The security measures can be applied and enforced at any layer, yet the user remains the main weak link in the security management chain.

Cyber-terrorism

Nowadays, there are two types of war that are silently growing. One is the economic war, whose main actors are countries, corporations, and the mob. An important component of this war is related

443

to the cyber-war. Maintaining global equilibrium is difficult enough, but some rules do exist due to the fact that the main purpose is to incorporate the enemy, not to destroy it. The other type of war is more dangerous, because its basis is religious. Typical of this war is the fact that nothing but total destruction of the enemy is accepted [3]. The main idea here is to destroy the enemy, regardless of the cost. This can have a major impact on local economies and sometimes even on the global economy because of globalization.

"Cyber-terrorism" is a relatively new term in the area of computing. It was first defined by Collin [4], who suggested that cyber-terrorism appears at the convergence between the cyberspace and terrorism. Hoffman [5] further clarified the concept. In his view, cyber-terrorism represents a form of violence or a threat of violence that has a political purpose and uses computer-related techniques. The importance of this new threat was partially neglected until the events of September 11, 2001.

After analyzing all the information collected about the September 11 events, the experts proved that the terrorist cells used information technologies to hide and coordinate their activities [6]. Since then, in the United States, cyber-terrorism began to represent a serious problem, and many resources were diverted to create new strategies for fighting it. In this context, US security agencies have found that local organizations such as the ones who fight for the supremacy of white American Christians, for protecting the environment, or for animal rights, have also begun to adopt these new tactics [7]. The fight against information technology(IT)-related criminal activities has escalated, and a new concept of cyber-warfare has emerged.

In Europe, compared to the US and Asia, these problems have been perceived as less important. As a result, mechanisms to fight cyberterrorism have been slow to develop. In Great Britain, cyber-warfare has been considered a problem only since 2008. This was the moment when the UK government began to develop and introduce a set of laws related to information security problems. The concept of digital police emerged in the process [8].

Some authors feel that the new wave of cyber-criminal activity is related to the great changes that appeared after the destabilization of the USSR and the fall of the Berlin Wall [9]. One possible explanation of this phenomenon is that the mass of high skilled IT programmers trained in the former Soviet Union began to be used by the Russian mob. However, this is not enough to justify the new magnitude of the attacks. In fact, the increase in cyber-criminality simply marks the transition from the tactics and techniques of the Cold War, to the arms of the newly adopted information society model.

A shift from the Cold War paradigm to a cyber-warfare paradigm is not a surprise, since war is conducted using current available technologies, and nowadays many highly developed societies are informational. The surprise is that the security measures taken when most of the vital systems were designed have been insufficient. In most cases, the reason is not the lack of procedures or know-how, but the pressure to decrease the costs. Nowadays, this cost optimization to the detriment of security are proving very dangerous, since the new tactics used in modern cyber-warfare can drive a society to an insurmountable level of loss. An example is the economic problems of Japan after the nuclear facilities used in electricity production were closed for other reasons than an attack. The effects on the Japanese economy were disastrous and are still not completely managed.

Cyber-attacks can be targeted to any available level of cyberspace model, depending on the final objective of the attackers. For example, the economic loss caused by the September 11 events was negligible, but the psychological impact was huge. This was a clear guerrilla tactic, where a small force produced significant results. Other types of attacks may target critical economic objectives like the energy system, production systems, or, in the worst case, the military infrastructure. These could lead to immediate results having huge costs.

A particularly insidious kind of attack is the economic one. Here, the cyber-warfare hot spot is shifted in most cases from governmental organizations to corporations. This is because transnational corporations administer funds and research facilities that are often greater than what most countries in the world can afford.

There are, in fact, two overlapping areas of cyber-war. One is related to cyber-terrorism, which is usually specific to Islamic fundamentalist groups or other organizations that use guerilla tactics. The other, broader war is for resources of any kind (raw, but also informational) that have two main objectives: economic and informational. Between the two, the more important one is the informational war, because winning access to raw materials is also, finally, a question of having the right information at the right moment.

A security paradigm shift in cyberspace

Within an organization, different types of risks can be identified: strategic, safety, program management and reputation, supply chain, legal, political, investment, budgetary risk, and, finally, information security risk [2]. It is difficult to justify the request for more organizational resources to be assigned for handling information security risks, since the other risks, in most cases, have the same (or maybe greater) importance. And the organization's staff must maintain a balance in addressing all the types of risks. Yet there is a need to increase the resources for IT security. In the short term, nothing significant can be done. The only solution is to change the environment and the long-term organizational politics related to informational risks so the increased costs can be distributed over a longer period of time. Yet this approach may still prove insufficient if changes are not made in the paradigm used to control the security risks.

How should the paradigm shift be conducted? The basic ideas are not new.

Under the Federal Information Management Act (FISMA), risk management of information security overlaps many other activities, including the enterprise architecture, capital planning, investment control, and system development [2]. This centralized approach has the advantage of establishing and maintaining a tight control. Yet at the federal level or international corporation level, the organizational complexity is so high that it is almost impossible to have a detailed representation, from the security point of view, about what is happening everywhere. This is due to the human lack of ability to handle large amounts of information without the risk of excluding some critical aspects from analysis. Introducing an *intelligent agent* into the equation may help experts at any organizational level in maintaining tight control. The agent-based approach can be integrated into FISMA.

Until now, a consistent part of Internet protection strategy was based on users' presumed knowledge about the subject. But most cyber-attacks that succeed are successful due to users' lack of knowledge or disregard of security protocols. The human-computer interface already tries to adapt people to computers and also to the use of expert systems. So, creating a *cyber-assistant* for any user should be more efficient than trying to increase the user's knowledge regarding the subject.

Intelligent agents in security auditing

The use of artificial intelligence is not new in the field of security. The first uses of an expert system in risk evaluation were related to business needs; the main interest was in sales optimization and it was designed to help the manager [10]. Intelligent agents have already been used for risk assessment with good results [11]. Another application, at the organizational level, of intelligent agents concerns multi-agent self-organization models with applications in operational enterprise management [12]. There are also tools for document flow processing used to help organization managers in decision making [13,14].

In the past decade, new concepts like Agent Based Artificial Immune System (ABAIS) have emerged in security-related research [15]. Regarding Internet security, all of the important techniques from the field of AI have been used. The increase in available computing power gives designers the possibility of analyzing a combination of two or more AI algorithms, in order to improve the response of the system in antivirus detection [16]. Any Internet security solution also includes a firewall. As a result, some research has been done on improving the monitoring of the information flow using intelligent agents. Here, the idea of cooperation among various intrusion detection systems (IDSs) was introduced [17]. Some approaches are intended to make estimations about the global information threat level for a system or organization [18].

The main parties involved in the security cycle are the chief information security officer, the stakeholder review team, and the executive decision maker [19]. An intelligent agent system may be deployed at any of these levels. The centralized approach can be used in expert system implementation as part of an larger information retrieval system, but its limits are especially related to the speed of inserting new rules in the database and also to their diversity. As the IT integration of a society increases, so do its dynamics. An approach based on a local expert system will not give the speed and flexibility required to quickly adapt to the changes in cyberspace.

Security cyber-assistant system

The cyber-assistant system may be used by any category of users, no matter their expertise in information security field. For the common user, the system will interact with its local internet security solution and offer supplementary information (even portions of current laws) when a decision regarding system security or law breaking must be made. A common use of the system may be when the user accesses sites that index media content that is prohibited to free distribution. Also, downloading illegal applications or keys for them may enter in the area of system messages.

For experts, such as the chief of IT-related security or other security staff, the system will act significantly differently. At their level, there are already databases with knowledge and specific security protocols that must be applied. So the system will provide periodic executive summaries generated by combining data mining from local databases with information retrieval from official or unofficial security-related channels.

Of course the system may be used, if legal agreements allow, to report any suspicious activity by a common user. In special cases, laws like the Electronic Communications Privacy Act in US and its variation in the UE or UK give the government full access to people's communications. User surveillance would be done mostly in organizations, because the normal user of the Internet may reject this option. Yet the advantage of the system in decreasing common user cyber-criminality is enough to justify its consideration.

The proposed system will have two goals. One is to search and retrieve from the Internet any news related to security breaches. The other is to gather or extract facts and rules for the inference engine that supports security management of the organization, or the user.

Regarding first functionality of the system, it may seem unnecessary to search and retrieve information related to security of information, especially of new breaches, when there are a lot of national and international organizations (e.g., CERT) with these goals. Unfortunately, there is another world outside these organizations that is more dynamic and more dangerous: the hacker's world. Most of the security-related approaches are based on the fixed idea that if enough force is used and enough constraints are enforced, the activity of the hackers can be really controlled. This seems to be a classical military approach. Years of efforts have already proven its lack of efficiency. A more diplomatic solution will be to discreetly intercept the hackers' social networks where the latest news related to security breaches appears. With this time advantage, a contingency plan within the organization can be developed. As a result, the system must search (using intelligent agents) any underground network that can be accessed or intercepted using an application.

This is possible because the idea is not to discover the real origin of information, the agent will have no problem using http or https over the anonymizer proxies that are used in most cases by the underground. The simulation of a browser signature in order to trick a target system that a real user is behind the request is already a common task. The second source of information, but with lower quality and a high volume of data, is related to the social networks. The ENCHELON system uses the same approach, but no organization can afford its operational costs [20]. As a result, new, cheaper ways of performing the same task must be found (e.g., like using intelligent agents). A filtered file containing a digest of all news will be provided by joining all the data extracted from any source.

As is previously mentioned the other goal of the system will be to help the security officer in better handling the increased flow of news, laws, and regulations related to his work. To do this, an intelligent agent will be placed at the output of any information source. This is necessary because, otherwise, the problem of translating natural language will make the solution unfeasible. The agent will have a dictionary with key terms and some knowledge about the format of the document. In this case, there is a good chance that the most important facts are isolated and extracted from the document. This will lead to an executive summary of the critical information.

In Figure 26.1, the structure of an intelligent agent that will provide the officer with the needed information is presented. As can be seen, the structure is very simple. The agent can be executed without problems on any type of computing node, including mobile devices.

The informational flow that must be analyzed by the main system (see Figure 26.2) is the document library, which contains all the security policies, laws, and regulations used by the company. A quick index table of all the documents will be created.

In Figure 26.2, the main structure of system is presented. It is created around the intelligent agent framework. The framework will provide dedicated agents to do information retrieval, interfacing with users, data mining, and other tasks needed to maintain the system's scalability, such as the agent for load balancing or the agent for communication security.

The other module is the communication one. In this approach, a communication agent and a communication module are proposed as separate entities in order to increase security, since this

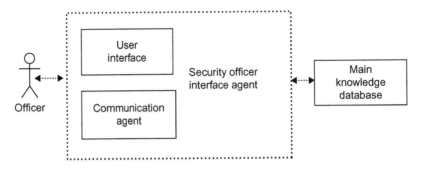

FIGURE 26.1

Security officer interface agent.

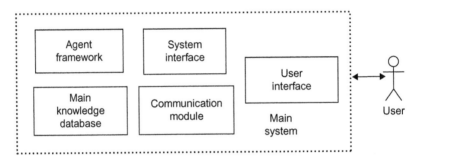

FIGURE 26.2

Main system structure.

solution will involve supplementary security check points in the communication workflow. For the same reason, access to the rest of the system will be not direct but through a separate system interface module. The user interface will provide all that is needed to maintain and set the application to its administrator.

The administrator of the system will configure each dedicated agent according to the data stream that must be acquired. Then the agent begins to search the Internet to find the desired data stream. When the agent comes to a node and finds something, it will search the master list to see if that source is already being processed. If the answer is no, the agent will clone itself and move on to another location. The clone will remain locally and begin to mine information from the data stream. From time to time, each miner will report the newly acquired information to the central base of the system.

The original agent is deployed at the central base and has the role of continuously gather the reports that come from each active clone on the internet. From time to time, it will generate a report specific to the managed resource. All these reports are then combined by a different agent that also handles the knowledge data base index and begins to cross-reference the received reports with the existing knowledge. This removes most of the redundancy, and the news that remains contain links to internal organizational knowledge.

In the case of a common user, the cost of having access to a system such as the one just presented for the corporation is not feasible. Yet there is the possibility that the market will come up with a business that makes this type of system available to common users. Each user would pay on a regular basis for the information that his or her own interface agent will provide. The user would also be able to to customize his or her intelligent agent and give it, if necessary, access to his or her own knowledge. Producers of Internet solution software have already adopted the idea of creating a network of knowledge about attacks. Their approach is simple, based on a combination of a centralized knowledge database that provides minimum help for the user and operator-based help. This software gives the user the possibility of setting new rules, but most users do not have the required skills. So the most advanced providers (such as Norton) automatically update the knowledge database about the threats and the "safe applications list."

The proposed approach has the flexibility of the AI methods. It would give the user interface agent, shown in Figure 26.3, the possibility to gather knowledge about the user's habits on the Internet and also to improve the help offered to the user.

There would be three types of users according to their skill levels in computer security. The basic level user would have fully automated support from the agent. The intermediate level user would be able to select security sources for analysis and set some rules. The third level user would have full access to the interface allowing him or her to customize all the functions of his or her interface agent.

The system will require a central base where the main knowledge repository is located. The advantage of the approach is that transnational corporations and federal administrations would not need to maintain centralization. The local central nodes will be located at the regional nodes, and, by the use of some dedicated intelligent agents, a distributed database can be maintained at the upper levels of the organization.

The information retrieval agent presented in Figure 26.4 has the most complex job in the system. It analyzes the data streams and extracts the basic information, minimizing redundancy as much as possible. In case of mobile node, which has fewer computing resources, the optional modules may not be loaded in order to avoid system overload.

From the point of view of law enforcement, the system will provide two types of enforcement. One is passive, or indirect, enforcement. This is due to the paradigm shift already discussed. From the outside point of view, there are small differences between a security expert and a user coupled

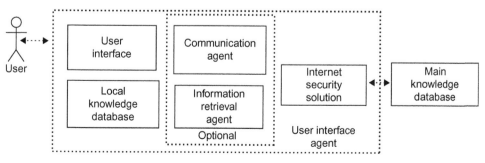

FIGURE 26.3

User interface agent structure.

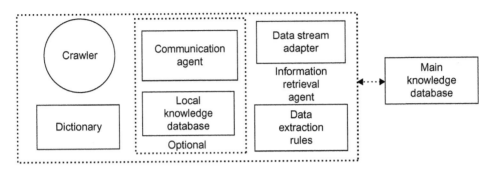

FIGURE 26.4

Information retrieval agent structure.

with a cyber-assistant that helps the user virtually in each decision related to the security of the user's system. Of course, the user may choose to ignore the suggestion from the system. This situation may be neglected if the system provides quotes from current laws regarding the problem in question. Experience shows that, in most cases, the users neglect the law because they either don't know it or don't understand the consequences. If the percentage of users that fully comply with Internet regulations increases, the activity of a real hacker will be much easier to detect.

The other form of enforcement is an active and direct. If the system dynamically retrieves news from various sources that are also used by hackers to disseminate the latest knowledge about detected security weaknesses or the latest methods for attacking a system or a class of applications, then the reaction speed of a security officer will be significantly improved.

SUMMARY

In this chapter, the concept of cyber-terrorism was analyzed in the context of global political changes. In the context of globalization, many societies have begun to adopt the information society paradigm. This will lead to an exponential increase in Internet complexity. Also, the classical form of war is changing, adapting to the new informational environment. In this context, a paradigm shift in assuring cyber-security is proposed. A multi-agent system may offer the solution for this paradigm change. This is possible because the increasing computing power and available broadband needed by this approach is beginning to be available in most situations at the cyberspace level. Finally, a system based on intelligent agents that provide a security cyber-assistant to help the common user or the information security staff in handling the increasing informational flow regarding security problems is proposed.

References

[1] Prucher J. Brave new words: The Oxford Dictionary of Science Fiction. Oxford University Press. New York: Oxford University Press; 2007.

[2] Gantz SD, Philpott DR. FISMA and the risk management framework-The new practice of federal cyber security. Waltham: Syngress; 2013.

[3] Gerdes A. Al-Qaeda on Web 2.0: Radicalization and recruitment strategies. In: Dudley A, Braman J, Vincenti G, editors. Investigating cyber law and cyber ethics: Issues, impacts and practices. York: Information Science Reference; 2012.

[4] Collin B. CJC Publications CJI-Archives. [Internet]. [retrieved 2013 Jun 10]. Retrieved from: <http://www.cjimagazine.com>: <www.cjimagazine.com/archives/cji4c18.html?id=415>; 1997

[5] Hoffman B. Inside terrorism. New York: Columbia University Press; 1998.

[6] Colarik AM. Cyberterrorism: Political and economic implications. London: Idea Group, Inc; 2006.

[7] Hoffman B. Inside terrorism. New York: Columbia University Press; 2010.

[8] Mitra A. Digital security: Cyber terror and cyber security. New York: Infobase Publishing; 2010.

[9] Gragido W, Pirc J. Cybercrime and espionage: An analysis of subversive multivector threats. Burlington: Syngress; 2013.

[10] McGregor GC. The risk advisor expert system. Proceedings of 4th Portuguese Conference on Artificial Intelligence. Berlin Heidelberg: Springer; 1989. p. 297−307

[11] Shikha Selvarani R. An efficient method of risk assessment using intelligent agents. Second International Conference on Advanced Computing & Communication Technologies (ACCT). New York: IEEE CPS; 2012. p. 123−126

[12] Gorodetskii VI. Self-organization and multiagent systems: II. Applications and the development technology. Journal of Computer and Systems Sciences International archive 2012;51(3):391−409.

[13] Godlewska M. Agent system for managing distributed mobile interactive documents. Transactions on Computational Collective Intelligence VI 2012;121−45.

[14] Delias P, Doulamis A, Matsatsinis N. What agents can do in workflow management systems. Artificial Intelligence 2011;35(2):155−89.

[15] Ramakrishnan S, Srinivasan S. Intelligent agent based artificial immune system for computer security-A review. Artificial Intelligence Review 2009;32(1−4):13−43.

[16] Wang X-B, Yang G-Y, Li Y-C, Liu D. Review on the application of artificial intelligence in antivirus detection systems. IEEE Conference on Cybernetics and Intelligent Systems. Washington: IEEE; 2008. p. 506−509

[17] Sanz-Bobi MA, Castro M, Santos J. IDSAI: A distributed system for intrusion detection based on intelligent agents. Fifth International Conference on Internet Monitoring and Protection. Washington: IEEE; 2010. p. 1−6.

[18] Hall A. Creating an expert system risk assessment tool for precursor analysis. In RAMS. Proceedings Reliability and Maintainability Symposium. New York: IEEE CPS; 2011. p. 1−4.

[19] Bayuk JL, Healey J, Rohmeyer P, Sachs MH, Schmidt J, Weiss J. Cyber security policy guidebook. Hoboken: John Wiley & Sons, Inc; 2012.

[20] O'Neil J. Enchelon: Somebody's listening. Tarentum: World Asociation Publisher; 2005.

Methods

Counter Cyber Attacks
By Semantic Networks

27

Peng He
University of Maryland, Baltimore, MD, USA

INFORMATION IN THIS CHAPTER

* Cyber threats
* Semantic networks
* Similarity measures
* Bayesian probability

INTRODUCTION

Nowadays, intrusion detection is one of the most challenging tasks for, and of highest priority in, the cyber-security field. As more and more security sensors are being deployed in the network and used to analyze and detect attacks, these sensors generate a huge volume of alerts with different event granularities and semantics [1]. Such a huge amount of alerts makes a network attack correlation process quite complex and uncertain. On the other hand, attack correlation has become an essential part in most intrusion detection systems (IDSs), since it can enhance the detection rate and provide more accurate attack strategies [2]. Thus, a better technique for attack analysis and correlation is vital for promoting the current network security.

We propose to identify and predict relevant attacks by using semantic networks. In the creation of a semantic network, each node represents an attack and the edges connect relevant attacks.

Specifically, our contributions are as follows: (1) We automatically construct a first mode semantic network from characterizing features of network attacks using similarity. (2) The first mode semantic network is kept adjusted by adding external semantic rules provided by domain expertise that could adjust it, in order to generate a more adaptable second mode semantic network. (3) We have applied several similarity measures, including Anderberg, Jaccard, Simple Matching, and a traditional correlation coefficient to create semantic networks. (4) Finally, we evaluated, through experiments, the various similarity measures and discovered that using the similarity coefficient Anderberg performs better in terms of precision and recall compared to existing correlation approaches in the cyber-security domain.

The rest of the chapter is organized as follows: The following section describes related work. "Methodology" outlines our approach using two modes of semantic networks. "Experiments" presents our experiments. The last section concludes the chapter.

Related work

In this section, related works on Attack Correlation, Semantic Networks, and the Bayesian probability model will be discussed separately.

Related work on attack correlation

In a situation where there are intensive attacks, not only will actual alerts be mixed with false alerts, but the amount of alerts will also become unmanageable [3]. The actual experience of intrusion detection practitioners indicates, "Encountering 10–20,000 alarms per sensor per day is common" [4]. Therefore, it is challenging to analyze intrusion alerts without the help of an alert correlation process, particularly due to the large amount of alerts produced by IDSs. Some previous methods are limited, in that they are restricted to known attack scenarios or those that can be generalized from known scenarios. While the authors in [3] propose to correlate the alerts generated by IDSs using prerequisites and consequences of the corresponding attacks, intuitively, the prerequisite of an attack is the necessary condition for the attack to be successful. The results show that their correlation method not only correlates related alerts and uncovers the attack strategies, but also provides a way to differentiate between alerts.

Other research suggests using appropriate attack correlation techniques to handle large collections of alerts, such as in [1], where the authors have developed a two-layered PA-based (primitive attack-based) correlation approach to tackle the problem. The first layer does PA construction by integrating related alerts into proper PAs. The second layer is the attack subplan-based correlation layer, which attacks a scenario correlation from recognized PAs by employing attack subplan templates to guide the correlation process. In [5], the authors indicate that alert correlation techniques effectively improve the quality of alerts reported by intrusion detection systems and are sufficient to support rapid identification of ongoing attacks. The research focuses on ways to develop the intrusion alerts correlation system according to the authors' XSWRL ontology-based alert correlation approach.

Related work on semantic networks

A *semantic network* or *net* is a graphic notation for representing knowledge in patterns of interconnected nodes and arcs. Computer implementations of semantic networks were first developed for artificial intelligence and machine translation, but earlier versions have long been used in philosophy, psychology, and linguistics. Sowa gives a descriptive outline on the types and use of semantic networks in different disciplines in [6,7]. Semantic networks have long been used to represent relationships [8]. Pearl used probabilities in semantic networks and performed extensive work in applying statistics and probability in causal semantic networks [9,10] to derive such networks from observed data. What is common to all semantic networks is a declarative graphic representation that can be used to either represent knowledge or support automated systems for reasoning about knowledge. Some versions are highly informal, while other versions are formally defined systems of logic.

There are some applications on applying semantic networks in different domains. The work in [11] describes a new metadata approach to elicit semantic information from environmental data and implement semantics-based techniques to assist users in integrating, navigating, and mining multiple environmental data sources. Another paper [12] has applied semantics in the domain of software engineering and provided methods to discover relevant software artifacts to increase software reuse and reduce the cost of software development and maintenance. It proposes a metadata approach with Semantic Networks that convey existing relationships between software artifacts. This approach reveals additional relevant artifacts that the user might have not been aware of. In this chapter, we discuss how to apply semantic networks in identifying related network attacks in the cyber-security domain and how it is used to increase the precision in detecting probable attacks with probability of occurrence.

Related work on the Bayesian probability model

Bayesian networks have been established as a ubiquitous tool for modeling and reasoning under uncertainty [13], and there are several existing applications in which the Bayesian probability model has been applied to intrusion detection systems [14−16].

One recent paper [17] presents work on justifying uncertainty modeling for cyber-security, with initial evidence indicating that it is a useful approach. The authors report their current efforts on identifying the important types of uncertainty and on using Bayesian networks to capture them for enhanced security analysis. They also build an example Bayesian network based on a current security graph model and justify their modeling approach through attack semantics. Experimental study shows that the resulting Bayesian network is not sensitive to parameter perturbation. Their work serves as a good foundation for us to apply the Bayesian network as our probability model on a cyber-security dataset, and use it to find out initial attacks located in our semantic network with a high probability of occurrence. In other words, the Bayesian probability model is used to predict the starting node in our semantic network, and then we can identify other relevant attacks with a high probability of occurrence in the current network situation.

Methodology

To avoid the intricate task of manually constructing and maintaining the semantic network, we adopt an approach for the construction of semantic networks in an automatic manner The construction consists of two layers: first mode and second mode networks. The first mode network identifies relevant attacks based on similarity measures, and the second mode network is modified based on the first mode and adjusts it by adding domain expertise, as shown in Figure 27.1.

Similarity-based semantic network

Let $X = \{x_1,....x_n\}$ be the set of network attacks, where each $x_i \in X$ is associated with a set of characterizing attributes $a_1 = \{a_{i1},.... a_{im}\}$. These attributes may be mixed with numeric values and categorical values. By applying discretization, the numeric values of these features can be transformed

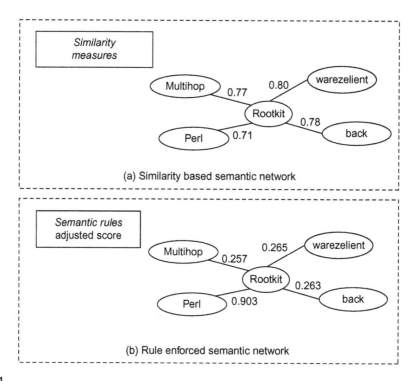

FIGURE 27.1

Constructing a semantic network.

into categorical values (binary) and form a feature vector $f_1 = \{f_{i1},\dots f_{im}\}$. In order to automatically create a similarity-based network, we first need to generate the feature vector associated with each attack. These feature vectors are used to determine how similar the attacks are in terms of the attributes characterizing them; they are then utilized to generate the semantic network. Especially in this research, the weighted frequency feature values in attack feature vectors are used to prepare for the binary feature vector, and the absolute cutoff data transformation [18] has been used to convert weighted frequency feature values into binary values of 0 and 1. Since each attack has more than one attribute that formed as one feature vector, in order to determine the similarity between attacks by taking consideration of different attributes, the union of all feature vectors creates a universal vector (V) that containing all attack attributes, which is $V = \{a_{i1} \cup a_{21,\dots} \cup a_{im}\}$. And then V will be used for the similarity-based semantic network creation.

We then use different similarity coefficients to quantify the similarity among universal feature vectors of the attacks. Based on the similarity coefficients, we connect similar nodes using edges and start creating the first mode semantic network.

Given a pair of nodes x_p and x_q, such that there exists a similarity between the two nodes, the probability w_{pq} of traversing from node x_p to x_q is:

$$w_{pq} = \frac{S_{pq}}{\deg_p} \text{ where } \deg_p = \sum_{s=1}^{k} S_{pj}$$

S_{pq} is one of the similarity coefficients between the feature vectors of attacks (nodes) x_p and x_q. S_{pj} is the weighted degree of the node p, and k is the number of incident edges on p. Thus, based on the similarity and probability computations, we automatically construct a first mode semantic network, as shown in Figure 27.1(a), which we refer to as a *Similarity Based Semantic Network*.

Below, we formally define the first mode semantic network as follows:

Definition 1 [Similarity Based Semantic Network]: Let $X = \{x_1,... x_n\}$ be the set of attacks, where each $x_i \in X$ has a feature vector $f_1 = \{f_{i1},.... f_{im}\}$, then a first mode similarity based network $N^{sn}(V^{sn}, E^{sn})$ is a directed graph where V^{sn} is a set of nodes and E^{sn} is a set of edges, such that $V^{sn} \subseteq X$ and $|V^{sn}| \subseteq |X|$, and each edge links two relevant attacks $<v_i, v_j>$ and has a probability score $w(v_i,v_j)$ where $0 < w(v_i,v_j) \le 1$. Definition 2 [Similarity Coefficient]: Similarity coefficients serve as an effective tool for measuring the similarity among objects in a dataset. In [19], the authors surveyed 35 different coefficients composed of four variables: a, b, c, and d. When objects o_i and o_j are evaluated for similarity, each object is associated with features $f_1, \ldots, f_n$ having values 0 or 1. The concept is illustrated in Figure 27.2.

In Figure 27.2, (a) represents the number of positive matches such that o_i and o_j both have a value of 1, (b) indicates the number of mismatches such that o_i has a value of 1 and o_j has a value of 0, (c) represents the number of mismatches such that o_i has a value of 0 and o_j has a value of 1, and (d) represents the number of negative matches such as o_i and o_j both have a value of 0.

Based on the empirical evaluation results from [19], we select three similarity coefficients that have high accuracy, precision, and recall: Anderberg, Jaccard/Tanimoto, and Simple Matching. These are used in creating different similarity based semantic networks in order to compare the performance of the similarity coefficients methods applied in cyber-security field. Their calculation formulas are defined as following (the symbols a, b, c, and d refer to those described in Figure 27.2):

Anderberg:
$$\frac{a}{a + 2(b + c)}$$

Jaccard/Tanimoto:
$$\frac{a}{a + b + c}$$

Simple Matching:
$$\frac{a + d}{a + b + c + d}$$

Pearson's correlation coefficient is also chosen to create another kind of Semantic Networks in our research, since it has been widely used in the cyber-security domain. Pearson's correlation

	f_1	f_2	f_3	f_4
O_i	1	1	0	0
O_j	1	0	1	0

(a) Column f_1 represents a 1–1 positive match;
(b) Column f_2 represents a 1–0 mismatch;
(c) Column f_3 represents a 0–1 mismatch;
(d) Column f_4 represents a 0–0 negative match.

FIGURE 27.2

Objects associated with feature values in similarity coefficient.

Table 27.1 Pair-Wise Jaccard Similarity Scores

Node 1	Node 2	Similarity Score
1	6	0.9
2	5	0.2
3	4	0.2
4	5	0.2
6	2	0.9
6	3	0.2

coefficient between two objects is defined as the covariance of the two objects "cov (X, Y)" divided by the product of their standard deviations "$\sigma_X \cdot \sigma_Y$." The formula is shown as:

$$pX, Y = \frac{\text{cov}(X, Y)}{\sigma_X \sigma_Y} = \frac{E[(X - \mu_X)(Y - \mu_Y)]}{\sigma_X \sigma_Y}$$

We next describe how to generate a relevance score "**rs**," based on one of above similarity coefficients.

Definition 3 [Relevance Score]: If v_i and v_j are two nodes in a semantic network N (E, V), there are k paths $p_1, \ldots, p_k$ between v_i and v_j, where path p_l ($1 \leq 1 \leq k$) consists of nodes $v_{11}, \ldots, v_{1|pl|+1}$ ($|p_l|$ is the length of path p_l). The relevance score rs, defined between v_i and v_j, is

$$rs = \max(\prod_{1 \leq i \leq |pl|} w(v_{l_i}, v_{1_{i+1}}))$$

This formula computes the relevance score between v_i and v_j as the maximum relevance score of all paths connecting v_i and v_j. For each such path, the relevance score between the two endpoints is computed as the product of relevance scores for all edges along the path.

Here we give a concrete example to explain how we generate relevance score "rs" based on one of similarity coefficients, "Jaccard." Suppose we have six objects, and according to Jaccard's coefficient calculation, we get pair-wise similarity scores stored, as shown in Table 27.1. One example pair of the objects' relevance score in a semantic network computed between object 1 and object 2 is the maximum relevance score of all paths connecting object 1 and object 2. Thus, a relevance score of 0.81 by object 1 and object 2 in Table 27.2 indicates that rs (1, 2) = rs (1, 6) * rs (6, 2) = 0.9 * 0.9 = 0.81.

Rule enforced semantic network

The automatically created first mode semantic networks—by using only similarity measures—do not include any of the semantic information that domain experts usually expect. Particularly in the cyber-security domain, this type of additional semantic information can be described as *semantic rules*. *Semantic rules* explicitly identify the connectivity relationship between two network attacks, which can be extracted from domain knowledge and represented as taxonomy and ontology. Some connectivity relationships described by semantic rules among attack nodes may not be the same as

Table 27.2 First Mode Semantic Network

Node 1	Node 2	Relevance Score
1	2	0.81
1	3	0.18
1	5	0.162
1	6	0.9
2	5	0.2
3	4	0.2
4	5	0.2
6	2	0.9
6	3	0.2
...	...	...

the results by similarity measures in the first mode semantic network, so we use semantic rules to adjust our previous attack correlation results to generate a *rule-enforced semantic network*.

Definition 4 [Semantic Rule]: Given two attack nodes x_p and x_q, a semantic rule "s" is defined as: x_p, x_q, where s_{pq} is the semantic score associated with these two attacks, extracted from domain expertise such as taxonomy. If two attack nodes x_p and x_q fall into same category of network attacks defined by taxonomy, we set the value of s_{pq} equal to 1. Otherwise, when x_p and x_q do not belong to the same attack category, the value of s_{pq} is set to 0.

Next, s_{pq} will be used to adjust the previous relevance score rs_{pq} given by a predefined threshold σ from domain experts. When the absolute value of $| s_{pq}\text{-}rs_{pq} | > \sigma$, it indicates that rs_{pq} needs to be updated by semantic rules, and the degree of the adjustment noted as ad_Degree, below, will also be customized by domain experts in order to reflect the most appropriate relevance score among attacks in the current network environment . Hence, there are two possible ways to update the previous relevance score:

(a) If the value of $(s_{pq}\text{-}rs_{pq}) > 0$, the updated relevance score is $RS'_{pq} = rs_{pq} + |s_{pq}\text{-}rs_{pq}| \times$ ad_Degree.

(b) If the value of $(s_{pq}\text{-}rs_{pq}) < 0$, the updated relevance score is $RS'_{pq} = rs_{pq} - |s_{pq}\text{-}rs_{pq}| \times$ ad_Degree.

Experiments
Experiment data

We selected the KDD CUP 99 data set [20] that was made available at the Third International Knowledge Discovery and Data Mining Tools Competition. This training dataset was originally prepared and managed by MIT Lincoln Labs [21], and the objective was to survey and evaluate research in intrusion detection. There are 494,021 network connection events in this dataset and among them, 75 percent of the data is used to build our semantic network and train our Bayesian probability model, and the other 25 percent of the data is used to evaluate the performance of our approach. In addition, a set of 41 different features is used to decide whether a selected sequence of events is an attack or a normal behavior. Twenty-three attack types were used in this data set. Among these network connection records, 20 percent of them represent normal patterns.

We next give some sample sequences of network connection events in the dataset we used in our research, as shown in Table 27.3:

The seven columns represent features that describe these network connection events. We only show a random seven features out of a total 41 features in the entire dataset. The labels in the last column indicate whether the sequence of events is a normal behavior or a kind of network attack, such as Guess_password or Load Module. These labels are also used to verify the performance of our four different similarity-based semantic networks.

Experiment process

We create four different semantic networks using the same network connection dataset through a two-step approach mentioned in the section titled "Methodology": (1) Four different similarity based semantic networks were created based on four kinds of similarity measures, including Anderberg, Jaccard, Simple Matching, and Correlation Coefficient. (2) We use domain expertise from a well-known attack taxonomy as semantic rules in our research. This attack taxonomy defined attack categories by consequence at MIT Lincoln Lab [22], as shown in Table 27.4. We next use it to adjust each similarity based semantic network from step 1, and finally, we generate four-rule enforced semantic networks, respectively.

The Bayesian probability model is also applied to sequences of the network connection event dataset to calculate the probability of occurrence for all attacks. In our experiments, we utilize the Bayesian probability model to identify attacks with a high probability of occurrence for every

Table 27.3 Sample Sequences of Network Connection Events

Protocol	Service	Flag	Source_ bytes	Destination _ bytes	Number_ failed_login	Attack/Normal Label
TCP	SMTP	SF	3170	329	0	Normal
TCP	HTTP	SF	297	13787	0	Normal
TCP	HTTP	SF	291	3542	0	Normal
TCP	TELNET	SF	295	753	1	Guess_password
TCP	TELNET	SF	281	1301	0	Load module

Table 27.4 A Taxonomy That Defines the Attack Category by Consequence

Attack Category	Attack Name
Denial of Service(DoS)	smurf, neptune, back, teardrop, pod, land
Remote to Local(R2L)	warezclient, guess_passwd, warezmaster, imap, ftp_write, multihop, phf, spy
User to Root(U2R)	buffer_overflow, rootkit, loadmodule, perl
Probe	satan, ipsweep, portsweep, nmap

sequence. After we get these initial attack prediction results, we can locate them as initial nodes in our semantic networks to find other relevant attacks. Figure 27.3 shows the steps of initial attack predicted by the Bayesian probability model in our research process.

Next we give a concrete example of how our semantic network can be used to identify relevant attacks with a high probability of occurrence in the current network situation. We see in Table 27.5, for the ID = 73727 sequence of events, a Bayesian prediction model is first used to identify the attack type "Rootkit" as the highest probability of occurrence in the network. We then locate "Rootkit" as an initial node in our rule-enforced semantic network shown in Figure 27.1(b). Our approach automatically indicates other attack types relevant with "Rootkit" and connects them with corresponding relevance scores. The second column, "Actual Label" is used to verify the performance of the semantic network. In this case, the attack "Perl" is predicted by the semantic network with the highest relevance score, and it is just the right attack label for sequence ID = 73727. Thus, for this case, the semantic network performs very well to increase the precision in detecting probable attacks with a high probability of occurrence.

Performance measures

Three metrics—precision, recall, and F-measure—have been applied to evaluate our approach as follows:

$$\text{Precision} = \frac{(\text{Relevant query answers}) \cap (\text{Retrieved answers})}{\text{Relevant answers}}$$

$$\text{Recall} = \frac{(\text{Relevant query answers}) \cap (\text{Retrieved answers})}{\text{Retrieved answers}}$$

$$\text{F} - \text{measure} = \frac{2 * \text{Precision} * \text{Recall}}{\text{Precision} + \text{Recall}}$$

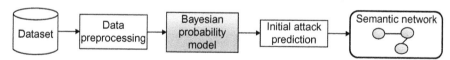

FIGURE 27.3

Initial attack predicted by Bayesian probability model in our approach.

Table 27.5 A Concrete Example of Semantic Network

ID	Actual Label	Bayesian Prediction	Relevant Attacks	Relevance Score
73727	**Perl**	Rootkit	**Perl**	**0.903333**
			warezclient	0.265921
			back	0.263353
			multihop	0.256667

Experiment results

We evaluate the four different semantic networks based on four various similarity measures, including Anderberg, Jaccard, Simple Matching, and Correlation Coefficient.

One important parameter in our approach is the user-defined threshold **t** for the relevance score in the semantic network. Only these attacks, which are relevant with a relevance score above **t**, are included in the semantic network recommendation results. We did experiments by varying threshold **t** in the range from 0 to 1; the observed values of Precision, Recall, and F-measure are presented in Figures 27.4, 27.5 and 27.6 as follows:

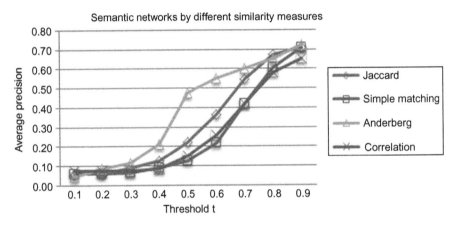

FIGURE 27.4

Average precision graphs for different semantic networks.

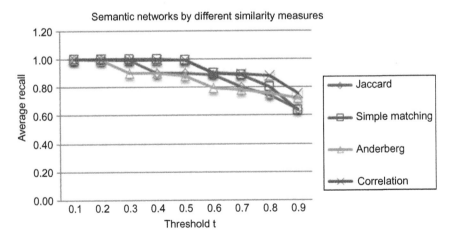

FIGURE 27.5

Average recall graphs for different semantic networks.

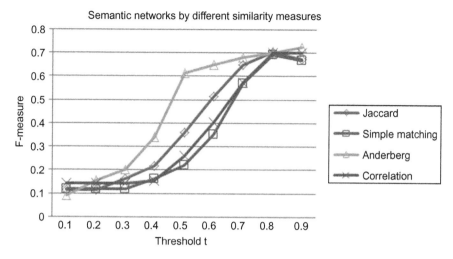

FIGURE 27.6

F-measure graphs for different semantic networks.

The evaluation results of average precisions for four different semantic networks based on four various similarity measures are shown in Figure 27.4. Among these, an Anderberg-based semantic network performs best in terms of precision when we vary the threshold **t** determined by the relevance score. The average precision for a Jaccard-based semantic network is in the second place, while the results of other two, Simple Matching and Correlation based semantic networks, are close, but they are lower than the Anderberg and Jaccard results.

At the same time, we drew average recall graphs for these four different semantic networks. We found that their average recall results perform similarly, and they are all in the range of 60 percent to 100 percent when we vary the threshold **t**.

We also discovered that 0.8 is the optimal threshold value as a relevance score for the best performance of all the semantic networks. We used the F-measure, which is a metric combining precision and recall results, shown in Figure 27.6. Our experiment results shown in the graphs also clearly indicate that the performance of Anderberg is superior to other similarity measures, including the traditional correlation coefficient in the cyber-security domain.

CONCLUSION AND FUTURE WORK

In order to handle the complex and uncertain network attack correlation tasks nowadays, and to increase the precision in detecting probable attacks with probability of occurrence on the current network environment, in this research, we use semantic networks that convey relationships among network attacks and assist in automatically identifying and predicting related attacks. Our contributions in this chapter are an extended work on an abstract paper [23], as following: we used four different similarity measures to automatically create the first mode semantic networks and adjust them with semantic rules provided by domain expertise. A Bayesian probability model is utilized to identify initial attacks located in our semantic network with a high probability of occurrence. We considered four different similarity measures, including Anderberg, Jaccard, Simple Matching, and a traditional correlation coefficient to automatically create semantic networks; and finally, by experiments, we discover that a semantic network using the similarity measure Anderberg performs better in terms of precision and recall compared to the existing correlation approach in the cyber-security domain.

We are confident that our approach can be used to tackle zero-day attacks, which is one of the most essential problems in cyber-security nowadays. A zero-day attack is a computer threat that tries to exploit computer application vulnerabilities that are unknown to the software developers, and its exploits are used or shared by attackers before the developer of the target software knows about the vulnerability. In fact, our approach has used several feature vectors from sequences of network events, and once some zero-day attacks had several feature vectors matching existing types of attacks embedded in them, these attacks should have been automatically constructed as attack nodes in our semantic network based on the attack features' similarity measures. The next step is how to identify them in our semantic network, and more studies will be addressed on this particular issue in our future works.

One of our recent publications [24] on AMCIS 2012 proposes to utilize domain knowledge in the form of taxonomy and ontology to improve attack correlation in cyber-security. In addition, we expect that the attack correlation results of machine-learning techniques can be used to refine the original attack taxonomy. The findings of the experiments suggest that domain knowledge and machine-learning techniques should be used together on attack classification tasks.

In the future, we plan to investigate additional similarity coefficients that can be used to create semantic networks. Additionally, we would like to apply context filters above the current semantic network technique in order to further increase the precision of attack correlation results. We also plan to experiment and validate our approach with more real network connection datasets.

Acknowledgments

This research is partially supported by Northrop-Grumman Corporation.

References

[1] Chien S-H, Chang E-H, Yu C-Y, Ho C-S. Attack subplan-based attack scenario correlation. Proceedings of the Sixth International Conference on Machine Learning and Cybernetics; 2007; Hong Kong.

[2] Yan W, Hou E, Ansari N. Extracting attack knowledge using principal-subordinate consequence tagging case grammar and alerts semantic networks. LCN'04. Proceedings of the 29th Annual IEEE International Conference on Local Computer Networks 2004.

[3] Ning P, Cui Y, Reeves DS, Xu D. Techniques and tools for analyzing intrusion alerts. ACM Transactions on Information and System Security 2004;7(2):274–318.

[4] Manganaris S, Christensen M, Zerkle D, Hermiz K. A data mining analysis of RTID alarms. Comput Netw 2000;34:571–7.

[5] Li W, Tian S. An ontology-based intrusion alerts correlation system. Expert System with Applications 2010;37:7138−46.

[6] Sowa JF. Semantic networks. [Internet]. Retrieved from: <http://www.jfsowa.com/pubs/semnet.htm>; [accessed 01.13].

[7] Sowa JF. Semantic networks. In: Shapiro SC, editor. Encyclopedia of Artificial Intelligence. New York: Wiley; 1992. p. 1493−511.

[8] Masterman M. Semantic message detection for machine translation. Using an interlingua. NPL 1961;438−75.

[9] Pearl J. Probabilistic reasoning in intelligent systems: Networks of plausible inference. San Francisco: Morgan Kaufmann; 1988.

[10] Pearl J. Causality: Models, reasoning, and inference. Cambridge: Cambridge University Press; 2000.

[11] Chen Z, Gangopadhyay A, Karabatis G, McGuire M, Welty C. Semantic integration and knowledge discovery for environmental research. Journal of Database Management 2007;18(1):43−68.

[12] Karabatis G, Chen Z, Janeja VP, Lobo T, Advani M, Lindvall M, et al. Using semantic networks and context in search for relevant software engineering artifacts. Journal on Data Semantics 2009; XIV:74−104.

[13] Darwiche A. Bayesian networks. Commun ACM 2010 Dec;53:12.

[14] Garcia Bringas P. Intensive use of Bayesian belief networks for the unified, flexible and adaptable analysis of misuses and anomalies in network intrusion detection and prevention systems. In: 18th International Conference on Database and Expert Systems Applications; 2007.

[15] Kruegel C, Mutz D, Robertson W, Valeur F. In: ACSAC, editor. Bayesian event classification for intrusion detection. 2003.

[16] Valdes A, Skinner K. Adaptive, model-based monitoring for cyber attack detection. In: RAID 'OO; 2000.

[17] Xie P, Li JH, Ou X, Liu P, Levy R. Using Bayesian networks for cyber security analysis. IEEE/IFIP International Conference on Dependable System & Networks (DSN) 2010.

[18] Pensa R, Leschi C, Besson J, Boulicaut J. Assessment of discretization techniques for relevant pattern discovery from gene expression data. BIOKDD 2004: In the 4th Workshop on Data Mining in Bioinformatics; 2004.

[19] Lewis DM, Janeja VP. An empirical evaluation of similarity coefficients for binary valued data. International Journal of Data Warehousing and Mining (IJDWM) 2011;7:2.

[20] KDD CUP 1999 Intrusion detection dataset. [Internet]. Retrieved from: <http://kdd.ics.uci.edu/databases/kddcup99/kddcup99.html>; [accessed 01.13].

[21] The DARPA intrusion detection data sets by MIT Lincoln Lab. [Internet]. Retrieved from: <http://www.ll.mit.edu/mission/communications/ist/corpora/ideval/data/index.html>; [accessed 01.13].

[22] Lippmann R, Fried D, Graf I, Haines J, Kendall K, McClung D, et al. Evaluating intrusion detection systems: The 1998 DARPA off-line intrusion detection evaluation. Proceedings of the DARPA Information Survivability Conference and Exposition 1998;12−26.

[23] He P, Karabatis G. Using semantic networks to counter cyber threats. ISI 2012: Poster abstract in Proceedings of IEEE International Conference on Intelligence and Security Informatics; 2012 Jun; Washington, DC, USA. p. 184. Link: 10.1109/ISI.2012.6284294.

[24] He P, Zhou L, Karabatis G. Using domain knowledge to faciliate cyber security analysis. AMCIS 2012 Proceedings; Paper 19. [Internet]. 2012 Jul 29. Retrieved from: <http://aisel.aisnet.org/amcis2012/proceedings/ISSecurity/19>.

Man-in-the-Browser Attacks in Modern Web Browsers

28

Sampsa Rauti and Ville Leppänen
University of Turku, Turku, Finland

INFORMATION IN THIS CHAPTER

- Web security
- Online fraud
- Man-in-the-browser attacks
- Flow of data through software layers when executing browser applications
- Malware countermeasures
- Obfuscation
- Building trust between software layers using cryptographic protocols

INTRODUCTION

As financial organizations and their customers move online, cybercriminals have started to operate low-risk and profitable online crime business. One sophisticated method they use is the man-in-the-browser attack.

Man-in-the-browser is a Trojan that infects a Web browser. It is able to change the contents of Web pages and tamper with network traffic. The malware acts between the server and the user. Neither the server nor the user can detect anything unusual, because the malware delivers fallacious information to both parties.

The Trojan waits for the user to log in to a specific Web page. When the user inputs sensitive data, for example data related to a money transfer, the Trojan alters this data before it is sent, without the user noticing. When the server sends back a confirmation of the data input by the user, the malware again alters this information so that the unsuspecting user sees what is expected. An important difference from online fraud attacks of previous generations is that a man-in-the-browser attack is practically impossible for the user to notice. Also, the user does absolutely nothing wrong, in the sense that there are not any security problems with the user's own actions. No modern authentication scheme works against this attack, because man-in-the-browser acts in the GUI, in the program logic, or in the browser's network traffic processing level, not on the authentication

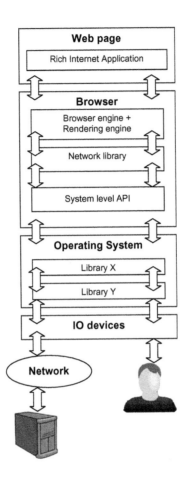

FIGURE 28.1

The flow of data from a server to the user and vice versa.

level. It just waits for the user to log in and uses the user's legitimate session to do its business. Thus, it is not surprising that the amount of Trojans intercepting and manipulating user input has increased rapidly in recent years [1] and that this business has been profitable for the attackers [2].

A man-in-the-browser attack can be implemented in many ways. Probably the easiest and most popular way is to implement a browser extension that secretly intercepts the network traffic, but other attack methods on other software layers also exist. Many of these layers are shown in Figure 28.1. This chapter sheds light on various attack vectors that exist on software layers of the browser and operating system libraries.

Chapter overview

In this chapter we examine typical browser architecture and explain the flow of data from the user to the server. We give a detailed description of attack vectors, that is, the points or components where attacks can take place. Based on these attack vectors, we study the different man-in-the-browser attacks grouped according to the software layers at which they take place. This helps to better understand the nature of the man-in-the-browser problem and to develop ideas for counter-measures against it. We then briefly explore possible countermeasures against the attacks described. A conclusion summarizes the chapter.

Related work

The man-in-the-browser attack has been discussed in detail by Dougan and Curran [3] and Gühring [4]. In [2], Ståhlberg describes various banking Trojans and some of the attack methods they use. The functionalities of malicious browser extensions have been studied by Sook and Enbody in [5] and by Ter Louw, Lim, and Venkatakrishnan in [6]. We analyze malicious browser extensions in [7] and present an obfuscation-based solution to the man-in-the-browser attack in Ajax applications [8]. Bandhakavi, King, Madhusudan, and Winslett [9] study vulnerabilities in benign browser extensions. Grosskurth describes different browser architectures in [10].

Browser architecture

To understand where vulnerabilities and attack vectors are located, we will briefly look at typical browser architecture, using Firefox's architecture as an example. The main components of this architecture are shown in Figure 28.2. Arrows show interaction and data flow between components.

The user interacts with the user interface, which handles the user's commands. The browser engine provides a high-level interface used to query and manipulate the rendering engine. The rendering engine handles parsing and lays out HTML documents, which are possibly styled with CSS. In Firefox, these two are bundled into the Gecko engine [10].

To parse HTML documents, and more generally XML, the rendering engine uses the XML parser. Mozilla's JavaScript engine, SpiderMonkey, executes JavaScript on Web pages. The networking subsystem, Necko, handles all network traffic in the browser. The rendering engine and user interface use a display backend for drawing. The graphic libraries provide primitives for drawing and windowing, user interface, widgets, and fonts. Data persistence in Firefox is provided by Mozilla's profile mechanism. This data store contains all data such as bookmarks, cookies, and page caches.

Cross Platform Component Object Model (XPCOM) is Mozilla's cross-platform component model, which is similar to Microsoft's COM. XPCOM makes practically all of Gecko's functionality available as a series of components [10].

XPConnect enables JavaScript objects to use and manipulate XPCOM objects. JavaScript objects can also implement XPCOM-compliant interfaces to be called by XPCOM. Thus, objects communicating on different sides of XPConnect do not need to know about the implementation language of the other side.

Finally, the system level API, NSPR, is a platform-neutral interface for system-level functions. Using this interface, other components like XPCOM and Necko can use the operating system's resources.

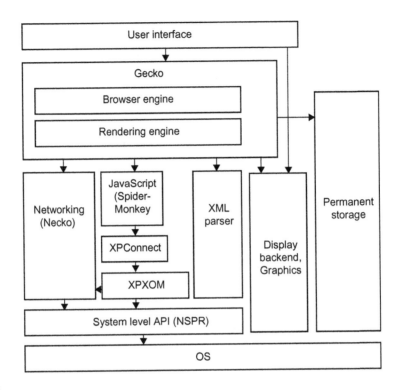

FIGURE 28.2

The architecture of the Firefox Web browser. *Adapted from [10].*

Firefox browser extensions are powerful enhancements that extend the browser's core function-ality. These extensions, written in JavaScript, use the services of Gecko, Necko, and NSPR through the interfaces provided by XPCOM. Firefox browser extensions have full privileges in the browser and can use practically all browser functionality, like intercepting HTTP requests and responses or modifying any Web page. Sandboxing that restricts the functionality of normal JavaScript on Web pages is not applied to browser extensions.

Man-in-the-browser attacks on different layers

In this section, we present man-in-the-browser attacks taking place at different layers and targeting various points in the data flow. In a sense, we analyze these attacks from the top down. First, we explore the attacks related to browser and rendering engines, then cover the network component and the system level API. Finally, we study the attacks associated with the operating system's net-working APIs. One can consider this as covering one possible path of data flow, when the user gives data as an input and this data is sent to the server.

Web page DOM and scripts

We can think of a Web page containing JavaScript code as the highest software layer. The man-in-the-browser attack can be implemented at this level either by modifying a Web page's DOM (Document Object Model) tree, by changing the Web page's JavaScript code, or by modifying the Ajax application's data transmission mechanism. The two latter techniques work if the attacker's target is an Ajax application. Because these three attacks change the structure of HTML and JavaScript code, they are actually attacks against the Gecko engine. In what follows, we take a look at these attacks and the methods used to achieve them.

Modifying the DOM tree

An easy method for modifying the input from the user is to use JavaScript to manipulate elements in a Web document's DOM tree. Consider a situation where the adversary wants to secretly change the value of a text field that will be sent to the server. The following steps could be used:

- A malicious browser extension listens to the click events in the document body. If a text field is clicked, it is immediately made "invisible" using CSS-style definitions, and its value is changed according to the wishes of the attacker.
- A new, identical text field is put in place of the original, now-invisible text field. The focus is set on the new element.
- The user types input into the new text field without noticing anything suspicious.
- When the data is submitted, the value of the original text field is sent to the server and the new text field filled by the user is saved for later use.

When the modified text is sent back from the server, the attacker again replaces it with the user's original input before it is displayed to the user. This can again be achieved by manipulating the DOM and replacing the changed value with the one the user expects. In an Ajax application, for example, the attacker can listen to a *DOMNodeInserted* event and immediately replace the new element's *innerHTML* property when it is inserted.

Modifying a DOM tree to fool the user is a relatively easy attack to implement, and some existing Trojans use this approach. However, it requires knowledge about how the Web page or Web application works and what kind of elements it contains.

Modifying the JavaScript functionality on a web page

Using JavaScript, we can replace and add script elements on a Web page to modify its JavaScript functionality. This method can be considered a special case of modifying the DOM tree. However, in this scenario, the visible elements in the tree are not altered. The attacker simply uses JavaScript to add and modify the existing script elements on a Web page.

The goal of an adversary is to change the JavaScript functionality of a Web page to secretly edit the input given by the user before it is sent as an HTTP request. The malicious code can be added to existing JavaScript functions, or functions can be replaced altogether with a new malicious implementation that tampers with the data given by the user. DOM provides *replaceChild*, *removeChild* and *appendChild* methods that can be used to achieve the replacement.

For example, the adversary could find out what the *XMLHttpRequest* object's "send" function (which Ajax applications usually use to send HTTP requests) is called and replace the data given as an argument to this function. The adversary would simply make a string replacement to the code in the original script element and replace this old element with a new script element containing the modified content. Alternatively, the adversary can overwrite entire functions by appending a new script element containing the function's new implementation. When there are two function declarations with the same name in JavaScript, the first one gets overwritten.

Modifying the Ajax transmission mechanism

XMLHttpRequest is a JavaScript API available in JavaScript. In Ajax applications, it is used to send HTTP or HTTPS requests to a server and to receive responses from the server.

In JavaScript, objects are created based on prototypes. If the attacker overrides *XMLHttpRequest*'s prototype implementation, the attacker can modify the payload of any Ajax request. An attacker can modify *XMLHttpRequest*'s prototype by adding malicious code as a part of send function:

```
XMLHttpRequest.prototype.originalSend = XMLHttpRequest.prototype.send;
var evilSend = function(data) {
// Modify the data here
this.originalSend(data);
};
XMLHttpRequest.prototype.send = evilSend;
```

All *XMLHttpRequest* objects now use the new implementation of the "send" function. Each time a request is sent, this code silently modifies the data and then passes it to the original send function.

The *XMLHttpRequest* object's callback function, *onreadystatechange*, is used to receive responses from the server. Again, an attacker can replace this function with the attacker's own implementation that alters the incoming data:

```
XMLHttpRequest.prototype.onreadystatechange = evilHandler;
```

Here, the function handler is assumed to be the malicious implementation that handles the data sent by the Web server before it is shown to the user. That is, this function simulates the Web page or Web application's normal behavior, fooling the user.

As in the previous two attacks, the adversary needs to have a good understanding of the website or application being attacked. However, especially in the case of Ajax applications, this is easily possible because the source code is kept on the client side and is totally visible to the attacker.

Accomplishing the example attacks

All three attacks we have discussed require JavaScript code to be inserted on a target Web page. How do attackers achieve this? There are two main methods to execute harmful JavaScript on a Web page: Cross-Site Scripting (XSS) attacks and browser extensions.

An XSS attack becomes possible if a Web application is vulnerable so that an attacker can inject the malicious code into a trusted website. The attacker uses normal functionality in a Web application to deliver the harmful code to another end user as a browser side script. Any

Web application that uses unsanitized input from a user in the output the application shows on a Web page is susceptible to this attack. The attacker gives the malicious code as an input, which is then executed on another user's machine when the user visits the appropriate page. The user's Web browser, of course, thinks that the harmful script originates from a trusted source. After all, it is the benign website or Web application that delivers the malicious code to the browser.

Once the adversary can slip the malicious code into a Web application, it is easy to perform the man-in-the-browser attack. The attacker uses some of the three previously described methods: manipulating the DOM tree, modifying the Ajax application's functionality, or subverting the Ajax transmission mechanism to attack an application or a website.

If the attacker is able to run browser extensions in the victim's browser, it is even easier to launch the previously described attacks, because browser extensions can freely manipulate content on any Web page in any way they want. With a malicious extension at the attacker's disposal, the attacker does not have to worry about finding vulnerabilities.

Even if the attacker does not have a malicious extension in the user's browser, it may still be possible to run code with full privileges if the attacker knows about a vulnerable point in some benign extension. This can happen if a malicious script is injected into a benign Web page using an XSS attack, or if the user visits some evil Web page containing a malicious script. This kind of privilege escalation can happen, for example, if an extension uses JavaScript's *eval()* function to execute a string taken from a Web page's source code or a string that can otherwise be altered by the attacker. This will usually lead to arbitrary code execution that enables the attacker to do practically anything in the browser. Using *eval()* is a bad practice, but it is still used in extensions from time to time. Other functions, such as *setTimeout()*, may also make privilege escalation possible.

In addition to using browser extensions, the attacker could also use XPCOM components from outside the browser to achieve the very same functionality as the extensions. While building an extension is much easier, infecting the browser provides an even better hiding place for a malicious piece of code.

Networking library and system-level API

Malware can intercept Firefox's HTTP requests and the server's responses by abusing either the networking library (Necko) or the system level API (NSPR). Necko can easily be compromised by malicious browser extensions. On the other hand, malware not residing in the browser can use NSPR that is located on a lower software layer.

Necko

Firefox browser extensions can easily use Necko's components through XPCOM interfaces. This allows the extensions to observe and modify all HTTP requests the browser makes and the responses it receives. In practice, this happens by implementing a listener interface called *nsIObserver*. A malicious extension implementing this interface then receives a notification each time a request or response takes place.

Assume an evil browser extension wants to tamper with outgoing traffic. Each notification has a topic that tells whether it deals with a request or a response. In the case of incoming traffic, malware listens to a notification with the *http-on-modify-request* topic. Associated with each arriving notification is an HTTP channel that implements the *nsIHttpChannel* interface.

The *nsIHttpChannel* interface includes an upload channel, *nsIUploadChannel*. The malware can use the upload stream of this channel to obtain the data it wants to modify. The modified data is put back in the HTTP channel and the request can resume normally.

Similarly, all incoming HTTP responses in the browser can be captured by listening to notifications with the *http-on-examine-response* topic. The payload included in a response can then be read and modified using the *nsITraceableChannel* interface, for example.

Naturally, Necko's previously mentioned interfaces can also be hooked by an external program, but building a browser extension is probably much easier, at least in Firefox's case. Internet Explorer uses *wininet.dll* for networking functionality. Zeus, which is a real-world example of a Trojan containing man-in-the-browser functionality, hooks WinInet in order to spy on and tamper with network traffic [11].

NSPR

NSPR can be attacked by hooking the *PR_Write* function. This is a function that writes a specified number of bytes to a file or socket. It is responsible for delivering outgoing HTTP requests. For example, Zeus Trojan hooks this function to intercept outgoing HTTP requests from Firefox [11]. Similarly, the *PR_Read* function in NSPR handles incoming responses from the server.

Network APIs

The malware on a user's computer can intercept HTTP requests the browser issues by using Windows network APIs without residing in the browser. Figure 28.3 shows a simplified sketch of these network-related interfaces.

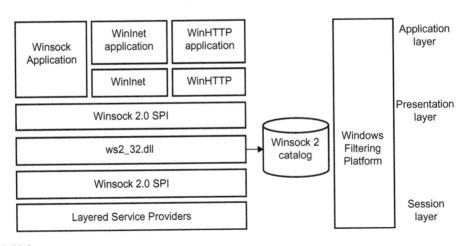

FIGURE 28.3

Windows network APIs. *Adapted from [12].*

Winsock is a technical specification defining how software should access network services in Windows. Winsock defines a standard interface between a client application, for example, a Web browser, and the underlying TCP/IP protocol stack.

WinInet and WinHTTP are basically wrappers built on top of Winsock and can be used to modify outgoing and incoming HTTP traffic. WinHTTP provides some HTTP-specific features, while WinInet is a more general API that also supports FTP, for example. Using these simplified interfaces makes an attacker's job simpler and less error-prone. However, if a Web browser uses Winsock directly, these APIs cannot be used to modify packets.

Introduced with Windows Vista, a new architecture called Windows Filtering Platform (WFP) allows applications to intercept and modify network traffic [13]. This can happen at several layers of the TCP/IP stack, as shown in Figure 28.3. WFP makes applications tampering with network traffic easier to implement and even provides an engine for choosing packets using predefined filtering conditions.

One solution that allows malware to easily hook API functions is Microsoft Detours. Detours intercepts Win32 functions by rewriting the in-memory code for target functions. The Detours package also provides tools for attaching DLLs and data segments to any Win32 binary [14].

A Layered Service Provider (LSP) is a feature of the Winsock 2 interface. It is a DLL that uses Winsock APIs to insert itself into the TCP/IP protocol stack. These LSPs intercept Winsock 2 commands before they get processed by *ws2_32.dll*. This means they can modify or remove commands, or simply store the data for later use. In a way, an LSP acts as a proxy between the application and Winsock 2. Malware may insert itself as an LSP in the network stack in order to make modifications to the outgoing and incoming data. Layered Service Providers use the Winsock SPI interface. The order of these providers is stored in the Winsock catalog.

It is noteworthy that encryption with Transport Level Security (formerly Secure Sockets Layers, or SSL) does not affect the malware making use of the APIs discussed above. This is because Winsock operates above the transport layer [12], where the data is encrypted. Malware modifies outgoing data before it is encrypted and incoming data after it is decrypted. HTTPS and the lock symbols in the browser can therefore give users a false sense of security.

Modifying network traffic and hooking API functions can sometimes be troublesome for malware, though, as anti-virus programs often consider such activity malicious. On the other hand, browser extensions are often deemed totally safe by antivirus programs and are not even checked for malicious behavior [5].

Countermeasures

There are no guaranteed countermeasures against man-in-the-browser attacks, as all existing methods to prevent them have been more or less effectively circumvented. Therefore, only partial solutions exist and we can, at best, try to considerably mitigate the problem.

The modern browser is like an operating system in the sense that it has many separate software layers and the user's applications are run on the top of this stack. The problem is that the adversary can freely and easily manipulate these layers or extend the browser by adding the attacker's own malicious code.

The countermeasures we propose are as follows:

- Building trust between software layers
- Using cryptographic protocols
- Using obfuscation

Building trust between software layers

We advocate the idea of building trust between different software layers and components by using cryptography. This is not yet a concrete solution, but a concept. In our approach, each component or layer would be run as a separate process. An ID could then be given to each component and the components would use cryptographic protocols to interact with each other. The idea is to make sure that the components really know who they are interacting with.

This idea is somewhat similar to the security scheme used in the Symbian OS. In Symbian, a process needs to hold a specific token (e.g., an unforgeable data value) in order to use a system resource [15]. Each resource is guarded by a service process to which other processes have to present their tokens.

Of course, the malware might find out the communication mechanism and try to use it to impersonate some component of the system. That is, the malware might learn to use the cryptographic protocol. This is why the integrity of the separate components should be checked regularly by a separate monitor.

In general, loading external dynamic libraries into a running process can be considered a very weak solution from the security point of view. This is why we propose a model where libraries are replaced by processes that use cryptographic protocols and possess unforgeable IDs. That is, the service interfaces should not be put behind passive libraries, but behind process interfaces that actively monitor the usage of resources.

Using cryptographic protocols

On the Web application level, encrypting user input may provide some advantages. For example, if user input is encrypted, malware that intercepts the HTTP request using the operating system's network APIs would not be able to easily manipulate or spy on the data. At the very least, some knowledge about the Web application's functionality and structure would be needed.

However, there would still be several components in the browser that would be able to see this data in plaintext. For example, if the data is encrypted using JavaScript, the interpreter can see data in both plaintext and encrypted form. This is why we ultimately need to build trust between software layers and monitor their integrity.

Using obfuscation

As noted previously, encrypting user input moves attacks to the upper layers such as the Web application layer. To protect Web applications, we can obfuscate their source code and the code that is being executed. Obfuscation refers to transforming the code into a form that is functionally equivalent to the original code. However, transforming the code makes it more difficult to understand or de-obfuscate using automatic tools. Obfuscated code will not be impossible to de-obfuscate, but the time and cost of de-obfuscating and understanding the code can be increased. In this sense, obfuscation bears some resemblance to encryption.

Obfuscating and randomizing a Web application's JavaScript and HTML code provide some protection against automated large-scale attacks that target a Web application's source code or the DOM structure of a Web page. Targeting these attack points in an automated large-scale attack requires much more work from the attacker if the application's source code and DOM structure are uniquely obfuscated for each session.

Furthermore, the Web application's code may also be changed dynamically during its execution [8]. In modern Web applications, this is made possible by Ajax techniques that allow for changing the contents of a Web page—and an Ajax application's source code—dynamically without the need to reload the whole page.

This is similar to building trust between software layers; we are not trying to block all the security holes here. Instead, we are aiming to make it very difficult for the malware to call the resources it needs, especially in the large scale.

Miscellaneous observations

It is noteworthy that the three techniques presented here, building trust between software layers, using cryptographic protocols, and using obfuscation, differ in their implementation requirements. Building trust between software layers requires replacing the layers in the Web browser with independent processes, so software has to be rewritten. Encryption and obfuscation in the Web application's code, however, only require the code to be modified by an obfuscating engine. That is, the programmer does not have to worry about obfuscation, which is a great advantage. Moreover, none of the three techniques require any user involvement.

Obfuscation might not only be useful on the Web application level, but on other software layers as well. Obfuscating lower layers like operating system libraries makes it possible to build trust between all software layers. Naturally, this requires an open source operating system, but the idea is still very interesting.

The integrity of browser extensions is also a concern. Firefox allows signed browser extensions, but hardly anyone uses this feature. Moreover, this signature is only used to check that the extension is genuine and really comes from the right source. Consequently, the integrity of signed extensions is not checked at runtime, so malware could still change them as it pleases after installation.

Therefore, the scheme we described above should also be applied to extensions to verify their integrity. At the same time, the privileges of browser extensions should be considerably restricted and their runtime actions should be monitored, even though this would probably cause some performance losses. Antivirus vendors should always treat browser extensions as possible threats to the browser and the user.

CONCLUSION

In this chapter, we examine a browser's components and possible attack vectors that malware can target to perform man-in-the-browser attacks. We also propose a conceptual, threefold solution that makes use of cryptographic identification and integrity monitoring of software components, encryption, and source code obfuscation.

There are many possible points of attack in a browser that this chapter has not covered in detail. After all, there is a huge number of functions in the call stack the malware could attach itself to. Still, we hope it is clear to the reader that a large number of possible points of attack exist in different software layers and components. This further emphasizes the fact that the man-in-the-browser attack is a serious threat to online security.

Even though the adversary, with enough hard work, can probably always find some way to alter online transactions, it is a decent goal to be able to prevent at least automated and generic large-scale man-in-the-browser attacks in the future.

References

[1] RSA. Making sense of man-in-the-browser attacks: Threat analysis and mitigation for financial institutions. [Internet]. Retrieved from: <http://www.rsa.com/products/consumer/whitepapers/10459_MITB _WP_0611.pdf>; 2011.

[2] Ståhlberg M. The Trojan money spinner. In: Virus Bulleting Conference; 2007.

[3] Dougan T, Curran K. Man-in-the-browser attacks. International Journal of Ambient Computing and Intelligence 2012;4(1):29–39.

[4] Gühring P. Concepts against man-in-the-browser attacks. [Internet]. Retrieved from: <http://www.cacert.at/svn/sourcerer/CAcert/SecureClient.pdf>; 2006.

[5] Sook AK, Enbody RJ. Spying on the browser: Dissecting the design of malicious extensions. Network Security 2011;5:8–12.

[6] Ter Louw M, Lim JS, Venkatakrishnan VN. Enhancing web browser security against malware extensions. Journal in Computer Virology 2008;4(3):179–95.

[7] Rauti S, Leppänen V. Browser extension-based man-in-the-browser attacks against Ajax applications with countermeasures. Proceedings of the 13th International Conference on Computer Systems and Technologies 2012;251–8.

[8] Rauti S, Leppänen V. Resilient JavaScript and HTML obfuscation and code protection for Ajax applications against man-in-the-browser attacks. Under review; 2013.

[9] Bandhakavi S, King ST, Madhusudan P, Winslett M. Vex: Vetting browser extensions for security vulnerabilities. Commun ACM 2011;54(9):91–9.

[10] Grosskurth A. A reference architecture for web browsers. Proceedings of the 21st IEEE International Conference on Software Maintenance 2005;661–4.

[11] IOActive. Reversal and analysis of Zeus and SpyEye banking Trojans. [Internet]. <http://www.ioactive.com/pdfs/ZeusSpyEyeBankingTrojanAnalysis.pdf>.

[12] Russinovich M, Solomon DA. Windows internals Part 1. 6th ed. Waypoint Press; 2012.

[13] Microsoft Developer Network. Windows filtering platform. [Internet]. 2012. <http://msdn.microsoft.com/en-us/library/windows/desktop/aa366510>(v = vs.85).aspx.

[14] Hunt G, Brubacher D. Detours: Binary interception of win32 functions. Proceedings of the 3rd conference on USENIX Windows NT Symposium 1999;14.

[15] Heath C, Symbian OS. platform security. Wiley & Sons Ltd; 2006.

Improving Security in Web Sessions: Special Management of Cookies

29

Nicolás Macia and Fernando G. Tinetti

The National University of La Plata, La Plata, BA, Argentina

INFORMATION IN THIS CHAPTER

* Web session management
* Alternative proposal to enhance security and privacy of Web sessions avoiding cookies
* Experimental verification of the proposed mechanism for Web session management

INTRODUCTION

Since its inception, HTTP (HyperText Transfer Protocol) has been a protocol for the rapid distribution of information [1,2]. Through simple requirements-responses, the protocol provides access to text, images, audio, HTML (HyperText Markup Language), and other resources. The protocol was created following the premise of a stateless one, with individual requests for specific resources replied with concrete answers providing either the resource or an indication of failure. HTTP rapidly became established as the quintessential application protocol due to massive Internet use, and evolved to what is known today as the World Wide Web. Over time, the need for different types of Web applications emerged (shopping sites, Webmail sites, home banking, etc.), and with them the need for a mechanism that allows the management of user sessions. Up to that point, the stateless nature of the HTTP protocol made it almost impossible to associate several requests of a Web application to the single user that originated those requests.

In order to be able to implement Web applications as those described above, a mechanism for HTTP session management was developed [3]. This mechanism enabled Web applications to have what is known as user sessions or Web sessions. Web session management does not alter in any way the HTTP protocol, since the mechanism is based on the use of additional HTTP headers exchanged between the client browser and the Web application server to associate the request with a particular user/session. The first proposal that allowed HTTP sessions called "cookies" to this additionals headers. The term remained in future recommendations to the IETF (Internet

Engineering Task Force), which were introduced in order to standardize the management of HTTP sessions [4−7]. Currently, the basic operation for the establishment of a Web session, when a user enters a particular site (i.e., makes a Web application request), can be explained as follows:

- The server sets a cookie and sends the cookie to the client in an HTTP header in the HTTP response.
- When the client receives the HTTP response, the client extracts the session cookie and stores it for the next HTTP requests to the same site.
- Every future requirement from the client to the previously visited site includes the stored HTTP cookie.
- The server is able to associate a request with a user session by inspecting the value of the header where the cookie is found.

Thus, the mechanism for Web session management enabled Web applications to set the association of a specific client with the requirements that the client has previously made. Basically, the use of cookies allowed for managing user sessions, which, in turn, allowed Web applications to authenticate users, authorize access to resources, and even to audit the actions performed by the users at the application level. However, cookies also introduced problems associated with security and user privacy [8,9]. Cookies could be stolen by different techniques, and other cookie-related issues in the development of Web applications further exposed the security of these types of applications and users. In this regard, note that when a cookie is stolen, it is possible to carry out session hijacking attacks, which can lead to identity theft attacks, denial of service, etc.

OWASP (Open Web Application Security Project) became a source of reference in different aspects of Web application security [10], and mainly focused on the development of secure Web applications. OWASP provides various guidelines for the safe development of Web applications, verification of Web application security, and code review, among others [11−14]. OWASP also provides another valuable resource to the Internet user community: a document called OWASP Top Ten Project, which describes the ten most dangerous security vulnerabilities in Web applications. The document was initially written in 2004 and was updated in 2007, 2010, and 2013 [15]. Many of the security problems identified by OWASP are related to the previously described session management via HTTP cookies.

We propose a new technique for Web session management, which transparently avoids exchanging HTTP cookies between a Web client and a Web server interconnection. Thus, there is no need for redesign or reimplementation of current Web applications to work under the proposed mechanism.

The rest of the chapter is organized as follows: The section titled "Related Work" introduces a summary related to session security, specifically focusing on cookie-related vulnerabilities; in "Proposed Mechanism for Web Session Management," the proposal for the special management of cookies is conceptually explained; "Implementation and Experiments" details the proof of concept implementation as well as the experimentation results on some specific Web applications; "Conclusions and Further Work" is devoted to conclusions and includes suggestions for future lines of research and work.

Related work

As explained above, the current mechanism for Web session management implies exchanging cookie/s between the client and the server of a Web application. Because of the very definition of the mechanism, the issue of user privacy was a topic of debate. The use of cookies and HTTP headers like Referer leads to situations where a third party is able to set up user profiles and determine, for a large set of users, which sites are visited by each of them, at what time of day, etc. Since the proposal for and creation of cookies, there have been several warnings published about a large loss of privacy, even from one of the authors of the RFC, which defined cookies as part of the HTTP headers for session management [8,9]. Besides the problems that cookies represent for user privacy, the security of Web applications can be affected by various problems, allowing for unauthorized access or identity fraud through manipulation or stolen cookies. Several Web session attacks are shown in [16], including those using SSL (Secure Sockets Layer), leading to the conclusion that (a) part of the problem is that HTTP is a stateless protocol, and (b) a solution would be to replace HTTP for something more suitable. Our approach does not include changing the protocol; it involves operating differently in order to avoid cookies while maintaining backward compatibility (i.e., no Web applications recoding/fixing).

OWASP has been working to enhance Web applications security in the current scenario of HTTP usage (including cookies). Also, OWASP explicitly identifies commercial initiatives working on Web security [17]. Several Web application security vulnerabilities included in OWASP Top Ten Project [15] are directly related to cookies, such as:

- "A2 Broken Authentication and Session Management," which is possible once a session cookie has been stolen or by session fixation attacks [18]. The stolen cookie can be used to steal the complete session, which, in turn, allows a third party/user to act as the real/original user.
- "A3 Cross-Site Scripting," or XSS, which allows stealing session cookies. Even if the HttpOnly attribute is used for cookies, another attack, XST (Cross-Site Tracing) [19], which can be considered as an XSS variant, allows stealing of cookies. The XST attack is possible only when the "harmless" HTTP Trace method is available. Enabling the HTTP Trace method could be considered as part of another OWASP top ten vulnerability: "A5 Security Misconfiguration."
- "A6 Sensitive Data Exposure," which also allows stealing session cookies. Some sites do not use SSL at all or use SSL only for exchanging user/password information, while all other data exchange is transferred as plain text. Non-encrypted data is easily recovered by means of sniffing techniques.

A summary of Web applications security actions/arrangements, taking into account [11−13] (specifically development and testing guides), can be done by different groups of people:

- Developers:
  - Verify all application inputs in order to prevent XSS attacks ("A3 Cross-Site Scripting").
  - Implement several controls related to cookies that are specifically oriented to prevent "A2 Broken Authentication and Session Management," such as:
    - Set a short time for cookies to expire, or expire them when the browser is closed.
    - Set the HttpOnly and Secure attributes to cookies.
    - Set the proper Domain and Path attributes to cookies.
    - Verify that every cookie maintains the same source IP.
    - Invalidate cookies after ending a session.
    - Always generate non-predictable cookies at the server side.
    - Renew cookies after a user/application privilege level change.
    - Use random tokens in order to avoid CSRF attacks: "A8 Cross-Site Request Forgery."

- Web server managers/administrators:
  - Disable dangerous HTTP methods: Trace, Connect, Delete, and Put, as suggested in OWASP Testing Guide (Put and Trace are the most dangerous).
  - Always use HTTPS in sites requiring user authentication and sensitive data transfer (cookies are one of the sensitive data, most of the time) so to reduce "A6 Sensitive Data Exposure."
- Security team:
  - Perform security tests to find possible gaps in the system.

As expected, OWASP suggestions do not imply that a site must be absolutely free of security concerns the suggestions are to reduce the number of possible issues as well as increase the complexity of eventual security/privacy attacks.

Proposed mechanism for web session management

Given that Web session management can be defined as the capability of maintaining a record of the succession of requests a Web client (user) has made, the proposed mechanism is based on the association

$$\text{client session} <==> \text{TCP connection}$$

in order to take advantage of the HTTP 1.1 keep-alive capabilities to persist the TCP connection used between Web client and server. The core of the proposed mechanism is the identification of a user session through the TCP connection, instead of the transfer of cookies set at the server side between client and server. The concept is not completely new; different application protocols transported over TCP, such as SSH, imap, pop, rdesktop, and so on, give meaning to the session while the corresponding TCP connection is established. If the TCP connection is interrupted, the session is lost or canceled. Two important problems have to be solved at this point:

- The proposed mechanism should be able to keep the state of a user/Web client session. The Web application has no way of determining whether successive requirements that come from the same TCP connection correspond to the same user a priori, since HTTP is a stateless protocol.
- The proposed mechanism should be transparent to existing Web applications. Currently, Web sessions are implemented as defined in RFC 6265. Although the proposed mechanism avoids cookie exchange with the client side, the Web application will maintain cookie usage (as *coming from* Web clients).

If these problems were solved, it would be possible to maintain backward compatibility with Web applications currently in production, as well as to avoid cookie/s exchange between Web clients and Web applications.

Conceptually, the proposed mechanism is based in a Web server filter/module capable of managing cookies so that:

- one HTTP session will be associated to the (client/server) TCP connection used at the transport layer.
- cookies are neither sent to nor received from Web clients. Instead, the filter module completely manages cookies.

- every cookie is associated with a Web client using its TCP connection to the Web server.
- the Web application software still receives the cookies as being sent by the Web client; that is, *transparently*.

Figure 29.1 shows schematically how the proposed scheme works, and in fact the proof of concept implemented and reported in this work follows exactly that description, taking advantage of the Apache Web server modular software architecture. Note that a cookie is necessary at the client side just to be returned in each following HTTP request (as described in RFC 6265), now the server replaces the usage of cookies by the TCP connection established by the client. However, given that current Web applications still use/need cookies at the server side, the intermediate filter in Figure 29.1 not only associates a persistent TCP connection to a Web session but also associates the persistent TCP connection to the corresponding cookie.

The cookie association with a persistent TCP connection is easily implemented by means of a database, as shown in Figure 29.1, which allows:

- the storage of cookies set by the server side, along with the corresponding persistent TCP connection.
- retrieval of the session cookie corresponding to a (persistent TCP connection) Web session by issuing a simple SQL query.

Note that the database stored at the server side is small: only data corresponding to open TCP connections have to be stored. Once a TCP connection is closed, the corresponding data is deleted from the database.

Specifically, the intermediate filter/module implementing the proposed Web session mechanism carries out very simple tasks on demand (for each HTTP request/response):

- When the Web application at the server side provides a response by setting a cookie, that cookie is stored in a local database by the filter/module. Data storage is minimal: each cookie

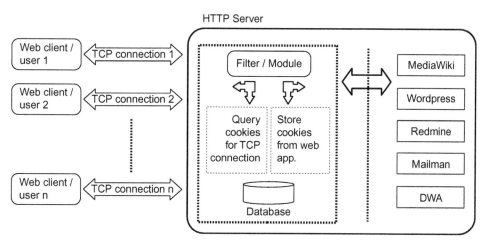

FIGURE 29.1

Management of cookies at a filter module in the Web application server.

and its corresponding persistent TCP connection, which is the TCP connection used to send the HTTP response, is stored. Also, the cookie is not included in the TCP response sent to the Web application client, since the Web application client (i.e., a browser) does not need the cookie.
- Every cookie is deleted from Web client requests; no cookies are used as received from Web clients. In this sense, there is no need to trust the client cookies, since every cookie is locally managed at the server side.
- Every Web client request generates a query on the local database, looking for cookies associated with the Web client persistent TCP connection. Every cookie provided by the database query is attached as part of the HTTP request headers sent to the Web application server. Thus, the Web application server receives the requests with the right cookies—those set by the server—which identifies user/Web session.

Clearly, several other adaptations/changes are also needed at the server side and in Web browsers for implementing client/user identification by its TCP connection.

- At the Web server side:
  - Set KeepAlive connections.
  - Adapt session time (usually a large one).
  - Set the number of requirements received through a connection to a large one.
- At the client (Web browser) side:
  - Set KeepAlive connections.
  - Set to 1 the number of simultaneous connections to the server.
  - Adapt session time (usually a large one).

The next section provides more details, as there are implementation-specific configurations/settings, depending on the Web server application and the browser, used at the Web client application side.

Implementation and experiments

As a proof of concept, the proposed mechanism has been implemented using Apache 2 HTTP server, taking into account its popularity (and its large market share of sites in production), efficiency, and extensibility. Clearly, Apache versatility has been one of the major reasons for its wide installation market share at the production level, and certainly its modular software architecture provides an excellent base for implementing proposals, such as the one in this work. More specifically, the filter/module was implemented as an Apache mod_perl.

At the client side, the Mozilla Firefox Web browser was used with various specific configuration details (non-*default* configuration). Other browsers were considered, but they were not used for various reasons:

- Google Chrome: the maximum number of simultaneous connections to the server is not configurable in this browser. Recall that the maximum number of TCP connections to the server should be 1.
- Opera: Despite being specifically configured for persistent HTTP 1.1 connections, this browser operates connections in a way similar to that expected by non-persistent connections in HTTP

Table 29.1 Tested Web Applications

Application	Version	Language
DVWA	1.0.7	Php
MediaWiki	1.20.4	Php
Wordpress	3.5.1	Php
Redmine	2.3.1	Ruby on Rails
Mailman	2.1.15	Python + C
Meran	0.9.4	Perl

1.0. It was found that the browser closes the connection and starts another one relatively soon. It was not found how to configure the browser to avoid this behavior.

As another part of the proof of concept, several Web applications were tested, taking into account several languages at the server side, as shown in Table 29.1.

Web applications were selected to represent well known applications maintaining some language heterogeneity at server side. Also, the first application, DVWA, has been specifically included because of its well-known number of vulnerabilities, so that it is possible to verify that cookie-related ones are fixed.

Experimental environment

Different configurations were performed on the server and browser to enable persistent connections. The server runs on a Linux Debian Stable (Wheezy), installed with the advanced packaging system (apt command), package apache2-mpm-prefork, HTTP Server: Apache/2.2.22. Specific configuration options to allow persistent TCP sessions

```
/etc/apache2/apache2.conf include:
#
# KeepAlive: Whether or not to allow persistent connections (more than
# one request per connection). Set to "Off" to deactivate.
#
KeepAlive: On
#
# KeepAliveTimeout: Number of seconds to wait for the next request from the
# same client on the same connection. 10 minutes = 600 seconds
#
KeepAliveTimeout: 600
#
# MaxKeepAliveRequests: The maximum number of requests to allow
# during a persistent connection. Set to 0 to allow an unlimited amount.
# We recommend you leave this number high, for maximum performance.
#
MaxKeepAliveRequests: 0
```

The client runs on a Linux Ubuntu 13.04 (Raring Ringtail), with Web browser Mozilla Firefox 22.0 installed with the). Specific configuration options to allow persistent TCP sessions (about: config) were set to:

```
network.http.keep-alive.timeout 600
network.http.max-connections-per-server 1
network.http.max-persistent-connections-per-server 1
network.http.keep-alive true
network.http.pipelining true
network.http.use-cache false
```

Note that the configuration option "network.http.use-cache false" does not affect the connection persistence itself, but it is used in order to avoid testing on modified scenarios due to cache contents/state.

Results and application-specific details

In general, the Web applications shown in Table 29.1 were successfully tested; that is, there were no problems detected while it was used. It is worth noting that the Web browser was not changed (only specifically configured) and the Web application remained unchanged (with only one minor exception, explained below). The main (and only) problem identified in the experimentation phase is related to the browser-side behavior: close the persistent HTTP connection and open another one. While this is acceptable in the current HTTP definition, it completely broke the proposed Web session management, since a new connection implies a brand new Web session. Several Web browser and Web client issues have been identified:

- Firefox implementation of Ctrl-F5: Reloading a page without using a cache in Firefox causes the TCP connection to be regenerated (Firefox closes the current connection and opens a new one). This is clearly an issue related to the browser implementation, since it was found that another browser such as Google Chrome does not regenerate the connection every time the Ctrl-F5 sequence is entered.
- Browser cache: The browser cache threatens normal use of the proposed mechanism. A cached page could be the cause of a malfunction in a Web application. Refreshing all pages using the Ctrl-F5 sequence goes against the proposed mechanism because it causes the use of a new connection. It also makes the debugging tasks much more difficult.
- A 500 HTTP response error code: Every HTTP response type 500 implies the current session should be closed. This is not necessarily a problem, since it would be wise to reset the connection once the server has identified and reported a problem.
- Issues related to HTTP pipelining/pending requests: When too many requests are generated and pipelined, the persistent HTTP connection is reset abruptly and the browser generates a new connection, even though previous responses to previous requests are expected. Clearly, this was found as a result of several stress experiments and depends on the browser implementation details specifically related to HTTP pipelining.
- Large amounts of data: This item is probably related to the previous problem, but problems were found when a page requires a large data transfer from the server. More specifically, Meran

has a configurable homepage that, by default, issues 37 requests, implying a total space of 1.6 MB. After setting and configuring the homepage, 34 requests were necessary, implying a total of 319 KB of space, and no more problems were found.

- DVWA hyperlinks different pages using simultaneously HTML $<a>$ tag and javascript object "window.location" to the linked page, as in

```
<li onclick = "window.location = '...site here.../.?page = include.php'" class>
<a href = "...site here.../.?page = include.php" >File Inclusion</a>
</li>
```

which was changed to

```
<li class>
<a href = "...site here.../.?page = include.php" >File Inclusion</a>
</li>
```

and the application functionality and usability did not change at all.

Most of the problems are related to Web browser implementation choices and are expected to be easily solved. Some application-specific issues, such as that explained above in the context of the DVWA application, are not possible to guess in advance and should be analyzed carefully for each application. DVWA was not chosen because it is easily fixed, though. Performance details such as pipelining, delayed responses, or exchange of large amounts of data could affect the proposed mechanism, as reflected in the above comments and explanations.

In general, as a result of the tests, it was found that the proposed mechanism is immune to all security problems that could be introduced by non-enforcement of security policies provided by OWASP for safe management of user sessions [20]. On the other hand, OWASP policies for authentication management of a Web application [21] are equally useful in both the current mechanism and the proposed mechanism.

CONCLUSION AND FURTHER WORK

It was proposed an alternative mechanism for web sessions management that does not require storage of cookies on browser-side. The proposed mechanism was successfully tested in a proof of concept on a set of Web applications based on different scripting languages. OWASP current security suggestions that should be taken into account (as explained above) by developers and server administrators would be reduced to: (1) prevent CSRF attacks and (2) use HTTPS connections. A browser using the proposed mechanism and specifically implemented for access to Web applications could help prevent CSRF problems on those Web applications. In the extreme scenario in which the World Wide Web uses only the proposed mechanism, there would be no issues about user privacy. However, despite being a utopian idea—that popular sites taking advantage of advertisement would use the proposed mechanism—this mechanism may be appropriate for home banking websites, as well as any other website that provides users access to critical functionality aor critical information.

To summarize, Web applications that use the proposed mechanism for session management would enhance security and privacy, since:

- no session cookies are stored at the client side, thus improving privacy. However, the proposed method does not solve every privacy issue since, for example, Referer usage would be almost forbidden or not used.
- all OWASP recommendations related to session management are not needed under the proposed mechanism.
- several vulnerabilities become harmless under the proposed method for session management:
  - XSS (Cross-Site Scripting).
  - XST (Cross-Site Tracing).
  - Broken authentication and session management:
    - Session fixation
    - Cookie attributes problems
- Web session stealing/tampering/denial of service would be possible only via the more difficult TCP connection stealing/tampering/denial of service. Notice that the use of secure protocols such as HTTPS makes stealing and tampering practically impossible.

There are several future lines of work, some related to current Web application analysis (checking for backward compatibility) and others related to client-side enhancements with respect to the use of different Web browsers. Since Web applications are now so heterogeneous, possibly including RIA (Rich Internet Applications), the analysis of the proposed techniques as a case-by-case job would be too complex. Several tests should be defined and done almost automatically so as to reduce such complexity. At the client side, it would be possible to implement a proxy that enables the use of any browser for Web access. Such a proxy should maintain only one connection with the server while it accepts requests of any Web browser on one or multiple (TCP) connections. If two or more users request access to the same Web application, the proxy should open one connection to the server for every user. If requests come from a NAT network, it could be useful to configure user authentication.

References

[1] Fielding R, Gettys J, Mogul J, Frystyk H, Masinter L, Leach P, et al. RFC 2616—Hypertext transfer protocol—HTTP/1.1; 1999.
[2] W3C. Http-Hypertext transfer protocol. [Internet]. Retrieved from: <http://www.w3.org/Protocols/>; [accessed 06.13].
[3] Netscape. Persistent client state-http cookies. [Internet]. Retrieved from: <http://curl.haxx.se/rfc/cookie_-spec.html>; [accessed 06.13].
[4] Kristol D, Montulli L. RFC 2109-Http state management mechanism. 1997.
[5] Moore K, Freed N. RFC 2964-Use of http state management. 2000.
[6] Kristol D, Montulli L. RFC 2965-Http state management mechanism. 2000.
[7] Barth A. RFC 6265-Http state management mechanism. 2011.
[8] Schwartz J. Giving Web a memory cost its users privacy. The New York Times. [Internet]. Available at: <http://www.nytimes.com/2001/09/04/business/giving-web-a-memory-cost-its-users-privacy.html>; 2001 [accessed 06.13].

[9] Kristol DM. Http cookies: Standards, privacy, and politics. ACM Transactions on Internet Technology (TOIT) 2001;1(2):151−98.

[10] OWASP. The open web application security project . [Internet]. Retrieved from: <http://www.owasp.org>; [accessed 06.13].

[11] OWASP. OWASP guide project. [Internet]. Retrieved from: <http://www.owasp.org/index.php/Category:OWASP_ Guide_Project>; [accessed 06.13].

[12] OWASP. OWASP testing project. [Internet]. Retrieved from: <http://www.owasp.org/index.php/Category:OWASP_ Testing_Project>; [accessed 06.13].

[13] OWASP. OWASP code review project. [Internet]. Retrieved from: <http://www.owasp.org/index.php/Category: OWASP_Code_Review_Project>; [accessed 06.13].

[14] OWASP. Cheat sheets. [Internet]. Retrieved from: <https://www.owasp.org/index.php/Cheat_Sheets>; [accessed 06.13].

[15] OWASP. OWASP top ten project. [Internet]. Retrieved from: <http://www.owasp.org/index.php/Category:OWASP_ Top_Ten_Project>; [accessed 06.13].

[16] Böck J. Session-Cookies and SSL. Study research project at the EISS (European Institute for system security). [Internet]. Available at: <http://blog.hboeck.de/uploads/ssl-cookies.pdf>; 2008 [accessed 06.13].

[17] OWASP. OWASP testing project, appendix A: Testing tools. [Internet]. Retrieved from: <https://www.owasp.org/index.php/Appendix_A:_Testing_Tools#Commercial_Black_Box_Testing_tools>; [accessed 06.13].

[18] OWASP. Session fixation. [Internet]. Retrieved from: <https://www.owasp.org/index.php/Session_fixation>.

[19] OWASP. Cross site tracing. [Internet]. Retrieved from: <https://www.owasp.org/index.php/Cross_Site_Tracing>.

[20] OWASP. Session management cheat sheet. [Internet]. Retrieved from: <https://www.owasp.org/index.php/Session_Management_Cheat_Sheet>.

[21] OWASP. Authentication cheat sheet. [Internet]. Retrieved from: <https://www.owasp.org/index.php/Authentication_Cheat_Sheet>.

Leveraging Semantic Web Technologies for Access Control

30

Eugenia I. Papagiannakopoulou[1], Maria N. Koukovini[1], Georgios V. Lioudakis[1], Nikolaos L. Dellas[2], Dimitra I. Kaklamani[1], and Lakovos S. Venieris[1]

[1]*National Technical University of Athens, Athens, Greece*
[2]*SingularLogic Software and Integrated IT Solutions, Nea Ionia, Greece*

INFORMATION IN THIS CHAPTER

- Implementing RBAC with ontologies
- Semantically extending the XACML Attribute Model
- Ontology-based context awareness
- Ontological specification of user preferences
- Semantic access control in online social networks
- DEMONS Ontological Access Control Model

INTRODUCTION

Any security violation and breach certainly includes illicit access to some resources, being systems, data, or operations. In this context, the evolution of security policies has brought access control at the core of security, but also privacy protection. Therefore, beyond legacy access control models, such as the Discretionary Access Control (DAC), the Mandatory Access Control (MAC) [1], and the well-adopted Role-Based Access Control (RBAC) [2], a variety of systems have been proposed, introducing a manifold of additional features. Most of the prominent approaches typically propose enhancements to RBAC models in order to incorporate different criteria in access control decisions, rather than just *which user* holding *which role* is performing *which action* on *which object*. In that respect, access control models have adopted concepts such as organization [3], context [4], attributes [5], and Separation and Binding of Duty (SoD/BoD) [6], among others, whereas Privacy-Aware Access Control [7] has emerged as a research field fostering personal data protection

493

leveraging access control. The advent of the Semantic Web and the technologies it brings, such as semantic ontologies and reasoning mechanisms, have provided access control with new potentials. Therefore, several approaches have leveraged Semantic Web technologies in various ways, seeking expressiveness, formal semantics, and reasoning capabilities; as a starting point, the Web Ontology Language (OWL) [8] was used to develop policy languages for the Web, such as Rei and KAoS [9], as well as to provide interoperability while accessing heterogeneous databases, as in [10–12].

This chapter provides an overview of the most characteristic access control approaches that make use of Semantic Web technologies. The motivation, application domain, and usage patterns followed by the studied approaches vary significantly. Therefore, the following sections adopt a categorization that is by no means unique, but that highlights important differentiations among the approaches. Since currently RBAC constitutes the baseline for access control, "Implementing RBAC with Ontologies" investigates approaches targeting its ontological implementation, whereas the next three sections outline systems with more specific focus. In particular, "Semantically Extending the XACML Attribute Model" overviews approaches providing semantic extensions to the XACML attribute model, "Ontology-Based Context Awareness" investigates the use of Semantic Web technologies fostering context-awareness in access control, and "Ontological Specification of User Preferences" describes mechanisms for ontologically specifying access and usage control user preferences. The advent of online social networks fed access control with new challenges, so "Semantic Access Control in Online Social Networks" deals with the corresponding semantic approaches. In "DEMONS Ontological Access Control Model," the DEMONS model, developed by the authors, is outlined; it is a fully ontological approach, combining various features and providing several advantages. Finally, "Discussion" concludes the chapter with a comparative discussion on the basis of important trends and features of the studied access control approaches.

Implementing RBAC with ontologies

Recently, there have been several efforts to express RBAC [2] policies using OWL. In this context, ontologies are used to represent the main concepts of RBAC—Action, Subject, Object, Role, Permission—as well as role hierarchies and dynamic and static SoD constraints. An important work in this field is presented in [13], where Finin et al. have introduced R*OWL*BAC, proposing two different approaches regarding role representation: the first maps roles to classes and sub-classes to which individual subjects can belong, whereas the second represents roles as instances of the generic `Role` class. In both cases, actions, subject,s and objects are represented by the corresponding classes, while the disjoint `PermittedAction` and `ProhibitedAction` subclasses of `Action` are introduced in order to control access. In the first case, roles (and active roles) are represented as classes of users, and the role hierarchy relation is mapped to the subsumption relation in OWL. In addition, this approach maps static and dynamic SoD constraints to class disjointness constraints in OWL. The second approach, modeling roles as instances, uses the properties `role` and `activeRole` in order to bind users to their possible and active roles, respectively. In this case, role hierarchy is obtained by means of the `subRole` property and constraints are modeled through the specialized `ssod` and `dsod` properties. However, in the second approach, DL reasoning cannot be exploited for enforcing RBAC. Instead, rules need to be added in the ontology, thus degrading performance. Similar to R*OWL*BAC, Ferrini et al. present an approach referred to as XACML + OWL [14]. In this model, OWL is used in conjunction with XACML [15], with a view to decoupling the management of constraints and RBAC hierarchies from the specification and the enforcement of the actual XACML policies. Additionally, it addresses some shortcomings of R*OWL*BAC, like the inconsistency when two classes are at the same time included (according to the role hierarchy) and subject to SoD constraints. Subjects are represented as OWL individuals, information about which can be retrieved through *semantic functions* defined in the framework. Regarding dynamic SoD constraints, this approach goes further by adding `Resource` and `Permission` classes which, along with the `Action` class, can be used to specify more complex constraints involving not only subjects, but also actions and resources. XACML + OWL exploits the obligation mechanism of XACML for managing the dynamic SoD constraints, so that for each permission granted, a list of axioms is added to the ontology, thus reducing constraint evaluation to the problem of checking the consistency of an ontology.

Another approach in the same philosophy is presented in [16], where He et al. define a high level OWL DL ontology and rules expressed by means of the Semantic Web Rule Language (SWRL) [17], not only representing and extending the NIST Standard RBAC model, but also combining the latter with the Attribute Based Access Control (ABAC) paradigm [5], in order to implement access control for Web services. This approach obtains dynamic role assignments based on users' credentials and their attributes, as well as dynamic association of access privileges with roles through attributes associated with services. Likewise, RBAC is adopted by [18] in a similar way and extended with contextual attributes, resulting in an access control system for context-aware collaborative environments, designed and built using Semantic Web technologies. The defined RBAC ontology is in turn attached to a domain-specific ontology that captures the features of the application in order to take into account attributes during the definition of policies and the access control decision. The limited expressive power of Description Logic has been mitigated by introducing SPARQL queries [19] that can check additional constraints against an available knowledge base.

Semantically extending the XACML attribute model

Apart from XACML + OWL [14], presented in the previous section, several approaches have leveraged XACML together with ontologies, most of them targeting the expression limitations of the attribute-based paradigm. In this direction, the approach presented in [20] proposes an ontology-based inference engine, which extends XACML attribute management for simplifying the specification and maintenance of ABAC policies. The standard XACML architecture is enhanced with two extensions, namely the Inference Engine and the Ontology Administration Point (OAP). User, resource, and environment attributes are ontologically represented and delivered by the OAP, and the Inference Engine in turn performs mappings between different attributes and attribute conditions. Inference is obtained with the help of SWRL rules, and derived attributes can then be queried by the context handler with SPARQL requests.

The approach presented in [21] addresses the expressiveness limitations of XACML regarding knowledge representation; it extends it in order to support ontology-based reasoning and rule-based inference, while maintaining the usability of its original features. In that respect, an intelligent

XACML shell, based on a multi-layer semantic framework, is used to enhance the semantic and knowledge representation of XACML by leveraging Semantic Web technologies. It is noted that, as opposed to XACML, where the data type of an attribute is a primitive data type, this approach enables the data type to be mapped to an ontology class, thus inheriting semantic knowledge from a specific domain.

Likewise, in [22], an XML filter is created for regulating the disclosure of information, according to both the XML document structure and the semantics of its contents; this is achieved by directly integrating a knowledge base, which contains a description of the domain, in an XACML engine. In essence, the OWL files contain a description of the concepts and their relations, and of the mapping to the corresponding document elements. A Policy Semantic Point (PSP) acts as a bridge between the access control and the ontology model by executing SPARQL queries on the inferred knowledge base.

Ontology-based context awareness

An important aspect of access control is reflected by the concept of *context*, which generally refers to information describing a specific situation; context includes static and dynamic environmental characteristics such as temporal, spatial, and historical. Contextual parameters concerning the subject, object, or action of an access control request, usually affect the activation of a role or the enforcement of a rule. Specifying which parts of this context information are relevant for a specific authorization decision, and how the corresponding information may be elicited and defined in the associated models, constitute key aspects of access control. The significance of context in this domain is evident, as there have been proposed numerous extensions to well-established models in order to include it, such as the Extended RBAC Profile of XACML, presented in [23].

A prominent approach in this area constitutes the Temporal Semantic Based Access Control (TSBAC) model [24], which enhances the specification of user-defined authorization rules by constraining time interval and temporal expressions over users' history of accesses, which are stored in a History Base. Indeed, the concept of history of accesses constitutes a parameter of significant importance, for example, for cases when the disclosure of some data must exclude the future access on the same or other data. This model uses logical time, rather than real time, in its authorization rules, while also providing a formal semantics specification for temporal authorizations. As TSBAC is an extension of the Semantic Based Access Control (SBAC) model [25,26], it is also based on the use of OWL ontologies for modeling access control entities along with their semantic interrelations, thus defining a *Subjects-Ontology*, an *Objects-Ontology*, and an *Actions-Ontology*. The most important contribution of SBAC has been the efficient propagation of policies—based on subsumption—through different semantic interrelations in the three levels of an ontology; *concept-level*, *property-level* and *individual-level*, where the semantic authorization flow can occur in each level or between different levels. The model proposed in [27] and referred to as GTHBAC is an extension of TSBAC, making use of real-time schemes as well; history-based constraints are integrated along with a generic access control model, thus increasing the expressiveness of the authorization rules while allowing temporal history-based decision and making it applicable to a wide variety of access control models.

Among the approaches comprising the family of context-aware semantic models, OrBAC [3,4,28] is rather the most mature, as it is the first approach to express all different types of context within a unique homogeneous framework. In particular, OrBAC defines a *Context Ontology* comprised not only of temporal, spatial, and historical context but also of *user-declared* and *application dependent* context; the latter depends on the characteristics that join the subject, the action, and the object and can be evaluated by querying the system database, whereas user-declared context allows for modeling contexts that are difficult to be described using environmental conditions. It is noted also that provisions targeting privacy protection can be implemented leveraging context, as proposed in [29], where the concept of purpose is modeled as a user-declared context. Starting from these elementary contexts, OrBAC allows for also defining conjunctive, disjunctive, and negative contexts. On the other hand, another specificity of the OrBAC ontology is that traditional triples <subject, action, object> are abstracted at the organizational level into triples <role, activity, view>; in particular, subjects are empowered in roles, objects are used in views, and actions implement activities, while forming hierarchies. In [30], ontologies to describe alerts and policies are defined, using inference rules to perform the mapping between concrete alerts and OrBAC contexts, which represent the necessary reaction that must be enforced when an alert is detected by the monitoring system.

Ontological specification of user preferences

Several access control approaches also incorporate in the decision-making process rules defined by the users, expressing in this way their own access and usage preferences. This trend is particularly met in privacy-aware access control [7], where XML-based languages, such as P3P [31] and APPEL [32], are used for formally representing preferences.

In order to increase the expressive power of such languages and enforce the semantics of a person's data protection intentions, researchers have leveraged ontologies. In this context, a model for privacy preferences representation and management, in which preference rules are represented in OWL, is described in [33]. This model includes formal descriptions of how requests and preference rules are defined, properties of a consistent rule-set that must be satisfied, how requests and preferences are matched, and how the consistency of the rule-set is ensured.

In [34], Sacco et al. present the Privacy Preference Ontology (PPO) along with the Privacy Preference Manager (PPM), allowing for fine-grained access control for the Web of Data. PPO provides a lightweight vocabulary for defining fine-grained privacy preferences for structured data, in combination with the Web Access Control (WAC) ontology,[1] while PPM allows users to create privacy preferences based on PPO and restricts access to their data to third-party users. `PrivacyPreference` constitutes the main class of PPO and various types of properties allow for defining: access restrictions to statements, resources, and named graphs; conditions to specify which particular statements, resources, and named graphs are being restricted; which access

---

[1]WAC-http://www.w3.org/ns/auth/acl.

privilege should be granted; and attribute patterns that must be satisfied by requesters. Specifically for the specification of attribute patterns, SPARQL ASK queries are leveraged.

In the same context, Hu et al. [35] propose that the semantic formal model for P3P can be enforced and expressed as a variety of ontologies and rules combinations, either by means of *homogeneous integration*, where all of the major terms are defined in ontologies and rules are used to overcome the expression limitations of ontologies, or through *hybrid integration*, where some of the terms in privacy protection policies are not explicitly declared or defined in ontologies but they are declared as predicates in each rule. Three types of ontologies are proposed, namely *data user ontology* categorizing the type of users, *data type ontology* describing personal profiles and digital traces, and *purpose ontology* to describe the intention of a data user to use a particular type of data.

Another approach leveraging P3P is [36], which relies on an ontology-based representation of the standard P3P base data schema, showing the internal structure of complex credentials in terms of fine-grained items. The P3P ontology is applied in order to automatically extend available XACML policies to include semantically equivalent additional conditions on users and resource description metadata. Augmented access control policies can be used as a replacement of the original ones, automatically incorporating ontology knowledge.

Semantic access control in online social networks

Online Social Networks (OSNs) have become a major type of online applications allowing information sharing among a large number of users, raising at the same time, however, new security and privacy concerns. The complex relations considered in such applications highlight the need for semantic organization of the contained knowledge and for semantic access control mechanisms.

In this context, Giunchiglia et al. [37] propose a Relation Based Access Control model (RelBAC), providing a formal model of permissions based on relationships among communities and resources. RelBAC can be used to model access control in terms of lightweight ontologies of users, objects, and permissions, allowing for automatically managing permissions. Similarly, the approach presented in [38] exploits relationships with the individuals and the community in order to determine the access restrictions to community resources. All this knowledge is represented in an ontology using OWL DL, while semantic rules are added on top of the ontology providing the sufficient expressivity and decidability to infer the indirect relationships.

Carminati et al. provide in [39] a much richer OWL ontology for modeling various aspects of online social networks, while also proposing *authorization, administration,* and *filtering* policies that depend on trust relationships among various users and are modeled using OWL and SWRL. In particular, the authors suggest modeling the following five important aspects of OSNs using Semantic Web ontologies: personal information, relationships among users, resources, relationships between users and resources, and actions.

A more detailed approach is presented in [40], which proposes the Ontology-based Social Network Access Control (OSNAC) model, encompassing two ontologies; the Social Networking systems Ontology (SNO), capturing the information semantics of a social network, and the Access Control Ontology (ACO), which allows for expressing the SWRL access control rules on the relations among concepts in the SNO. Finally, it captures delegation of authority and empowers both users and the system to express fine-grained access control policies.

DEMONS ontological access control model

In the context of the EU FP7 DEMONS project,[2] a novel ontological access control model has been proposed aiming at introducing privacy awareness into distributed processes [41,42]. It is the latest of a series of ontology-based access control models that our group has developed during the last years [43−47]. The DEMONS approach has been conceived with expressiveness in mind and combines several features, including context, attributes, privacy-awareness, SoD and BoD, and a variety of dependencies, while having been successfully applied in the automatic privacy-aware verification and transformation of distributed workflows. It consists of two OWL ontologies, namely the Information Model Ontology (IMO) and the Policy Model Ontology (PMO), with the former containing the domain knowledge and the latter providing all the necessary classes and properties for the ontological specification of access control rules. Knowledge extraction is performed by means of a targeted reasoning software library implemented in DEMONS.

The DEMONS model is grounded on the concept of *actions*, referring to the situation where an *actor* performs an *operation* on a *resource* within an *organization*, that is, an action is a structure $<a_i, op_i, res_i, org_i>$. Access control rules are used for defining *permissions*, *prohibitions*, and *obligations* over actions and can be specified at three abstraction levels: abstract, concrete, or semi-abstract. An *access control rule* is a structure:

$$\left.\begin{array}{l}Permission \\ Prohibition \\ Obligation\end{array}\right\}(pu, \ act, \ preAct, \ cont, \ postAct)$$

where *act* is the action that the rule applies to, *pu* is the purpose for which *act* is permitted/prohibited/obliged to be executed, *cont* is a structure of contextual parameters, *preAct* is a structure of actions that should have preceded, and *postAct* refers to the action(s) that must be executed following the rule enforcement. The basis for the access control rules specification is provided by the IMO, where the considered concepts comprise classes characterized by intra- and inter-class relations that are implemented as OWL object properties. The main intra-class properties are isA, isPartOf and moreDetailedThan that essentially comprise AND- and OR- hierarchies (e.g., purposes OR hierarchy; data types, roles, and operations AND and OR hierarchies, etc.), enabling inheritance, as well as dependencies specification. Inter-class relations describe associations between concepts of different classes, indicating, for instance, the roles that may act for a purpose, or the attributes characterizing a concept.

---

[2]DEcentralized, cooperative, and privacy-preserving MONitoring for trustworthinesS (DEMONS), homepage: http://fp7-demons.eu/.

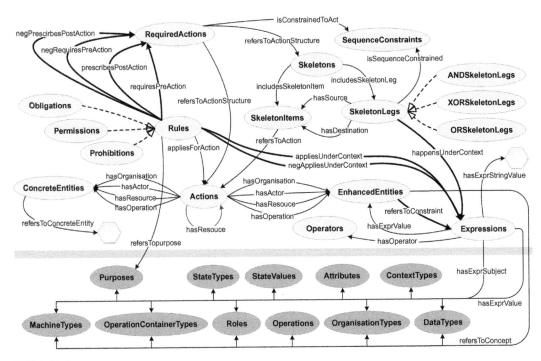

FIGURE 30.1

Policy model ontology (PMO). Dark-shaded ovals denote IMO classes.

The main components of access control rules are actions. As shown in Figure 30.1 depicting the PMO, actions are ontologically implemented as Actions class instances, with $<a_i, op_i, res_i, org_i>$ being reproduced by means of the corresponding object properties. Within actions, actor, operation, resource, and organization are defined at either the abstract or the concrete level; in that respect, for the representation of an action's elements at the abstract level, instances of the EnhancedEntities class are leveraged, constraining the referenced IMO semantic type with respect to its attributes and/or sub-concepts, while for the concrete level, the aforementioned properties point at instances of the class ConcreteEntities.

Two useful tools for defining constraints upon actions' elements, and also achieving rich expressiveness in general, are *expressions* and *logical relations*. The latter, implied by thick lines in Figure 30.1, allow specifying logical structures of concepts. Expressions enable the definition of contextual conditions and constraints on concepts (e.g., on an actor's attributes); they comprise ternary relations assigning a value to a subject through an operator, or logical structures of such triples.

Actions instances are used for specifying the main action and pre- and post-actions of a rule; in the latter cases this association is indirect, with the RequiredActions class mediating and enabling the specification of time and sequence constraints. Beyond such constraints, the DEMONS

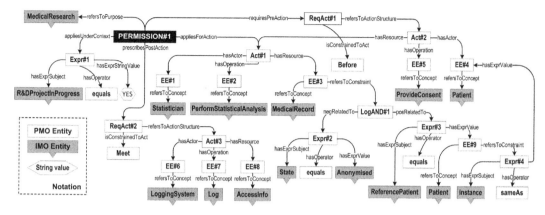

FIGURE 30.2

Example of ontological access control rule.

approach incorporates a mechanism for combining actions, so as to form complex structures thereof, referred to as *skeletons*, following various sequence patterns. Finally, dependencies among all the entities comprising the actions of a rule enable the specification of advanced SoD and BoD constraints, instead of relying only on role-/user- centric constraints.

Figure 30.2 illustrates the ontological representation of an example rule, inspired from guidelines for the health sector [48]: *"For the purpose of medical research and in the context of an ongoing R&D project, a statistician is allowed to perform statistical analysis on identifiable medical records of a patient, if the said patient has provided consent therefore; for accountability reasons, access should be immediately logged."*

In that respect, three actions are considered, corresponding to the statistical analysis (Act#1), the pre-action of consent provision (Act#2), and the post-action of logging (Act#3). The use of the SequenceConstraints instance Meet imposes a strict temporal constraint, prescribing that the end of the main action should coincide with the beginning of the post-action (Act#3), whereas Before implies a loose sequence constraint, meaning that the pre-action Act#2 should be executed sometime before the main action. Additionally, these actions involve various enhanced entities, most of which are unconstrained, such as EE#1 corresponding to the Statistician actor, or EE#2 reflecting the statistical analysis operation. On the other hand, EE#3 referring to the MedicalRecord resource has two constraints, described by expressions Expr#2 and Expr#3, and associated through an AND logical relation (LogAND#1). Specifically, Expr#2 implies identifiable data, through negation over Anonymised state, while Expr#3 is an example of concepts' binding. MedicalRecord, being the resource of statistical analysis (Act#1), is assumed to contain the ReferencePatient field, indicating the patient it refers to. Since Patient is a Roles instance, it has to be explicit that it is not any patient who has provided consent, but the one being the data subject of the MedicalRecord. In that respect, EE#9 is constrained by Expr#4, specifying that the reference patient instance should be sameAs the patient implied by EE#4.

Actions themselves may comprise resources of other actions. This is the case with Act#1, comprising the resource of Act#2, in the sense that the patient must have provided consent for Act#1 execution. Finally, the permission of Figure 30.2 applies for the purpose of `MedicalResearch`, given that an R&D project is in progress (`R&DProjectInProgress`).

Discussion

In the previous sections, some of the most representative state-of-the-art ontological access control models have been presented. Seeking the description of inheritance of authorizations and properties, as well as advanced reasoning capabilities, a common characteristic of these models is that they leverage ontologies in order to construct hierarchies of the considered concepts. Support of hierarchies may vary from simple role hierarchy (e.g., as in [13]) to hierarchies of all the concepts associated with the access authorization, such as purposes or operations (e.g., as in [41]).

Moreover, apart from the main features that they support, these models can be further evaluated against a set of key access control aspects; Table 30.1 provides an overview of the features that each of the afore-presented models supports, either directly or partially. The basic criterion for categorizing an access-control model as privacy-aware is whether it takes into consideration the purpose for which access to resources is requested during the access decision process; for instance, [33] and [41] explicitly base their authorizations upon the concept of purpose. Other approaches, such as [40], allow for the specification of usage policies by the owners of the requested resources, whereas other models, for example, [22], are characterized as privacy-aware for aiming at the minimization of data disclosure, this way addressing the *necessity*, *adequacy*, and *proportionality* privacy principles.

Most of the models studied use Semantic Web technologies for the specification of access control rules. In that respect, the majority of the presented models leverage SWRL for expressing the rules over the application domain ontologies, while some approaches, like [18] and [41], completely integrate access control with ontologies by introducing dedicated access control ontologies, and evaluate the access requests by means of reasoning over these ontologies. Lack of semantic rules support means that the model under consideration instead makes use of XML-based standards, such as the XACML policy language, for specifying the corresponding authorizations, leveraging though Semantic Web technologies for their semantic extension. In fact, supporting XACML is by itself an important feature, since this way, an access control model can be employed by systems already using the XACML standard, regardless of the technology used for the specification of access control rules.

Furthermore, a few models provide the means for specifying SoD constraints. Most of them support both static and dynamic SoD, constraining the actors of the access actions, while [30] and [41] allow for the specification of SoD and BoD constraints not only on the actor but also on every entity associated with the access action.

Finally, as *context* and *attributes* are not always treated as independent sets, we consider as attributes those parameters further characterizing the entities of an access action, while contextual information refers to all the external parameters. The purpose of using both these concepts in access control is similar, serving the need to further refine access control rules with parameters that are either dynamic and external or describe variants of similar concepts. Context and attributes provide for describing expressive policies, but also require high expressiveness from the underlying models;

Table 30.1 Comparative Overview of the Semantic Access Control Models

Semantic Models	Privacy-Aware	Context-Aware	Attribute-Based	Semantic Rules	SoD	XACML Support
ROWLBAC [13]	–	*	*	+	+	–
XACML + OWL [14]	–	*	+	–	+	+
He et al. [16]	–	*	+	+	+	–
Cruz et al. [18]	–	+	+	+	+	–
Priebe et al. [20]	–	+	+	–	–	+
Ching Hsu [21]	–	*	+	–	–	+
Rota et al. [22]	+	*	+	–	–	+
GTHBAC [24–27]	–	+	+	+	–	–
OrBAC [3,4,28–30]	*	+	+	+	+	–
Bodorik et al. [33]	+	*	–	+	–	–
PPO + PPM [34]	+	–	+	+	–	–
Hu et al. [35]	+	*	*	+	–	–
Ardagna et al. [36]	+	–	+	–	–	+
RelBAC [37]	+	*	–	+	–	–
Elahi et al. [38]	+	–	–	+	–	–
Carminati et al. [39]	+	–	*	+	–	–
OSNAC [40]	+	–	*	+	–	–
DEMONS [41]	+	+	+	+	+	–

The symbols " + ", "" and " – " indicate, respectively, direct, partial/indirect, and no support for the corresponding feature.*

in that respect, various approaches have leveraged Semantic Web technologies toward describing constraints on context and attributes, as also implied by the popularity of these aspects highlighted in Table 30.1.

Acknowledgments

The research of M. N. Koukovini is co-financed by the European Union (European Social Fund–ESF) and Greek national funds through the Operational Program "Education and Lifelong Learning" of the National Strategic Reference Framework (NSRF) —Research Funding Program: *Heracleitus II. Investing in knowledge society through the European Social Fund.* We also acknowledge partial support from the EU FP7 DEMONS and ARUM projects.

References

[1] Samarati P, di Vimercati SDC. Access control: Policies, models, and mechanisms. In: FOSAD 2000: Foundations of Security Analysis and Design, vol. 2171 of Lecture Notes in Computer Science; Springer; 2001. p. 137−196.

[2] Ferraiolo DF, Sandhu R, Gavrila S, Kuhn DR, Chandramouli R. Proposed NIST standard for role-based access control. ACM Trans Inf Syst Secur 2001;4:224−74.

[3] Abou-El-Kalam RE, Baida P, Balbiani S, Benferhat, F, Cuppens Y, Deswarte A, et al. Organization based access control. In Policy'03: 4th IEEE International Workshop on Policies for Distributed Systems and Networks; 2003 Lake Como, Italy. p. 120−131.

[4] Cuppens F, Cuppens-Boulahia N. Modeling contextual security policies. Int J Inf Secur 2008;7 (4):285−305.

[5] Yuan E., Tong J. Attributed based access control (ABAC) for Web services. In ICWS '05: Proceedings of the IEEE International Conference on Web Services; 2005.

[6] Botha RA, Elo JHP. Separation of duties for access control enforcement in workflow environments. IBM Syst J 2001;40(3):666−82.

[7] Antonakopoulou A, Lioudakis GV, Gogoulos F, Kaklamani DI, Venieris IS. Leveraging access control for privacy protection: A survey. In: Privacy Protection Measures and Technologies in Business Organizations: Aspects and Standards. Yee G, editor. IGI Global; 2012. p. 65−94.

[8] The World Wide Web Consortium (W3C). OWL web ontology language overview. W3C Recommendation. [Internet]. Retrieved from: <http://www.w3.org/TR/owl-features>; 2004.

[9] Tonti G, Bradshaw J, Jeffers R, Montanari R, Suri N, Uszok A. Semantic web languages for policy representation and reasoning: A comparison of KAoS, Rei, and Ponder. In: The SemanticWeb-ISWC 2003. Lecture Notes in Computer Science. Springer. 2003;2870: 419−437.

[10] Mitra P, Pan C-C, Liu P, Atluri V. Privacy-preserving semantic interoperation and access control of heterogeneous databases. In: ASIACCS '06: Proceedings of the 2006 ACM Symposium on Information, Computer and Communications Security; ACM; 2006. p. 66−77.

[11] Pan C-C, Mitra P, Liu P. Semantic access control for information interoperation. In: SACMAT '06: Proceedings of the 11th ACM Symposium on Access Control Models and Technologies. New York, NY; ACM, 2006. p. 237−246.

[12] Sun Y, Pan P, Leung H-F, Shi B. Ontology based hybrid access control for automatic interoperation. In: Xiao B, Yang L, Ma J, Muller-Schloer C, Hua Y, editors. Autonomic and Trusted Computing, 4610. Lecture Notes in Computer Science, Springer; 2007. p. 323−32.

[13] Finin TW, Joshi A, Kagal L, Niu J, Sandhu RS, Winsborough WH, et al. R*OWL*BAC: representing role based access control in OWL. In SACMAT '08: Proceedings of the 13th ACM Symposium on Access Control Models and Technologies; ACM; 2008. p. 73−82.

[14] Ferrini R, Bertino E. Supporting RBAC with XACML + OWL. In SACMAT '09: Proceedings of the 14th ACM Symposium on Access Control Models and Technologies; ACM; 2009. p. 145−154.

[15] Organization for the Advancement of Structured Information Standards (OASIS). eXtensible Access Control Markup Language (XACML) Version 2.0. OASIS Standard. [Internet]. Retrieved from: <http://docs.oasis-open.org/xacml/2.0/access_control-xacml-2.0-core-spec-os.pdf>; 2005.

[16] He Z, Huang K, Wu L, Li H, Lai H. Using semantic web techniques to implement access control for web service Information Computing and Applications In: Zhu R, Zhang Y, Liu B, Liu C, editors. Communications in Computer and Information Science, 105. Springer; 2011. p. 258−66

[17] Parsia B, Sirin E, Grau BC, Ruckhaus E, Hewlett D. Cautiously approaching SWRL. Tech Rep. University of Maryland; 2005.

[18] Cruz F, Gjomemo R, Lin B, Orsini M. A constraint and attribute based security framework for dynamic role assignment in collaborative environments. In: CollaborateCom 2008: Collaborative Computing: Networking, Applications and Worksharing, Bertino E, Joshi JBD, editors. Lecture Notes of the Institute for Computer Sciences, Social Informatics and Telecommunications Engineering, 10. Springer; 2008. p. 322−39.

[19] The World Wide Web Consortium (W3C). SPARQL query language for RDF. W3C Recommendation. [Internet]. <http://www.w3.org/TR/rdf-sparql-query>; 2008.

[20] Priebe T, Dobmeier W, Kamprath N. Supporting attribute-based access control with ontologies,. In ARES 2006: Proceedings of the First International Conference on Availability, Reliability and Security. IEEE Computer Society; 2006. p. 465−472.

[21] Hsu C. Extensible access control markup language integrated with Semantic Web technologies. Inf Sci 2013;238(0):33−51.

[22] Rota SS, Rahaman MA. XML secure views using semantic access control. In EDBT '10: Proceedings of the 2010 EDBT/ICDT Workshops. New York, NY; ACM; 2010. p. 5:1−5:10.

[23] Abi Haidar D, Cuppens-Boulahia N, Cuppens F, Debar H. An extended RBAC profile of XACML. In SWS '06: Proceedings of the 3rd ACM workshop on Secure web services. New York, NY; ACM; 2006. p. 13−22.

[24] Ravari AN, Amini M, Jalili R, Jafarian J. A history based semantic aware access control model using logical time. In ICCIT 2008: Proceedings of the 11th International Conference on Computer and Information Technology; 2008. p. 43−50.

[25] Javanmardi S, Amini M, Jalili R. An access control model for protecting Semantic Web resources. Web policy workshop 2006;32−46.

[26] Javanmardi S, Amini A, Jalili R, Ganjisafar Y. SBAC: A semantic-based access control model. In: NORDSEC-2006; 2006.

[27] Ravari AN, Jafarian J, Amini M, Jalili R. GTHBAC: A generalized temporal history based access control model. Telecommun Syst 2010;45:111−25.

[28] Preda S, Cuppens F, Cuppens-Boulahia N, Garcia-Alfaro J, Toutain L. Dynamic deployment of context-aware access control policies for constrained security devices. J Syst Softw 2011;84:1144−59.

[29] Ajam N, Cuppens-Boulahia N, Cuppens F. Contextual privacy management in extended role based access control model. In: Garcia-Alfaro J, Navarro-Arribas G, Cuppens-Boulahia N, Roudier Y, editors. Data Privacy Management and Autonomous Spontaneous Security, 5939. Lecture Notes in Computer Science. Springer; 2010. p. 121−35.

[30] Cuppens-Boulahia N, Cuppens F, Autrel F, Debar H. An ontology-based approach to react to network attacks. Int J Inf Comput Secur 2009;3(3):280−305.

[31] The World Wide Web Consortium (W3C). The platform for privacy preferences 1.1 (P3P1.1) Specification. [Internet]. Retrieved from: <http://www.w3.org/TR/P3P11>; 2006.

[32] The World Wide Web Consortium (W3C). A P3P preference exchange language 1.0 (AP- PEL1.0). [Internet]. Retrieved from: <http://www.w3.org/TR/P3P-preferences>; 2002.

[33] Bodorik P, Jutla D, Wang MX. Consistent privacy preferences (CPP): model, semantics, and properties. In SAC 2008: Proceedings of the 2008 ACM Symposium on Applied Computing; ACM; 2008. p. 2368−2375.

[34] Sacco O, Passant A, Decker S. An access control framework for the web of data. In: Proceedings of 2011 IEEE 10th International Conference on Trust, Security and Privacy in Computing and Communications (TrustCom); 2011. p. 456−463.

[35] Hu Y-J, Guo H-Y, Guang-DeLin. Semantic enforcement of privacy protection policies via the combination of ontologies and rules. In: Proceedings of IEEE International Conference on Sensor Networks, Ubiquitous and Trustworthy Computing (SUTC '08); 2008. p. 400−407.

[36] Ardagna C, Damiani E, De Capitani di Vimercati S, Fugazza C, Samarati P. Offline expansion of XACML policies based on P3P metadata. In: Lowe D, Gaedke M, editors. Web Engineering, 3579. Lecture Notes in Computer Science; Springer; 2005. p. 363–74.

[37] Giunchiglia F, Zhang R, Crispo B. Ontology driven community access control. In: SPOT2009-Trust and Privacy on the Social and Semantic Web; 2009.

[38] Elahi N, Chowdhury M, Noll J. Semantic access control in web based communities. In ICCGI 2008: Proceedings of the Third International Multi-Conference on Computing in the Global Information Technology; IEEE Computer Society; 2008. p. 131–136.

[39] Carminati B, Ferrari E, Heatherly R, Kantarcioglu M, Thuraisingham B. A semantic web based framework for social network access control. In SACMAT '09: Proceedings of the 14th ACM Symposium on Access Control Models and Technologies; ACM; 2009. p. 177–186.

[40] Masoumzadeh A, Joshi J. OSNAC: An ontology-based access control model for social networking systems. In SOCIALCOM '10: Proceedings of the 2010 IEEE Second International Conference on Social Computing. IEEE Computer Society; Washington, DC, USA; 2010. p. 751–759.

[41] Papagiannakopoulou EI, Koukovini MN, Lioudakis GV, Garcia-Alfaro J, Kaklamani DI, Venieris IS, et al. A privacy-aware access control model for distributed network monitoring. Computers & Electrical Engineering; 2012.

[42] Koukovini MN, Papagiannakopoulou EI, Lioudakis GV, Kaklamani DI, Venieris IS. A workflow checking approach for inherent privacy awareness in network monitoring. In DPM 2011: Proceedings of the 6th International Workshop on Data Privacy Management vol 7122 In: Garcia- Alfaro J, Cuppens-Boulahia N, Navarro-Arribas G, editors. of Lecture Notes in Computer Science. Springer; 2011

[43] Lioudakis GV, Koutsoloukas EA, Dellas NL, Tselikas N, Kapellaki S, Prezerakos GN, et al. A middleware architecture for privacy protection. Comput Netw 2007;51(16):4679–96.

[44] Lioudakis GV, Koutsoloukas EA, Dellas N, Kapitsaki GM, Kaklamani DI, Venieris IS. A semantic framework for privacy-aware access control. In: Proceedings of the 2008 International Multiconference on Computer Science and Information Technology. 3rd International Workshop on Secure Information Systems (SIS 2008); 2008 Oct 20–22; Wisła, Poland; 2008. p. 813–820.

[45] Lioudakis GV, Gogoulos FI, Antonakopoulou A, Kaklamani DI, Venieris IS. Privacy protection in passive network monitoring: An access control approach. In WAINA 2009: Proceedings of the IEEE 23rd International Conference on Advanced Information Networking and Applications (AINA) Workshops/Symposia; 2009 May 26–29; Bradford, UK. 2009. p. 109–116.

[46] Gogoulos F, Antonakopoulou A, Lioudakis GV, Mousas AS, Kaklamani DI, Venieris IS. Privacy-aware access control and authorization in passive network monitoring infrastructures. In CIT 2010: Proceedings of the 10th IEEE International Conference on Computer and Information Technology; 2010.

[47] Antonakopoulou A, Gogoulos FI, Lioudakis GV, Mousas A, Kaklamani DI, Venieris IS. An ontology for privacy-aware access control in network monitoring environments. Journal of Research and Practice in Information Technology; 2013.

[48] Data Protection Commissioner of Ireland. Data protection guidelines on research in the health sector. 2007.

Cyber Security Education: The Merits of Firewall Exercises

31

Evan Damon[1], Jens Mache[1], Richard Weiss[2], Kaleb Ganz[1], Claire Humbeutel[1], and Miles Crabill[1]

[1]Lewis & Clark College, Portland, OR, USA
[2]Evergreen State College, Olympia, WA, USA

INFORMATION IN THIS CHAPTER

- Firewall
- Computer science education
- Lab exercises
- Interaction
- Extensibility
- Approachability
- Competition

INTRODUCTION

Firewalls are an essential part of network defense, and studying them captures aspects of confidentiality and availability. Educating students about them is therefore an essential part of cyber-security education. In this chapter, we describe and evaluate three firewall exercises. We develop four criteria and assess how well each exercise meets the criteria we set out. Finally, we explore emerging trends in firewalls and firewall education, and we make recommendations based on our observations.

Firewalls remain a key element of computer security despite being among the oldest security strategies. Although they have become more sophisticated, port controls and packet inspection techniques are still a mainstay for defending the perimeter of a network. Firewalls originated as the relatively rare packet filter in the late 1980s; they have since become ubiquitous, existing in various forms on nearly every network-connected router, computer, and server. This widespread implementation makes firewalls an integral part of computer security. Strangely, though, firewall education was not emphasized in computer science until recently; firewalls and other security concepts were considered elective material in 2001 [1]. This was probably due to a multitude of factors, such as the lack of a universal firewall syntax and the difficulty of setting up a security laboratory for simulating computer networks and firewalls. Some exercises did exist, but they were not particularly deployable; one exercise required a set of laptops to be transported and set up on-site [2]. The seeming dearth of educational firewall exercises leaves computer security students without a complete understanding of computer networks. Knowledge of firewalls, how they work, and how they are administered is imperative to understanding and practicing computer security.

It is for these reasons that we have evaluated the current state of firewall education. Firewall exercises do exist, after all. The three exercises we selected were chosen for their availability and deployability within an existing classroom or laboratory setting. These exercises came from varied sources. The first was a standalone simulation designed by Professor Ken Williams [3]. This tool, called FireSim, pits players against each other in a competitive simulation. Players assume the role of a firewall administrator and write rules that prevent other players from potentially compromising the security of their network. Simultaneously, they conduct probes against each other, taking advantage of vulnerabilities in the firewall. The second exercise was from Vincent Nestler's *Principles of Computer Security*[4] and used a cloud-based virtual network, called the RAVE. The RAVE exercises give the user control over a virtual network of four machines. The students configure the firewall of one machine and test it from another. The third exercise, DETERlab [5], is also a cloud-based network. Designed by the University of South California's Information Sciences Institute in collaboration with the University of Utah, DETERlab allows students to remotely log in to the VMs. In our case, these were two machines running a Linux environment. One student works with iptables to configure the firewall to prevent unwanted access while allowing desirable services, while the other uses network tools, such as nmap, to test the effectiveness of their other machine's firewall. These three exercises are evaluated in more detail later. In addition, we discuss new firewall exercises by Palo Alto Networks and EDURange. EDURange can be used to create competitive, interactive exercises and is independent of platform.

Criteria for firewall education

In order to predict the educational effectiveness of firewall education exercises, we developed a set of criteria that have shown promising results in classroom environments. Exercises can engage students through interactivity and competition. To teach the security mindset, they should involve real-time problem-solving and analysis. These skills are necessary when configuring an enterprise firewall. Third, exercises should be extensible. That is, instructors or other users should be able to add scenarios or other features to the exercise in a reasonably simple manner. This ensures that the exercise remains up-to-date and teaching points or important concepts can easily be added. Finally, an exercise must be easy to use (approachable). The exercise should achieve the educational goals without adding complexities such as difficult-to-use syntax or tools. In summary, our criteria specifies that an exercise should be competitive, provide some manner of interactivity, have a degree of extensibility, and be easy for a student to understand without being too simplistic.

These criteria were heavily influenced by the curricular guidelines outlined by the Association for Computing Machinery (ACM) and the Institute of Electrical and Electronics Engineers (IEEE) [6]. These guidelines stipulate that firewall education is "generally essential" in undergraduate curricula. The guidelines advise that, at a minimum, eighty percent of the Tier-2 Core subjects (of which firewalls are an element) be covered. The criteria outlined above hopes to facilitate this goal.

Evaluation of firewall exercises

With the above criteria in mind, we evaluated the three previously mentioned exercises and assessed their educational strengths and weaknesses.

FireSim

FireSim was created using Java applets and XML files. The setup involves downloading a group of files to a networked machine that serves as the host machine. Players then connect to the host machine and choose a username. Once the administrator/instructor uses the GUI to start the game, players are able to conduct simulated attacks against one another in a competitive setting. Through the GUI, players select an attack and direct it at a particular opponent. If the attack is successful, the attacker receives a point while the defender loses a point. After 60 seconds, the same attack can be launched against the same opponent. Players write firewall rules using the Cisco firewall syntax. The goal is to create a list of firewall rules that filter specific packets. This can take many forms, but most rules block or allowed access to certain ports, depending on the source and destination IP addresses.

To introduce complexity, FireSim allows the administrator/ instructor to give players new "tasks" or injects. Tasks are stored in the XML files used by the simulation, allowing for more to be added. Each task may require players to create additional firewall rules that mitigate the new situation or vulnerability. The task is announced to the players, and after 60 seconds, players may begin to attack each other using it.

FireSim does many things well. It does a good job of simulating a real network and its network map includes many servers at specific IP addresses. This is one of FireSim's greatest strengths. The underlying network simulation gives the exercise a great deal of potential for further development.

FireSim has weaknesses as well. The tasks are not as clear as they could be. Some are "trick" tasks that do not require additional firewall rules. These are intended to show the user that, when creating a firewall, extending your whitelist too far is dangerous. However, this is not obvious to the user. If a player does nothing and is impervious to attack, they may not learn this lesson. On the other hand, players who incorrectly extend the whitelist may have difficulty understanding why they lose points. Firesim could be made more effective by providing more feedback to the students for them to achieve a deeper understanding.

The scenarios are often about blocking access to a particular service, which is easy enough. However, the zero-sum nature of the point system may promote an offensive strategy, where players spend time attacking other players as frequently as possible. For some players, this may take emphasis away from the firewall configuration and place much of it on attacking. In summary, FireSim is moderately successful as a firewall exercise. It is competitive, since players test each other's firewalls and try to expose vulnerabilities. The competitive structure, though, is a zero-sum structure. This puts a great deal of emphasis on offensive strategies, while the educational goal should concentrate on defense. FireSim does a good job of giving the students hands-on experience. The simulation puts players in full control of a firewall. The main shortcoming is that some of the scenarios are less than successful, but that can be remedied. The simulation offers some extensibility through its XML files, which store the tasks and actions available to players. Finally, FireSim is fairly approachable. The only confounding factors are the syntax and lack of feedback. The feedback level is relatively low, but further development of FireSim or a similar exercise could provide better feedback.

The RAVE

The RAVE lab firewall exercises are designed to teach students how to configure a firewall in Linux. Each student accesses their own virtual machines on which they can configure iptables. The steps for the lab are explicitly spelled out. The goal of the firewall lab is to teach students how to use iptables (using the Uncomplicated Firewall (UFW) [7] syntax) and the effects of different rules through hands-on work.

The advantages of this approach are mostly found in its simplicity, resistance to mistakes, and opportunity to practice what the student are learning about in the related book [4]. The instructions are easy to understand and follow, and they progress in a logical manner. The pictures that are provided make it easy to check how the lab is progressing and to find any part of the GUI that the lab requires.

The use of virtual machines that can be quickly restored from snapshots gives the exercise resistance to mistakes. That way, if a firewall is misconfigured and the student is locked out, the problem can be corrected by restoring the previous state.

A major disadvantage is the lack of scalability. If a number of people are connecting at the same time, the servers can become overloaded. Also, it requires an Internet connection. The RAVE lab does not meet all of our criteria. The exercises are not competitive. Students explore defensive scenarios, but there is no adversary to find their mistakes. RAVE is also not particularly extensible; the configuration is hidden from the instructor. However, RAVE is interactive. The exercise guides the players through the steps, allowing the players to apply what they learn. Unfortunately, this advantage is somewhat diminished by the simplicity of the exercises. The step-by-step nature helps to show the user how to proceed, but does not require the user to apply much analysis. The RAVE is extensible since it is based on virtualization. Currently, most instructors do not have the tools for creating their own exercises or modifying the existing one.

DETERlab

DETERlab offers an exercise in which users configure a firewall on live Linux machines. The DETERlab exercise that covers firewalls also covers UNIX file permissions. The tasks for the two are independent of each other, but descriptions for the two are intermixed. This can make it lengthy to find relevant information for each of the tasks on the walkthrough web page. This section of the chapter focuses exclusively on the firewall aspects of the exercise.

The firewall tutorial portion of this exercise starts out with a description of stateless and stateful firewalls, what the difference between them is, and a little bit of history behind the development of the two. A description follows of how a firewall policy should be designed and how to implement one using iptables, the default Linux firewall. It briefly covers the syntax and a few example rules. The lab then goes on to describe four different network tools. These are nmap, ifconfig, telnet, and netcat. Each of these has about a sentence- to a paragraph-long description and an example of what the tool returns in the terminal when used.

The interactive portion of the lab is done on two remotely accessed nodes. Accessing these nodes requires the user to connect to their DETERlab account through Secure Shell (SSH), then from SSH into the two control nodes. Each of these two nodes serves a different function. One node is their firewall. The other is a machine through which users test the firewall rules they have implemented on their server node.

The firewall rules are applied using a script. The user writes the rules, then runs the script to enable the firewall using those rules. It is also easy for the user to turn off all rules and remove them by running another script that is provided on the server node. The tasks that the lab asks the user to do are: write a rule that prevents spoofing; allow access to OpenSSH, Apache, and MySQL on their standard ports; allow UDP access to specified ports; allow ICMP ping requests; allow all established and related traffic; and lastly, to drop all other traffic to any unspecified port. If the user accidently configures iptables in a way as to get locked out, the user must reboot the instance, which can take some time. The user can test the firewall by using nmap or telnet to a port in question; however, there is no test provided that allows the user to determine if the user's anti-spoofing rules are functional.

The best feature of using this DETERlab exercise is that it is realistic. Since it uses common firewall syntax, students must remotely connect to the environment to make changes, and they have a broad spectrum of network testing tools at their command. It is also possible for the instructor to create new scenarios that require the students to modify their firewalls to fit this new situation. Many of the advantages of using this exercise for learning and teaching firewall rules have the potential to also be disadvantages, depending on the proficiency of the students and instructor. Iptables has a complex syntax. Also, the possibility that students may lock themselves out of the environment is both an advantage and a disadvantage in that it teaches them about the possibility of doing so in a real IT position; but it takes time to reboot the system and can be frustrating. Other disadvantages are that some overhead is required to set up the experiment, and students must wait for the systems to become available to connect to them.

Based on the criteria stated above, DETERlab falls short in its competitive aspects and its approachability. The exercise poses no competition, as it is in an isolated environment in which the student is working alone, and as such, doesn't capture the real-world situation of defending against an attacker in real time. Due to the range of network tools available and the complicated syntax of iptables, this exercise can be challenging as a first approach to learning about firewalls and writing firewall rules. However, this exercise fulfills our criteria for interactivity, since the students have full control over how they wish to set up their firewalls to complete the tasks and the order in which they wish to tackle them. DETERlab is highly extensible due to the way that the network/device configuration is done. Its system uses specific .ns files that allow the instructor to specify the number of nodes and how they are connected, as well as other network configuration specifics.

Satisfying the criteria

It is desirable to provide students with an active learning environment that focuses on analysis skills. We still need to think about what we can teach and how to provide laboratory exercises for undergraduate students. There are also some pedagogical issues. While the exercises received high scores on student interest [8], they only had moderate coverage of the security education principles that instructors value. This suggests the need for additional work to extend the scope and intellectual complexity of these exercises.

One option is EDURange, an in-development tool intended to be an extensible framework for creating interactive and competitive cyber-security scenarios. Implemented on cloud-based computing platforms (currently Amazon Web Services' Elastic Compute Cloud [9]), it is simple to set up a virtual network. Each student uses SSH to login to a gateway VM and from there logs in to their own VM. The student can use either UFW syntax or iptables to create firewall rules and can then use network testing tools to probe the firewalls of fellow students. By using UFW's syntax, the scenario becomes much more approachable than either FireSim or the DETERlab exercise, which use the more complicated iptables or Cisco syntax. This allows students to focus on comprehension of the concepts of firewalls without having to master the syntax. Also, having all of the students in the same network space, and giving them tools to test and potentially penetrate their fellow students' machines, adds a component of competition to the scenario. EDURange is designed to be extensible. Instructors can modify which services the students' firewalls should allow or deny. The network configuration can also be changed. These changes are made by editing a configuration file, written in YAML [10], which is parsed using Ruby scripts. This file sets up the network and machines as specified by the instructor. These YAML files can even be used to create a variety of virtual network configurations to suit different types of scenarios. The instructor does not need to manually change network configurations or write any scripts to do so. For example, the scripts can be parameterized so that the instructor could choose the size of the network and the services running on the hosts.

Another option is firewall exercises by Palo Alto Networks. The Palo Alto device is a so-called "next generation" firewall, which has recently become more prevalent. Palo Alto's approach involves the control of general service categories, such as a "file-sharing" category, as opposed to specific ports and services. For example, it can detect that a host is sending an IRC message over an sftp port. It also makes use of innovative prevention measures, such as traffic classification and data filtering. The classifications of the traffic logs are used to examine what services on the network are being used, and if any are harmful. To train students to use their firewall devices, Palo Alto offers lab modules [11]. These modules lead students through step-by-step labs to accomplish different tasks such as creating user groups and blocking specific types of websites. These labs cover firewall administration, network interface configuration, network layer configuration, application identification, content identification, and packet decryption. The lab modules are not competitive; in most cases, two students use a single router and must work together. However, competition could easily be introduced through time limits, scoring, or direct competition between an attacker and defender, provided the network is isolated from the Internet.

Future exercises and projects like EDURange and Palo Alto's educational modules can take the identified criteria into account as they are developed. As has been discussed, the inclusion of hands-on, competitive aspects in cyber-security education promotes understanding and the development of analysis skills. In order to better teach cyber-security students about firewalls (and thereby general network functions and security), educators and exercise designers can incorporate some of the strengths found in FireSim, RAVE, DETERlab, and the Palo Alto activities. To reiterate, these strengths were the competitive structure and approachable layout found in FireSim and the hands-on approach found in the DETER and RAVE labs.

Figure 31.1 summarizes the strengths and weaknesses of the different exercises (EDURange is excluded because it has not reached a usable level of completion).

	FireSim	DETERlab 7	Rave/Nestler 7.3	Palo Alto
Competitive	Yes	No, but possible	No	No, but possible
Interactive	Yes, control of firewall rules	Yes, full control of machines	Yes, full control of machines	Yes, limited control using a GUI
Extensibility	Possible (XML file supplements)	.ns files to build environments	Maybe possible (virtual machine images)	Possible (fully-functional commercial product)
Approachability	Simple	Complex	Very simple (step-by-step instructions)	Simple (step-by-step instructions)
Syntax	Cisco	iptables	UFW	Graphical Interface
Scenarios	ftp, dns, http, snmp, ntp, instant messaging netbios	ssh, http, sql, mail, ping, udp	ssh, http, ftp	Pre-configured service categories
Setup	LAN (need at least n+2 computers for n players)	Cloud (access through ssh)	Cloud (access through vSphere)	Needs router and internet access
Documentation	Present but not extensive	A long webpage (interleaved with Unix permissions exercise)	Lab book	Lab pamphlet
In-class vs. Homework	LAN setup (most likely requires classroom usage)	Possible as homework, but might require help from instructor	Easy steps make for a good homework assignment	In-class; students would have to take the device home
Best feature	Competitive	Realism	Step-by-step	Realism
Disadvantage	Lack of feedback, bugs	Realism (places student in large, breakable environment)	Slow (needs bandwidth for remote desktop), simplistic	Requires expensive physical hardware

FIGURE 31.1

Comparison of Exercises for Teaching Firewall Configuration.

As can be seen in 31.1, some of the exercises are more appropriate than others in teaching cyber-security students about firewall configuration. Particularly of note are the possibilities offered by Palo Alto's exercises and fully functional hardware, though this is currently off-set by the high cost of the devices. Also of note is that FireSim was the only exercise to involve competition as a feature.

Emerging trends in firewall education

Various trends have become apparent in personal and commercial firewalls. Firewall companies like Palo Alto, Cisco, and Barracuda have begun to use new strategies when defending networks. Barracuda [12] and Palo Alto [13] offer virtual implementations of their firewalls. Both companies have also introduced "next-generation" firewall techniques, primarily emphasizing application awareness: Palo Alto's App-ID [14] and Barracuda's NG Firewall [15] can identify applications by their traffic signature and can control traffic on the application layer (e.g., allow Skype calls but prevent Skype file transfers). Though virtualization and application awareness are beyond the scope of a personal firewall, firewall software has become part of general security suites. Commercial anti-virus suites like those offered by Kaspersky [16] and Norton [17] include firewalls; free software like Microsoft Security Essentials [18] and the open-source Snort IDS function as firewalls and even include some application layer functionality [19].

These trends may begin to appear in firewall education tools. Application awareness may be difficult to simulate, but the virtual firewall implementations could allow students to use them in isolated, special purpose virtual environments. Companies like Palo Alto offer training programs; if educational licenses of their virtual firewalls are available, instructors may be able to use them to educate their students on the emergent firewall technologies. However, this would be a proprietary system, and we are interested in teaching analytical skills not just tools. Many of the features such as identifying signatures for applications are not open, but the student could write their own regular expression recognizer. EDURange could also potentially utilize the power of regular expressions as part of iptables.

CONCLUSION

In 2001, the ACM and IEEE's curriculum guidelines listed firewalls and additional security concepts as optional. In the 2013 guidelines, firewall knowledge was elevated to a core topic. Recently, training platforms have been created that allow students to work with firewalls without the need for physical devices [20].

Based on undergraduate students' experience with three of these firewall training exercises, we concluded that all three are workable firewall education tools, but they all could be improved. FireSim is competitive, interactive, and entertaining, but the educational aspects are limited by the low levels of feedback and guidance. DETERlab was the most realistic of the exercises, involving fully configured machines. However, accessing and following the exercise was rather involved, and could be daunting for introductory-level students. This could be improved with additional tutorials.

Finally, the RAVE labs are focused and accessible. The exercises are well-written, easy to follow, and educational. Since they run on virtual machines, students can recover from mistakes using snapshots. A Web connection is required, as well as the vSphere client running on Windows, before students can begin to use RAVE.

Each exercise had strengths and weaknesses. We recommend RAVE for beginning security students; the simple instructions and stable setup give introductory students a good environment to work in. DETERlab is useful for more advanced students. The structure gives students greater access to the command-line interface and software management, which may be daunting for beginning students. Students must also be aware of security pitfalls (e.g., blocking SSH from within an SSH session) and other problems, meaning introductory-level users could easily have trouble. FireSim is the only competitive exercise of these three; we recommend it as an in-class exercise. Finally, although Palo Alto's lab exercises may require expensive hardware, instructors could consider them for actual hands-on experience with newer trends in the firewall market. Eventually, virtual devices may be available.

Of course, every exercise has issues. No "silver bullet" exists for firewall education. Some exercises sacrifice simplicity for realism, while others exchange educational depth for approachability. Future firewall exercises will have to take this into account along with the recent developments in firewall configuration. For example, the EDURange project attempts to utilize cloud-based virtual machines for availability. Hopefully, future projects will be able to balance the competition, interactivity, extensibility, and approachability.

Acknowledgments

Partial support for this work was provided by the National Science Foundation's "Transforming Undergraduate Education in Science, Technology, Engineering and Mathematics (TUES)" program under Awards No. 1141314 and 1141341, by the John S. Rogers Science Research Program of Lewis & Clark College, and by the James F. and Marion L. Miller Foundation. We would also like to thank Michael Locasto and Stefan Boesen for their contributions.

References

[1] Computing Curricula: Computer Science. Association for Computing Machinery. [Internet]. Retrieved from: < http://www.acm.org/education/curric_vols/cc2001.pdf > ; 2001 [accessed 06.13].

[2] A Portable Computer Security Workshop. ACM Digital Library. [Internet]. Retrieved from: < http://dl.acm.org/citation.cfm?doid=1248453.1248456 > ; 2006 [accessed 06.13].

[3] Firewall Simulation. Williams.comp.ncat.edu. [Internet]. Retrieved from: < http://williams.comp.ncat.edu/FireSim/index.htm>; [accessed 05.13].

[4] Nestler V, White G. Conklin WMA. Principles of computer security: CompTIA Security+ and beyond. Lab Manual. McGraw Hill; 2011.

[5] About DeterLab. DeterLab.net. [Internet]. Retrieved from: < http://info.deterlab.net/about > ; [accessed 05.13].

[6] Computer Science Curricula. Stanford AI Lab. [Internet]. Retrieved from: < http://ai.stanford.edu/users/sahami/CS2013/ironman-draft/cs2013-ironman-v1.0.pdf > ; 2013 [accessed 06.13].

[7]   UFW. Community Ubuntu Documentation. [Internet]. Retrieved from: < https://help.ubuntu.com/community/UFW > ; 2013 [accessed 07.13].

[8]   Weiss R, Mache J, Nilsen E. Top 10 hands-on cybersecurity exercises. Journal of Computing Sciences in Colleges 2013;29(1).

[9]   Amazon Elastic Compute Cloud. Amazon Web Services. [Internet]. Retrieved from: < http://aws.amazon.com/ec2/ > ; 2013 [accessed 05.13].

[10] YAML Ain't Markup Language. YAML 1.2. [Internet]. Date of article [accessed on year mon day]. Retrieved from: <http://www.yaml.org/>; 2011 [accessed 05.13].

[11] Firewall Configuration Essentials 101 Course. [Internet]. Retrieved from: https://support.paloaltonetworks.com/101_course/player.html.

[12] Next Generation Firewall Vx. Barracuda Networks. [Internet]. Retrieved from: < https://www.barracuda.com/products/ngfirewall/vx > ; 2013 [accessed 07.13].

[13] Virtualized Firewalls. Palo Alto Networks. [Internet]. Retrieved from: <https://www.paloaltonetworks.com/products/platforms/virtualized-firewalls/vm-series/overview.html> ; 2013 [accessed 06.13].

[14] App-ID. Palo Alto Networks. [Internet]. Retrieved from: < https://www.paloaltonetworks.com/products/technologies/app-id.html > ; 2013 [accessed 06.13].

[15] Next Generation Firewall - Features. Barracuda Networks. [Internet]. Retrieved from: https://www.barracuda.com/products/ngfirewall/features; 2013 [accessed 06.13].

[16] Internet Security 2014. Kaspersky Lab. [Internet]. Retrieved from: http://usa.kaspersky.com/products-services/home-computer-security/internet-security; 2013 [accessed 07.13].

[17] Internet Security. Norton. [Internet]. Retrieved from: < http://us.norton.com/internet-security/# > ; 2013 [accessed 07.13].

[18] Microsoft Security Essentials Product Information. Windows. [Internet]. Retrieved from: < http://windows.microsoft.com/en-us/windows/security-essentials-product-information#tabs1=features > ; 2013 [accessed 07.13].

[19] SNORT - First Line of Defense for Web application attacks. Packet Storm Security. [Internet]. Retrieved from: < http://dl.packetstormsecurity.net/papers/IDS/snort-firstline.pdf > ; [accessed 07.13].

[20] Weiss R, Mache J, Nestler V, Dodge R, Hay B. Teaching cybersecurity through interactive exercises using a virtual environment. J Comput Sci Colleges 2012;28:10.

Case Study

Surveillance without Borders: The Case of Karen Refugees in Sheffield

Geff Green and Eleanor Lockley

Sheffield Hallam University, Sheffield, UK

INFORMATION IN THIS CHAPTER

- The surveillance imaginary
- Virtual/material spaces of surveillance
- Liminal spaces
- Borderlands and surveillance Local/Global geographies of Surveillance
- Surveillance, identity and becoming

INTRODUCTION

Although it is not a new phenomenon for immigrant communities to carry inter-ethnic or inter-religious disputes with them across the world, there appears to be very little literature about this phenomenon, especially in relation to the dimensions that digital communication might bring to this type of situation. This chapter provides an account of a recent skirmish that carried many of the historical characteristics of exported inter-ethnic, politico-military conflicts while also bearing new markers whose dimensions are a consequence of 21st century communication technologies. This particular incident is also marked by its relationship to past events, uneven power relationships, and a long-running political and military campaign for self-government.

We initiated a community project to work with Burmese refugees in the Sheffield area of the UK that involved the use of various aspects of social media as well as the more traditional journalistic techniques and approaches, developing media practices with the aim of developing students' skills as community journalists. This project arose from a stated desire by certain members of the exiled Burmese community to become reporters on human rights abuses and political oppression being enacted by the Burmese regime across their country of origin. The project took place from September, 2009 to April, 2010. Some of the participants were from various Burmese ethnic minorities, while the majority of the participants were ethnic Karen, reflecting the large number of Karen refugees who had moved to the UK between 2005 and 2007 under the Gateway Protection Scheme, which works with the UNHCR. Certain members of this group of Karen became the targets of the hacking and flaming attacks that we relate below.

This chapter outlines and discusses how local conflicts can be manifested at great distance, aided by new media and its surveillance. In the case presented, we encountered a local conflict that was based in a completely different location from the place of origin. It was also characterized by confusion about the extent to which the offending and offensive communication was inter-local or locally based. How fear and trauma can be reignited far from their place of origin are also addressed. We focus on one particular case study, and in doing so, we identify the methods used, the source of terror, and the relationship between the tools of physical oppression and the evocation of them through the use of a variety of media and surveillance activities. We demonstrate how this was done through a combination of opportunism and calculated psychological oppression to hound individuals. One tool we use is a critical discourse analysis of some of the material directed at the Karen.

This critique is informed particularly in relation to knowledge of the historical and political background of the events, but also in relation to aspects of Karen identity and culture that allow what could be seen as more general discourse of threat and insult to be understood in terms of its specific significance to this community and its experiences, history, and identity. In particular, the way cultural taboos are exploited in this type of information warfare to undermine the credibility of key figures through rumor and allegation is highlighted, as well as how a message of "We are watching you despite your physical distance from us" is sent through colonizing virtual spaces used by a refugee community, establishing what we describe as "inverse reach." It is therefore relevant to provide some literature and theory relating to these events, while the methodological issues relating to our positions as researchers (and participant observers) are also addressed.

The purpose of this case study is not to investigate or identify perpetrators but to analyze the events, the relationship between real and virtual worlds, and how online events translate into real-world actions and local consequences. This work does not seek to explore the broader questions about who is the terrorist and who is the terrorized, as this conflict cannot always be understood in terms of aggressor and victim. However, we look at one particular dimension of cyber terror and surveillance when it is used as a tool of oppression against one's own citizens [1] and against refugees who have left their country of origin [2].

Background

This case study helps to provide insight into the mechanics of a kind of online warfare and the ways in which its impetus originates in real-world conflict and extends into real events and ramifications after taking place in a virtual space through hacking. A key background activity to this work is understanding the pre-existing ethnic sensitivities and constructions of identity alongside those expressed through online media by both sides in the conflict. Without this background, it is difficult to understand the context for trauma, the responses of the Karen community, and the discourse of the cyber-attacks themselves. The unique situation of the Karen also explains how some of the hacking took place.

Significance of Karen identity and its construction

It is important to understand a few key issues relating to the identity of the Karen without getting into a discussion about the complex range of factors that influence identity in general [3]. In this instance, ideas about identity cannot be entirely removed from psychological factors (which we discuss below), especially with regard to the importance of stories of hardship forming a certain type of badge of identity. It can be said that the Karen collective identity is not primarily a cultural, religious, or ethnic issue, but rather a political one. It has developed against a background of ethnic conflict and competition that has a long history in Burma [4], capitalized upon by the British [5], and further reified in post-colonial conflicts continuing since the establishment of the Burmese state until the present day.

A number of researchers have explored aspects of identity and its modern practices, particularly among refugees and migrants in the borderlands between Thailand and Burma, where many have fled or migrated [6–10].

There has been an on-going project to demarcate, simplify, and to some extent define a common ground among the Karen that would allow them to unite against the Burmese regime under a common flag. The work of Comaroff and Comaroff [11], undertaken in other ethnic contexts, focuses on this type of convenient and deliberate repackaging of identity for a common political or commercial purpose. In actual fact, the Karen spread from the so-called Karen territories to other regions and have several different linguistic groups and religious affiliations, ranging from brands of Christianity to Buddhism and Animism. Linguistically, the Karen dialects all supposedly belong to the same linguistic family [12], although they are sometimes "mutually unintelligible" [9]. Some no longer speak the original dialects and many live in urban areas or are migrant workers in other countries and are essentially apolitical [13]. However, the refugee camps and surrounding areas have become a focus of the work of the Karen National Union (KNU), which has included the migration of some key activists to other countries such as the United States, Australia, the United Kingdom, New Zealand, Canada, and Japan. The community we were working with could largely be equated with the KNU and their activities, and the people targeted were the more active members of the community as well as participants in our training scheme.

Certain events and activities such as the Karen New Year are particularly important assertions of a form of hybrid constructed Karen identity drawing on a range of traditional practices and putting them together as a show of unity both for their own community and for the benefit of host communities and opponents. Markers of identity comprise songs, woven garments, dances, and particular annual rituals and events. Sheffield's Karen community is largely Christian and most are Baptists, but they have been at pains to present a message of pantheistic tolerance and cooperation, although the reality of Buddhist Karen presents a contradictory challenge to those who equate the Burmese regime and the Burman ethnicity with Buddhism.

Insights from our engagement with the Karen

Education has an important role in Karen community culture, and the lengths to which the community has gone to organize systems and programs or education, particularly within the context of the

Christian Karen, are notable. This is relevant to our later analysis of the type of language used in the cyber-attack on the Karen. Kuroiwa and Verkuyten [9] have highlighted a particular type of leadership scheme of education in their study of the Karen, and our own media project highlighted this emphasis through film produced by Karen parents featuring their children talking about school.

Our participants also gave us a number of examples about surveillance in Burma. For instance, we were told of how, in the Internet cafés in Rangoon, the Burmese government would take over the mouse control just to let people know that they were being watched. So some of the community group were already aware of the government's capability for digital spying.

Another important factor that has come out of our research is the desire among many to use communication media, surveillance, and information to report on the "invisible war" that has been going on in the jungles of the Karen territories [14]. However, as we have found out, the counter-surveillance has taken new and unexpected forms enabled by new technologies, which subverted our community's attempts to fight the Burmese regime with information and reporting, a form of counter-power [15].

Shared trauma

Collective and individual trauma is a sensitive subject to explore in most cultural contexts, and this is no different with the Karen. Our work with respondents, especially community leaders, together with the collection of stories related to us about atrocities and human rights abuses inflicted on them, their friends, and families, has drawn quite a clear picture of unresolved trauma among the community [14]. This community is now confronted with a new cultural context in the UK of health care and general societal practices and attitudes that put added stresses on individuals [16]. Many have witnessed murder, destruction, rape, slavery, displacement, or their results, and the younger members of the community have grown up with these stories. Although the telling of the stories may in certain ways be cathartic [10], the threats made, which in fairly specific ways reference the types of violence and oppression they have experienced, can have a particularly powerful impact.

Our study does not allow us to independently make a mental health assessment of this community, and indeed it is not the primary aim of this chapter. Yet the mechanics suggested by Beiser and others [17,18] back up our observations regarding the potentially devastating results of psychological warfare undertaken through surveillance and cyber-attack upon those who have already been physical or emotional victims of a conflict situation. Although we have not undertaken direct mental health assessments of the group in Sheffield, our discussions with community leaders and their particular profiles suggest a high risk and indeed presence of mental illness associated with trauma such as Post-Traumatic Stress Disorder (PTSD).

We do not enter into the debates around defining and diagnosing mental illness in a context of cultural relativism, but instead work with the idea broadly drawn by Beiser [17] that mental illness/trauma is a shared physiological experience potentially moderated by culture but negatively impacting all who experience it in similar ways, even if it is not entirely expressed or admitted in the same manner. Similarly, the fears and paranoias that can be associated with and amplified by those experiences, plus the effect of hostile referencing to those fears through surveillance and subsequent verbal attacks, should not be underestimated in their importance.

Methodological issues
Access to the community

The original research aims were to understand the transnational and local communication practices of the Burmese and Karen communities as a whole, with a focus on new information and communication technologies (ICTs). The approach was not originally constructed to investigate specific questions around ethnic conflict [14]. However, the events that occurred toward the latter part of the project cast a shadow over the original research intentions and provided a scenario worthy of analysis and further investigation, along with unique data whose context and content would not normally be easy to observe or capture. The online presence of blogs that continue to attack this community have subsequently been monitored.

One limitation to this project was language. There has been a heavy dependency upon translation to deliver the training and to understand many of the outputs. The need to translate into both Burmese and Karen languages was the first indication of the political and ethnic sensitivities that required attention. This need resulted in using two different interpreters for two basic language groups: the Burman and Sgaw Karen. Much of the understanding of the attacks on the Karen community relies on the translations of the posts by the community themselves. However, there is no question of the validity of the translations, as they would have no reason to raise such unpleasant allegations about their own community.

At the beginning of the project we considered the problems associated with how revealing individual identities within the Karen community in Sheffield as journalistic participants online might put them or their families at a certain level of risk, especially since the project members highlighted the Burmese government's dislike of Internet use. Their participation in various online journalistic activities was approached with sensitivity, but it is now perhaps clearer that the community did not fully understand the virtual inverse reach of the Burmese regime. Their resettled positions as refugees in a new country turned out to be not as secure as they had thought.

Ethnography

The ethnographic approach was important but had its limitations. As previously mentioned, this was due to language differences and our research being based around specific joint activities and events, without being entirely embedded in their extended communal and individual activities, as would be the case in a traditional anthropological study of a rural co-located community [19]. Becoming familiar with and getting to know the communities occurred through the training events, visits to homes, interviews, and various public events such as Karen New Year, Teachers Day, a wedding, church services, and a wrist-tying ceremony. The survival strategies taken by Karen communities displaced to Western countries seeking to preserve their social and cultural identity in a foreign environment have been highlighted, as well as the routine and less routine threats that exist to their activities and status [20].

The media training project provided an excellent opportunity to learn about the community through their stories, their aims, their anxieties, and their impediments. The method of engagement with this community was designed to build a relationship of trust, friendship, and exchange of knowledge. Although artificial in certain respects, this project allowed the Karen and Burman to reveal their attitudes and opinions through their engagements with specific tasks. This also helped in the analysis and understanding of the series of events that arose when the group's project blog was hacked. From an ethnographic point of view, the situation observed took place in a shared virtual environment whose ownership and control came into question at the point of being hacked. Our insight into the community through contact with community leaders, participants in our training, media created for the project, and observations provided important background knowledge for interpreting and making sense of the hacking attack.

Analyzing discourse

Although there was quite extensive material posted on the blog, the material focused on here has been selected by one of the community informants for the attention of the project organizers. The editorial decisions in presenting these as particularly important made them significant in terms of their impact and meaningfulness to the Karen community. The names used in the flaming incident have been concealed to protect their identities and to avoid further dissemination of the allegations and threats made to specific individuals.

We have provided a discourse analysis of this key textual material from these events, which helps to dissect the language of terror within the rubric of actual collective and individual community experience. This approach helps to explain why the threats, insults, and insinuations were experienced as very real. A discourse was reified and combined with lived experience to recall traumas of the past and create new ones in an apparently safe and free context.

The hacking incident

Toward the end of the project, there was a substantial amount of audio, video, and text content that the community had created and displayed on a blog site. At this point, a concerned Karen community leader alerted us to an abuse of the project blog. This constituted an online smear campaign toward community members and activists from the Karen community, many of whom were also participants in the training project.

Although we were aware at the outset that there were possible sensitivities and suspicions that could arise with the ethnic mix of students, we expected that any Burmese government interference might be taken against the university or perhaps the collective group of participating students. The specific ways in which conflict occurred was surprising to us in its nature, form, and consequences, illustrating how difficult it is to predict or control the way that media use develops in any particular situation.

Initially these concerns were raised alongside the idea that the abuse had been done by someone in the group who was a spy. The reasoning behind this, from the community leader's perspective, was that the messages and content contained personal information that only the community could know. Another justification in support of the spy suspicion was that a video of the group during the very first session (which was not on the blog) had been uploaded onto YouTube. However, a video of the session was uploaded on a different website by an external project coordinator and was probably accessed by the hackers in this way. The Karen community was not aware of this, nor were

Sheffield Hallam University staff (who were co-delivering the training with the external contractors), until after the project had finished. This also shows how surveillance of our online activities began at quite an early stage.

The event sent waves though the community, partly because of the nature of the comments and partly because of the trust community members felt they had given to the university. Also, importantly, it connected with their previous experiences with the Burmese government and military. In fact, it was surprising that they continued to attend the final few sessions (although in admittedly fewer numbers). An investigation by university information networking technology experts indicated the IP (Internet Protocol) address of the hacker was in Thailand. However, from the community members' point of view, this was a dramatic manifestation of the long arm of the Burmese regime. They understood this to be part of the psychological and physical warfare that extended from the ethnic cleansing of Karen communities in Burma, now extended to a newer, "virtual" location. It raised the question of whether there was someone in the community who had tipped off the hackers in Thailand or whether the hackers just found the project information from random search engines (the project particularly highlighted and advertised its purpose online, which was to provide journalistic skills to the Karen community). From the community's perspective, whether there was an informant in the group or someone was posting messages from Thailand, it highlighted a threat that spies continued to monitor and harass them.

Community leaders were asked to translate some of the messages to help provide the project co-ordinators with a clearer understanding of the incident. The hacked accounts posted sexual images and derogatory content (see translations in the appendix). One participant reported receiving an email threatening the participant's family and including specific names and personal information. Another participant reported receiving threatening emails and text messages to a mobile phone—again about the participant's family—and that the details in the email threats included information that only the community could know. User names on the blog were email addresses, so hackers had the email addresses to target the participants directly. Notably, they did not target any of the staff email accounts, nor did they target the Burman participants.

This further fueled the belief that the spy in the group was a Burman participant, not part of the Karen community. Petty tensions between the Karen and Burman groups around the provision of dual language interpreters appeared to move to a new level.

What the community had failed to appreciate was that the audio blog posts, which contained personal information, were spoken in their native tongue and possibly accessed (and invariably understood) by the hackers, and rather the e-mail and test threats was perhaps just a consequence of the hackers making use of the technology and searching through the previous blog posts. The nature of the comments also alleged unfounded rumors of sexual behavior directed specifically at a female activist with a high international profile as a political campaigner. Comments were also directed at her daughter. These came in the form of text messages as well as messages on the blogging site used by the media training project to post media and comments. Login identities, including those of lecturers, were taken over and used to post other lewd and insulting messages. These messages could be seen as immature and ineffectual, but the impact they had was very strong and was seized upon by the Karen as evidence confirming their mistrust of Burmans. It also caused hesitation about using the Internet in any way without the risk of being monitored or attacked.

At the outset of the project we had discussed with some of the group that their online presence as part of the project would make them visible and identifiable in new ways, and despite being in a

UK context, engaging in journalistic activities could potentially have ramifications for their friends and relatives in their home countries. However, they were adamant that reporting and publicizing their cause was a priority for them as a community, and by being in another, freer country, they would be able to get their message to the outside world. Ultimately, though, they were shocked by the degree of inverse reach that the new media eventually afforded their opponents in Thailand and Burma. This was a lesson to them (and to us) about the recoiling nature of modern digital communication technologies and how borders of the traditional nation-state afford little protection against this kind of activity.

Later discussions about the incident with Sheffield's Burmese refugee community identified a significant part of what had happened. A disaffected member of Sheffield's Karen community (which, not surprisingly, has its own internal tensions, disputes, disagreements, and power struggles), was unburdening to a friend in Burma by phone, and the call was hacked, monitored, and recorded. The details of the gossip were then used as ammunition in the cyber-attacks, both to upset particular prominent community members and to damage their standing and reputations in their immediate community and the wider campaigning KNU community of which they were an active part. An edited version of the phone call also appeared on a Burmese government−monitored website. This was how the community member was eventually identified. We have to rely on the anecdotal evidence of our respondent regarding the technical details of this account, but it explains the availability of sordid gossip, sexual threat, and allegations, along with derogatory comments on aspects of ethnic identity in later blogs and emails.

In the early days of the World Wide Web, flaming was frowned upon and often criticized as a practice [21]. But the modern manifestation of this practice that we encountered had more incendiary and sinister implications than the online bickering that usually characterized such exchanges in the past. Although the nature of the insults, threats, rumors, and allegations were crude and even adolescent, the way these attached to the background of the Karen community in terms of both real practices and tacit threats meant that they needed to be taken seriously as representing more than immature hacking by disenfranchised individuals. It also meant that the ramifications and echoes of this cyber-attack in terms of its emotional and psychological impact were significant [18].

After recently checking a BlogSpot that featured the community video, it is clear that the Karen community in Sheffield are still being targeted. At the time of checking (September, 2011), one particular member of the community had been targeted for being in a relationship with a man from a different ethnic background. The BlogSpot includes personal photographs of the community member and the partner. This approach of undermining ethnic cohesion through allegations of miscegenation is also apparent in the hacked email messages on our project blog. This raises the question of where the personal photographs were accessed from. One answer could be a social networking site such as Facebook, which is used quite widely by some of the younger members of the community. Several of the community members who we built relationships with now have social network profiles, and it would seem that this is a good method of keeping in contact with their family and friends across the world—presumably those located either in the western zones or in the Thai refugee camps. This example demonstrates how material of a personal nature shared on a social networking site and intended for a small circle of friends and family can be subverted and more widely circulated in a recontextualized form to create a distorted narrative by employing the conservative cultural taboos of the community at large, including the global diaspora and its networks of political activists. This recontextualization is perhaps familiar to celebrities and the tabloid press, but increasingly, it can apply to anyone with a media presence who might have affiliations to more than one society or clique.

"We are Watching You": Analysis of discourse messages posted

Our analysis of the messages posted focuses primarily on the pieces of text contained in the appendix, but our interpretation of them draws on our wider experience and knowledge of this community, as well as other theories and research pertinent to this case study. We have divided the key themes of the allegations made against the Karen community as follows:

- Corruption (sins)
  - moral
  - exploitative
  - financial (theft, embezzlement)
  - religious
- Sexual misconduct (sins)
  - rape
  - adultery
  - incest
  - miscegenation
  - sexual license
- Lack of education/culture

A key element of the analyzed material plays upon anxieties and male disempowerment by initially discrediting males through alleging corrupt or immoral behavior. However, another key element in the texts focuses on money. The religious dimension to these allegations also should not be underestimated, as they could be evaluated within a framework of the Ten Commandments. Religious credibility is of supreme importance among the Christian Karen, so any damage to reputations within this biblical rubric can be a powerful weapon of insult.

The psychological disempowerment is further enacted through symbolic rape of wives and daughters (mirroring actual human rights abuses in Burma). When aimed toward women or children, the pattern is to predatorily portray them as sexual targets but also as sexually immoral—more specifically, making allegations of interracial sexual bonds specifically aimed at their daughters. The hackers make use of and play on classic taboos such as miscegenation [22,23], which threaten the future ethnic purity [8] of an isolated community, regardless of whether there is any truth in the allegations. It also builds on anxieties the community holds about the disappearance of their cultural identity through unintentional cultural assimilation. Men, as guardians of culture and identity, are particularly being targeted by these types of allegations (although this is not to diminish the feeling of threat experienced by the women concerned). These anxieties are genuine and possibly well-founded in the longer term, and thus the nature of the threats and allegations are quite sophisticated in manipulating collective community anxieties while at the same time seeking to create community divides.

The systematic way in which these taboos were employed shows a broad strategy for discrediting a carefully chosen list of active individuals who are a threat to the Burmese regime because of their networking, affiliation, leadership, and, more crucially, freedom to communicate—characteristics not previously (or barely) tolerated in Burma. Both female and male members of the community were targeted, primarily community leaders and KNU activists who were also participants in the training we provided, so digital material from them in Karen, English, and some Burman was available online from which details and information were extracted, reprocessed, and used as part of the attack.

Although the financial aspects of the discourse appear as a subcategory under the more general terminology of corruption (above), they are worthy of note because of their frequency in the texts. Our discussions with the Karen indicated that those in the refugee camps, who sometimes receive financial aid from overseas family members despite those family members' own hardships in the West, tend to hold high expectations of financial opportunities in the UK. These expectations are mainly of perceived opportunities to work, as well as social safety nets that the UK appears to present, even though these perceptions are not entirely accurate. The general struggle for any kind of financial gain among the Karen internationally means that a strategy implying greed and financial corruption, especially at others' expense, will also play on prejudice to undermine the credibility of those being targeted by the servants of the Burmese regime among their broader constituency.

The third theme of allegations we identified relates to being uncultured and uneducated. Although this may seem trivial in relation to allegations of rape and murder, for instance, the power of insult carried by this allegation in an Asian context should not be underestimated, especially among the Christian Karen, who place a particularly high value on education. Illiteracy or a "fish paste" accent implies a lack of authenticity and credibility in terms of potential leadership.

Motivations behind the threats

The exact motivation of the cyber-attacks on members of the community cannot be identified. They could have been coordinated attempts to target activists by representatives of the Burmese secret services, or perhaps a collection of renegade acts by disaffected individuals. Possible motivations we have identified are as follows:

- Disaffected Karen (unlikely, although this was key in terms of surveillance)
- Jealousy (that the Sheffield community has escaped the regime)
- Refugee camp politics
- Displaced immigrant community politics

In fact, all of these are dimensions of the surveillance and cyber-attack scenarios we have observed. The fact that, as a standard practice, the Burmese government targets all Internet communication from those who have escaped the regime in an attempt to show those who are living in Burma the wrath of their power and control leads to a variety of methods, and agents. In the case of the refugee/activist diaspora, the surveillance is borderless, limited by the level of visibility of those activists, the methods they take to protect data and online identities, and the content of their public digital imprint. This systematic approach is an extension, across borders, of practices followed in Burma through the inverse reach afforded by digital communication technologies. It's often not personal, but various techniques are used to make people believe it is. Attacks are three-pronged in terms of the damage they seek to inflict. The first is the damage to reputation, credibility, and standing among the international constituency and perhaps the local community of those being attacked. The second is the potential schism that can be created between competing dissident groups. The third is direct psychological attack against the individuals concerned and the community at large through referencing their fears and prior traumas.

Methods used

The attacks intended to incite the following ideas:

- Surveillance: accessing rumors and exaggerating and disseminating them
- Fear: terrorizing and amplifying trauma
- "Divide and rule": targeting Karen and Burman dissidents, which encouraged mutual suspicion and lack of unity among diverse resistant groups

The surveillance took several forms: hacking into and recording phone conversations as well as broader online monitoring and gathering of online discourse from the Karen community. This information was used to create a fictional narrative that drew upon taboos, prejudices, and sensitivities among the Karen to attack them. In particular, the attacks relied on trauma derived from experiences testified to in the media pieces the Karen produced for us and in other conversations we have had with them.

The work of Marshall et al. [18] deals with a longer-term study of Cambodian refugees in the United States. The similarities between the two communities' experiences are striking; the factors listed in [18] match exactly with those experiences of the Karen we have mentioned above. Even more interesting, Beiser outlines what he calls the "re-emergence of risk-inducing painful memory" ([17] p. 556). This is directly induced by the online attackers.

It is significant that although the video uploaded to YouTube included Burmese as well as Karen participants, it was the Karen who were targeted. This relates to the "divide and rule" aspect of the methods used. Many postcolonial nations previously under British rule inherited methods of divide and rule along ethnic lines. The Burmese use of these methods is illustrated in the surveillance and attack methods we witnessed and the predictable inter-ethnic suspicions and accusations that resulted between Karen and Burman exiles.

Impact on the community

Our research confirmed a whole range of stories the Karen community had to tell about things that had happened to them and their relatives over many years at the hands of the Tatmadaw (Burmese military). Although these stories represented a certain badge of identity (if not pride in survival), they also revealed a weakness of lived memories and the possibilities of future online attacks, through which they could continue to be threatened. What perhaps needs to be remembered is that, in cases of post-traumatic stress [24], the reality of the imagined or remembered events and associated psychological states can, at times, seem more real than the prosaic reality of the present moment.

The impact that this cyber-attack had on the community is most significant as it relates to their collective and individual experiences. They saw it implicitly as the Burmese government attempting to intimidate them at long distance; since the government was unable to physically oppress them, it sought to do so psychologically. The intimidation was accomplished by using new media and, to some extent, by turning against the Karen the tools of communication used to highlight their stories. It also raised suspicions that were directed toward non-Karen Burmese in Sheffield, specifically those undertaking the training, partly because of their non-Karen status. However, a discussion with one of the community leaders also indicated that the possibility of a member of the Karen community being in the pay of the Burmese government could not be ruled out. This indicates the level of collective paranoia that can be induced by a cyber-attack that is underpinned by decades of war and oppression.

Because totalitarianism relies on fear as much as on the physical repression that leads to fear [25], these types of events are important even though they don't make a physical mark. The fact that they were directed at women mirrored the community's inability to protect children and women from the actions of Burmese soldiers in the Karen territories [8], thereby reminding the community of real events experienced by them, their relatives, or their friends. In response, as was clear from our discussions with community representatives, the community wanted to identify local perpetrators. This brought the physical threat connected to the virtual threats closer, and made it possible to consider acting on the threat in ways they could more easily conceptualize—through identifying and punishing a local perpetrator, as well as asking the university to take responsibility for the fact that the blogging software we had used had been hacked by outsiders. This desire to identify and blame became a tactic of empowerment against the disempowering discourse of the attackers.

CONCLUSION

There is a danger that the Karen are portrayed as passive recipients of media attacks. However, although naivete on the part of some individuals had allowed the attacks to develop, the very reason that community members had engaged the media training was that they understood the power and necessity of media methods to counter the actions and discourse of those who had for so long held power over them. Their desire to create a counter-power [15] through new media, and their freedom to do so in a Western context, clearly presented a threat to the Burmese regime, which led to these cyber-attacks.

It is not possible to completely untangle the events that took place, nor is it the job of academics to identify the perpetrators. However, through this incident we gained important insight into the reality, nature, and mechanics of a specific set of events leading from surveillance to online attacks. We also saw firsthand the effects of these events in tapping the paranoia and trauma held by the community at large, originating in the long-term domination of the Karen by the Burmese political regime.

We have termed the ability to strike back through the very channels of resistance as "inverse reach." Inverse reach enables authoritarianism to reach across national boundaries to discredit and undermine individuals and their efforts to work toward political aims outside the regime's physical purview. Paradoxically, in this case, while ICTs in the hands of the oppressed were demonstrated as offering advantages—especially as tools for empowerment, enabling voices of resistance—they were turned on the users as further tools of oppression.

Targeting specific individuals makes the threat seem more personal—"We know who you are" —and constitutes a tangible and effective form of intimidation. Intellectually, the Karen know they can't be physically reached, yet the threat of being monitored from a distance is still felt by many members of the community and results in what can seem to be a very tangible experience of attack.

Use of sexual threats and innuendo as tools of manipulation was a predominant aspect of this cyber-terrorism. Using specific names and targeting specific individuals added the dimension of surveillance to the attack. On one hand, the discourse is crude gutter language; on another, it shows a deep understanding of the kinds of anxieties held by the community and how they can be played upon. The online discourse also linked to the Tatmadaw's known actions against the Karen. Some discourses, such as the accusation of rape, were inversions of acts committed against the Karen.

Notably, the community regarded this event as much more alarming than the local, more reified racial harassment they have experienced in their neighborhoods in the UK, which they also discussed with our researchers. This is a clear indication of the effectiveness of fear as a tool of authoritarianism over long distances. At the same time, the refugee activists can see that they are being effective, in that they are being targeted. There is still a live website that specifically serves to attack the Karen communities in the UK.

With the ceasefire declared between the Karen National Union (KNU) and the Burmese government in 2012, it is possible that the cyber-attacks may cease. However, the historical precedent for a cold war indicates that a "war of words" and background military maneuvers and posturing may continue despite the cessation of physical hostilities. The situation in Burma since the ceasefire appears to herald the possibility of longer-term peace between the majority Burman regime and ethnic minority communities such as the Karen. However, the apparatus of surveillance and oppression has not yet been dismantled. The memories of past persecution and atrocities are always available to be rekindled and exploited through new forms of psychological warfare, using new media methods to monitor communication and to reach individuals in threatening and intrusive ways far from the zones of physical conflict.

Appendix

The following messages were received by the Karen community who then translated them into English:

- KCA UK is a beggar organisation and they are a bunch of English lackeys.
- Karen refugees in Sheffield are all fake refugees.
- [Eight people—four group members and four associated with the KNU] are racist and making money from the government by organizing demonstration using the community name.
- [Five of the same people named in the previous message—two group members and three associated with the KNU] who work as an interpreter speaks with 90% fish paste assent and making money from the community who can't even read ABCD.
- [One person, a group member, also named in the previous messages,] came from Ohm Pham refugee camps and he make money while he was in-charge of the aids in the refugee camps. [Name] is living on government doe so he got little money that's why he forms several groups and creating projects to make money. His eldest daughter got pregnant with one Iraqi animal and run away with him. His other daughter is having a fling with one Iranian animal.

- [Name of male group member] is always looking to have a fling with other men's wife.
- [Name of a different male group member] is a rapist.
- Name of male who is a group member and KNU member] is fxxxing his own adopted mom. They are fake mom and son. They are really a couple.

Messages from the attackers to the community were also posted on the website: http://liar-peoples.blogspot.com/.

References

[1] OpenNet Initiative. Internet Filtering in Burma in 2005: A country study, OpenNet initiative. [Internet]. Retrieved from: http://opennet.net/studies/burma#toc2d>; 2005 [accessed 07.02.12].

[2] Nagaraja S, Anderson R. The snooping dragon: social-malware surveillance of the Tibetan movement. Technical Report no 746. University of Cambridge Computer Laboratory; 2009.

[3] Routledge Handbook of Identity Studies. Elliott A, editor. Routledge, London; 2011.

[4] Lieberman VB. Ethnic politics in eighteenth-century Burma. Mod Asian Stud 1978;12(3):455−82.

[5] Heikkilä-Horn ML. Imagining 'Burma': a historical overview. Asian ethnicity 2009;10(2):145−54.

[6] Cheesman N. Seeing "Karen" in the Union of Myanmar. Asian Ethnicity 2002;(3):199−220.

[7] Harriden J. Making a name for themselves: Karen identity and the politicization of ethnicity in Burma. Journal of Burma Studies 2002;7:84−144.

[8] Horstmann A Confinement and mobility: Transnational ties and religious networking among Baptist Karen at the Thailand-Burma Border. MMG Working papers 10-16. Max Planck Institute for the Study of Religious and Ethnic Diversity; 2010.

[9] Kuroiwa Y, Verkuyten M. Narratives and the constitution of a common identity. The Karen in Burma. Identities 2008;15(4):391−412.

[10] Dudley S. Materialising exile: material culture and embodied experience among Karenni refugees in Thailand. New York & Oxford: Berghahn Books; 2010.

[11] Comaroff JL, Comaroff J. Ethnicity, Inc. Chicago Studies in Practises of Meaning. Chicago & London: University of Chicago Press; 2009.

[12] Bradley D. Tibeto-Burman languages and classification. In: Bradley D, editor. Papers in Southeast Asian Linguistics No. 14: Tibeto-Burman Languages of the Himalayas, 14. the Australian National University: Pacific Linguistics; 1997. p. 1−72.

[13] Thawnghmung AM The Karen revolution in Burma: Diverse voices, uncertain ends. East-West Center, Policy Studies 45 (Southeast Asia), USA; 2008.

[14] Green G, Lockley E. Communication practices of the Karen in Sheffield: Seeking to navigate their three zones of displacement. Asian J Commun 2012;22(6):566−83.

[15] Castells M. Communication, power and counter-power in the network society. Int J Commun 2007;1:238−66.

[16] Hynes P, Thu YM. To Sheffield with love. Forced migration review 2008;30:49.

[17] Beiser M. Resettling refugees and safeguarding their mental health: Lessons learned from the canadian refugee resettlement project. Transcult Psychiatry 2009;46:539.

[18] Marshall GN, Schell TL, Elliott MN, Berthold SM, Chun CA. Mental health of cambodian refugees 2 decades after resettlement in the United States. J Am Med Assoc 2005;3(5):294.

[19] King T, Wilder WD. The Modern anthropology of South East Asia: An introduction. London: Routledge /Curzon; 2003.

[20] Cho NV (2009) New media and Burmese diaspora identities in New Zealand. [dissertation]. Auckland University of Technology: Pacific Media Centre, School of Communication Studies; 2009.

[21] Gackenbach J. Psychology and the Internet: Intrapersonal, interpersonal, and transpersonal implications. London: Academic Press; 2007.

[22] Fanon F Black skin, white masks. 1986 ed. (First ed. 1952). Pluto Press.

[23] Foeman AK, Nance T. Reviewed from miscegenation to multiculturalism: Perceptions and stages of interracial relationship development. J Black Stud 1999;29(4):540−57.

[24] Ringold S, Burke A, Glass RM. Refugee Mental Health. JAMA:. J Am Med Assoc 2005;294(5):646.

[25] Skidmore M. Darker than midnight: Fear, vulnerability, and terror making in urban Burma (Myanmar). Am Ethnol 2003;30(1):5−21.

Further Reading

Anon Report. Burma, Bureau of Democracy, Human Rights, and Labor. US Department of State. [Internet]. 2008 Mar 11. Retrieved from: http://www.state.gov/g/drl/rls/hrrpt/2007/100515.htm.

Ball D. Security developments in the Thailand-Burma borderlands. Working paper. Australian Mekong Resource Centre; 2003 (9).

Chowdhury M. The Role of the Internet in Burma's Saffron revolution. The Berkman Centre for Internet and Society. Internet Case Study Series; 2008.

Colaric AM, Janczewski LJ. Cyber warfare and cyber terrorism. Information Science Reference. London: An imprint of IGI Global; 2007.

Crane A. In the company of spies: When competitive intelligence gathering becomes industrial espionage. Bus Horiz 2005;48:233−40.

Danitz T, Strobel WP. Networking dissent cyber activists use the Internet to promote democracy in Burma. In: Arquilla J, Ronfeldt D, editors. Networks and Netwars: The Future of Terror, Crime, and Militancy. USA: Rand; 2001.

Dudley S. A sense of home in exile. Forced Migration Review 2008;30:23.

Refugee health: an approach to emergency situations. In: Hanquet G, editor. Medecins Sans Frontieres. MacMillan Education Ltd. London; 1997. p. 286−291.

Johnson HL. Click to donate: Visual images, constructing victims and imagining the female refugee. Third World Q 2011;32(6):1015−37.

Krekel B. Capability of the People's Republic of China to conduct cyber warfare and computer network exploitation. US-China Economic & Security Review Commission; 2009.

Lenner K. Beyond the republic of Fear: Symbolic domination in Ba'thist Iraq. Robert Schuman Centre for Advanced Studies. Mediterranean Programme Series. 2007/32.

Nesdale D, Rooney R, Smith L. Migrant ethnic identity and psychological distress. J Cross Cult Psychol 1997;28:569−88.

Sandhu JA. Burmese case study: Far from inherent−democracy and the Internet. The McMaster Journal of Communication 2011;7(1).

Sharples R. Technology in the borderlands. Forced Migration Review 2008;30:24.

The Karen Women's Organisation. State of terror: Women at risk. Forced Migration Review. 2008;(30):12.

Wortzel L. (2010) China's approach to cyber operations: Implications for the United States. [Internet]. 2010 [accessed 03.11]. Retrieved from: http://www.internationalrelations.house.gov/111/wor031010.pdf.

Focus Topics: From Online Radicalisation to Online Financial Crime

Theory

A Framework for the Investigation and Modeling of Online Radicalization and the Identification of Radicalized Individuals

33

Petra Saskia Bayerl[1], Andrew Staniforth[2], Babak Akhgar[3], Ben Brewster[3], and Kayleigh Johnson[3]

[1]*Erasmus University, Rotterdam, The Netherlands*
[2]*North East Counter Terrorism Unit, West Yorkshire Police, West Yorkshire, UK*
[3]*Sheffield Hallam University, Sheffield, UK*

INFORMATION IN THIS CHAPTER

- Aspects to consider in modeling online radicalization
- Approaches to measure radical online behavior

INTRODUCTION

On May 22, 2008, British citizen Nicky Reilly made his way to the Giraffe restaurant in Exeter, South England, with a rucksack containing six bottles full of nails and home-made explosives. He ordered a drink and then made his way to the lavatory, taking his rucksack with him. There the device detonated prematurely. None of the 44 guests present was injured, but it damaged the restaurant and caused injuries to Reilly. A note left at his home revealed his actions as a tribute to Osama bin Laden and declared that violence would continue until "the wrongs [done by 'the West' to the Muslim world] have been righted." Appearing at court as Mohammed Abdulaziz Rashid Saeed, Reilly pleaded guilty to offenses of attempted murder and preparing for acts of terrorism and was subsequently sentenced to life imprisonment. While the actions of Reilly were clearly abhorrent, many would come to view him as a victim of terrorism himself. Recruited online in chat rooms, extremists had molded a home-grown terrorist, had directed him to bomb-making websites, and had discussed what his target should be. Reilly became, if not an outright victim, then at least an instrument to serve the terroristic purposes of others, manipulated by anonymous terrorists online.

The threat from contemporary terrorism is both serious and enduring, being international in scope and involving a variety of individuals, groups, and networks that are driven by extremist beliefs. No country, community, or citizen should consider themselves immune from the global reach of international terrorists who believe they can advance their political, religious, or ideological aims through acts of violence. Tackling the terrorist threat remains a national security priority for many governments across the world.

In this context, online radicalization has become a pertinent issue. As the introductory example demonstrates, the Internet has changed—and continues to change—the very nature of terrorism [1]. The Internet is well-suited to the nature of terrorism and the psyche of the terrorist. In particular, the ability to remain anonymous makes the Internet attractive to the terrorist plotter [2]. Terrorists use the Internet to propagate their ideologies, motives, and grievances. The most powerful and alarming change for modern terrorism, however, has been its effectiveness for attracting new terrorist recruits, very often the young and most vulnerable and impressionable in our societies. Modern terrorism has rapidly evolved, becoming increasingly non-physical, with vulnerable "home-grown" citizens being recruited, radicalized, trained, and tasked online in the virtual and ungoverned domain of cyberspace. With an increasing number of citizens putting more of their lives online, the interconnected and globalized world in which we now live provides an extremely large pool of potential candidates to draw into the clutches of disparate terrorists groups and networks [3].

The indoctrination of our citizens by online radicalizers and recruiters is a pressing concern for all in authority. The Internet has become crucial in all phases of the radicalization process, as it provides conflicted individuals with direct access to unfiltered radical and extremist ideology, which drives the aspiring terrorist to view the world through this extremist lens. When combined with widely marketed images of the holy and heroic warrior, the Internet becomes a platform of powerful material, communicating terrorist visions of honor, bravery, and sacrifice for what is perceived to be a noble cause [3].

The prevention of online radicalization remains an ambitious undertaking, and still we must find new and innovative ways in which to expose and isolate the apologists for violence, and protect the people and places where they operate. Intelligence and law enforcement agencies across the world have come to learn more about how the processes of radicalization develop, but their collective understanding remains far from perfect. If preventive measures are to have a chance in interdicting at least the most savage excesses of online extremism, counter-measures need to be informed by better definitions of online radicalization and improved modeling of its causal mechanisms. The framework outlined in this chapter provides intelligence and law enforcement agencies with a structured framework for the investigation and modeling of online radicalization. It further provides a systematic approach for the identification of individuals radicalized online to support the prevention of terrorism and violent extremism.

In addressing the security challenge of online radicalization, the objectives of our framework are two-fold:

1. Provide a systematic basis with which to model causal mechanisms of online radicalization in the form of an Radicalization-Factor Model.
2. Provide an approach for the empirically derived identification of radicalized individuals based on behavioral indicators.

Its application is intended to support the following functions:

- *Inform the choice of concepts and evaluate the completeness of modeling approaches*: The quality of modeling approaches relies on the correct and complete choice of concepts. Our framework provides a matrix covering all relevant aspects pertinent to online radicalization. This matrix can be used to inform the choice of factors and judge whether all pertinent areas are included in the model.
- *Represent interactions of disparate factors within a common framework*: Considerations of online radicalization tend to focused on only a specific set of factors. Our framework creates a common matrix to raise awareness about and represent the interconnectedness of causal factors.
- *Support analysts in devising strategies to detect and prevent radicalization by providing guidance on the factors that are shown to enhance or discourage it*: Models based on our framework provide analysts with structured guidance on which areas to target for detecting and preventing online radicalization and radicalized individuals, especially in advocating a clear operationalization of behavioral indicators.
- *Provide a roadmap to indicate gaps in our knowledge on online radicalization*: Inserting known factors into our framework, the matrix provides a systematic view on factors and their relationships under-represented in the current work on online radicalization.

Systematic consideration of influencing factors: The radicalization-factor model

Nobody suddenly wakes up in the morning and decides that they are going to make a bomb. Likewise, no one is born a terrorist. Conceptualizations of radicalization have increasingly recognized that becoming involved in violent extremism is a process: it does not happen all at once [4]. Similarly, the idea that extremists adhere to a specific psychological profile has been abandoned, as has the view that there may be clear profiles to predict who will follow the entire trajectory of radicalization [1].

Instead, empirical work has identified a wide range of potential "push" and "pull" factors leading to (or away from) radicalization. This starts with the fact that terrorist groups can fulfill important needs: they give a clear sense of identity, a strong sense of belonging to a group, the belief that the person is doing something important and meaningful, and also a sense of danger and excitement [4]. For some individuals, and particularly young men, these are very attractive factors. At-risk individuals share a widely held sense of injustice. The exact nature of this perception of injustice varies with respect to the underlying motivation for violence, but the effects are highly similar [4]. Personal attitudes such as strong political views against government foreign policies regarding conflicts overseas can play an important role in creating initial vulnerabilities.

Terrorism is a minority-group phenomenon, not the work of a radicalized mass of people [1]. People are often socialized into this activity, leading to a gradual deepening of their involvement over time [4]. Radicalization is thus a social process, which requires an environment that enables and supports a growing commitment. The process of radicalization begins when these enabling environments intersect with personal "trajectories," allowing the causes of radicalism to resonate with the individual's personal experience [1]. Some of the key elements in the radicalization process are thus related to the social network of the individual (e.g., who is the person spending time with, and who are his or her friends?) [4].

As this short overview demonstrates, past research has identified a wide range of influencing factors. Still, despite an impressive amount of work on radicalization, consensus on the process and the relevant factors leading to online radicalization, or radicalization more generally, remains elusive [5]. Moreover, existing theoretical models use disparate lenses and mechanisms to explain why (online) radicalization takes place in some people and not in others (e.g., [6–8]).

For this reason we argue for a theory-independent approach that enables the aggregation of empirical findings into a common framework. We suggest the Radicalization-Factor Model (RFM) as such a framework that allows the integration of known causal factors on online radicalization.

The model considers four interlinked factors:

1. *Characteristics of the radicalized individual*: This aspect refers to features of the individual that are linked with a weaker or stronger vulnerability for radicalization in general or a preference for specific ideologies as well as specific patterns of online and radical behaviors. These can include aspects from demographic information to norms, values, or personal experiences.
2. *Characteristics of the environment*: This aspect refers to the environment(s) in which not only the individual, but also the ideological groups, operate. The environmental(s) can be analyzed with respect to political, economic, social, technological, and legal characteristics (political system, societal diversity, general level of education, religious observance, Internet penetration rate, legal system, etc.).
3. *Characteristics of the radical groups and ideologies*: Terrorism comes in many forms based on political, religious fundamentalist, nationalist-separatist, social revolutionary, and extreme right-wing ideologies [9]. Other typologies of terror include state-sponsored terrorism and single-issue terrorism; the latter very often committed by the lone actor or "lone wolf" terrorist [10]. Identifying the specific genre of terrorism is an important factor in determining the most effective counter-measures to deploy.
4. *Characteristics of the technologies related to online radicalization*: Technologies differ greatly in the extent to which they may lend themselves for online radicalization or for terroristic behaviors (indicators). Relevant aspects are here, for instance, the degree of anonymity for users, the speed with which information can be send/accessed, or the number of users to be reached at the same time.

RFM further includes the usage of technologies by the individual as well as the usage of technologies by the ideological group(s) the individual belongs to or is influenced by. These two aspects consider inter-linkages between technology (factor 4) and the individual (factor 1) and radical groups (factor 3), respectively. With this, RFM allows to represent knowledge about specific online behaviors increasing or decreasing radicalization (e.g., radicalizing individuals tend to exclusively access networks that adhere to their own ideology, which, in turn, leads to exaggerated views of public support for their own view [11]). In including technology features as well as technology usage patterns, our framework thus explicitly addresses the context of online radicalization.

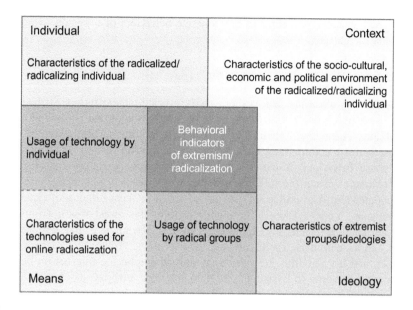

FIGURE 33.1

The Radicalization-Factor Model (RFM).

The complete Radicalization-Factor Model (RFM) is presented in Figure 33.1.

Identification of radicalized individuals: Behavioral indicators

While RFM provides the matrix to outline the causal pathways toward online radicalization, a second crucial element is to clarify what online radicalization and radicalism exactly entails. In our view, without a clear definition, it is impossible to unequivocally link influencing factors to online radicalization. Further, only with a clear view on which behaviors can serve as indicators is it possible to identify radicalized (or radicalizing) individuals. Such conceptual clarity is also relevant to allow differentiation between radicalized individuals, who may pose an actual/acute threat, from mere sympathizers. Of course, the transition from sympathizer to active terrorist is not a distinct step [12]. Still, omitting the specification of clear criteria can result in a dangerous blurring of the concept and thus increase the risk to unsystematically expand the group of targeted individuals (risk of false positives). Moreover, the clear specification of indicators enables the comparison of definitions of online radicalization as well as comparability of empirical results. Therefore, *a precise operationalization of online radicalization* is needed in every application case.

We propose three ways of operationalizing online radicalization/extremism:

(a) single behavioral indicators
(b) combinations of behavioral indicators
(c) intensity of one or more behaviors

By "behavioral indicators" we refer to the concrete behaviors of a person, which indicate that he or she has been radicalized.

Single behavioral indicators

Some behaviors are very clear and can by themselves indicate radicalization. Such single indicators are best defined as online behaviors that crossed the legal threshold; that is, the individual has committed criminal acts of inciting racial hatred and violence, encouraged terrorist activity, or is directly concerned in the commission, preparation, or instigation of acts of terrorism. If a person shows one of these behaviors, it can be assumed with some certainty that radicalization has occurred. To illustrate, consider the following example:

When UK counter-terrorism police officers raided a flat in West London in October, 2005, they arrested a young man, Younes Tsouli. The significance of this arrest was not immediately clear, but investigations soon revealed that the Moroccan-born Tsouli was the world's most wanted "cyber-terrorist." In his activities, Tsouli adopted the user name "Irhabi 007," (Irhabi meaning "terrorist" in Arabic), and his activities grew from posting advice on the Internet on how to hack into mainframe computer systems to assisting those in planning terrorist attacks. Tsouli trawled the Internet, searching for home movies made by US soldiers in the theaters of conflict in Iraq and Afghanistan that would reveal the inside layout of US military bases. Over time, these small pieces of information were collated and passed to those planning attacks against military bases. This virtual hostile reconnaissance provided insider data, illustrating how it was no longer necessary for terrorists to conduct physical reconnaissance if relevant information could be captured and meticulously pieced together from the Internet. Police investigations subsequently revealed that Tsouli had €2.5million worth of fraudulent transactions passing through his accounts, which he used to support and finance terrorist activity.

Pleading guilty to charges of incitement to commit acts of terrorism, Tsouli received a sixteen-year custodial sentence to be served at Belmarsh High Security Prison in London where, perhaps unsurprisingly, he has been denied access to the Internet. The then National Coordinator of Terrorist Investigations, Deputy Assistant Commissioner Peter Clarke, said that Tsouli "provided a link to [...] the heart of al Qa'ida and the wider network that he was linking into through the Internet [...]what it did show us was the extent to which they could conduct operational planning on the Internet. It was the first virtual conspiracy to murder that we had seen."

Tsouli exhibited a range of behaviors that clearly demonstrated the high degree of his involvement in terrorist activities, from providing information to assist in the planning of terrorist attacks to their financial support. Any one of these behaviors constitutes a single behavioral indicator for radicalization.

Combinations of behavioral indicators

Other behaviors are less clear; for example, reading radical blogs can come from different motivations (a person is studying the topic for a high school paper, may simply be curious, or indeed be trying to obtain access to a radical group). Some behaviors are thus not unambiguous enough to identify online radicalization. In this case, a combination of specific behaviors (i.e., two or more actions occurring together) may still provide a clear indication that radicalization is taking or has taken place.

In June of 2006, Hammad Munshi, a 16-year-old school boy from Leeds, United Kingdom, was arrested and charged on suspicion of committing terrorism-related offenses. He remains the youngest person in Europe to be formally charged and convicted of terrorist offenses. Following his arrest, police searches were conducted at his family home, where his wallet was recovered from his bedroom. It was found to contain hand-written dimensions of a sub-machine gun. At the time, Munshi had excellent information technology skills; he had registered and run his own website on which he sold knives and extremist material. He passed on, for example, information on how to make napalm as well as how to make detonators for improvised explosive devices (IED). At the time of his arrest, Munshi was still a schoolboy and had been directly influenced by being exposed to extremist rhetoric and propaganda on the Internet from the comfort of his bedroom, unbeknownst to his family, friends, and wider social network.

While the individual actions by Munshi certainly are problematic, in this case the full degree of radicalization becomes apparent only in their combination. Considering pertinent combinations of behavioral indicators may thus support identification of at-risk individuals at a stage when radicalization is still at a lower level. Taken alone, single online activity may provide such a weak signal to authorities that it barely leaves a trace on their monitoring mechanisms, but amplifying this signal to make it stronger by grouping it together with other combinations of behavioral and contextual factors can provide a more comprehensive picture from which authorities can inform their assessments of potential risk, threat, and harm to society.

Intensity of one or more behaviors

In addition to the types of behaviors, their intensity can provide important indications for the degree of radicalization. Intensity here refers to how often or how rapidly a certain behavior occurs. As a simple example, observing a person posting daily blog or forum discussion entries may indicate a higher level of radicalization than a person posting only once a month. While single indicators or indicator combinations consider the qualitative aspects of radicalization, intensity thus takes into account the quantitative aspects of behaviors.

Application of the framework

For investigators and analysts the proposed framework has multiple applications to support the prevention of terrorism and the pursuit of terrorists. The primary operational challenge for conducting complex investigations and analysis of online radicalization is setting a tight and focused strategy.

Our approach provides a framework and parameters within which an online investigation can be methodically progressed, tracked and monitored. The framework and model ensures a holistic approach as practitioners give due consideration to the four inter-linked factors, including the characteristics of the radicalized individual, the environment, the radical groups and ideologies and the technologies related to online radicalization. Working within this framework, counter-terrorism practitioners can identify weak signals, early indicators and emerging behaviors of individuals on the path towards radicalization. Such early signals of online activity can be assessed and appropriately prioritized by existing intelligence and law enforcement agency tasking and coordination mechanisms. Appropriate action can then be taken where considered necessary, leading to early preventative interventions, continued monitoring or executive action.

For the adequate representation of causal mechanisms the linkage between the radicalization-factor model and behavioral indicators is crucial. Starting with a precise definition (operationalization) of online radicalization the framework asks for the informed selection of influencing factors that are known to impact the chosen operationalization of radicalization. In this way the framework enforces a clear and concise representation of causal pathways reducing the temptation to include 'all-and-every possible variable just in case'. The consistent approach to tackle online radicalization investigation through the application of the proposed framework serves to shed light on causal variables. This provides valuable information for further analysis to identify emergent behaviors, trends and patterns of those being recruited and radicalized online. From this data, new evidenced-based policies and strategies can emerge to push the current investigation of online radicalization beyond the current state of the art.

The practical value of RFM lays also in highlighting gaps in our collective knowledge and understanding of online radicalization. It can provide evidence of behavioral and environmental factors which may inform best practice guidance for online radicalization instigative techniques and support the development of a new doctrine for contemporary counter-terrorism practice. Identification of gaps also opens new avenues for multi-disciplinary academic research, especially within the human factor, psychological and technology domains.

While the proposed model and framework in isolation makes a positive contribution to the prevention and detection of online radicalization, its greater value to the protection of the public is its full integration and adoption into existing investigative machinery. As part of the contemporary counter-terrorism tool-kit, our framework helps to ensure that all in authority are better informed today to tackle the online radicalization challenges of tomorrow.

References

[1] Schmid AP. The Routledge handbook of terrorism research. Oxon: Routledge; 2011.
[2] Bongar B. Psychology of terrorism. New York: Oxford University Press; 2007.
[3] Davies L. Educating against extremism. Trentham: Stoke-on-Trent; 2008.
[4] Silke A. Terrorists, victims and society—Psychological perspectives on terrorism and its consequences. Chichester: Wiley; 2006.
[5] Sedgwick M. The concept of radicalization as a source of confusion. Terrorism and Political Violence 2010;22:479—94.
[6] McCauley C, Moskalenko S. Mechanisms of political radicalization: pathways toward terrorism. Terrorism and Political Violence 2008;20:415—33.
[7] Sageman M. Leaderless Jihad: Terror networks in the twenty-first century. Philadelphia: University of Pennsylvania Press; 2008.
[8] Wiktorowicz Q. Radical Islam rising: Muslim extremism in the West. Lanham: Rowman & Littlefield; 2005.

[9]   Hudson RA. The Sociology and psychology of terrorism: Who becomes a terrorist and why? Library of Congress, Federal Research Division. [Internet]. Retrieved from: <http://www.loc.gov/rr/frd/pdffiles/Soc_Psych_0 f_Terrorism.pdf>; 1999.

[10] Awan I, Blakemore B. Policing cyber hate, cyber threats and cyber terrorism. Surrey: Ashgate; 2012.

[11] Wojcieszak ME. Computer-mediated false consensus: radical online groups, social networks and news media. Mass Commun Soc 2011;14:527−46.

[12] Moskalenko S, McCauley C. Measuring political mobilization: the distinction between activism and radicalism. Terrorism and Political Violence 2009;21:239−60.

Preventing Terrorism Together: A Framework to Provide Social Media Anti-Radicalization Training for Credible Community Voices

34

Andrew Staniforth[1] and Holger Nitsch[2]

[1]*North East Counter Terrorism Unit, West Yorkshire Police, West Yorkshire, UK*
[2]*Fachhochschule fur Offenttliche Verwaltung und Rechtspflege in Bayern, Bavaria, Germany*

INFORMATION IN THIS CHAPTER

- Counter-terrorism
- Online radicalisation
- Counter-extremism
- Counter-terrorism strategy
- Anti-radicalization training
- Social media
- Community credible voices

INTRODUCTION

At 2:20 pm on May 22, 2013, British soldier Drummer Lee Rigby of the Royal Regiment of Fusiliers was walking outside his barracks in Woolwich, southeast London [1]. As he made his way onto Artillery Place, a vehicle deliberately swerved from the road onto the pavement and struck him. Two occupants got out of the car and viciously attacked and killed him with a cleaver and a knife [2]. With no prior warning of the ambush, unarmed Drummer Rigby had little chance to defend himself or to make his escape. After the initial attack, his lifeless body was moved to the center of the road, where it was left while the two attackers, Michael Adebowale, 22, and Michael Adebolajo, 28, engaged in conversation with the public as they walked by, encouraging them to look at what had happened [3]. As armed police officers arrived at the scene of the incident, the attackers ran toward them, brandishing their weapons. Police officers shot and detained the two suspects, arresting them for the murder of the British soldier. The horrific public death of Drummer Lee Rigby on the streets of London was greeted with shock across the United Kingdom. The injuries inflicted upon the victim were so severe the 25-year-old had to be formally identified by a forensic dentist [4]. His brutal murder amplified the amorphous threat from non-hierarchical terrorist cells of radicalized individuals affiliated to al Qa'ida.

Citizens who witnessed the killing of Drummer Rigby served as freelance journalists and evidence gatherers, reporting images from the scene of the attack to television and social networks. They captured the terrorists' justification and motivation for the murder of the British soldier on their smart mobile devices. Just moments following the attack, a frenzy of social media communications from online users provided commentary of the incident, condoning the senseless killing of a young man. The vast majority of citizen comments and media reporting was mature, balanced, and measured, given the terror that had taken place. The incident sparked online debate, but it was a conversation that was quickly joined by violent extremists from all sides of the political spectrum pushing their own rhetoric and ideologies. The posting of extreme and hard-line views did little to help the public's understanding of the emerging terrorist incident.

While extremists used the attack to further promote their specific cause and draw attention to their particular grievances, other online users published comments that would have damaging consequences. One such online message was posted by Deyka Ayan Hassan, a 21-year-old English and politics undergraduate student of Kingston University [5]. Hassan contacted the police after receiving hundreds of tweets from people threatening to rape and kill her in the aftermath of Drummer Rigby's murder. However, police officers later arrested Hassan as she admitted to sending a tweet, which she said was a joke, about the design of the clothing worn by Drummer Rigby that was mentioned in citizens' reporting of the attack. At the time of his murder, Drummer Rigby was wearing a "Help the Heroes" T-shirt, which was given out by a charitable organization established to support the return home of armed forces personnel from theaters of conflict overseas. Hassan had posted a message on Twitter that said: "To be honest, if you wear a Help for Heroes t-shirt you deserve to be beheaded" [6]. The tweet received a furious backlash from British far-right organizations; there were threats so severe that Hassan feared for her safety, resulting in her reporting the matter to the police.

Appearing at Hendon Magistrates' Court in London during June, 2013, Hassan was ordered to undertake 250 hours of community service after admitting the charge of sending a malicious electronic message. Magistrate Nigel Orton, chairman of the bench, said Hassan could have been jailed by the court for what she had done but the court had accepted her claim that, at the time she had posted the offending tweet, she did not know it was a soldier who had been killed. Mr Orton said: "The tragic events in Woolwich that day have created a context which made this tweet appear extreme. It had a huge impact and clearly caused offence and distress. We accept you didn't intend to cause harm and you felt it was a joke. Your act was naive and foolish and without regard to the general public at a time of heightened sensitivity" [7]. The court also heard Hassan's father was working for charities that combat extremism and had previously been an associate advisor for policing diversity to the Metropolitan Police Service [8].

In the aftermath of the terrorist murder in London, an online platform was created by extremist groups and individuals to espouse their harmful views. A battleground between the voices of good and evil had been established, and while some online voices could be heard to rebut the extremist protagonists, their collective voice was weak and lacked the volume and credibility to fight back against the online onslaught of extremists who supported the slaying of the British soldier. Extremists had hijacked appropriate and proportionate online discussions and debate. Those whose intentions served to divide communities rather than unite them during a time of crisis occupied the space provided by social media. The attack of a British soldier on home soil had provided an opportunity for cyber terrorist recruiters to reach out and radicalize the vulnerable members of the online community.

Online radicalization

The terrorist murder of Drummer Lee Rigby confirmed to security authorities across Europe what they already knew: that the threat from contemporary terrorism now emerges from numerous sources and is being imported into individual member states, as well as coming from within its own borders. The incubation of the home-grown threat had already been identified by many intelligence agencies within Europe, and the "neighbor terrorist"—drawn from the very communities the counter-terrorism apparatus of member states were attempting to protect—continued to flourish, despite the successful intervention of numerous terrorist plots and the concerted efforts of law enforcement agencies.

The primary challenge of tackling contemporary terrorism across Europe remains the increasing impact of the Internet upon terrorist recruitment, radicalization, and attack planning. The terrorist threat has become virtual, with terrorists being recruited, radicalized, trained, and tasked online with little deterrent or cyber presence from law enforcement. The policing of political violence—traditionally categorized as intelligence-led and politically sensitive—has historically generated structures that had been remote, secretive, and specialist. Yet the contemporary evolution of terrorism has spawned important new trends and demanded a new policing response. Contemporary terrorism now involves embedded citizens as much as foreign extremists [9]. The way in which members of communities across Europe are being influenced by the extreme single narrative of the religious ideology promoted by al Qa'ida remains a critical concern for the European Union. This single narrative, when combined with a complex malaise of social and economic factors, serves to manipulate individuals toward extremist perspectives, cultivating a home-grown terrorist threat. While security authorities across member states understand that terrorism comes in many forms, the primary threat continues to emerge from al Qa'ida, whose support and Islamist network is propagated online.

No community should consider themselves immune from the global reach and connectivity of Islamist groups following in the footsteps of al Qa'ida. Many member states across Europe share similar security challenges, including the identification of potential terrorist suspects operating within their communities and the need to understand the factors that lead to the development of extremist views.

In Germany, the case of Dennis Mamadou Cuspert brought home to security forces the reality of violent extremist online radicalization. Cuspert, who was born in 1975 in Berlin, in the borough of Kreuzberg, had a German mother. His father, who originated from Ghana, left the family shortly after Cuspert's birth [10]. Cuspert had a troubled childhood and an argumentative relationship with his stepfather, a former member of the United States armed forces. At the age of only eight,

Cuspert embarked upon his criminal career by stealing toy cars. As a teenager, he and his gang were involved in dealing drugs and committing armed robberies. After shooting a friend in the face with a gas pistol, Cuspert was sentenced to three years' imprisonment, during which time he decided to start a new career as a rap musician [11].

In 2002, upon his release from prison, Cuspert changed his name to Deso Dogg and became a successful "gangster rapper." His new-found career lasted until 2009, and although he never reached the top rankings of fellow musical artists, he was well-known and respected among his peers and enjoyed a dedicated fan base. During his musical career he forged contacts with radical Islamist groups including the Turkish Kaplan Group, the Hizb ut-Tahrir, and the Tablighi-Jamaat [12]. In 2010, Cuspert announced his retirement from music in order to continue his work as an Islamic preacher. He again changed his name, this time calling himself Abu Maleeq. Leading salafist preachers in Germany, including Pierre Vogel, believed Cuspert provided a unique opportunity, given his fame as a musician, to promote their cause and engage in their missionary work. The salifist preachers expected that Cuspert's former music fans would continue to follow him and convert to the salifist interpretation of Islam [13]. Guided by extremist preachers, Cuspert became increasingly radical and forged close associations with Abu Nagie, from the organization, "Wahre Religion" (true religion). He began to produce propaganda *nasheeds* (religious chants) to glorify jihad, which were broadcast on the Internet.

Now immersed within the Islamist ideology, Cuspert continued producing salafist online propaganda for the jihadist movement, extending his efforts to working for an organization called Millatu Ibrahim [14]. It was during this time that his activity came to the attention of the police. Following an incident in May, 2012 in Bonn, where a police officer was seriously injured by a knife wielded by an Islamist extremist during a clash with members of the right-wing party "pro Köln," police conducted 80 raids of premises suspected to be occupied by members of the extreme salafist movement. In one of the raided flats, officers discovered a vest filled with explosives, which had been prepared by Cuspert. While forensic examinations revealed that the improvised device would not have detonated, it provided a clear signal to authorities that Cuspert was preparing to pursue his extremist believes through acts of violence [15].

In Germany, the public disorder between extreme salifists and right-wing groups brought about the ban of *Millatu Ibrahim*. Unfortunately for German authorities, Cuspert disappeared along with associates shortly after the raids and was suspected of making his way to Egypt [16].

In September, 2012, Cuspert published a video online in which he asked all Muslims in Germany to fight against the German government and threatening to bring jihad to Germany. Reflecting on Cuspert's radicalization development process, authorities were concerned at the speed at which he had adopted such extreme views, most likely as a result of the high level of support and influence he received from leading Islamist preachers. His online *nasheeds* and propaganda videos would have damaging consequences, serving to radicalize others to the Islamist cause. In February, 2011, Arid Uka, 22, a Muslim ethnic Albanian who grew up in Germany, killed two United States soldiers at Frankfurt Airport [17]. At his trial, Uka revealed that he had been radicalized by jihadist propaganda videos he had watched online. As part of their investigations, German authorities examined his Facebook profile and found that, just days before the shooting, Uka had written alongside one of Cuspert's videos, "I love you for Allah Abu Maleeq" [18]. Authorities could not deny the influence of Cuspert as an online terrorist recruiter and radicalizer, nor could they ignore the power of the Internet, which continues to transform the very nature of terrorism.

Collaboration in counter-terrorism

Understanding why citizens across Europe are moving toward extremist perspectives, and creating an alternative to allow them to resist such views, is a priority for the counter-terrorism apparatus of individual member states. The need for credible and actionable intelligence to monitor and prevent terrorism has come to the fore and has been added to the more traditional tactics of the pursuit of terrorists through criminal justice processes. The imperative to refocus and react to new trends is central to many member states' counter-terrorism strategies across Europe, reflecting concerns for increased preventive activity. Bringing the prevention of terrorism to community-focused policing across Europe has produced palpable moves toward expansion and localism in the policing of political violence.

Preventing terrorism and violent extremism at a local and national level was recognized by the Justice and Home Affairs Council of the European Union who, in December, 2005, established the European Union Counter-Terrorism Strategy. The strategy was divided into four pillars—Prevent, Protect, Pursue, and Respond, and was welcomed by the heads of member states and governments. This pan-European strategy sought to take the agenda of work that was set out at the March, 2004 European Council (constituting the European Union Action Plan on Terrorism) into the next phase. The strategy committed the European Union "to combat terrorism globally while respecting human rights, and to make Europe safer, allowing its citizens to live in an area of freedom, security and justice" [19].

Recognizing that international terrorism is a trans-national phenomenon by definition, the role of the European Commission is to facilitate and coordinate intensified cooperation between European Union member states. Efforts of the European Commission have included the orientation and facilitation of the emergence, identification, and exchange of good, local practices in countering terrorist radicalization. The role of the European Commission recognizes the need to protect citizens from new and emerging terrorist tactics but most importantly, it recognizes that all in authority require a united and combined response across the European Union, which has to be tough on terrorism and on the causes of terrorism. Though absolutely necessary for citizen safety, this level of protection continues to be an ambitious undertaking and one that serves to encourage the "mainstreaming" of counter-terrorist policy and action. Concepts such as community involvement, multi-agency working, and public assurance—now widely accepted and practiced in local policing across numerous member states—have migrated into the policing of political violence. All police officers, and not just those specialist counter-terrorism officers, now share in these tasks. Counter-terrorism policing has thus become a matter for all police departments, for all their strategic partners, and for all the public.

In order to tackle the phenomenon of online radicalization, especially the opportunity provided by social media following a terrorist event, five organizations across European member states have combined their efforts and are progressing research supported by the Prevention of and Fight against Crime Programme of the European Commission Directorate-General Home Affairs.

Bringing their own expertise to bear in concert with one another, the North East Counter Terrorism Unit of West Yorkshire Police in the UK; the European Institute of Bulgaria; the Police and Border Guard of Estonia; the Ministry of Interior, Counter Terrorism Center in Hungary; and Fachbereich Polizei in Germany are working together to find innovative solutions to strengthen communities' online resilience to harmful terrorist rhetoric. The strategic aim of their collaborative efforts is reflected in the title of the research project: Social Media Anti-Radicalization Training for Credible Voices (SMART-CV). The purpose of SMART-CV is to develop a table-top community consequence exercise. The exercise shall increase the awareness of the benefits of harnessing the power and influence of social media to prevent radicalization of individuals following a local, national, or global counter-terrorism-related incident. The aim of this research meets the Prevention of and Fight Against Crime Programme of the European Commission objectives by stimulating, promoting, and developing horizontal methods and tools necessary for strategically preventing and fighting terrorism. By providing a counter-narrative, members of communities who attend SMART-CV exercises will help to prevent online radicalization. While social media is abused by those who are recruiting individuals from our communities for terrorist activities, SMART-CV will utilize the same networks to address community tensions, provide public reassurance, and counter harmful single narratives.

Credible voices

Recognizing that members of local communities can play an important part in preventing the radicalization of individuals, SMART-CV's essential elements are the identification, support, and training of "Credible Voices" within local communities. A Credible Voice is a person, a group, or an organization that is able to genuinely and openly represent a community, or part of community, by effectively communicating key positive messages. Credible Voices shall leverage the full potential of their reach, influence, position, and social standing to establish counter-narratives, thereby promoting and raising awareness of alternative perspectives and encouraging a positive discourse and exchange of information between law enforcement agencies and the communities they serve. Examples of Credible Voices include local religious or faith leaders; local charitable organizations or groups whose work is recognized as contributing to local communities; local volunteers who may manage youth clubs or groups, or provide local services and support to communities; as well as professionals such as teachers, youth services workers, and health workers who work within a local area. While this is not an exhaustive range of example Credible Voices, this list provides a broad indication of just some of the individuals and groups that may be able to support the prevention of online radicalization. Credible Voices shall be able to provide unique local perspectives and positive support to counter potentially damaging online narratives as part of the broader community contingency response to a terrorist incident.

The outcomes from this collaborative research will serve to improve the positive impact of counter-terrorism measures and avoid the unnecessary escalation of extremist online rhetoric through the presence and amplification of online Credible Voices. Their efforts shall strengthen community cohesion and resilience to such extremist propaganda and provide a moderate and measured alternative narrative.

CONCLUSION

The approach to implement preventive counter-terrorism action by governments across European Union member states has by no means been welcomed and supported by all. In developing the preventive aspects of counter-terrorism policy at a local community level, governments have entered uncharted waters. Never before have national and central government counter-terrorism policies been directly linked to local community issues in this way. That being said, the notion that communities can defeat terrorism by refusing to accept extremist rhetoric is now understood by law enforcement agencies as a primary part of their counter-terrorism efforts—an approach that underpins the unique collaborative research methodology of SMART-CV.

While the free movement of citizens has accelerated the phenomenon of online radicalization across the European Union, it has also rapidly progressed as a direct result of the increasing use of new social media, which serves to erode traditional physical boundaries. At the same time, terrorist events and other contemporary crises no longer conform to geographical boundaries. As a direct result, European citizens now require a coordinated and consistent approach to the protection of their community, wherever their locality.

Collaboration in counter-terrorism provides the key to tackling online radicalization. No single law enforcement agency or government can protect its communities alone. All in authority must recognize the need to actively encourage increased collaborative efforts and support the engagement and participation in applied research that maximizes the opportunity for future citizen safety. Law enforcement practitioners are now tackling the phenomenon of online radicalization by working together and sharing challenges and approaches. But it is not law enforcement agencies that shall defeat terrorism; it is communities. Harnessing and supporting their efforts, while focusing on the development of online Credible Voices, shall serve to stop more members of our communities from choosing the destructive road of radicalization.

References

[1] British Army. [Internet]. Available at: <http://www.army.mod.uk/news/25536.aspx>; [accessed 28.06.13].

[2] Daily Mail. [Internet]. Available at: <http://www.dailymail.co.uk/news/article-2331079/Woolwich-murder-Distraught-family-widow-murdered-soldier-Lee-Rigby-visit-street-died.html>; [accessed 03.07.13].

[3] BBC. [Internet]. Available at: http://www.bbc.co.uk/news/uk-22644857>; [accessed 06.06.13].

[4] Express. [Internet]. Available at: <http://www.express.co.uk/news/uk/405880/Student-in-court-for-vile-beheading-Twitter-post-after-the-death-of-Drummer-Lee-Rigby>; [accessed 11.06.13].

[5] Express. [Internet]. Available at: <http://www.express.co.uk/news/uk/405880/Student-in-court-for-vile-beheading-Twitter-post-after-the-death-of-Drummer-Lee-Rigby>; [accessed 11.06.13].

[6] Express. [Internet]. Available at: <http://www.express.co.uk/news/uk/405880/Student-in-court-for-vile-beheading-Twitter-post-after-the-death-of-Drummer-Lee-Rigby>; [accessed on 11.06.13].

[7] Express. [Internet]. Available at: <http://www.express.co.uk/news/uk/405880/Student-in-court-for-vile-beheading-Twitter-post-after-the-death-of-Drummer-Lee-Rigby>; [accessed 11.06.13].

[8] Express. [Internet]. Available at: <http://www.express.co.uk/news/uk/405880/Student-in-court-for-vile-beheading-Twitter-post-after-the-death-of-Drummer-Lee-Rigby>; [accessed on 13.06.13].

[9] Staniforth A. Routledge companion to UK counter-terrorism. Oxon. Routledge; 2012.

[10] Dantschke C., Mansour A., Müller J., Serbest Y. Ich lebe nur für Allah—Argumente und Anzeihunskraft des Salafismus. ZDK—Gesellschaft Demokratische Kultur. Berlin; 2011.

[11] Lambert S. Mit8 Jahren wurde "Deso Dogg" aus Kreuzberg kriminell-jetzt kämpft er um seine Zukunft. Berliner Zeitung (27.06.2004). Berlin.

[12] Dantschke C, Mansour A, Müller J, Serbest Y. Ich lebe nur für Allah—Argumente und Anzeihunskraft des Salafismus. ZDK—Gesellschaft Demokratische Kultur. Berlin; 2011.

[13] Dantschke C, Mansour A, Müller J, Serbest Y. Ich lebe nur für Allah—Argumente und Anzeihunskraft des Salafismus. ZDK—Gesellschaft Demokratische Kultur. Berlin; 2011.

[14] Berliner Morgenpost. Anklage gegen Berliner Rapper Deso Dogg. 2011 Apr 17.

[15] Flade F. Polizei findet Sprengstoffweste bei Ex-Rapper. 2012.

[16] Welt Die. Axel. Berlin: Springer Verlag; 2012.

[17] BBC [Internet]. Available at: <http://www.bbc.co.uk/news/world-europe-16984066>; [accessed 26.06.13].

[18] Frankfurter Rundschau. Prüfstelle für jugendgefährdende Medien setzt islamistische Kampflieder auf den Index. 2012.

[19] The European Union Counter Terrorism Strategy [Internet]. Available at: <http://register.consilium.eu.int/pdf/en/05/st14/st14469-re04.en05.pdf>; [accessed 01.07.13].

Methods

Investigating Radicalized Individual Profiles through Fuzzy Cognitive Maps

Babak Akhgar[1], Fahimeh Tabatabayi[2], Petra Saskia Bayerl[3], Samir M.R. Nasserzadeh[4], and Andrew Staniforth[5]

[1]*Sheffield Hallam University, Sheffield, UK*
[2]*MehrAlborz University, Tehran, Iran*
[3]*Erasmus University, Rotterdam, The Netherlands*
[4]*University of Tehran, Tehran, Iran*
[5]*North East Counter Terrorism Unit, West Yorkshire Police, West Yorkshire, UK*

INFORMATION IN THIS CHAPTER

- Review of current models on radicalization: How can it happen?
- Overview of analysis methods for online radical profiles
- Fuzzy Cognitive Mapping as an approach to model causality in online radicalization

INTRODUCTION

The openness and freedom of the Internet unfortunately supports "self-radicalization," that is, the radicalization of individuals without direct input or encouragement from others. The role of the Internet in both radicalization and the recruitment into terrorist organizations has therefore become a growing source of concern. The Internet allows individuals to find people with shared views and values and to access information to support their radical beliefs and ideas. The unregulated and ungoverned expanse of the Internet knows no geographical boundaries, thus creating a space for radical activists to connect across the globe. This is especially problematic as the easy access to like-minded people helps to normalize radical ideas such as the use of violence to solve problems [1,2].

Yet, solving the issue of radicalization by simple processes (e.g., the suggestion of "cleaning up" the Internet) is impossible [3]. Part of the problem is that claims that terrible things are happening on extremist websites and in Internet chat-rooms are difficult to verify [1,4]. Consequently, many of the current policy proposals to address this security challenge are either unrelated to the issue or lack a sound empirical basis. We argue that this requires an alternative and more comprehensive approach that takes the complex nature of the problem into account and that can be integrated into any policy aimed at tackling online radicalization.

Identifying radicalized individuals is a complex task. There is still scant research in this field, and the automatic and semi-automatic models presented thus far are not capable of identifying individuals and their profiles in a comprehensive manner. In this chapter we introduce Cognitive Maps and Web mining as techniques for an alternative approach to the classification of online radicalized individuals. In the first part of this chapter, we review current models on the radicalization process, which provide the basis for the modeling of online radicalization. The second part of the chapter outlines the use of data mining and artificial intelligence methods in this context.

The radicalization process: How can it happen?

In a recent review on the radicalization process, Christmann [5] identified eight important models or perspectives on the subject of the radicalization process:

1. Marc Sageman's four-stage process
2. Taarnby's eight-stage recruitment process
3. The Prevent Pyramid, developed by the Association of Chief Police Officers (ACPO)
4. The New York Police Department's four-stage radicalization process
5. Gill's pathway model
6. Wiktorowicz's al-Muhajiroun model
7. McCauley and Moskalenko's 12 mechanisms of political radicalization
8. The staircase to Terrorism

Marc Sageman's four-stage process

According to Sageman [6], the radicalization process progresses in four steps that reinforce each other. The process commences with "moral outrage," which is then "interpreted in a specific way" by the person (e.g., through interactions on online forums). The third step demands that radical ideas "resonating with own personal experiences" are supported by interactions with like-minded people. These ideological groups give the inividual and other groups further self-confidence by justifying their ideologies, actions, and beliefs. In the final step, individuals may be "mobilized through a network" [7]. Although called a four-stage model, these stages are not necessarily considered as sequential.

Taarnby's eight-stage recruitment process

Drawing heavily on Sageman's [8,9] work, Taarnby [10] outlines the structure of a recruitment process in eight stages:

1. Individual alienation and marginalization
2. A spiritual quest
3. A process of radicalization
4. Meeting and associating with like-minded people
5. Gradual seclusion and cell formation
6. Acceptance of violence as a legitimate political means
7. Connection with a gatekeeper in the know
8. Going operational

The prevent pyramid

In the Prevent Pyramid, developed by the Association of Chief Police Officers (ACPO), radicalization is described as a gradual change from being part of a broad base of sympathizers to becoming an active terrorist [11]. What is notable in this model is a linear development across four tiers (see Table 35.1). This linear view stands in contrast to other authors such as Bartlett, Birdwell, and King [12], who believe that radicalization is an unforseeable and non-linear phenomenon.

Table 35.1 The Prevent Pyramid Model		
Tiers	**Level of Radicalization**	**Description**
Tier 1	All members of the community (Universal approach)	Wider community; unclear how broad this group actually is
Tier 2	The vulnerable (Targeted approach)	Not committing any violent acts, but providing tacit support to the top of the pyramid
Tier 3	Moving toward extremism (Interventionist approach)	Support group; larger group than the group who belongs to the 4th tier
Tier 4	Actively breaking the law (Enforcement approach)	Active terrorists; relatively few in number

The New York police department's four-stage radicalization process

The New York Police Department (NYPD) [13] proposed a four-stage process from pre-radicalization to jihadization. This model is based on the systematic examination of eleven in-depth case studies of "Al Qa'ida-influenced radicalization and terrorism." Details of the four phases are presented in Table 35.2.

Table 35.2 The NYPD Four-Stage Radicalization Process	
Stages of the Process	**Description of the Stages**
Pre-radicalization	A person's life situation before radicalization creates a vulnerability to radicalization ("at risk" group; comparable to Tier 3 in the Prevent Pyramidal model).
Self-identification	Beginning of association with like-minded individuals and adoption of the ideology as their own. A "cognitive opening" acts as a catalyst in this stage. Individuals leave their previous beliefs and are ready to accept new idealogies.
Indoctrination	Intensifying of individuals' beliefs, and finally, whole-hearted adoption of the ideology. This stage is faciliated by a "spiritual sanctioner" and association with like-minded people to deepen the beliefs (comparable to Tier 3 in the Prevent Pyramidal model).
Jihadization	The operational phase in which members may carry out acts of violence and terrorist attacks.

Gill's pathway model

Gill [14] proposed a pathway model for an individual's development across four key stages on the way to becoming a suicide bomber. The stages are summerized in Table 35.3.

Table 35.3 Gill's Pathway Model

Stages of the Process	Description
Broad socialization process	Exposure to propaganda that tends toward violence
Catalysts	Catalysts motivate joining an extremist organization
Pre-existing ties to aid recruitment	Kinship and friendship ties faciliate recruitment phase
Suicide bombers	Internalization of the group's norms and values

Wiktorowicz's al-Muhajiroun model

Wiktorowicz [15] focused on the role that social influences play in leading a person to join a radicalized Islamic group. He proposed his model in a four-stage process from cognitive opening to socialization, as shown in Table 35.4.

Table 35.4 Wiktorowicz's al-Muhajiroun Model

Stage of the Process	Description
Cognitive opening	Where a person can gain new ideas and world views
Religious seeking	Where a person seeks meaning through a religious framework
Frame alignment	Where the public representation offered by the radical group "makes sense" to the seeker and attracts the initial interest
Socialization	Where a person experiences religious instruction that facilitates indoctrination, identity-construction, and value changes

McCauley and Moskalenko's 12 mechanisms of political radicalization

Instead of suggesting a process model, McCauley and Moskalenko [11] identified twelve "mechanisms" of political radicalization. These mechanisms operate across three levels: individual, group, and "the mass." The mechanisms are listed in Table 35.5.

The staircase to terrorism

Moghaddam [16] offers a sophisticated "multi-causal approach" with the aim "to understand suicide terrorism [foregoing] the pathway metaphor in favour of the analogy of a narrowing 'staircase to terrorism'" ([5] p. 16). The model is composed of three levels, but suggests to focus on the individual (dispositional factors), organizations (situational factors), and the environment (sociocultural, economic, and political forces). The radicalization process progresses in six steps using

Table 35.5 McCauley and Moskalenko's 12 Mechanisms

Level of Radicalization	Mechanisms	Description
Individual	1. Personal victimization 2. Political grievance 3. Joining a radical group—the slippery slope 4. Joining a radical group—the power of love 5. Extremity shift in like-minded groups	Refers to the role of personal dissatisfaction in the decision to radicalize
Group	6. Extreme cohesion under isolation and threat 7. Competition for the same base of support 8. Competition with state power 9. Within-group competition—fissioning	Refers to political grievances based on political events or trends
Mass	10. Jujitsu politics 11. Hatred 12. Martyrdom	Refers to activities such as joining a radical group and starting with small tasks and finally leading to violent actions

the metaphor of a staircase (see Table 35.6). As Christmann [5] explains the model, "Moghaddam's metaphor is of a staircase housed in a building where everyone lives on the ground floor, but where an increasingly small number of people ascend up the higher floors, and a very few reach the top of the building to carry out a terrorist act."

Table 35.6 Staircase of Terrorism

	Description
Ground floor	Psychological interpretation of material conditions
First floor	Perceived options to fight unfair treatment
Second floor	Displacement of aggression
Third floor	Moral engagement
Fourth floor	Categorical thinking and the perceived legitimacy of the terrorist organization
Fifth floor	The terrorist act and sidestepping inhibitory mechanisms

A psychological model for the process of radicalization by Davis et al.

A variety of additional theories to the ones reviewed by Christmann [5] strive to depict the extremism and the radicalization process. Biological theories, for instance, address age and gender-related factors affecting vulnerability to radicalization (e.g., [17,18]. Social theories consider the effects of deprivation and segregation, political crises, social bands and networks, and the role of religion [5,19], while psychological theories refer to the attributes forming the terrorist personality through a review of pathological processes.

Integrating multiple case studies, Davis, Atran, Sageman, and Rijpkema [20] developed a psychological model for the process of radicalization. Their model considers three aspects:

1. Radicalization as changing moral priorities
2. Cognitive dissonance and individual radicalization
3. Vicarious cognitive dissonance and network radicalization

The model thus focuses on the relationship between ideas and behaviors at both the individual and the network levels. The assumptions of this social-cognitive model can be summarized as follows (cp. [20]:

- There is no reliable demographic pattern describing those who become radicalized; instead, highly developed group bonds seem important precursors of collective radical action.
- A sophisticated ideological basis for radical action is not a necessary precursor of radical action, and violent networks are not distinguishable from the communities they are embedded within by a special sense of moral outrage.
- A formal process of recruitment and "brainwashing" is not a necessary feature of radicalization.
- The pathway to violence is typically a gradual one, on both individual and collective levels.

The central concept of this model is that cognitive dissonance occurs across networks of individuals observing each other, demonstrating how radicalization may spread through networks [19].

The suite of models designed to better understand the phenomenon of radicalization covers a broad range of perspectives. While the complexity of addressing the security challenges of radicalization are shown in the sheer number of models, they also provide evidence that our collective understanding of the radicalization process remains far from perfect. Still, the models do share common traits. For example, there appears to be strong recognition in all models that becoming involved in violent extremism through radicalization is a process: it does not happen all at once. Similarly, the idea that there is a simple psychological profile to describe terrorists has been abandoned. Reviewing the models, it becomes clear that there have been substantial steps forward to understanding the development of individuals into terrorists. Still, the inconsistencies across models also demonstrate that immense gaps in understanding of the radicalization process remain and that considerably more research is required to identify the factors that influence online radicalization.

Investigating radical online profiles: A short overview of existing methods

Nowadays all prominent extremist groups have established at least one form of presence on the Internet [21]. The increasing sophistication and interactivity of extremists online has led to considerable challenges in detecting radical online content; among them the coverage of content, the often ephemeral nature of the content, and the diversity of data formats. The rise of social media has increased the challenge only further [21,22]. Accordingly, robust methods are needed to identify radical online profiles. A number of methods have been suggested over the last years to tackle this task. Table 35.7 provides a short summary of existing approaches based on general Web mining methods. Table 35.8 summarizes approaches specializing in online radicalization.

Table 35.7 Overview of General Web Mining Methods

Method	Description of the Method	Sources
Resource mobilization	The process of securing control over resources needed for collective action such as communications, money, information, human assets, and specialized skills	[23]
Web harvesting (or Web mining/Web farming)	The process of gathering and organizing unstructured information from pages and data on the Web using manual, semi-automatic, or automatic approaches to harvesting Web content in specific domains.	[21,24]
Web content harvesting	This approach is concerned with the specific content of documents such as HTML files, images, and email messages. Since such documents are scattered throughout the Web, the approach aims to exploit the semantic of known structures and to map these to a data model.	[25–27]
Web structure harvesting (Web link analysis)	This technique is based on the analysis of hyperlink structures and is used to discover hidden relationships among Web communities. The approach takes advantage of popular links from other sources, which point to a certain Web entity (i.e., Web pages, HTML or XML tags). As an important indicator, it uses the popularity and the frequency of visitors of the page.	[28,29]
Web usage harvesting	This harvesting technique uses data about usage patterns of Web pages (i.e., IP addresses, page references, the date and time of use) recorded and stored by Web servers to investigate, track, and evaluate user behavior and Web structures.	[30,31]

Table 35.8 Overview of Methods for the Mining of Online Radicalized Profiles

Method	Description	Source
Content and link analysis	1. *Dark Web collection building* Identification of terrorist groups from reliable sources; identification of group URLs and in-/out-link expansion 2. *Dark Web content analysis* Attribute-based content analysis of communications, propaganda, virtual communities, etc.; synthesis of resource allocation patterns 3. *Dark Web link analysis* Hyperlink extraction and link analysis; website clustering and classification	[2]
Network analysis and visualization	1. *Blog spider program* Downloading of relevant pages from the entities of interest using standard HTTP protocol; extracting URLs and storing into a queue 2. *Information extraction* Extraction of information from the user profiles, including date of creation, linkages, comments, subscription, etc. Since blogs hosted on the same hosting site could have different formats, pattern matching or entity extraction techniques can be applied (e.g., rule-based algorithms, structural, contextual, or lexical and machine learning).	[32]

(Continued)

Table 35.8 (Continued)

Method	Description	Source
	3. *Network analysis* This step includes three types of analysis: a. Topological analysis is used to ensure the network extracted from links between bloggers is not random, i.e., contains meaningful information to perform the centrality and community analysis. Three techniques are applied to categorize the extracted networks: average shortest path length,[1] average clustering coefficient,[2] degree distribution.[3] b. Centrality analysis is used to identify the key nodes in a network. Three traditional centrality measures can be used: degree,[4] betweenness,[5] and closeness.[6] c. Community analysis is used to identify social groups in a network. 4. *Visualization* The final step aims to visualize the extracted network using various types of network layout methods. Two common methods are multidimensional scaling (MDS) and graph layout approaches.	
Manual method and link analysis	This method includes four steps: 1. *Manual identification of terrorist group(s)*, e.g., from government reports or research centers. 2. *Manual identification of terrorist/extremist group(s) through seed URLs* from authoritative sources/experts, literature, or terrorism keyword lexica to query major search engines on the Web. 3. *Expansion of terrorist/extremist URL set* through: a. In/out links: Out-links are extracted from the HTML contents of "favorite link" pages under the seed websites; in-links are extracted from Google in-link search service through Google API. b. Forum analysis: Using a program logging into the forums of interest and downloading of the dynamic forum contents (multilingual and multimedia Web contents). c. URL filtering: As bogus or unrelated websites can disrupt the collection, a robust filtering process is used. 4. *Dark Web content analysis* based on three attributes: technical sophistication with 13 attributes, content richness with five attributes, and Web interactivity with 11 attributes.	[24]
Social network analysis	This study contains two interactive visualization techniques using 2D graphs that dynamically facilitate the exploration of complex networks. Authors tried to introduce a method facilitating the analysis of networks automatically instead of using investigators or by manual method. They applied fisheye views[7] and fractal views[8] to visualize terrorist networks. 1. *General representation of community members*	[33] [34]

(Continued)

Table 35.8 (Continued)

Method	Description	Source
Algorithm for identification of key members	Creation of a reduced/filtered representation of the inner social community by aligning the representation to community's goals and interaction of members. 2. *Identification of key members* Application of an algorithm to identify the key members of a virtual community based on their topics of interest.	

General approach for broad profile search using content analysis	1. *Search space definition*
	   a. Major blog sites containing political and international contents (using Google).
	   b. Major video sharing sites (using Youtube due to its popularity and tagging features).
	   c. Virtual world (using Second Life due to its leadership position in virtual worlds).
	2. *Access and registration*
	3. *Content analysis and interpretation*
		[35]

[1] *The average of the lengths of the shortest paths between all pairs of nodes in a network.*
[2] *The number of links that actually exist among node i's neighbors over the possible number of links among these neighbors.*
[3] *The probability that an arbitrary node has exactly k links.*
[4] *"Degree is defined as the number of direct links a node has. 'Popular' nodes with high degree scores are the leaders, experts, or hubs in a network. It has been shown that these popular nodes can be a network's 'Archilles' Heel,' whose failure or removal will cause the network to quickly fall apart."*
[5] *"Betweenness of a node is defined as the number of geodesics (shortest paths between two nodes) passing through it. Nodes with high betweenness scores often serve as gatekeepers and brokers between different communities."*
[6] *"Closeness is the sum of the length of geodesics between a particular node and all the other nodes in a network."*
[7] *"Fisheye view is a kind of nonlinear magnification technique. It maintains the same screen size by magnifying the region surrounding the focus while compressing the distant regions without losing the global structure of the network."*
[8] *"Fractal view identifies a focus's context based on its associations with other nodes. It enhances the view of focus and its context by reducing less relevant information."*

Fuzzy cognitive mapping of factors for self-radicalization as an alternative approach

Our approach is based on Cognitive Mapping (CM). CMs are a means to visualize the causal relationships between concepts in a particular domain. In our approach, we employ Fuzzy Cognitive Maps (FCMs), as they also provide feedback mechanisms to support decision-making. In the following, we detail the application of FCMs as a promising approach for the modeling, identification, and extraction of factors affecting online behavior of radicalized individuals or groups and the simulation of e-radicalization.

Methodological background

From an artificial intelligence perspective, FCMs constitute neuro-fuzzy systems, which are able to incorporate expert knowledge. This is a soft computing technique, which is capable of dealing with complex situations representing how humans reason about a domain [36,37].

The most pronounced features of FCMs are their flexibility in system design, model, and control as well as the possibility for comprehensive operation and abstractive representation of behaviors within complex systems. FCMs are signed graphs, which capture cause-effect relationships in an integrated system. The nodes of the graph (also referred to as concepts) represent the key factors and attributes of the modeled system such as inputs, outputs, states, events, actions, goals, and trends. Variables that cause a change are called *Cause Variables*, while those that undergo the effect of the change in the cause variable are called *Effect Variables*. Signed weighted arcs describe the causal relationships among nodes in the graph. The causal relationships link nodes to each other in either a positive or a negative way. If the relationship is positive, an increase or decrease in a cause variable results in a change of the effect variable(s) in the same direction. The weight in the signed arc determines the degree of causality (i.e., change) between the linked concepts. The resulting graph of nodes and arcs provides a clear representation of how concepts influence each other and how high the degree of influence is [36,38−40].

FCM nodes are named concepts forming the set of C = {C1, C2, ... ,Cn}. Arcs (Cj, Ci) are oriented and represent causal links between concepts, i.e., they indicate in which way concept Cjinfluences concept Ci. Arcs are elements of the set A = {(Cj, Ci)ji} ∪ C×C. Weights of arcs are associated with a weight value matrix $W_{n \times n}$, in which each element of the matrix wji∈ [−1,1] ∪ R, such that if (Cj, Ci)∉A, then wji = 0 − the weights for excitation (respectively inhibition) causal links from concept Cj to concept Ciare wji > 0 (respectively wji < 0). The proposed methodology framework assumes that [−1, 1] is a fuzzy bipolar interval, in which bipolarity represents a positive or negative relationship [37,41].

In every cycle, the value i^{th} of each concept C_i is computed. By combining the impacts of all concepts related to a concept C_i and by squashing the overall impact using a barrier function f, we obtain the following rule for determining the value of C_i after each new cycle:

$$C_i^{t+1} = f\left[C_i^t + \sum_{i=1, i \neq j} W_{ji}C_j^t\right]$$

where C_i^{t+1} and C_i^t are the values of concept i at times $t+1$ and t respectively, Wjiis the weight value of the directed interconnection from concept j to concept i, and f is the barrier function used to restrict the concept value into the range [0,1] [36,42−44].

In general, the design of FCMs requires experts who have knowledge of the modeled domain and at the same time knowledge about the FCMs formalism. However, since even medium-sized models involve a large number of parameters such as concepts and weights, it is often difficult to obtain satisfactory performance and accuracy. At times, a group of experts is used to design a FCM. In this case, additional parameters such as credibility coefficients for each individual expert need to be estimated, which adds to the complexity of the design process [37]. Also, experts are not always able to express their expertise in explicit terms.

Therefore, new ways of capturing knowledge, such as learning algorithms, have been defined to improve the capabilities of FCMs [36,45]. In this method, not only casual relations between nodes, but also the strength of each edge, is determined based on historical data, which is extracted by computational procedures. During the learning process, the weight of edges in an FCM are modified to find the desired connection matrix. The values of all edges connected to a node will be

Table 35.9 Review of FCM Studies

Authors	Context	Approach to Develop FCM	Computational Method
[46]	Supervision of multi-agent systems	Numerical-based	Dynamical Fuzzy Cognitive Map (DFCM)
[29]	Web-mining inference	Numerical-based	WEMIA[1] mechanism in three phases: extracting association rules from Web-logs, transforming association rules into causal knowledge via FCMs, applying inference amplifications to the causal knowledge
[30]	Knowledge base of news information to predict interest rates	Expert-based + numerical-based	Developing a knowledge-based news miner (KBN) to search
[44]	Classifying patterns	Numerical-based	FCM-per learning algorithms (SGA & ANNs)
[36]	Training fuzzy cognitive maps	Numerical-based	Active Hebbian learning algorithm (AHL)

[1]Web mining inference amplification.

modified as soon as the value of a concept changes, allowing the model to behave in a dynamic manner [45]. The value of this method for the development of FCMs for the Web has been demonstrated in several studies. Table 35.9 provides some examples.

Application of FCMs for the analysis of the online radicalization process

We used the clear benefits of FCMs to develop a new mathematical method to enable the causal modeling of self-radicalization processes. This new CM is based on mapping factors known to encourage or discourage individuals to become self-radicalized. The factors are chosen based on reviews of the empirical literature. Table 35.10 provides an overview of important influencing factors established through a literature review of nearly twenty journal papers, reports, and working papers. This table can be used as direct input for the development of FCMs to model online radicalization. The development of FCMs is conducted in three steps, which are outlined in Figure 35.1.

Our FCM-approach considers variables determining alternative paths for online radicalization as well as the relationships among the variables. Each mutual relationship can include one linguistic fuzzy weight, which determines the accuracy of the expert choice. For each relationship, planners should answer the following question during the modeling: *How strongly, do you believe, is the causal relationship between variable (X) and variable (Y)?* The influence of one concept on another is interpreted as a linguistic variable taking values in the universe $U = [-1,1]$, for which its term set T(influence) could be: T(influence) = {negatively strong, negatively medium, negatively weak, zero, positively weak, positively medium, positively strong} [39]. For our purposes, we define the quantity space of the weight relationships Q(w) as the set:

Table 35.10 Factors Affecting Online Self-Radicalization

Online Self-Radicalization Factors (Concepts) (C1)	Polarity (+/−) No relation	Authors
Increasing radical-content Web forums (C2)	+	[1,35,47−49]
Posting e-mail containing radical messages (C3)	+	[1,35,50−53]
Downloading and sharing radical-content videos and images (C4)	+	[1,35,54−58]
Using panels of chat (i.e., echo chatrooms) causes creation of homogeneous groups (C5)	+	[1,59,35,50,53,52, 47,49]
Disseminating radical documents through the Web (i.e., a variety of instructional materials, ideologies, and propaganda) (C6)	+	[1,35,54−56,58,60]
Violent online games websites (C7)	+	[35,56,49]
Anonymization (the Internet creates an anonymous sphere to depersonalize participants (C8)	+/No relation	[5,47,49]
Age group and gender (youth are more vulnerable than adults) (C9)	+/No relation	[61,56]
Strengthening international inter-agency cooperation (C10)	−	[57,60,48]
The promotion of media educational discussions (C11)	−	[56]
Using symbolism and slogans (to attract younger users) (C12)	+	[62,56]
Using Web 2.0 platforms; i.e., social networks and video platforms (in order to approach younger users) (C13)	+	[35,53,56]
Multimedia trends on the websites (C14)	+	[7,47,58]
Propaganda on the Internet to attract youth ("Dehumanizing ideas wrapped in fun and entertainment") (C15)	+	[62,60,48,49]
Recruitment and training (C16)	+	[62,21,58]
Command and control (C17)	+	[21,58]
Technical sophistication (basic HTML techniques, advanced HTML, and dynamic Web programming used to enable users to remain anonymous) (C18)	+	[57,58]
Web interactivity tools (one-to-one interactivity, community-level interactivity, transaction-level interactivity) (C19)	+	[47,57,58]

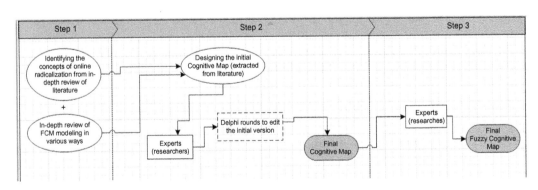

FIGURE 35.1

The FCM development process.

Q(w): {Undefined; Weak; Moderate; Strong} assuming the following order for Q(w): {Weak < Moderate < Strong} [63].

The resulting FCM represents the belief planners share with regard to the existence of certain relationships, yet not the magnitude of the change a variable may undergo because of its causal relationship with all connected variables. To aggregate the answers collected from experts, the Mamdani fuzzy operator is applied [64,65]. Aggregating the expert judgments with the aid of the fuzzy toolbox in the MATLAB software, a signed, directed CM of online self-radicalization results. An example for such a graph, based on the information in Table 35.10, is shown in Figure 35.2.

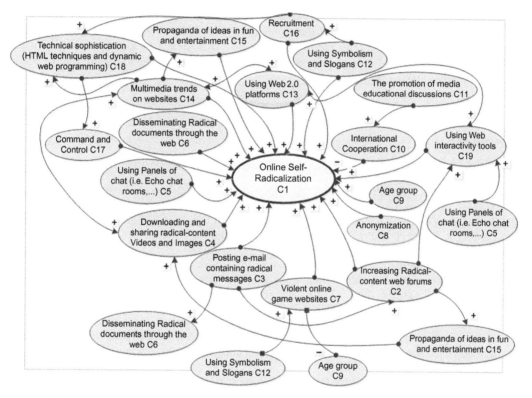

FIGURE 35.2

Signed concept map of online self-radicalization.

CONCLUSION

The world in which we now live is increasingly interconnected and interdependent. The tremendous growth in Internet use and mobile connectivity has provided widespread security concerns from government and security agencies. While the Internet has provided positive advances in communications, there remains a small number of individuals who seek to destroy our democratic values by harnessing the power and influence of the Internet to progress their own extremist causes. Innovative approaches are needed to identify and prevent online radicalization and activities that may lead to insecurity.

As the tools of radicalization are increasingly being disseminated via the Internet, security practitioners are seeking techniques to recognize the common profiles of self-radicalized individuals and indications of radicalization to prevent those vulnerable to radicalization from adopting extremist views and to pursue those who seek to harm others. In this chapter, we present Fuzzy Cognitive Maps as an approach for the modeling and visualization of causal relationships among factors affecting online radicalization. With their sound mathematical underpinnings, Fuzzy Cognitive Maps created in this rigorous fashion allow analysts to confidently assess the causes of self-radicalization. They can further support the development of better strategies to prevent online self-radicalization. This serves to provide security practitioners with better opportunities to protect the communities they serve from the threats arising from individuals radicalized online.

References

[1] Institute for Strategic Dialogue. I. f. Radicalisation: The role of the Internet: A working paper of the Ppn. Institute for Strategic Dialogue. n.d.

[2] Zhou Y, Reid E, Qin J, Chen H, Lai G. U.S. Domestic Extremist Groups on the Web: Link and Content Analysis. Intelligent Systems 2005;20(5):44−51.

[3] Stevens T, Neumann R. Countering Online Radicalisation A Strategy for Action. London: ICSR; 2009.

[4] Pantucci R, Rubin H. A Typology of Lone Wolves: Preliminary Analysis of Lone Islamist Terrorists. London: ICSR; 2011.

[5] Christmann K. Preventing religious radicalisation and violent extremism: A systematic review of the research evidence. Youth Justice Board for England and Wales 2012.

[6] Sageman M. Leaderless Jihad. Terror Networks in the 21st Century. Philadelphia, Pennsylvania: University of Pennsylvania Press; 2008.

[7] Tabatabayi F, Nasserzadeh SMR, Yates S, Akhgar B, Lockely E, Fortune D From local to global: Community-based policing and national security. Akhgar B, Yates S, editors. In: Strategic Intelligence Management: National Security Imperatives and Information and Communications Technologies. Elsevier; 2013. p. 85−92.

[8] Sageman M. Understanding Terror Networks. Philadelphia: University of Pennsylvania Press; 2004.

[9] Sageman M. A Strategy for Fighting International Islamist Terrorists. Ann Am Acad Pol Soc Sci 2008;618(1):223−31.

[10] Taarnby M. Recruitment of Islamist Terrorists in Europe: Trends and Perspectives. Danish Ministry of Justice 2005.

[11] McCauley C, Moskalenko S. Mechanisms of political radicalization: pathways toward terrorism. Terrorism and Political Violence 2008;20(3):415−33.

[12] Bartlett J, Birdwell J, King M. The Edge of Violence. Demos 2010.

[13] NYPD. Radicalisation in the West: The Homegrown Threat. New York; 2007.

[14] Gill P. Suicide Bomber Pathways Among Islamic Militants. Policing: A Journal of Policy and Practice 2008;4(2):414−22.

[15] Wiktorowicz Q. Joining the Cause:Al-Muhajiroun and Radical Islam. The Roots of Radical Islam, Department of International Studies, Rhodes College, 2004.

[16] Moghaddam FA. From the terrorists' point of view: Toward a better understanding of the staircase to terrorism. In: Stritzke WGK, Lewandowsky S, Denemark D, Clare J, Morgan F, editors. Terrorism and Torture: An Interdisciplinary Perspective. New York, United States: United States of America by Cambridge University Press; 2009. p. 10624.

[17] Bakker E. Jihadi terrorists in Europe, their characteristics and the circumstances in which they joined the Jihad: An exploratory study. The Hague: Netherlands Institute of International Relations; 2006.

[18] Wadgy L. The psychology of extremism and terrorism: A Middle-Eastern perspective. Aggression and Violent Behaviour 2007;12(2):141−55.

[19] Rijpkema R. Theoretical frames on pathways to violent radicalization. Office of Naval Research 2009.

[20] Davis R, Atran S, Sageman M, Rijpkema R. Theoretical Frames on Pathways to Violent Radicalization. Office of Naval Research 2009.

[21] Correa D. Solutions to detect and analyze online radicalization. IIITD; 2011.

[22] MacKinnon L, Bacon L, Gan D, Loukas G, Chadwick D, Frangiskatos D. Cyber security counter-measures to combat cyber terrorism. In: Akhgar B, Yates S, editors. In: Strategic Intelligence Management: National Security Imperatives and Information and Communications Technologies. Elsevier; 2013. p. 234−57.

[23] Gustavson T, Sherkat DE. Elucidating the web of hate. The ideological structuring of network ties among right wing hate groups on the Internet. Annual Meetings of the American Sociological Association 2004.

[24] Qin J, Zhou Y, Reid E, Lai G, Chen H. Analyzing terror campaigns on the internet: technical sophistication,content richness, and Web interactivity. Int J Hum Comput Stud 2007;65:71−84.

[25] Kay R. Web Harvesting. Computer World. [Internet] Jun 21. Retrieved from: <http://www.computer-world.com>; 2004.

[26] Reilly B, Tuchel G, Simon J, Palaima C, Norsworthy K, Myrick L. Political Communications Web Archiving: Addressing Typology and Timing for Selection, Preservation and Access, 3rd ECDL Workshop on Web Archives, Trondheim, Norway, 2003. Available online from: <http://old.diglib.org/pubs/news05_01/nyunews5.htm>.

[27] Gerstenfeld PB, Grant DR, Chiang C. Hate online: a content analysis of extremist internet sites. Analysis of Social Issues and Public Policy 2003;3(1):29−44.

[28] Borgman L, Furner J. Scholarly communication and bibliometrics. In: Cronin B, editor. Annual Review of Information Science and Technology. Information Today; 2002.

[29] Chang Lee K, Sung Kim J, Ho Chang N, Jea Kwon S. Fuzzy cognitive map approach to web-mining inference amplification. Expert system with application 2002;22:197−211.

[30] Hong T, Han I. Knowledge-based data mining of news information on the Internet using cognitive maps and neural networks. Expert System with Application 2002;23:1−8.

[31] Srivastava J, Cooley R, Deshpande M, Tan P. Web usage mining: Discovery and applications of usage patterns from Web data. SIGKDD Explorations 2000;1(2):1−12.

[32] Chau M, Xu J. Mining communities and their relationships in blogs: a study of online hate groups. Int J Hum Comput Stud 2006;65(1):57−70.

[33] Yang CC, Liu N, Sageman M. Analyzing the terrorist social networks with visualization tools. Intelligence and Security Informatics 2006;3975:331−42.

[34] L'Huillier G, Alvarez H, Rios A, Aguilera F. Topic-based social network analysis for virtual communities of interests in the dark web. SIGKDD Explorations 2010;12(2):66−73.

[35] Chen H, Thoms S, Fu T. Cyber extremism in Web 2.0: An exploratory study of international Jihadist. Taipei: IEEE; ISI; 2008. p. 98−103.

[36] Papageorgiou EI, Stylios CD, Groumpos PP. Active Hebbian learning algorithm to train fuzzy cognitive maps. International Journal of Approximate Reasoning 2004;37:219−49.

[37] Stach W, Kurgan L, Pedrycz W, Reformat M. Genetic Learning of Fuzzy Cognitive Maps. Fuzzy Sets and Systems 2005;153:371−401.

[38] Craiger JP, Goodman DF, Weiss RJ, Butler A. Modeling Organizational Behavior with Fuzzy Cognitive Maps. International Journal of Computational Intelligence and Organisations 1996;1:120−3.

[39] Groumpos PP. Fuzzy cognitive maps: basic theories and their application to complex systems. In: Dr. Glykas M, editor. Fuzzy Cognitive Maps Advances in Theory, Methodologies, Tools and Applications. Springer-Verlag Berlin Heidelberg Publishers; 2010. p. 1−22.

[40] Wei Z, Lu L, Yanchun Z. Using fuzzy cognitive time maps for modeling and evaluating trust dynamics in the virtual enterprises. Expert Systems with Applications 2008;35:1583−92.

[41] Xirogiannis G, Glykas M. Intelligent modeling of e-business maturity. Expert Systems with Applications 2007;32:687−702.

[42] Stach W, Kurgan L, Pedrycz W. Expert-Based and Computational Methods for Developing Fuzzy Cognitive Maps. In: Dr. Glykas M, editor. Fuzzy Cognitive Maps Advances in Theory, Methodologies, Tools and Applications. Springer-Verlag Berlin Heidelberg Publishers; 2010. p. 23−41.

[43] Kosko B. Fuzzy Cognitive Maps. Int J Man Mach Stud 1986;24:65−75.

[44] Papakostas GA, Koulouriotis DE. Classifying patterns using fuzzy cognitive maps. In: Glykas M, editor. Fuzzy Cognitive Maps Advances in Theory, Methodologies, Tools and Applications. Springer; 2010. p. 291−306.

[45] Alizadeh S, Ghazanfari M. Learning FCM by chaotic simulated annealing. Chaos, Solitons and Fractals 2009;41:1182−90.

[46] Aguilar J. Dynamic Fuzzy Cognitive Maps for the Supervision of Multiagent Systems. In: Dr. Glykas M, editor. Fuzzy Cognitive Maps Advances in Theory, Methodologies, Tools and Applications. Springer-Verlag Berlin Heidelberg Publishers; 2010. p. 307−24.

[47] Preece J. Online communities: Designing usability, supporting sociability. New York City: Wiley; 2000.

[48] Thompson R. Radicalization and the use of social media. Journal of Strategic Security 2011;4(4):167−90.

[49] Yunos Z, Hafidz S. Cyber terrorism and terrorist use of ict and cyberspace. In: Searcct, Ramli DP, editors. Searcct's Selection Of Articles. Kuala Lumpur, Malaysia: Southeast Asia Regional Centre for Counter-Terrorism (SEARCCT). 2011 (vol 2.)

[50] Kahne J, Middaugh E, Lee N, Feezell JT. Youth online activity and exposure to diverse perspectives. New Media and Society 2011;1−21. doi:10.1177/1461444811420271.

[51] Kelley J. Terror groups hide behind encryption. USA Today. [Internet]. Available at: <http://www.usa-today.com/tech/news/2001-02-05-binladen.html>; 2001.

[52] Livingstone S, Bober M. Regulating the Internet at home: contrasting the perspectives of children and parents. In: Buckingham D, Willett R, editors. Digital generations: Children, young people and new media. Mahwah, NJ: Lawrence Erlbaum; 2004. p. 93−113.

[53] Lee E. When and how does depersonalization increase conformity to group norms in computer-mediated communication?. Communic Res 2006;33:423−47. doi:10.1177/0093650206293248.

[54] Coll S, Glasser SB. Terrorists turn to the Web as base of operations. Washington Post 2005;7.

[55] Jenkins BM. World becomes the hostage of media-savvy terrorists: Commentary. USA Today. [Internet]. Available at: http://www.rand.org/>; 2004.

[56] Mainz. Right-wing extremism online−Targeting teenagers with stylish websites. [Internet]. Available at: jugendschutz.net; 2009.

[57] Qin J, Zhou Y, Reid E, Lai G, Chen H. Analyzing terror campaigns on the Internet: Technical sophistication,content richness, and Web interactivity. Int J Hum Comput Stud 2007;65:71−84.

[58] Weimann G. www.terror.net: How modern terrorism use the Internet. Special Report, US Institute of Peace. [Internet]. Available at <http://www.usip.org/pubs/specialreports/sr116.pdf>; 2004.

[59] Becker A. Technology and terror: The new modus operandi. Frontline. [Internet]. Available at: <http://www.pbs.org/wgbh/pages/frontline/shows/front/special/tech.html>; 2004.

[60] Reid E, Qin J, Zhou Y, Lai G, Sageman M, Weimann G, et al. Collecting and analyzing the presence of terrorists on the web: a case study of Jihad websites. Intelligence and Security Informatics 2005;3495:402−11.

[61] Ashour O. Online de-radicalization? countering violent extremist narratives: Message, messenger and media strategy. Perspectives on Terrorism. Terrorism Research Initiative 2010;15−20.

[62] ISTS. Examining the cyber capabilities of Islamic terrorist groups. Report, Institute for Security Technology Studies. [Internet]. Available at: <http://www.ists.dartmouth.edu/>; 2004.

[63] Axelrod R. Structure of decision: The cognitive maps of political elites. Princeton, NJ: Princeton University Press; 1976.

[64] Mendel. (2008). A short fuzzy logic tutorial. IEEE; 2008.

[65] Tabatabaei F, Akhgar B, Nasserzadeh SMR, Yates S. Semulating online customer satisfaction using fuzzy cognitive mapping. ITNG 2012;540−7.

Financial Security against Money Laundering: A Survey

36

Girish Keshav Palshikar and Manoj Apte

Tata Consultancy Services Limited, Pune, MH, India

INFORMATION IN THIS CHAPTER

- What is Money laundering?
- Anti-money laundering efforts
- Estimating the extent of ML
- Data mining techniques for ML detection

Money laundering

Money laundering (ML) is a serious problem for the economies and financial institutions around the world. As a recent example, a global bank paid a fine of $1.9 billion to the US government in a large ML case[1]. As another example, recently an online global currency exchange company was accused by the US government of laundering over $6 billion in seven years through 55 million transactions for millions of customers worldwide[2]. Financial institutions get used by organized criminals and terrorists as vehicles of large-scale money laundering, which presents them with challenges such as complying with regulations, maintaining financial security, preserving goodwill and reputation, and avoiding operational risks like liquidity crunch and lawsuits. With its connections to organized crimes as well as terrorist financing, ML has become a serious issue worldwide and has been receiving considerable attention from national governments and international bodies such as the United Nations (UN), the International Monetary Fund (IMF) and the World Bank [1−4]. In this paper, we begin with an overview of the problem of ML and discuss some commonly used methods of ML and the anti-ML efforts worldwide. After surveying some analytics techniques used to estimate the extent of ML, we survey some data-mining techniques reported in the literature for detection of ML episodes (instances).

---

[1]http://www.reuters.com/article/2012/12/11/us-hsbc-probe-idUSBRE8BA05M20121211
[2]http://www.nytimes.com/2013/05/29/nyregion/liberty-reserve-operators-accused-of-money-laundering.html?pagewanted=all&_r=0

ML refers to activities performed with the aim of enabling the use of illegally obtained ("dirty") money for legal purposes, while hiding the true source of the money from government authorities. Dirty money often comes from *predicate* (underlying) *crimes* such as drug trafficking, illicit arms trades, smuggling, prostitution, gambling, corruption and bribery, fraud, piracy, robbery, currency counterfeiting, and other organized crimes. In some cases, it may also come from incomes of legal businesses that need to be hidden for evading taxes. ML enables the conversion of cash from the *underground* (shadow) *economy* into monetary instruments of the *legal economy*.

Hiding the true source of the dirty money (activities, locations, people, and organizations) is a crucial requirement for ML. The destinations (i.e., the receivers) of the laundered money (i.e., the dirty money brought into the legal economy) are often known legal entities, such as registered businesses and legal citizens, though sometimes these are shell companies or nonexistent persons. The laundered money is often in the form of legal instruments (e.g., cash, bonds) or legal assets (stocks, real estate, jewelry, etc.) held by these legal entities. Sometimes, ML methods attempt to "mix" the dirty money into the legal income of these entities, with the aim that they should appear indistinguishable from each other. In this sense, hiding the true destination of the laundered money is also an important requirement for ML. This is also the case when ML is being done for terrorist financing.

Apart from the social costs arising out of the prevalence of organized crimes, ML also has adverse effects on the legal economy. ML undermines the integrity of the financial institutions: arrival of large sums of laundered money at financial institutions and their sudden disappearance can cause liquidity problems as well as loss of reputation and goodwill. ML may cause inexplicable changes in money demand, supply, increased volatility of international capital flows, and interest and exchange rates, which makes it difficult for countries to control their economic policies. Money launderers are more interested in protecting their proceeds and not necessarily in getting returns from the investment. Thus they invest in activities that are not necessarily economically beneficial; for example, they invest in construction or hotels not because of any demand but because of their short-term interests.

Criminals keep devising complex schemes (or methods) to perform ML, which involve multiple jurisdictions (or countries), dummy (or shell) companies, stolen or fake identities, (mis)use of financial institutions (banks, credit cards, stock market, and insurance), as well as auxiliary businesses such as real estate, shipping, and jewelry. Figure 36.1 shows a broad classification of the steps involved in a typical ML method. The authors of [5] survey emerging ML methods that use virtual reality role-playing games (e.g., Second Life, World of Warcraft) and online multi-player games for ML, because these environments offer opportunities that allow large sums of money to be moved across national borders without restriction and with little risk of detection or tracing.

With the advent of the Internet and online banking and investments, new financial services have made it much easier to conduct international transactions as well as to hide or steal true identities. Since the types and volumes of legal transactions are very large, and often the individual transactions involved in an ML episode appear superficially legal, it is not easy to detect entire ML episodes, particularly because criminals may be using innovative and unknown schemes. Hence automated data mining techniques are needed, which can be coupled with experts' domain knowledge about financial transactions and criminal investigations for effective ML detection.

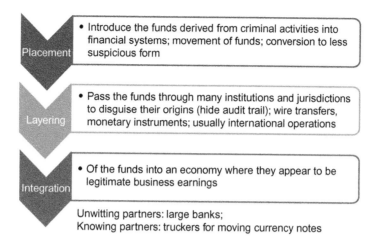

FIGURE 36.1

Broad steps in an ML method.

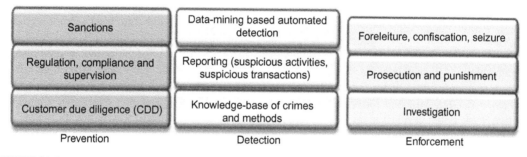

FIGURE 36.2

Pillars of AML efforts.

Anti-money laundering efforts

Realizing the gravity of ML, various nations have started a number of *anti-ML (AML)* activities, along with cooperative international efforts, for the prevention, detection, and control of ML. The main goals of an AML regime are: (i) reduce the illegal drugs trade and other organized crimes (blue/white collar), (ii) protect the integrity of the core financial system, and (iii) control corruption and terrorism-related activities. AML activities mainly consist of passing ML-related legislation, establishing financial crime investigation units, establishing compliance norms for financial institutions, etc. (Figure 36.2) [2]. The UN General Assembly established an action plan against ML in 1996, and in 1998 urged the member states to adopt national money laundering legislation and programs. Many other countries also have similar laws; for example, the Prevention of Money Laundering Act passed in 2003 in India.

Key issues in investigating an ML episode are: identifying the *modus operandi*, identifying monetary instruments and institutions involved, identifying parties and beneficiaries involved, proving the unlawful origins of the money, tracing the transactions, proving liabilities and intent, proving violations of particular laws, and prosecution. AML also includes preventive actions (audits, employee training) and detection and regulatory compliance steps (e.g., reporting suspicious transactions), etc.

International cooperation in AML activities

International cooperation is crucial in controlling ML, primarily because most large-scale ML methods involve moving money across national borders and making use of international financial institutions. Advent of the Internet-related financial services (e.g., for payments) has allowed criminals to come up with new ML methods. Criminals often take advantage of weak regulations or weak enforcement authorities in some geographies and make extensive use of such "havens" to devise complex ML methods. Hence, international cooperation is crucial for ensuring a smooth exchange of information about ML methods as well as coordination of anti-ML actions; for example, data integration and sharing, knowledge sharing, AML regime compliance, surveillance and monitoring, investigation, prosecution, etc.

In addition to the UN, the World Bank and IMF also take interest in the control of ML and establishment of effective national AML regimes. The Egmont Group (http://www.egmontgroup. org) is an international consortium of the national Financial Investigation Units (FIUs) of over 100 countries, which cooperate in collecting knowledge and exchanging information about individuals, organizations, ML methods, etc. Some global banks have formed the Wolfsberg Group for establishing standards and policies for the financial services industry, with a focus on the *customer due diligence (CDD)*, ML, and terrorist financing [6] (www.wolfsberg-principles.com). The Financial Action Task Force (FATF) is an international consortium of 33 countries (including India) established in 1989 with the aim to "set standards and promote effective implementation of legal, regulatory and operational measures for combating money laundering, terrorist financing and other related threats to the integrity of the international financial system" (www.fatf-gafi.org). FATF periodically issues a set of comprehensive recommendations for coordinating and strengthening the AML regimes in its member countries (1996, 2001, 2003, 2012) [7−10]. The recommendations cover a gamut of AML activities: enforcement (confiscation), prevention and detection (CDD and record-keeping, reporting of suspicious transactions), investigation and compliance (regulation, supervision, dealing with non-compliance with AML standards, transparency), and international cooperation. Some example recommendations are:

- Do not allow anonymous accounts or accounts in obviously fictitious names.
- Identify the customer and verify the customer's identity using reliable, independent source documents, data, or information.
- Take reasonable measures to verify the identity of the beneficial owner.
- Obtain information on the purpose and intended nature of the business relationship.

FATF identifies some ML havens (offshore financial centers ([OFC]) as: Seychelles, Lichtenstein, Nauru, Myanmar, Bahamas, Bahrain, Cayman Island, Mauritius, Luxembourg, the Netherlands, Antilles, and Antigua.

Implementation of an AML regime

Most AML regimes require financial institutions to file various reports such as the Suspicious Activity Report (SAR), suspicious Currency Transaction Report (CTR), and reports on suspicious entities; in the United States, for example, a suspicious CTR involves cash of $10,000 or more, and an SAR involves participation of entities from known ML havens. It is usually the responsibility of banks, stock markets, and other financial institutions to detect, investigate, and prevent ML and to report suspicious cases to appropriate authorities, such as the FinCEN (Financial Criminal Enforcement Network) in United States and the Financial Investigation Unit in India (http://fiuindia.gov.in). Implementing an AML regime and ensuring compliance with the relevant legislations and international commitments are large and complex tasks. It is difficult to sift through the suspicious transaction reports and identify the true instances of ML. Some of the challenges include:

- A high volume of transactions (> $1000 trillion p.a. worldwide; millions of wire transfer/Internet payments daily);
- Transactions around the world involving millions of people and companies, complex instruments and products (checks, credit cards, investments, etc.), transaction types (wire transfer, cash, etc.), and channels (ATM, Internet);
- Very low transaction volumes for actual ML (< $1 trillion p.a.); most transactions are "normal";
- Unknown and evolving modus operandi; and
- Partial and incomplete data, knowledge, and investigation skills in any one institution (need for cooperation across multiple agencies).

As a rough estimate, financial institutions spent about $500 million in 2012 on AML products and services. Geiger and Wuensch [11] shed light on the costs and benefits of ML efforts and discuss the possible reasons for failure of AML to fight the predicated crimes and collateral damage caused by AML and call for a thorough review of the current approach followed by the world governing bodies for AML. Much practical advice is available in white-papers from several vendors for implementing an effective AML regime [12–15]. See [16] for a comparative evaluation of several AML products.

Estimating the extent of ML

Estimates of the annual total amounts of money laundered worldwide vary considerably. In one case, it is estimated to be several hundred billion dollars, or alternatively, as high as two to five percent of the global economy. Many techniques have been developed to estimate the extent of ML within a national economy [17–26], which may be defined as the amount of dirty money brought into the legal economy of a particular country; we survey some of them. It is difficult to directly estimate the actual amounts of money being laundered (say, in a year in a particular country). An indirect approach has often been used to infer an estimate of the extent of ML. One approach estimates the extent of the "shadow economy" and then, assuming that some known fraction of the shadow economy is converted into legal economy, we get an estimate of the extent of ML.

So we need to first define what is meant by a shadow economy. Several related definitions are in common use. Feige [18] defines shadow economy as all currently unregistered economic activities that contribute to the officially calculated (or observed) Gross National Product (GNP). Smith [23] defines it as market-based production of goods and services, whether legal or illegal, that escapes detection in the official estimates of GDP. Tanzi [25] discusses the incentives for a country to report inflated or deflated GNP numbers and the need and some limitations of the techniques used for estimating the size of the shadow economy. Frey and Schneider [19] and Schneider and Enste [21] debate on the causes of any increase of the shadow economy and effects of the same on the official economy. They also discuss different approaches for estimating the size of the shadow economy. Direct approaches use surveys and samples based on voluntary replies or tax auditing and other compliance methods to estimate the size of the shadow economy. Indirect approaches use discrepancies between observed and expected values of selected variables to estimate the extent of the shadow economy. Some indirect methods include:

a. The discrepancy between national expenditure and national income statistics
b. The discrepancy between official and actual labor force
c. The transactions approach
d. The currency demand approach
e. The physical input (electricity consumption) method
f. The modeling approach

We discuss some of these approaches here.

Discrepancy between national expenditure and income

As a principle of accounting, the income in the GNP of a country should equal the expenditure in the economy. So if an independent estimate of expenditure is available, then the gap between the expenditure and the officially reported income of the economy can be considered as constituting the shadow economy. This approach can yield good results if an accurate independent estimate of the expenditure is available. However, there is a risk of just finding out the discrepancies of the accounting statistics rather than actually getting the size of the shadow economy using this approach.

The currency demand approach

This is a commonly used econometric method to estimate the size of a shadow economy. This approach assumes that the shadow economy transactions happen in cash payments and so there is a direct relationship between the demand for currency and the size of the shadow economy. An excessive increase in the currency demand is attributed to a rising tax burden and the thriving of the shadow economy. This approach usually assumes that the size of the shadow economy is zero in the base year. Moreover, not all transactions in the shadow economy are actually carried out in cash and may involve barter, gold, and real estate holdings as alternate forms of currency. Another limitation is that this approach attributes all the increased demand for currency to the emergence of the shadow economy, which may not be correct.

Tanzi [24] has used the currency demand approach for estimating the size of the shadow economy. He modeled the currency demand by a regression equation, as follows:

$$\ln\left(\frac{C}{M_2}\right) = \beta_0 + \beta_1 \ln(1 + TW) + \beta_2 \ln\left(\frac{WS}{NI}\right) + \beta_3 \ln\left(\frac{NI}{N}\right) + \varepsilon$$

Here, M_2 is one possible indicator for the money supply. Methods to compute the quantity M_2 vary from country to country and depend on the nature of monetary instruments available. Roughly, M_2 includes the physical money in circulation + demand deposits + other checkable deposits + savings deposits + time deposits + traveler's cheques. It does not include, for example, cash in bank vaults, cash reserves of banks, large time deposits, or money market funds (e.g., investments in stocks, mutual funds, etc.). TW is a weighted average tax rate, NI is the national income, WS/NI is the proportion of wages and salaries in the national income, NI/N is the per capita income, R is the interest paid on savings and time deposits (to capture the opportunity cost of holding cash), C/M_2 is the ratio of cash holdings (currency in circulation) to money in current and deposit accounts, and ε is an error term.

The factors on the right are all known to affect the C/M_2 ratio. For example, the sign of β_1 is expected to be positive because, as the tax rates increase, tax evaders shift to tax-evading activities that require currency (rather than traceable monetary instruments such as checks). The sign of β_4 is expected to be negative, because as the economic development increases (as proxied by an increase in per capita income), more activities would use checks over cash, leading to a fall in demand for cash. Tanzi used US economy data from 1929 to 1980 to estimate the regression coefficients and got $\beta_0 = -5.0262$, $\beta_1 = 0.2479$, $\beta_2 = 1.7303$, $\beta_3 = -0.1554$, $\beta_4 = -0.2026$.

These can now be used to estimate the predicted value of the ratio C/M_2, and since M_2 is already known, the predicted value C_1 for C is known. Then Tanzi re-estimated the regression coefficients assuming zero tax rates (i.e., assuming $TW = 0$), and used them to get another estimate, C_2, for C. The difference between C_1 and C_2 is an estimate of the "illegal money," IM. The difference between the money supply indicator M_1 (obtained by excluding savings deposits and time deposits from M_2) and IM gives an estimate of the "legal money," L. Dividing the GNP by L gives an estimate of the income velocity V of the legal money. Assuming that the velocity of the illegal money is the same as V, an estimate of the size of the underground economy is obtained as $IM \cdot V$. Tanzi got the value of \$21.75 billion (in terms of 1972 dollars) as the estimate for the size of the underground economy for the United States in 1980. See [17] for more modern versions of this approach; see [22] for more modern estimates of the shadow economy for various countries.

The electricity consumption approach

Several approaches have been devised to use resource consumption patterns to estimate the extent of the shadow economy. We review here the approach used by Lacko [20]. Lacko assumes that a part of the shadow economy is associated with the non-industrial consumption of electricity and that a part of the household electricity consumption is actually used by the shadow economy. In her model, the electricity consumption is affected by factors such as the GDP, the share of the industrial sector in GDP, the unemployment rate, and the fraction of electricity consumed by the industry. In fact, Lacko uses the year 1989 as the base year and the value of an independent variable (as on 1994) is really the difference between its values in 1994 and 1989. Lacko's equation is

$$\Delta E = d_1 \Delta G + d_2 \Delta GI + d_3 \Delta EI + d_4 \Delta U + d_5$$

where ΔE is the change in electricity consumption between 1989 and 1994, ΔG is the change of the official GDP between 1989 and 1994, ΔGI is the change of the share of industry in the GDP between 1989 and 1994, ΔEI is the difference between the change of electricity consumption by the industry and the change in total electricity consumption between 1989 and 1994, and ΔU is the maximal rate of unemployment between 1989 and 1994. The regression coefficients are estimated using the data for various post-socialist countries. Once an estimate of the electricity used by the shadow economy was obtained for a particular country, it was mapped to the fraction of that country's GDP using a simple baseline method. While this and similar approaches do have merit, they may not be reliable for power-deficient economies of developing countries. It is not clear if the equation is economically justified when using the data of the variables for a particular country over a number of years (rather than over multiple countries in the same year).

Modeling approach

A particular indirect method uses a specific indicator for the shadow economy and defines a model (usually, a regression model) that defines its dependence on various causes. Confirmatory factor analysis (CFA) techniques [27] offer a more general statistical framework, where one can define a model that explicitly identifies the dependencies among multiple indicator and cause variables (which are observed) and multiple factor variables (which are hidden). Structural equation modeling (SEM) is commonly used as the modeling formalism, which allows the modeler to define dependencies among multiple observed indicators, multiple observed causes, and multiple hidden factors (the MIMIC model). Dell'Anno [26] defines shadow economy as the single hidden factor η; six causes, namely, government employment in the labor force (X_1), tax burden (X_2), subsidies (X_3), social benefits paid by government (X_4), self-employment (X_5), and unemployment rate (X_6); and two indicators, namely, real Gross Domestic Product index (Y_1) and labor force participation rate (Y_2). The structural equations relating them are:

$$\eta = \alpha + \gamma_1 X_1 + \gamma_2 X_2 + \gamma_3 X_3 + \gamma_4 X_4 + \gamma_5 X_5 + \gamma_6 X_6 + \zeta$$
$$Y1 = \delta_1 + \lambda_1 \eta + \varepsilon_1$$
$$Y2 = \delta_2 + \lambda_2 \eta + \varepsilon_2$$

The last two equations relate the factors to the observed indicators and hence are called the measurement model. The model identification algorithm (usually based on maximum likelihood) estimates the coefficients and the variances and covariances of the independent variables using the sample data, and using them, estimates the population covariance matrix (which should be reasonably close to the observed sample covariance matrix, if the model is a good fit). Several test statistics, such as the χ^2-test, the comparative fit index (CFI), and the root mean square error of approximation (RMSEA) are used to estimate the goodness of fit of the model to the given data. Once the values of η are estimated, Dell'Anno then computes the extent of the shadow economy as a percentage of GDP by converting the index of the shadow economy estimated by the first structural equation (17.6 percent of the GDP in 1994 for Portugal).

Data mining techniques for ML detection

A number of data mining and statistical techniques have been used for detection of ML instances. The input data is usually either the various suspicious reports (CTR, SAR, etc.) or the dataset of all transactions within a financial institution. The output is the set of highly suspicious transactions or highly suspicious entities (e.g., persons, organizations, or accounts). Supervised classification techniques (such as support vector machines) are not that suitable because of general unavailability of reliably proven ML instances as labeled training data, as well as severe class imbalance, since the number of known ML instances are likely to be far fewer than normal transactions. Unsupervised techniques such as profiling, clustering, anomaly detection, link analysis, and data visualization have been used for ML detection. Knowledge representation techniques such as expert systems or Bayesian networks can be used to capture and use the domain knowledge of experts; for example, see [28], which uses agent-oriented ontology to capture anti-ML knowledge. Many good surveys are available that review the use of data mining techniques for general fraud detection (not necessarily ML) [29–32]. The authors of [33,34] survey AI/data-mining techniques that can be applied to ML detection.

A common approach for ML detection as used within a financial institute (e.g., a bank) is to first segment the entities (e.g., accounts) into clusters, using a suitable similarity measure and business knowledge. Then a suitable set of summary features (profile) is computed for each entity (based on domain knowledge) using their transaction histories. These profile features are usually nonlinear functions of the transaction data and are designed to be highly representative of the suspiciousness for entities (e.g., based on withdraw/deposit frequencies, transaction amount deviations, transaction volumes and velocities, etc.). Finally, the entities are prioritized on the basis of their profile features and top-k (few) are selected for in-depth investigations.

Senator et al. [35] from FINCEN have created the FINCEN AI system (FAIS) that links and evaluates reports of large cash transactions to identify potential ML and has been in operation at FINCEN since 1993. The objective is to detect previously unknown, potentially high-value entities (transactions, subjects, accounts) for possible investigation. The model supports three belief levels: Reported, Accepted, and Hypothesized. The reported transactions are at the belief level of Reported. These transactions are consolidated in clusters. Summary data like Subject and Account clusters, computed from the sets of reported transactions, represent the next belief level (Accepted). At these levels, certain derived attributes are computed that are necessary for evaluating the data-driven suspiciousness based on information discovered by analysts, including the linkages among the clusters. The highest level of belief (Hypothesized) is used for higher level abstractions like cases and patterns. FAIS has integrated the Alta Analytics NETMAP link-analysis package, which uses the "wagon-wheel" displays. FINCEN uses both wagon-wheel displays and traditional "link-and-edge" charts for analysis. FAIS has attempted use of techniques like Case-based Reasoning (CBR) and data mining (nearest neighbor, decision trees), which were not very successful due to the lack of many labeled examples. Even unsupervised learning algorithms were found to be not so reliable because of difficulties in deriving appropriate features due to poor data quality and the need for background knowledge. These techniques were found to be useful as knowledge engineering aids. Analysts have used FAIS to generate the suspiciousness score and evaluated the subjects through research and analysis of the data available from all the sources for development of valid leads. These leads are then fully researched and analyzed by the law enforcement agencies. FINCEN uses the feedback from these agencies to make improvements in the system.

Given the fact that only a few entities will be known as having participated in ML, active learning can be used to reduce the need for labeled data. At each step, an active learning method selects one data point for manual labeling by the user and uses it to refine its classification model. Deng et al. [36] use active learning via sequential design for detecting money laundering. For simplicity, we assume that each account in the same cluster has two features, denoted $(x_1, x_2)^T$. Define a convex combination $z = wx_1 + (1 - w)x_2$ to convert the data to the univariate form, where $w \in [0, 1]$ is the unknown weight. The suspiciousness of an account is defined by the Logit function $F(z \mid \theta) = \mathbf{P}(Y = 1 \mid z, \theta) = \frac{e^{(z-\mu)/\sigma}}{1 + e^{(z-\mu)/\sigma}}$ which has three unknown parameters, $\theta = (\mu, \sigma, w)^T$, and Y denotes the class label. At the end, given a threshold α (e.g., $\alpha = 0.8$), we identify all accounts z for which $F(z) \geq \alpha$, that is, the threshold hyperplane is $L_\alpha = \{x = (x_1, x_2)^T : \frac{z-\mu}{\sigma} = \log(\frac{\alpha}{1-\alpha}), where z = wx_1 + (1 - w)x_2\}$. Given the current pool of labeled data used so far (starting with one labeled data point), the new value for θ is estimated using a maximum-likelihood technique. Then, since $F(z)$ is known only through a few noisy labeled data points, a stochastic approximation algorithm for finding roots of $F(z)$ [37] is used to find k_0 points closest to the current hyperplane. Among these candidates, the point with the maximum value for the Fisher information matrix is selected and presented to the user for manual labeling.

Observed financial transactions can be summarized as a graph with entities (e.g., accounts) as nodes. Graph mining techniques can be used to identify suspicious money flows across the edges of such a graph. Zhang et al. [38] propose a new Link Discovery based on Correlation Analysis (LDCA) on timeline data to identify communities in the absence of explicit link information. The correlation between two persons is defined through a correlation function between their financial transaction history vectors. If both are part of the same ML episode, they should exhibit similar financial transaction patterns, and thus, one expects a higher correlation value for them. Michalak and Korczak [39] propose a graph mining method for the detection of subgraphs corresponding to suspicious transaction patterns (e.g., a lattice-like sender-intermediaries-receiver pattern). Their method takes into consideration dependencies between individual transfers that may be indicative of illegal activities; see also [40].

Chang et al. [41] have presented a set of coordinated visualization metaphors including heatmap, search by example, keyword graphs, and strings and beads, which are based on identifying specific keywords within the wire transactions. This set of visualizations helps analysts to detect accounts and transactions that exhibit suspicious behaviors. Huang et al. [42] propose a two-step visualization-based solution for fraud detection in stock markets, where first they use 3D treemaps to monitor the real-time stock market performance and to identify a particular stock that produced an unusual trading pattern. Then they perform social network visualization to conduct behavior-driven visual analysis of the suspected pattern, identify the entities involved in the fraud, and further attack plans.

Zdanowicz [43] applies statistical outlier detection techniques to detect ML episodes in import and export trades data, since overvaluing imports or undervaluing exports is a common ML method. Kingdon [44] has developed a set of active agents ("Sentinels"), along with probabilistic methods, to detect unusual events and entities indicative of ML. Wand et al. [45] present two interesting unsupervised techniques to identify suspicious entities. In peer group analysis, an entity (e.g., account) is selected as a target and is compared with all other entities in the database, and a peer group of entities most similar to the target object is identified. The behavior of the peer group is then summarized at each subsequent time point, and the behavior of the target entity is compared with the summary of its peer group. Those target entities exhibiting behavior most different from their peer group summary behavior are flagged. Break point analysis (BPA) slides a window over the sequence of transactions of an account and uses statistical tests to compare a window with earlier ones to detect any sharp changes in the transaction patterns (e.g., frequency, amounts). Zengan [46] developed a cluster-based outlier detection algorithm to identify suspicious ML transaction patterns.

Ju and Zheng [47] have proposed a supervised decision tree algorithm for ML detection, combined with a privacy preserving strategy (Inner Product Protocol) to protect the identity of the account owners, in case they are not identified as part of suspicious ML. Gao and Ye [48] discuss a methodology for AML, in which many steps make use of various data-mining techniques such as outlier detection, link analysis, and community detection. Considering the huge transaction volumes, [49] discusses the use of data-warehousing and OLAP cube technology in AML applications. Phua et al. [50] developed a fraud detection method to predict criminal patterns from skewed data, which uses a single meta-classifier (stacking) to choose the best base classifiers (naïve Bayes, C4.5, and back-propagation), and combines their predictions (bagging) to improve cost savings (stacking-bagging). Given the scarcity of labeled data, generating and using synthetic transactions data that can contain known suspicious patterns is important for validating the ML detection algorithms; see [51].

CONCLUSION

Financial institutions get used by organized criminals and terrorists as vehicles of large-scale money laundering, which presents these institutions with challenges of regulatory compliance, maintaining financial security, preserving goodwill and reputation, and avoiding operational risks like liquidity crunch and lawsuits. Hence prevention, detection, and control of ML is crucial for the financial security and risk management of financial institutions. In this chapter, we began with an overview of the problem of ML and discussed some commonly used methods of ML and the anti-ML efforts worldwide. After surveying some analytics techniques used to estimate the extent of ML, we surveyed some data-mining techniques that have been reported in the literature for detection of ML episodes (instances). Data-mining and statistical techniques play a crucial role in sifting through enormous volumes of financial transactions data to identify potentially suspect entities. While much has been done, there is a need to continue to develop more effective ML detection techniques, particularly in the face of class imbalance, lack of many labeled examples, evolution of newer ML methods (e.g., those involving identity theft or online games), availability of faster, newer, and more anonymous financial services over the Internet, and the need to capture and use domain and investigative knowledge. Unlike most other applications, the evaluation of ML detection techniques is hampered by publicly available labeled data about known ML episodes. Nevertheless, a recent spate of high-profile ML detection cases, in the United States and in other countries such as India, is a clear pointer toward the effectiveness of AML regimes. Newer technologies such as big data analytics, text mining, social networks analysis, and anomaly detection should be explored for more effective ML detection.

References

[1] Madinger J. Money Laundering: A guide for criminal investigators. 3rd ed. CRC Press; 2012.
[2] Truman EM, Reuter P. Chasing dirty money: Progress on anti-money laundering. Peterson Institute; 2004.
[3] Turner JE. Money laundering prevention: Deterring, detecting, and resolving financial fraud. Wiley; 2011.
[4] Woods BF. Art and science of money laundering: Inside the commerce of international narcotics trafficking. Colorado: Paladin Press; 1998.
[5] Irwin ASM, Slay J. Detecting money laundering and terrorism financing activity in Second Life and World of Warcraft. Proceedings of the 1st International Cyber Resilience Conference. Edith Cowan University; Perth Western Australia; 2010.
[6] Hinterseer K. The Wolfsberg anti-money laundering principles. Journal of Money Laundering Control 2001;5(1):25−41.
[7] Financial Action Task Force (FATF) on money laundering, the forty recommendations; 2003.
[8] Financial Action Task Force (FATF) on money laundering, report on money laundering typologies 2002−2003; 2003.
[9] Financial Action Task Force (FATF) on money laundering, money laundering using new payment methods; 2010.
[10] Financial Action Task Force (FATF) on money laundering, special recommendations on terrorist financing; 2003.
[11] Geiger H, Wuensch O. The fight against money laundering. Journal of Money Laundering Control 2007;10:1.
[12] Deloitte Financial Advisory Services LLP. Anti-money laundering services: Helping clients implement anti-money laundering detection and compliance programs around the globe; 2008. www.deloitte.com.
[13] Menon R, Kumar S. Understanding the role of technology in anti money laundering-compliance: A strategic model for financial institutions; 2005. www.infosys.com.
[14] Prasanna G. Enterprise-wide anti-money laundering and KYC initiatives. Tata Consultancy Services; 2012. www.tcs.com.
[15] SAS Institute. Reducing the cost of AML compliance; 2011. www.sas.com.
[16] Ray A, Katkov N. Evaluating the enterprise-wide compliance vendors: Solutions for anti-money laundering and anti-fraud; 2012. www.celent.com.
[17] Bhattacharyya DK. On the economic rationale of estimating the hidden economy. Econ J. 1999; 109(456):348−59.
[18] Feige EL. The underground economies: Tax evasion and information distortion. Cambridge: Cambridge University Press; 1989.
[19] Frey BS, Schneider F. Bd 12 Economics Informal and Underground economy. International Encyclopedia of Social and Behavioral Science. Elsevier Science; 2000.

[20] Lacko M. Do power consumption data tell the story? Electricity Intensity and Hidden Economy in Post-Socialist Countries. Budapest Working Papers on the Labour Market 9902. Institute of Economics; Hungarian Academy of Sciences; 1999.

[21] Schneider F, Enste DH. Shadow economies: Size, causes and consequences. J Econ Lit 2000; XXXVIII:77−114.

[22] Schneider F, Buehn A, Montenegro C. New estimates for the shadow economies all over the world. International Economic Journal. Korean International Economic Association 2010;24(4):443−61.

[23] Smith P. Assessing the size of the underground economy: The statistics Canada perspectives. Canadian Economic Observer 1994;7:316−33.

[24] Tanzi V. The underground economy in the United States: Annual estimates, 1930−1980. IMF Staff Papers 1983;30(2):283−305.

[25] Tanzi V. Uses and abuses of estimates of the underground economy. The Economic Journal 1999;109: F338−47.

[26] Dell'Anno R. The shadow economy in Portugal: An analysis with the MIMIC approach. Journal of Applied Economics 2007;X(2):253−77.

[27] Thompson B. Exploratory and confirmatory factor analysis: Understanding concepts and applications. American Psychological Association; 2004.

[28] Wang Y, Wang H, Gao S, Xu D, Ye K. Agent-oriented ontology for monitoring and detecting money laundering process. In InfoScale '07: Proceedings of the 2nd International Conference on Scalable Information Systems, Article 81. Institute for Computer Sciences. Social-Informatics and Telecommunications Engineering (ICST). Brussels, Belgium; 2007.

[29] Bolton R, Hand D. Statistical Fraud detection: A review. Statistical Science. 2002;17(3):235−55.

[30] Fawcett T, Foster T, Provost F. Adaptive fraud detection. Data Mining and Knowledge Discovery 1997;1:291−316.

[31] Phua C, Lee V, Smith K, Gayler R. A comprehensive survey of data mining-based fraud detection research. Artificial Intelligence Review; 2005.

[32] Yue D, Wu X, Wang Y, Li Y, Chu C-H. A review of data mining-based financial fraud detection research. Int Conference on Wireless Communications. Networking and Mobile Computing; 2007. p. 5519−22.

[33] US Congress Office of Technology. Information technologies for the control of money laundering. OTA-ITC-630; 1995.

[34] Watkins RC, Reynolds KM, Demara R, Georgiopoulos M, Gonzalez A, Eaglin R. Tracking dirty proceeds: Exploring data mining technologies as tools to investigate money laundering. Police Practice and Research 2003;4(2):163−78.

[35] Senator TE, Goldberg HG, Wooton J, Cottini MA, Umar Khan AF, Klinger CD, et al. The financial crimes enforcement network AI system (FAIS): Identifying potential money laundering from reports of large cash transactions. AI Magazine. 1995 Winter;16(4):21−39.

[36] Deng X, Joseph VR, Sudjianto A, Jeff Wu CF. Active learning via sequential design with applications to detection of money laundering. J Am Stat Assoc 2009;104(487):969−81.

[37] Kushner HJ, Yin GG. Stochastic approximation and recursive algorithms and applications. Springer-Verlag; 2003.

[38] Zhang Z, Salerno JJ, Yu PS. Applying data mining in investigating money laundering crimes. SIGKDD'03 2003;747−72.

[39] Michalak K, Korczak J. Graph mining approach to suspicious transaction detection. Federated Conference on Computer Science and Information Systems 2011;69−75.

[40] Moll L. Anti money laundering under real world conditions-Finding relevant patterns [MS thesis]. Department of Informatics: University of Zurich; 2009.

[41] Chang R, Lee A, Ghoniem M, Kosara R, Ribarsky W, Yang J, et al. Scalable and interactive visual analysis of financial wire transactions for fraud detection. Information Visualization 2008;7(1):63−76.

[42] Huang ML, Liang J, Nguyen QV. A visualization approach for frauds detection in financial market. In: Proc 13th Int Conference on Information Visualisation; 2009. p. 197−202.

[43] Zdanowicz JS. Detecting money laundering and terrorist financing via data mining. Communications of the ACM 2004;47(5):53−5.

[44] Kingdon J. AI fights money laundering. IEEE Intell. Syst 2004;19(3):87−9.

[45] Bolton RJ, Hand DJ. Unsupervised profiling methods for fraud detection. Proc Credit Scoring and Credit Control VII 2007;5−7.

[46] Zengan G. Application of cluster based local outlier factor algorithm in anti money laundering. In MASS '09: Proc Int Conference on Management and Service Science; 2009. p. 1−4.

[47] Ju C, Zheng L. Research on suspicious financial transactions recognition based on privacy preserving of classification algorithm. In ETCS '09: 1st Int Workshop on Education Technology and Computer Science 2009;2:525−8.

[48] Gao Z, Ye M. A framework for data mining-based anti-money laundering research. Journal of Money Laundering Control 2007;10(2):170−9.

[49] Korczak J, Marchelski W, Oleszkiewicz B. A new technological approach to money laundering discovery using analytical SQL server. In AITM 2008: Advanced Information Technologies for Management. In: Korczak J, Dudycz H, Dyczkowski M, editors. Research Papers, 35. Wroclaw University of Economics; 2008. p. 80−104.

[50] Phua C, Alahakoon D, Lee V. Minority report in fraud detection classification of skewed data. SIGKDD Explorations 2004;6(1):50−9.

[51] Barse E, Kvarnström H, Jonsson E. Synthesizing, test data for fraud detection systems. In: Proceedings of the 19th Annual Computer Security Applications Conference; 2003. p. 384−95.

Intelligent Banking XML Encryption Using Effective Fuzzy Logic

37

Faisal T. Ammari[1], J. Lu[1], and Maher Aburrous[2]
[1]*University of Huddersfield, Huddersfield, UK*
[2]*Al Hoson University, Abu Dhabi, UAE*

INFORMATION IN THIS CHAPTER

- Introduction
- Literature review
- System model and design
- Experiments and results
- Summary

INTRODUCTION

The eXtensible Markup Language (XML) [1] has been widely adopted in many financial institutions in their daily transactions; this adoption was due to the flexible nature of XML providing a common syntax for systems messaging in general and in financial messaging in particular [2]. Excessive use of XML in financial transactions messaging created an aligned interest in security protocols integrated into XML solutions in order to protect exchanged XML messages in an efficient yet powerful mechanism. There are several approaches proposed by researchers to secure XML messages.

Many models have been proposed to protect exchanged messages both on the network level [3,4] and on the XML level. Among the proposed models, W3C played a major role, providing standardized forms to represent XML data in a secure and trusted method. W3C introduced XML Encryption [5], XML Signature [6], and XML Key Management [7].

The XML Encryption standard defines how to encrypt the XML message. This can involve fully encrypting the entire message, partially encrypting it by selecting parts of each message, or even encrypting external elements attached to the message itself. Although this model is able to secure

XML messages, some issues arose concerning performance and inefficient memory usage [8,9], leaving room for more improvements and enhancements.

However, financial institutions (i.e., banks) perform large volume of transactions on a daily basis that require XML encryption on a large scale. Encrypting a large volume of messages in full will result in performance and resource issues. Therefore, an approach is needed to encrypt specified portions of an XML document, syntax for representing encrypted parts, and processing rules for decrypting them. W3C XML encryption has a feature to encrypt parts of an XML document called element-wise encryption, which is the process of encrypting parts of the XML document. To avoid any performance or resources issues, a mechanism should be considered to choose which parts of the XML document are to be encrypted on the fly, whereby those parts are selected upon intelligent criteria detecting sensitive information within the XML document.

The Fuzzy Logic (FL) [10] approach can be used here to distinguish sensitive parts within each XML document. FL provides a simple way to arrive at a definite conclusion based upon vague, ambiguous, imprecise, noisy, or missing input information. FL's approach to control problems mimics how a person would make a faster decision. FL incorporates a simple, rule-based "If X and Y then Z" approach to solving a control problem, rather than attempting to model a system mathematically. The FL model is empirically-based, relying on an operator's experience rather than on technical understanding of the system.

The fuzzy logic approach is quantified based on a combination of historical data and expert input. Fuzzy logic has been used for decades in the computer sciences to embed expert input into computer models for a broad range of applications. The advantage of the fuzzy approach is that it enables processing of vaguely defined variables and variables whose relationships cannot be defined by mathematical relationships. Fuzzy logic can incorporate expert human judgment to define those variables and their relationships. The model can be closer to reality and be more site specific than some of the other methods [11].

Literature review

Flexibility, expressiveness, and usability of XML have formed a motive for researchers to shed more light on XML security. Researchers have focused their interests on securing XML data due to the increased usage of XML in many business and educational cases. Efficient models have been proposed [3–7,12] to add a secure layer over exchanged XML data. The models' main purpose is to ensure data confidentiality and authenticity. Many XML threats [8] have been considered, such as Oversized Payload, Schema Change, XML Routing, and Recursive Payload. Such threats have forced researchers to pay more attention to securing exchanged XML messages.

W3C XML Encryption Working Group [5] is developing a method for XML encryption and decryption. The group used XML syntax to represent the secured elements in XML. Their approach is able to encrypt the whole message, full nodes, and sub-trees; however, it is not able to encrypt an element while keeping the descendants of the same node unchanged, and also it cannot handle attribute encryption. Therefore, a solution has been proposed [9] to handle this limitation. Ed Simon proposed changing the attribute so that it is encrypted with the *EncryptedDataManifest* attribute and includes any other details inside the element. Another solution proposed was to use XSLT for attribute transformation into elements to perform the encryption process. However, this suggested solution was not successful, as the decrypted parts need to be transformed back to the original attributes for message validation against the corresponding XML schema.

A system has been proposed by [13] for pool encryption, which has the capability of removing sensitive information from the output file. Their basic idea is to parse the XML message that needs encryption into a DOM tree, where each node in the tree is labeled and all information related to its position is attached to the corresponding node. Then each node is encrypted individually with a node-specific encryption key. These nodes are removed from their original position in the XML message into a pool that contains all other encrypted nodes. The pool can be saved into the original message or in a different message. The sender determines the decryption capabilities of different users by distributing the collection of node keys to the receiver. This collection of node keys is encrypted with the recipients' key before final submission. Although this model solves the issue of removing confidential material from the main message and hides the size of the encrypted content, it has the following disadvantages: (1) The original position for each individual node needs to be attached, due to the addition of "the position information," (2) a decent increase in message size is noticed, due to the pool of node keys, (3) a decent increase in message size is noticed, (4) there is high resource usage and bandwidth allocation, (5) more storage and more processing power is needed, and (6) a unique node key has to be generated for each node.

The authors of [14] introduced an XML access control (XAC) that is a server-side access control, and a trusted access control processor, allowing security policies and procedures to be established. Based on the policies, XAC presents a way to control access of users to specific portions of the full XML document that is stored on a server. XAC encrypts an XML element with the ability to exclude its descendants. This specific feature gives the advantage of XAC over XEnc because XEnc requires the encryption of a full sub-tree.

The authors of [15] presented an approach to incorporate fuzziness in XML. Their approach tried to identify the potential entities in XML that can have fuzzy values. They analyze the structure of an XML document to identify the portions that can be handled using fuzziness; then they specify the appropriate mechanism to incorporate fuzziness. Their approach focused on XML being structured (logical and physical) and well-formed language.

The authors of [16] introduced a fuzzy XML data model to manage fuzzy data in XML, based on possibility distribution theory, by first identifying multiple granularity of data fuzziness in UML and XML. The fuzzy UML data model and fuzzy XML data model that address all types of fuzziness are developed. Further, they developed the formal conversions from the fuzzy UML model to the fuzzy XML model, and the formal mapping from the fuzzy XML model to the fuzzy relational databases.

The authors of [17] presented an XML methodology to represent fuzzy systems for facilitating collaborations in fuzzy applications and design. DTD and XML Schema are proposed to define fuzzy systems in general. One fuzzy system can be represented in different formats understood by different applications using the concept of XSLT stylesheets. With an example, they represent that given fuzzy system in XML and transform it to comprehensible formats for Matlab and FuzzyJess applications.

The authors of [18] proposed an approach along with an automated tool called FXML2FOnto for constructing fuzzy ontologies from fuzzy XML models. They also investigated how the constructive fuzzy ontologies may be useful for improving some of the fuzzy XML applications (i.e., reasoning on fuzzy XML models).

System model and design

Our model consists of two major parts. Each part has a discrete scope that acts as an independent unit and forms an essential part of the whole system. Content is classified using a set of fuzzy classification techniques [19] and encrypted using an element-wise encryption on selected parts within each XML message. The fuzzification phase is performed before the XML messages are submitted to the next phase, which is responsible for securing message content. The process of fuzzy classification is mainly responsible for defining an attribute value and assigning it to an existing XML tag named "ImportanceLevel." The assigned value is used to define the security level needed in the next phase. The next phase involves applying element-wise encryption to different parts within each XML message. Encryption could be for the whole message or elements of an XML message. The "Importance Level" value assigned in the fuzzification phase is also used to decide which type of encryption and key size is to be deployed. Element-wise encryption is based on W3C's recommendation [5]. Figure 37.1 illustrates the system model and basic components used to form our model.

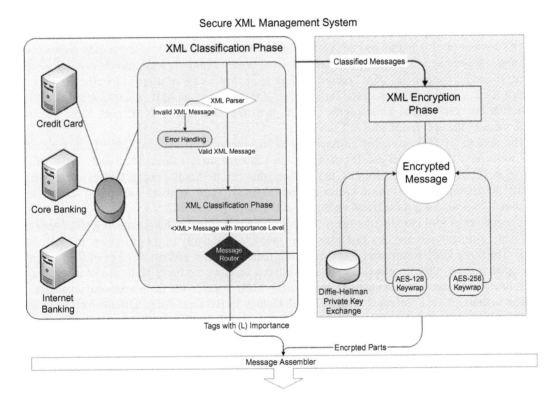

FIGURE 37.1

System design and components.

As seen in the figure, the main two components are displayed as two separate units; each act as an independent unit performing a set of operations that is used as input to the other phase.

The system core has been built based on two major phases. Phase one involves performing a set of fuzzy classification techniques on XML messages. The fuzzy classification process is designed mainly for determining the similarity of different standards within the same message. Basically, the main target is to describe how semantic concepts are evaluated and explained by the provided XML content. Upon fuzzy classification, a new value is generated and assigned to an existing XML tag.

We assigned the name "ImportanceLevel" to the mentioned tag so we can use it as an identifier for the next phase. Phase two involves applying element-wise encryption to different parts within each XML message. Encryption could be for the whole message, some elements, or some attributes of an element of an XML message. The ImportanceLevel value assigned in phase one is used to decide which type of encryption is performed; it also decides which parts of the XML message are to be encrypted. We base our encryption on W3C's recommendation [5]. The following stages form the system life cycle in detail.

Fuzzy classification phase

In our fuzzy classification phase, we categorized 10 transaction characteristics into three different layers according to their type. The characteristics were chosen after exploring different experts' opinions and backgrounds, reviewing financial analysis tools, reviewing technical reports, researching different online and offline financial systems conducted within the financial institution, and performing a set of internal surveys among banking group heads. We categorized these 10 transaction characteristics extracted from the XML message into three layers (Account Segment, Details Segment, and Environment Segment). Grouping will facilitate and simplify the process of fuzzy classification.

This phase is responsible for assigning a new value, which is the importance level for each XML tag. The main idea is to distinguish which parts of the message are to be encrypted using an AES-128-bit key encryption, and which are to be encrypted using an AES-256-bit key. Usage of the key depends on the importance level value (high, medium or low), whereby we deploy the 128-bit key on tags with "Medium" importance level and the 256-bit key on tags with a "High" importance level value. Tags with a "Low" importance level value are forwarded directly to the message assembler, where no encryption is performed. The phase uses fuzzification techniques of a set of input variables based on 10 characteristics extracted from the XML message, all depending on the previous knowledge, experience, and expertise backgrounds. The 10 characteristics are defined in detail as follows:

1. Transaction amount: Financial institutions set pre-defined transaction limits. The limits allow users to perform transactions with specified limits on a daily basis. The range of transaction limits is defined based on the local policy within each institution. Banks normally treat the transaction amount as an alert to any critical transaction; the amount is used in most banks to measure the weight of total transaction performed. Source, destination, and amount all combine to act as an alert that is already pre-defined based on the bank's policy. Large

transaction amounts will affect the importance of the transaction itself, which can be used in our model as a measurement item in our importance level evaluation.

2. Transaction currency: We use a well-defined list of allowed currencies that can be used online or offline. Each currency has its own set of risk variables, depending on usage and importance. Foreign currency uses exchange rates, operational interference, and market value for the transaction the moment it occurred. Banks treat each FX transaction with high importance, because it involves buying and selling with the bank's rate. We have used this factor in our importance evaluation

3. Account type: Accounts are segmented within each institution. Segmentation is performed to enable the application of a set of internal rules on selected segments. Each segment has its own value and weight; for example, corporate account segments are listed with high importance and priority because most of the transactions are large volume, which can benefit the bank for each transaction. We used this factor due to its role in deciding the importance level for the whole transaction.

4. Transaction notes: Exceptions are placed on unusual activity on a specific account, and such exceptions will raise a flag in any transaction being processed to handle the exception before the process is completed. Having a flagged transaction will raise the importance level and trigger an alert to monitor that specific transaction due to its importance; we have used this factor to measure the importance level in term of transaction critical weight.

5. Profile ID: This is a unique identifier for the destination account owner; the value is set during the system integration and profile creation process. Companies or individuals with custom profile IDs have a high potential to be monitored for transactions. Monitoring is based on the transaction amount after classifying each profile ID, whereby a range of IDs are listed in the high importance zone, all after deploying a bank's methods and procedures.

6. Account tries: This refers to how many times the account is used in the system; more usage means more trust, whereby the history of the account is known and trusted. A historical log is kept and evaluated on a regular basis to confirm trusted accounts and suspicious ones. Evaluation will result in a set of important ranges of trusted accounts to be used in a transaction evaluation and setting an importance level.

7. Incorrect password tries: This is the number of times a user enters the password incorrectly to try to complete the financial transaction. This factor adds a slight importance level for each transaction; a high rate of incorrect tries gives an indication of high importance.

8. Time spent on the service: This refers to the time spent navigating the service before performing a transaction. The time range is set based on the bank's policy, taking into consideration peak hours. This factor is considered a technical factor to measure the importance level of the transaction based on non-financial elements.

9. Daily transactions: this refers to how many transactions are performed before the financial transaction is carried out. The number of daily transactions puts a weight on the overall importance level for the transaction itself, whereby the number of transactions to be performed is set based on the bank's policy within the allowed ranges.

10. Transaction time: The financial day is categorized into three periods: peak period, normal hours, and dead zone. Periods are defined by the financial institution based on local policy and historical transaction periods. Each period has its own value, which adds an importance level,

and how the occurrence of any transaction is affected by the time of occurrence. Ranges are set to weigh an importance level when the transaction is performed.

Fuzzy methodology

Our fuzzy classification phase is based on Mamdani [19] fuzzy inference and performs the four basic steps shown in Figure 37.2.

Step 1 (Fuzzification): Take the crisp input X and input Y and determine the degree to which these inputs belong to, and where they fit into, the fuzzy set. Figure 37.3 illustrates an example of a linguistic variable used to represent one factor, which is the transaction currency. The x-axis represents the range of the transaction amount. The y-axis represents the degree of each value in the linguistic descriptor.

Transaction Currency (Non-Sensitive, Normal, Sensitive)

Variable used: Transaction amount

Ranges:

- Non-Sensitive: [0, 0, 6, 8]
- Normal: [6,9,12]
- Sensitive: [10,12,18,18]

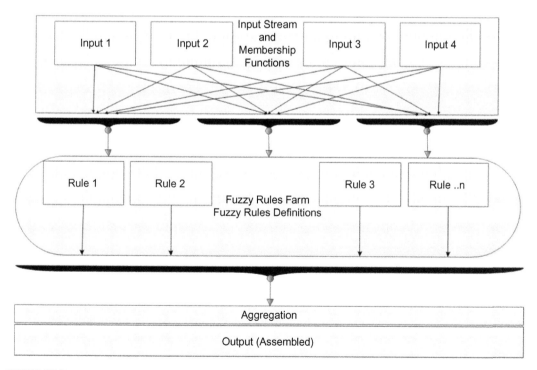

FIGURE 37.2

Mamdani fuzzy inference system.

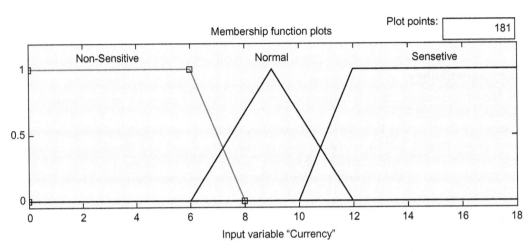

FIGURE 37.3

Input variables in the fuzzification step.

Step 2 (Rule evaluation): Take the fuzzy inputs and apply them to the qualified fuzzy rules. The fuzzy operators (AND/OR) are used in case of any uncertainty to get a single value. The outcome value is called the "Truth Value," which will be applied to the membership function for rule evaluation.

Step 3 (Aggregation of the rule outputs): Process of unification of the outputs of all the rules. Combining scaled rules into a single fuzzy set for each variable.

Step 4 (Transforming the fuzzy output into a crisp output): Figure 37.4 illustrates an example of an expected crisp output [Low, Medium, and High].

The output should have a clear, crisp value where it will be assigned to each tag classified.

Low: This tag means the importance level is low and less attention should be paid to the value. The root element and child tags should be forwarded directly to the message assembler, skipping the encryption phase.

Medium: This tag is important to some extent, and the tag attribute is assigned the value of medium, so an element-wise encryption will be applied using the AES algorithm with a 128-bit key on selected parts.

High: This tag is to be handled with high importance and encrypted in the next phase using the AES algorithm with a 256-bit key.

Detection module

To perform the fuzzy inference system, we have categorized the XML tags within each message into 10 characteristics distributed into three layers, each with its own weight and criteria. The layers are account layer, details layer, and environment layer. Figure 37.5 represents the layers distribution.

After giving a weight to each layer, the calculation of overall weight is based on the following criteria:

$$\text{Importance Level: Sum(Layer Weight} * \text{Layer Member)}$$

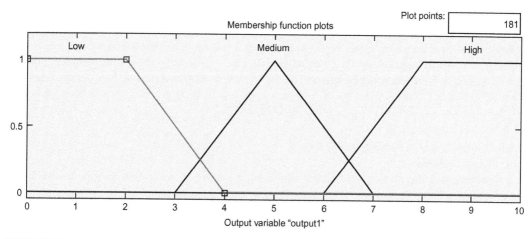

FIGURE 37.4

Sample output of classification rate importance level.

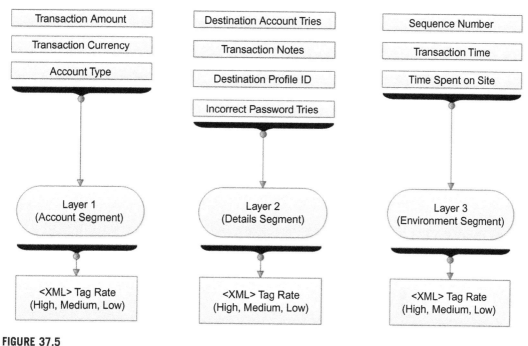

FIGURE 37.5

The 10 characters distribution over three layers.

Rule Base: Each layer has a set of rules defined, based on input variables within each layer. The rule is based on the "if-then" rule. The rule base should contain a number of entries depending on how many layer members exist. For example, layer 1 has three members and we have three outputs expected, so the entries should be calculated as $(3^3) = 27$ entries presenting the rules for that layer. The final evaluation is dependent on finding the center of gravity, as shown in Equation 1.

$$COG = \frac{\int \mu_i(x)xdx}{\int \mu_i(x)dx} \tag{1}$$

$\mu i(x)$: Aggregated membership function.

x: Output variable.

After deploying the fuzzy classification methodology on the three layers, we then have a list of classified tags with an importance level attribute defined and assigned.

Encryption module

The encryption phase has two possibilities: the first one is to perform an element-wise encryption using the AES algorithm with a 256-bit key size, while the second is to perform an element-wise encryption using the AES algorithm with a 128-bit key size. Key size is determined by the importance level value assigned in the fuzzy classification phase. Figure 37.6 illustrates the process of encryption. Tags with "Low" importance level will be forwarded directly to the message composition stage without any type of encryption being performed.

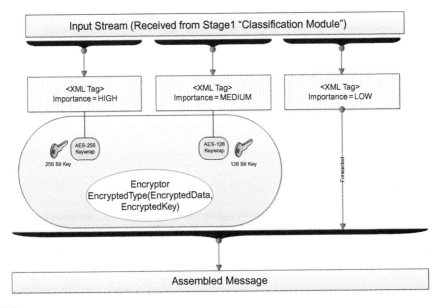

FIGURE 37.6

Encryption module layout.

```
<TransactionDetails src='/paymentsystem.xml'>
  <Account ImportanceLevel="High">
          <AccHolder>Faisal Ammari</AccHolder>
          <AccountNumber>120130101144343401</AccountNumber>
          <Amount>32200</Amount>
          <Currency>USD</Currency>
          <Type>Indivisual</Type>
  </Account>
  <AccountDetails ImportanceLevel="Low">
          <AccountUsage>3</AccountUsage>
          <PasswordTries>1</PasswordTries>
          <ProfileID>0028827</ProfileID>
  </AccountDetails>
</TransactionDetails>
```

FIGURE 37.7

Sample XML message after fuzzy classification.

Tags related to the parent tag are also encrypted using the same level of encryption. Child tags behavior is taken from the parent "ImportanceLevel" value. Figure 37.7 illustrates the XML message after the fuzzy classification phase, where the "ImportanceLevel" attribute is assigned a value.

Figure 37.8 illustrates the same XML message after encryption, depending on the fuzzy classification performed earlier.

Tags related to the parent tag are also encrypted using the same level of encryption. Child tags behavior is taken from the parent "ImportanceLevel" value. In Figure 37.7, Account Holder, Account Number, Amount, Currency, and Type tags are encrypted using AES encryption with a 256-bit key size, as per their parent "Account" layer. Basically, we inherit the encryption behavior from parent to child as per our categorization process, and the categorization process in our model is built based on relevance and parent tag evaluation.

Keys used during the encryption process should be transferred to the decryptor in the destination using a secure and private method. We use Diffie-Hellman [20] key exchange for the handover of keys between source and destination. Figure 37.9 illustrates how to exchange keys between source and destination.

Experiments and results

We have performed our evaluation using two sets of XML messages; each set represents a period in which the messages were extracted. Each set has a number of XML messages to test. Collected XML messages present online banking service transactions fetched from Jordan Ahli Bank, one of the leading banks in Jordan. We have selected to deploy full and partial encryption on selected sets

```
<TransactionDetails src='/paymentsystem.xml'>
    <Encrypted_Data src='xmlenc#'>
    <EncryptionMethod Algorithm='xml#AES'/>
    <Key_Info src='XML_Sig'>
      <Key_Name>AMD</Key_Name>
    </Key_Info>
    <Ci_Data>
      <Ci_Value>54544464fsdf?:#</Ci_Value>
    </Ci_Data>
    </Encrypted_Data>
  <AccountDetails ImportanceLevel="Low">
      <AccountUsage>3</AccountUsage>
      <PasswordTries>1</PasswordTries>
      <ProfileID>0028827</ProfileID>
  </AccountDetails>
  </TransactionDetails>
```

FIGURE 37.8

Sample XML message after fuzzy classification stage.

of XML messages, whereby we will deploy full encryption on the first set of XML messages and partial encryption on the second set of XML messages.

The two sets have been selected randomly, taken over a period of seven months (between January, 2012 and August, 2012), and specifically representing financial transactions. In the first set, we collected 1,000 random XML messages taken over a period of three months (between January, 2012 and March, 2012). In the second set we used 1,500 XML messages taken over a period of four months (between April, 2012 and August, 2012). Sample sets were collected after receiving the necessary approvals and authorizations from the bank's concerned departments. Table 37.1 illustrates the two sets of XML messages in detail.

Figure 37.10 illustrates an actual XML message fetched from one of the XML messages in set 1.

Table 37.2, Table 37.3, and Table 37.4 illustrate a sample of the data provided in set 1, segregated into three layers.

To ensure that we are evaluating our model in a fair and comprehensive manner, we divided our evaluation into two stages. Evaluation stages are compared against W3C XML encryption recommendations. In each stage, there are two experiments performed; each experiment presents an encryption using different key sizes. In the first stage, we have deployed full message encryption

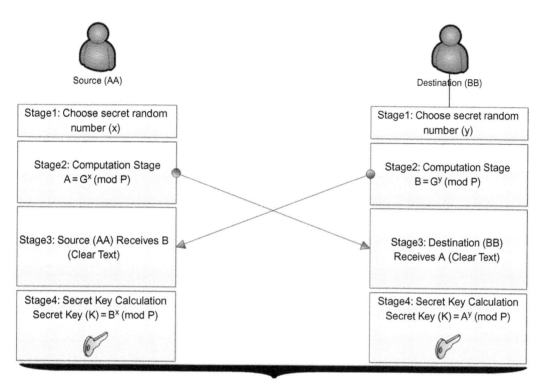

FIGURE 37.9

Key exchange using D-H method.

Set	Messages	Nodes	Size	Period	Encryption
Table 37.1 Experiment Set Details					
1	1,000	4,000	947 KB	3 Months Jan 12–Mar 12	Full
2	1,500	6,000	1380 KB	4 Months Apr12–Aug 12	Partial

using W3C encryption standard with different key sizes. In the second stage, we have deployed partial encryption using W3C encryption standard with different key sizes.

Results from both stages are compared against our model, which uses element-wise encryption and a mixture of key sizes. Table 37.5 illustrates the evaluation details for Stage 1.

Stage 1: The evaluation for this stage has been conducted by performing two experiments; the first experiment was deployed by performing full encryption using the W3C XML encryption standard with a 128-bit key size deployed on the first set of 1,000 XML messages. SXMS uses the same sample of XML messages to deploy element-wise encryption. The SXMS model uses

```
<?xml version="1.0"?>
<Transfers>
  - <Transaction ImportanceLevel="High" xmlns="http://example.org/paymentv2" Segment="Account">
      <TransactionAmount>2500</TransactionAmount>
      <Transaction_Currency Code="USD">001</Transaction_Currency>
      <Account_Type Code="001">Corporate</Account_Type>
    </Transaction>
  - <Transaction ImportanceLevel="Medium" xmlns="http://example.org/paymentv2" Segment="Details">
      <Transaction_Notes>154</Transaction_Notes>
      <Profile_ID>44</Profile_ID>
      <AccountTries>01</AccountTries>
      <PasswordTries>02</PasswordTries>
    </Transaction>
  - <Transaction ImportanceLevel="Medium" xmlns="http://example.org/paymentv2" Segment="Environment">
      <Posting_Date>2011/01/08</Posting_Date>
      <Transaction_Time>14:22:12</Transaction_Time>
      <Time_On_Service>00:25:13</Time_On_Service>
      <Daily_Transactions>2</Daily_Transactions>
      <Customer_Language>A</Customer_Language>
    </Transaction>
  - <Transaction xmlns="http://example.org/paymentv2" Segment="Additional">
      <IPAddress>128.2000.3.10</IPAddress>
      <From_Account>321456987456321457</From_Account>
      <To_Account>96325874193214587</To_Account>
    </Transaction>
</Transfers>
```

FIGURE 37.10

Actual XML message from set 1.

Table 37.2 Experiment Set Details

Transaction Amount	Transaction Currency	Account Type	Account Segment
Non-Sensitive	Non-Sensitive	Non-Sensitive	Low
Normal	Normal	Sensitive	Medium
Sensitive	Non-Sensitive	Sensitive	High
Normal	Non-Sensitive	Sensitive	Medium
Sensitive	Non-Sensitive	Non-Sensitive	Low

Table 37.3 Experiment Set Details

Transaction Notes CODE	Destination ProfileID	Destination Account Tries	Incorrect Password Tries	Details Segment
Normal	Sensitive	Non-Sensitive	Non-Sensitive	Medium
Sensitive	Non-Sensitive	Non-Sensitive	Non-Sensitive	Medium
Non-Sensitive	Normal	Non-Sensitive	Normal	Low
Non-Sensitive	Sensitive	Sensitive	Sensitive	High
Normal	Sensitive	Non-Sensitive	Non-Sensitive	Medium

Table 37.4 Experiment Set Details

Time On Site	Daily Transactions	Transaction Time	Transaction Level
Sensitive	Normal	Sensitive	**High**
Non-Sensitive	Sensitive	Sensitive	**High**
Normal	Non-Sensitive	Normal	**Medium**
Sensitive	Non-Sensitive	Sensitive	**High**
Non-Sensitive	Normal	Sensitive	**High**

Table 37.5 Stage 1 Set Details

Stage	XML Messages	Model	Experiment 1 Key Used	Experiment 2 Key Used
1	**1,000 Messages** 4,000 Nodes	W3C **Full Encryption**	**128 bit**	**256 bit**
		SXMS **Element-Wise**	**128** bit or **256** bit or NO Encryption	**128** bit or **256** bit or NO Encryption

Table 37.6 Appearances for Each Classification Layer

Classification Layer	"High" Appearances	"Medium" Appearances	Percentage (High + Medium)
Layer 1 (Account)	267	62	32.9%
Layer 2 (Details)	401	410	81.1%
Layer 3 (Environment)	250	421	67.1%

symmetric AES encryption with mixed key values (128-bit, 256-bit). Key size used in the encryption process depends on the importance level attribute value assigned by the fuzzification stage for a selected set of tags within each XML message. Our model's main goal is to optimize and increase encryption-processing time; therefore, we have listed the number of occurrences for "High" and "Medium" importance levels, which require an encryption process to secure existing content. Table 37.6 represents the number of occurrences for transactions marked "High" and "Medium" across the three layers.

As seen in Table 37.6, the highest occurrences for "High" and "Medium" importance levels combined is 32.9 percent in layer 1, which means only 32.9 percent of the 1,000 XML messages require an encryption processing using either a 128-bit key or a 256-bit key, leaving 67.1 percent of the sample data to be forwarded directly to the message assembler without the need of the encryption process. In brief, instead of performing full encryption for the whole XML message, or even performing partial encryption on pre-selected parts, we were able to produce secured, optimized, and utilized messages, performing encryption only on needed parts selected using our fuzzy

```
<?xml version="1.0"?>
- <Transfers>
    - <Transaction ImportanceLevel="Low" xmlns="http://paymentv2">
        <Transaction_Notes>002</Transaction_Notes>
        <Profile_ID>92</Profile_ID>
        <AccountTries>02</AccountTries>
        <PasswordTries>01</PasswordTries>
      </Transaction>
    - <Transaction ImportanceLevel="Low" xmlns="http://paymentv2">
        <Posting_Date>2011/01/07</Posting_Date>
        <Service_ID>WWW60</Service_ID>
        <Customer_Language>E</Customer_Language>
      </Transaction>
    - <Transaction ImportanceLevel="Medium" xmlns="http://paymentv2">
        <TransactionAmount>755</TransactionAmount>
        <Transaction_Currency Code="JOD">001</Transaction_Currency>
        <Account_Type Code="001">Indivisual</Account_Type>
      </Transaction>
    - <Transaction ImportanceLevel="High" xmlns="http://paymentv2">
        <IPAddress>128.200.3.212</IPAddress>
        <From_Account>390230101401043000</From_Account>
        <To_Account>120130101155414000</To_Account>
      </Transaction>
  </Transfers>
```

FIGURE 37.11

Classified XML message taken from first implementation.

Table 37.7 Performance Evaluation for Stage 1, Experiment 1

Stage 1, Experiment 1 (Full Encryption)	Processing Time		File Size	
XML Message Set	SXMS Model	W3C128 bit	XML Messages	SXMS Model
1 XML File	0.0018 ms	0.0023 ms	1 XML File	0.0018 ms
300 XML	0.562 ms	0.702 ms	300 XML	0.562 ms
600 XML	0.873 ms	1.264 sec	600 XML	0.873 ms
900 XML	1.271 sec	1.825 sec	900 XML	1.271 sec
1,000 XML (Set 1)	1.625 sec	2.456 sec	1,000 XML (Set 1)	1.625 sec

classification techniques. Figure 37.11 shows an actual XML message after the fuzzy classification phase, where we notice the importance level value assigned per root node in each XML message.

Table 37.7 illustrates the time needed and the resulting file size to encrypt the XML message set using our model compared against the W3C XML encryption model using a 128-bit key size and encrypting each message in full.

We have encrypted the XML messages in chunks of 1, 300, 600, 900, and 1,000 messages. Our SXMS model processed the XML chunks with a measurable improvement in processing time

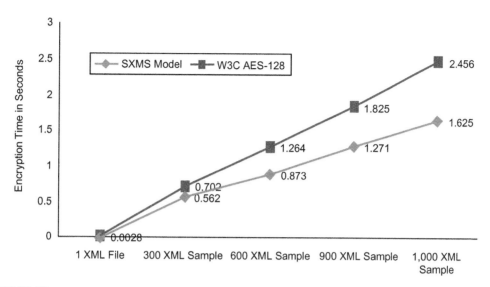

FIGURE 37.12

Comparison chart between SXMS and W3C model using a 128-bit key.

compared to the W3C XML encryption model, which uses a 128-bit key size to encrypt the whole XML message. SXMS uses a 128-bit key in the cases where the importance level attribute value equals "Medium" and a 256-bit key is used when the importance level attribute value equals "High." As seen in Table 37.7, the encryption process for all 1,000 XML messages using the W3C encryption standard with a 128-bit key size took 2.456 seconds to complete, compared to 1.625 seconds using the SXMS model. The result reflects a 33.8 percent improvement in processing time for the 1,000 messages. Figure 37.12 illustrates the comparison between the two models and performance improvement using SXMS.

Table 37.7 also illustrates file size reduction by encrypting XML messages using the SXMS model. The table shows a measurable reduction in file size, whereby the total size of the 1,000 encrypted XML messages was 988 KB using the W3C model with a 128-bit key size and encrypting each XML message in full. SXMS achieved smaller sizes for the same set of 1,000 encrypted XML messages, which is 652.4 KB, showing a size reduction of 34 percent from the encrypted file size using the W3C model. Such improvement can save a measurable amount of space and bandwidth on a large scale. Figure 37.12 illustrates the processing time needed to encrypt the sample messages in the first experiment compared to our model.

As seen in Figure 37.12, the x-axis represents the number of XML messages being processed, while the y-axis represents the processing time in seconds to encrypt the XML messages. Figure 37.13 shows the file size comparison for the encrypted XML messages using SXMS and W3C XML encryption syntax and processing model using a 128-bit key size and performing full message encryption.

The second experiment has been conducted performing full encryption using the W3C XML encryption standard with a 256-bit key deployed on the same 1,000 sample XML messages.

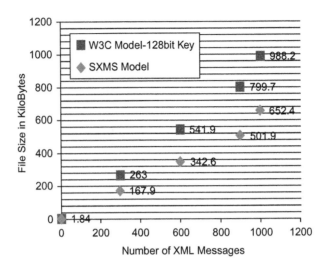

FIGURE 37.13

Comparison chart between SXMS and W3C model using a 128-bit key

Table 37.8 Performance Evaluation for Stage 1, Experiment 2				
Stage 1, Experiment 2 (Full Encryption)	**Processing Time**		**File Size**	
Message Set	SXMS Model	W3C 256 bit	SXMS Model	W3C 256 bit
1 XML File	0.0018 ms	0.0027 ms	1.14 KB	1.98 KB
300 XML	0.562 ms	0.811 ms	167.9 KB	283.4 KB
600 XML	0.873 ms	1.591 sec	342.6 KB	601 KB
900 XML	1.271 sec	2.137 sec	501.9 KB	864.8 KB
1,000 XML	**1.625 sec**	**2.8 sec**	**652.4 KB**	**1112 KB**

SXMS uses the same sample of XML messages to deploy element-wise encryption. Later we compare results for both experiments against results from our model. Table 37.8 illustrates the time needed and the resulting file size to encrypt the XML message set using our model compared against the W3C XML encryption model using a 256-bit key size and encrypting each message in full.

We have encrypted the XML messages in chunks of 1, 300, 600, 900, and 1,000 messages. Our SXMS model processed the XML chunks with a measurable improvement in processing time compared to the W3C XML encryption model, which uses a 256-bit key size to encrypt the whole XML message. SXMS uses a 128-bit key in the cases where the importance level attribute value equals "Medium" and a 256-bit key is used when the importance level attribute value equals "High."

In the second experiment of Stage 1, we deployed the W3C encryption standard to fully encrypt the same sample of 1,000 XML messages, but this time using a 256-bit key size. SXMS used the same sample of XML messages to deploy element-wise encryption. The SXMS model uses symmetric AES encryption with mixed key values (128-bit, 256-bit). Key size used in the encryption process depends on the importance level attribute value assigned by the fuzzification stage for a selected set of tags within each XML message. Table 37.8 represents the time needed for each model performing the encryption process on the selected sample of messages.

As seen in Table 37.8, the encryption process for the whole message using the W3C encryption standard with a 256-bit key size took 2.8 seconds to complete, compared to 1.625 seconds using the SXMS model. The result reflects a 41.9 percent improvement in processing time for the 1,000 messages.

Table 37.8 also illustrates the file size reduction encrypting XML messages using the SXMS model The table shows a measurable reduction in file size, whereby the total size of the encrypted 1,000 XML messages was 1112 KB using the W3C model with a 256-bit and encrypting each XML message in full. SXMS achieved smaller sizes for the same set of 1,000 encrypted XML messages, which is 652.4 KB, showing a size reduction of 41.3 percent from the encrypted file size using the W3C model. Such an improvement can save a measurable amount of space and bandwidth on a large scale. Figure 37.14 illustrates the performance comparison between the SXMS model and the W3C encryption standard using a 256-bit key size. Figure 37.15 shows a file size comparison for the encrypted XML messages using SXMS and the W3C XML encryption syntax and processing model, using a 256-bit key size.

Finally, Figures 37.16 and 37.17 illustrate the final performance and file size reduction comparison between SXMS and the W3C model for both experiments, which uses a 128-bit key and a 256-bit key, performing full encrypting for each XML message in the first message set. Figure 37.16 presents a measurable amount of performance improvement using the SXMS model.

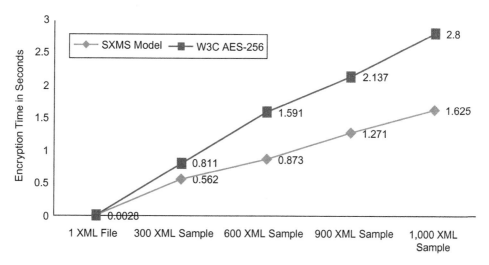

FIGURE 37.14

Comparison chart between SXMS and W3C model using a 256-bit key.

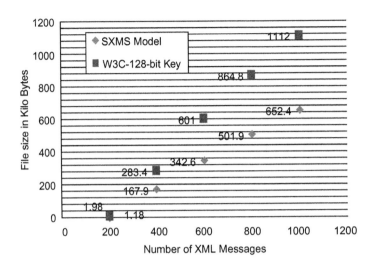

FIGURE 37.15

File size comparisons between SXMS and W3C model using a 256-bit key.

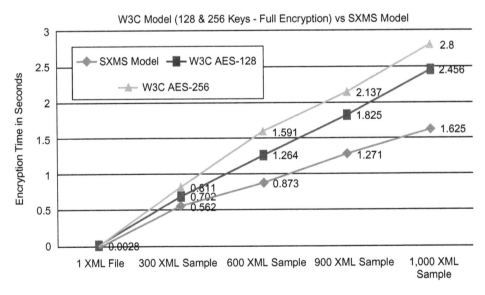

FIGURE 37.16

Performance comparisons between SXMS and XML using a 256-bit key.

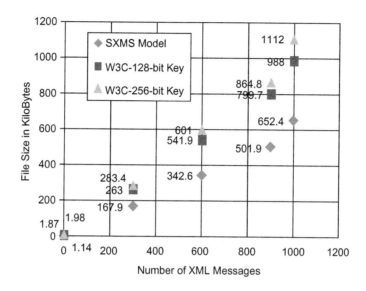

FIGURE 37.17

Performance comparisons between SXMS and W3C using an AES-as 128-bitkey.

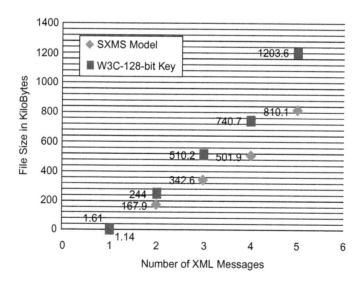

FIGURE 37.18

Performance comparisons between SXMS and W3C using an AES-as 128-bit key.

Figure 37.18 shows a file size comparison for the encrypted XML messages using SXMS and the W3C XML encryption syntax and processing model using a 128-bit key size performing partial message encryption.

Table 37.9 Performance Evaluation for Stage 2, Experiment 2

Stage 2, Experiment 2 (Partial Encryption)	Processing Time		File Size	
Message Set	SXMS Model	W3C 128 bit	SXMS Model	W3C 128 bit
1 XML File	0.0018 ms	0.0021 ms	1.14 KB	1.72 KB
300 XML	0.562 ms	0.687 ms	167.9 KB	269 KB
600 XML	0.873 ms	1.42 sec	342.6 KB	588.4 KB
900 XML	1.271 sec	2.026 sec	501.9 KB	813.9 KB
1,500 XML	**1.963 sec**	**2.899 sec**	**810.1 KB**	**1399.6 KB**

In the second experiment of Stage 2, we deployed the W3C encryption standard to partially encrypt the XML messages to a sample of 1,500 XML messages, but this time using a 256-bit key size. SXMS used the same sample of XML messages to deploy element-wise encryption. The SXMS model uses symmetric AES encryption with mixed key values (128-bit, 256-bit). Key size used in the encryption process depends on the importance level attribute value assigned by the fuzzification stage for a selected set of tags within each XML message. Table 37.9 represents the time needed for each model performing the encryption process on the selected sample of messages.

As seen in Table 37.9, the encryption process for part of the message using the W3C encryption standard with a 256-bit key size took 2.899 seconds to complete, compared to 1.963 seconds using the SXMS model. The result reflects a 32.2 percent improvement in processing time for the 1,500 messages. Table 37.9 also illustrates file size reduction encrypting XML messages using the SXMS model. The table shows a measurable reduction in file size, whereby the total size of the 1,500 encrypted XML messages was 1399.6 KB using the W3C model with a 256-bit key size and encrypting parts of the XML message. SXMS achieved smaller sizes for the same set of 1,500 encrypted XML messages—810.1 KB—showing a size reduction of 42.1 percent from the encrypted file size using the W3C model. Such improvement can save a measurable amount of space and bandwidth on a large scale.

Figure 37.19 illustrates the comparison between the SXMS model and the W3C encryption standard using a 256-bit key size and encrypting parts of the XML message for the second sample set.

Figure 37.20 shows a file size comparison for the encrypted XML messages using SXMS and the W3C XML encryption syntax and processing model using a 256-bit key size and performing partial message encryption.

Finally, Figure 37.21 and Figure 37.22 illustrate performance improvements and a file size reduction comparison between the SXMS model and the W3C model for both experiments in Stage 2, showing a measurable performance improvement and size reduction on a large scale using the SXMS model.

Summary

In this chapter, a novel approach for securing financial XML messages using intelligent mining fuzzy classification techniques has been proposed.

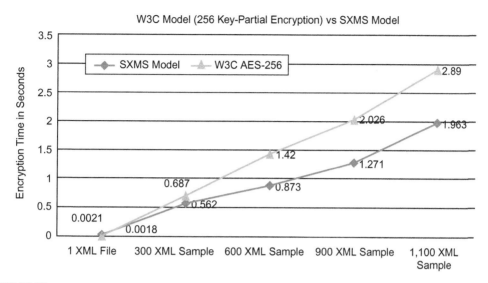

FIGURE 37.19

Comparisons between SXMS and W3C standard using an AES-256-bit key.

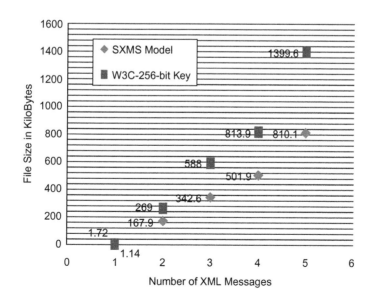

FIGURE 37.20

File size comparisons between SXMS and W3C model using a 256-bit key.

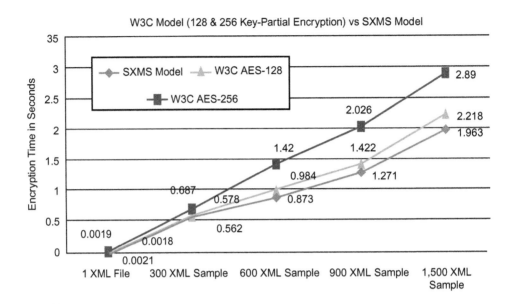

FIGURE 37.21

Comparisons between SXMS and W3C standard using different keys.

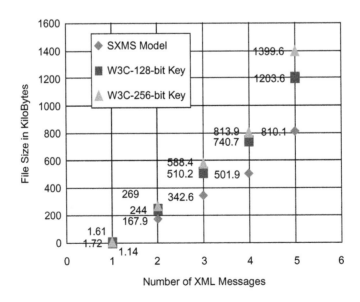

FIGURE 37.22

File size comparisons between SXMS and W3C standard using different keys.

Mining fuzzy classification techniques have been used to evaluate and measure the data sensitivity level within each XML message to find a degree of sensitivity for each tag in the message. The mining fuzzy classification process allowed us to assign a value to a new attribute added to the parent XML nodes. A value is determined by applying a set of classification processes based on Mamdani inference. A new value has been used to determine which type of encryption algorithm is being performed on selected tags, allowing us to secure only the needed parts within each message, rather than encrypting the whole message. XML encryption is based on the W3C XML recommendation. Nodes that are assigned an importance level value of "High" are encrypted using the AES encryption algorithm with a 256-bit key size to ensure that maximum security is performed. Nodes that are assigned an importance level value of "Medium" are encrypted using the AES encryption algorithm with a 128-bit key size . An implementation was performed on a real-life environment, using online banking systems to demonstrate the model's flexibility, feasibility, and functionality. Our experimental results with the new model verified tangible enhancements in encryption efficiency, processing time reduction, and financial XML message utilization.

Each unit in our SXMS model acts independently as a separate system. Taking into consideration such a flexible nature allows for and motivates future work and enhancements. The following points describe the future work on each unit within our SXMS model:

- Fuzzy classification phase: We can utilize supervised machine learning techniques to automate the fuzzy rule generation process in order to reduce the human expert knowledge intervention and increase performance of the phishing detection system. This can be achieved by generating classification rules using well-known classifiers. For example, we can use: PRISM [21], C4.5 Decision Tree [22], Ripper [23], k-nearest neighbor classification (kNN) [24], naïve Bayes classification [25], linear least squares fit mapping [26], and the vector space method [27]. These mining association classification rules can be combined with a fuzzy logic inference engine to provide efficient and competent techniques for importance level extraction.
- Encryption phase: We can utilize a different encryption scheme; asymmetric algorithms can be deployed. We have deployed symmetric encryption due to the efficiency and processing time outperforming asymmetric encryption algorithms. We can even change the symmetric encryption algorithm to something else, like DES, triple DES, or Blowfish. Researchers will be able to test and measure performance for any replaced encryption algorithm. Also, usage of the encryption keys can be change to reflect a different key size for each importance level assigned. For example, we can assign an encryption key of 192 bits instead of 256 bits for the importance level "High" value.
- We can create multiple instances of SXMS whereby it handles XML messages based on a load balancer designed to distribute XML messages on multiple SXMS instances. By performing this distribution, processing speed will be boosted by two times or even more, depending on the new instances created and used. However, such initiative might be a high cost on the resources used.

References

[1] Bray T, Paoli J, Sperberg-McQueen CM. Extensible markup language (XML). 1.0. W3C; 1998.
[2] Fan M, Stallaert J, Whinston AB. The Internet and the future of financial markets. Commun ACM 2000;43(11):83−8.

[3] Organization for the Advancement of Structured Information Standards (OASIS). Extensible access control markup language (XACML) V2.0; 2005.

[4] ContentGuard. XrML: The digital rights language for trusted content and services. [Internet]. Available at: <http://www.xrml.org/>; 2001.

[5] XML encryption syntax and processing (W3C Recommendation); 2003.

[6] XML-signature syntax and processing (W3C/IETF Recommendation); 2002.

[7] XML key management specification (XKMS 2.0). [Internet]. Available at: <http://www.w3.org/TR/2005/PR-xkms2-20050502/>; 2005.

[8] Juric M, Sarang P, Loganathan R, Jennings F. SOA approach to integration. Packt Publising; 2007.

[9] Simon E. XML encryption: Issues regarding attribute values and referenced. External Data. W3C XML-Encryption Minutes; Session 3. Boston, MA; 2000.

[10] Zadeh LA. Fuzzy sets, information and control; 1965.

[11] Mahant N. Risk assessment is fuzzy business — Fuzzy logic provides the way to assess off-site risk from industrial installations. Australia: Bechtel; 2004.

[12] Oasis security services (saml) tc. [Internet]. Available at: < http://www.oasis-open.org/committees/security/>.

[13] Geuer-Pollmann C. XML pool encryption. ACMWorkshop on XML Security. University of Siegen; Institute for Data Communications Systems; 2002.

[14] Rosario R. Secure XML an overview of XML encryption; 2001.

[15] Gaurav A, Alhajj R. Incorporating fuzziness in XML and mapping fuzzy relational data into fuzzy XML. Proceedings of the 2006 ACM Symposium on Applied computing. Dijon, France; 2006.

[16] Ma Z, Fuzzy XML. data modeling with the UML and relational data models. Data & Knowledge Engineering 2007;63:972–96.

[17] Tseng C. Universal fuzzy system representation with XML. Computer Standards and Interfaces 2005;28:218–30.

[18] Fu Zhang ZM, Ma LY. Construction of fuzzy ontologies from fuzzy XML models. Knowledge-Based Systems: 2013;42:20-39. ISSN 0950-7051. Avaiable from http://dx.doi.org/10.1016/j.knosys.2012.12.015.

[19] Liu M, Chen D, Wu C. The continuity of Mamdani method. International Conference on Machine Learning and Cybernetics 2002;3:1680–2.

[20] Diffie W, Hellman ME. New directions in cryptography. IEEE Trans on Information Theory IT-22 1976;6:644–54.

[21] Cendrowska J. PRISM: an algorithm for inducing modular rules. Int J Man Mach Stud 1987;27(4):349–70.

[22] Quinlan J. Improved use of continuous attributes in c4.5. Journal of Artificial Intelligence Research 1996;4(1):77–90.

[23] Cohen W. Fast effective rule induction. Proceedings of the twelveth International Conference on Machine Learning. CA, USA; 1995. p. 115–23.

[24] Guo G, Wang H, Bell D, Bi Y, Greer Y. Using kNN model for automatic text categorization. Journal of Soft Computing. Verlag Heidelberg: Springer; 2004.

[25] McCallum A, Nigam KA. Comparison of event models for naive bayes text classification. In: AAAI-98 Workshop on Learning for Text Categorization; Madison, WI; 1998. p. 41–8.

[26] Yang Y, Chute CG. An application of least squares fit mapping to text information retrieval. In: Proceedings of the ACM SIGIR. Pittsburgh, PA; 1993. p. 281–90. 163.

[27] Gauch S, Madrid JM, Induri S, Ravindran D, Chadlavada S. KeyConcept: A conceptual search engine. Information and Telecommunication Technology Center; Technical Report: ITTC-FY2004-TR-8646-37. University of Kansas.

Further Reading

Shirasuna S, Slominski A, Fang L, Gannon D. Performance comparison of security mechanisms for grid services. Fifth IEEE/ACM International Workshop on Grid Computing. IEEE Computer Society; 2004. p. 360−4.

Park N, Kim H, Chung K, Sohn S, Won D. XML-Signcryption based LBS security protocol acceleration methods in mobile distributed computing. Computational Science and Its Applications; ICCSA 2006. Berlin/Heidelberg: Springer; 2006;3984:251−9.

Imamura, T, Clark, A, Maruyama, H. A stream-based implementation of XML encryption. In: XMLSEC 2002: Proceedings of the 2002 ACM Workshop on XML security. ACM Press; 2002. p. 11−17.

Hwang G-H, Chang T-K. An operational model and language support for securing XML documents. Computers & Security 2004;23(6):498−529.

Index

Note: Page numbers followed by "*f*" and "*t*" refer to figures and tables, respectively.

Printed and bound by CPI Group (UK) Ltd, Croydon, CR0 4YY

03/10/2024

01040323-0008